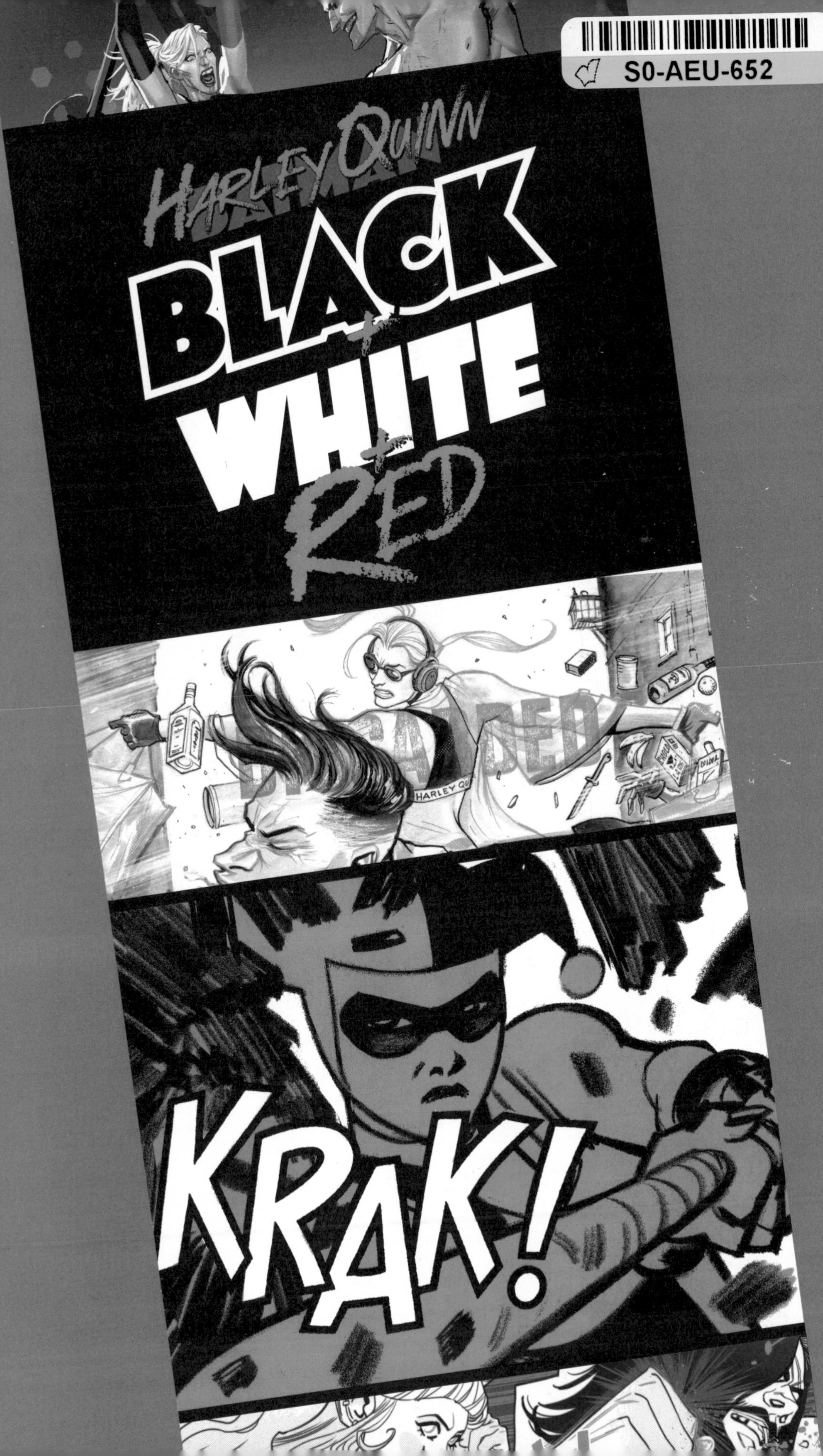
Harley Quinn
BLACK + WHITE + RED
KRAK!

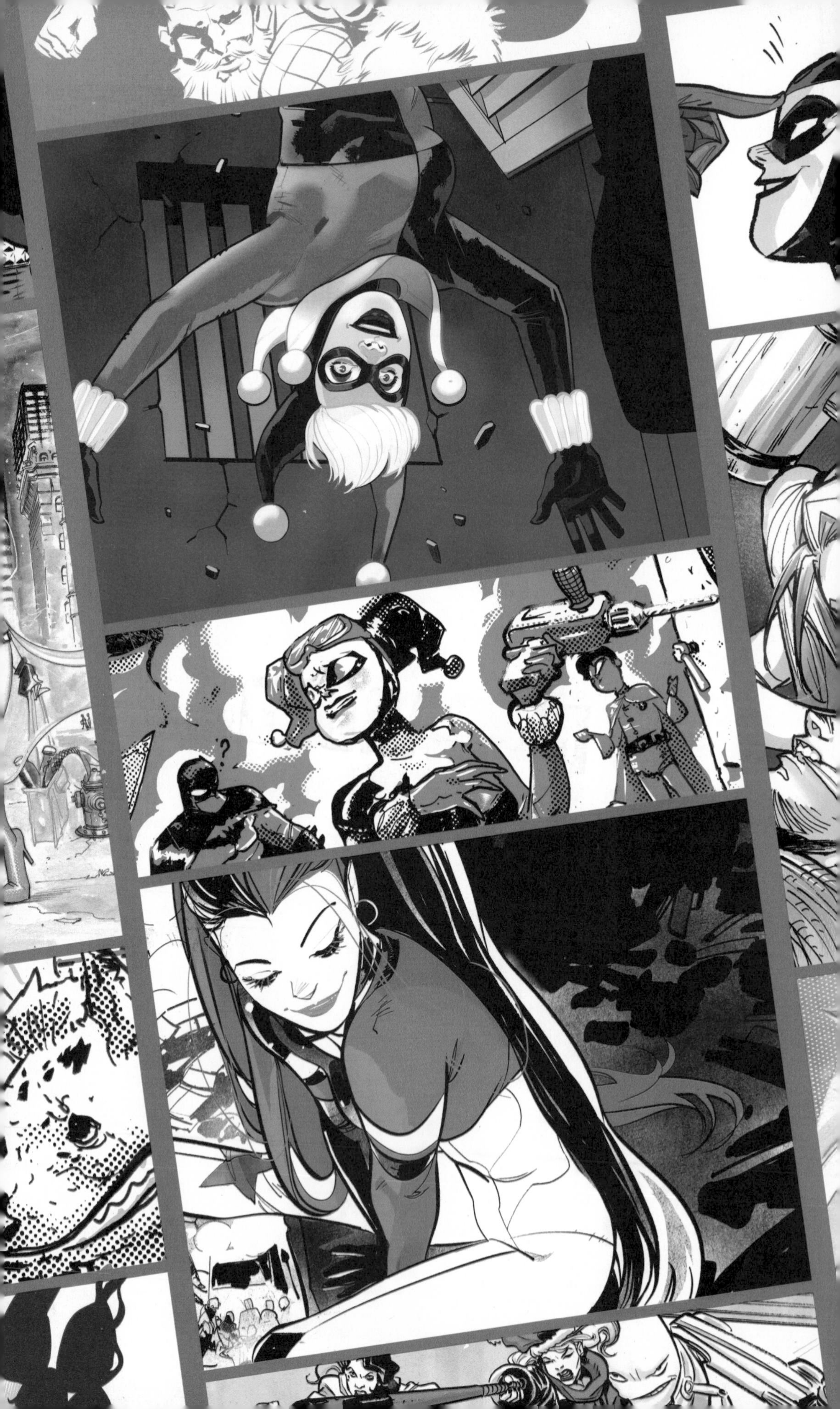

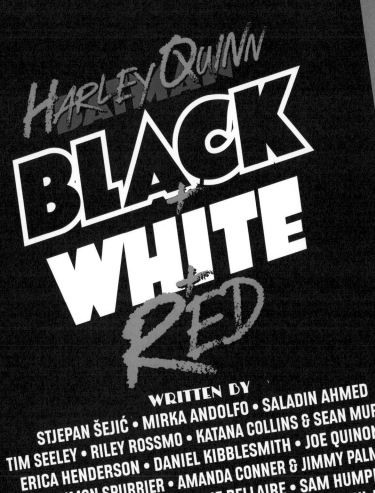

HARLEY QUINN
BLACK + WHITE + RED

WRITTEN BY

STJEPAN ŠEJIĆ • MIRKA ANDOLFO • SALADIN AHMED
TIM SEELEY • RILEY ROSSMO • KATANA COLLINS & SEAN MURPHY
ERICA HENDERSON • DANIEL KIBBLESMITH • JOE QUINONES
DANI • SIMON SPURRIER • AMANDA CONNER & JIMMY PALMIOTTI
PATRICK SCHUMACKER • JORDIE BELLAIRE • SAM HUMPHRIES
FRANK TIERI • LIZ ERICKSON • DAVID MANDEL • PAUL DINI

ART BY

STJEPAN ŠEJIĆ • MIRKA ANDOLFO • JAVIER RODRIGUEZ
JUAN FERREYRA • RILEY ROSSMO • MATTEO SCALERA
ERICA HENDERSON • MARGUERITE SAUVAGE • JOE QUINONES
DANI • OTTO SCHMIDT • CHAD HARDIN • ELEONORA CARLINI
GREG SMALLWOOD • STEPHEN BYRNE • TOM FOWLER
TOM DERENICK • ADAM HUGHES • KEVIN ALTIERI

ADDITIONAL COLORS BY

ENRICA EREN ANGIOLINI • BRIAN REBER

LETTERS BY

GABRIELA DOWNIE • JOHN J. HILL • CLAYTON COWLES
STEVE WANDS • DERON BENNETT • ANDWORLD DESIGN
ADITYA BIDIKAR • TOM NAPOLITANO • BECCA CAREY
TROY PETERI • DAVE SHARPE • JOSH REED

COLLECTION COVER ART BY JORGE JIMENEZ

HARLEY QUINN created by PAUL DINI & BRUCE TIMM
SUPERMAN created by JERRY SIEGEL and JOE SHUSTER.
By special arrangement with the Jerry Siegel Family

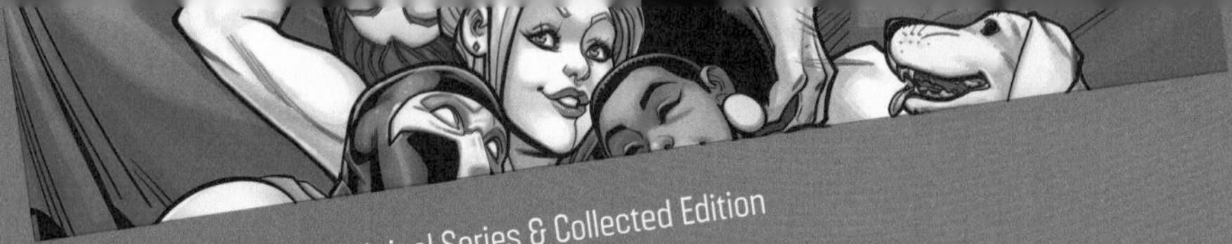

CHRIS CONROY Editor – Original Series & Collected Edition

ANDY KHOURI
MAGGIE HOWELL
AMEDEO TURTURRO Editors – Original Series
STEVE COOK Design Director – Books
AMIE BROCKWAY-METCALF Publication Design
SUZANNAH ROWNTREE Publication Production

MARIE JAVINS Editor-in-Chief, DC Comics

DANIEL CHERRY III Senior VP – General Manager
JIM LEE Publisher & Chief Creative Officer
DON FALLETTI VP – Manufacturing Operations & Workflow Management
LAWRENCE GANEM VP – Talent Services
ALISON GILL Senior VP – Manufacturing & Operations
NICK J. NAPOLITANO VP – Manufacturing Administration & Design
NANCY SPEARS VP – Revenue
MICHELE R. WELLS VP & Executive Editor, Young Reader

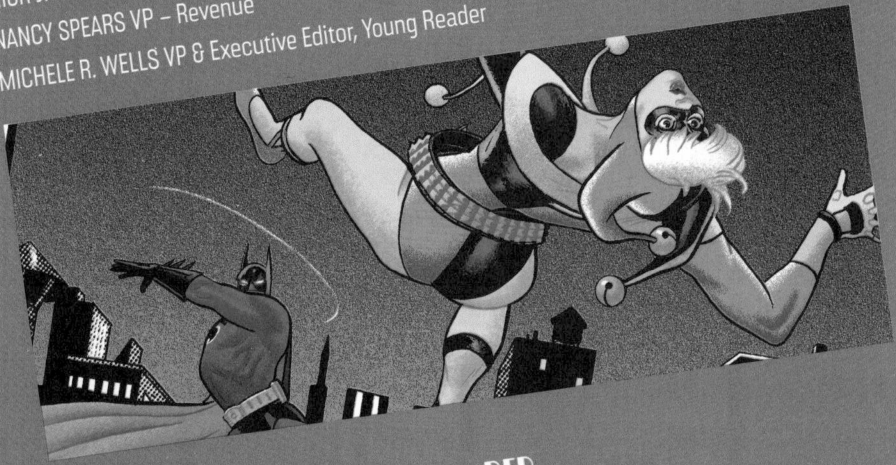

HARLEY QUINN BLACK + WHITE + RED

DC Comics, 2900 West Alameda Ave., Burbank, CA 91505

DC Comics, 2900 West Alameda Ave., Burbank, CA 91505
Printed by LSC Communications, Owensville, MO, USA. 4/2/21.
First Printing.
ISBN: 978-1-77950-995-6

Library of Congress Cataloging-in-Publication Data is available.

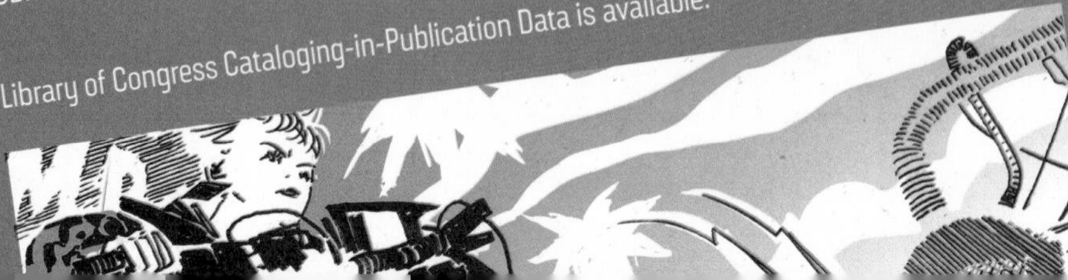

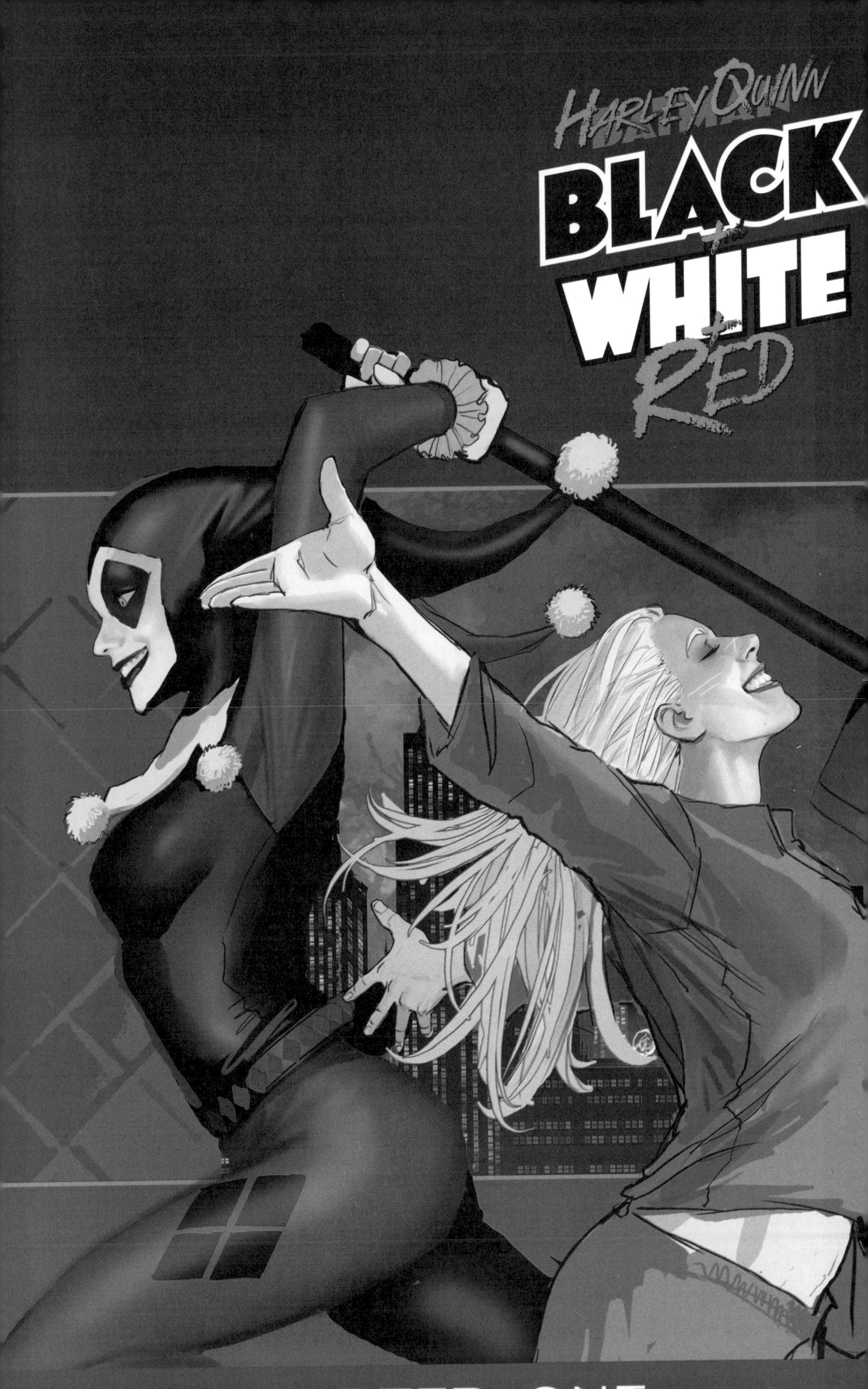
HARLEY QUINN
BLACK + WHITE + RED

CHAPTER ONE

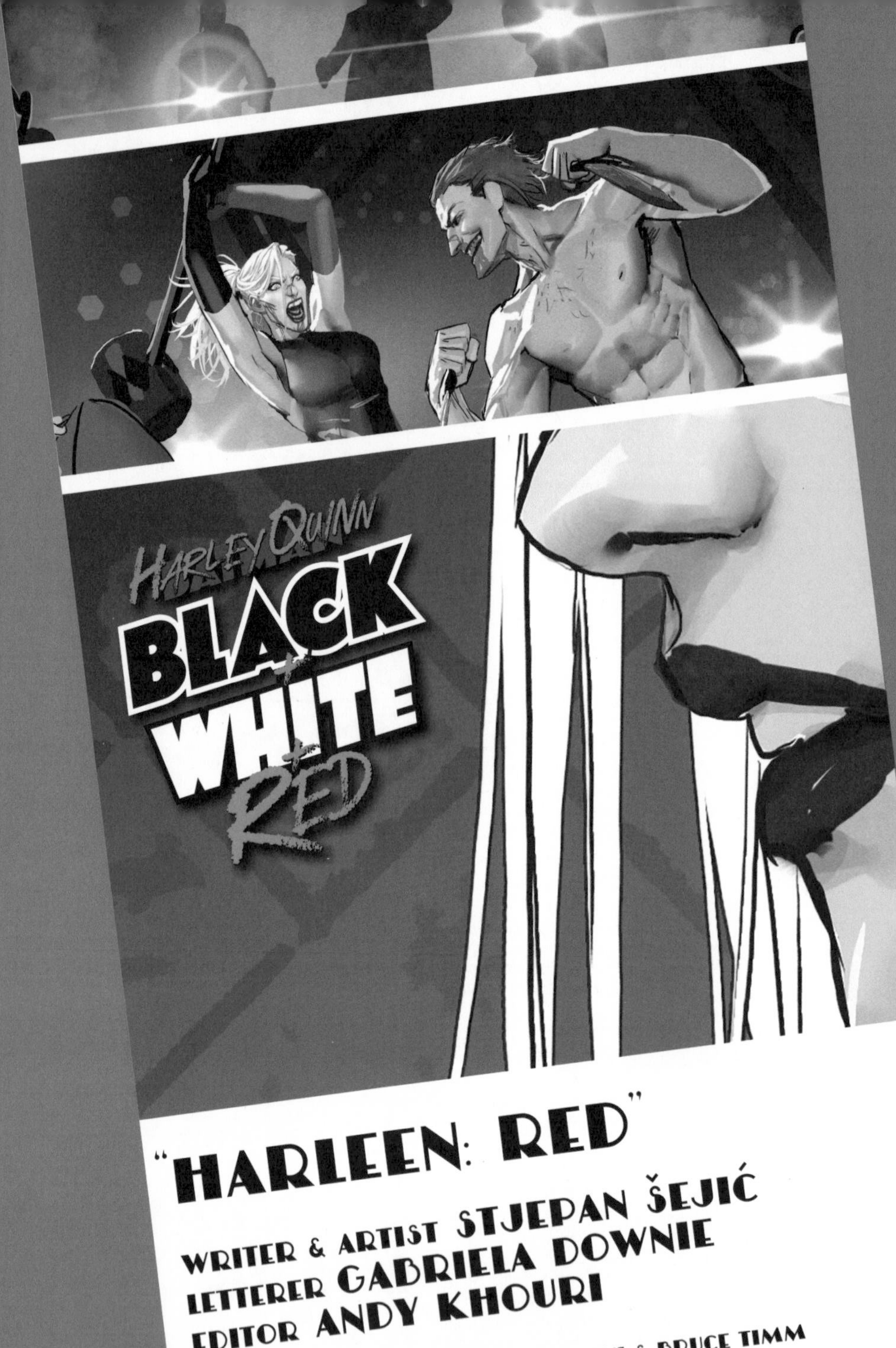
HARLEY QUINN
BLACK
+
WHITE
+
RED

"HARLEEN: RED"

WRITER & ARTIST STJEPAN ŠEJIĆ
LETTERER GABRIELA DOWNIE
EDITOR ANDY KHOURI

HARLEY QUINN CREATED BY PAUL DINI & BRUCE TIMM

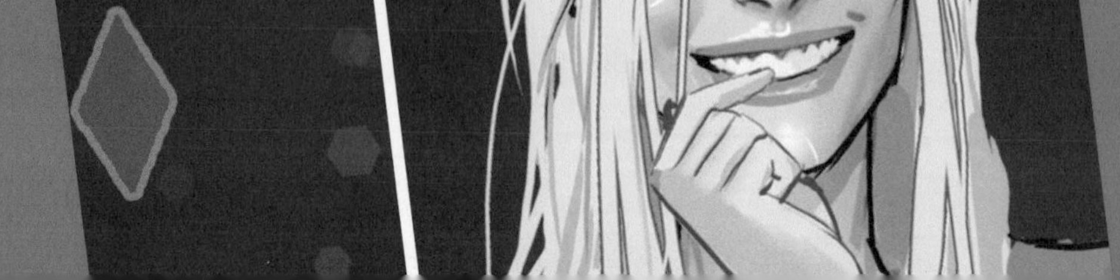

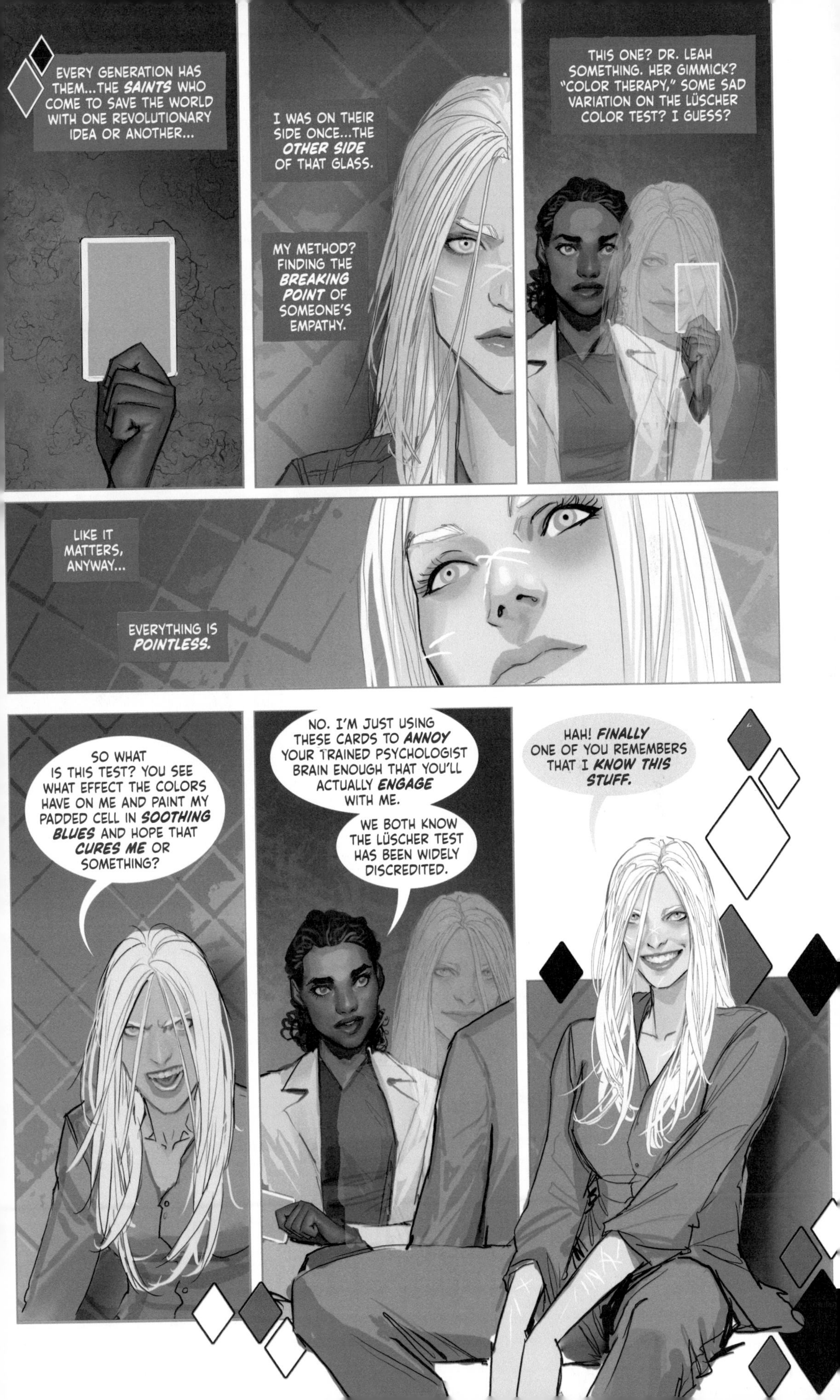
EVERY GENERATION HAS THEM...THE SAINTS WHO COME TO SAVE THE WORLD WITH ONE REVOLUTIONARY IDEA OR ANOTHER...
I WAS ON THEIR SIDE ONCE...THE OTHER SIDE OF THAT GLASS.
MY METHOD? FINDING THE BREAKING POINT OF SOMEONE'S EMPATHY.
THIS ONE? DR. LEAH SOMETHING. HER GIMMICK? "COLOR THERAPY," SOME SAD VARIATION ON THE LÜSCHER COLOR TEST? I GUESS?
LIKE IT MATTERS, ANYWAY...
EVERYTHING IS POINTLESS.
SO WHAT IS THIS TEST? YOU SEE WHAT EFFECT THE COLORS HAVE ON ME AND PAINT MY PADDED CELL IN SOOTHING BLUES AND HOPE THAT CURES ME OR SOMETHING?
NO. I'M JUST USING THESE CARDS TO ANNOY YOUR TRAINED PSYCHOLOGIST BRAIN ENOUGH THAT YOU'LL ACTUALLY ENGAGE WITH ME.
WE BOTH KNOW THE LÜSCHER TEST HAS BEEN WIDELY DISCREDITED.
HAH! FINALLY ONE OF YOU REMEMBERS THAT I KNOW THIS STUFF.

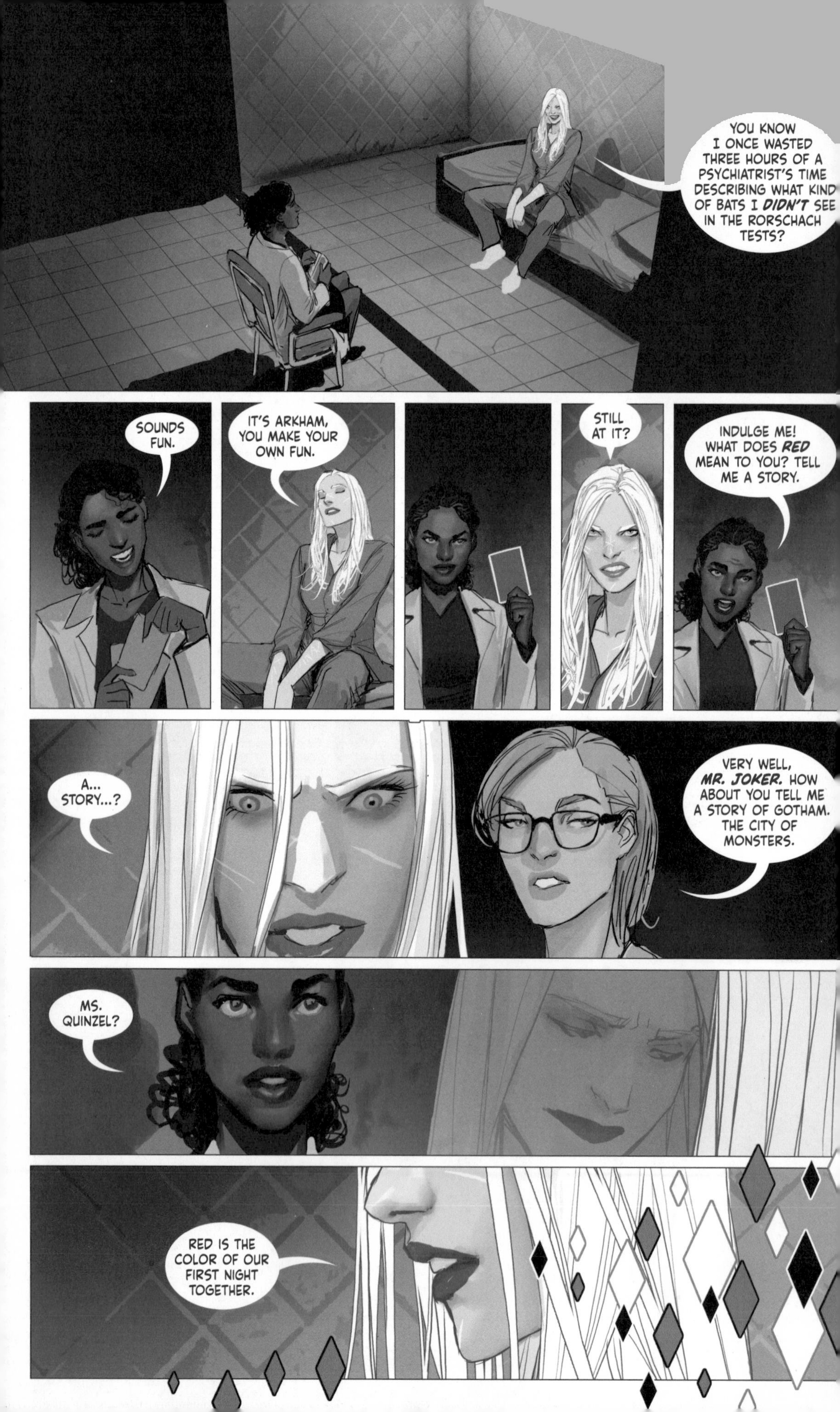

YOU KNOW I ONCE WASTED THREE HOURS OF A PSYCHIATRIST'S TIME DESCRIBING WHAT KIND OF BATS I *DIDN'T* SEE IN THE RORSCHACH TESTS?
SOUNDS FUN.
IT'S ARKHAM, YOU MAKE YOUR OWN FUN.
STILL AT IT?
INDULGE ME! WHAT DOES ***RED*** MEAN TO YOU? TELL ME A STORY.
A... STORY...?
VERY WELL, ***MR. JOKER.*** HOW ABOUT YOU TELL ME A STORY OF GOTHAM. THE CITY OF MONSTERS.
MS. QUINZEL?
RED IS THE COLOR OF OUR FIRST NIGHT TOGETHER.

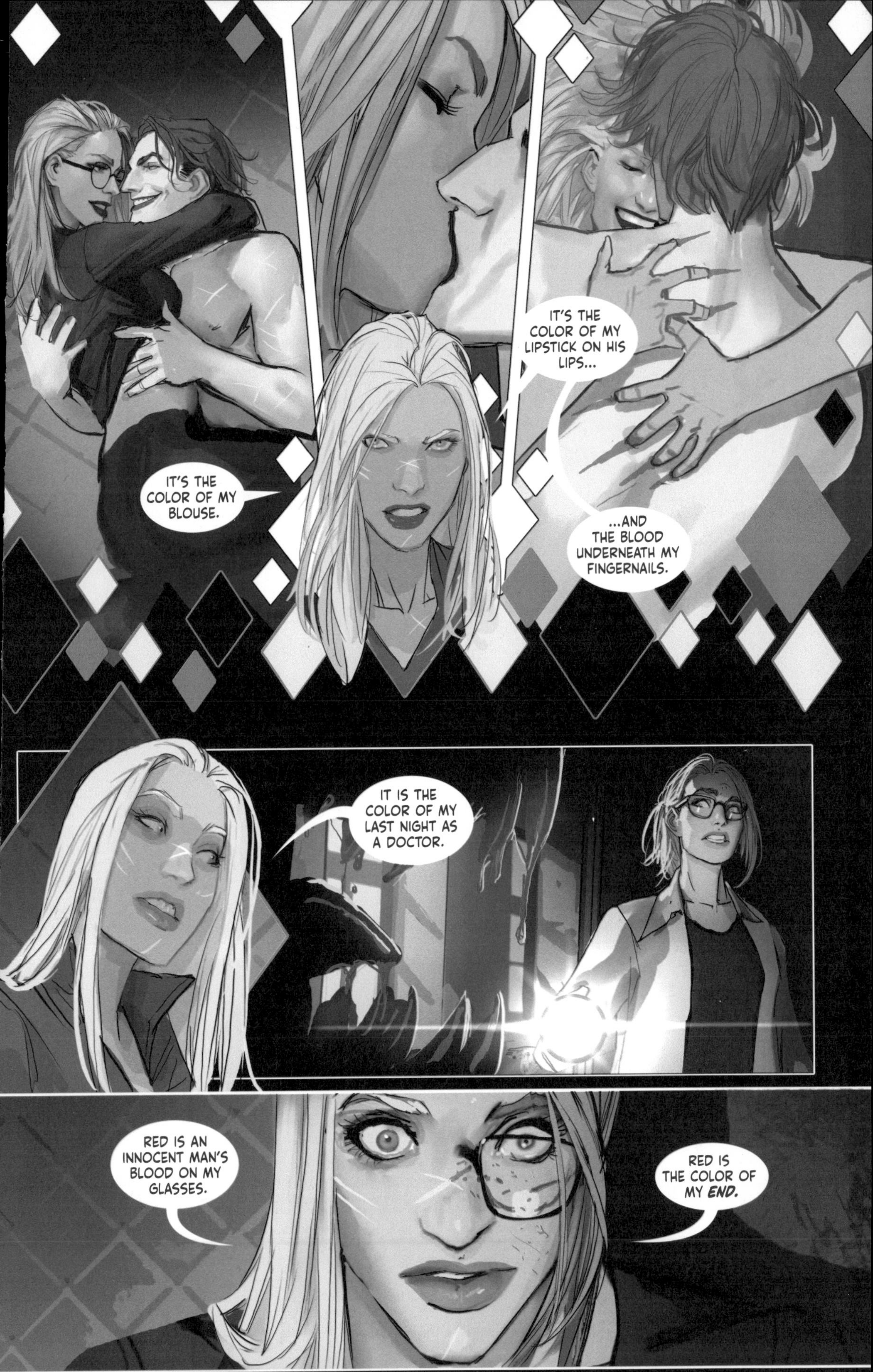
IT'S THE COLOR OF MY BLOUSE.
IT'S THE COLOR OF MY LIPSTICK ON HIS LIPS...
...AND THE BLOOD UNDERNEATH MY FINGERNAILS.
IT IS THE COLOR OF MY LAST NIGHT AS A DOCTOR.
RED IS AN INNOCENT MAN'S BLOOD ON MY GLASSES.
RED IS THE COLOR OF MY *END.*

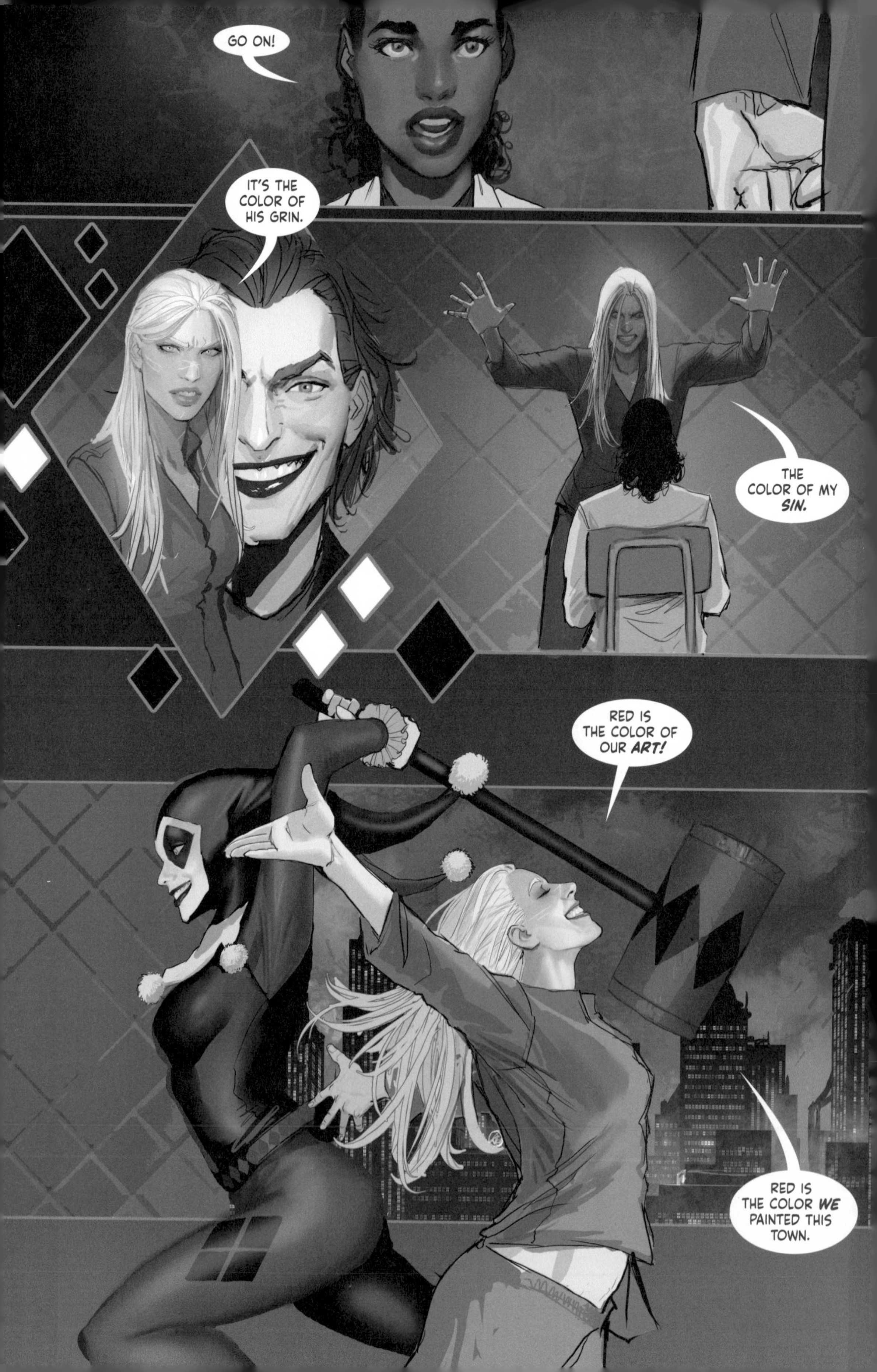
GO ON!
IT'S THE COLOR OF HIS GRIN.
THE COLOR OF MY *SIN.*
RED IS THE COLOR OF OUR *ART!*
RED IS THE COLOR *WE* PAINTED THIS TOWN.

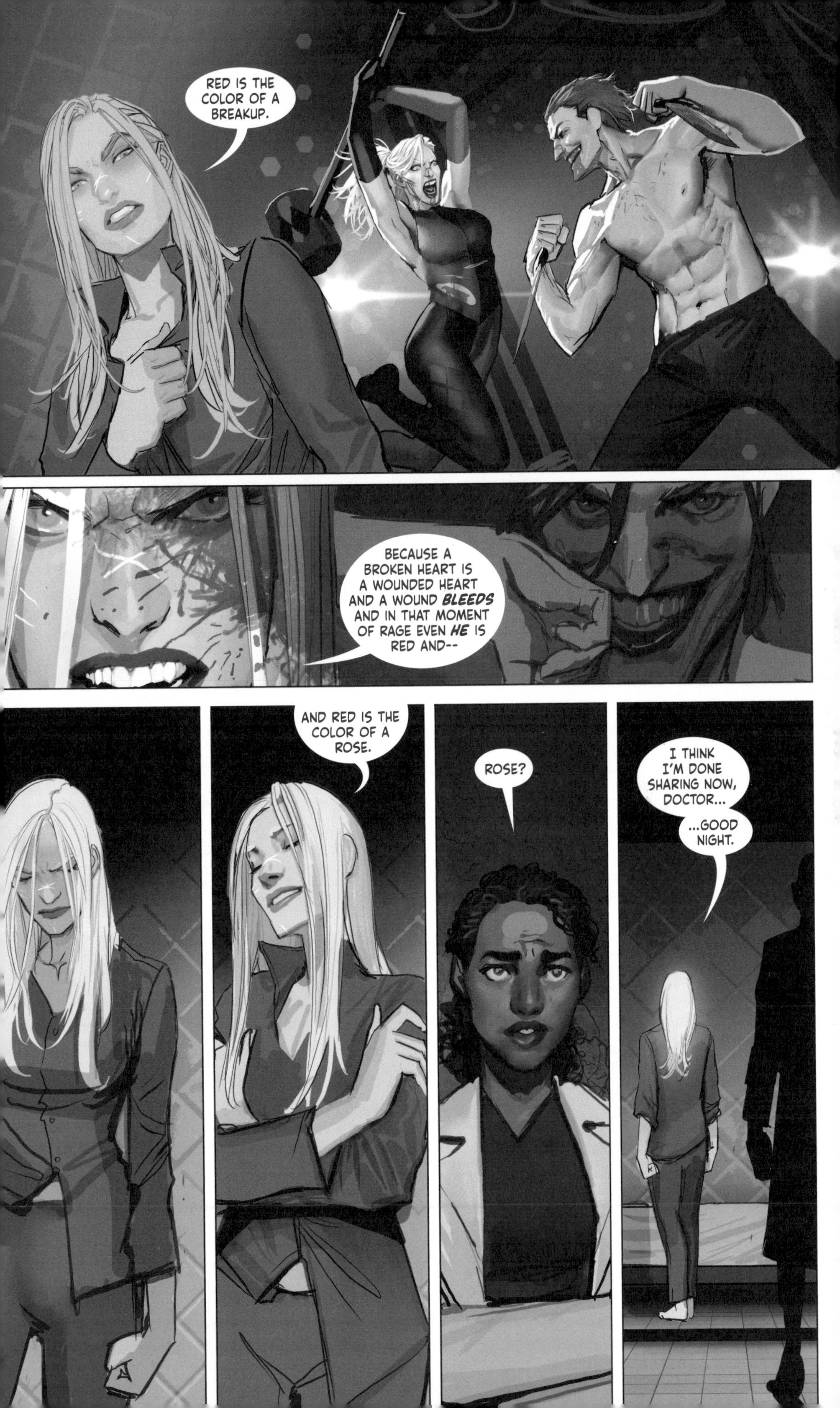

RED IS THE COLOR OF A BREAKUP.
BECAUSE A BROKEN HEART IS A WOUNDED HEART AND A WOUND **BLEEDS** AND IN THAT MOMENT OF RAGE EVEN **HE** IS RED AND--
AND RED IS THE COLOR OF A ROSE.
ROSE?
I THINK I'M DONE SHARING NOW, DOCTOR...
...GOOD NIGHT.

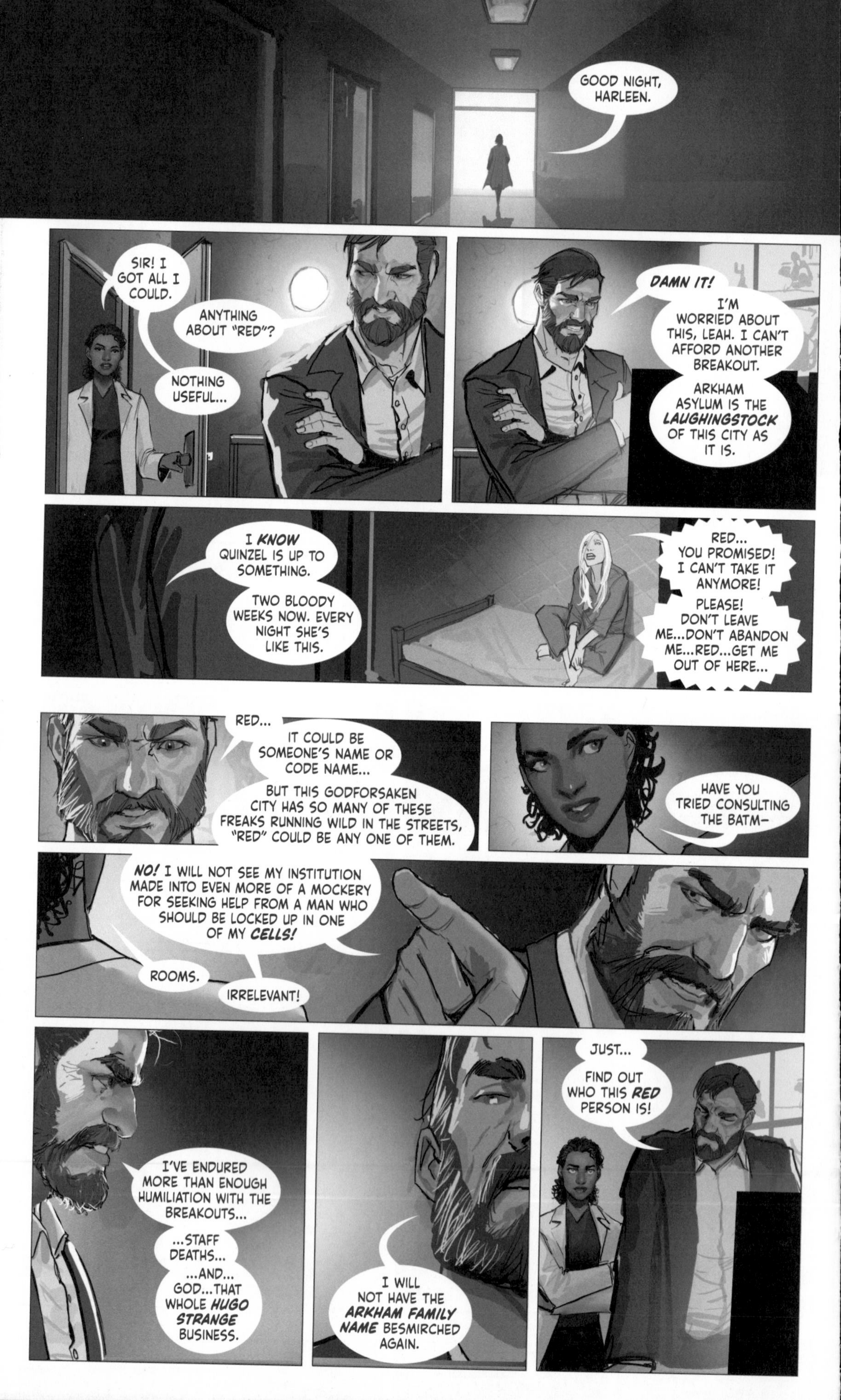
GOOD NIGHT, HARLEEN.
SIR! I GOT ALL I COULD.
ANYTHING ABOUT "RED"?
NOTHING USEFUL...
DAMN IT!
I'M WORRIED ABOUT THIS, LEAH. I CAN'T AFFORD ANOTHER BREAKOUT.
ARKHAM ASYLUM IS THE LAUGHINGSTOCK OF THIS CITY AS IT IS.
I KNOW QUINZEL IS UP TO SOMETHING.
TWO BLOODY WEEKS NOW. EVERY NIGHT SHE'S LIKE THIS.
RED... YOU PROMISED! I CAN'T TAKE IT ANYMORE!
PLEASE! DON'T LEAVE ME...DON'T ABANDON ME...RED...GET ME OUT OF HERE...
RED...
IT COULD BE SOMEONE'S NAME OR CODE NAME...
BUT THIS GODFORSAKEN CITY HAS SO MANY OF THESE FREAKS RUNNING WILD IN THE STREETS, "RED" COULD BE ANY ONE OF THEM.
HAVE YOU TRIED CONSULTING THE BATM—
NO! I WILL NOT SEE MY INSTITUTION MADE INTO EVEN MORE OF A MOCKERY FOR SEEKING HELP FROM A MAN WHO SHOULD BE LOCKED UP IN ONE OF MY CELLS!
ROOMS.
IRRELEVANT!
I'VE ENDURED MORE THAN ENOUGH HUMILIATION WITH THE BREAKOUTS...
...STAFF DEATHS...
...AND... GOD...THAT WHOLE HUGO STRANGE BUSINESS.
I WILL NOT HAVE THE ARKHAM FAMILY NAME BESMIRCHED AGAIN.
JUST...
FIND OUT WHO THIS RED PERSON IS!

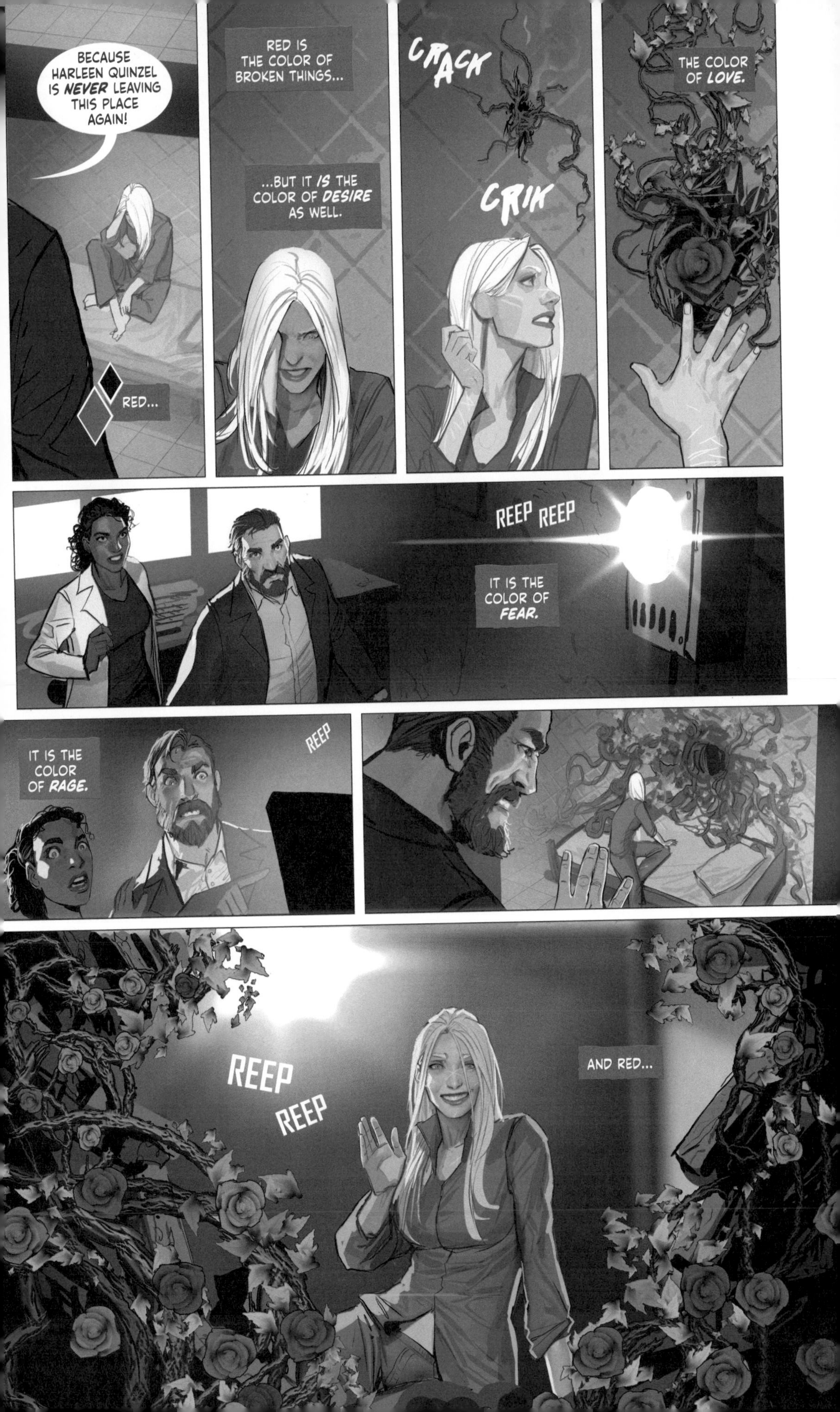
BECAUSE HARLEEN QUINZEL IS NEVER LEAVING THIS PLACE AGAIN!
RED...
RED IS THE COLOR OF BROKEN THINGS...
...BUT IT IS THE COLOR OF DESIRE AS WELL.
CRACK
CRIK
THE COLOR OF LOVE.
REEP REEP
IT IS THE COLOR OF FEAR.
IT IS THE COLOR OF RAGE.
REEP
REEP
REEP
AND RED...

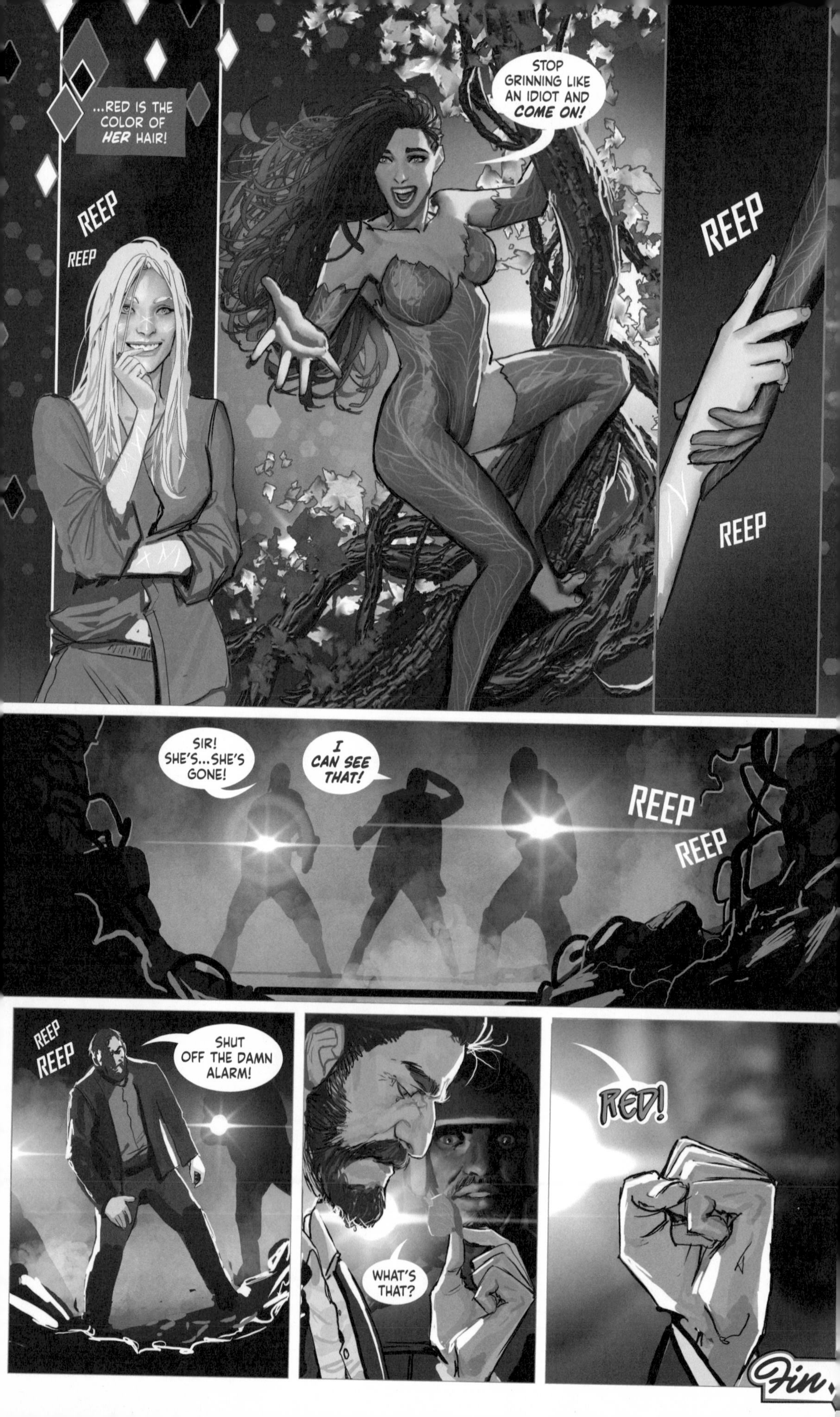
...RED IS THE COLOR OF *HER* HAIR!
REEP
REEP
STOP GRINNING LIKE AN IDIOT AND *COME ON!*
REEP
REEP
SIR! SHE'S...SHE'S GONE!
I CAN SEE THAT!
REEP
REEP
REEP
REEP
SHUT OFF THE DAMN ALARM!
WHAT'S THAT?
RED!
Fin.

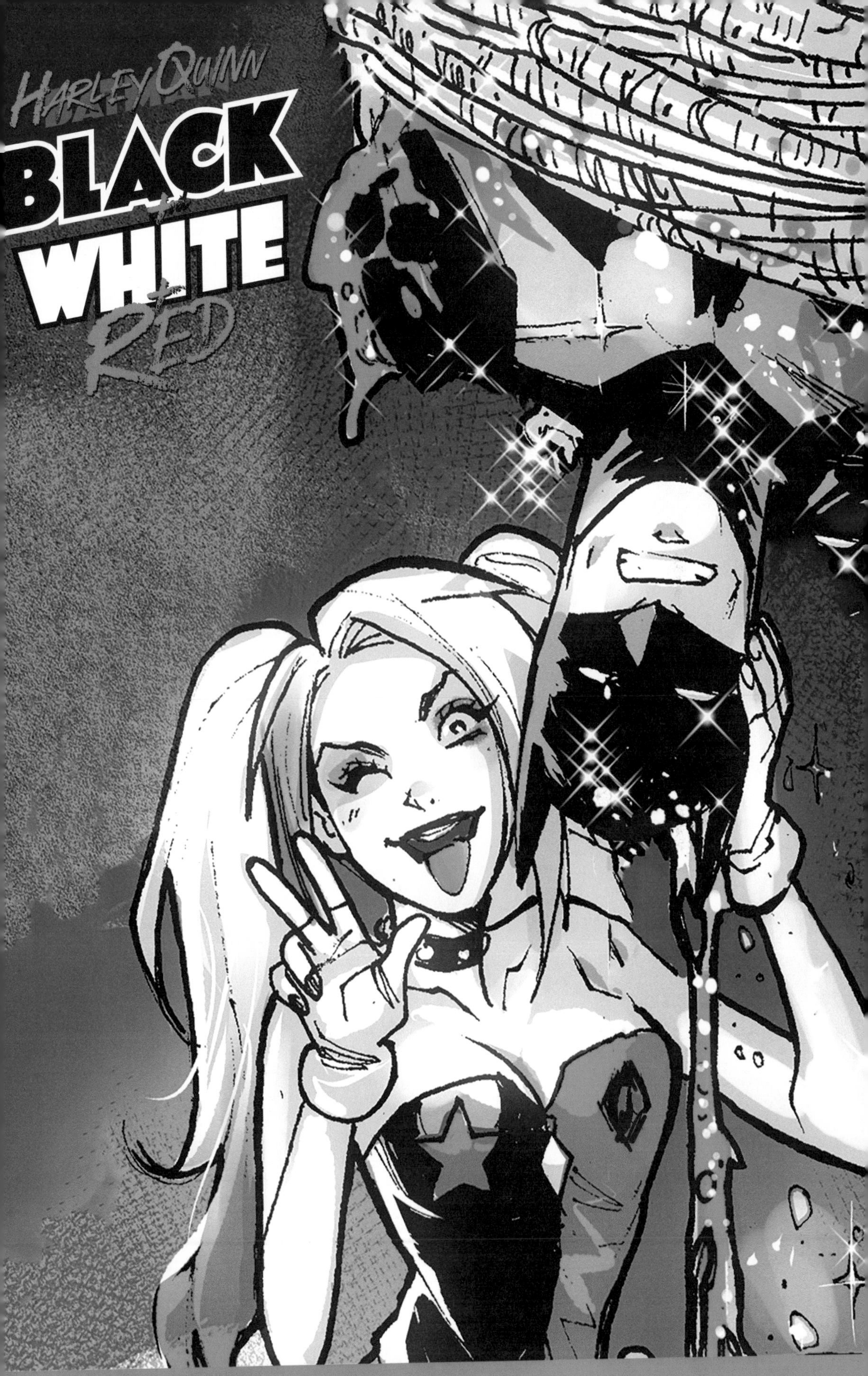
Harley Quinn
BLACK + WHITE + RED

CHAPTER TWO

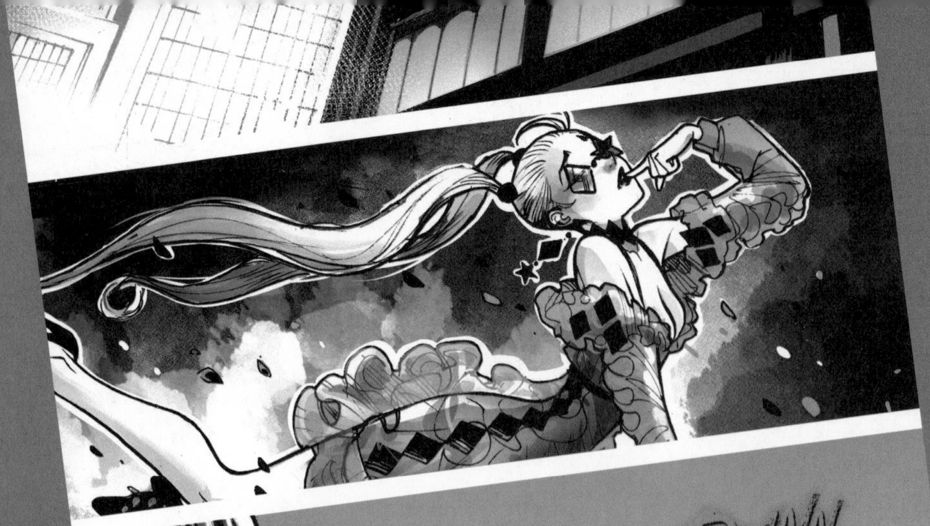

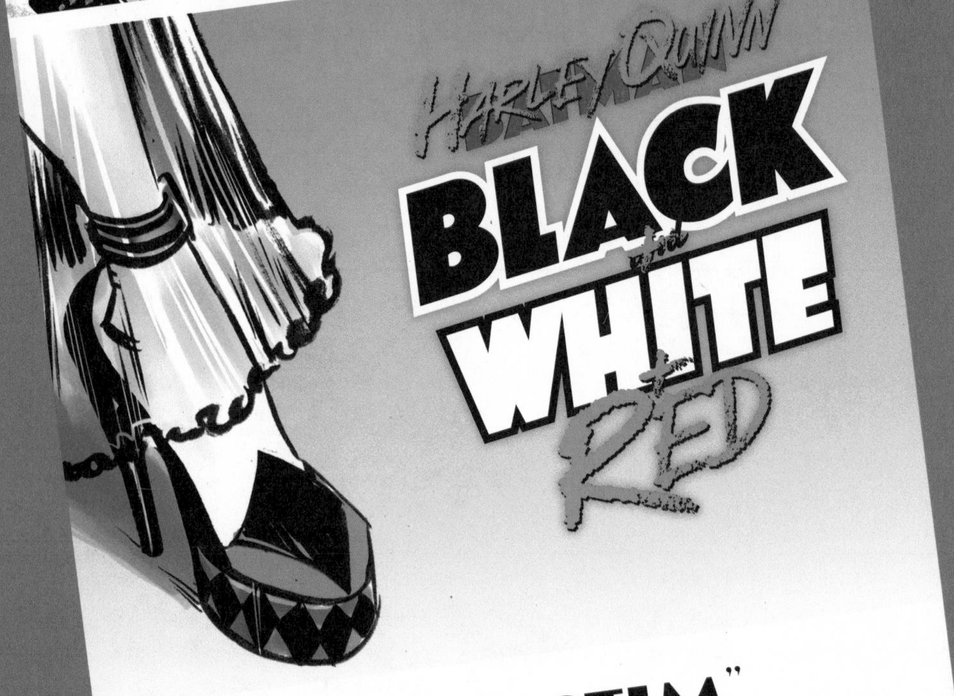
HARLEY QUINN
BLACK
WHITE
RED

"FASHION VICTIM"

WRITER & ARTIST **MIRKA ANDOLFO**
LETTERER **JOHN J. HILL**
EDITOR **MAGGIE HOWELL**

HARLEY QUINN CREATED BY PAUL DINI & BRUCE TIMM

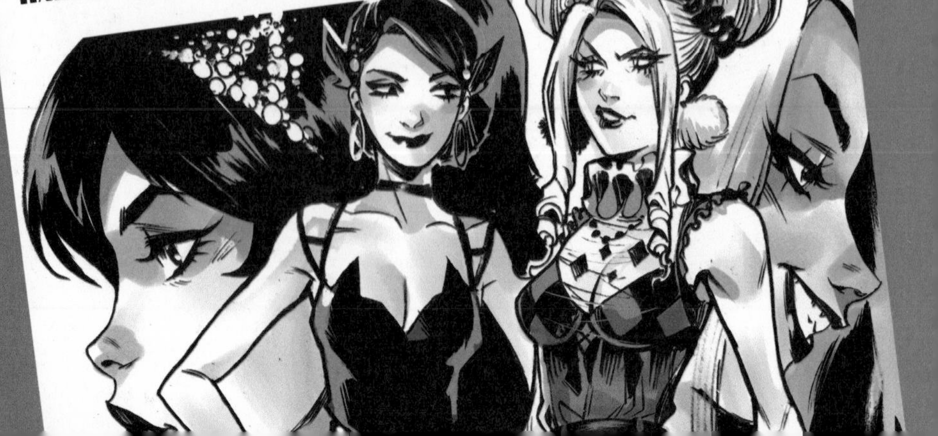

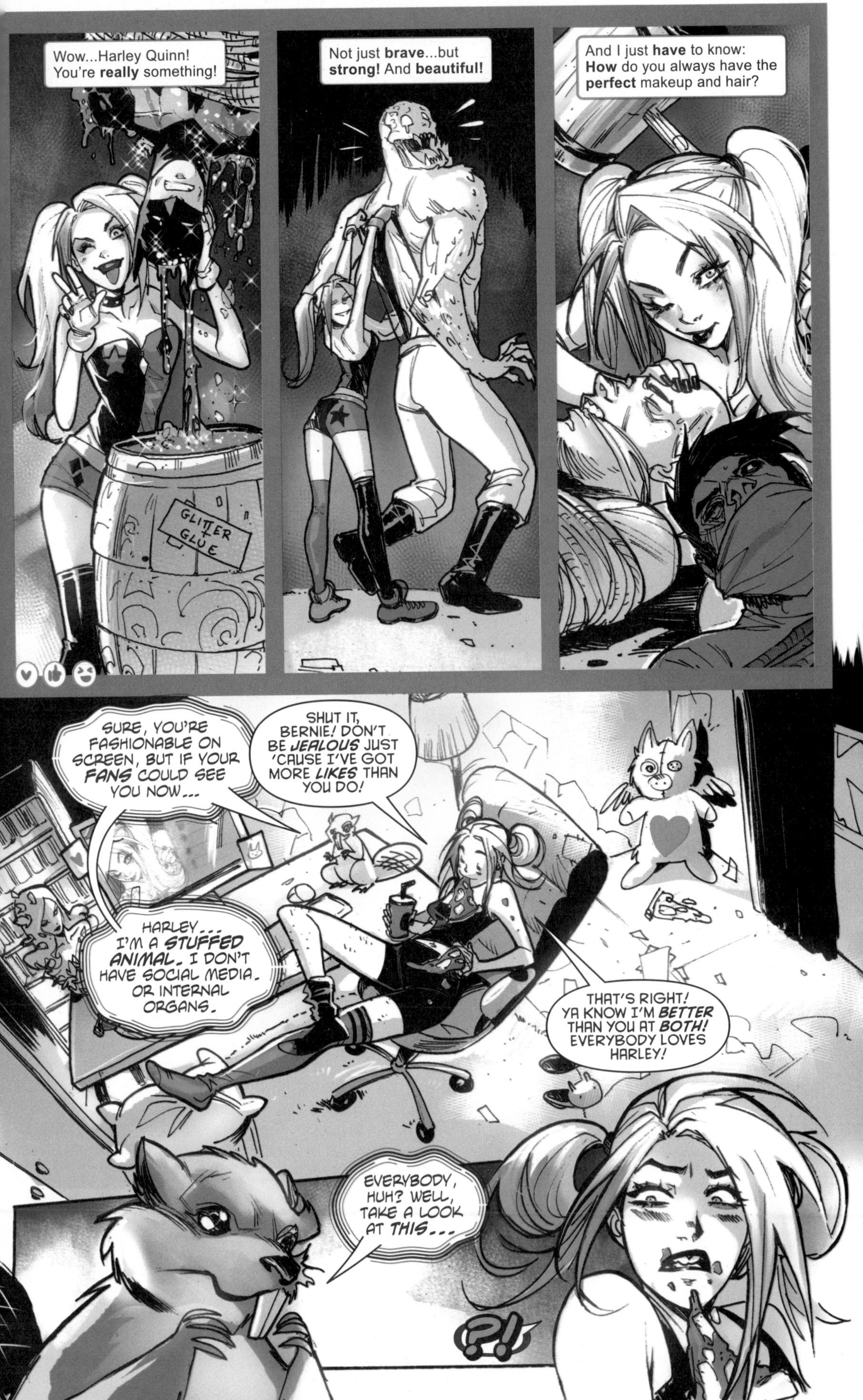
Wow...Harley Quinn! You're **really** something!
Not just **brave**...but **strong!** And **beautiful!**
And I just **have** to know: **How** do you always have the **perfect** makeup and hair?
GLITTER GLUE
SURE, YOU'RE FASHIONABLE ON SCREEN, BUT IF YOUR FANS COULD SEE YOU NOW...
SHUT IT, BERNIE! DON'T BE JEALOUS JUST 'CAUSE I'VE GOT MORE LIKES THAN YOU DO!
HARLEY... I'M A STUFFED ANIMAL. I DON'T HAVE SOCIAL MEDIA. OR INTERNAL ORGANS.
THAT'S RIGHT! YA KNOW I'M BETTER THAN YOU AT BOTH! EVERYBODY LOVES HARLEY!
EVERYBODY, HUH? WELL, TAKE A LOOK AT THIS...
?!

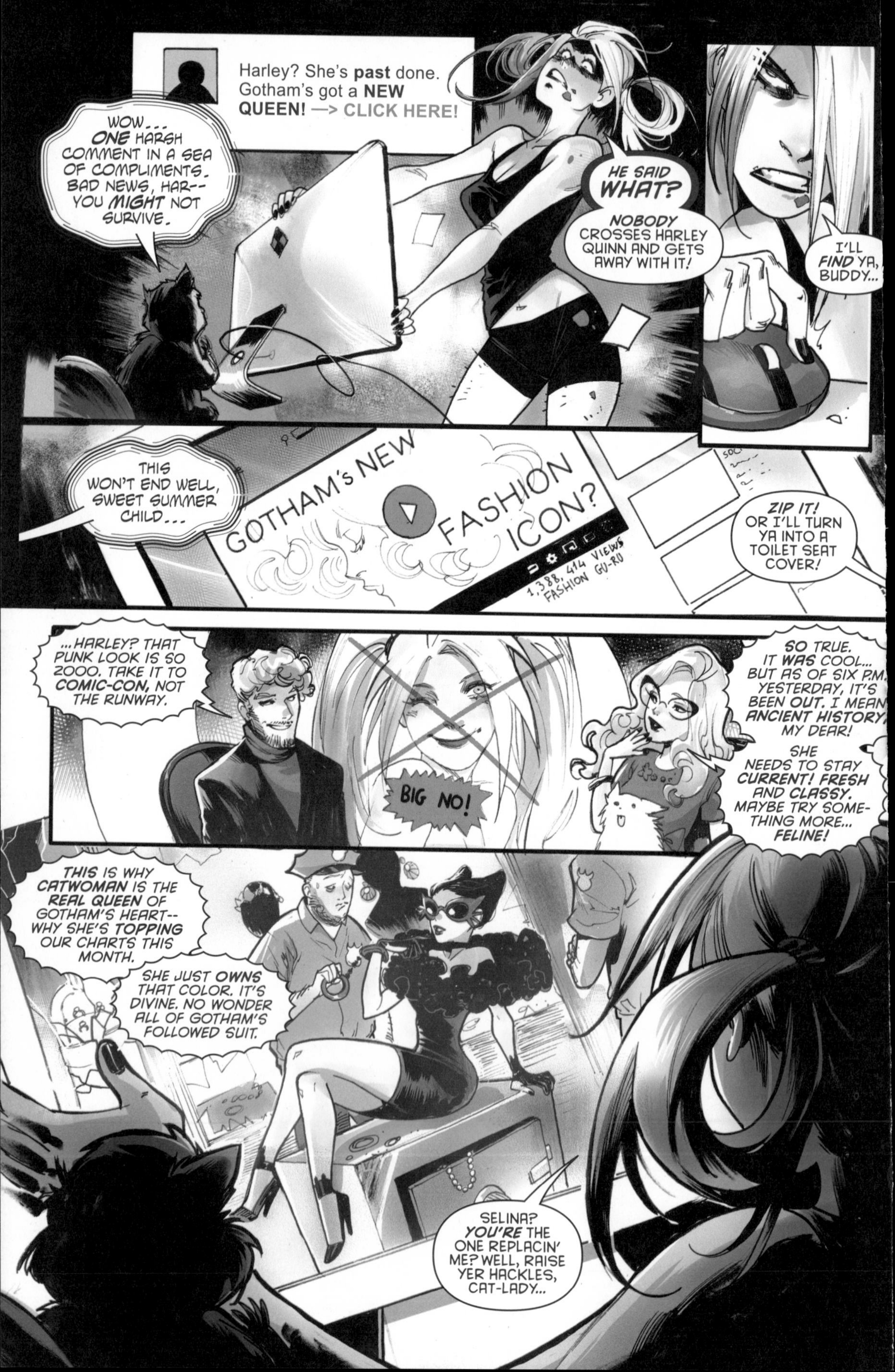

Harley? She's **past** done. Gotham's got a **NEW QUEEN!** —> **CLICK HERE!**
WOW... ONE HARSH COMMENT IN A SEA OF COMPLIMENTS. BAD NEWS, HAR-- YOU MIGHT NOT SURVIVE.
HE SAID WHAT?
NOBODY CROSSES HARLEY QUINN AND GETS AWAY WITH IT!
I'LL FIND YA, BUDDY...
THIS WON'T END WELL, SWEET SUMMER CHILD...
GOTHAM'S NEW FASHION ICON?
1,388,414 VIEWS
FASHION GU-RU
ZIP IT! OR I'LL TURN YA INTO A TOILET SEAT COVER!
...HARLEY? THAT PUNK LOOK IS SO 2000. TAKE IT TO COMIC-CON, NOT THE RUNWAY.
BIG NO!
SO TRUE. IT WAS COOL... BUT AS OF SIX P.M. YESTERDAY, IT'S BEEN OUT. I MEAN ANCIENT HISTORY, MY DEAR!
SHE NEEDS TO STAY CURRENT! FRESH AND CLASSY. MAYBE TRY SOME-THING MORE... FELINE!
THIS IS WHY CATWOMAN IS THE REAL QUEEN OF GOTHAM'S HEART-- WHY SHE'S TOPPING OUR CHARTS THIS MONTH.
SHE JUST OWNS THAT COLOR. IT'S DIVINE. NO WONDER ALL OF GOTHAM'S FOLLOWED SUIT.
SELINA? YOU'RE THE ONE REPLACIN' ME? WELL, RAISE YER HACKLES, CAT-LADY...

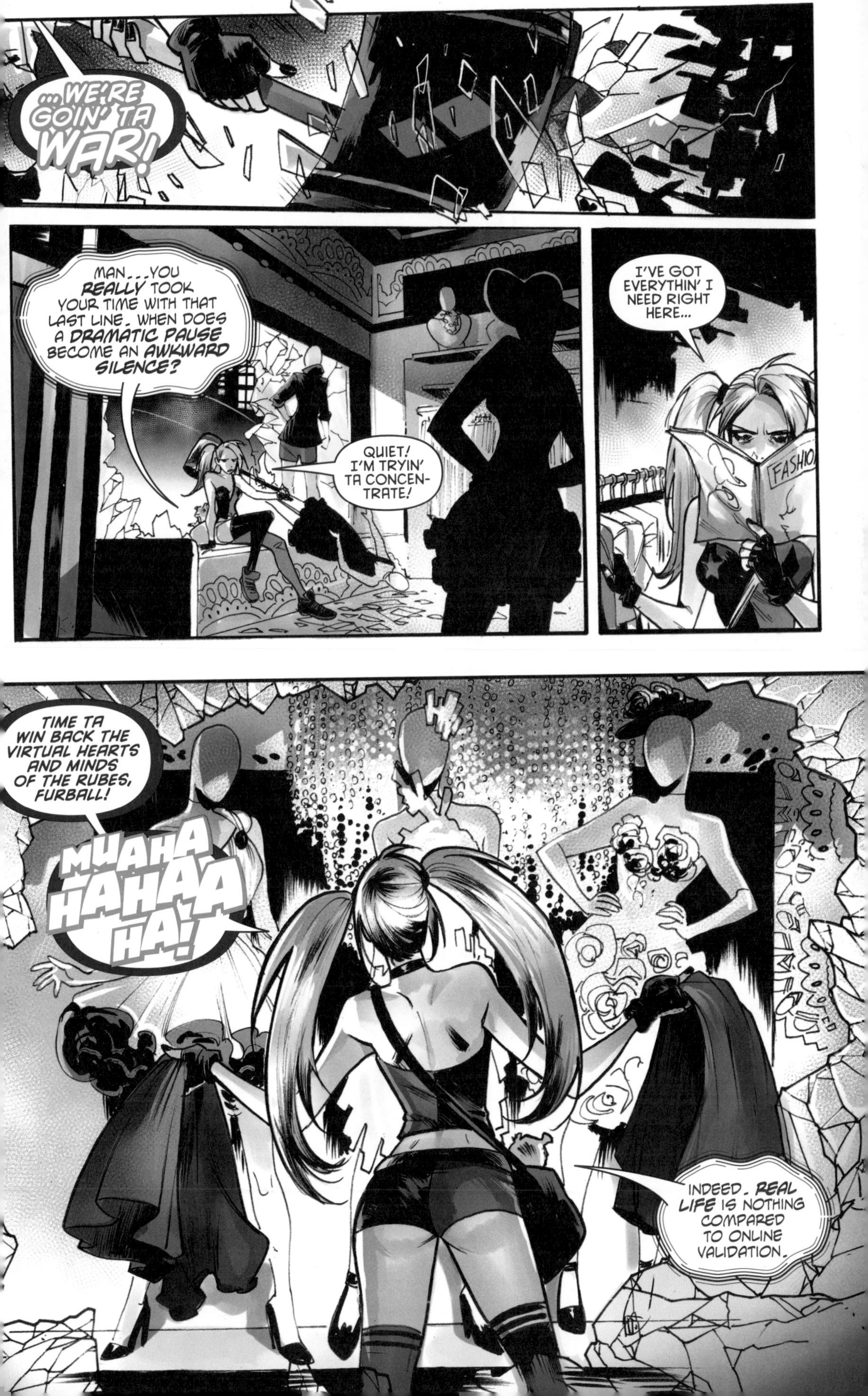
...WE'RE GOIN' TA WAR!
MAN...YOU REALLY TOOK YOUR TIME WITH THAT LAST LINE. WHEN DOES A DRAMATIC PAUSE BECOME AN AWKWARD SILENCE?
QUIET! I'M TRYIN' TA CONCENTRATE!
I'VE GOT EVERYTHIN' I NEED RIGHT HERE...
FASHIO
TIME TA WIN BACK THE VIRTUAL HEARTS AND MINDS OF THE RUBES, FURBALL!
MUAHA HAHAA HA!
INDEED. REAL LIFE IS NOTHING COMPARED TO ONLINE VALIDATION.

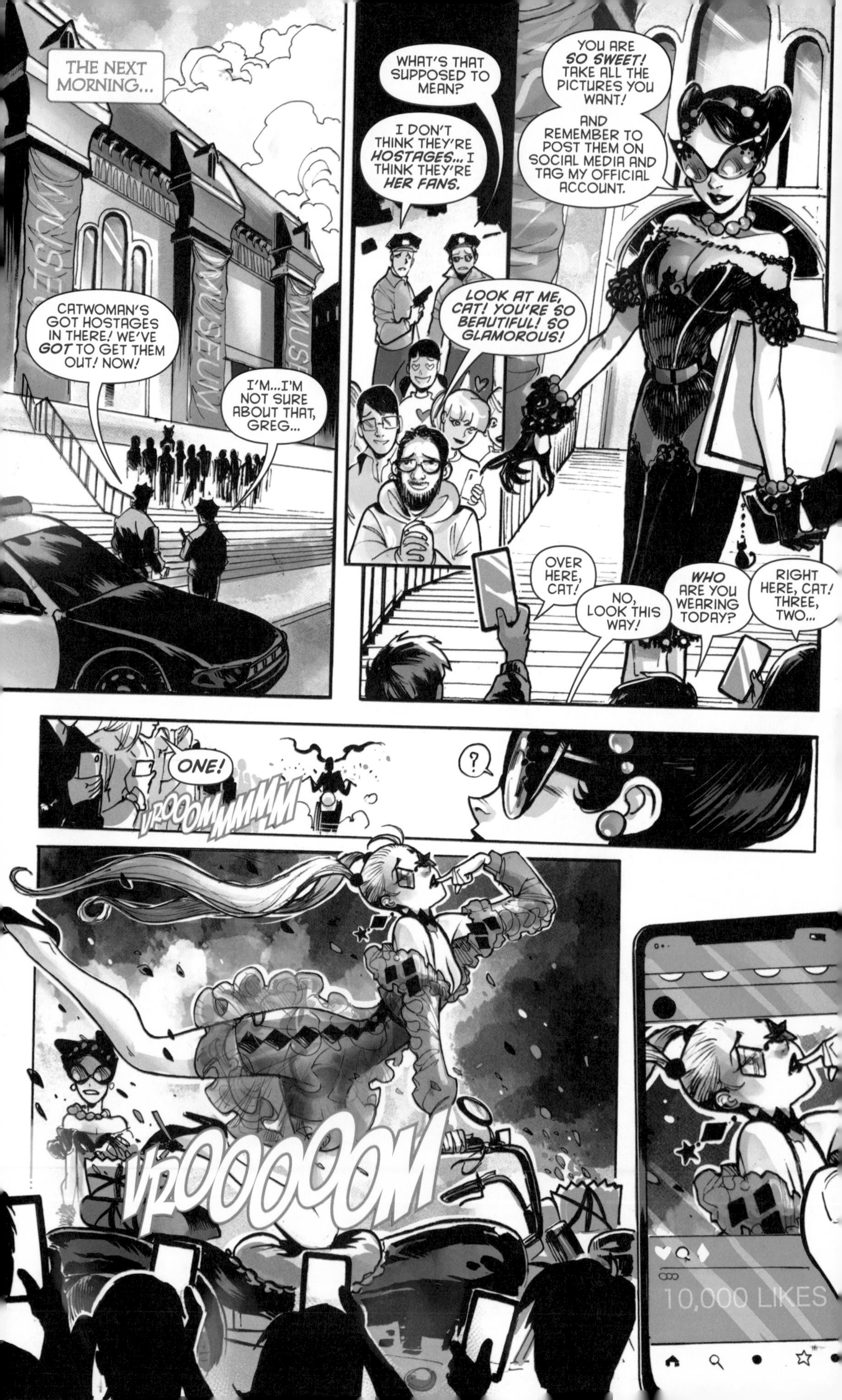
THE NEXT MORNING...
MUSEUM
MUSEUM
MUSEUM
CATWOMAN'S GOT HOSTAGES IN THERE! WE'VE GOT TO GET THEM OUT! NOW!
I'M...I'M NOT SURE ABOUT THAT, GREG...
WHAT'S THAT SUPPOSED TO MEAN?
I DON'T THINK THEY'RE HOSTAGES... I THINK THEY'RE HER FANS.
LOOK AT ME, CAT! YOU'RE SO BEAUTIFUL! SO GLAMOROUS!
YOU ARE SO SWEET! TAKE ALL THE PICTURES YOU WANT!
AND REMEMBER TO POST THEM ON SOCIAL MEDIA AND TAG MY OFFICIAL ACCOUNT.
OVER HERE, CAT!
NO, LOOK THIS WAY!
WHO ARE YOU WEARING TODAY?
RIGHT HERE, CAT! THREE, TWO...
ONE!
VROOOMMMMM
?
VROOOOOOM
10,000 LIKES

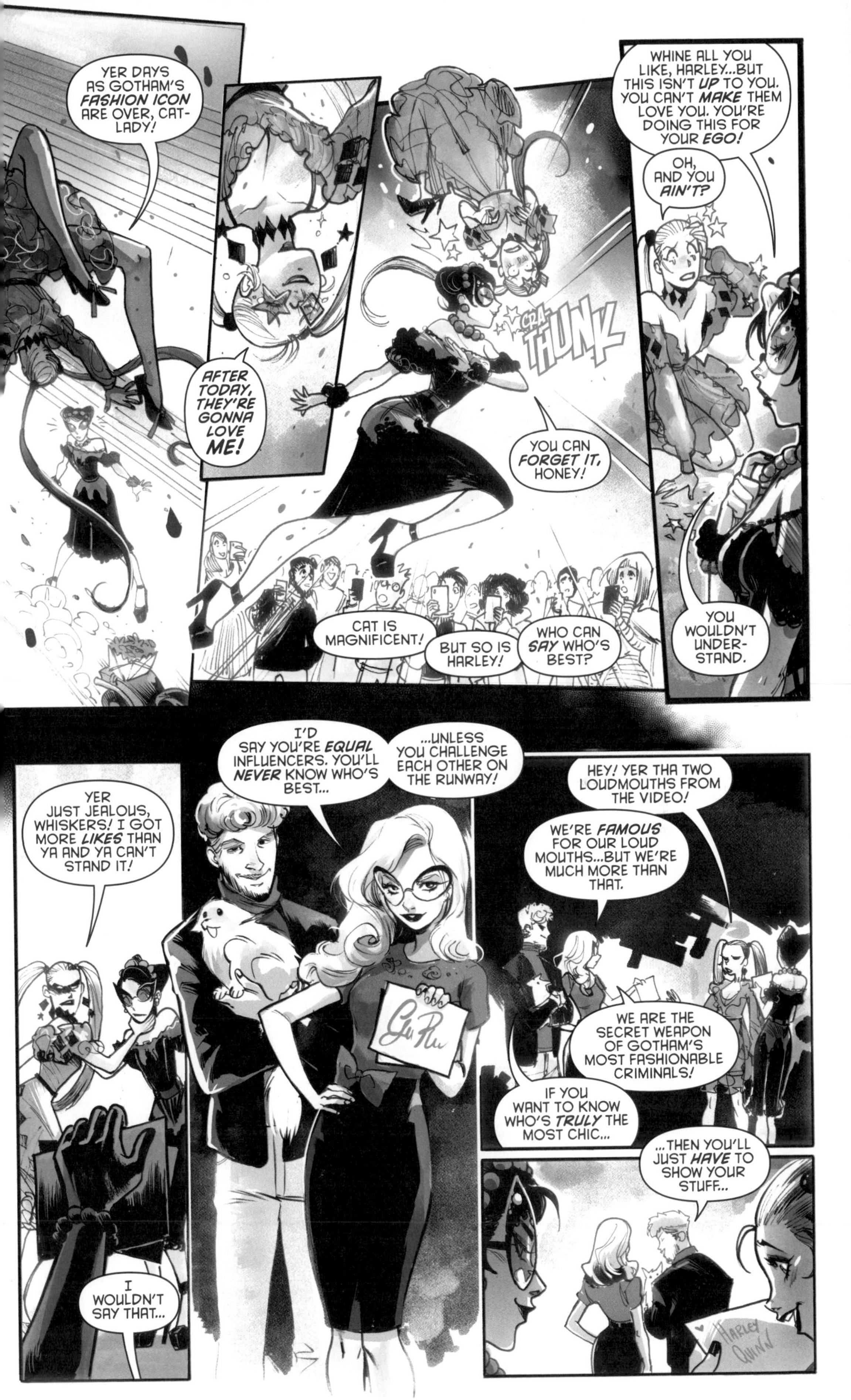
YER DAYS AS GOTHAM'S FASHION ICON ARE OVER, CAT-LADY!
AFTER TODAY, THEY'RE GONNA LOVE ME!
YOU CAN FORGET IT, HONEY!
CRA-THUNK
CAT IS MAGNIFICENT!
BUT SO IS HARLEY!
WHO CAN SAY WHO'S BEST?
WHINE ALL YOU LIKE, HARLEY...BUT THIS ISN'T UP TO YOU. YOU CAN'T MAKE THEM LOVE YOU. YOU'RE DOING THIS FOR YOUR EGO!
OH, AND YOU AIN'T?
YOU WOULDN'T UNDER-STAND.
YER JUST JEALOUS, WHISKERS! I GOT MORE LIKES THAN YA AND YA CAN'T STAND IT!
I WOULDN'T SAY THAT...
I'D SAY YOU'RE EQUAL INFLUENCERS. YOU'LL NEVER KNOW WHO'S BEST...
...UNLESS YOU CHALLENGE EACH OTHER ON THE RUNWAY!
HEY! YER THA TWO LOUDMOUTHS FROM THE VIDEO!
WE'RE FAMOUS FOR OUR LOUD MOUTHS...BUT WE'RE MUCH MORE THAN THAT.
WE ARE THE SECRET WEAPON OF GOTHAM'S MOST FASHIONABLE CRIMINALS!
IF YOU WANT TO KNOW WHO'S TRULY THE MOST CHIC...
...THEN YOU'LL JUST HAVE TO SHOW YOUR STUFF...
HARLEY QUINN

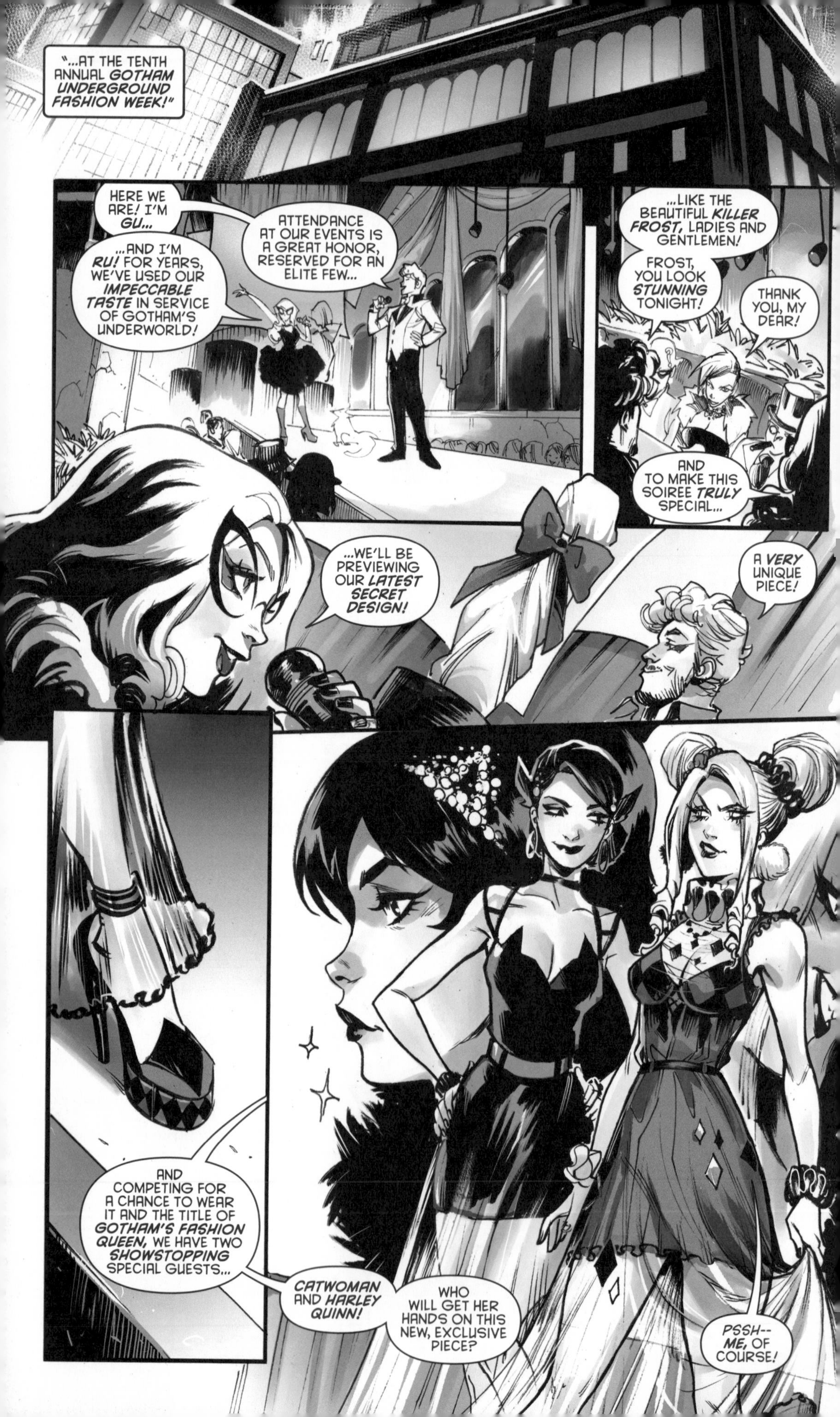
"...AT THE TENTH ANNUAL GOTHAM UNDERGROUND FASHION WEEK!"
HERE WE ARE! I'M GU...
...AND I'M RU! FOR YEARS, WE'VE USED OUR IMPECCABLE TASTE IN SERVICE OF GOTHAM'S UNDERWORLD!
ATTENDANCE AT OUR EVENTS IS A GREAT HONOR, RESERVED FOR AN ELITE FEW...
...LIKE THE BEAUTIFUL KILLER FROST, LADIES AND GENTLEMEN!
FROST, YOU LOOK STUNNING TONIGHT!
THANK YOU, MY DEAR!
AND TO MAKE THIS SOIREE TRULY SPECIAL...
...WE'LL BE PREVIEWING OUR LATEST SECRET DESIGN!
A VERY UNIQUE PIECE!
AND COMPETING FOR A CHANCE TO WEAR IT AND THE TITLE OF GOTHAM'S FASHION QUEEN, WE HAVE TWO SHOWSTOPPING SPECIAL GUESTS...
CATWOMAN AND HARLEY QUINN!
WHO WILL GET HER HANDS ON THIS NEW, EXCLUSIVE PIECE?
PSSH-- ME, OF COURSE!

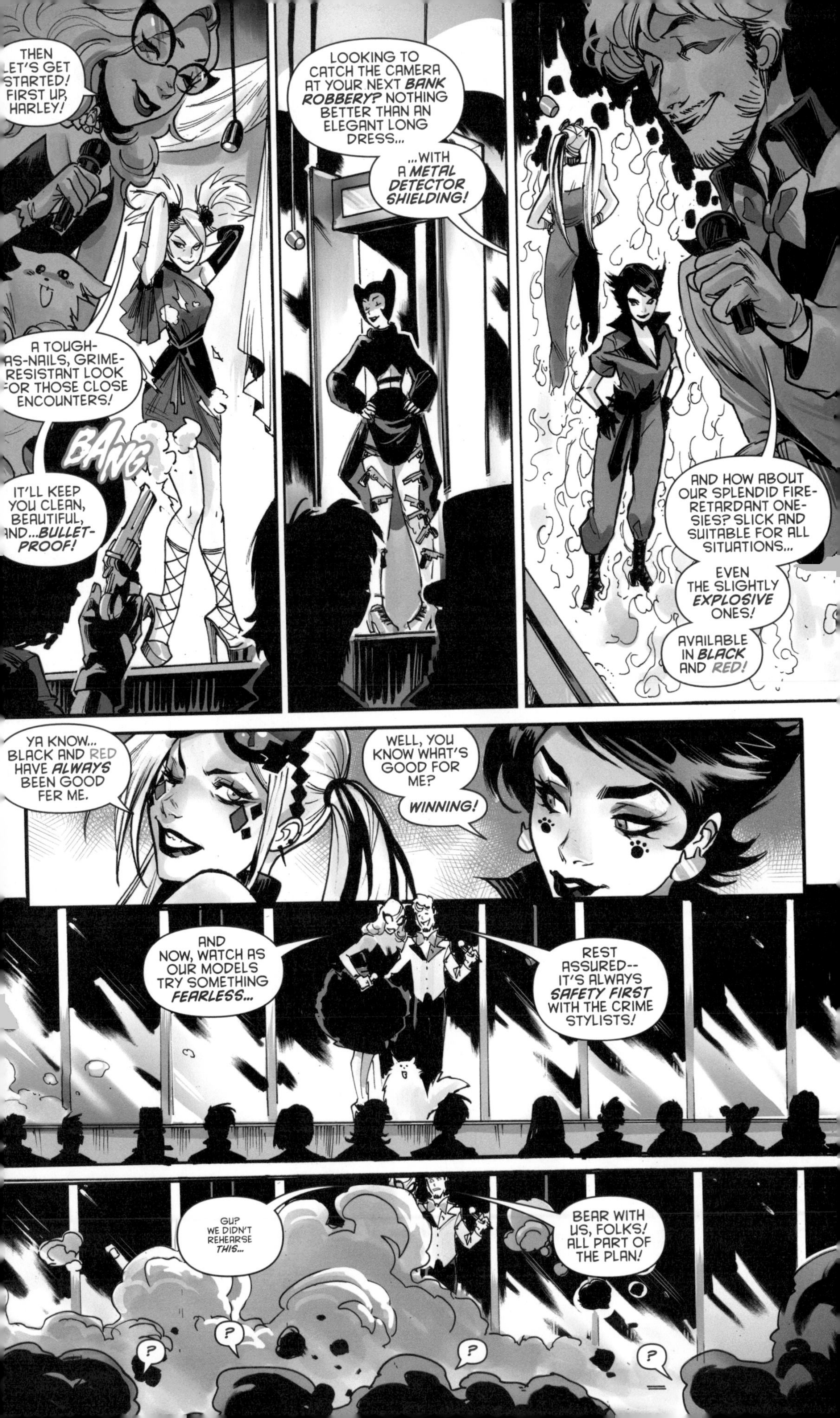

THEN LET'S GET STARTED! FIRST UP, HARLEY!
A TOUGH-AS-NAILS, GRIME-RESISTANT LOOK FOR THOSE CLOSE ENCOUNTERS!
BANG
IT'LL KEEP YOU CLEAN, BEAUTIFUL, AND...BULLET-PROOF!
LOOKING TO CATCH THE CAMERA AT YOUR NEXT BANK ROBBERY? NOTHING BETTER THAN AN ELEGANT LONG DRESS...
...WITH A METAL DETECTOR SHIELDING!
AND HOW ABOUT OUR SPLENDID FIRE-RETARDANT ONE-SIES? SLICK AND SUITABLE FOR ALL SITUATIONS...
EVEN THE SLIGHTLY EXPLOSIVE ONES!
AVAILABLE IN BLACK AND RED!
YA KNOW... BLACK AND RED HAVE ALWAYS BEEN GOOD FER ME.
WELL, YOU KNOW WHAT'S GOOD FOR ME?
WINNING!
AND NOW, WATCH AS OUR MODELS TRY SOMETHING FEARLESS...
REST ASSURED-- IT'S ALWAYS SAFETY FIRST WITH THE CRIME STYLISTS!
GU? WE DIDN'T REHEARSE THIS...
BEAR WITH US, FOLKS! ALL PART OF THE PLAN!
?
?
?
?

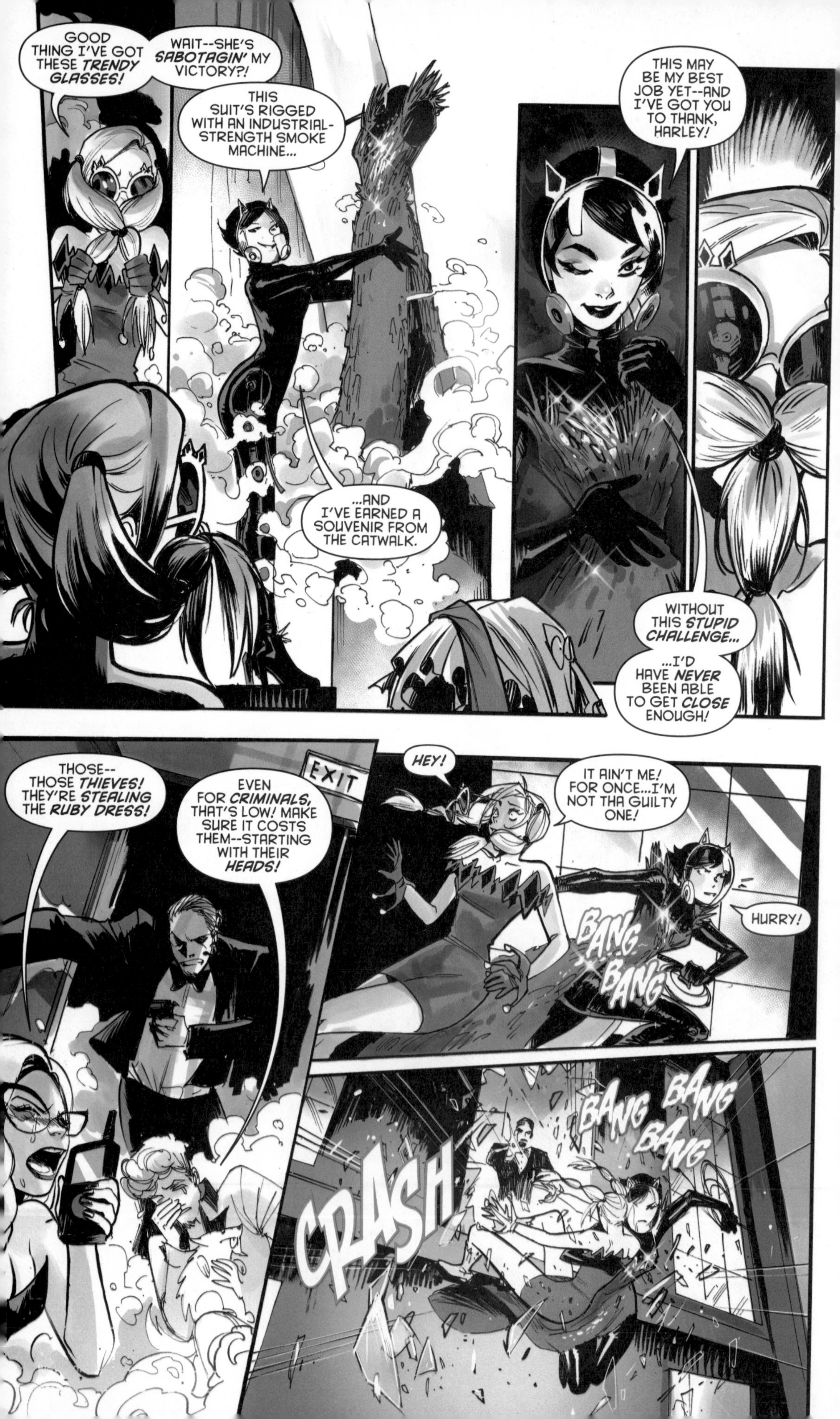

GOOD THING I'VE GOT THESE TRENDY GLASSES!
WAIT--SHE'S SABOTAGIN' MY VICTORY?!
THIS SUIT'S RIGGED WITH AN INDUSTRIAL-STRENGTH SMOKE MACHINE...
...AND I'VE EARNED A SOUVENIR FROM THE CATWALK.
THIS MAY BE MY BEST JOB YET--AND I'VE GOT YOU TO THANK, HARLEY!
WITHOUT THIS STUPID CHALLENGE...
...I'D HAVE NEVER BEEN ABLE TO GET CLOSE ENOUGH!
THOSE--THOSE THIEVES! THEY'RE STEALING THE RUBY DRESS!
EXIT
EVEN FOR CRIMINALS, THAT'S LOW! MAKE SURE IT COSTS THEM--STARTING WITH THEIR HEADS!
HEY!
IT AIN'T ME! FOR ONCE...I'M NOT THA GUILTY ONE!
HURRY!
BANG BANG
BANG BANG BANG
CRASH

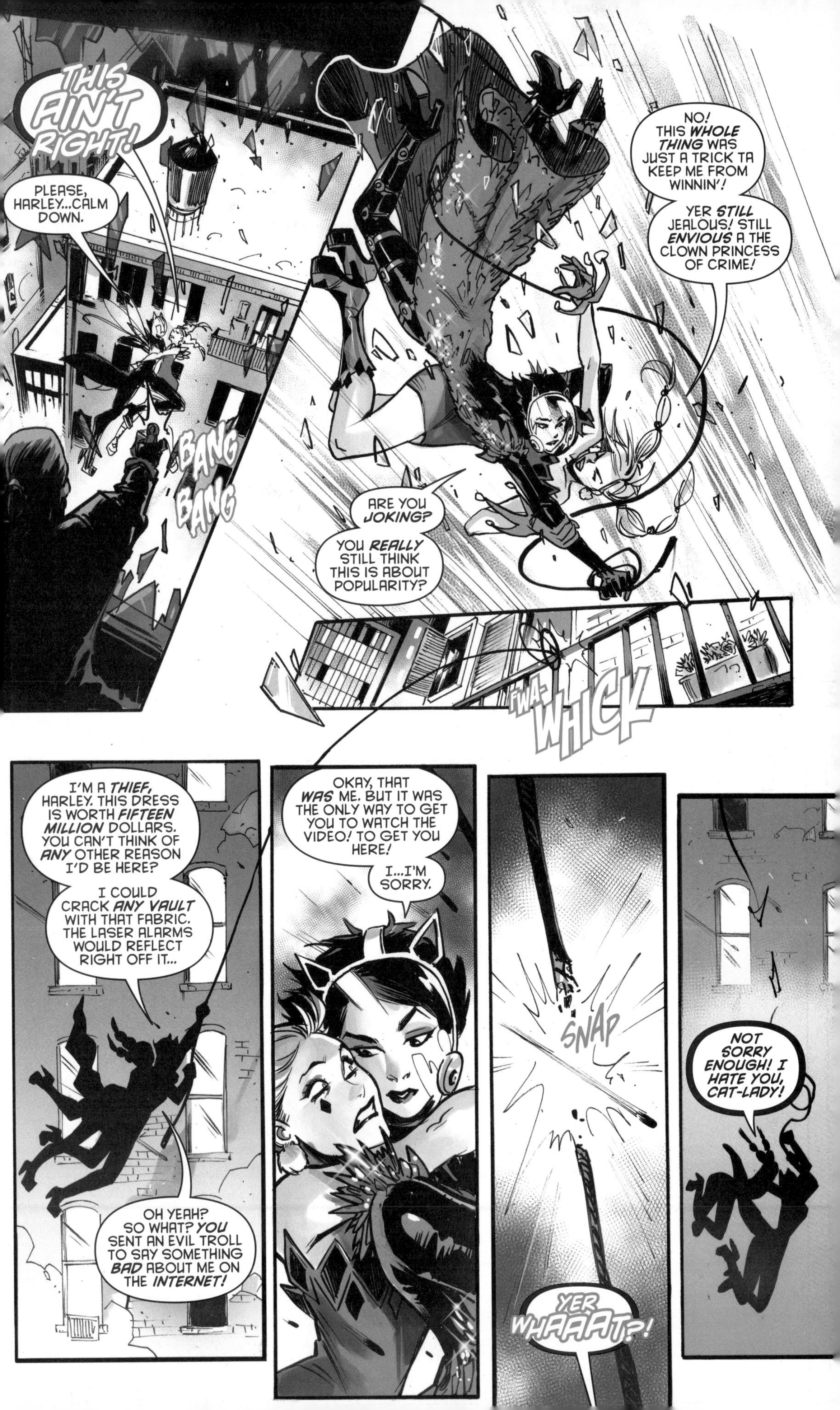
THIS AIN'T RIGHT!
PLEASE, HARLEY...CALM DOWN.
NO! THIS WHOLE THING WAS JUST A TRICK TA KEEP ME FROM WINNIN'!
YER STILL JEALOUS! STILL ENVIOUS A THE CLOWN PRINCESS OF CRIME!
BANG
BANG
ARE YOU JOKING?
YOU REALLY STILL THINK THIS IS ABOUT POPULARITY?
FWA-WHICK
I'M A THIEF, HARLEY. THIS DRESS IS WORTH FIFTEEN MILLION DOLLARS. YOU CAN'T THINK OF ANY OTHER REASON I'D BE HERE?
I COULD CRACK ANY VAULT WITH THAT FABRIC. THE LASER ALARMS WOULD REFLECT RIGHT OFF IT...
OH YEAH? SO WHAT? YOU SENT AN EVIL TROLL TO SAY SOMETHING BAD ABOUT ME ON THE INTERNET!
OKAY, THAT WAS ME. BUT IT WAS THE ONLY WAY TO GET YOU TO WATCH THE VIDEO! TO GET YOU HERE!
I...I'M SORRY.
SNAP
YER WHAAAT?!
NOT SORRY ENOUGH! I HATE YOU, CAT-LADY!

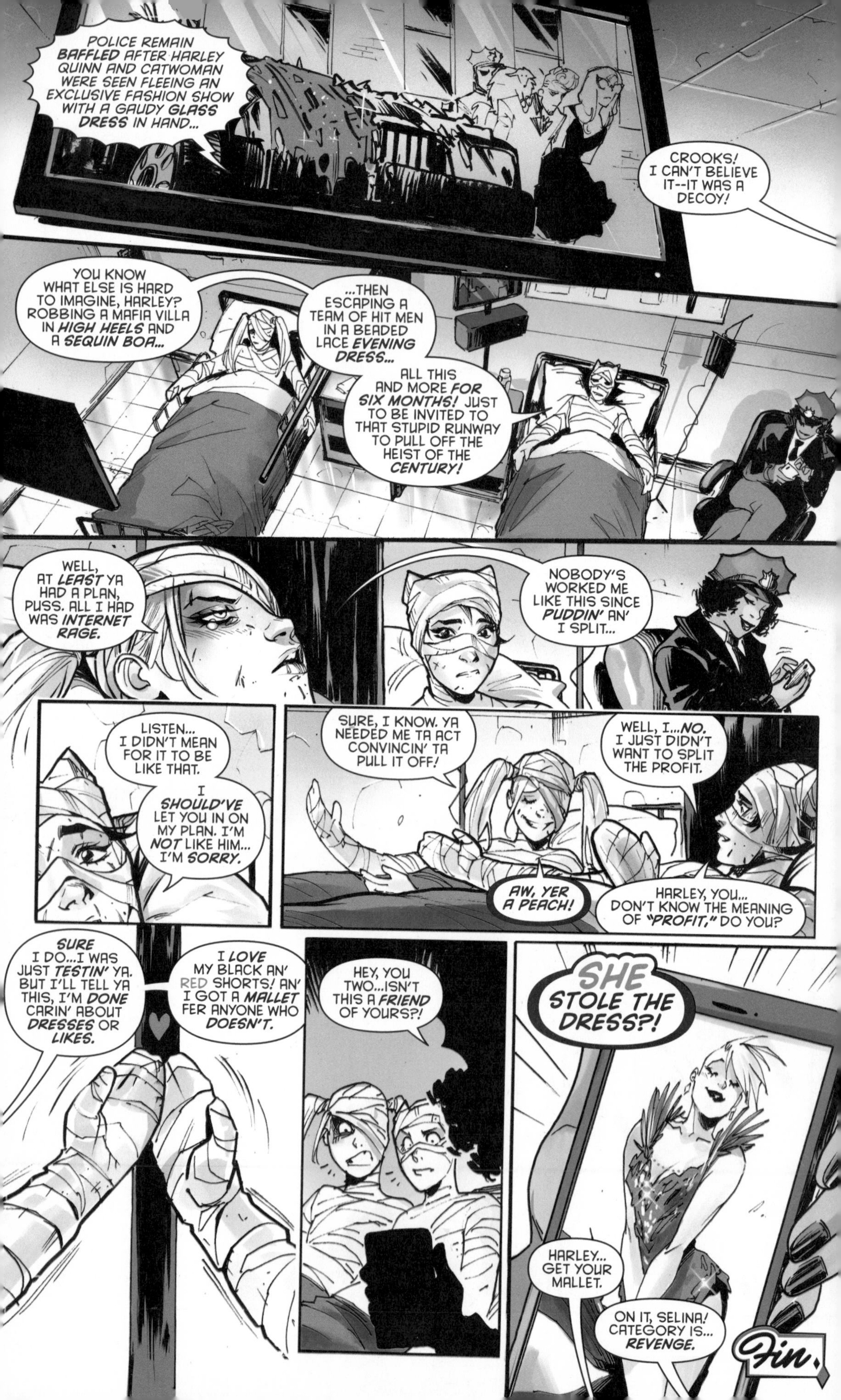
POLICE REMAIN BAFFLED AFTER HARLEY QUINN AND CATWOMAN WERE SEEN FLEEING AN EXCLUSIVE FASHION SHOW WITH A GAUDY GLASS DRESS IN HAND...
CROOKS! I CAN'T BELIEVE IT--IT WAS A DECOY!
YOU KNOW WHAT ELSE IS HARD TO IMAGINE, HARLEY? ROBBING A MAFIA VILLA IN HIGH HEELS AND A SEQUIN BOA...
...THEN ESCAPING A TEAM OF HIT MEN IN A BEADED LACE EVENING DRESS...
ALL THIS AND MORE FOR SIX MONTHS! JUST TO BE INVITED TO THAT STUPID RUNWAY TO PULL OFF THE HEIST OF THE CENTURY!
WELL, AT LEAST YA HAD A PLAN, PUSS. ALL I HAD WAS INTERNET RAGE.
NOBODY'S WORKED ME LIKE THIS SINCE PUDDIN' AN' I SPLIT...
LISTEN... I DIDN'T MEAN FOR IT TO BE LIKE THAT.
I SHOULD'VE LET YOU IN ON MY PLAN. I'M NOT LIKE HIM... I'M SORRY.
SURE, I KNOW. YA NEEDED ME TA ACT CONVINCIN' TA PULL IT OFF!
WELL, I...NO. I JUST DIDN'T WANT TO SPLIT THE PROFIT.
AW, YER A PEACH!
HARLEY, YOU... DON'T KNOW THE MEANING OF "PROFIT," DO YOU?
SURE I DO...I WAS JUST TESTIN' YA. BUT I'LL TELL YA THIS, I'M DONE CARIN' ABOUT DRESSES OR LIKES.
I LOVE MY BLACK AN' RED SHORTS! AN' I GOT A MALLET FER ANYONE WHO DOESN'T.
HEY, YOU TWO...ISN'T THIS A FRIEND OF YOURS?!
SHE STOLE THE DRESS?!
HARLEY... GET YOUR MALLET.
ON IT, SELINA! CATEGORY IS... REVENGE.
Fin.

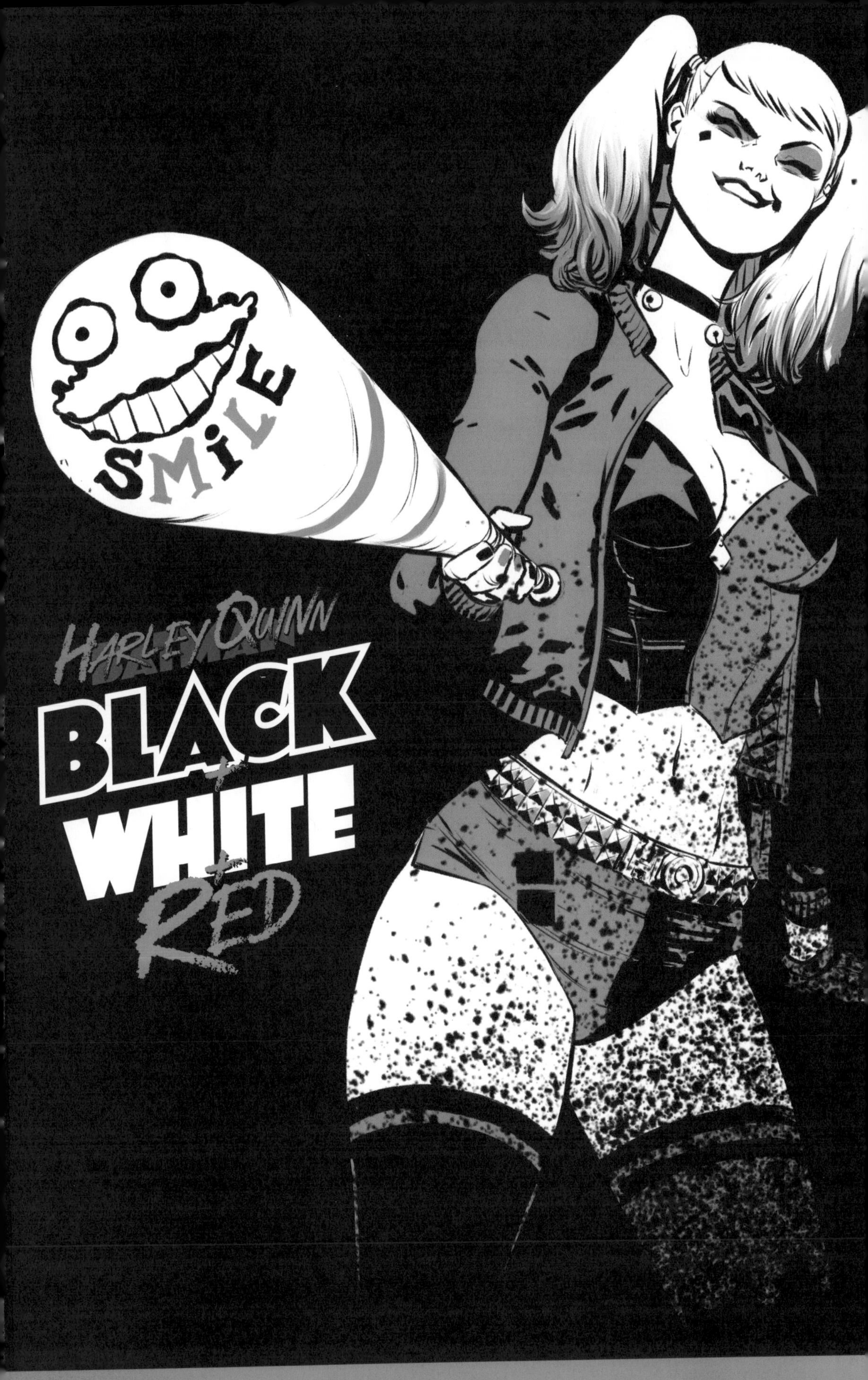
SMILE
HARLEY QUINN
BLACK + WHITE + RED

CHAPTER THREE

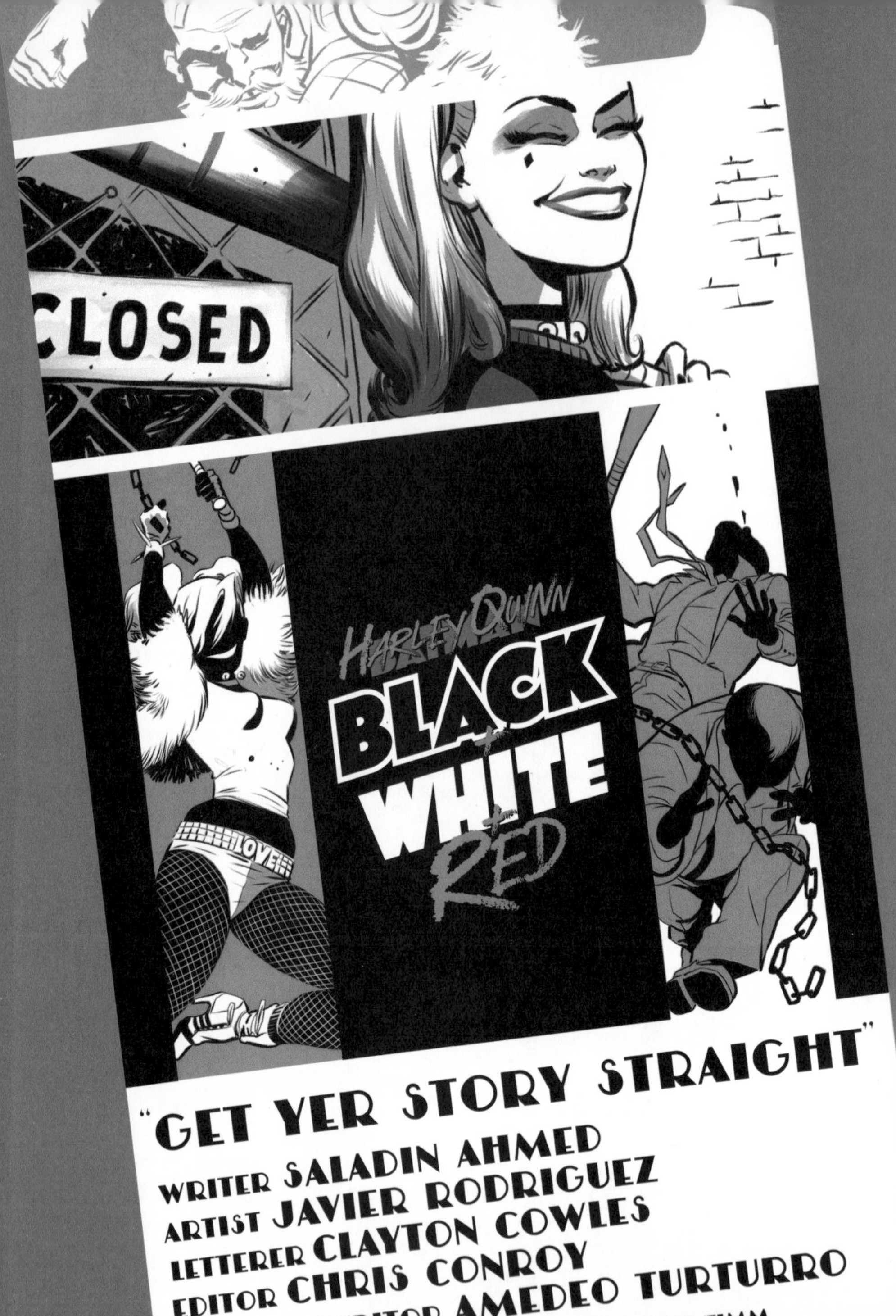
CLOSED
HARLEY QUINN
BLACK + WHITE + RED
LOVE

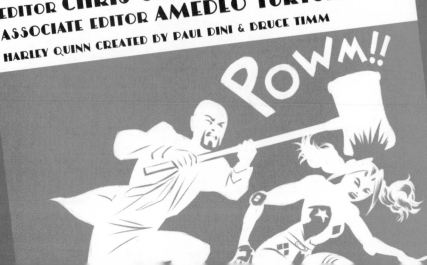

"GET YER STORY STRAIGHT"

WRITER SALADIN AHMED
ARTIST JAVIER RODRIGUEZ
LETTERER CLAYTON COWLES
EDITOR CHRIS CONROY
ASSOCIATE EDITOR AMEDEO TURTURRO

HARLEY QUINN CREATED BY PAUL DINI & BRUCE TIMM

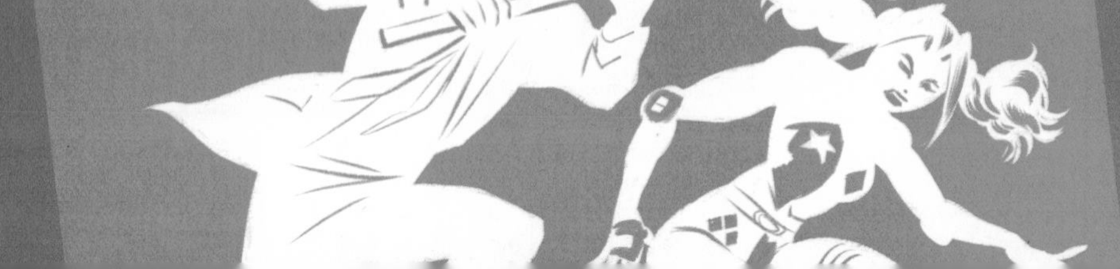
POWM!!

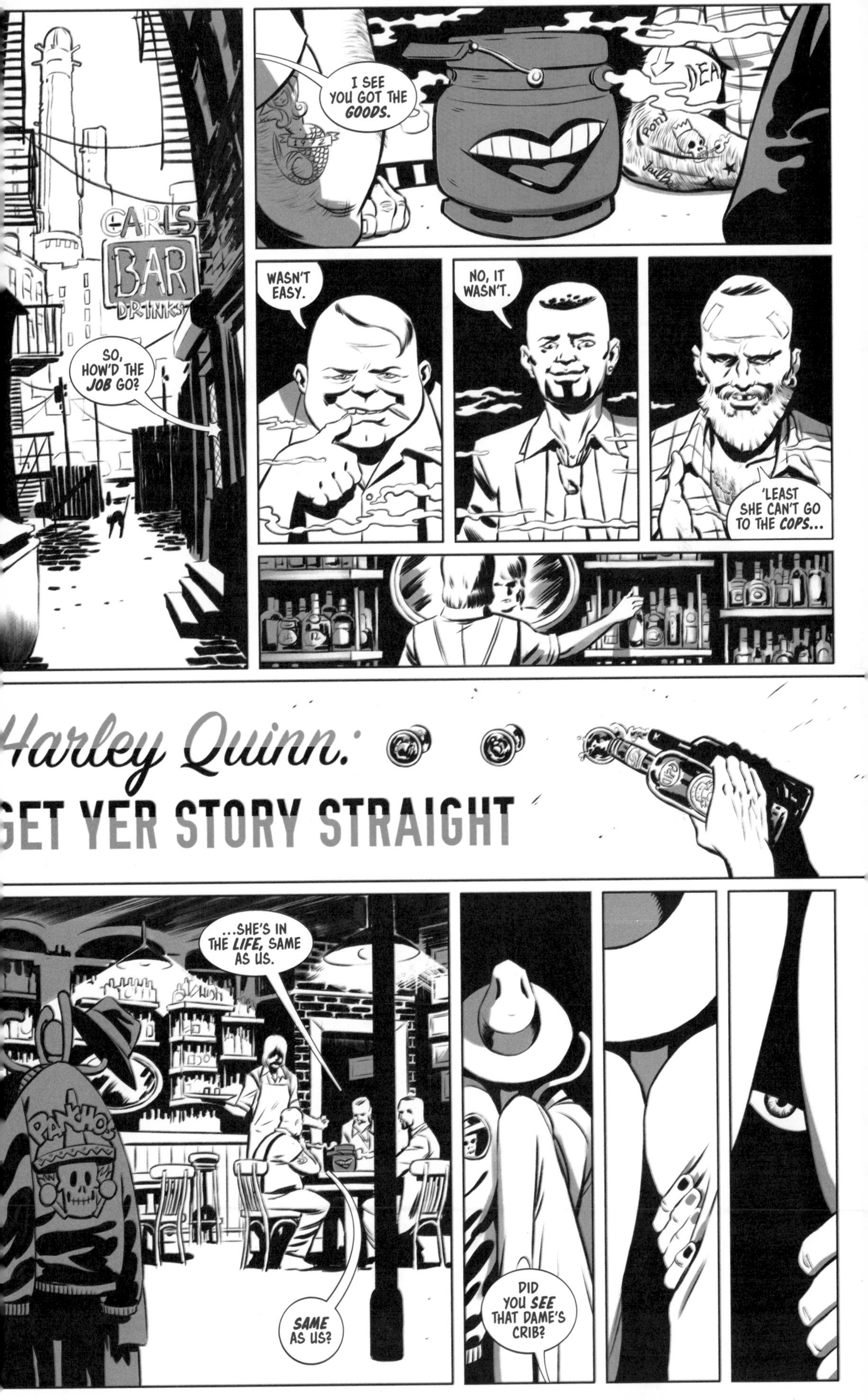
CARLS
BAR
DRINKS
SO, HOW'D THE *JOB* GO?
I SEE YOU GOT THE *GOODS.*
WASN'T EASY.
NO, IT WASN'T.
'LEAST SHE CAN'T GO TO THE *COPS*...
Harley Quinn:
GET YER STORY STRAIGHT
...SHE'S IN THE *LIFE,* SAME AS US.
PANCHO'S
SAME AS US?
DID YOU *SEE* THAT DAME'S CRIB?

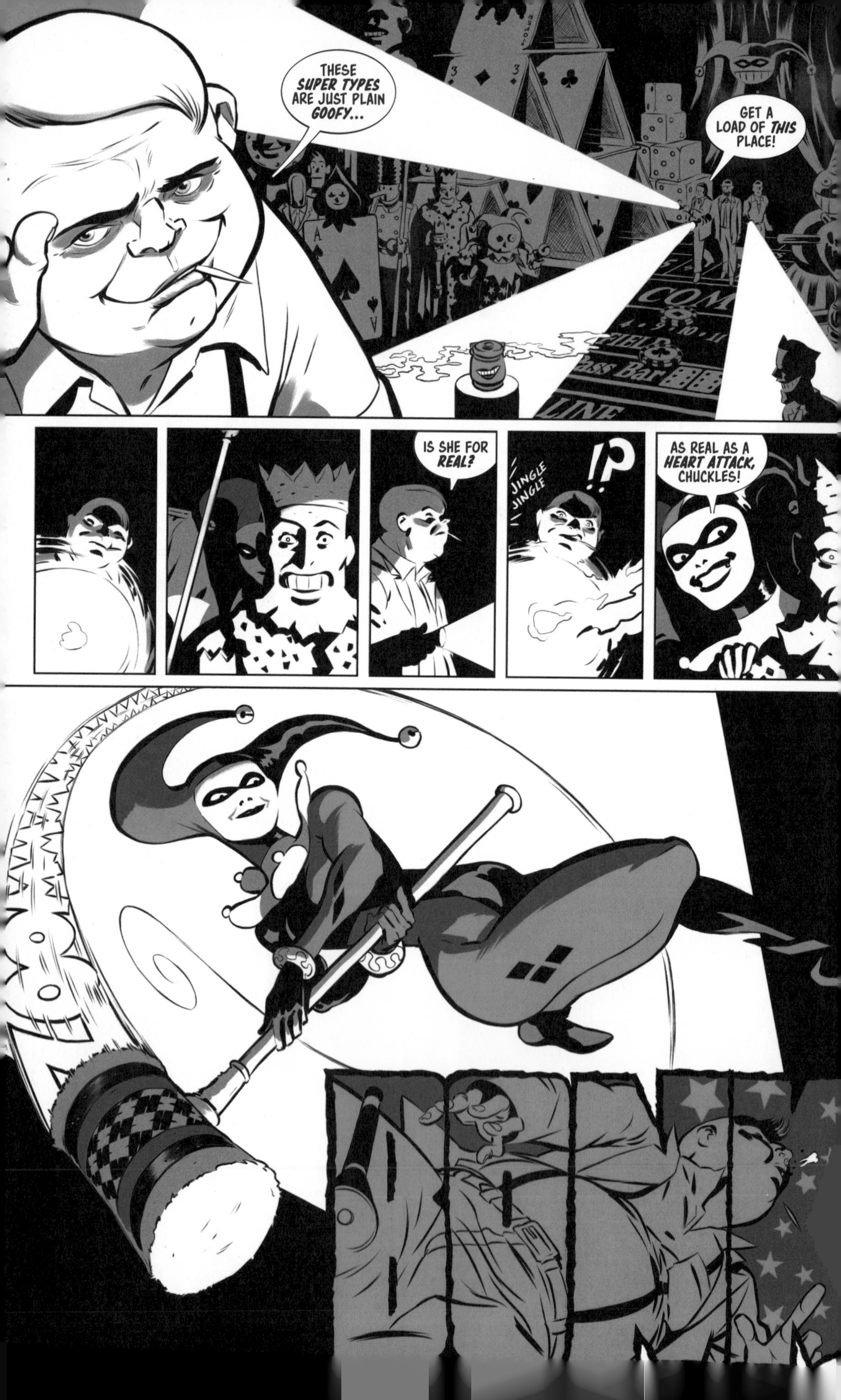

THESE SUPER TYPES ARE JUST PLAIN GOOFY...
GET A LOAD OF THIS PLACE!
IS SHE FOR REAL?
JINGLE JINGLE
!?
AS REAL AS A HEART ATTACK, CHUCKLES!

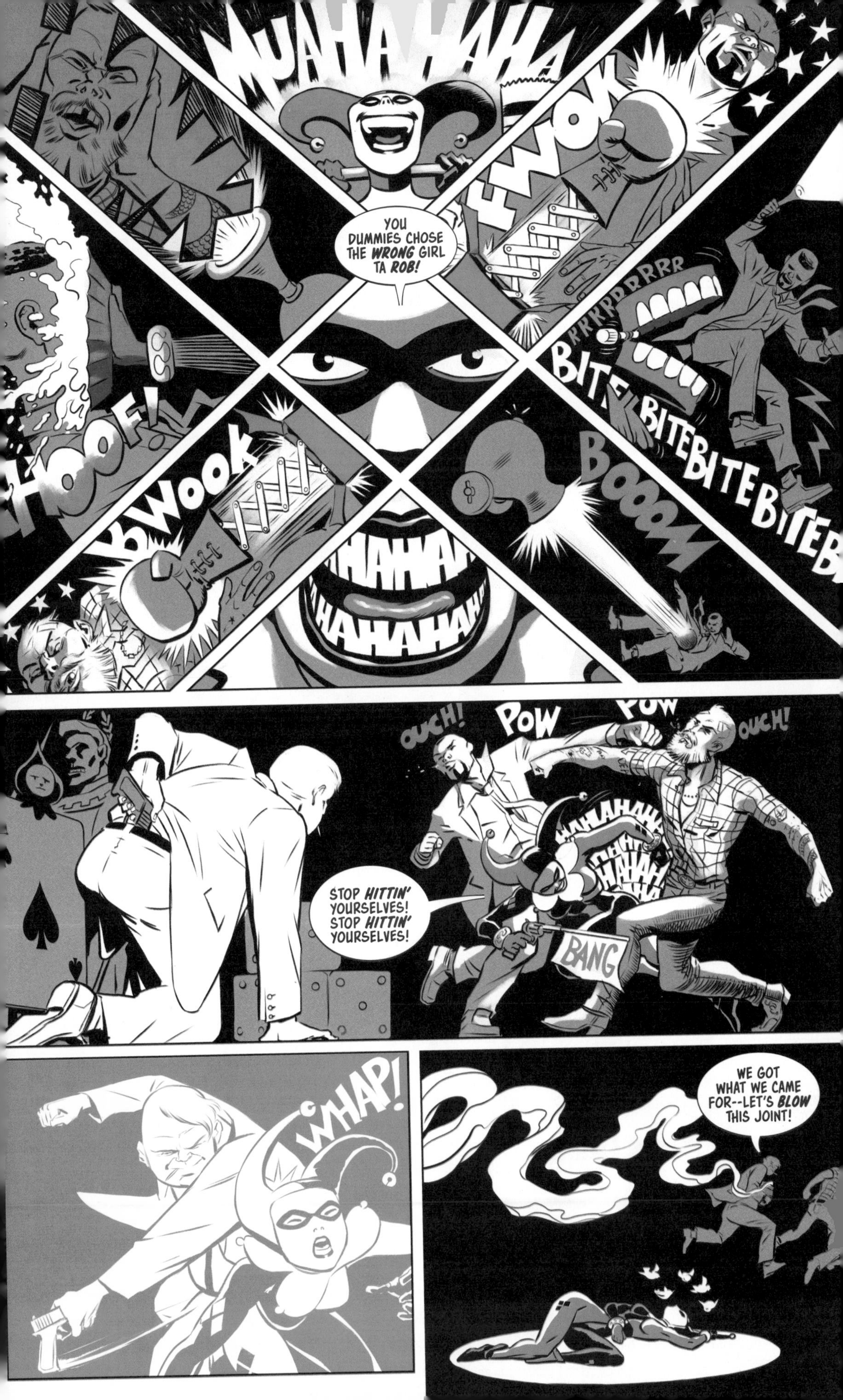
MUAHA HAHA
FWOK
YOU DUMMIES CHOSE THE *WRONG* GIRL TA *ROB!*
RRRRRRR
BITEBITEBITEB
BOOOOM
BWOOK
HOOF!
OUCH!
POW
POW
OUCH!
STOP *HITTIN'* YOURSELVES! STOP *HITTIN'* YOURSELVES!
BANG
WHAP!
WE GOT WHAT WE CAME FOR--LET'S *BLOW* THIS JOINT!

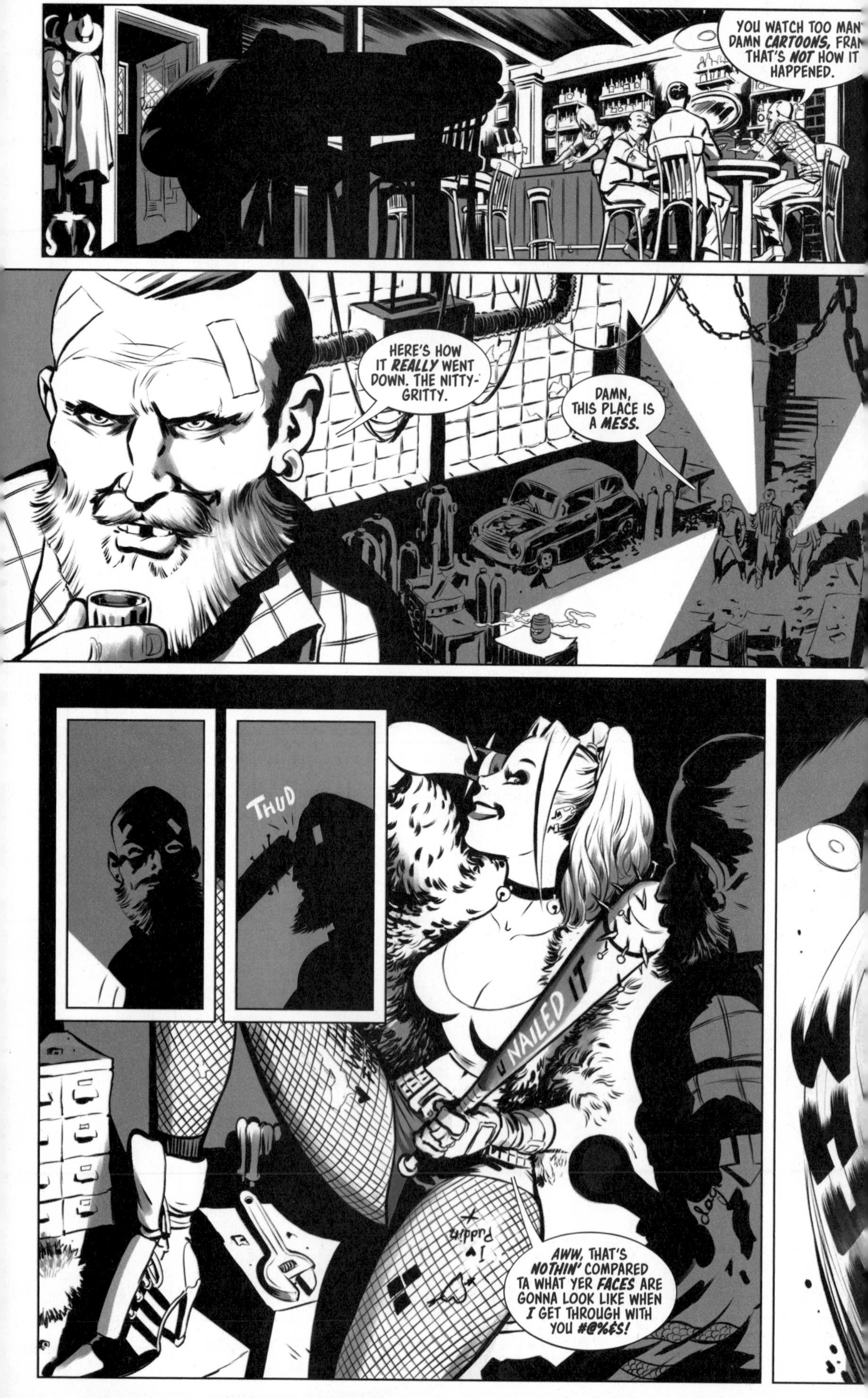
YOU WATCH TOO MANY DAMN CARTOONS, FRANK. THAT'S NOT HOW IT HAPPENED.
HERE'S HOW IT REALLY WENT DOWN. THE NITTY-GRITTY.
DAMN, THIS PLACE IS A MESS.
THUD
NAILED IT
I ♥ Puddin
AWW, THAT'S NOTHIN' COMPARED TA WHAT YER FACES ARE GONNA LOOK LIKE WHEN I GET THROUGH WITH YOU #@%£$!

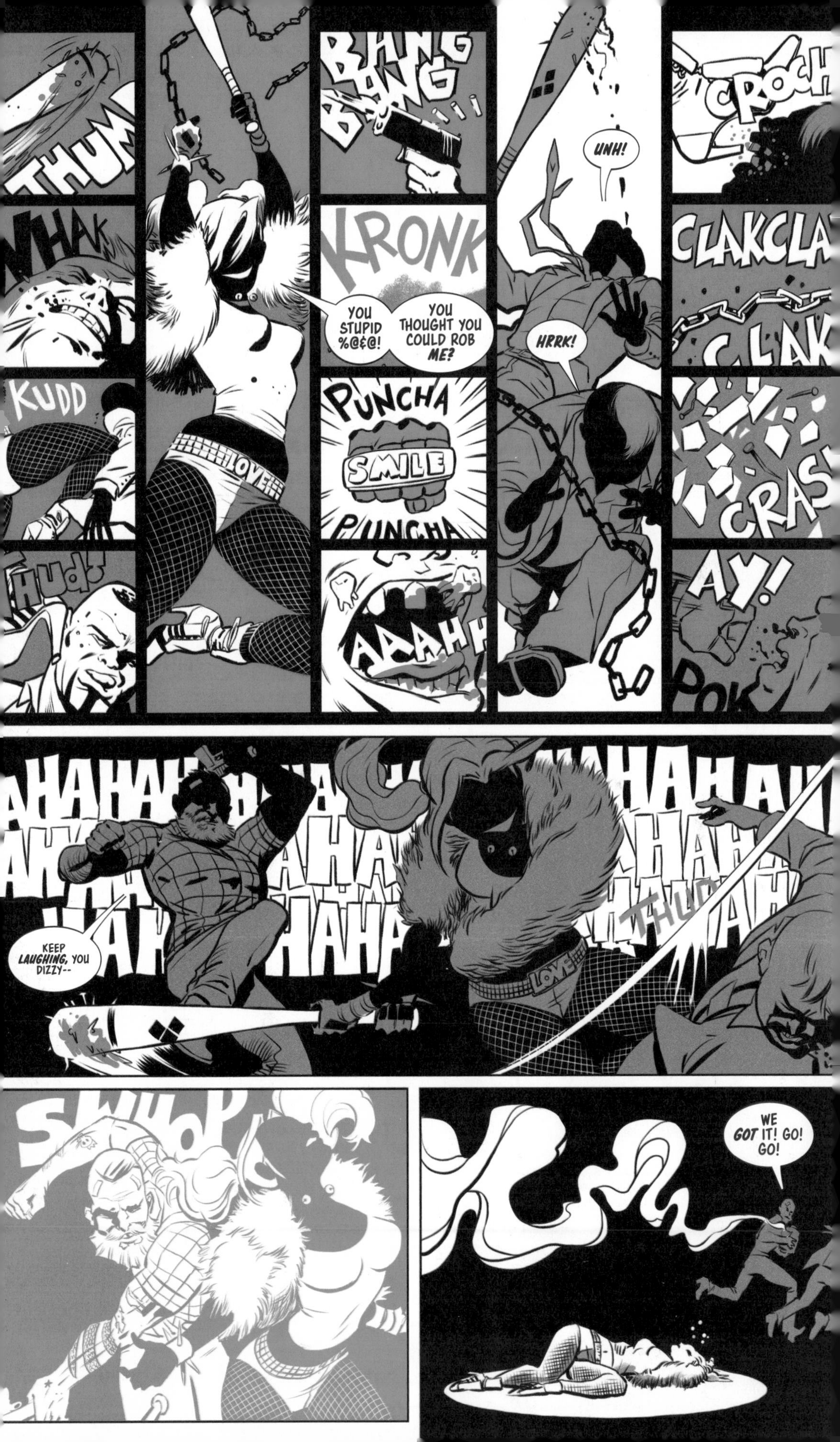
THUM
WHAK
KUDD
THUD!
BANG
BANG
KRONK
YOU STUPID %@&@!
YOU THOUGHT YOU COULD ROB ME?
PUNCHA
SMILE
PUNCHA
AAAHH
UNH!
HRRK!
CROCH
CLAKCLA
CLAK
CRAS
AY!
POK
LOVE
KEEP LAUGHING, YOU DIZZY--
THUD
SWOOP
WE GOT IT! GO! GO!

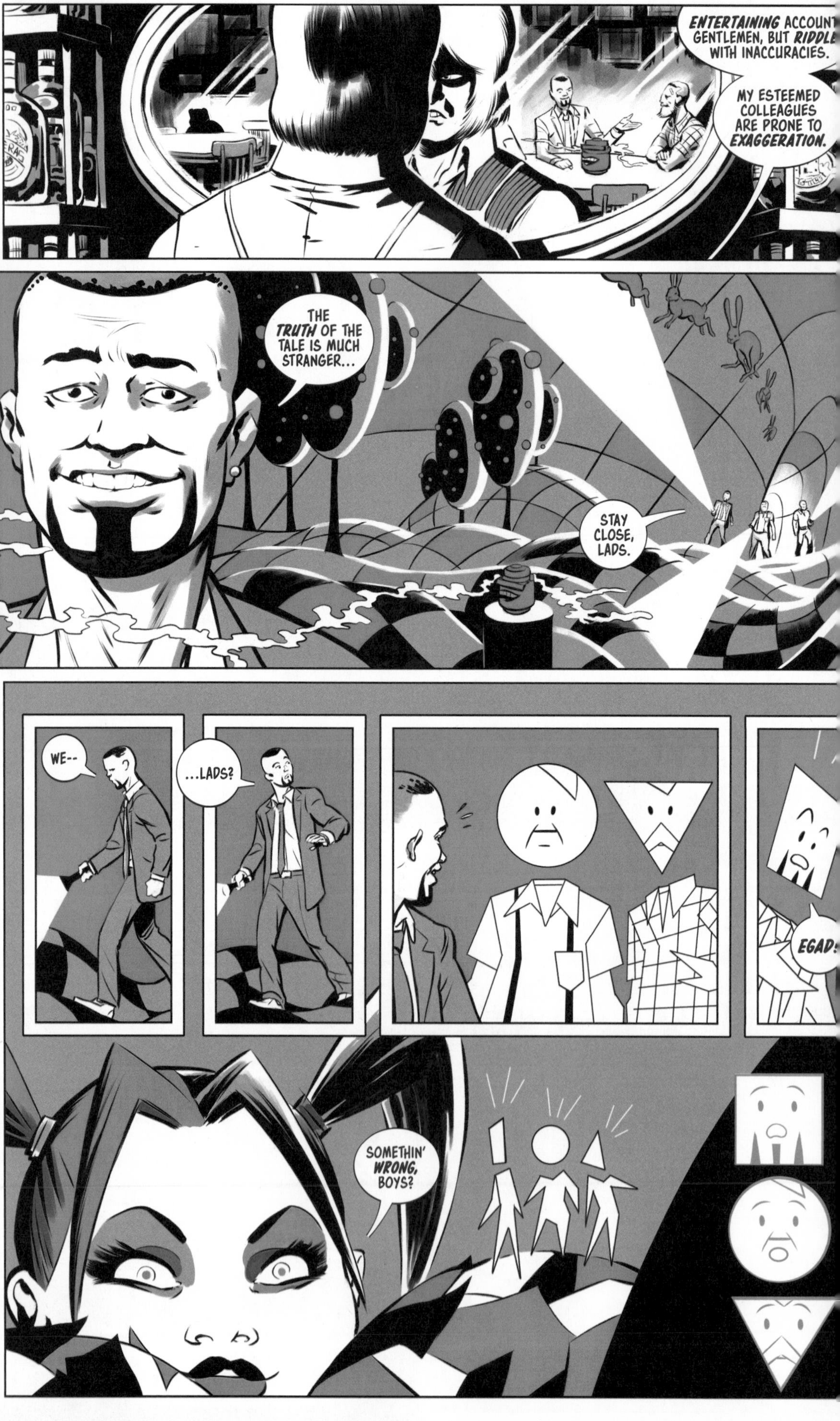
ENTERTAINING ACCOUNT, GENTLEMEN, BUT RIDDLED WITH INACCURACIES.
MY ESTEEMED COLLEAGUES ARE PRONE TO EXAGGERATION.
THE TRUTH OF THE TALE IS MUCH STRANGER...
STAY CLOSE, LADS.
WE--
...LADS?
EGAD!
SOMETHIN' WRONG, BOYS?

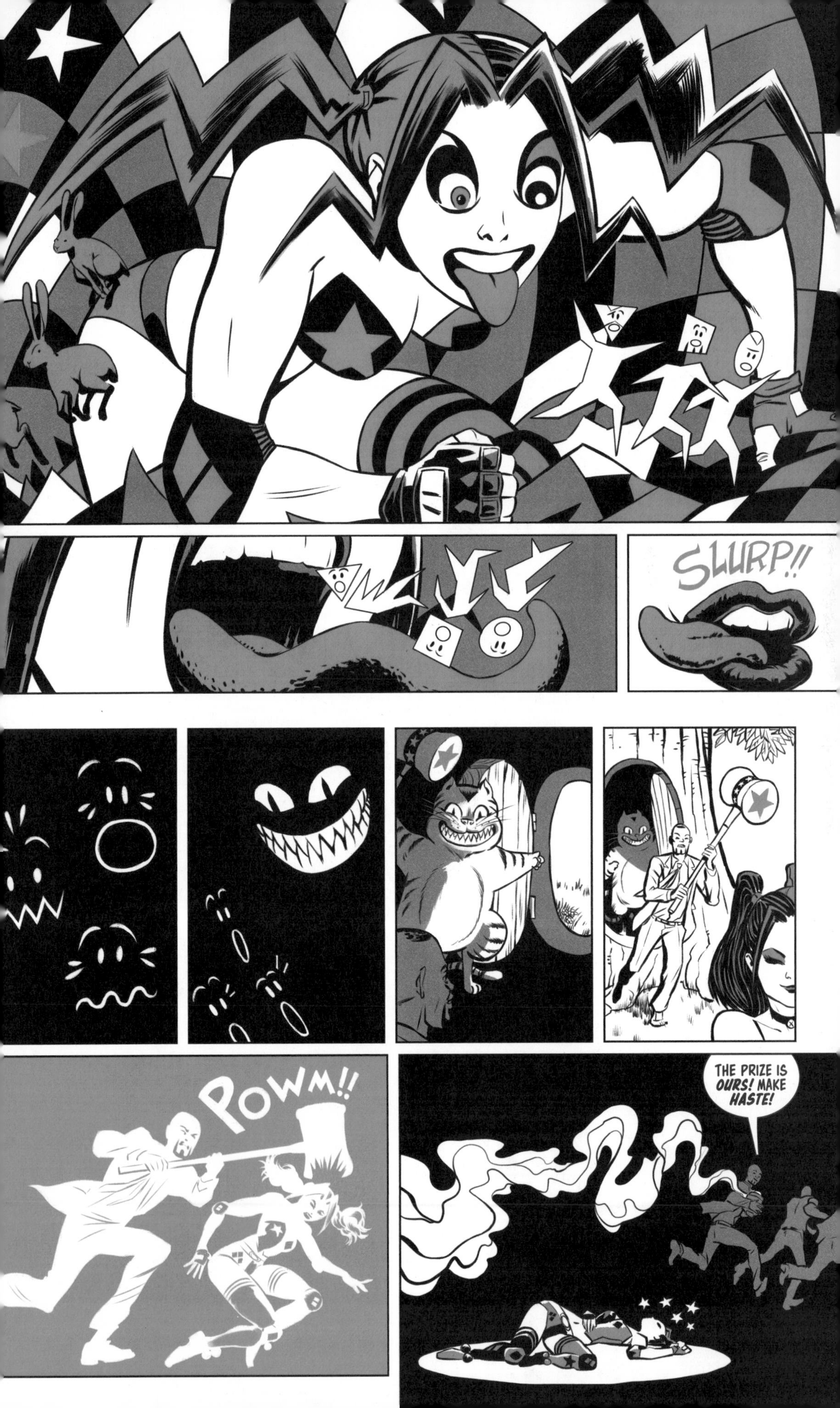
SLURP!!
POWM!!
THE PRIZE IS OURS! MAKE HASTE!

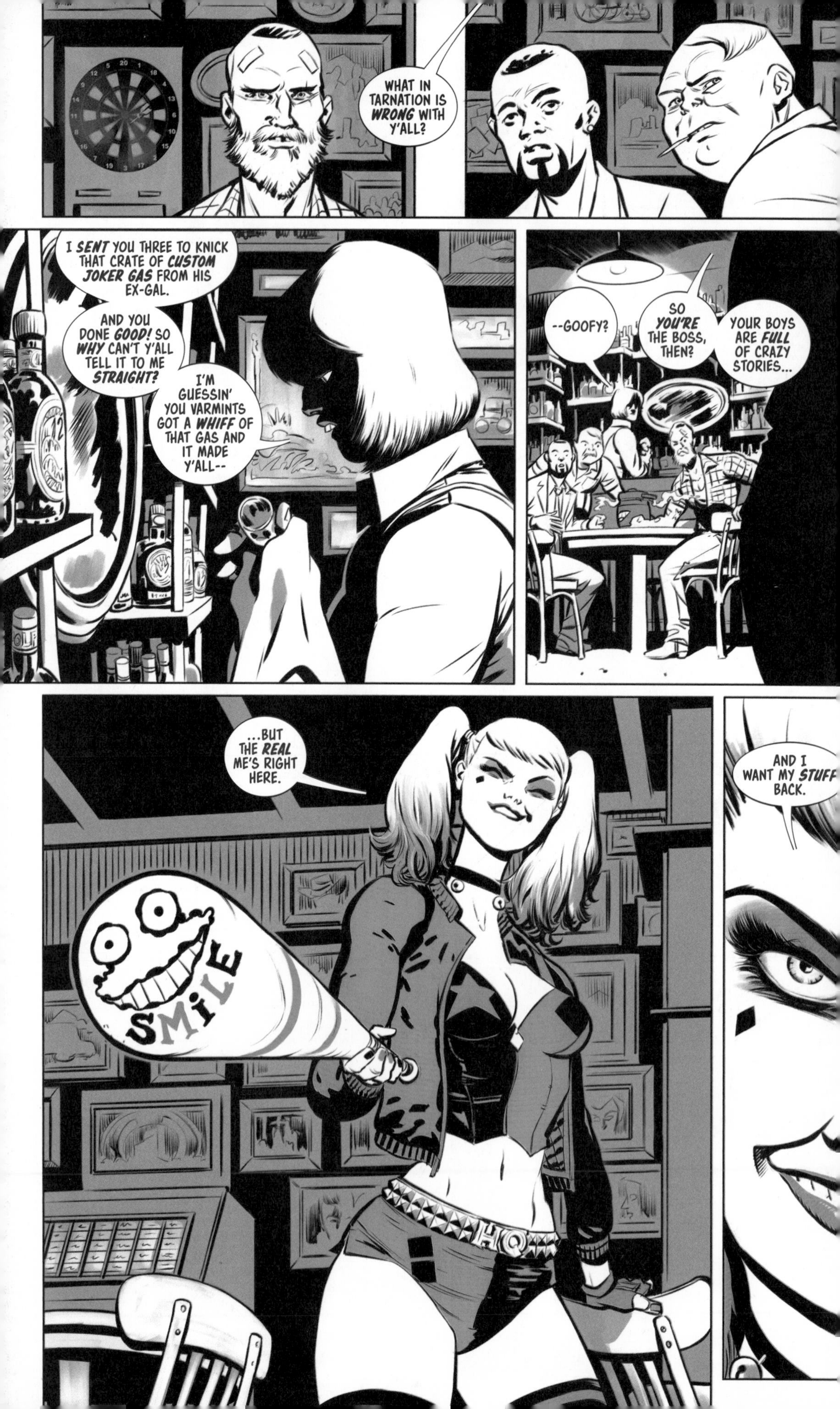
WHAT IN TARNATION IS WRONG WITH Y'ALL?
I SENT YOU THREE TO KNICK THAT CRATE OF CUSTOM JOKER GAS FROM HIS EX-GAL.
AND YOU DONE GOOD! SO WHY CAN'T Y'ALL TELL IT TO ME STRAIGHT?
I'M GUESSIN' YOU VARMINTS GOT A WHIFF OF THAT GAS AND IT MADE Y'ALL--
--GOOFY?
SO YOU'RE THE BOSS, THEN?
YOUR BOYS ARE FULL OF CRAZY STORIES...
...BUT THE REAL ME'S RIGHT HERE.
SMILE
HQ
AND I WANT MY STUFF BACK.

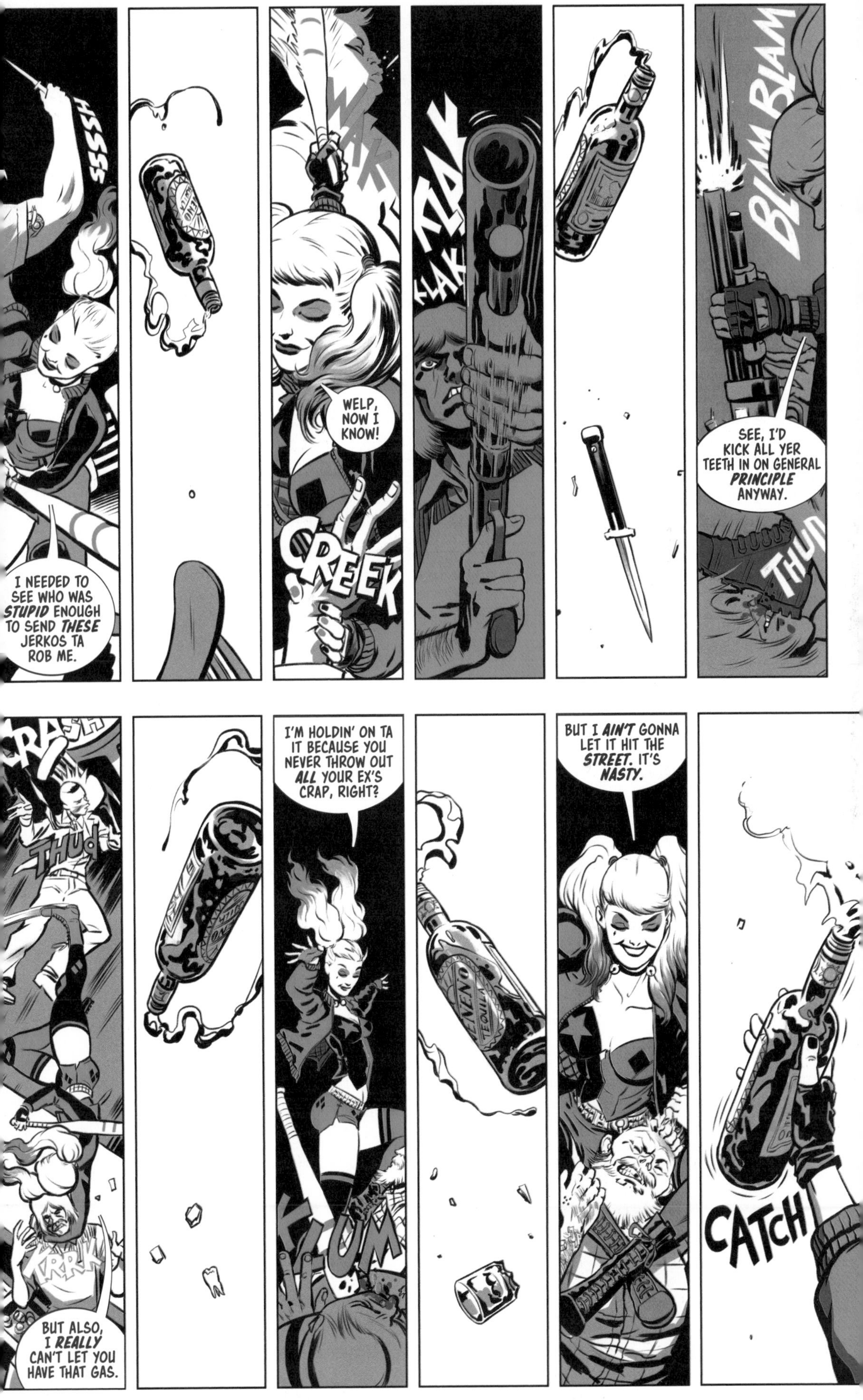
SSSSH
I NEEDED TO SEE WHO WAS STUPID ENOUGH TO SEND THESE JERKOS TA ROB ME.
WAK
WELP, NOW I KNOW!
CREEK
KLAK KLAK
BLAM BLAM
SEE, I'D KICK ALL YER TEETH IN ON GENERAL PRINCIPLE ANYWAY.
THUD
CRASH
THUD
BUT ALSO, I REALLY CAN'T LET YOU HAVE THAT GAS.
I'M HOLDIN' ON TA IT BECAUSE YOU NEVER THROW OUT ALL YOUR EX'S CRAP, RIGHT?
BUT I AIN'T GONNA LET IT HIT THE STREET. IT'S NASTY.
CATCH

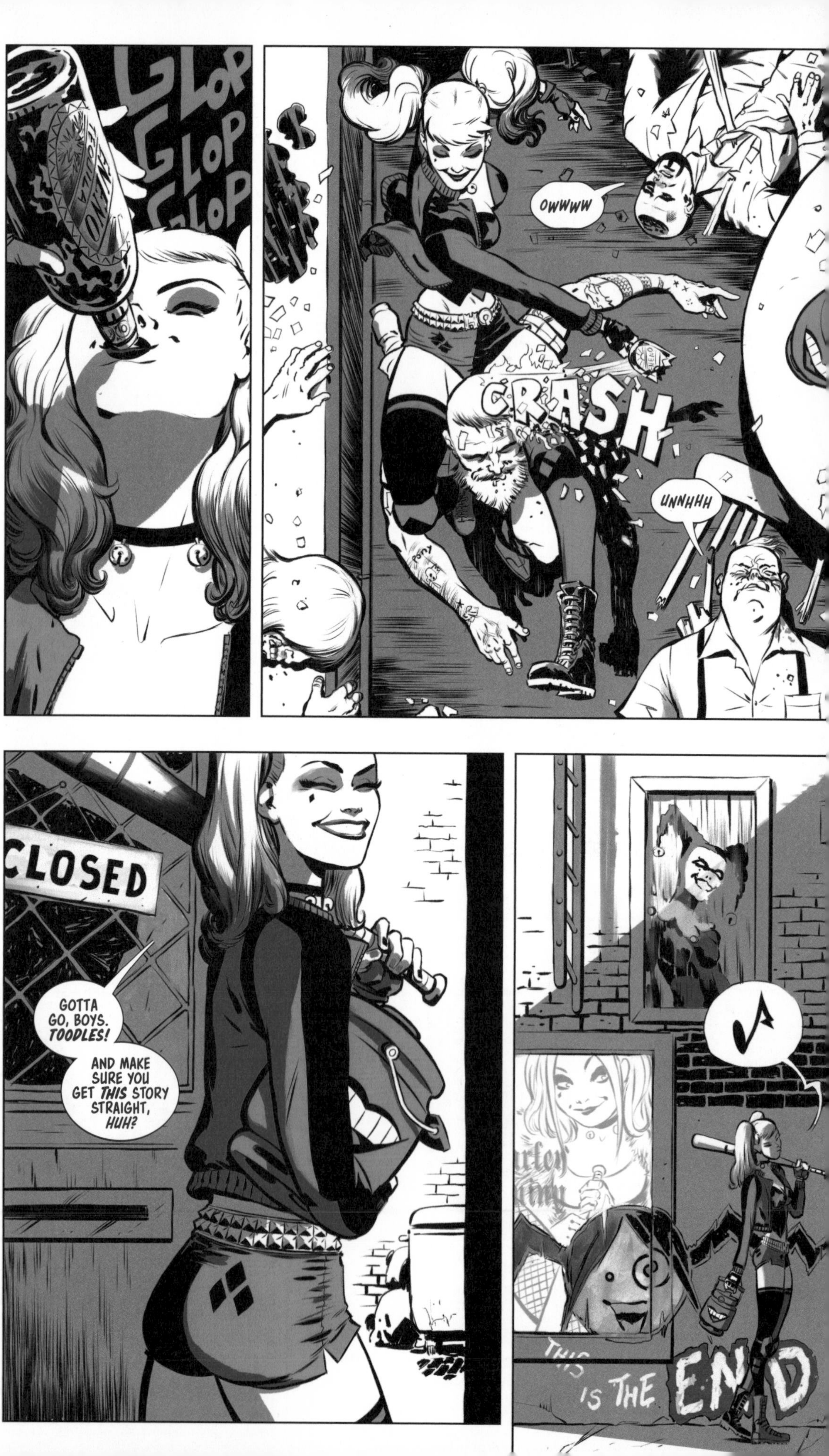
GLOP
GLOP
GLOP
OWWWW
CRASH
UNNHHH
GOTTA GO, BOYS. *TOODLES!*
AND MAKE SURE YOU GET *THIS* STORY STRAIGHT, *HUH?*
CLOSED
THIS IS THE END

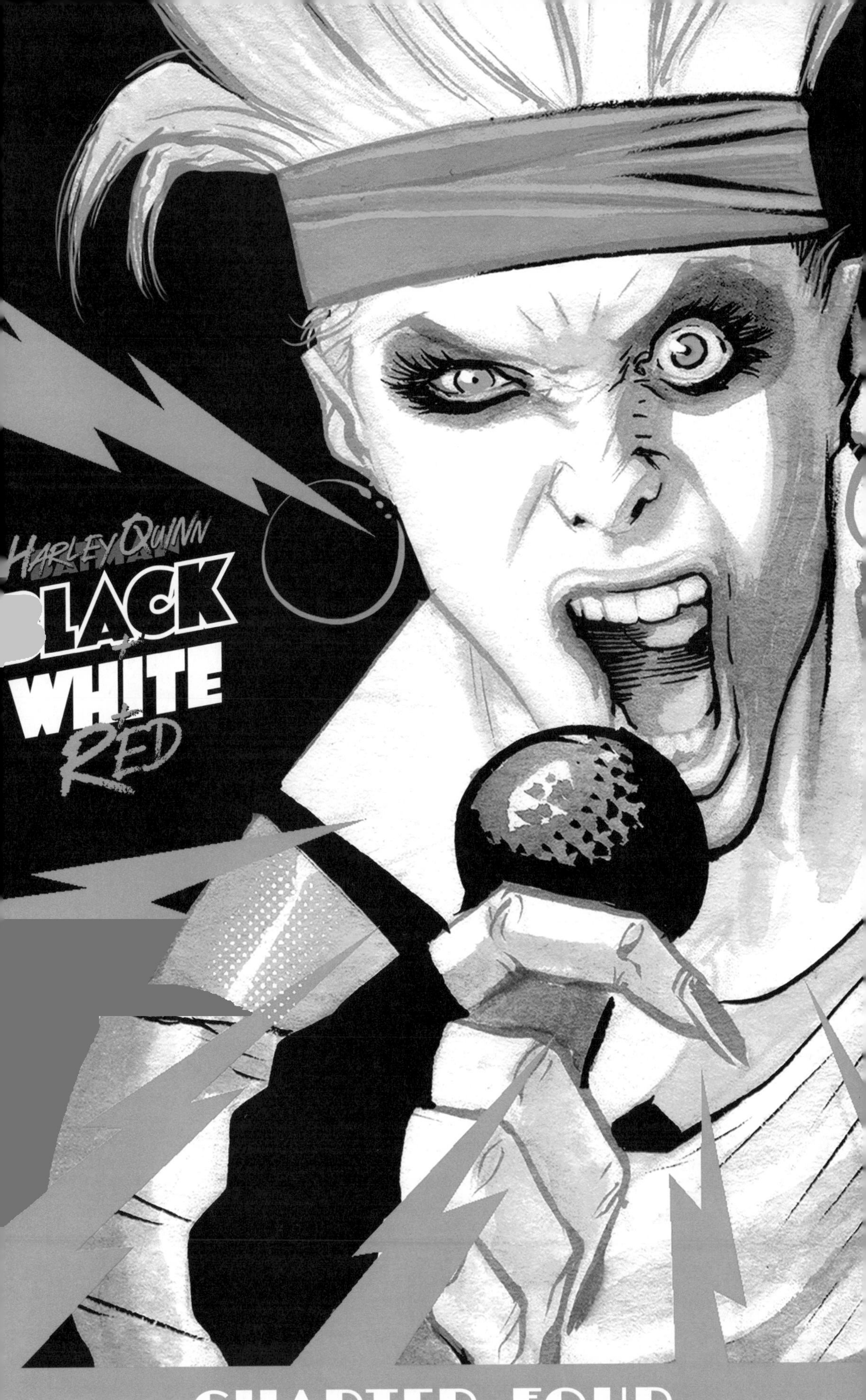
HARLEY QUINN
BLACK
+
WHITE
+
RED

CHAPTER FOUR

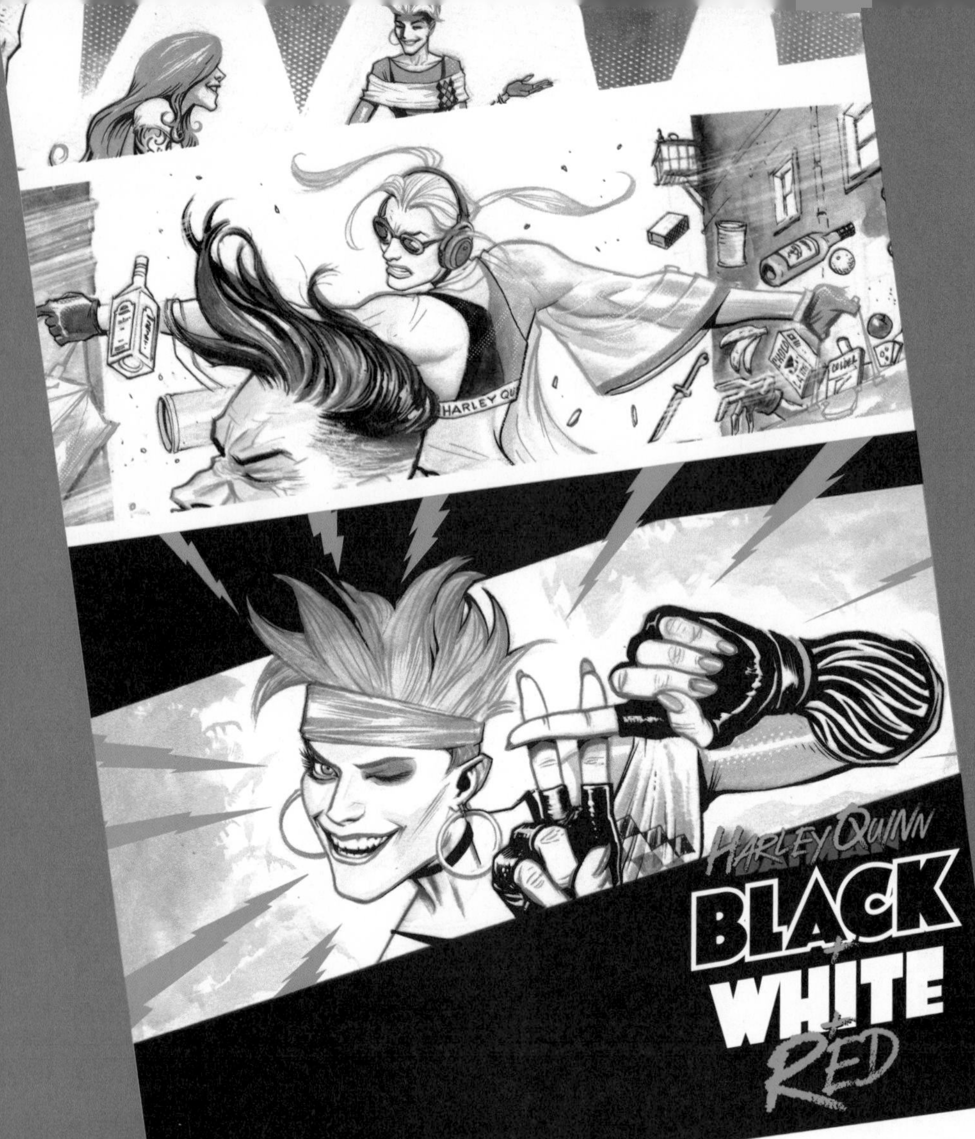
HARLEY QUINN
HARLEY QUINN
BLACK + WHITE + RED

"WHO DISS?"

WRITER TIM SEELEY
ARTIST JUAN FERREYRA
LETTERER STEVE WANDS
EDITOR ANDY KHOURI

HARLEY QUINN CREATED BY PAUL DINI & BRUCE TIMM

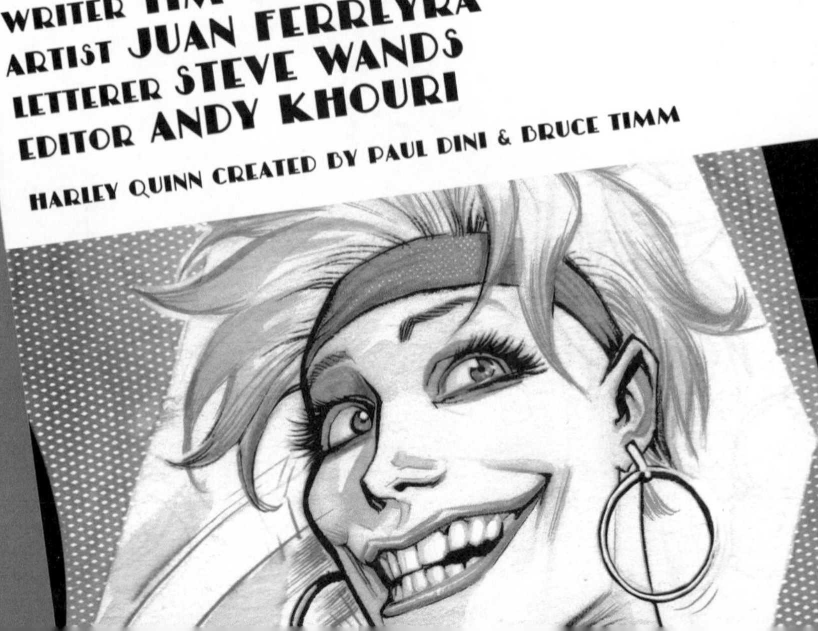

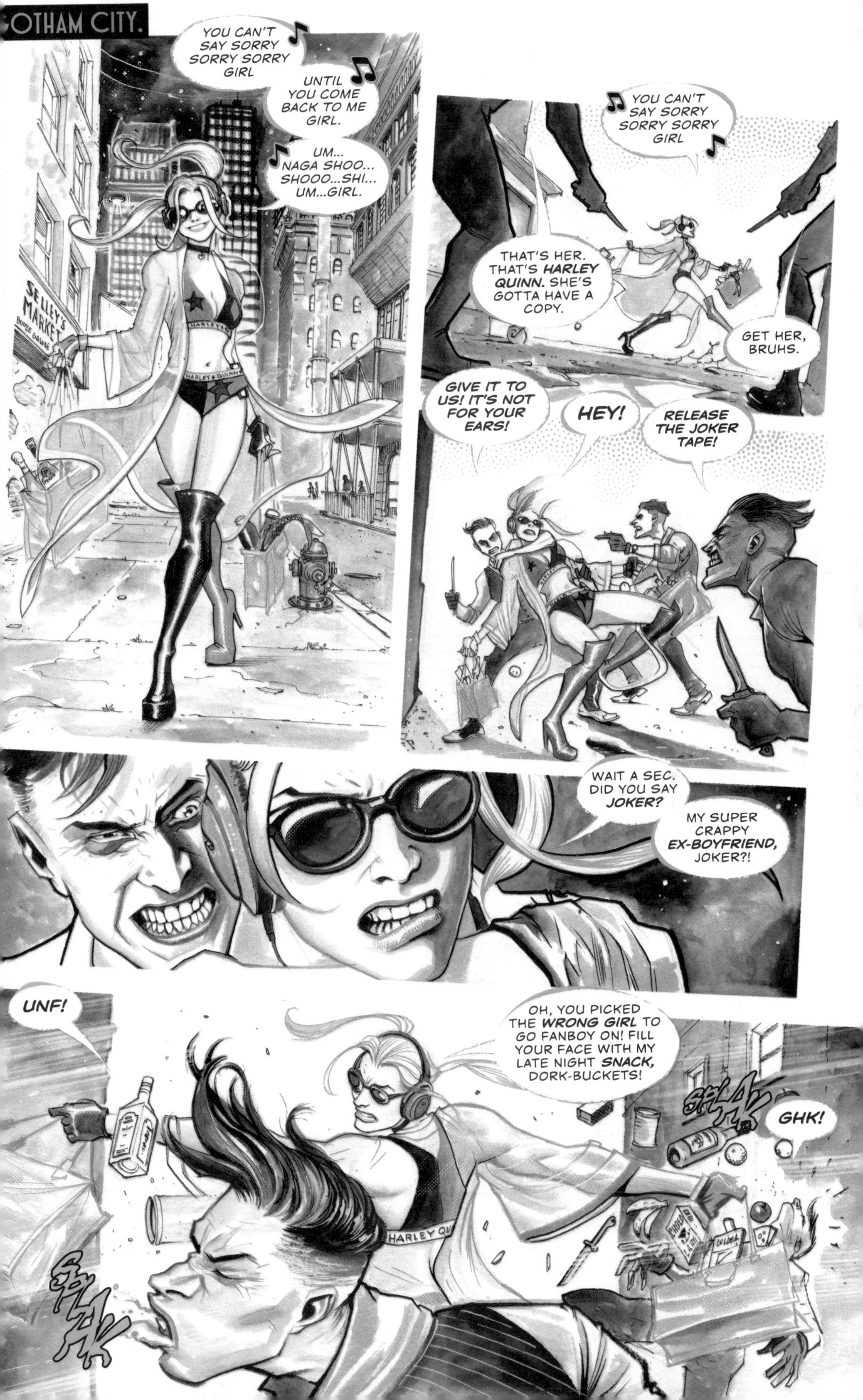

OTHAM CITY.
YOU CAN'T SAY SORRY SORRY SORRY GIRL
UNTIL YOU COME BACK TO ME GIRL.
UM... NAGA SHOO... SHOOO...SHI... UM...GIRL.
SELLEY'S MARKET
YOU CAN'T SAY SORRY SORRY SORRY GIRL
THAT'S HER. THAT'S HARLEY QUINN. SHE'S GOTTA HAVE A COPY.
GET HER, BRUHS.
GIVE IT TO US! IT'S NOT FOR YOUR EARS!
HEY!
RELEASE THE JOKER TAPE!
WAIT A SEC. DID YOU SAY JOKER?
MY SUPER CRAPPY EX-BOYFRIEND, JOKER?!
UNF!
OH, YOU PICKED THE WRONG GIRL TO GO FANBOY ON! FILL YOUR FACE WITH MY LATE NIGHT SNACK, DORK-BUCKETS!
SPLAK
GHK!

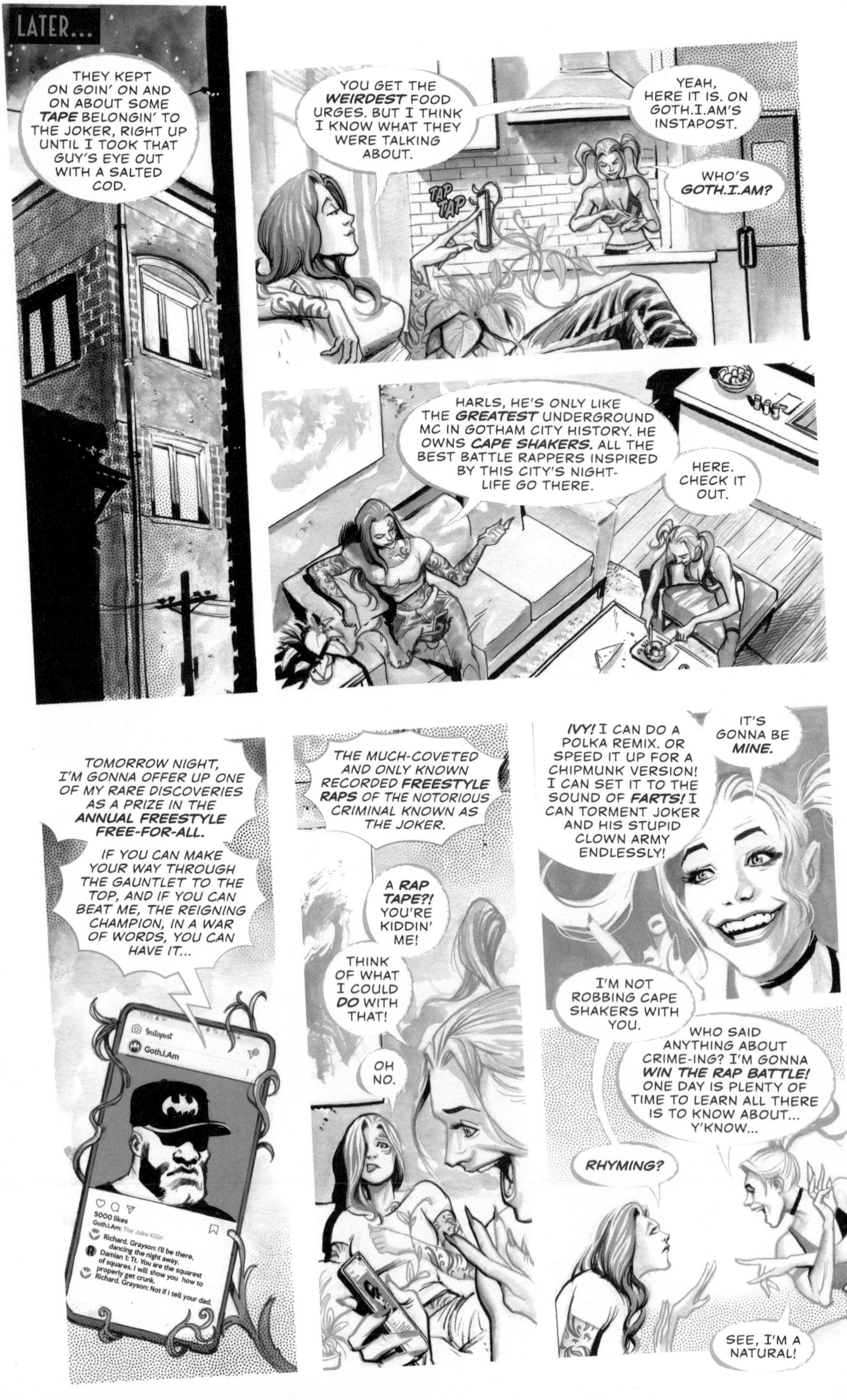
LATER...
THEY KEPT ON GOIN' ON AND ON ABOUT SOME TAPE BELONGIN' TO THE JOKER, RIGHT UP UNTIL I TOOK THAT GUY'S EYE OUT WITH A SALTED COD.
YOU GET THE WEIRDEST FOOD URGES. BUT I THINK I KNOW WHAT THEY WERE TALKING ABOUT.
TAP TAP
YEAH, HERE IT IS. ON GOTH.I.AM'S INSTAPOST.
WHO'S GOTH.I.AM?
HARLS, HE'S ONLY LIKE THE GREATEST UNDERGROUND MC IN GOTHAM CITY HISTORY. HE OWNS CAPE SHAKERS. ALL THE BEST BATTLE RAPPERS INSPIRED BY THIS CITY'S NIGHT-LIFE GO THERE.
HERE. CHECK IT OUT.
TOMORROW NIGHT, I'M GONNA OFFER UP ONE OF MY RARE DISCOVERIES AS A PRIZE IN THE ANNUAL FREESTYLE FREE-FOR-ALL.
IF YOU CAN MAKE YOUR WAY THROUGH THE GAUNTLET TO THE TOP, AND IF YOU CAN BEAT ME, THE REIGNING CHAMPION, IN A WAR OF WORDS, YOU CAN HAVE IT...
Instapost
Goth.I.Am
5000 likes
Goth.I.Am: The Joke Killin'
Richard. Grayson: I'll be there, dancing the night away.
Damian 1: Tt. You are the squarest of squares. I will show you how to properly get crunk.
Richard. Grayson: Not if I tell your dad.
THE MUCH-COVETED AND ONLY KNOWN RECORDED FREESTYLE RAPS OF THE NOTORIOUS CRIMINAL KNOWN AS THE JOKER.
A RAP TAPE?! YOU'RE KIDDIN' ME!
THINK OF WHAT I COULD DO WITH THAT!
OH NO.
IVY! I CAN DO A POLKA REMIX. OR SPEED IT UP FOR A CHIPMUNK VERSION! I CAN SET IT TO THE SOUND OF FARTS! I CAN TORMENT JOKER AND HIS STUPID CLOWN ARMY ENDLESSLY!
IT'S GONNA BE MINE.
I'M NOT ROBBING CAPE SHAKERS WITH YOU.
WHO SAID ANYTHING ABOUT CRIME-ING? I'M GONNA WIN THE RAP BATTLE! ONE DAY IS PLENTY OF TIME TO LEARN ALL THERE IS TO KNOW ABOUT... Y'KNOW...
RHYMING?
SEE, I'M A NATURAL!

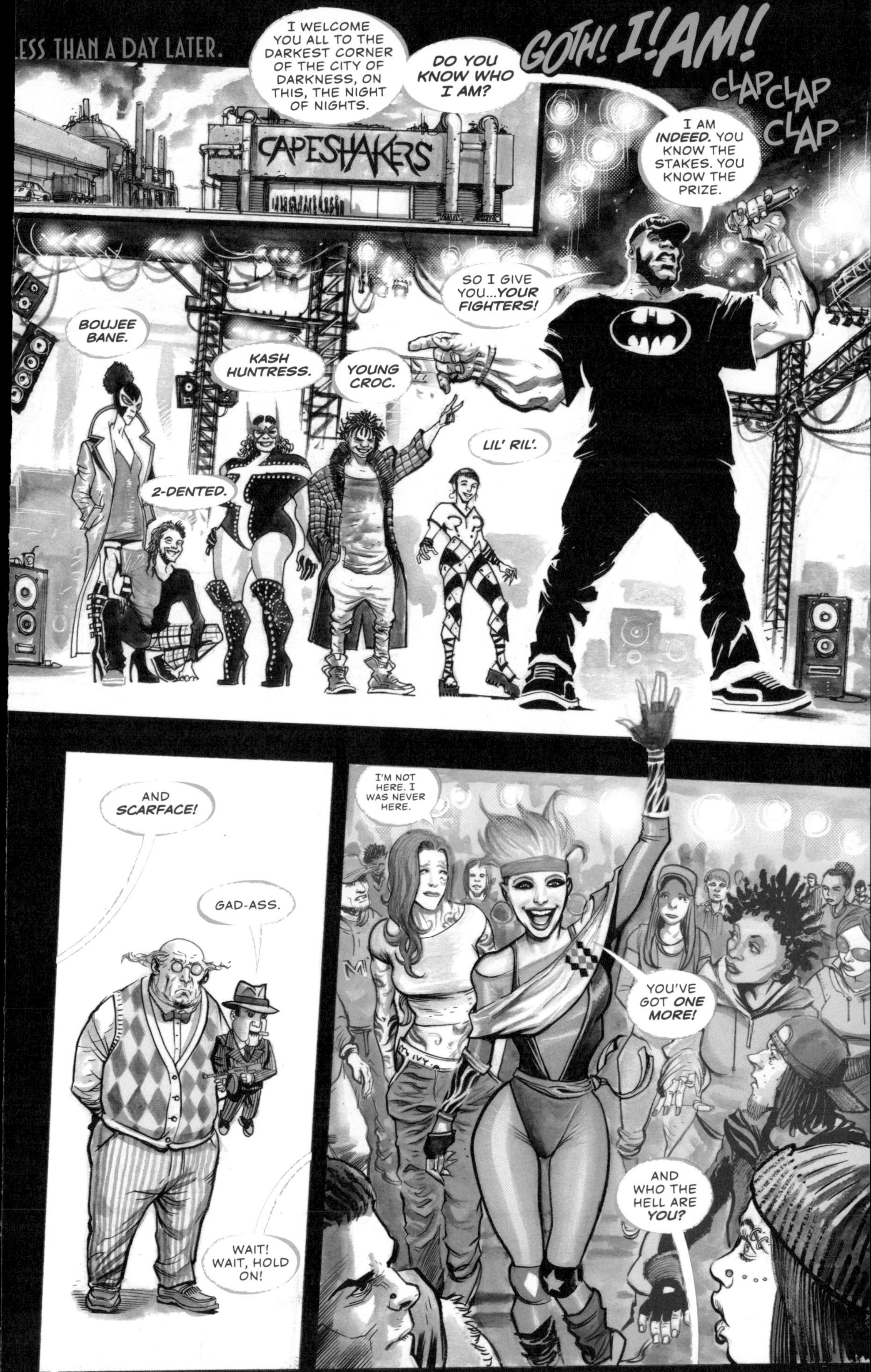

LESS THAN A DAY LATER.
I WELCOME YOU ALL TO THE DARKEST CORNER OF THE CITY OF DARKNESS, ON THIS, THE NIGHT OF NIGHTS.
DO YOU KNOW WHO I AM?
GOTH! I! AM!
CLAP CLAP CLAP
CAPESHAKERS
I AM INDEED. YOU KNOW THE STAKES. YOU KNOW THE PRIZE.
SO I GIVE YOU...YOUR FIGHTERS!
BOUJEE BANE.
KASH HUNTRESS.
YOUNG CROC.
LIL' RIL'.
2-DENTED.
AND SCARFACE!
GAD-ASS.
WAIT! WAIT, HOLD ON!
I'M NOT HERE. I WAS NEVER HERE.
YOU'VE GOT ONE MORE!
AND WHO THE HELL ARE YOU?

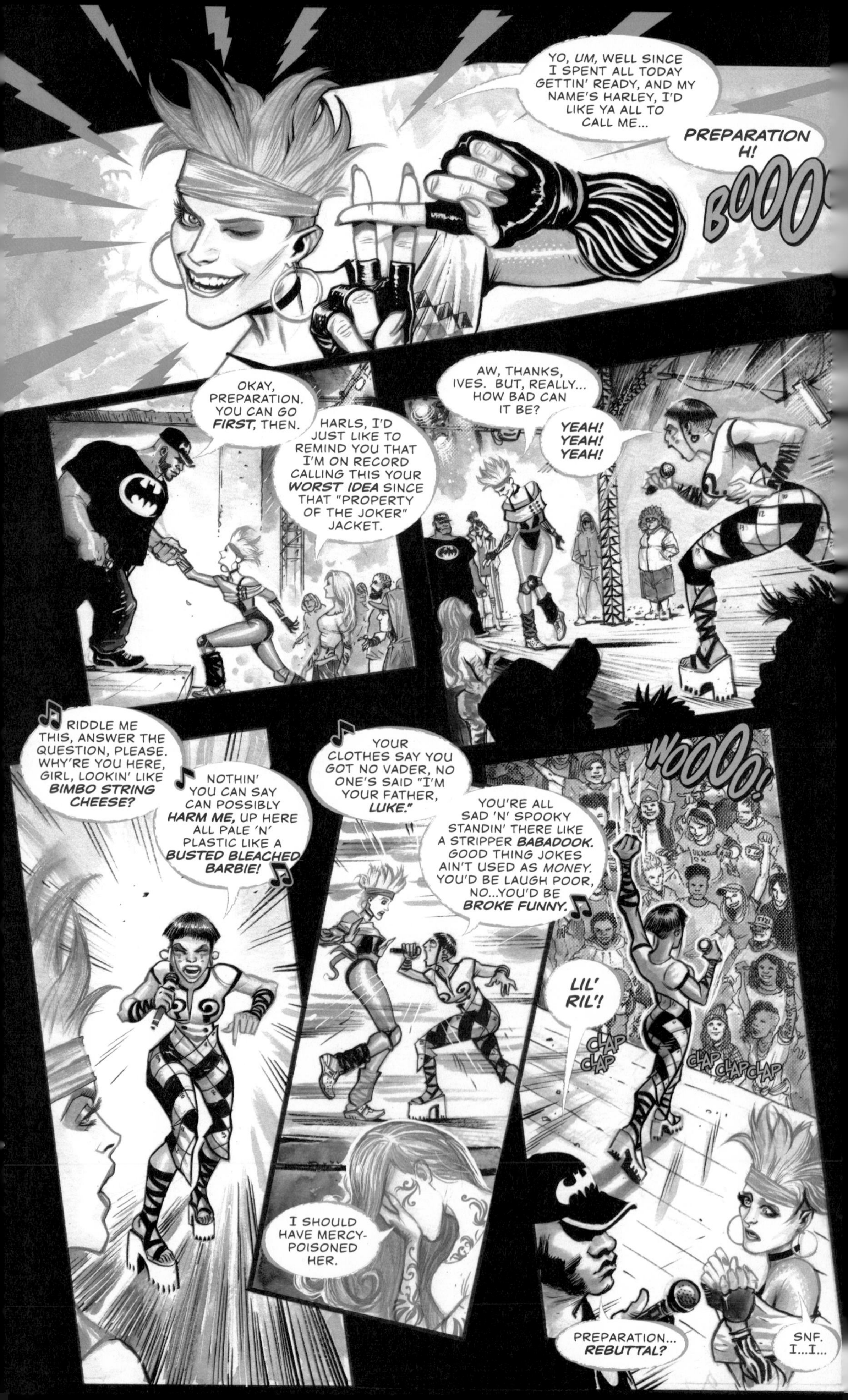

YO, UM, WELL SINCE I SPENT ALL TODAY GETTIN' READY, AND MY NAME'S HARLEY, I'D LIKE YA ALL TO CALL ME...
PREPARATION H!
BOOO
OKAY, PREPARATION. YOU CAN GO FIRST, THEN.
HARLS, I'D JUST LIKE TO REMIND YOU THAT I'M ON RECORD CALLING THIS YOUR WORST IDEA SINCE THAT "PROPERTY OF THE JOKER" JACKET.
AW, THANKS, IVES. BUT, REALLY... HOW BAD CAN IT BE?
YEAH! YEAH! YEAH!
RIDDLE ME THIS, ANSWER THE QUESTION, PLEASE. WHY'RE YOU HERE, GIRL, LOOKIN' LIKE BIMBO STRING CHEESE?
NOTHIN' YOU CAN SAY CAN POSSIBLY HARM ME, UP HERE ALL PALE 'N' PLASTIC LIKE A BUSTED BLEACHED BARBIE!
YOUR CLOTHES SAY YOU GOT NO VADER, NO ONE'S SAID "I'M YOUR FATHER, LUKE."
YOU'RE ALL SAD 'N' SPOOKY STANDIN' THERE LIKE A STRIPPER BABADOOK. GOOD THING JOKES AIN'T USED AS MONEY. YOU'D BE LAUGH POOR, NO...YOU'D BE BROKE FUNNY.
WOOOOO!
LIL' RIL'!
CLAP CLAP
CLAP CLAP CLAP
I SHOULD HAVE MERCY-POISONED HER.
PREPARATION... REBUTTAL?
SNF. I...I...

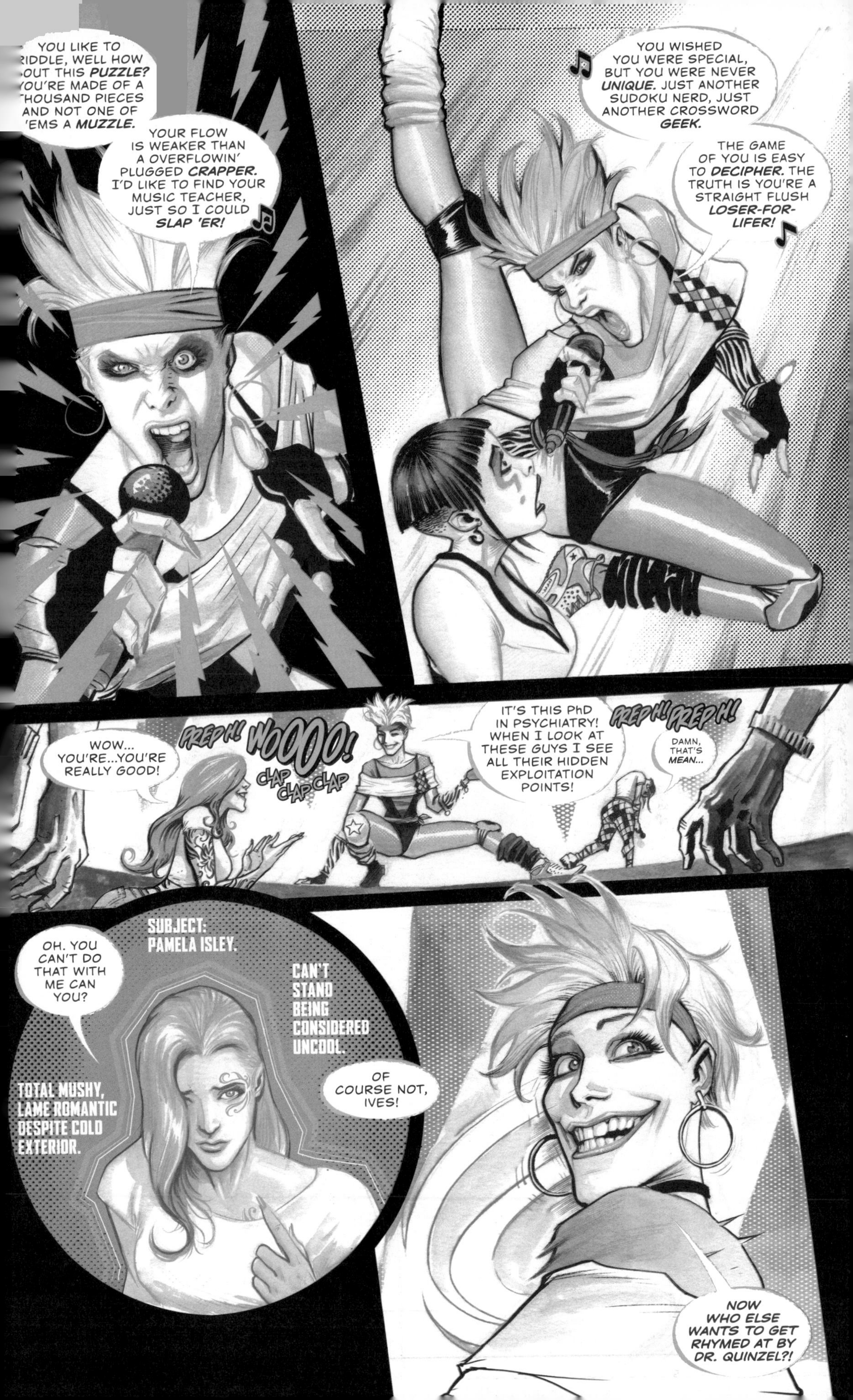
YOU LIKE TO RIDDLE, WELL HOW 'BOUT THIS PUZZLE? YOU'RE MADE OF A THOUSAND PIECES AND NOT ONE OF 'EMS A MUZZLE.
YOUR FLOW IS WEAKER THAN A OVERFLOWIN' PLUGGED CRAPPER. I'D LIKE TO FIND YOUR MUSIC TEACHER, JUST SO I COULD SLAP 'ER!
YOU WISHED YOU WERE SPECIAL, BUT YOU WERE NEVER UNIQUE. JUST ANOTHER SUDOKU NERD, JUST ANOTHER CROSSWORD GEEK.
THE GAME OF YOU IS EASY TO DECIPHER. THE TRUTH IS YOU'RE A STRAIGHT FLUSH LOSER-FOR-LIFER!
PREP H! WOOOO!
CLAP CLAP CLAP
WOW... YOU'RE...YOU'RE REALLY GOOD!
IT'S THIS PhD IN PSYCHIATRY! WHEN I LOOK AT THESE GUYS I SEE ALL THEIR HIDDEN EXPLOITATION POINTS!
PREP H! PREP H!
DAMN, THAT'S MEAN...
OH. YOU CAN'T DO THAT WITH ME CAN YOU?
SUBJECT: PAMELA ISLEY.
CAN'T STAND BEING CONSIDERED UNCOOL.
TOTAL MUSHY, LAME ROMANTIC DESPITE COLD EXTERIOR.
OF COURSE NOT, IVES!
NOW WHO ELSE WANTS TO GET RHYMED AT BY DR. QUINZEL?!

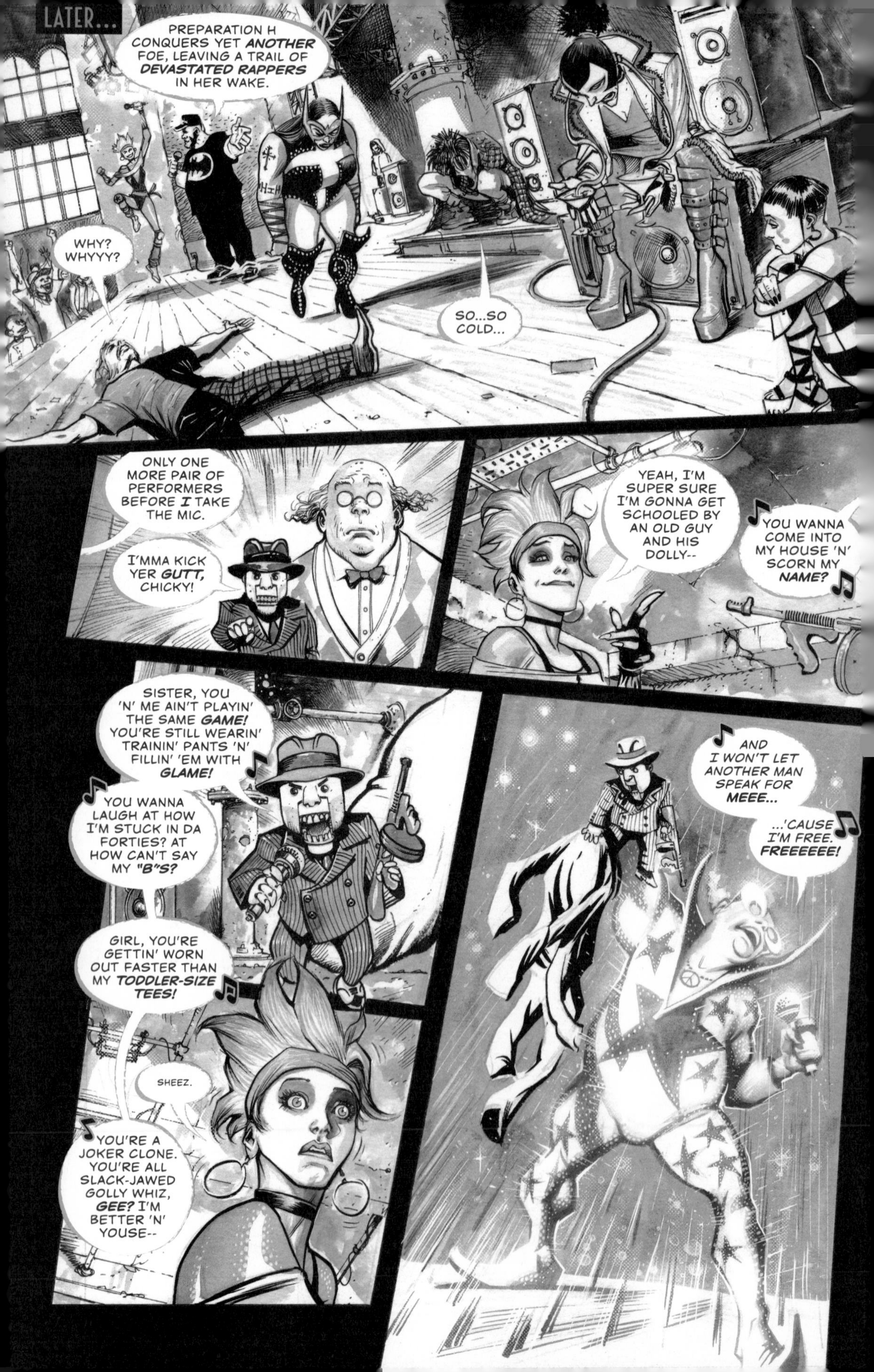
LATER...
PREPARATION H CONQUERS YET ANOTHER FOE, LEAVING A TRAIL OF DEVASTATED RAPPERS IN HER WAKE.
WHY? WHYYY?
SO...SO COLD...
ONLY ONE MORE PAIR OF PERFORMERS BEFORE I TAKE THE MIC.
I'MMA KICK YER GUTT, CHICKY!
YEAH, I'M SUPER SURE I'M GONNA GET SCHOOLED BY AN OLD GUY AND HIS DOLLY--
YOU WANNA COME INTO MY HOUSE 'N' SCORN MY NAME?
SISTER, YOU 'N' ME AIN'T PLAYIN' THE SAME GAME! YOU'RE STILL WEARIN' TRAININ' PANTS 'N' FILLIN' 'EM WITH GLAME!
YOU WANNA LAUGH AT HOW I'M STUCK IN DA FORTIES? AT HOW CAN'T SAY MY "B"S?
GIRL, YOU'RE GETTIN' WORN OUT FASTER THAN MY TODDLER-SIZE TEES!
SHEEZ.
YOU'RE A JOKER CLONE. YOU'RE ALL SLACK-JAWED GOLLY WHIZ, GEE? I'M BETTER 'N' YOUSE--
AND I WON'T LET ANOTHER MAN SPEAK FOR MEEE...
...'CAUSE I'M FREE. FREEEEEE!

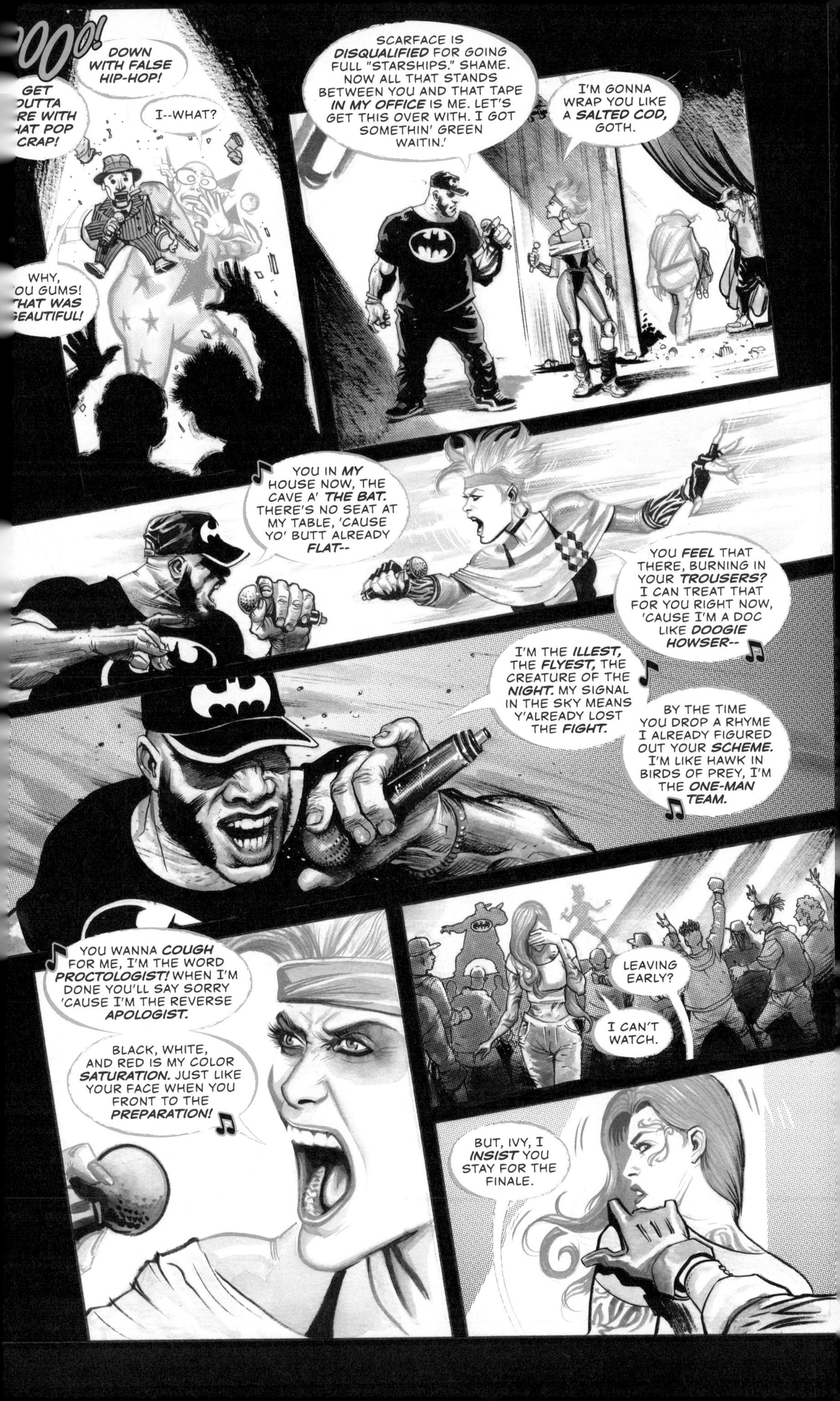
OOOO!
DOWN WITH FALSE HIP-HOP!
GET OUTTA ...RE WITH ...HAT POP CRAP!
I--WHAT?
WHY, ...OU GUMS! THAT WAS ...EAUTIFUL!
SCARFACE IS DISQUALIFIED FOR GOING FULL "STARSHIPS." SHAME. NOW ALL THAT STANDS BETWEEN YOU AND THAT TAPE IN MY OFFICE IS ME. LET'S GET THIS OVER WITH. I GOT SOMETHIN' GREEN WAITIN.'
I'M GONNA WRAP YOU LIKE A SALTED COD, GOTH.
YOU IN MY HOUSE NOW, THE CAVE A' THE BAT. THERE'S NO SEAT AT MY TABLE, 'CAUSE YO' BUTT ALREADY FLAT--
YOU FEEL THAT THERE, BURNING IN YOUR TROUSERS? I CAN TREAT THAT FOR YOU RIGHT NOW, 'CAUSE I'M A DOC LIKE DOOGIE HOWSER--
I'M THE ILLEST, THE FLYEST, THE CREATURE OF THE NIGHT. MY SIGNAL IN THE SKY MEANS Y'ALREADY LOST THE FIGHT.
BY THE TIME YOU DROP A RHYME I ALREADY FIGURED OUT YOUR SCHEME. I'M LIKE HAWK IN BIRDS OF PREY, I'M THE ONE-MAN TEAM.
YOU WANNA COUGH FOR ME, I'M THE WORD PROCTOLOGIST! WHEN I'M DONE YOU'LL SAY SORRY 'CAUSE I'M THE REVERSE APOLOGIST.
BLACK, WHITE, AND RED IS MY COLOR SATURATION. JUST LIKE YOUR FACE WHEN YOU FRONT TO THE PREPARATION!
LEAVING EARLY?
I CAN'T WATCH.
BUT, IVY, I INSIST YOU STAY FOR THE FINALE.

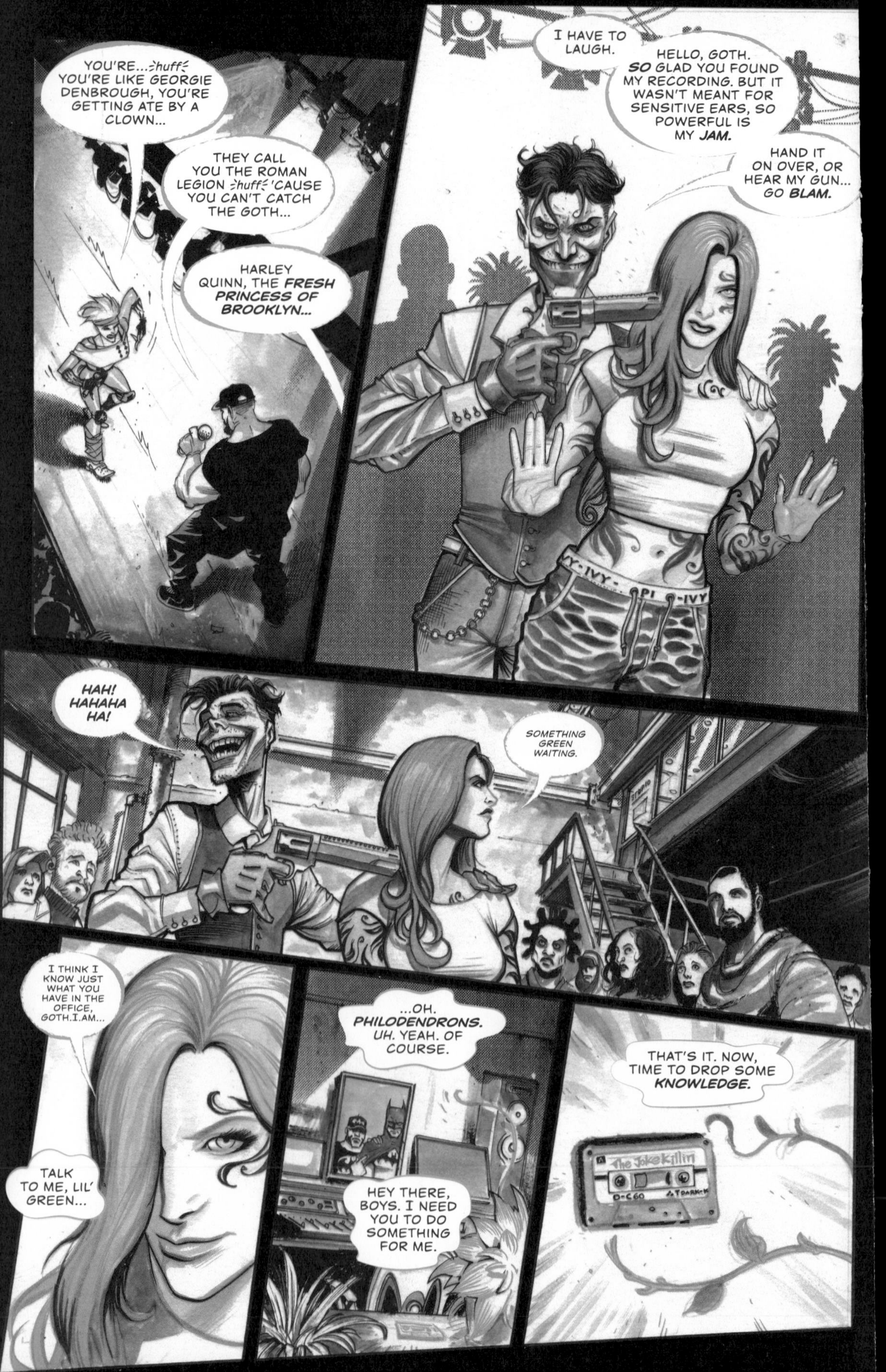
YOU'RE... *huff* YOU'RE LIKE GEORGIE DENBROUGH, YOU'RE GETTING ATE BY A CLOWN...
THEY CALL YOU THE ROMAN LEGION *huff* 'CAUSE YOU CAN'T CATCH THE GOTH...
HARLEY QUINN, THE ***FRESH PRINCESS OF BROOKLYN...***
I HAVE TO LAUGH.
HELLO, GOTH. ***SO*** GLAD YOU FOUND MY RECORDING. BUT IT WASN'T MEANT FOR SENSITIVE EARS, SO POWERFUL IS MY ***JAM.***
HAND IT ON OVER, OR HEAR MY GUN... GO ***BLAM.***
HAH! HAHAHA HA!
SOMETHING GREEN WAITING.
I THINK I KNOW JUST WHAT YOU HAVE IN THE OFFICE, GOTH.I.AM...
TALK TO ME, LIL' GREEN...
...OH. ***PHILODENDRONS.*** UH. YEAH. OF COURSE.
HEY THERE, BOYS. I NEED YOU TO DO SOMETHING FOR ME.
THAT'S IT. NOW, TIME TO DROP SOME ***KNOWLEDGE.***

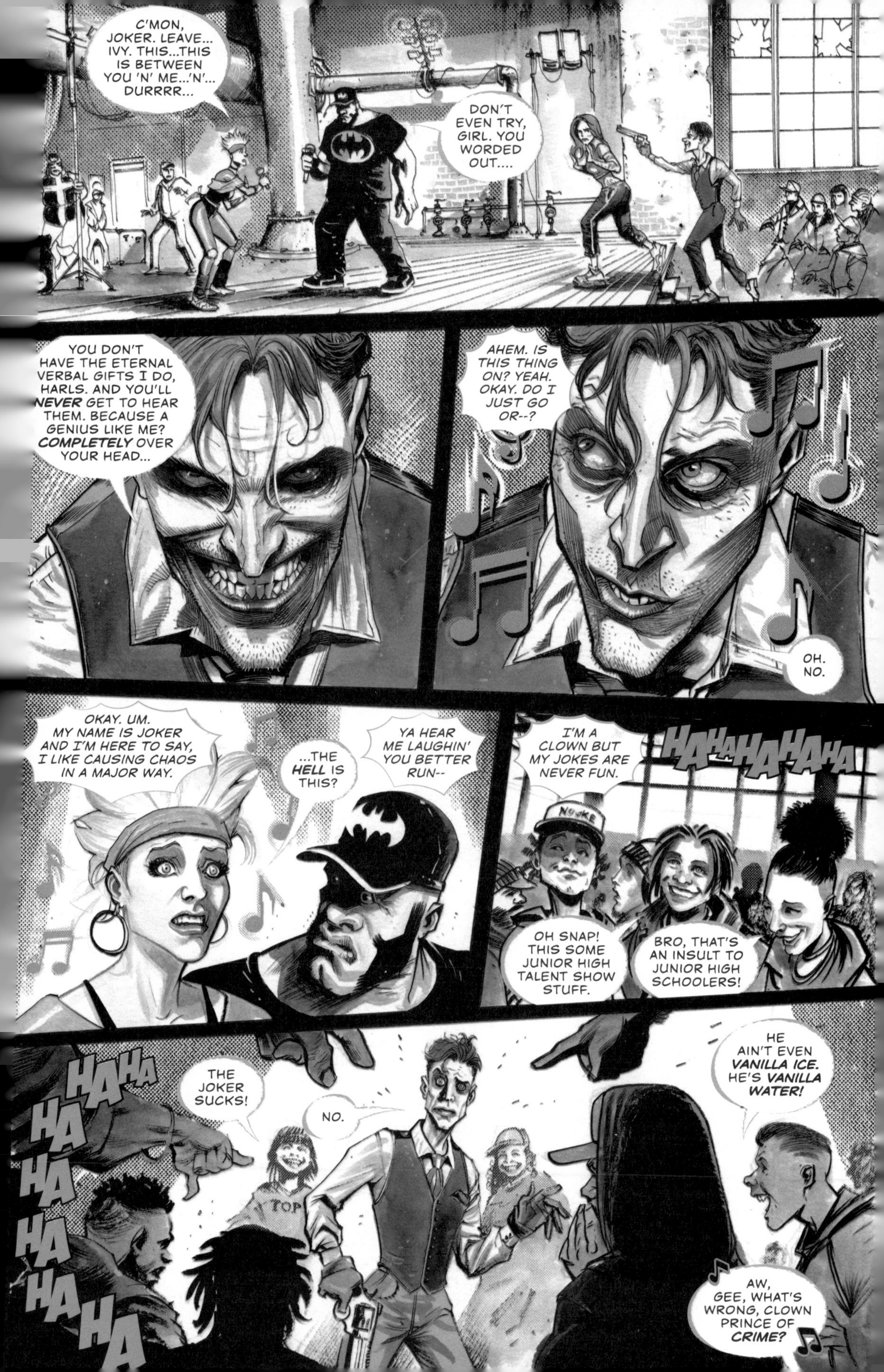
C'MON, JOKER. LEAVE... IVY. THIS...THIS IS BETWEEN YOU 'N' ME...'N'... DURRRR...
DON'T EVEN TRY, GIRL. YOU WORDED OUT....
YOU DON'T HAVE THE ETERNAL VERBAL GIFTS I DO, HARLS. AND YOU'LL NEVER GET TO HEAR THEM. BECAUSE A GENIUS LIKE ME? COMPLETELY OVER YOUR HEAD...
AHEM. IS THIS THING ON? YEAH. OKAY. DO I JUST GO OR--?
OH. NO.
OKAY. UM. MY NAME IS JOKER AND I'M HERE TO SAY, I LIKE CAUSING CHAOS IN A MAJOR WAY.
...THE HELL IS THIS?
YA HEAR ME LAUGHIN' YOU BETTER RUN--
I'M A CLOWN BUT MY JOKES ARE NEVER FUN.
HAHAHAHAHAHA
OH SNAP! THIS SOME JUNIOR HIGH TALENT SHOW STUFF.
BRO, THAT'S AN INSULT TO JUNIOR HIGH SCHOOLERS!
HAHA
HA
HA
HA
HA
HA
HA
THE JOKER SUCKS!
NO.
HE AIN'T EVEN VANILLA ICE. HE'S VANILLA WATER!
AW, GEE, WHAT'S WRONG, CLOWN PRINCE OF CRIME?

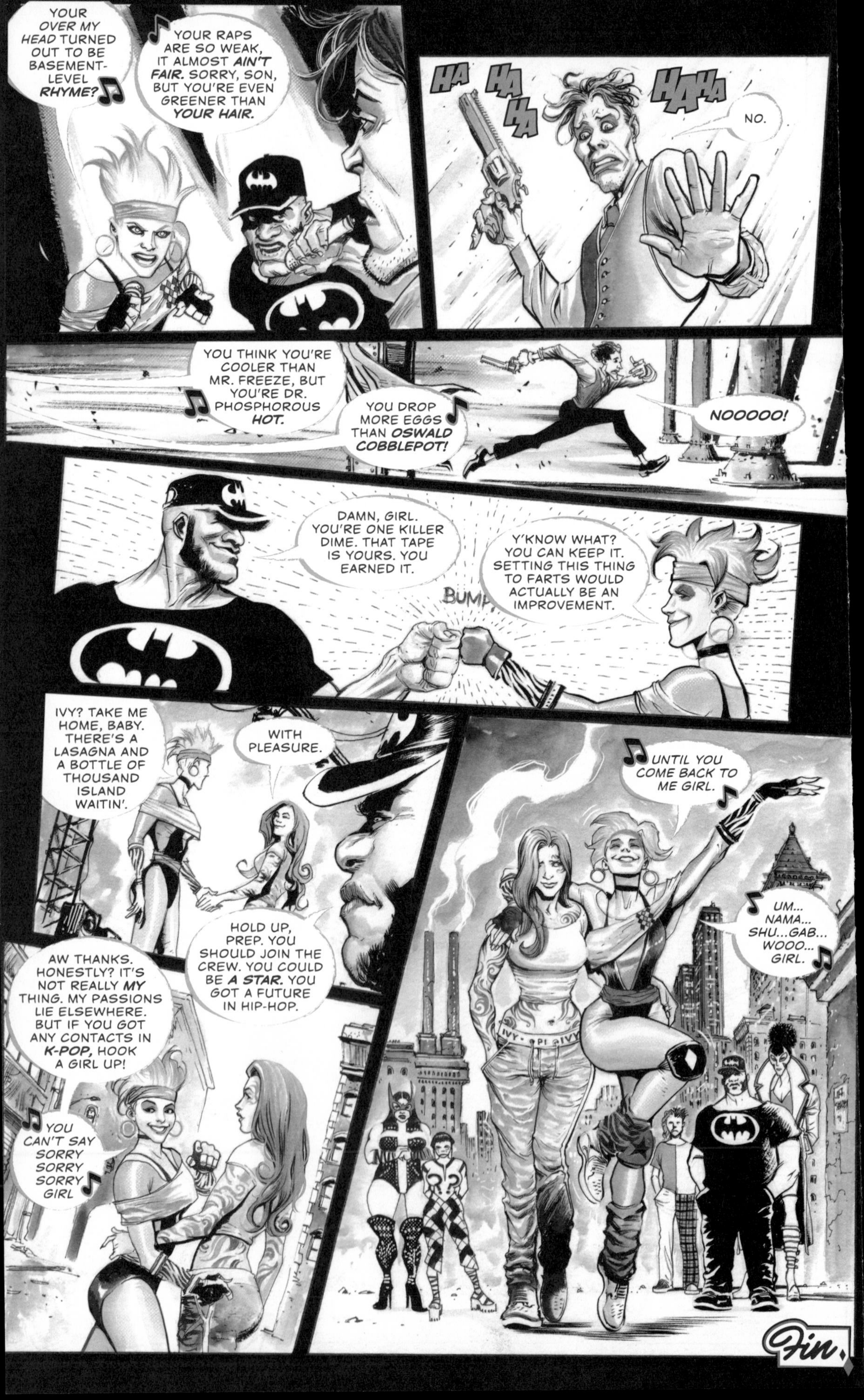
YOUR OVER MY HEAD TURNED OUT TO BE BASEMENT-LEVEL RHYME?
YOUR RAPS ARE SO WEAK, IT ALMOST AIN'T FAIR. SORRY, SON, BUT YOU'RE EVEN GREENER THAN YOUR HAIR.
HA HA HA HAHA
NO.
YOU THINK YOU'RE COOLER THAN MR. FREEZE, BUT YOU'RE DR. PHOSPHOROUS HOT.
YOU DROP MORE EGGS THAN OSWALD COBBLEPOT!
NOOOOO!
DAMN, GIRL. YOU'RE ONE KILLER DIME. THAT TAPE IS YOURS. YOU EARNED IT.
Y'KNOW WHAT? YOU CAN KEEP IT. SETTING THIS THING TO FARTS WOULD ACTUALLY BE AN IMPROVEMENT.
IVY? TAKE ME HOME, BABY. THERE'S A LASAGNA AND A BOTTLE OF THOUSAND ISLAND WAITIN'.
WITH PLEASURE.
HOLD UP, PREP. YOU SHOULD JOIN THE CREW. YOU COULD BE A STAR. YOU GOT A FUTURE IN HIP-HOP.
AW THANKS. HONESTLY? IT'S NOT REALLY MY THING. MY PASSIONS LIE ELSEWHERE. BUT IF YOU GOT ANY CONTACTS IN K-POP, HOOK A GIRL UP!
YOU CAN'T SAY SORRY SORRY SORRY GIRL
UNTIL YOU COME BACK TO ME GIRL.
UM... NAMA... SHU...GAB... WOOO... GIRL.
Fin.

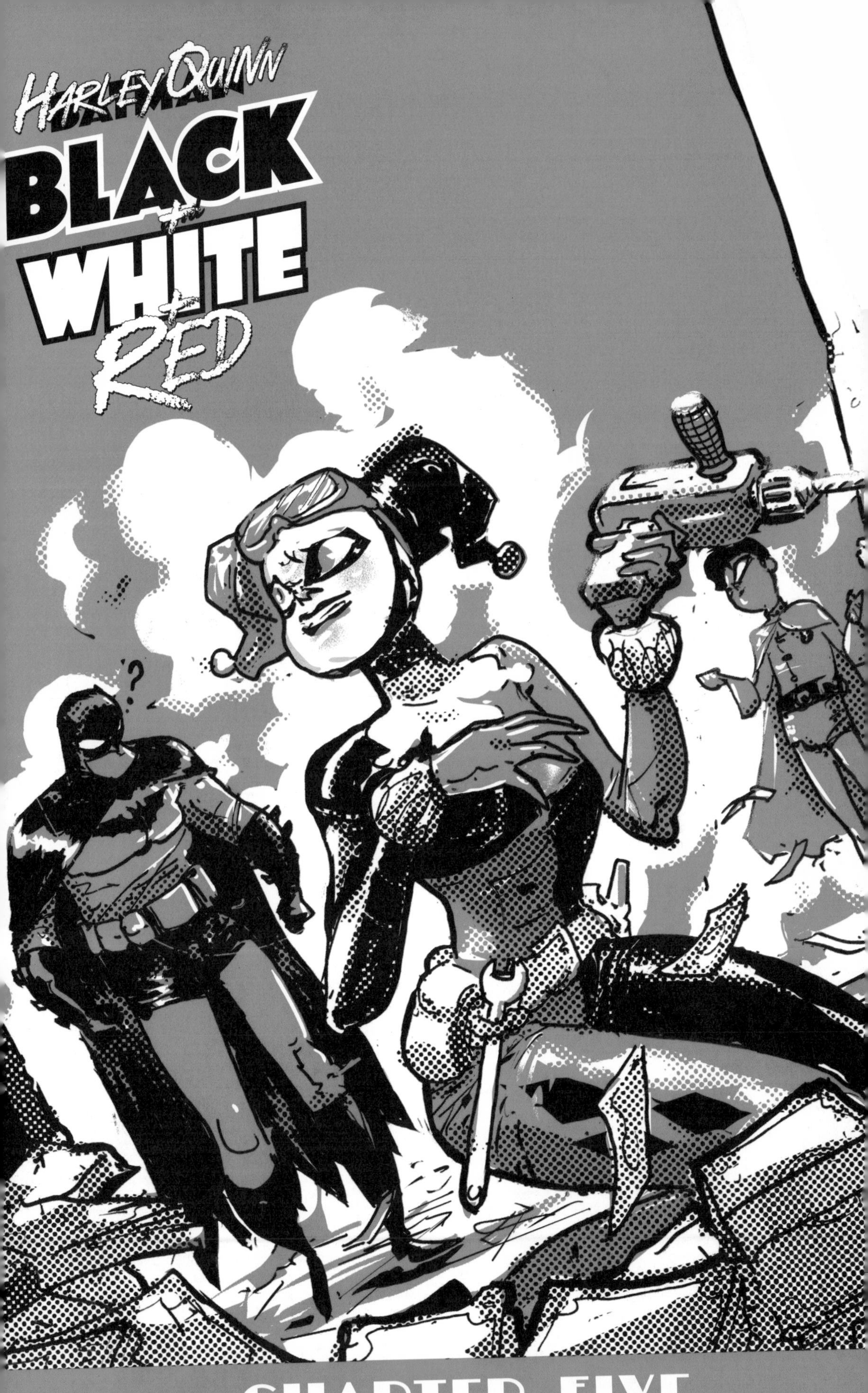
HARLEY QUINN
BLACK
+
WHITE
+
RED
?

CHAPTER FIVE

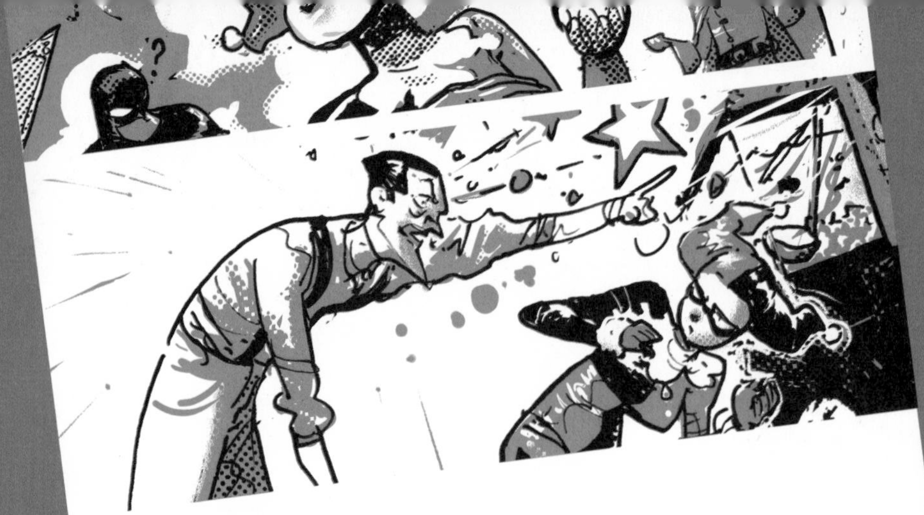

Harley Quinn
BLACK & WHITE & RED

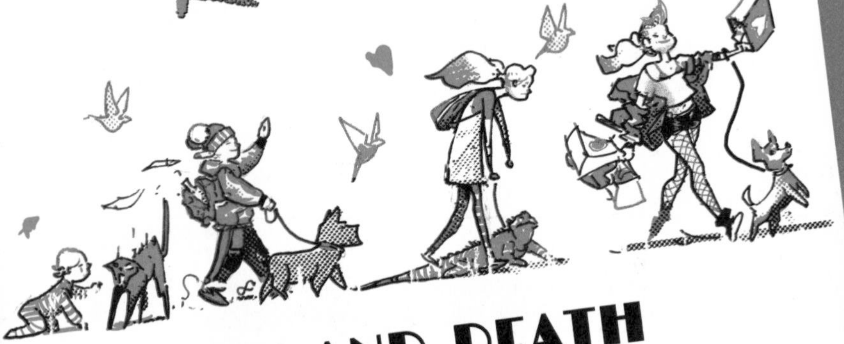

"THE LIFE AND DEATH OF HARLEY QUINN"

WRITER & ARTIST **RILEY ROSSMO**
LETTERER **DERON BENNETT**
EDITOR **AMEDEO TURTURRO**

HARLEY QUINN CREATED BY PAUL DINI & BRUCE TIMM
SUPERMAN CREATED BY JERRY SIEGEL AND JOE SHUSTER.
BY SPECIAL ARRANGEMENT WITH THE JERRY SIEGEL FAMILY

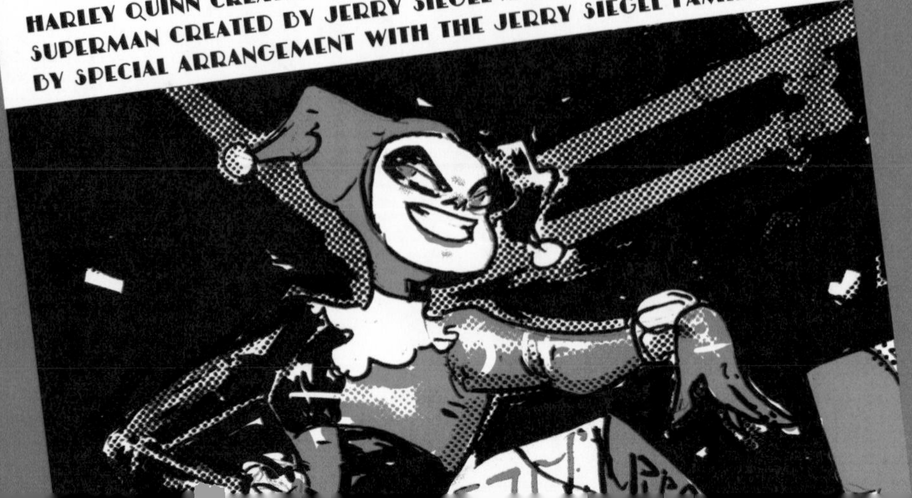

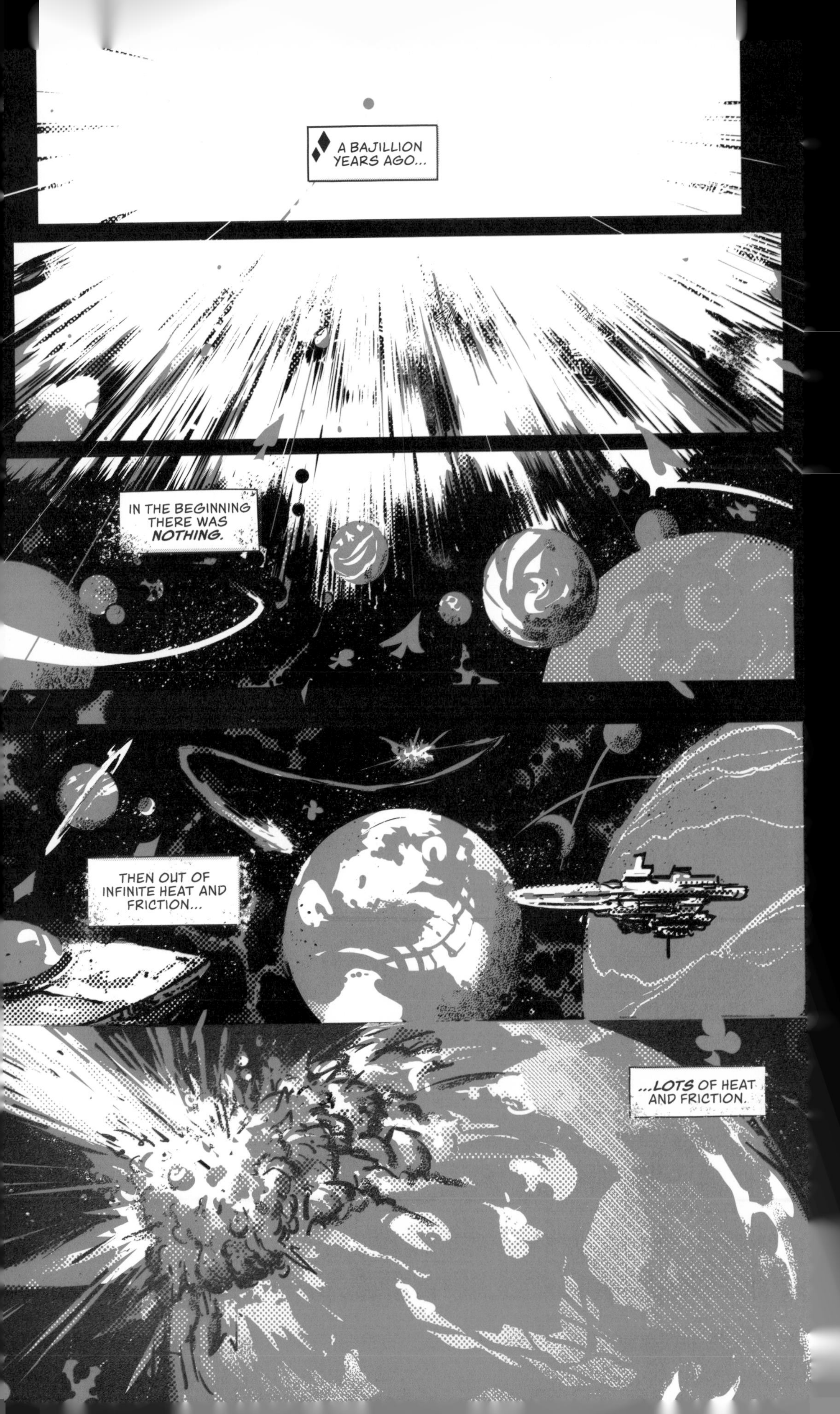
A BAJILLION YEARS AGO...
IN THE BEGINNING THERE WAS NOTHING.
THEN OUT OF INFINITE HEAT AND FRICTION...
...LOTS OF HEAT AND FRICTION.

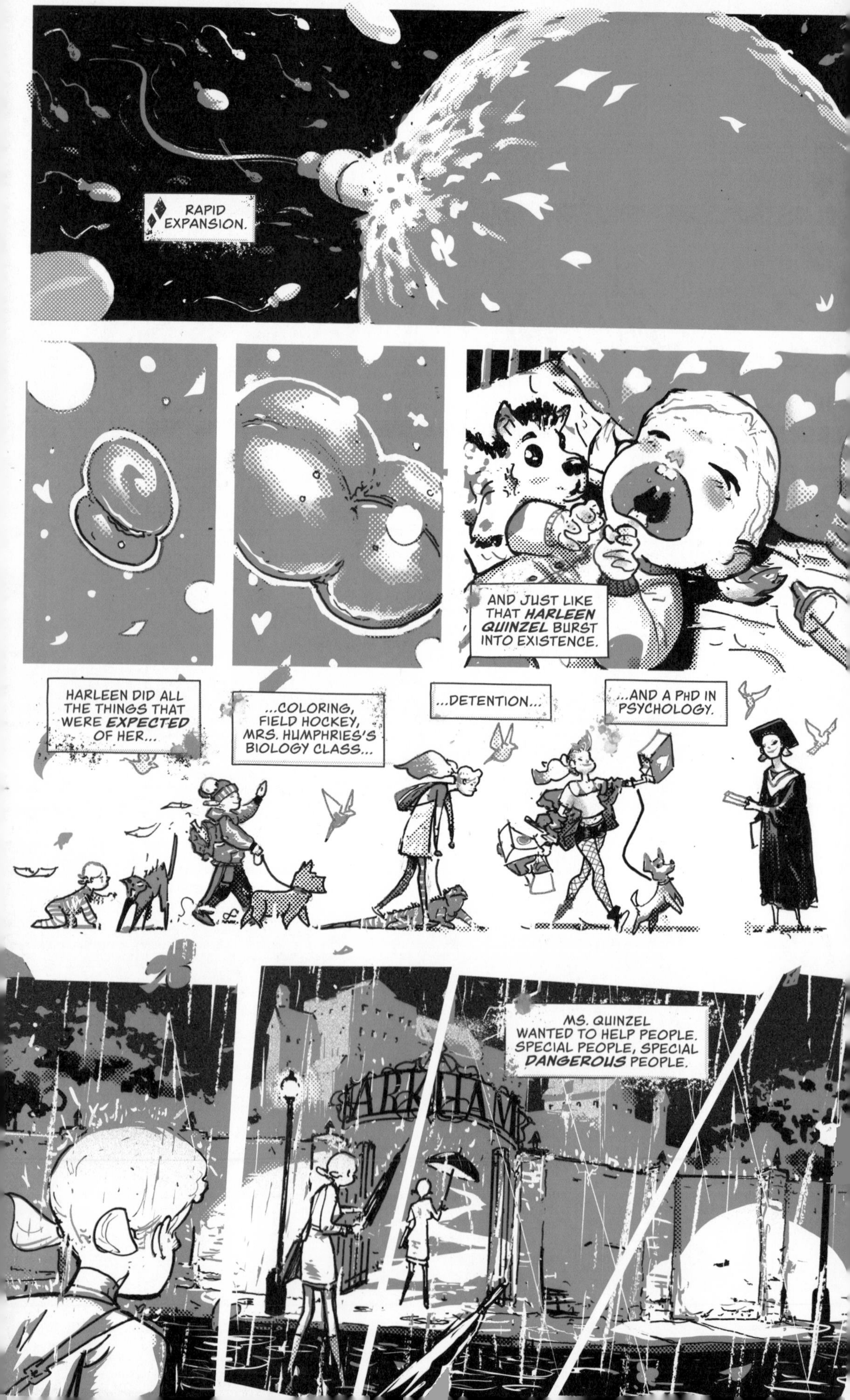
RAPID EXPANSION.
AND JUST LIKE THAT HARLEEN QUINZEL BURST INTO EXISTENCE.
HARLEEN DID ALL THE THINGS THAT WERE EXPECTED OF HER...
...COLORING, FIELD HOCKEY, MRS. HUMPHRIES'S BIOLOGY CLASS...
...DETENTION...
...AND A PHD IN PSYCHOLOGY.
MS. QUINZEL WANTED TO HELP PEOPLE. SPECIAL PEOPLE, SPECIAL DANGEROUS PEOPLE.

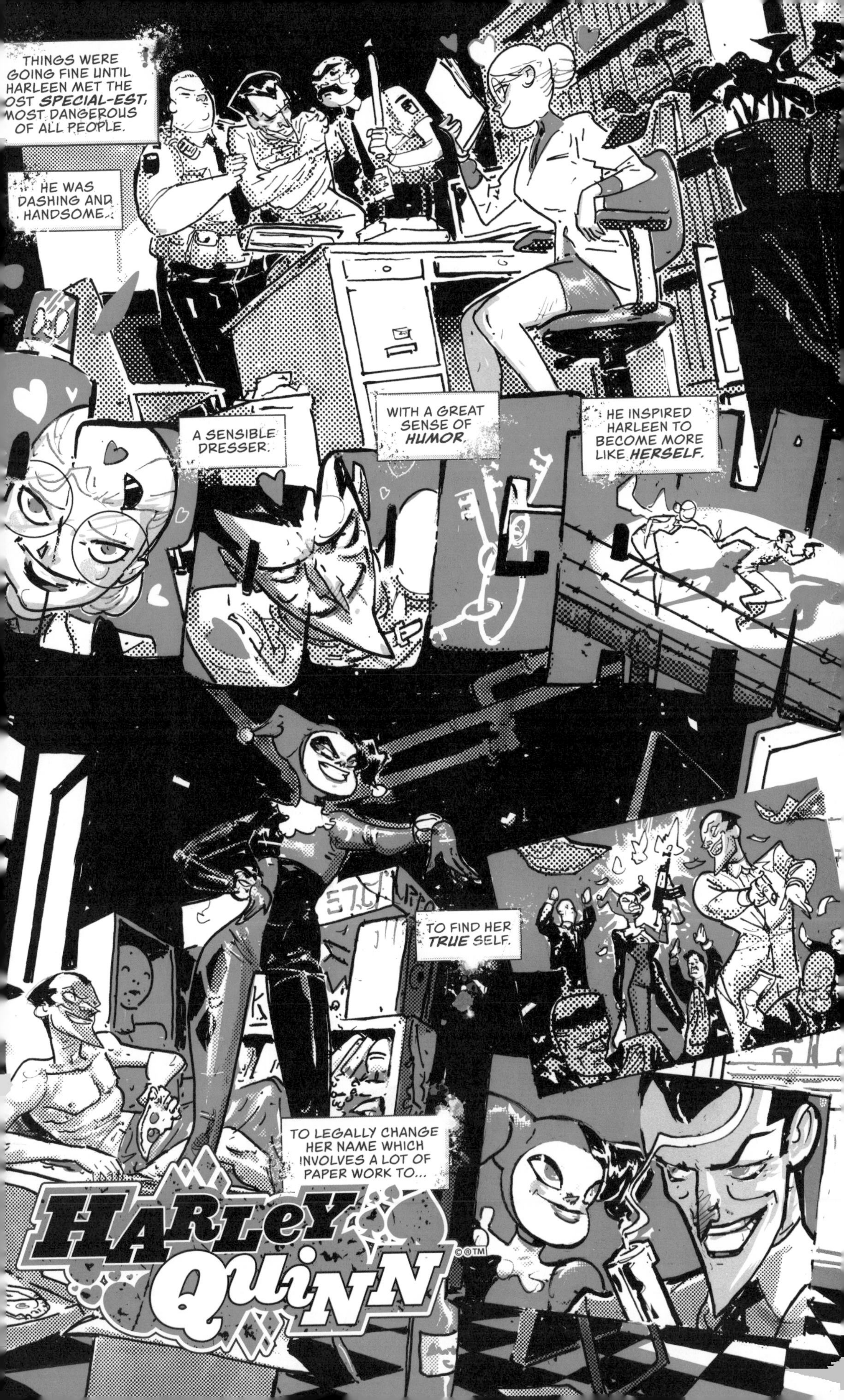
THINGS WERE GOING FINE UNTIL HARLEEN MET THE OST SPECIAL-EST, MOST DANGEROUS OF ALL PEOPLE.
HE WAS DASHING AND HANDSOME.
A SENSIBLE DRESSER.
WITH A GREAT SENSE OF HUMOR.
HE INSPIRED HARLEEN TO BECOME MORE LIKE HERSELF.
TO FIND HER TRUE SELF.
TO LEGALLY CHANGE HER NAME WHICH INVOLVES A LOT OF PAPER WORK TO...
HARLEY QUINN ©®TM

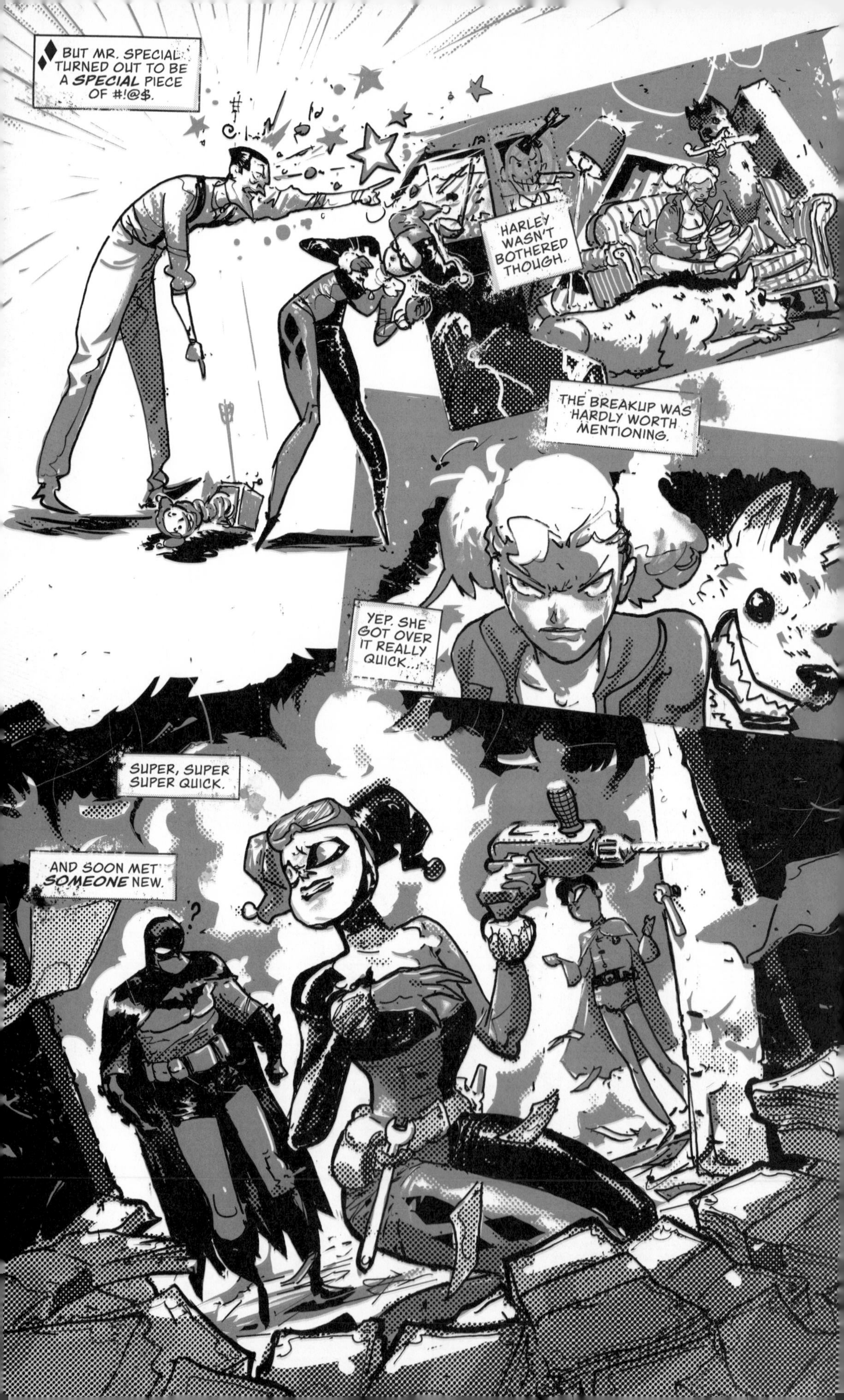
BUT MR. SPECIAL TURNED OUT TO BE A *SPECIAL* PIECE OF #!@$.
HARLEY WASN'T BOTHERED THOUGH.
THE BREAKUP WAS HARDLY WORTH MENTIONING.
YEP. SHE GOT OVER IT REALLY QUICK...
SUPER, SUPER SUPER QUICK.
AND SOON MET *SOMEONE* NEW.
?

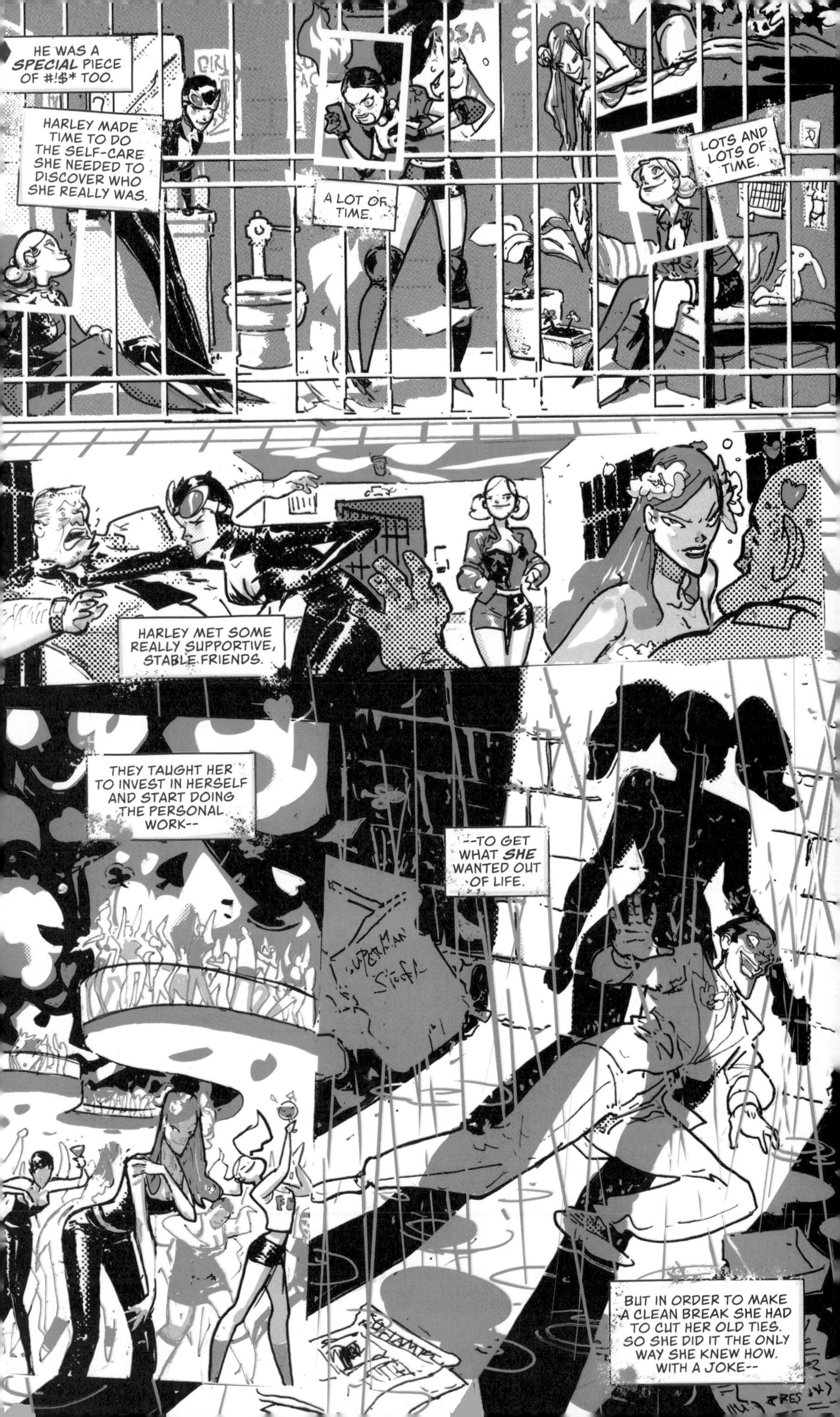
HE WAS A SPECIAL PIECE OF #!$* TOO.
HARLEY MADE TIME TO DO THE SELF-CARE SHE NEEDED TO DISCOVER WHO SHE REALLY WAS.
A LOT OF TIME.
LOTS AND LOTS OF TIME.
HARLEY MET SOME REALLY SUPPORTIVE, STABLE FRIENDS.
THEY TAUGHT HER TO INVEST IN HERSELF AND START DOING THE PERSONAL WORK--
--TO GET WHAT SHE WANTED OUT OF LIFE.
BUT IN ORDER TO MAKE A CLEAN BREAK SHE HAD TO CUT HER OLD TIES. SO SHE DID IT THE ONLY WAY SHE KNEW HOW. WITH A JOKE--

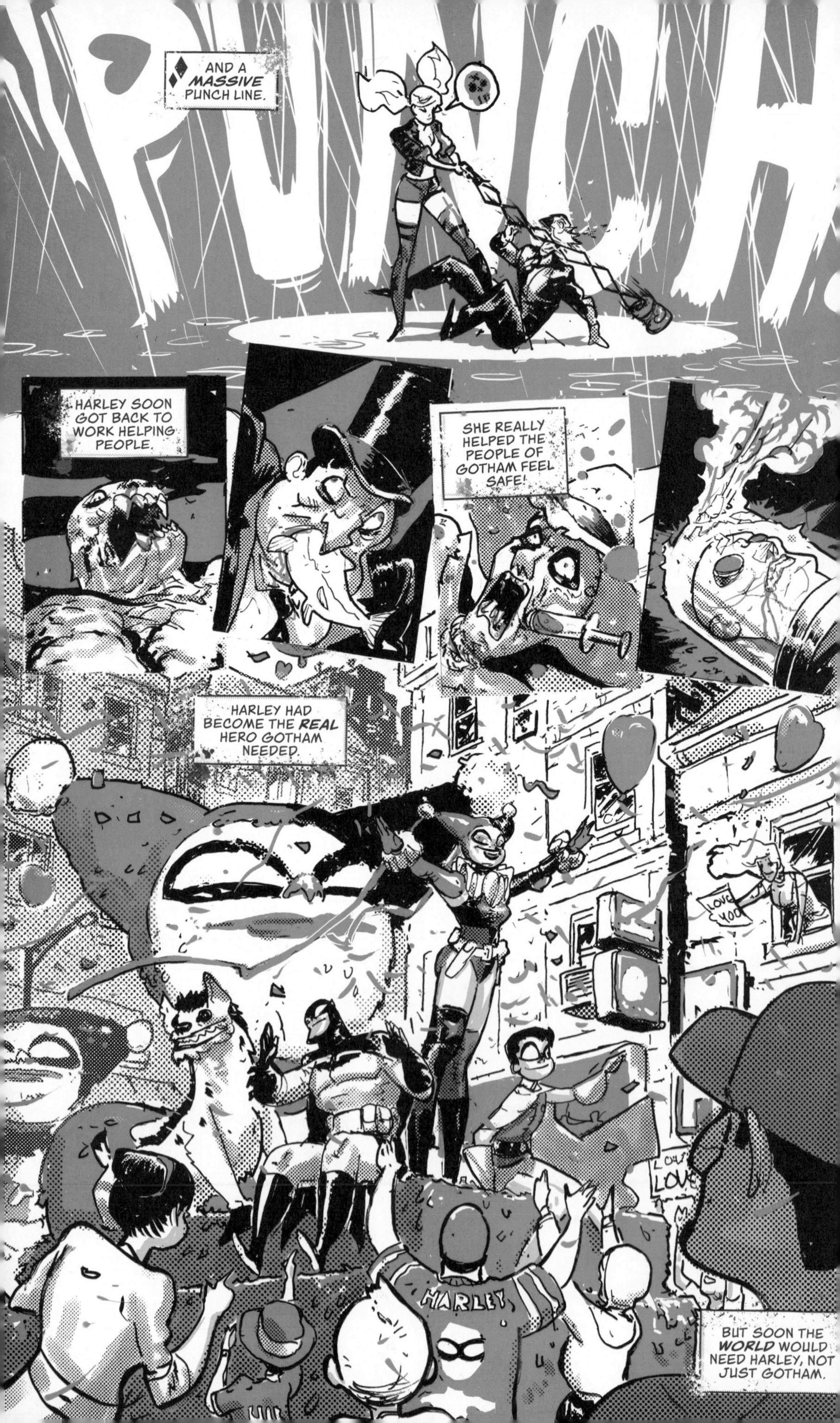
PUNCH!
AND A MASSIVE PUNCH LINE.
HARLEY SOON GOT BACK TO WORK HELPING PEOPLE.
SHE REALLY HELPED THE PEOPLE OF GOTHAM FEEL SAFE!
HARLEY HAD BECOME THE REAL HERO GOTHAM NEEDED.
LOVE YOU
LOVE
HARLEY
BUT SOON THE WORLD WOULD NEED HARLEY, NOT JUST GOTHAM.

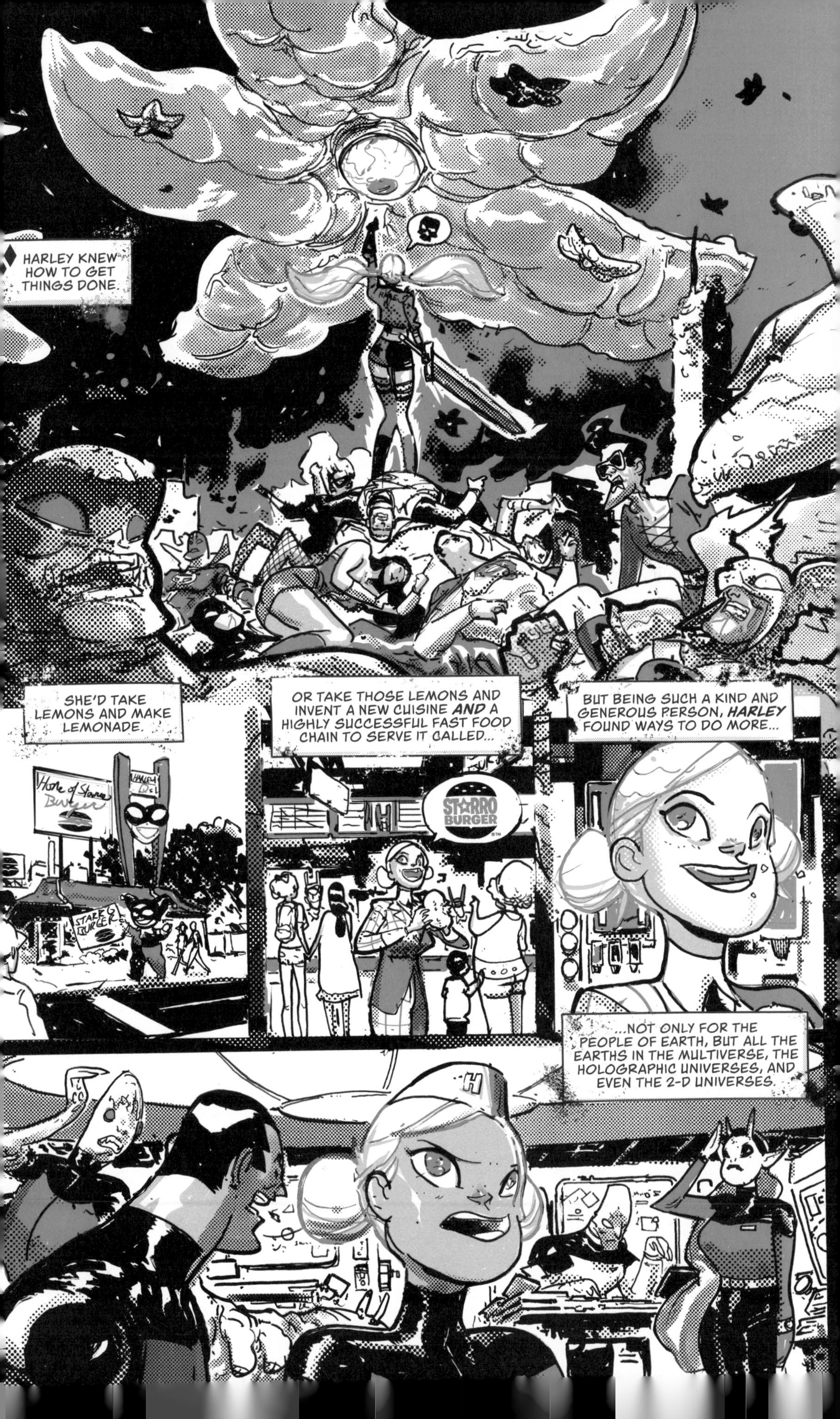
HARLEY KNEW HOW TO GET THINGS DONE.
SHE'D TAKE LEMONS AND MAKE LEMONADE.
OR TAKE THOSE LEMONS AND INVENT A NEW CUISINE AND A HIGHLY SUCCESSFUL FAST FOOD CHAIN TO SERVE IT CALLED...
STARRO BURGER
BUT BEING SUCH A KIND AND GENEROUS PERSON, HARLEY FOUND WAYS TO DO MORE...
...NOT ONLY FOR THE PEOPLE OF EARTH, BUT ALL THE EARTHS IN THE MULTIVERSE, THE HOLOGRAPHIC UNIVERSES, AND EVEN THE 2-D UNIVERSES.

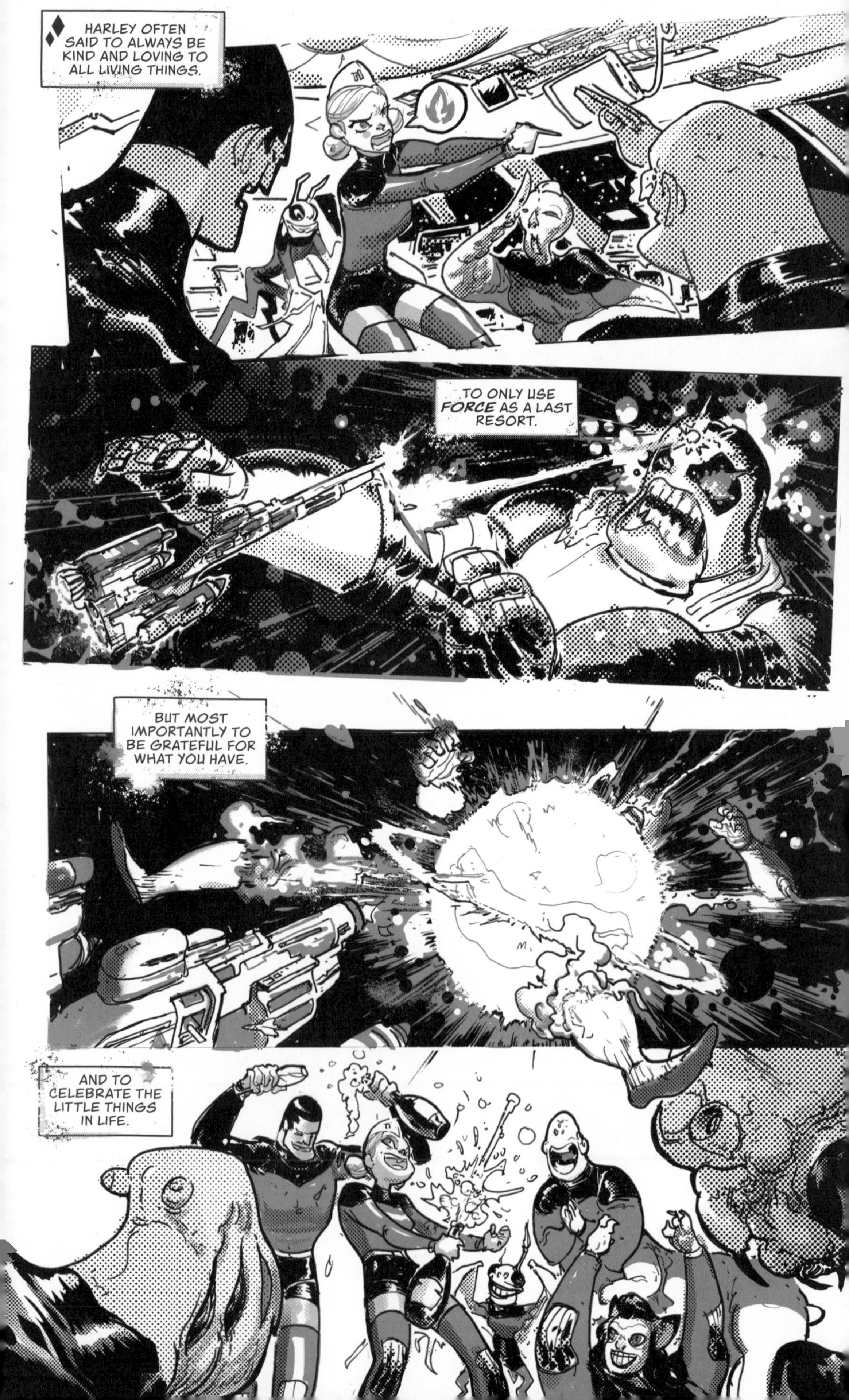
HARLEY OFTEN SAID TO ALWAYS BE KIND AND LOVING TO ALL LIVING THINGS.
TO ONLY USE *FORCE* AS A LAST RESORT.
BUT MOST IMPORTANTLY TO BE GRATEFUL FOR WHAT YOU HAVE.
AND TO CELEBRATE THE LITTLE THINGS IN LIFE.

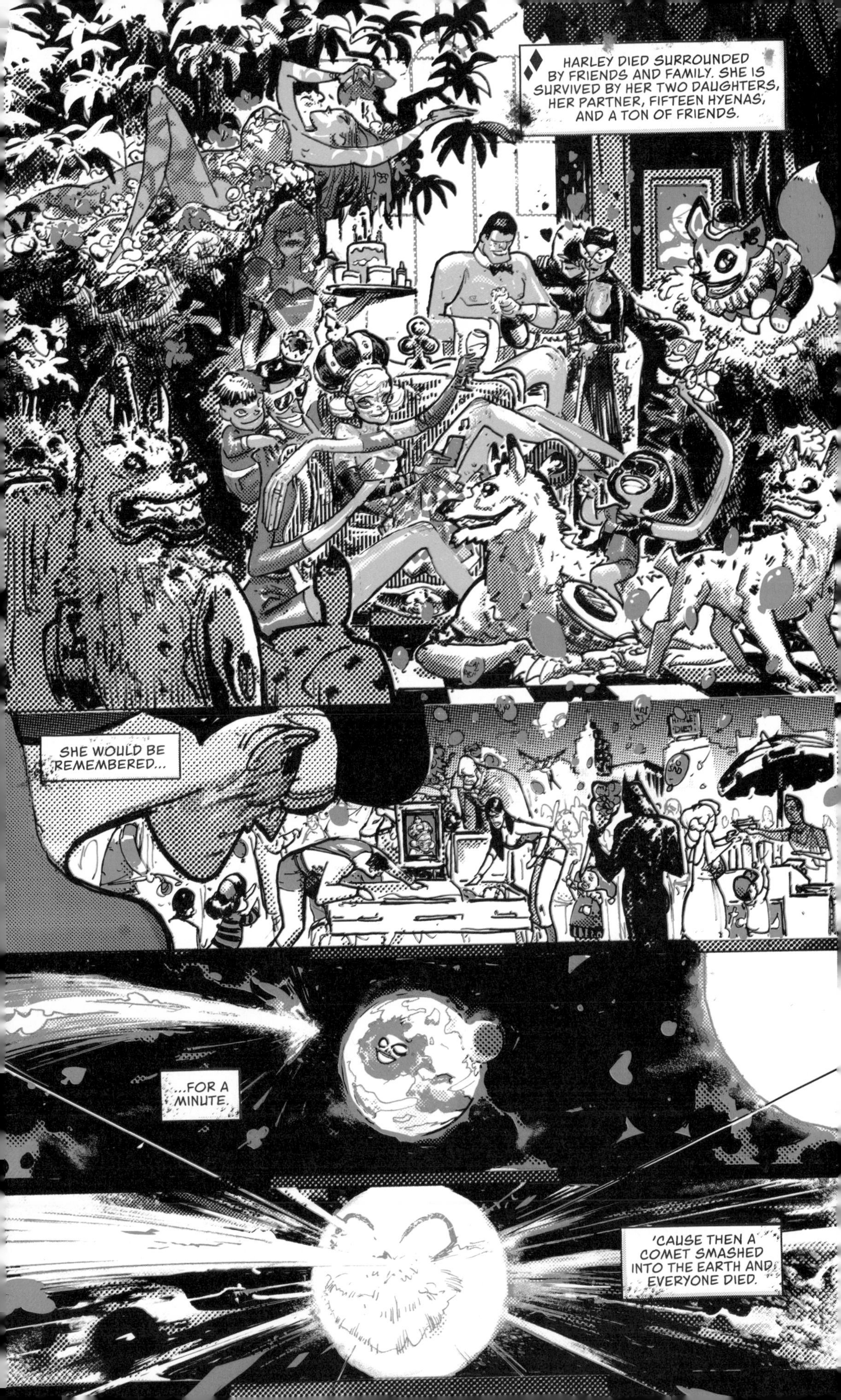
HARLEY DIED SURROUNDED BY FRIENDS AND FAMILY. SHE IS SURVIVED BY HER TWO DAUGHTERS, HER PARTNER, FIFTEEN HYENAS, AND A TON OF FRIENDS.
SHE WOULD BE REMEMBERED...
...FOR A MINUTE.
'CAUSE THEN A COMET SMASHED INTO THE EARTH AND EVERYONE DIED.

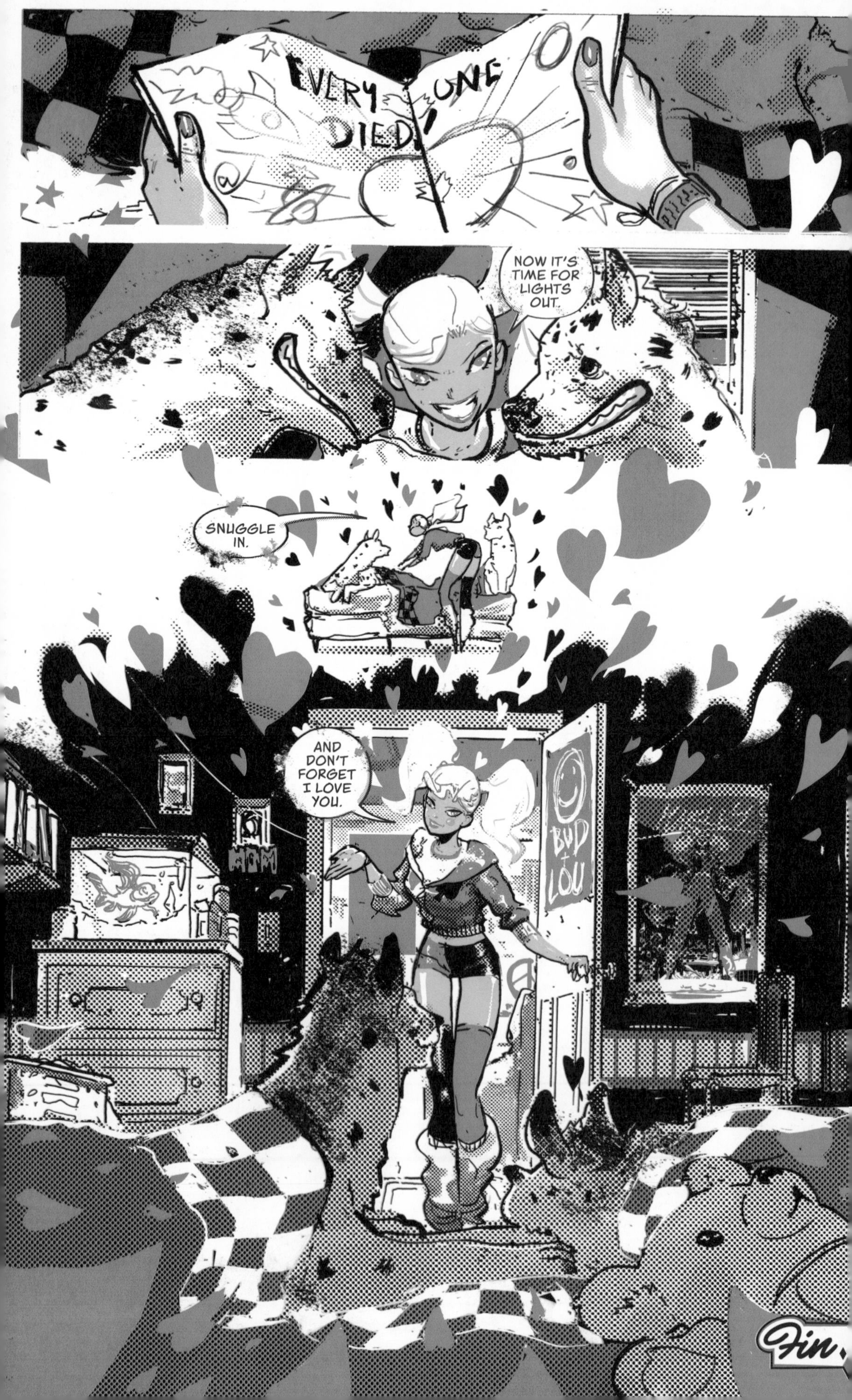

EVERY ONE DIED!
NOW IT'S TIME FOR LIGHTS OUT.
SNUGGLE IN.
AND DON'T FORGET I LOVE YOU.
BUD + LOU
Fin.

HARLEY QUINN BLACK and WHITE + RED

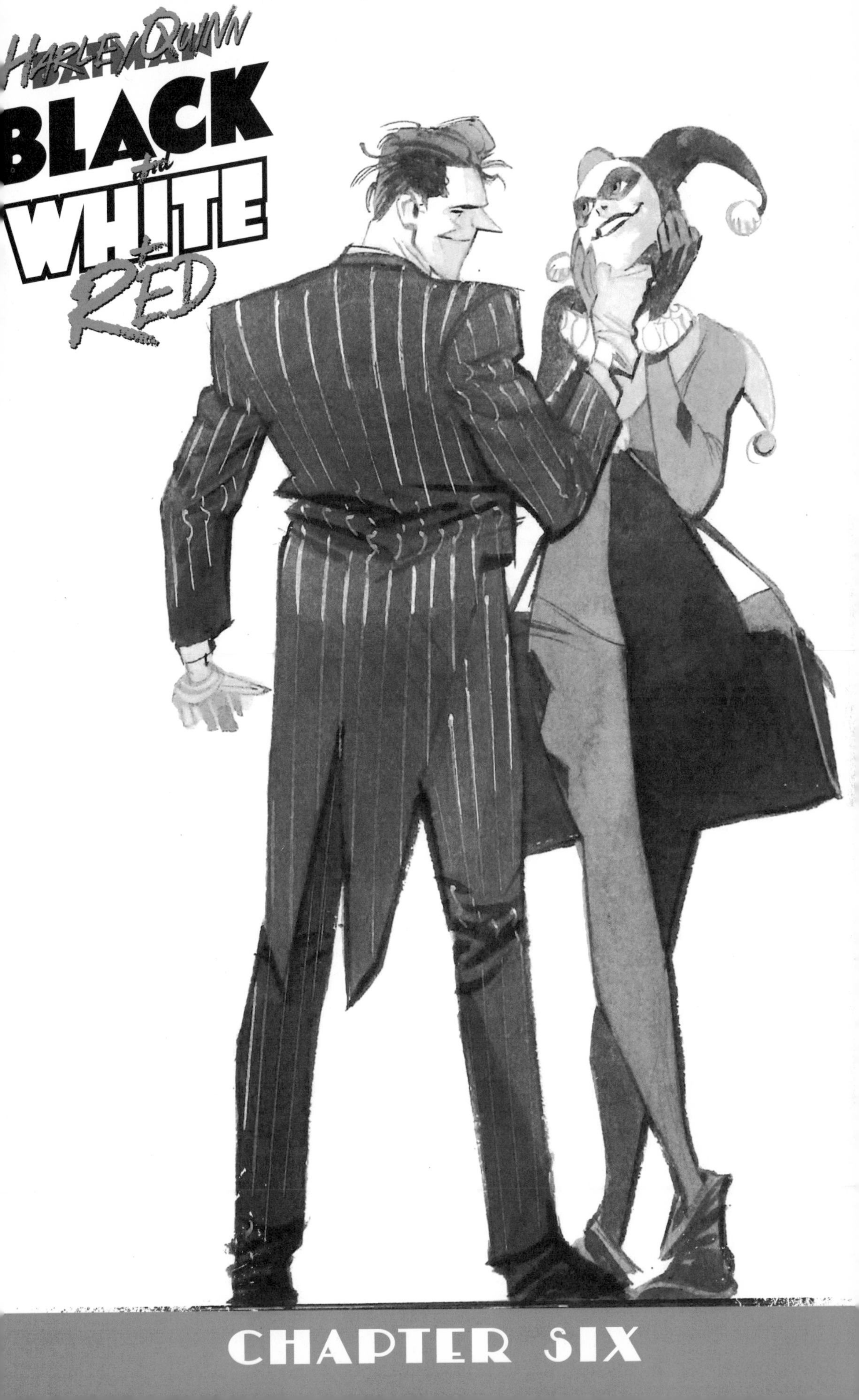

CHAPTER SIX

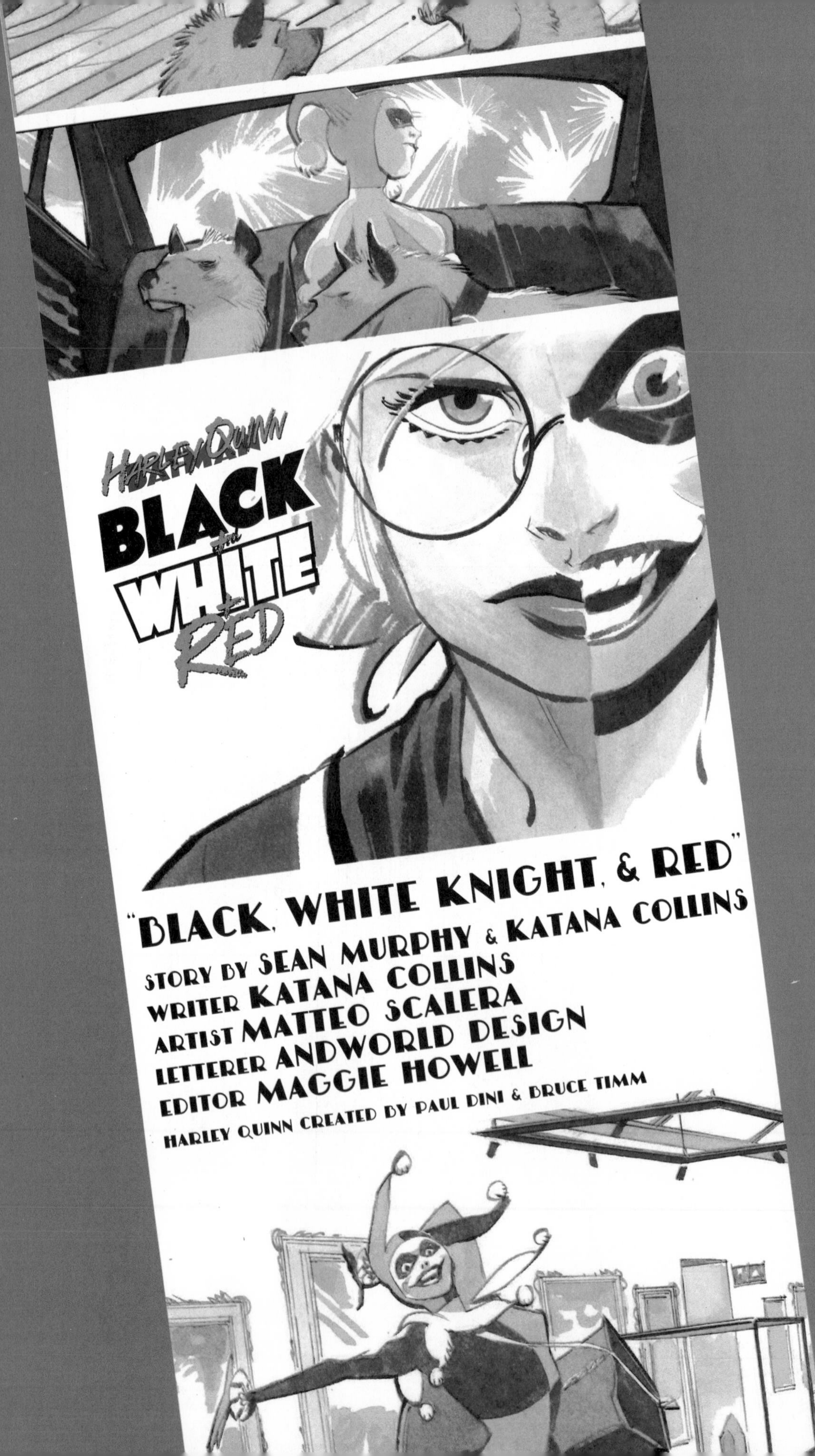
HARLEY QUINN
BLACK and WHITE + RED
"BLACK, WHITE KNIGHT, & RED"
STORY BY SEAN MURPHY & KATANA COLLINS
WRITER KATANA COLLINS
ARTIST MATTEO SCALERA
LETTERER ANDWORLD DESIGN
EDITOR MAGGIE HOWELL
HARLEY QUINN CREATED BY PAUL DINI & BRUCE TIMM

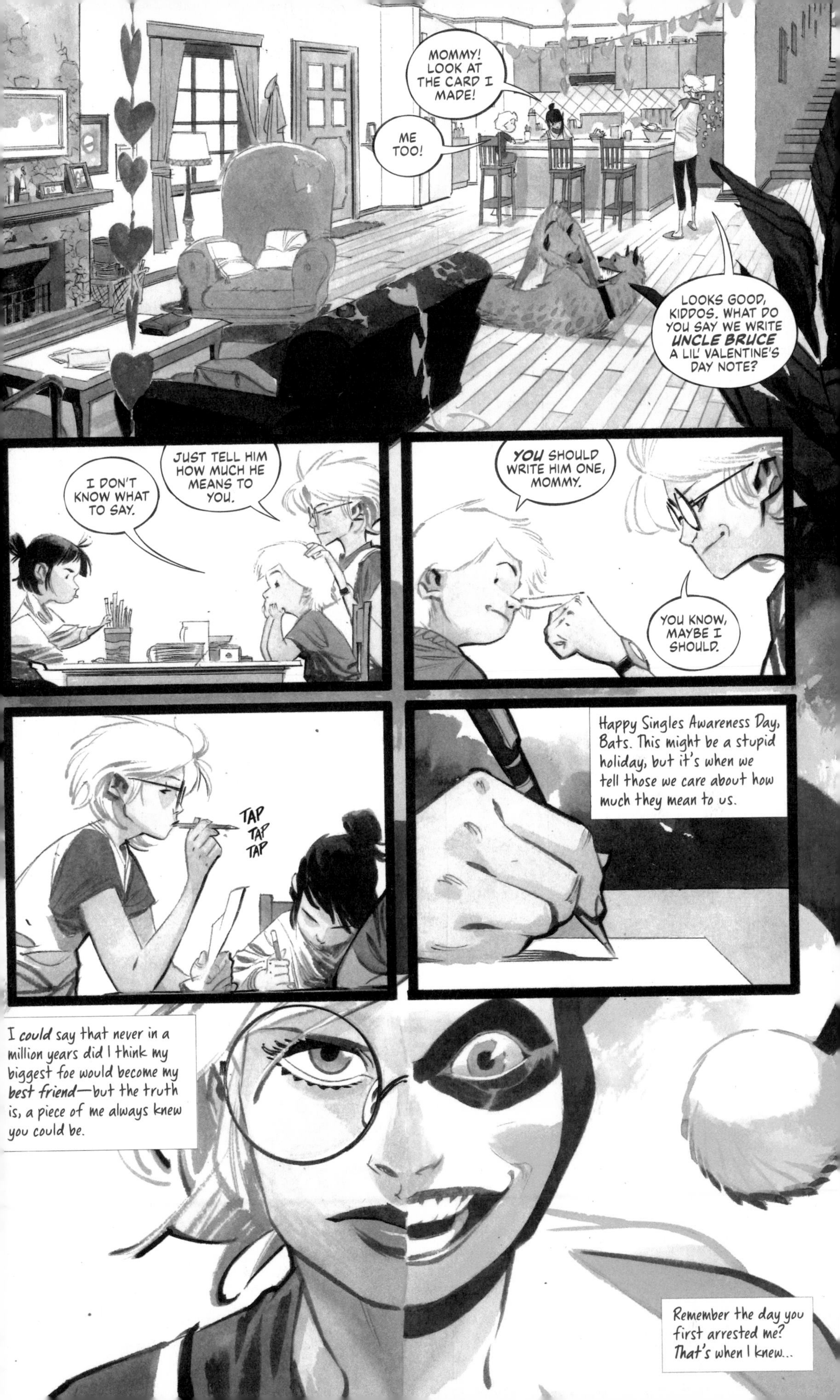
MOMMY! LOOK AT THE CARD I MADE!
ME TOO!
LOOKS GOOD, KIDDOS. WHAT DO YOU SAY WE WRITE UNCLE BRUCE A LIL' VALENTINE'S DAY NOTE?
I DON'T KNOW WHAT TO SAY.
JUST TELL HIM HOW MUCH HE MEANS TO YOU.
YOU SHOULD WRITE HIM ONE, MOMMY.
YOU KNOW, MAYBE I SHOULD.
TAP TAP TAP
Happy Singles Awareness Day, Bats. This might be a stupid holiday, but it's when we tell those we care about how much they mean to us.
I could say that never in a million years did I think my biggest foe would become my best friend—but the truth is, a piece of me always knew you could be.
Remember the day you first arrested me? That's when I knew...

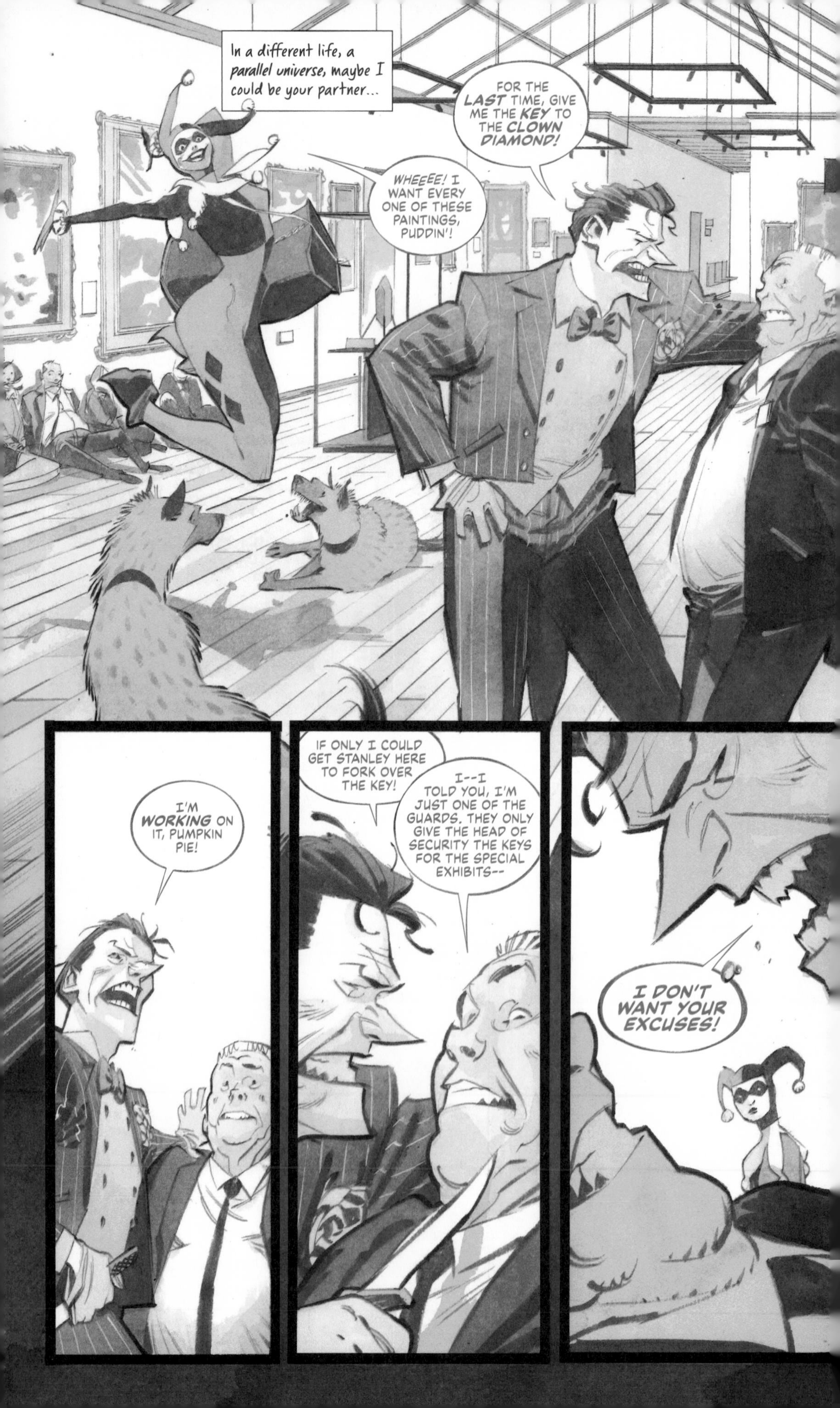

In a different life, a parallel universe, maybe I could be your partner...
FOR THE LAST TIME, GIVE ME THE KEY TO THE CLOWN DIAMOND!
WHEEEE! I WANT EVERY ONE OF THESE PAINTINGS, PUDDIN'!
I'M WORKING ON IT, PUMPKIN PIE!
IF ONLY I COULD GET STANLEY HERE TO FORK OVER THE KEY!
I--I TOLD YOU, I'M JUST ONE OF THE GUARDS. THEY ONLY GIVE THE HEAD OF SECURITY THE KEYS FOR THE SPECIAL EXHIBITS--
I DON'T WANT YOUR EXCUSES!

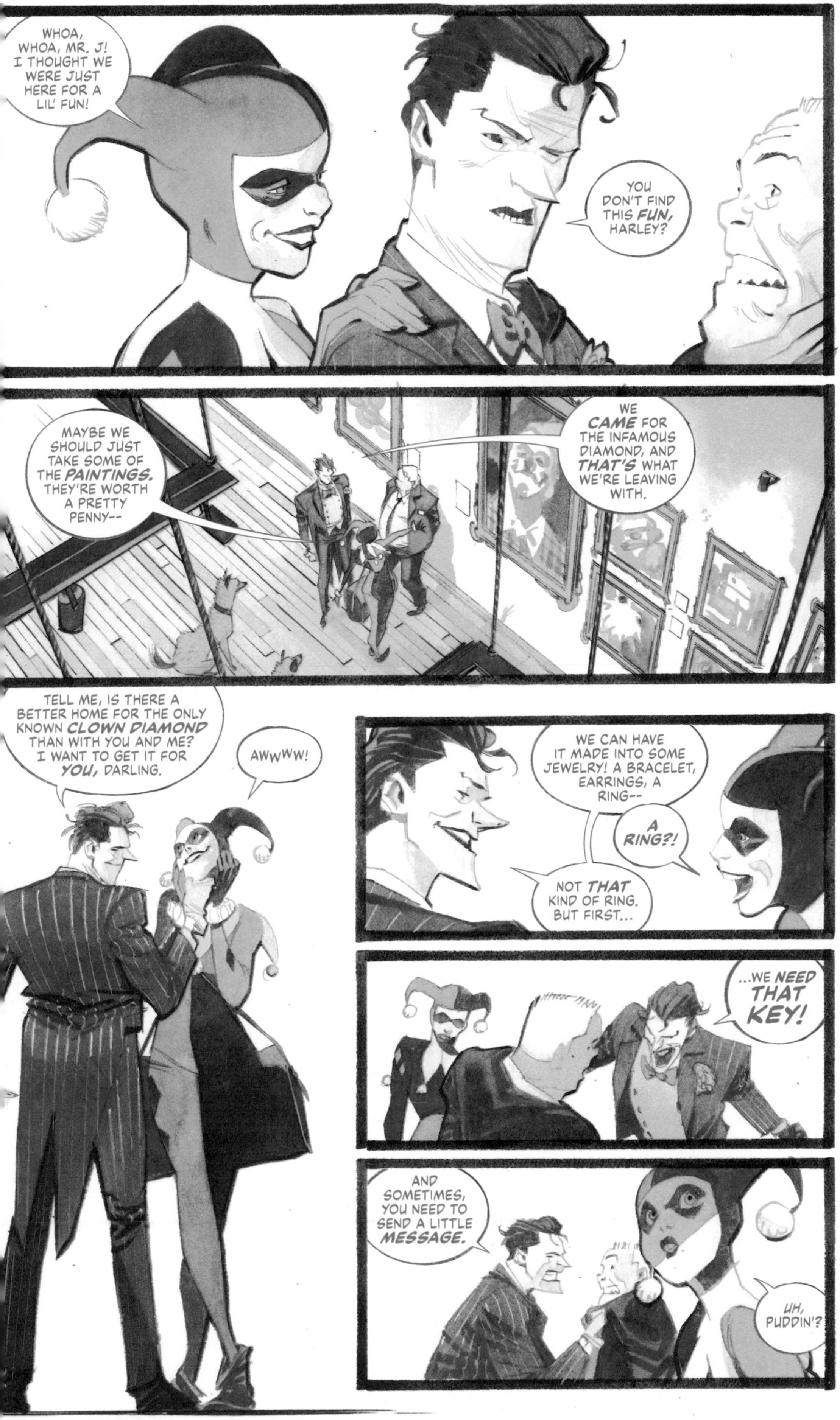

WHOA, WHOA, MR. J! I THOUGHT WE WERE JUST HERE FOR A LIL' FUN!
YOU DON'T FIND THIS FUN, HARLEY?
MAYBE WE SHOULD JUST TAKE SOME OF THE PAINTINGS. THEY'RE WORTH A PRETTY PENNY--
WE CAME FOR THE INFAMOUS DIAMOND, AND THAT'S WHAT WE'RE LEAVING WITH.
TELL ME, IS THERE A BETTER HOME FOR THE ONLY KNOWN CLOWN DIAMOND THAN WITH YOU AND ME? I WANT TO GET IT FOR YOU, DARLING.
AWWWW!
WE CAN HAVE IT MADE INTO SOME JEWELRY! A BRACELET, EARRINGS, A RING--
A RING?!
NOT THAT KIND OF RING. BUT FIRST...
...WE NEED THAT KEY!
AND SOMETIMES, YOU NEED TO SEND A LITTLE MESSAGE.
UH, PUDDIN'?

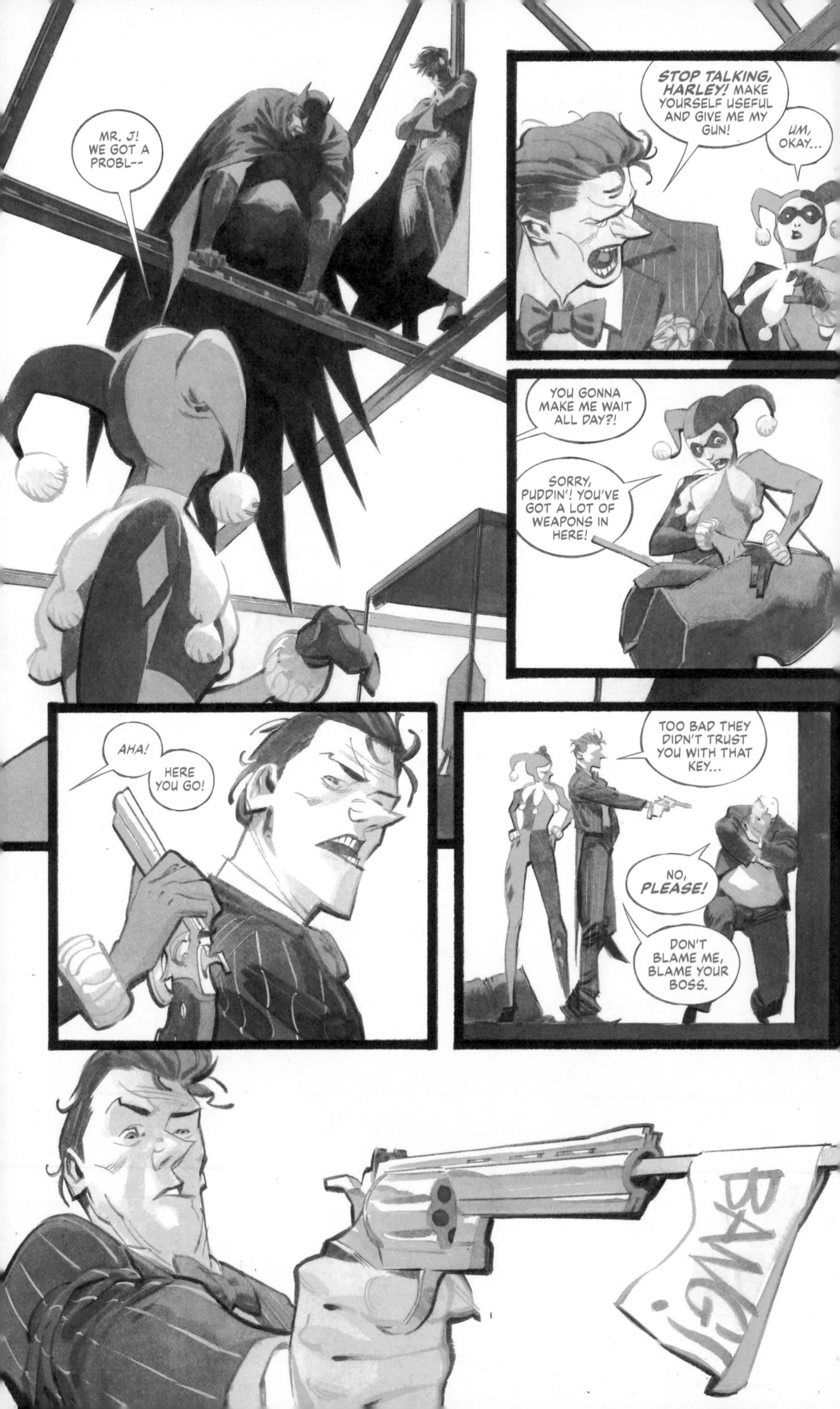
MR. J! WE GOT A PROBL--
STOP TALKING, HARLEY! MAKE YOURSELF USEFUL AND GIVE ME MY GUN!
UM, OKAY...
YOU GONNA MAKE ME WAIT ALL DAY?!
SORRY, PUDDIN'! YOU'VE GOT A LOT OF WEAPONS IN HERE!
AHA!
HERE YOU GO!
TOO BAD THEY DIDN'T TRUST YOU WITH THAT KEY...
NO, PLEASE!
DON'T BLAME ME, BLAME YOUR BOSS.
BANG!

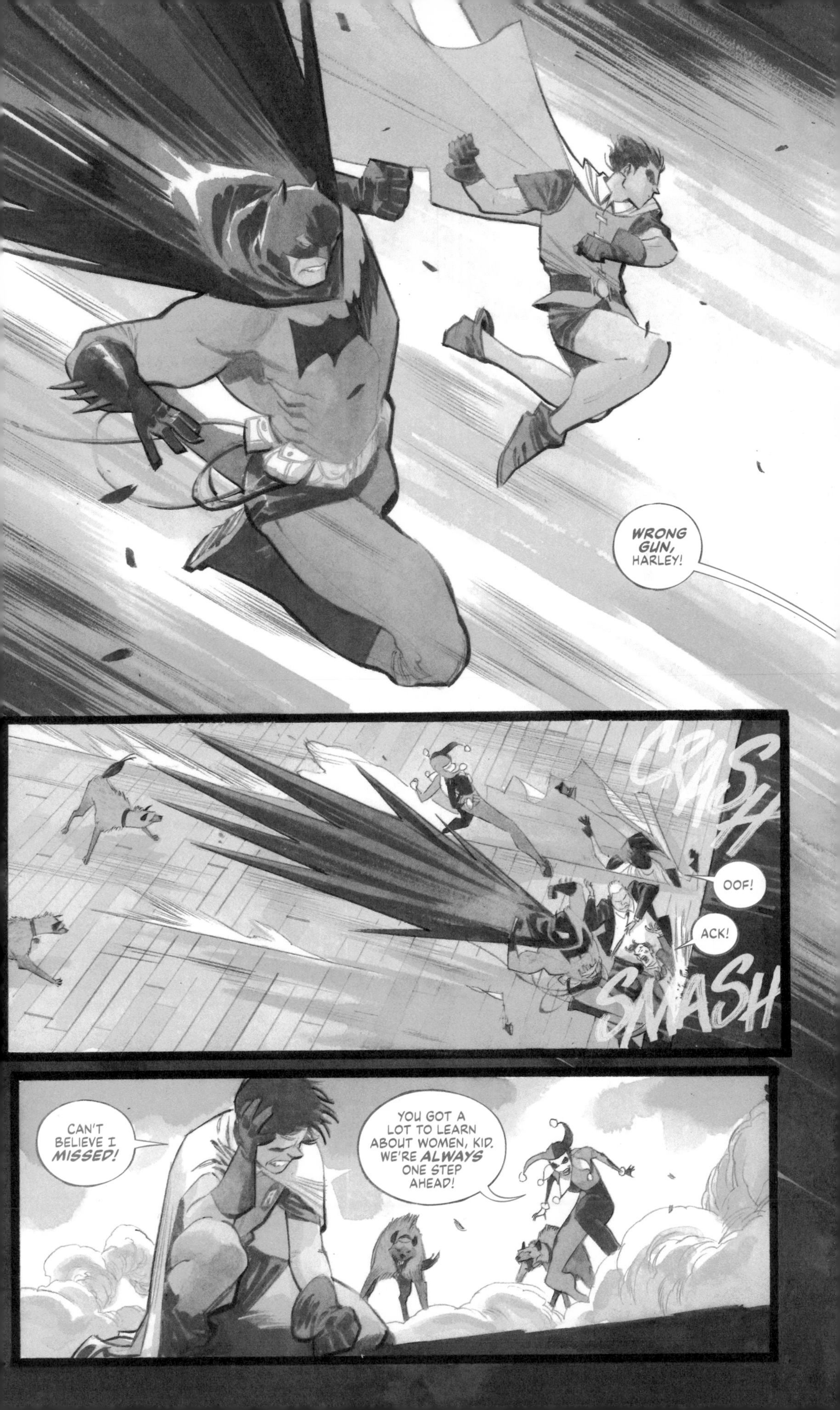
WRONG GUN, HARLEY!
CRASH
OOF!
ACK!
SMASH
CAN'T BELIEVE I MISSED!
YOU GOT A LOT TO LEARN ABOUT WOMEN, KID. WE'RE ALWAYS ONE STEP AHEAD!

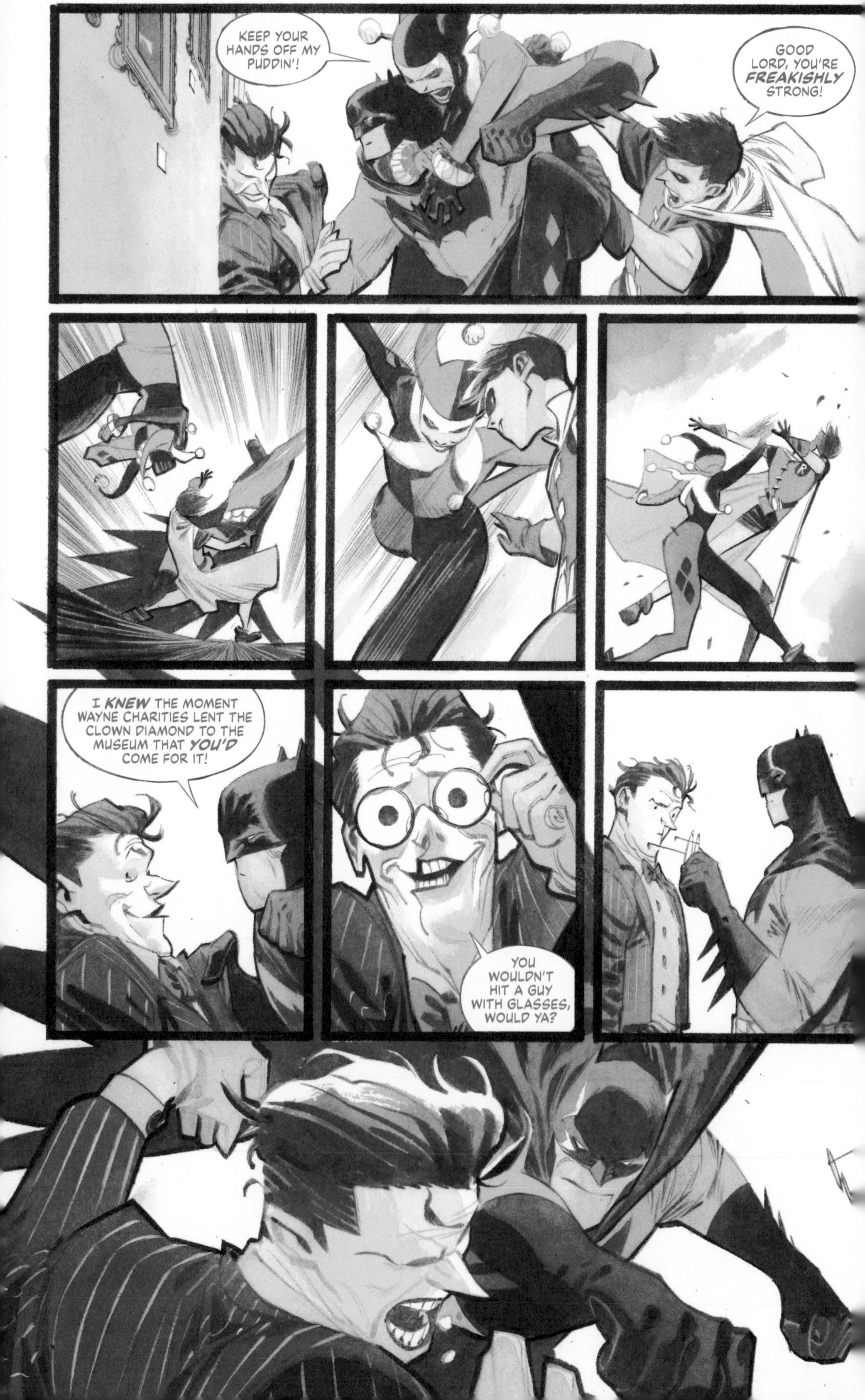
KEEP YOUR HANDS OFF MY PUDDIN'!
GOOD LORD, YOU'RE FREAKISHLY STRONG!
I KNEW THE MOMENT WAYNE CHARITIES LENT THE CLOWN DIAMOND TO THE MUSEUM THAT YOU'D COME FOR IT!
YOU WOULDN'T HIT A GUY WITH GLASSES, WOULD YA?

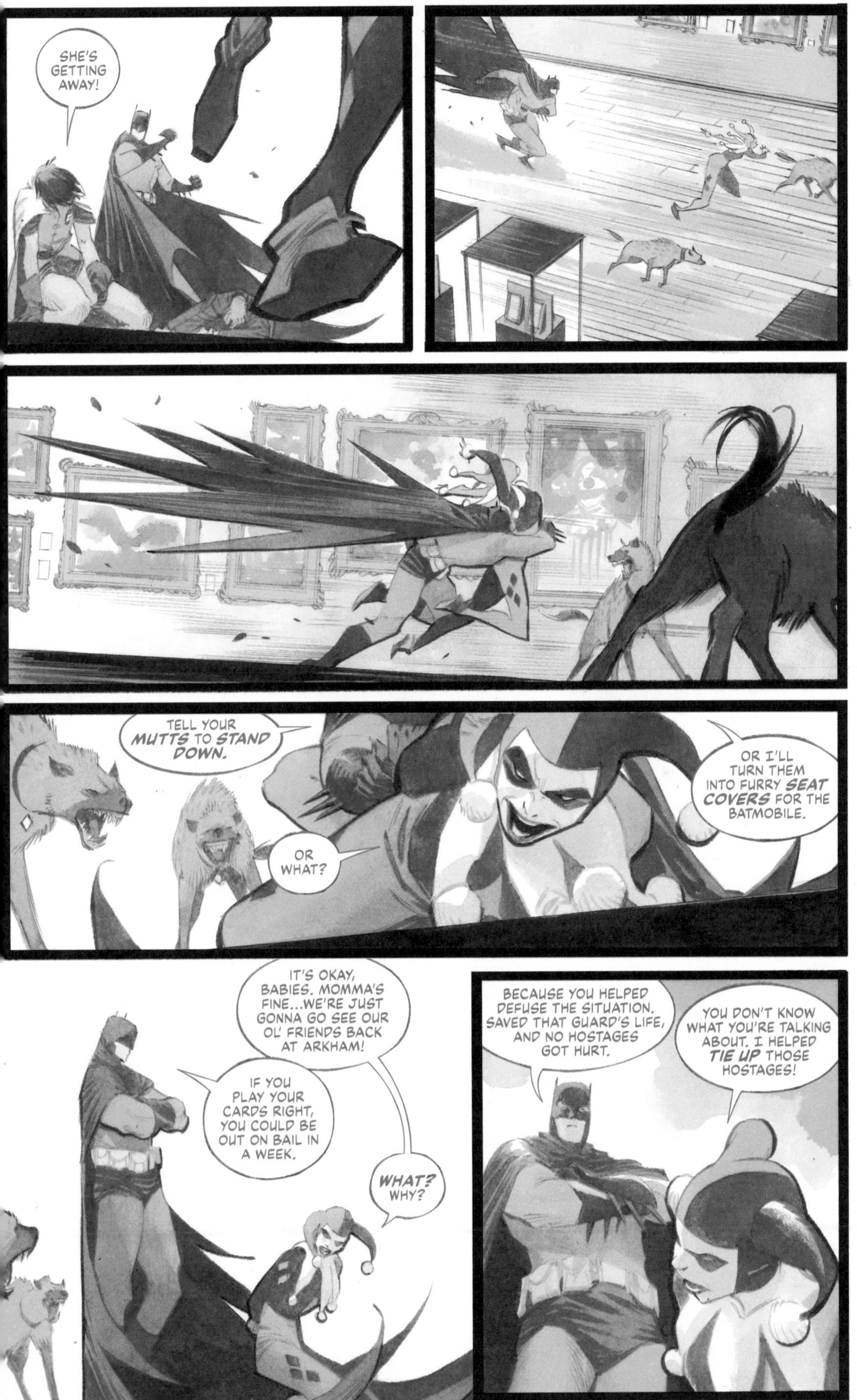
SHE'S GETTING AWAY!
TELL YOUR MUTTS TO STAND DOWN.
OR WHAT?
OR I'LL TURN THEM INTO FURRY SEAT COVERS FOR THE BATMOBILE.
IT'S OKAY, BABIES. MOMMA'S FINE...WE'RE JUST GONNA GO SEE OUR OL' FRIENDS BACK AT ARKHAM!
IF YOU PLAY YOUR CARDS RIGHT, YOU COULD BE OUT ON BAIL IN A WEEK.
WHAT? WHY?
BECAUSE YOU HELPED DEFUSE THE SITUATION. SAVED THAT GUARD'S LIFE, AND NO HOSTAGES GOT HURT.
YOU DON'T KNOW WHAT YOU'RE TALKING ABOUT. I HELPED TIE UP THOSE HOSTAGES!

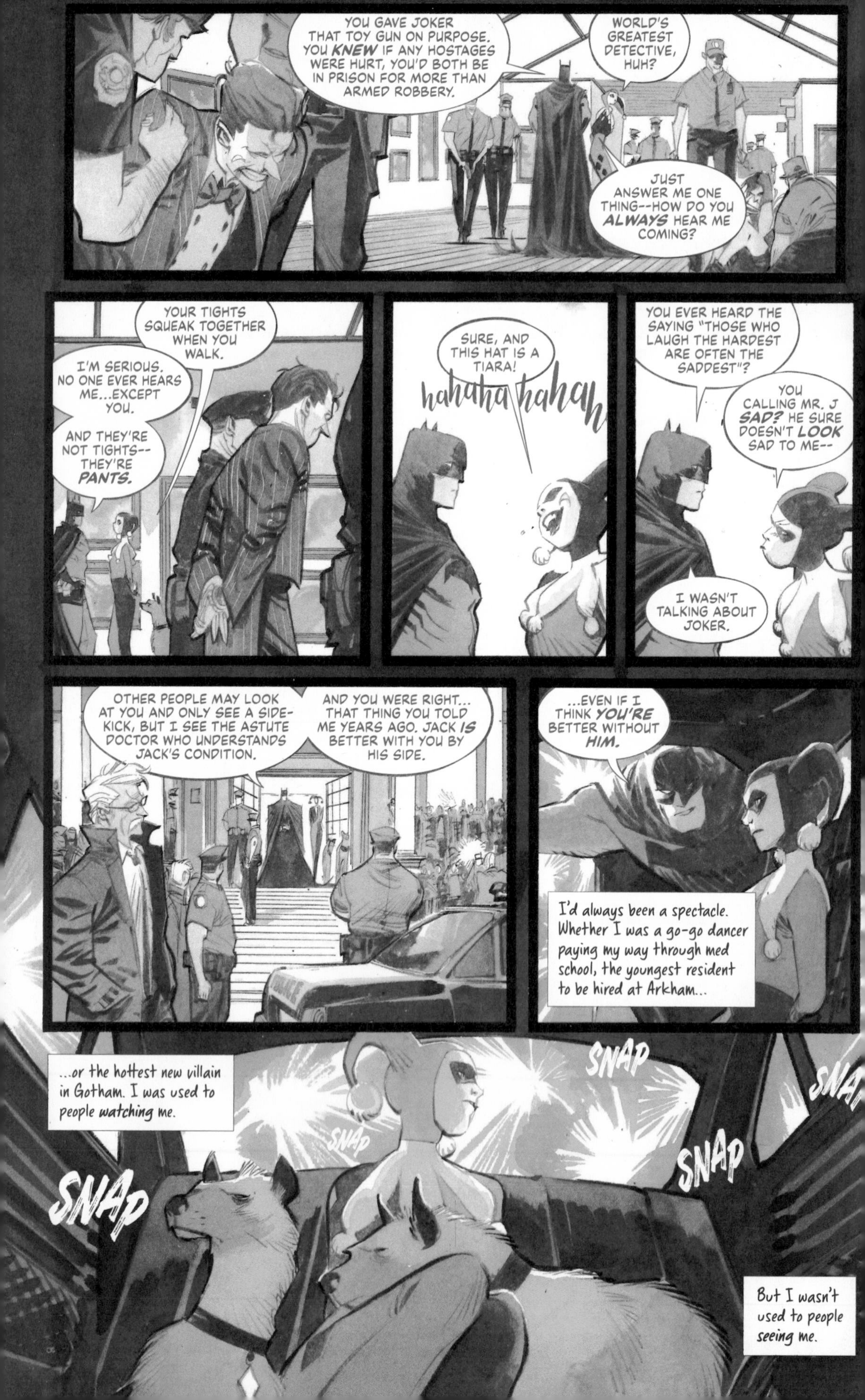
YOU GAVE JOKER THAT TOY GUN ON PURPOSE. YOU KNEW IF ANY HOSTAGES WERE HURT, YOU'D BOTH BE IN PRISON FOR MORE THAN ARMED ROBBERY.
WORLD'S GREATEST DETECTIVE, HUH?
JUST ANSWER ME ONE THING--HOW DO YOU ALWAYS HEAR ME COMING?
YOUR TIGHTS SQUEAK TOGETHER WHEN YOU WALK.
I'M SERIOUS. NO ONE EVER HEARS ME...EXCEPT YOU.
AND THEY'RE NOT TIGHTS-- THEY'RE PANTS.
SURE, AND THIS HAT IS A TIARA!
hahaha hahah
YOU EVER HEARD THE SAYING "THOSE WHO LAUGH THE HARDEST ARE OFTEN THE SADDEST"?
YOU CALLING MR. J SAD? HE SURE DOESN'T LOOK SAD TO ME--
I WASN'T TALKING ABOUT JOKER.
OTHER PEOPLE MAY LOOK AT YOU AND ONLY SEE A SIDE-KICK, BUT I SEE THE ASTUTE DOCTOR WHO UNDERSTANDS JACK'S CONDITION.
AND YOU WERE RIGHT... THAT THING YOU TOLD ME YEARS AGO. JACK IS BETTER WITH YOU BY HIS SIDE.
...EVEN IF I THINK YOU'RE BETTER WITHOUT HIM.
I'd always been a spectacle. Whether I was a go-go dancer paying my way through med school, the youngest resident to be hired at Arkham...
...or the hottest new villain in Gotham. I was used to people watching me.
SNAP
SNAP
SNAP
SNAP
But I wasn't used to people seeing me.

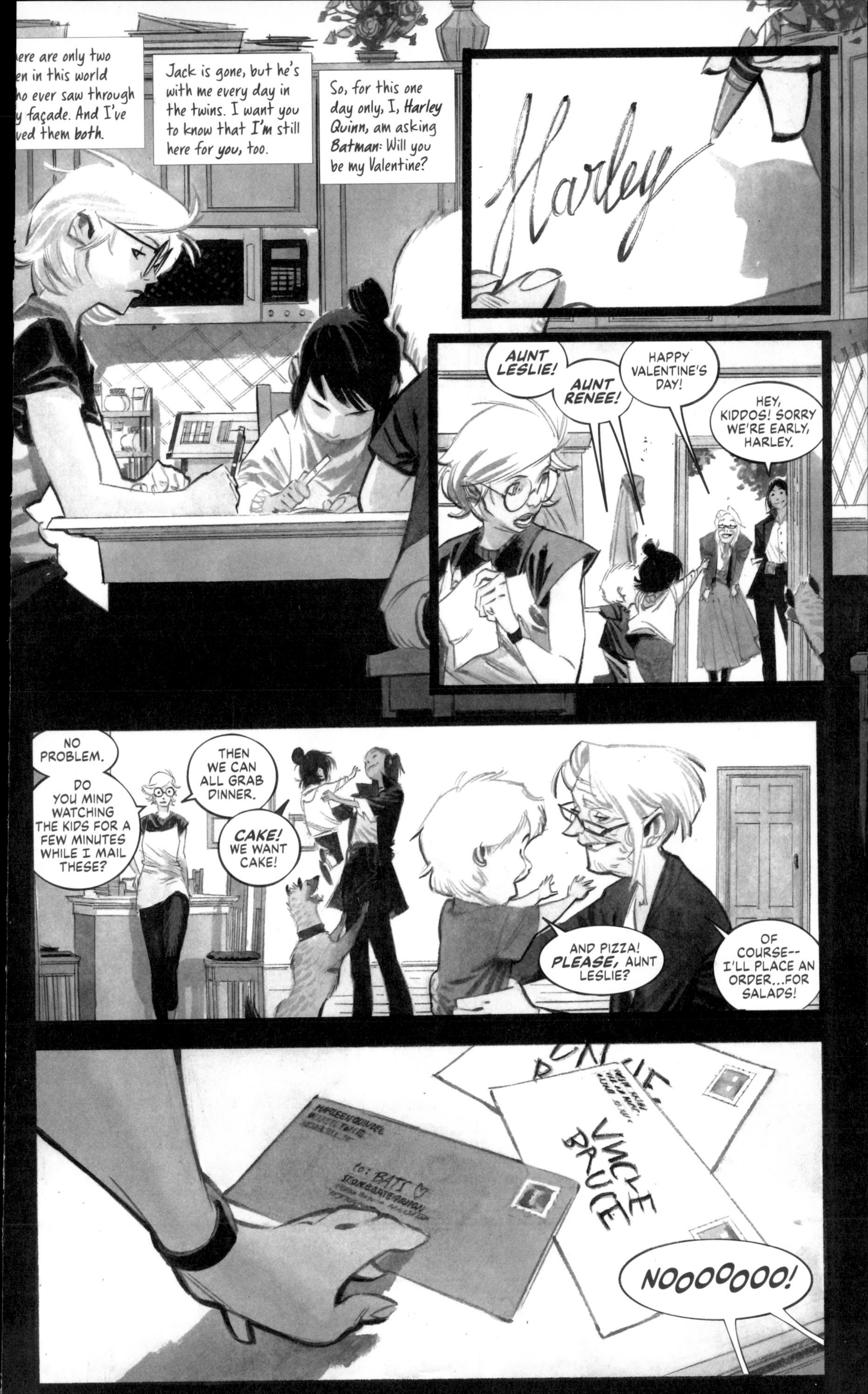
here are only two
en in this world
ho ever saw through
y façade. And I've
ved them both.
Jack is gone, but he's with me every day in the twins. I want you to know that I'm still here for you, too.
So, for this one day only, I, Harley Quinn, am asking Batman: Will you be my Valentine?
Harley
AUNT LESLIE!
AUNT RENEE!
HAPPY VALENTINE'S DAY!
HEY, KIDDOS! SORRY WE'RE EARLY, HARLEY.
NO PROBLEM.
DO YOU MIND WATCHING THE KIDS FOR A FEW MINUTES WHILE I MAIL THESE?
THEN WE CAN ALL GRAB DINNER.
CAKE! WE WANT CAKE!
AND PIZZA! PLEASE, AUNT LESLIE?
OF COURSE-- I'LL PLACE AN ORDER...FOR SALADS!
HARLEEN QUINZEL
to: BATS ♡
UNCLE BRUCE
NOOOOOOO!

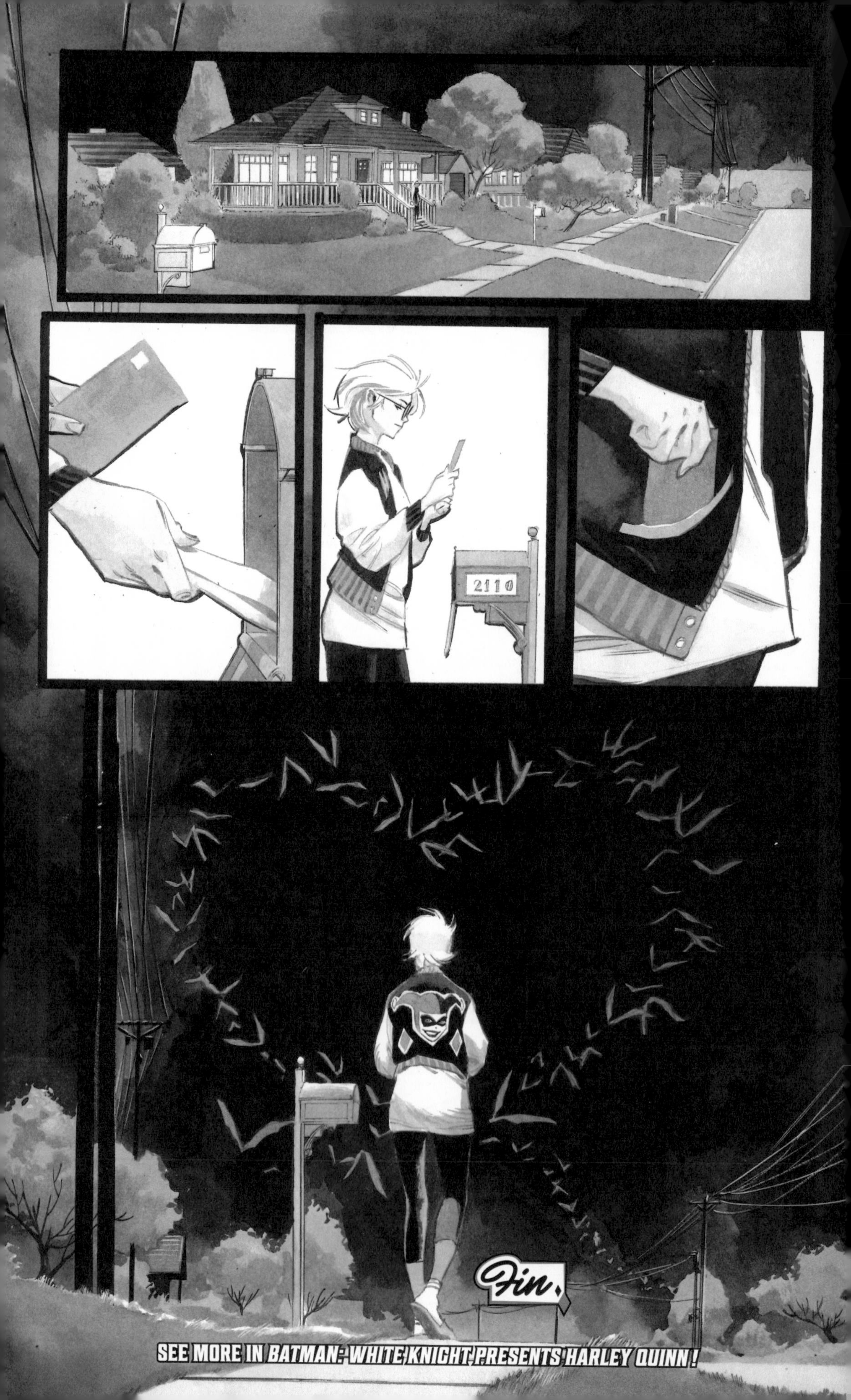
2110
Fin.
SEE MORE IN BATMAN: WHITE KNIGHT PRESENTS HARLEY QUINN!

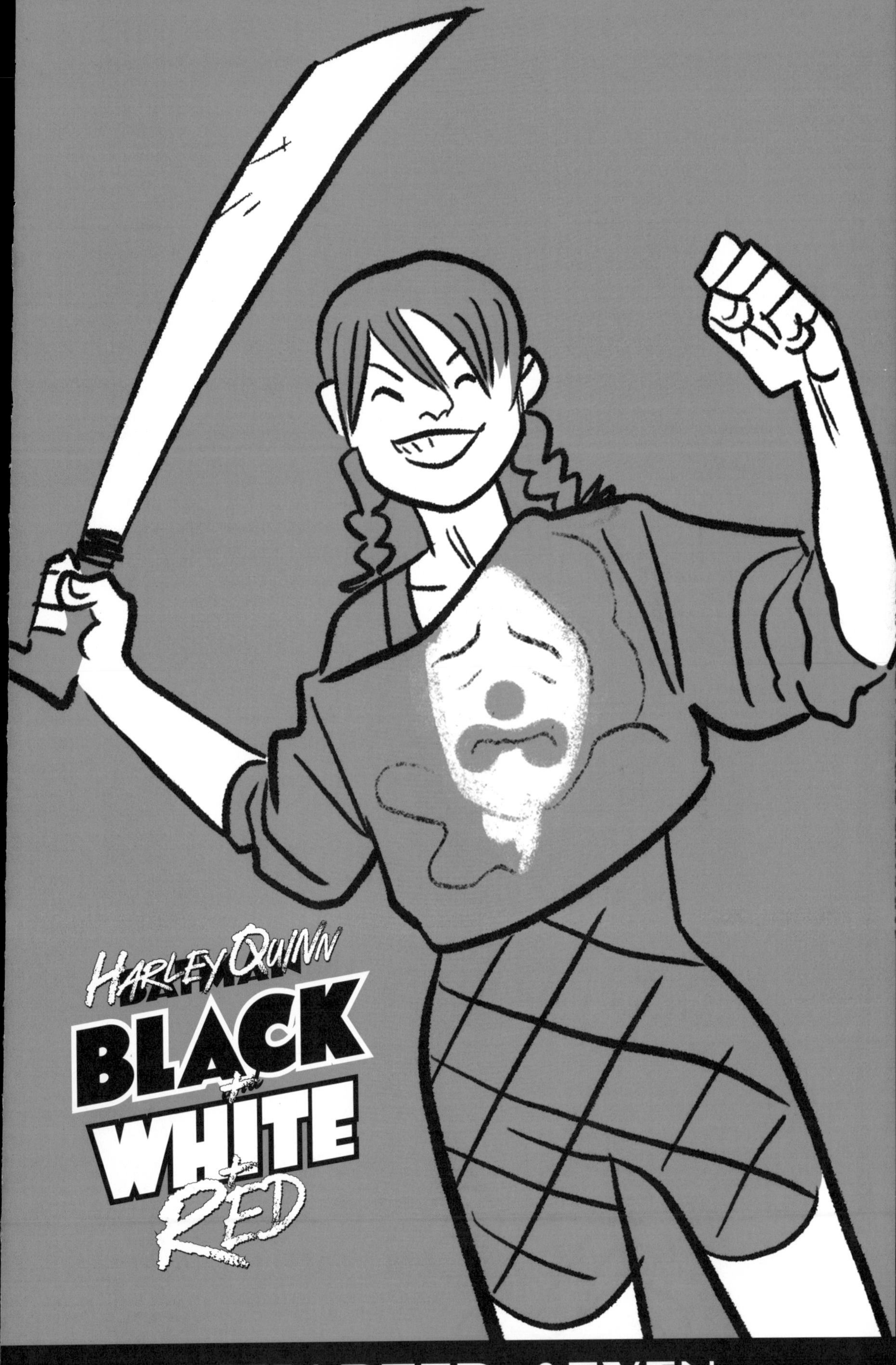
HARLEY QUINN
BLACK
+
WHITE
+
RED

CHAPTER SEVEN

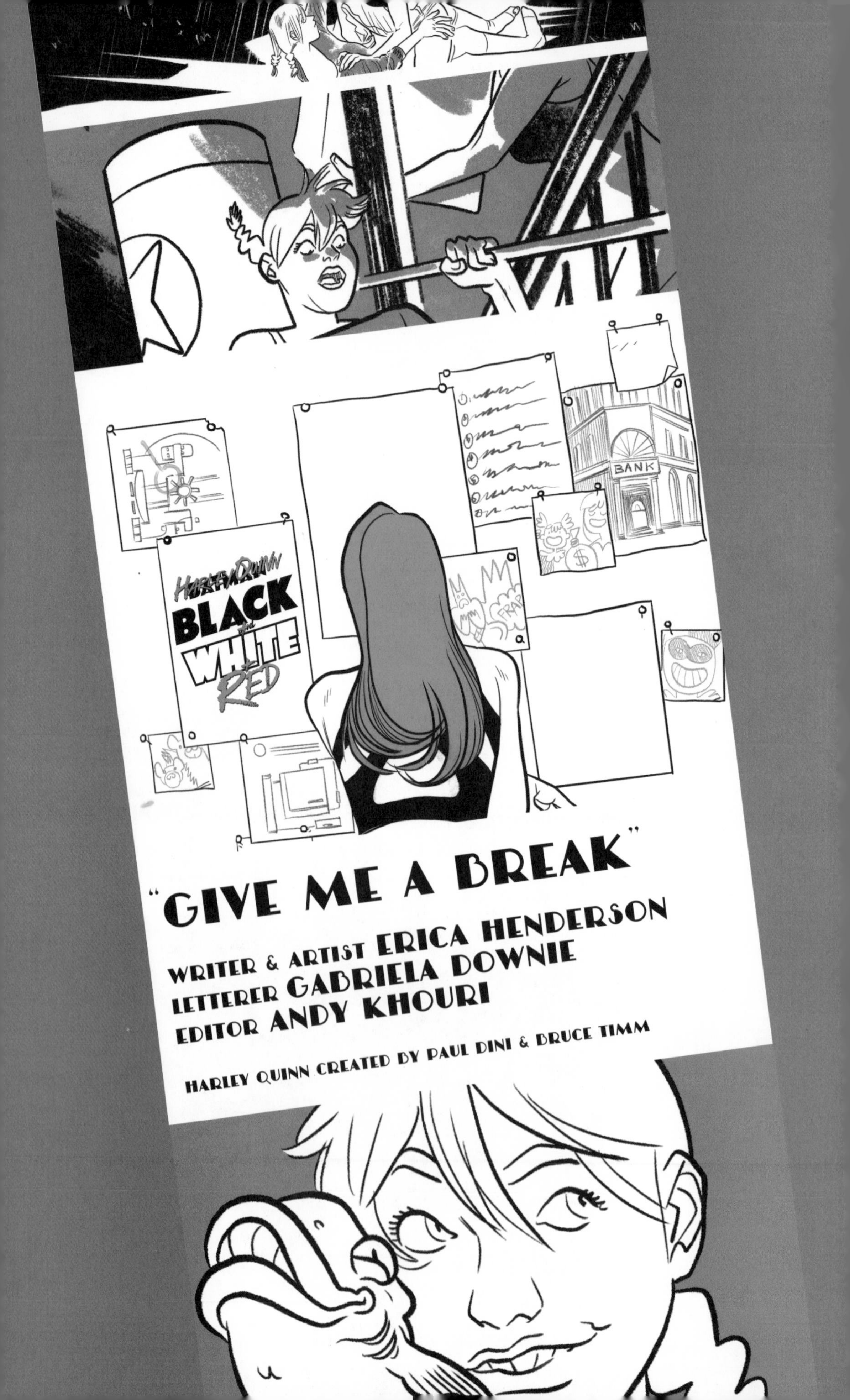
HARLEY QUINN
BLACK WHITE RED
BANK
FRAP
"GIVE ME A BREAK"
WRITER & ARTIST ERICA HENDERSON
LETTERER GABRIELA DOWNIE
EDITOR ANDY KHOURI
HARLEY QUINN CREATED BY PAUL DINI & BRUCE TIMM

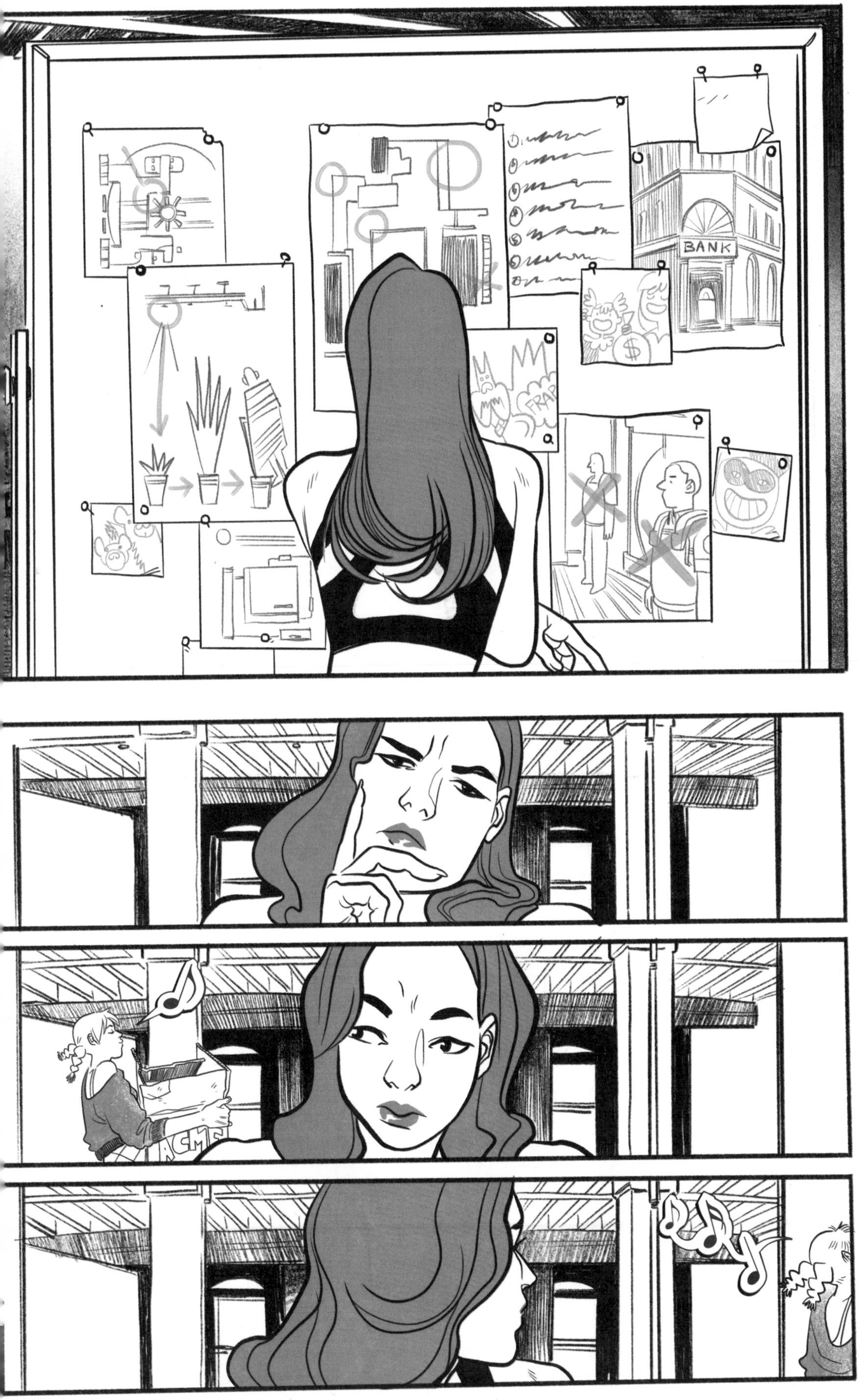
BANK
FRAP
ACME

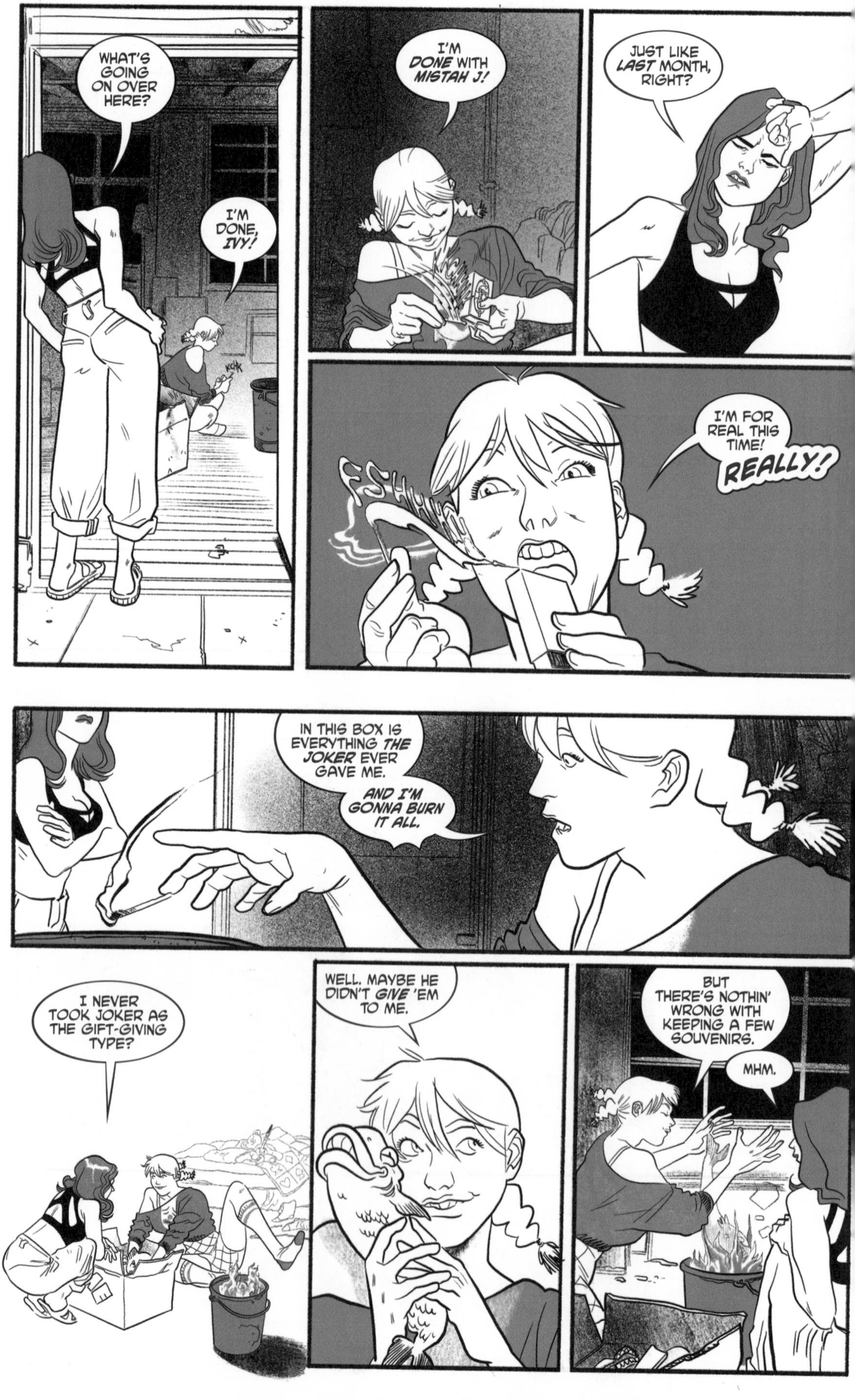
WHAT'S GOING ON OVER HERE?
I'M DONE, IVY!
KCHK
I'M DONE WITH MISTAH J!
JUST LIKE LAST MONTH, RIGHT?
I'M FOR REAL THIS TIME! REALLY!
FSHHH
IN THIS BOX IS EVERYTHING THE JOKER EVER GAVE ME.
AND I'M GONNA BURN IT ALL.
I NEVER TOOK JOKER AS THE GIFT-GIVING TYPE?
WELL. MAYBE HE DIDN'T GIVE 'EM TO ME.
BUT THERE'S NOTHIN' WRONG WITH KEEPING A FEW SOUVENIRS.
MHM.

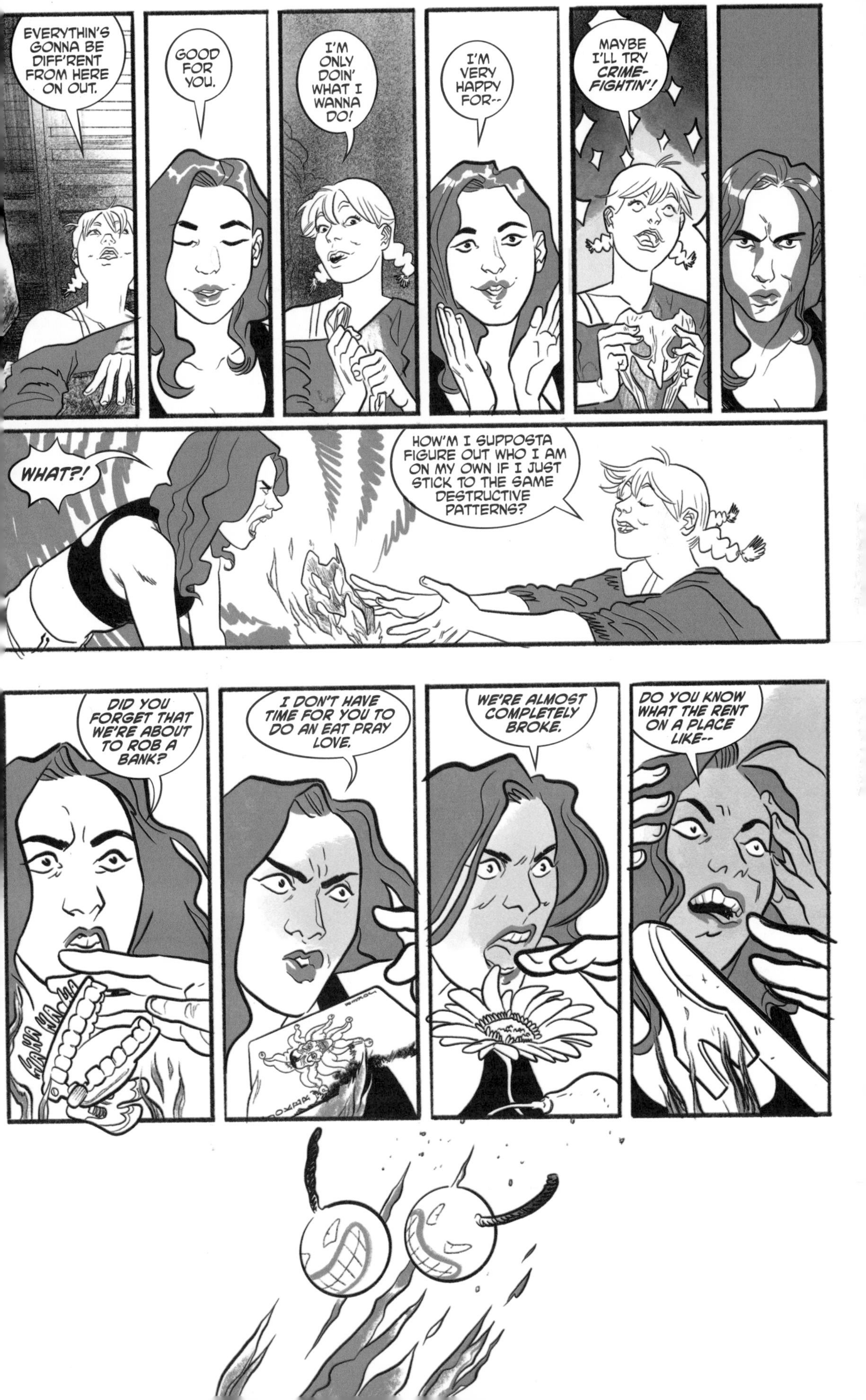
EVERYTHIN'S GONNA BE DIFF'RENT FROM HERE ON OUT.
GOOD FOR YOU.
I'M ONLY DOIN' WHAT I WANNA DO!
I'M VERY HAPPY FOR--
MAYBE I'LL TRY *CRIME-FIGHTIN'!*
WHAT?!
HOW'M I SUPPOSTA FIGURE OUT WHO I AM ON MY OWN IF I JUST STICK TO THE SAME DESTRUCTIVE PATTERNS?
DID YOU FORGET THAT WE'RE ABOUT TO ROB A BANK?
I DON'T HAVE TIME FOR YOU TO DO AN EAT PRAY LOVE.
WE'RE ALMOST COMPLETELY BROKE.
DO YOU KNOW WHAT THE RENT ON A PLACE LIKE--

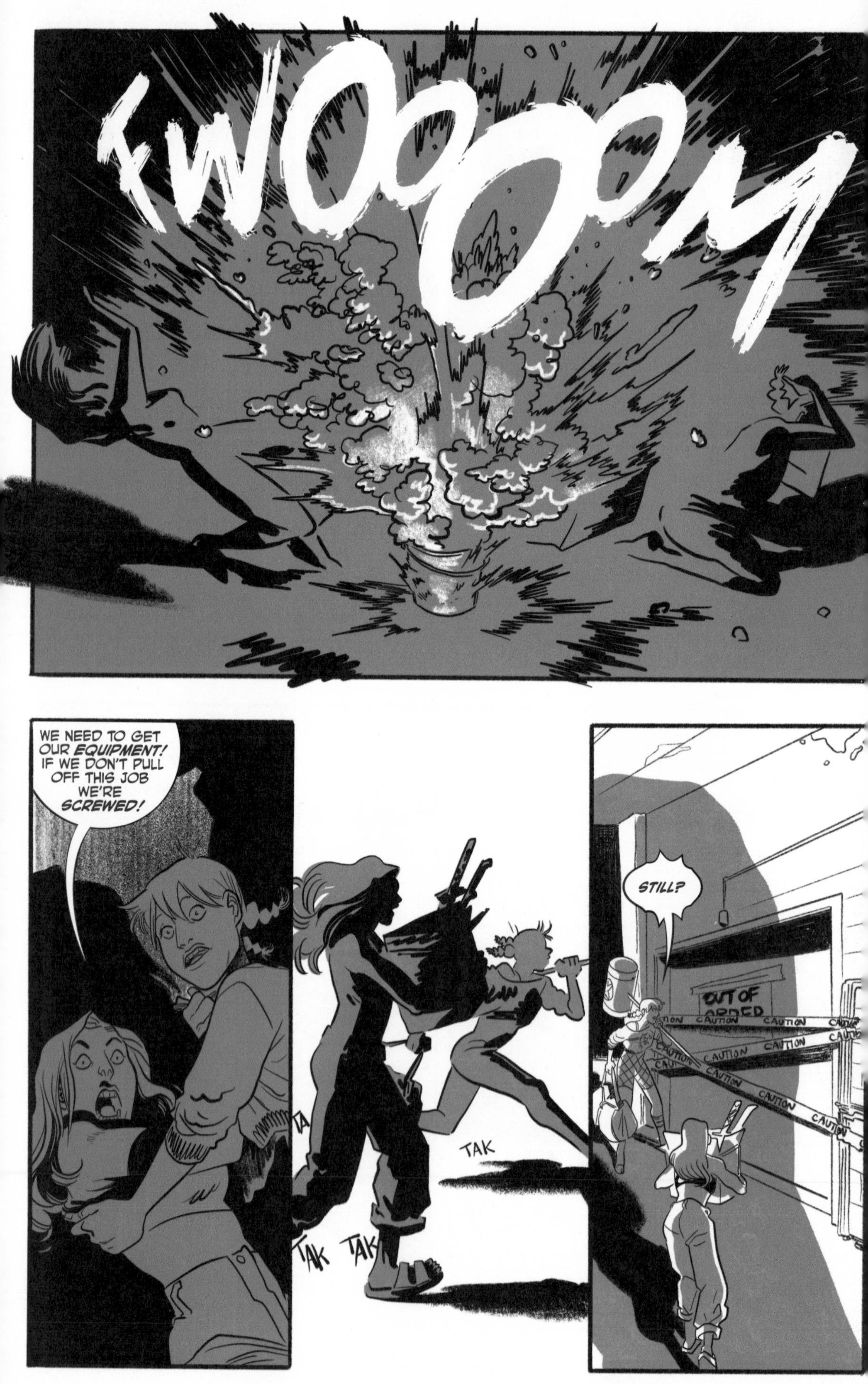
FWOOOOM
WE NEED TO GET OUR EQUIPMENT! IF WE DON'T PULL OFF THIS JOB WE'RE SCREWED!
TA
TAK
TAK TAK
STILL?
OUT OF
CAUTION

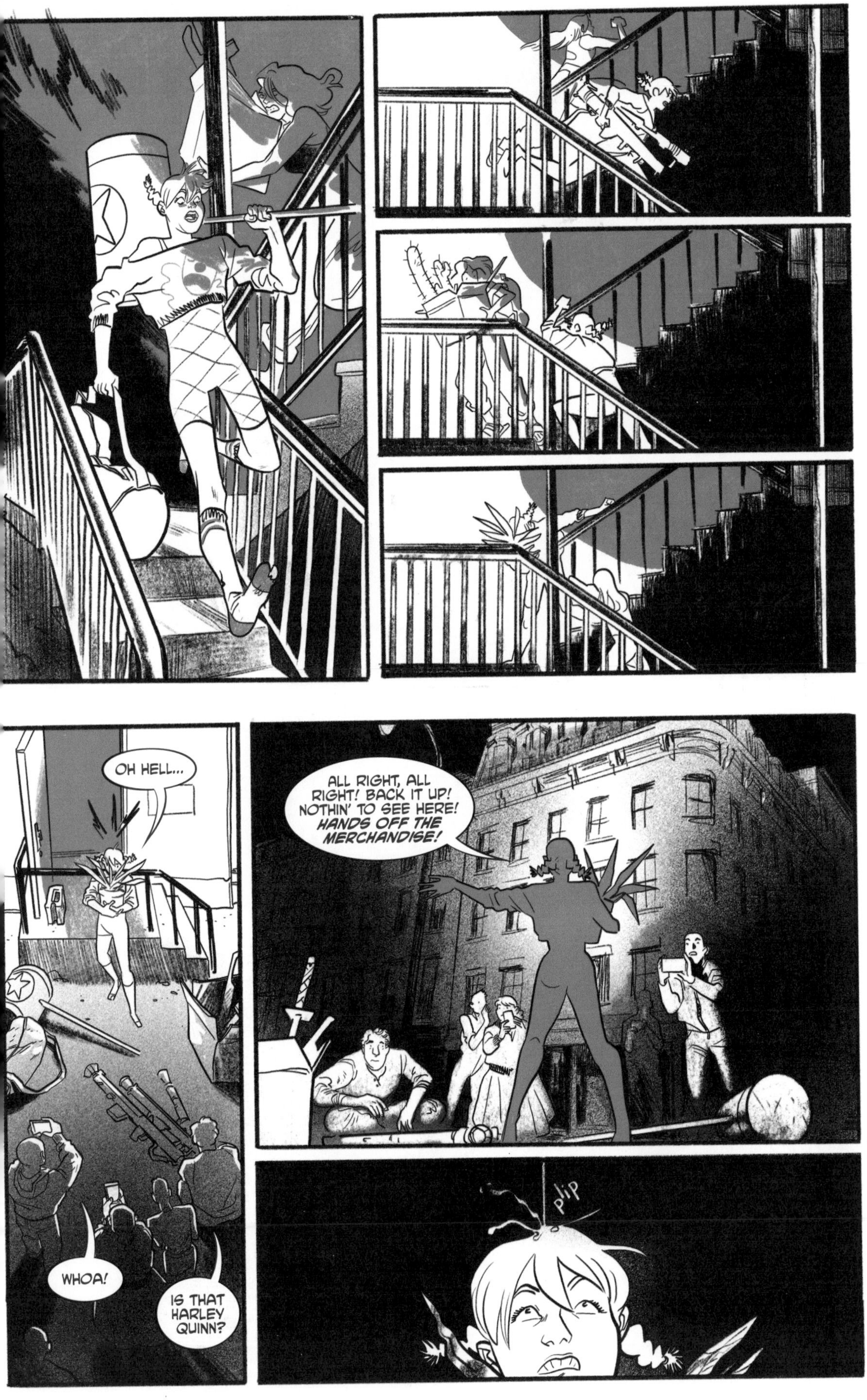
OH HELL...
WHOA!
IS THAT HARLEY QUINN?
ALL RIGHT, ALL RIGHT! BACK IT UP! NOTHIN' TO SEE HERE! HANDS OFF THE MERCHANDISE!
plip

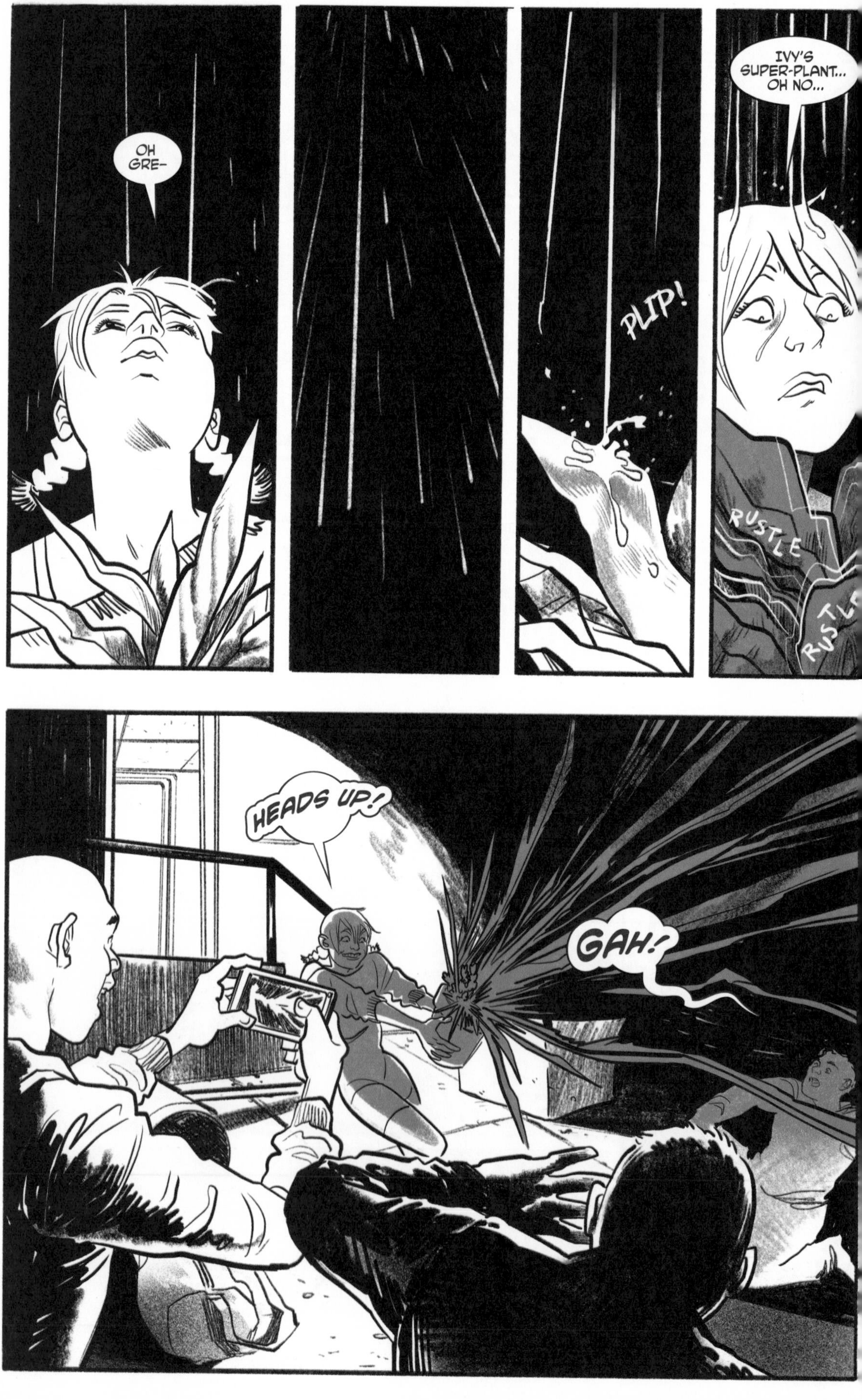
OH GRE-
PLIP!
IVY'S SUPER-PLANT... OH NO...
RUSTLE
RUSTLE
HEADS UP!
GAH!

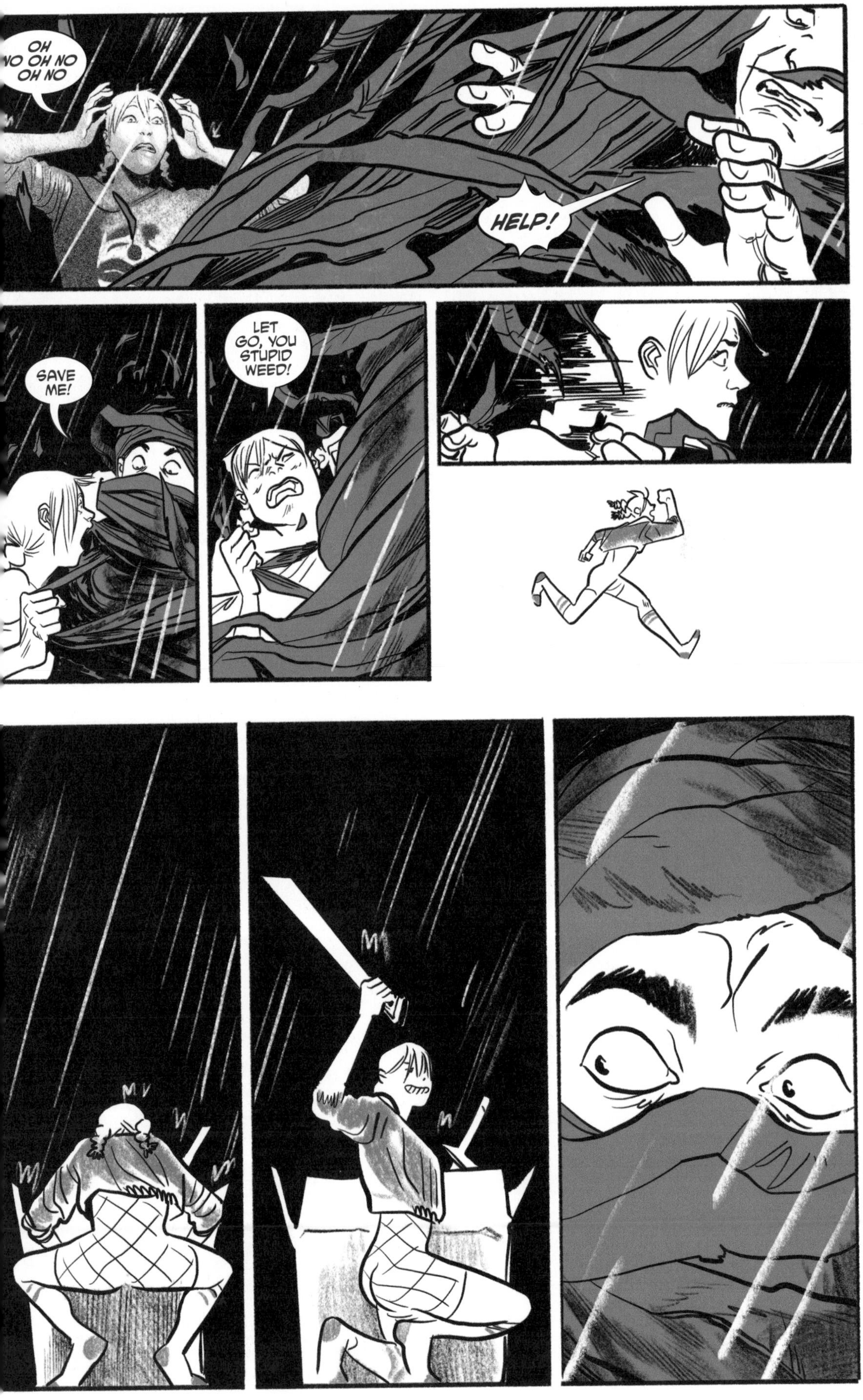
OH NO OH NO OH NO
HELP!
SAVE ME!
LET GO, YOU STUPID WEED!

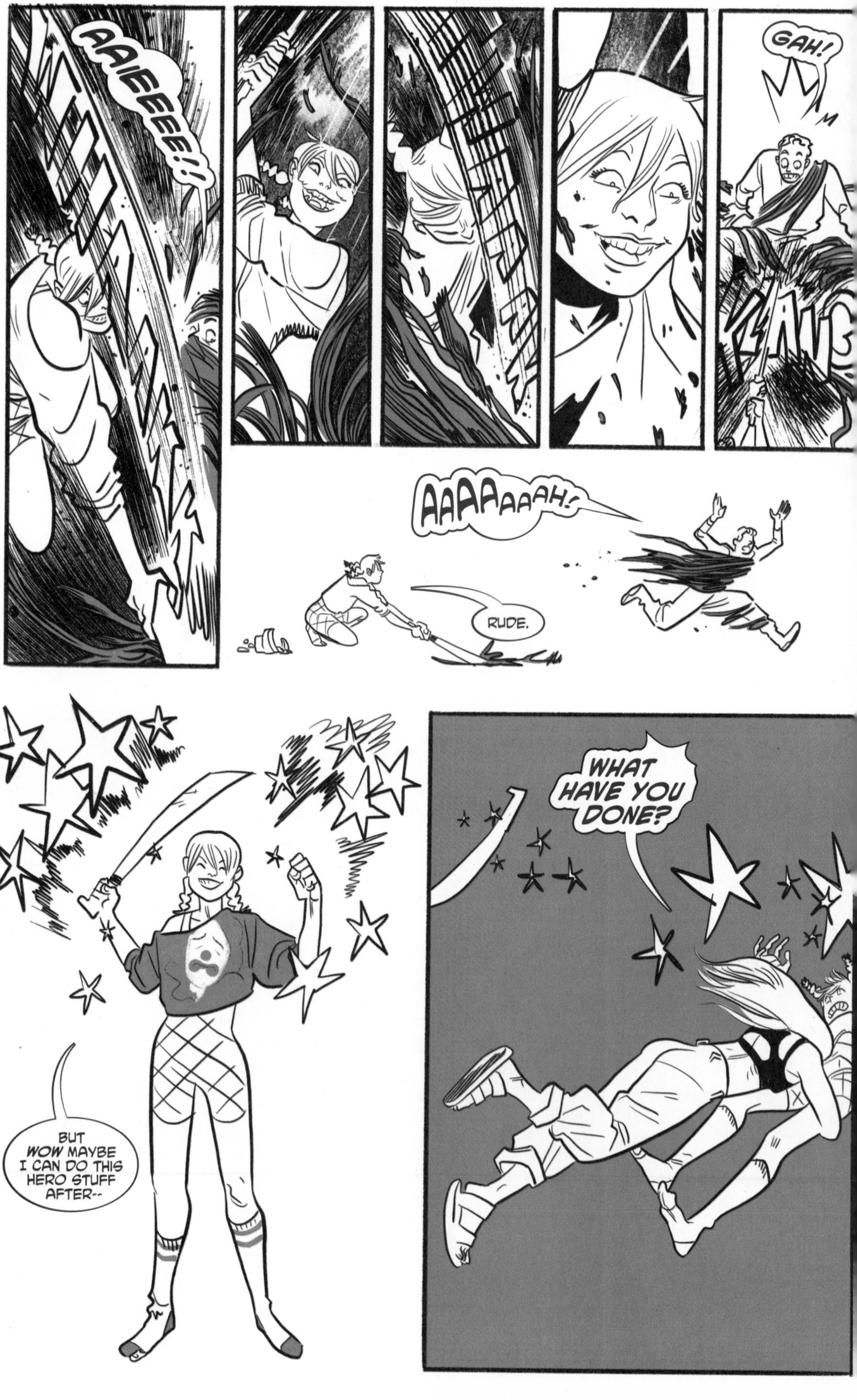
AAIEEEEE!!
GAH!
M
KLANG
AAAAAAAH!
RUDE.
BUT WOW MAYBE I CAN DO THIS HERO STUFF AFTER--
WHAT HAVE YOU DONE?

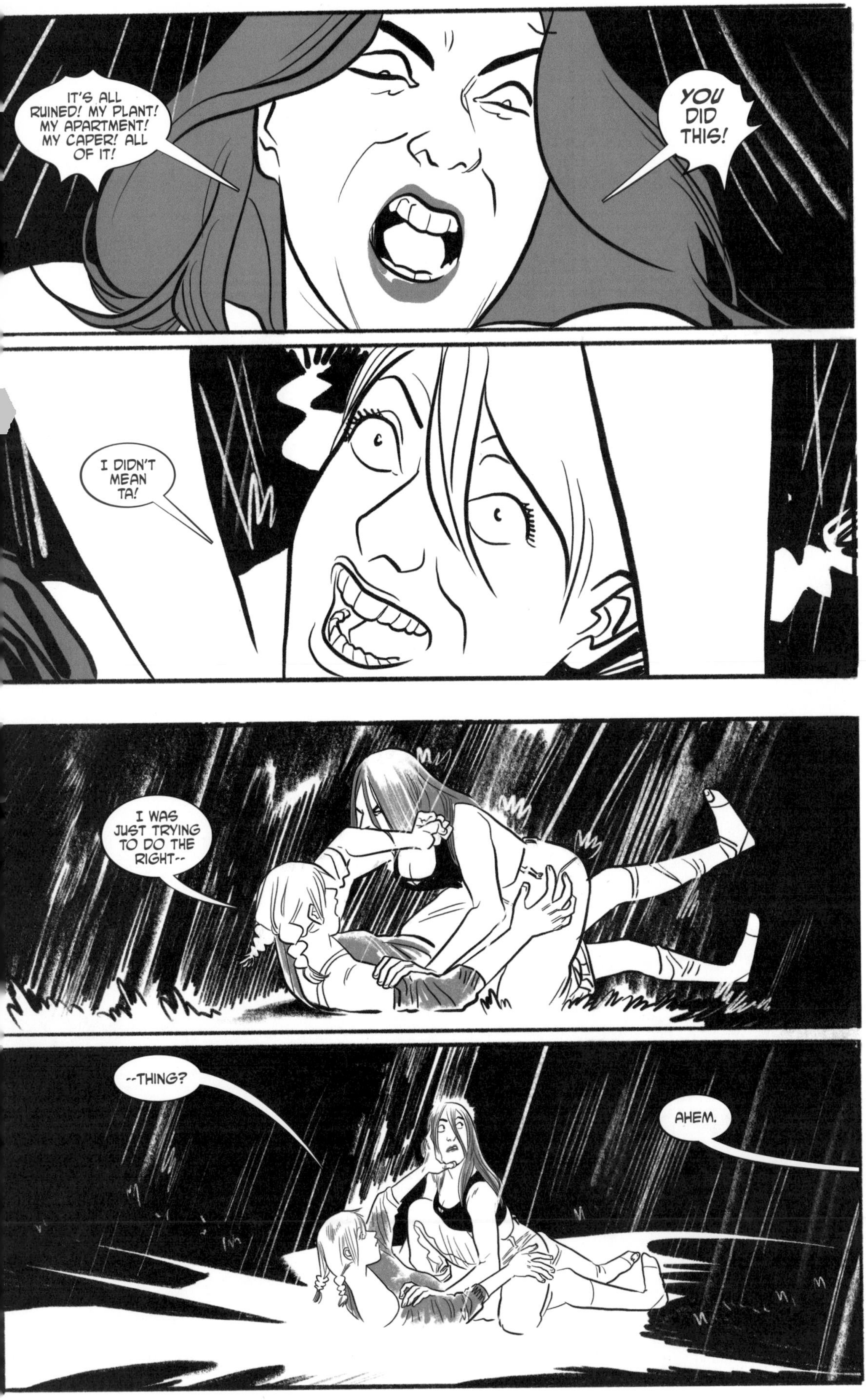
IT'S ALL RUINED! MY PLANT! MY APARTMENT! MY CAPER! ALL OF IT!
YOU DID THIS!
I DIDN'T MEAN TA!
I WAS JUST TRYING TO DO THE RIGHT--
--THING?
AHEM.

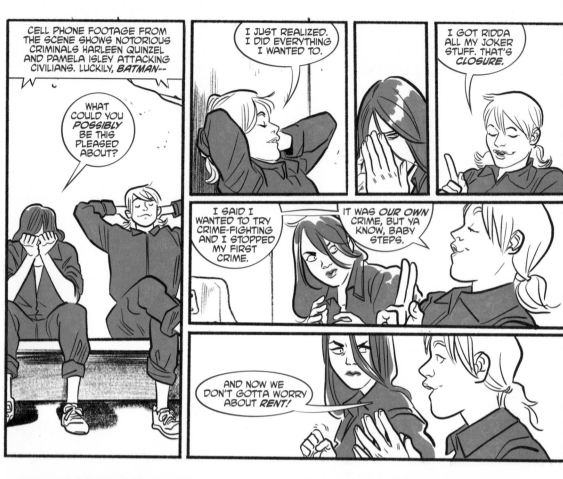

CELL PHONE FOOTAGE FROM THE SCENE SHOWS NOTORIOUS CRIMINALS HARLEEN QUINZEL AND PAMELA ISLEY ATTACKING CIVILIANS. LUCKILY, *BATMAN*--

WHAT COULD YOU *POSSIBLY* BE THIS PLEASED ABOUT?

I JUST REALIZED. I DID EVERYTHING I WANTED TO.

I GOT RIDDA ALL MY JOKER STUFF. THAT'S *CLOSURE.*

I SAID I WANTED TO TRY CRIME-FIGHTING AND I STOPPED MY FIRST CRIME.

IT WAS *OUR OWN* CRIME, BUT YA KNOW, BABY STEPS.

AND NOW WE DON'T GOTTA WORRY ABOUT *RENT!*

Fin.

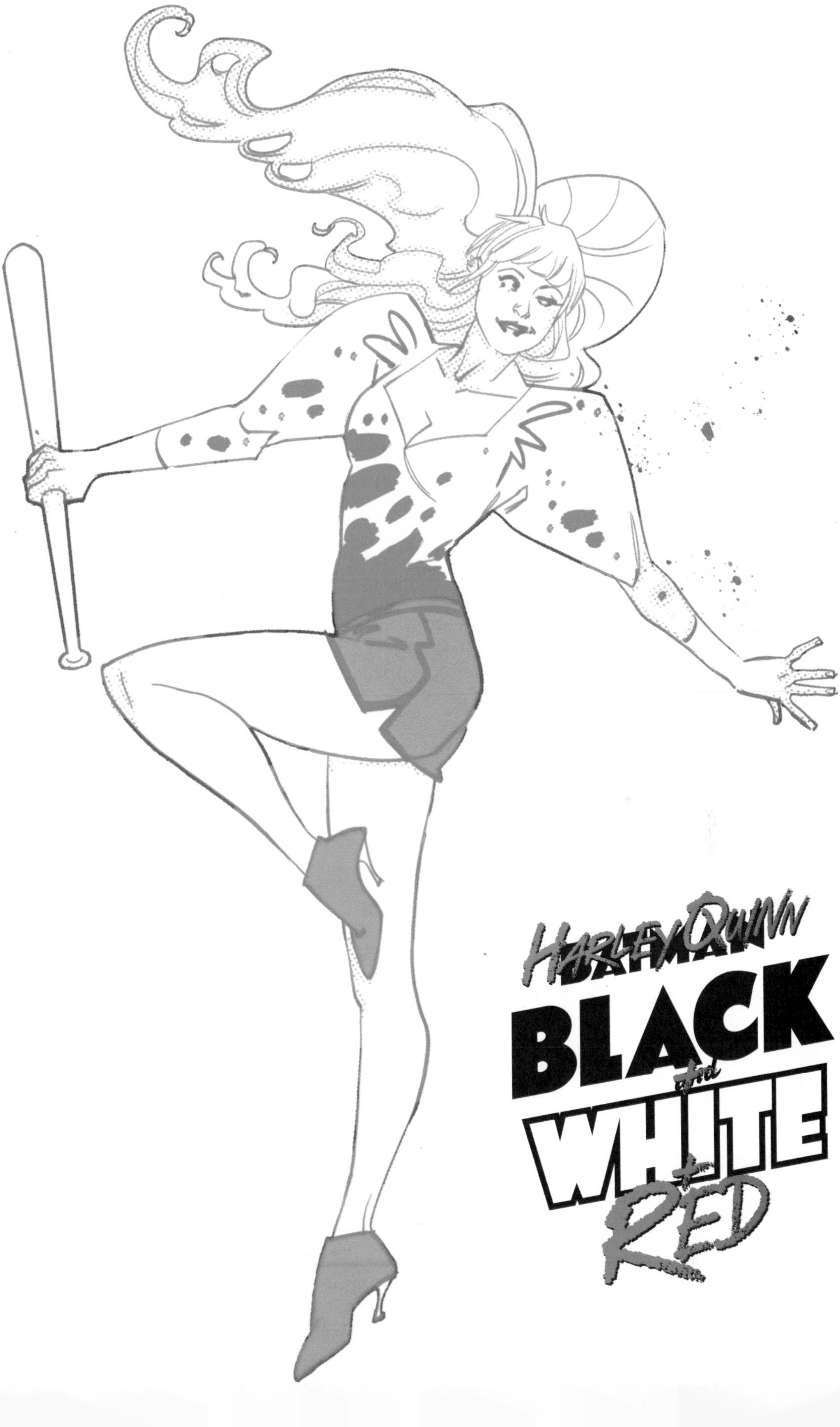

HARLEY QUINN
BATMAN
BLACK
and
WHITE
+
RED

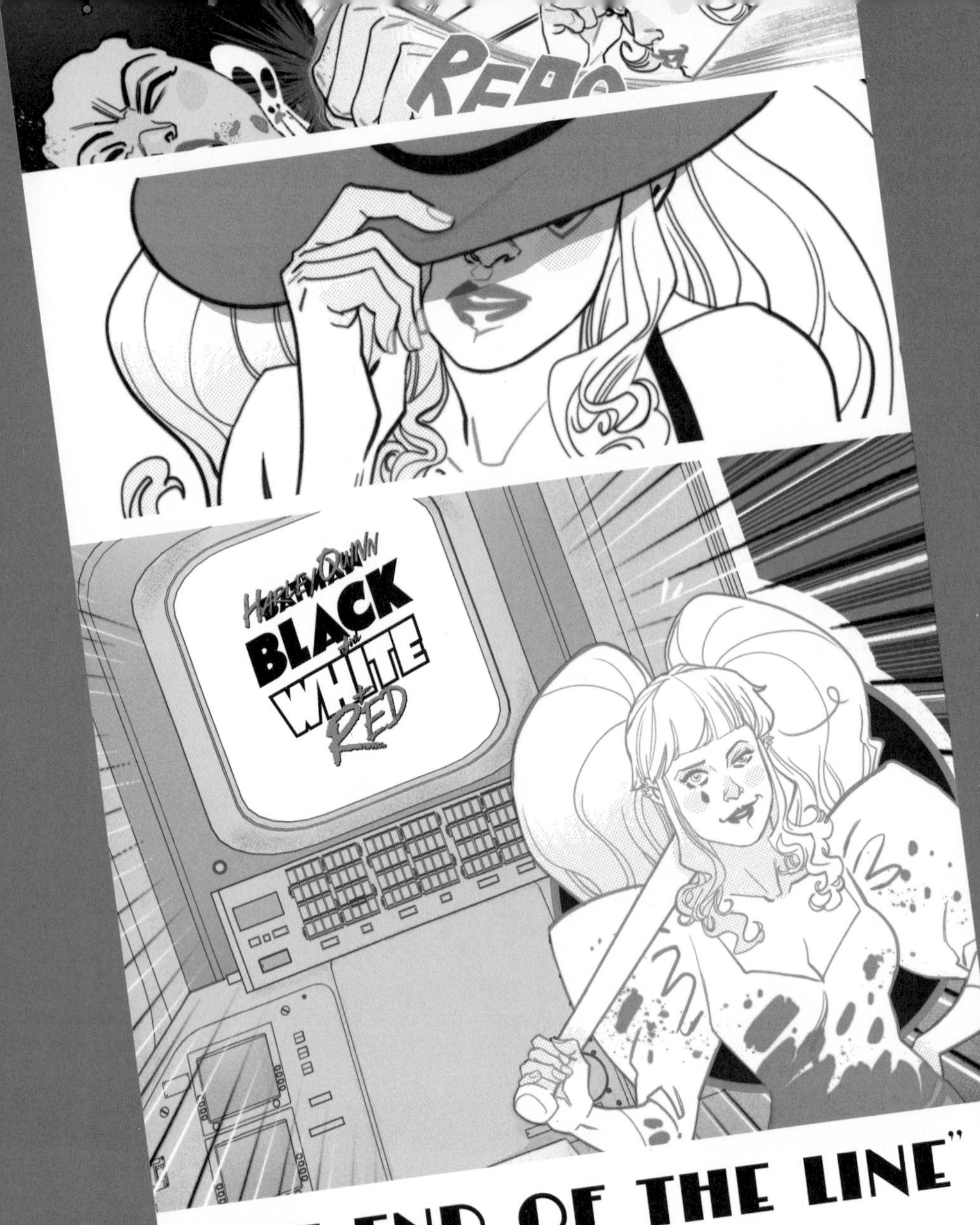
BLACK
WHITE
RED

"THE END OF THE LINE"

WRITER **DANIEL KIBBLESMITH**
ARTIST **MARGUERITE SAUVAGE**
LETTERER **ANDWORLD DESIGN**
EDITOR **CHRIS CONROY**
ASSOCIATE EDITOR **AMEDEO TURTURRO**
HARLEY QUINN CREATED BY PAUL DINI & BRUCE TIMM

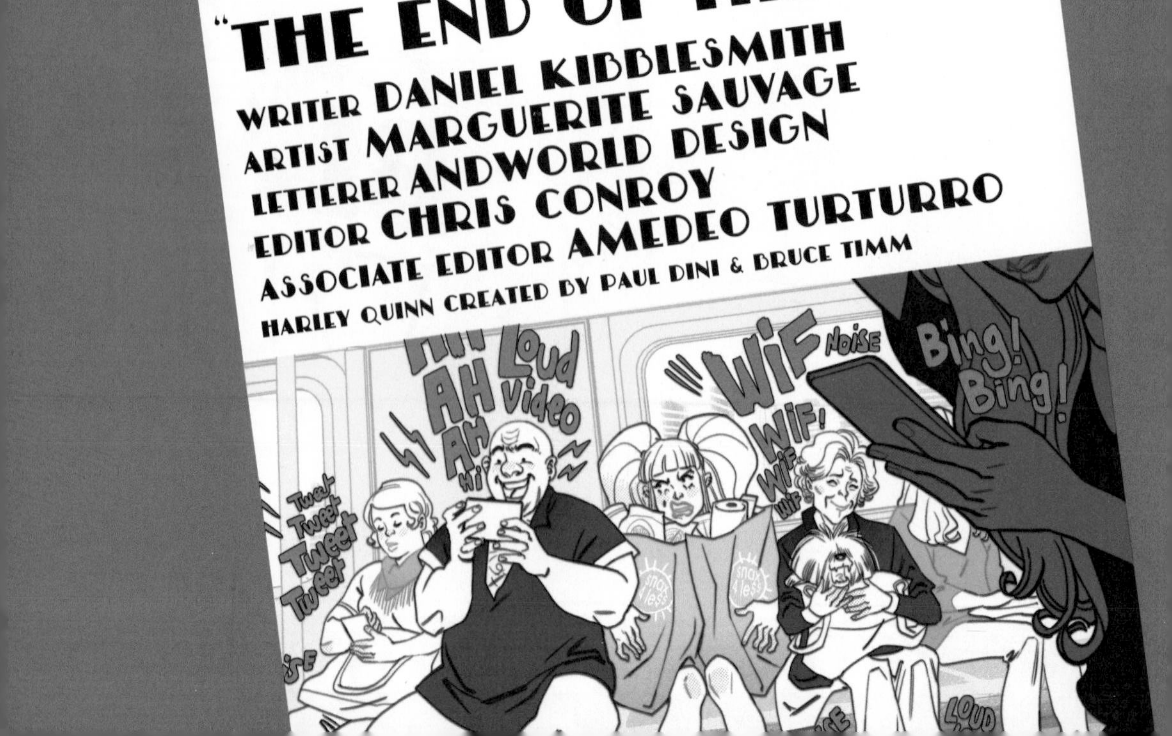
AH
AH
AH
Hi
Loud
video
WiF
Noise
WiF!
WiF
WiF
Bing!
Bing!
Tweet
Tweet
Tweet
Tweet
Tweet
snax 4 less
snax 4 less

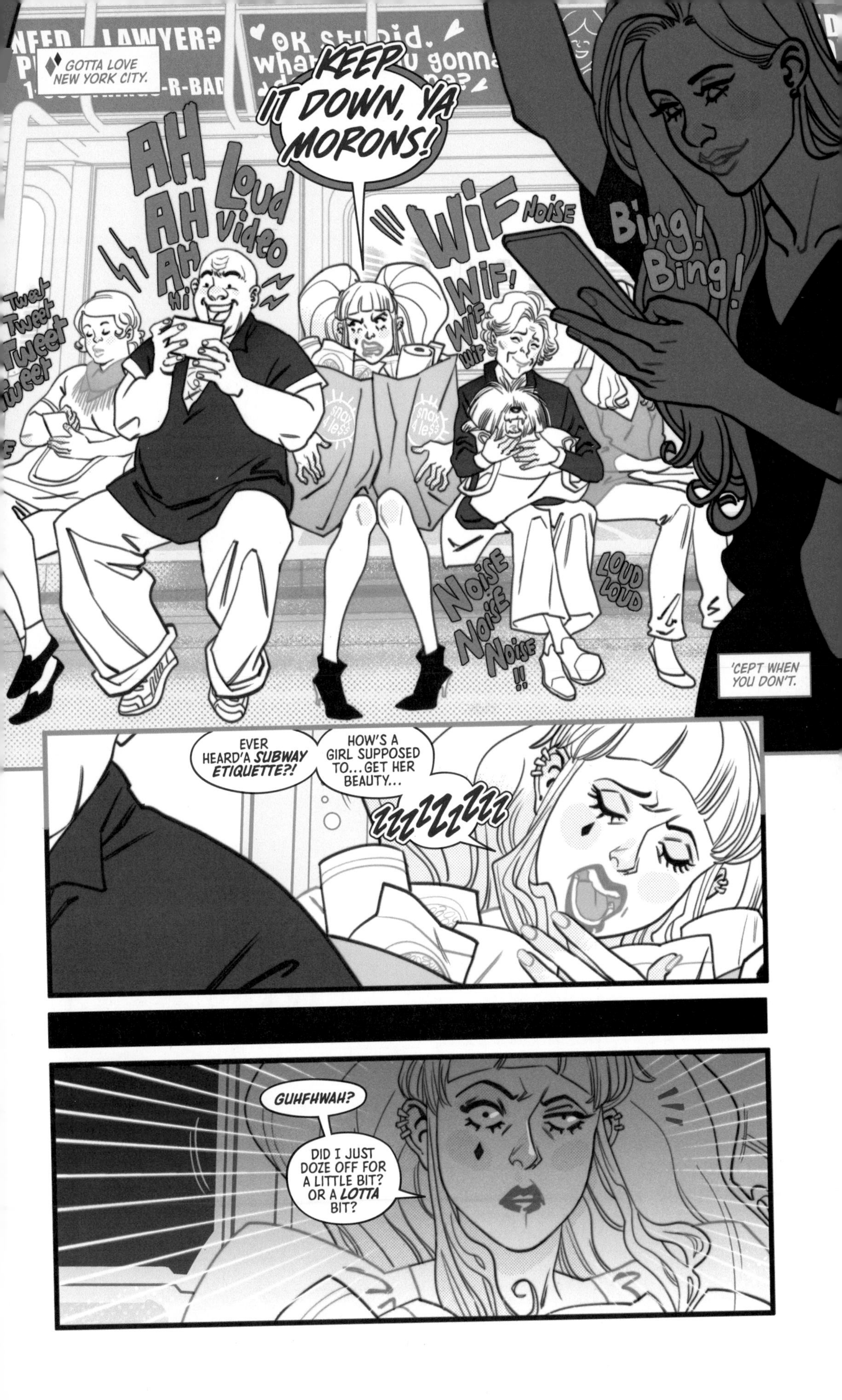

GOTTA LOVE NEW YORK CITY.
KEEP IT DOWN, YA MORONS!
AH AH AH HI
Loud Video
WIF NOISE
WIF!
WIF WIF
Bing! Bing!
Tweet Tweet Tweet Tweet
Noise Noise Noise!!
LOUD LOUD
'CEPT WHEN YOU DON'T.
EVER HEARD'A SUBWAY ETIQUETTE?!
HOW'S A GIRL SUPPOSED TO... GET HER BEAUTY...
ZZZZZZZZZ
GUHFHWAH?
DID I JUST DOZE OFF FOR A LITTLE BIT? OR A LOTTA BIT?

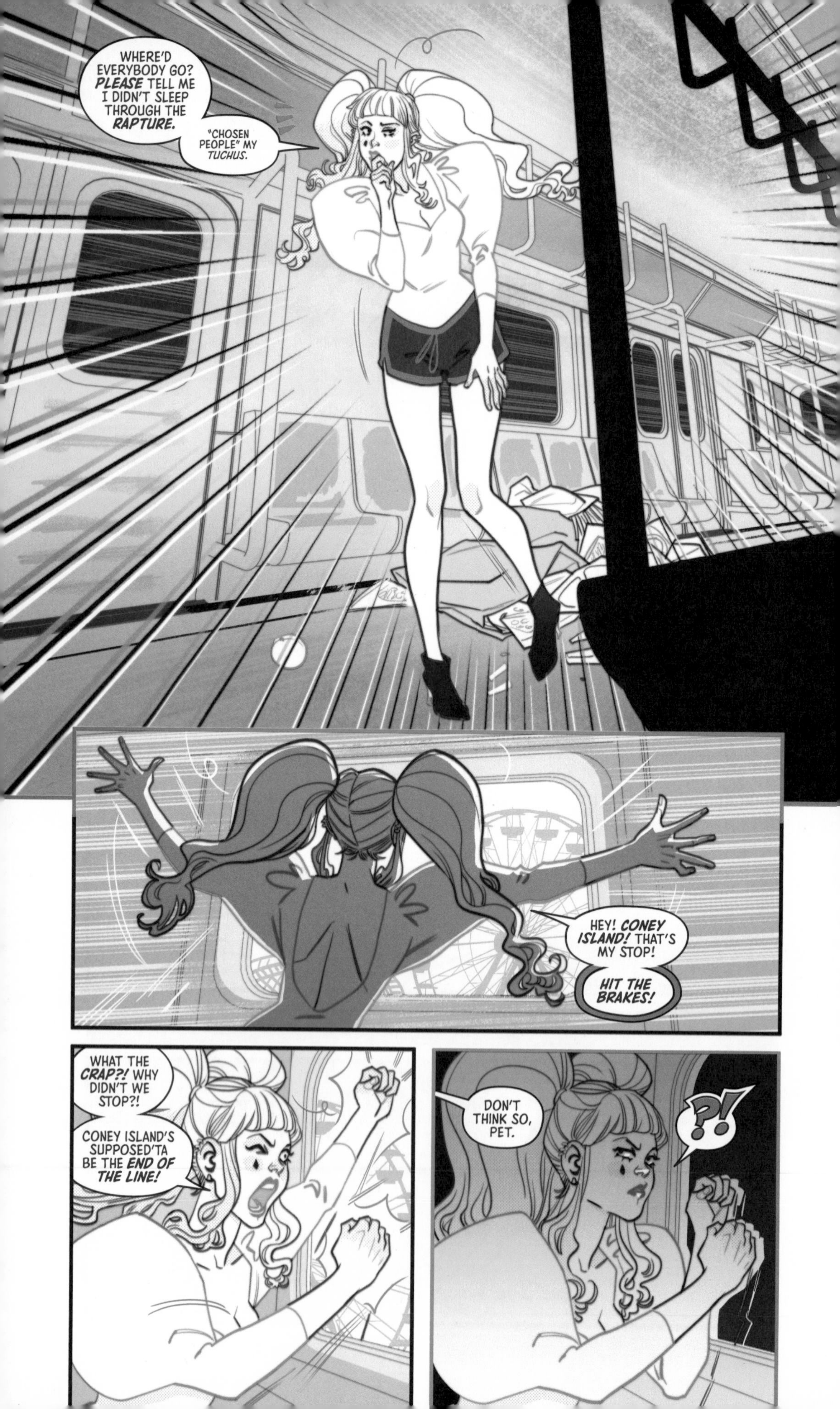
WHERE'D EVERYBODY GO? PLEASE TELL ME I DIDN'T SLEEP THROUGH THE RAPTURE.
"CHOSEN PEOPLE" MY TUCHUS.
HEY! CONEY ISLAND! THAT'S MY STOP!
HIT THE BRAKES!
WHAT THE CRAP?! WHY DIDN'T WE STOP?!
CONEY ISLAND'S SUPPOSED'TA BE THE END OF THE LINE!
DON'T THINK SO, PET.
?!

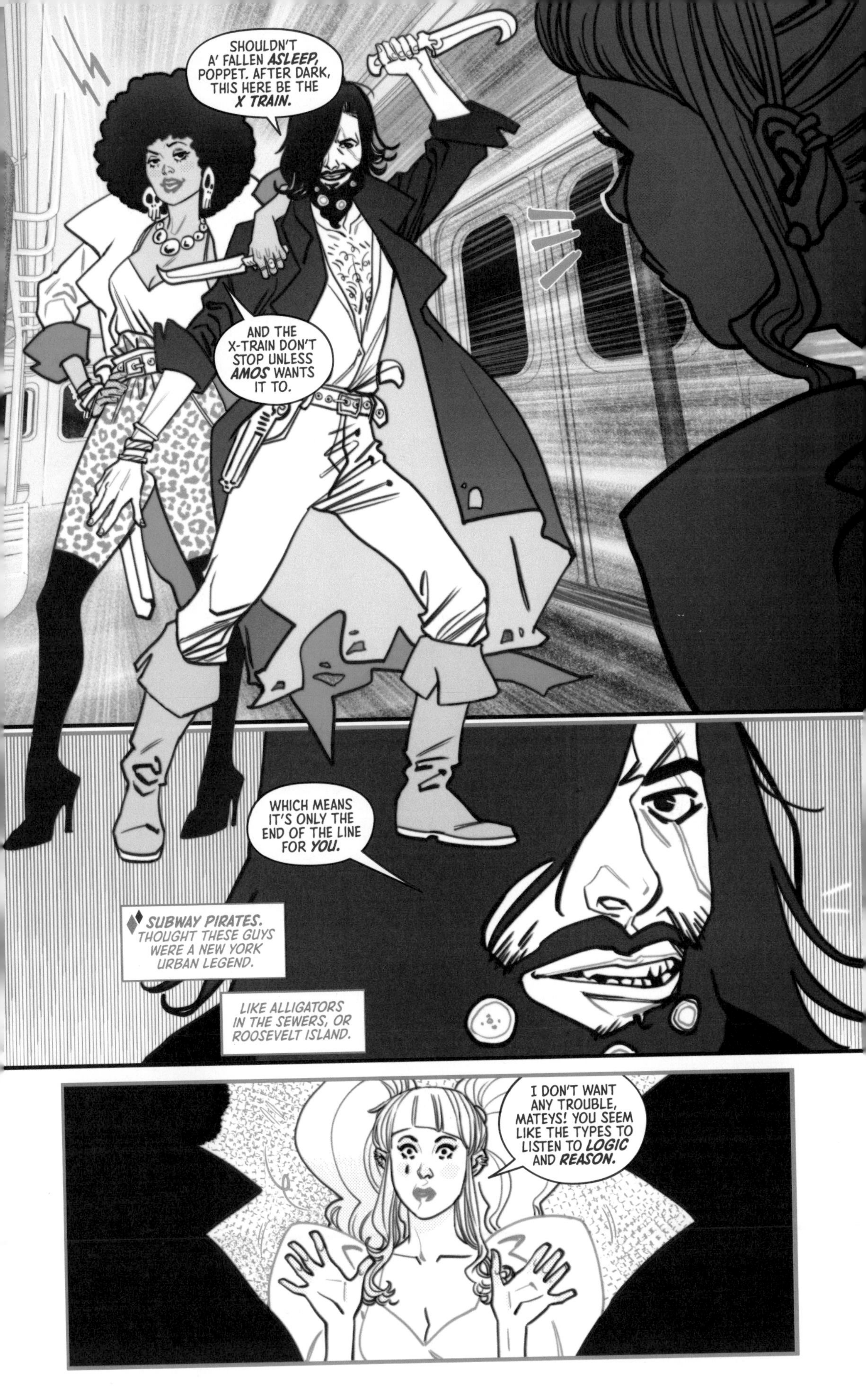
SHOULDN'T A' FALLEN ASLEEP, POPPET. AFTER DARK, THIS HERE BE THE X TRAIN.
AND THE X-TRAIN DON'T STOP UNLESS AMOS WANTS IT TO.
WHICH MEANS IT'S ONLY THE END OF THE LINE FOR YOU.
SUBWAY PIRATES. THOUGHT THESE GUYS WERE A NEW YORK URBAN LEGEND.
LIKE ALLIGATORS IN THE SEWERS, OR ROOSEVELT ISLAND.
I DON'T WANT ANY TROUBLE, MATEYS! YOU SEEM LIKE THE TYPES TO LISTEN TO LOGIC AND REASON.

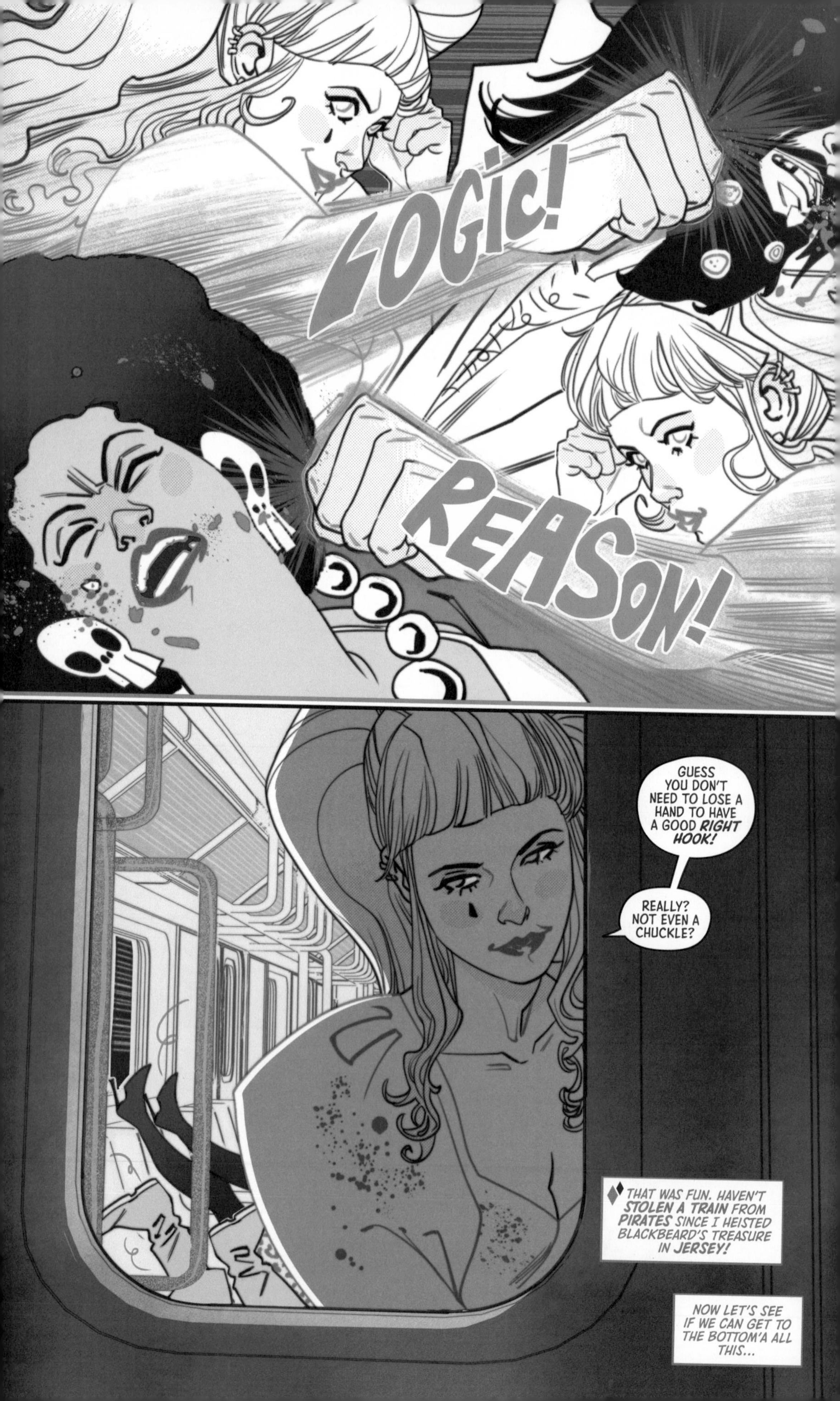
LOGIC!
REASON!
GUESS YOU DON'T NEED TO LOSE A HAND TO HAVE A GOOD RIGHT HOOK!
REALLY? NOT EVEN A CHUCKLE?
THAT WAS FUN. HAVEN'T STOLEN A TRAIN FROM PIRATES SINCE I HEISTED BLACKBEARD'S TREASURE IN JERSEY!
NOW LET'S SEE IF WE CAN GET TO THE BOTTOM'A ALL THIS...

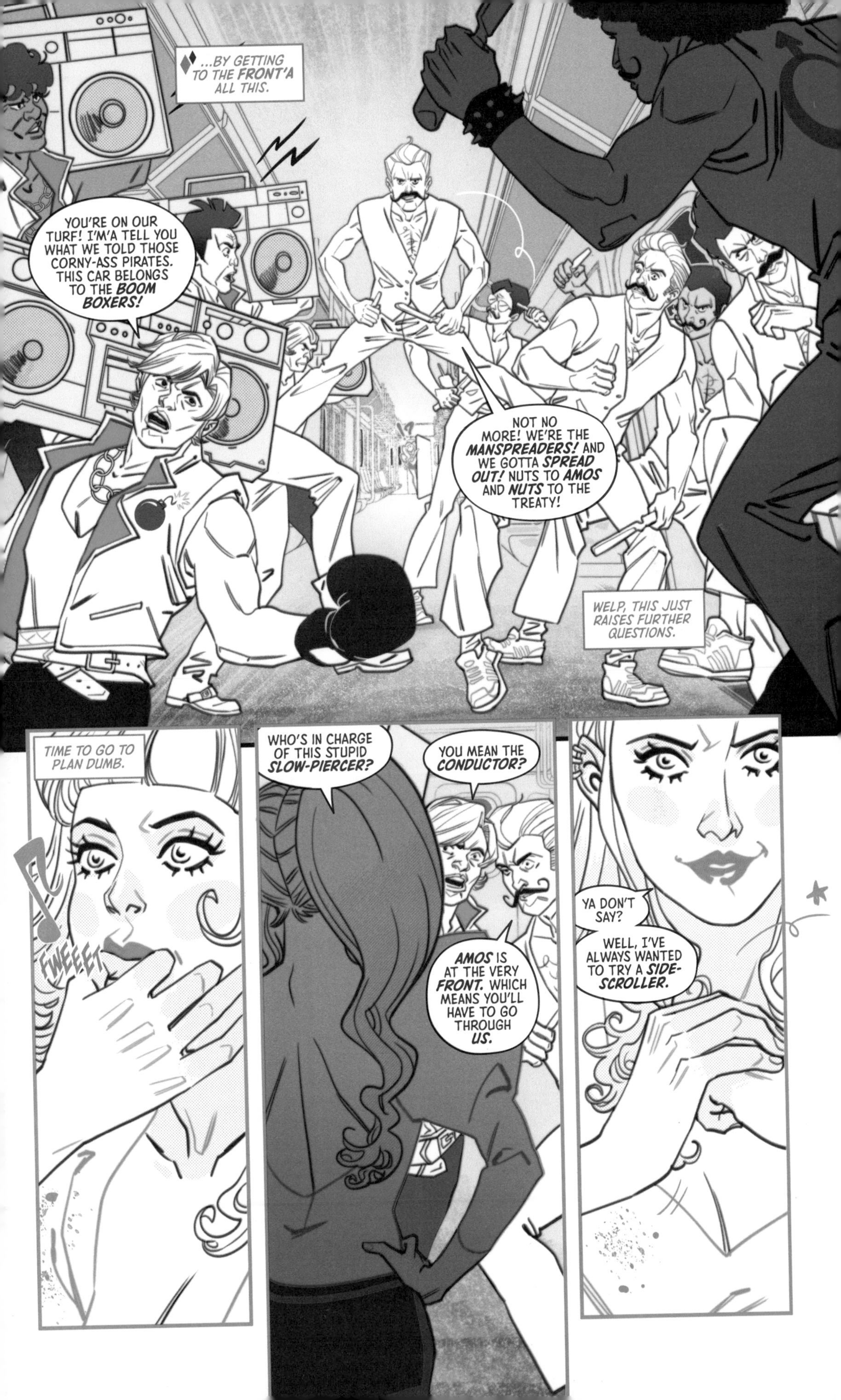
...BY GETTING TO THE FRONT'A ALL THIS.
YOU'RE ON OUR TURF! I'M'A TELL YOU WHAT WE TOLD THOSE CORNY-ASS PIRATES. THIS CAR BELONGS TO THE BOOM BOXERS!
NOT NO MORE! WE'RE THE MANSPREADERS! AND WE GOTTA SPREAD OUT! NUTS TO AMOS AND NUTS TO THE TREATY!
WELP, THIS JUST RAISES FURTHER QUESTIONS.
TIME TO GO TO PLAN DUMB.
FWEEET
WHO'S IN CHARGE OF THIS STUPID SLOW-PIERCER?
YOU MEAN THE CONDUCTOR?
AMOS IS AT THE VERY FRONT. WHICH MEANS YOU'LL HAVE TO GO THROUGH US.
YA DON'T SAY?
WELL, I'VE ALWAYS WANTED TO TRY A SIDE-SCROLLER.

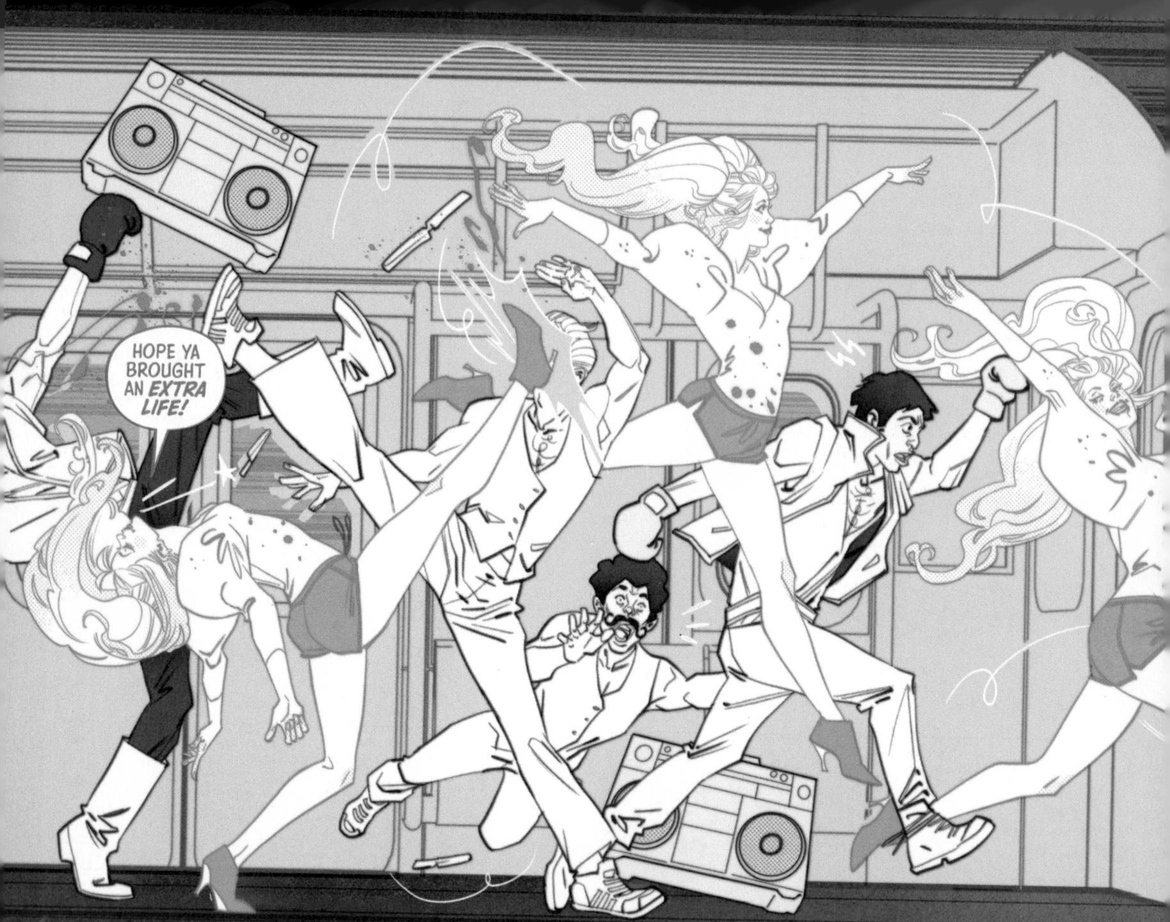
HOPE YA BROUGHT AN EXTRA LIFE!

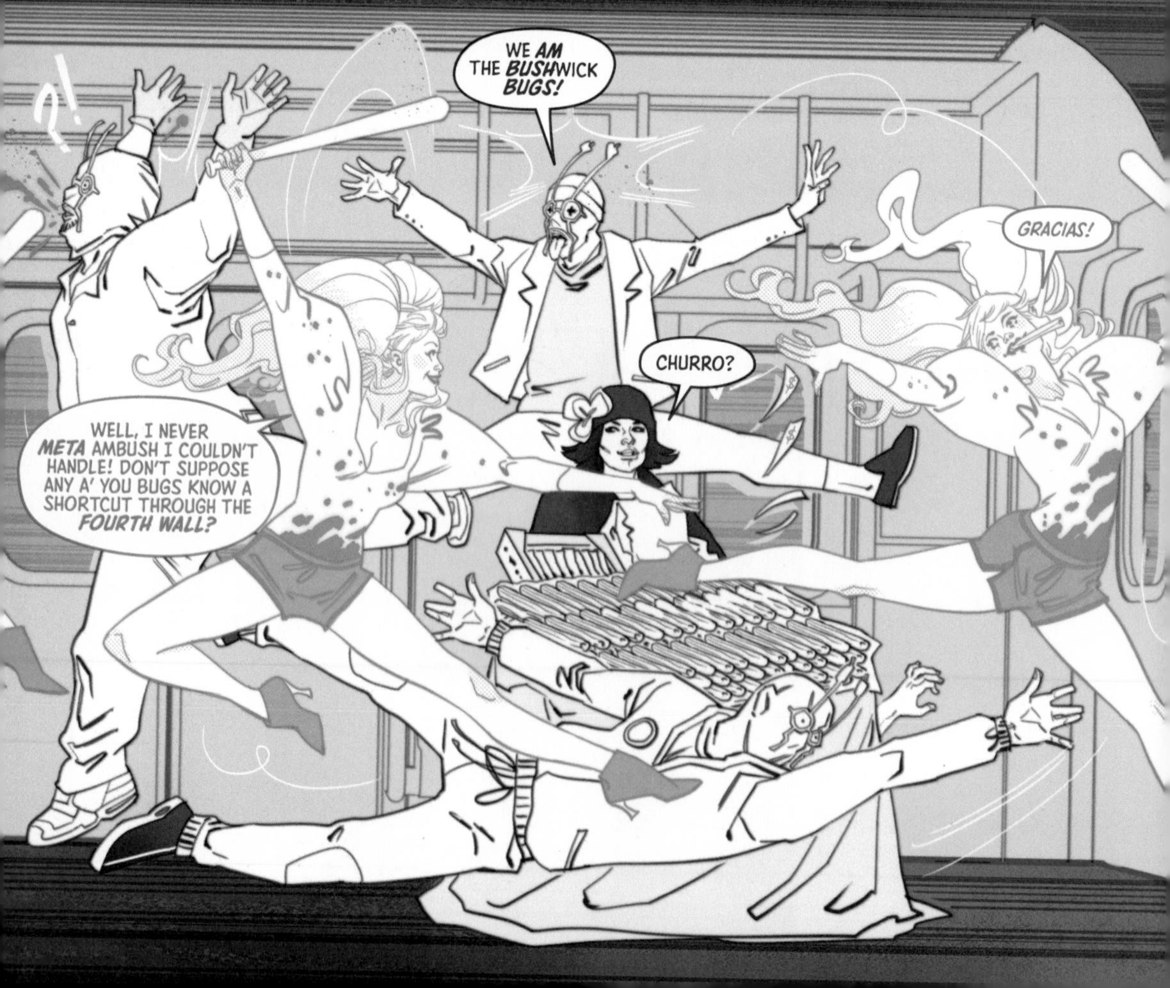
WE AM THE BUSHWICK BUGS!
GRACIAS!
CHURRO?
WELL, I NEVER META AMBUSH I COULDN'T HANDLE! DON'T SUPPOSE ANY A' YOU BUGS KNOW A SHORTCUT THROUGH THE FOURTH WALL?

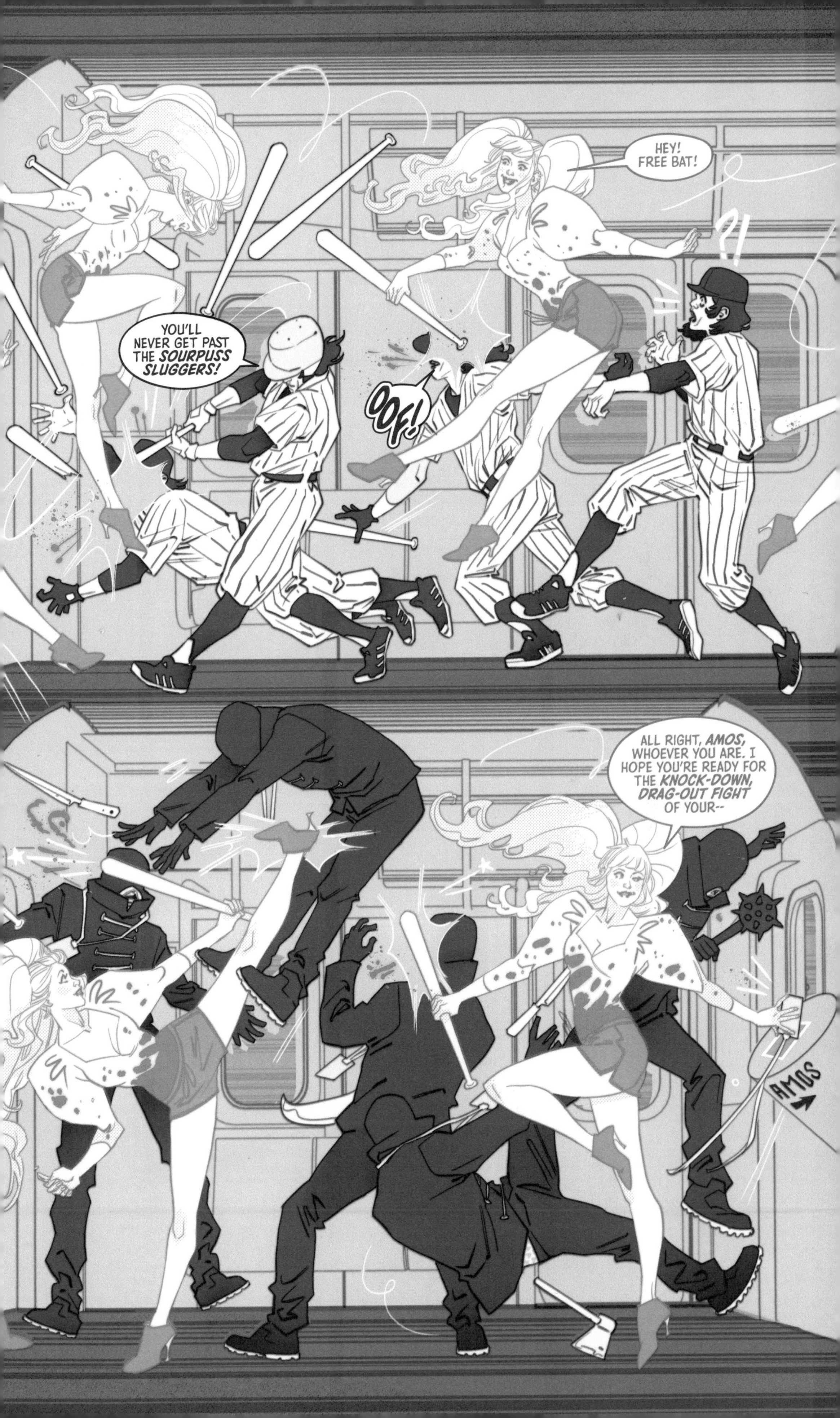
HEY! FREE BAT!
?!
YOU'LL NEVER GET PAST THE SOURPUSS SLUGGERS!
OOF!
ALL RIGHT, AMOS, WHOEVER YOU ARE. I HOPE YOU'RE READY FOR THE KNOCK-DOWN, DRAG-OUT FIGHT OF YOUR--
AMOS

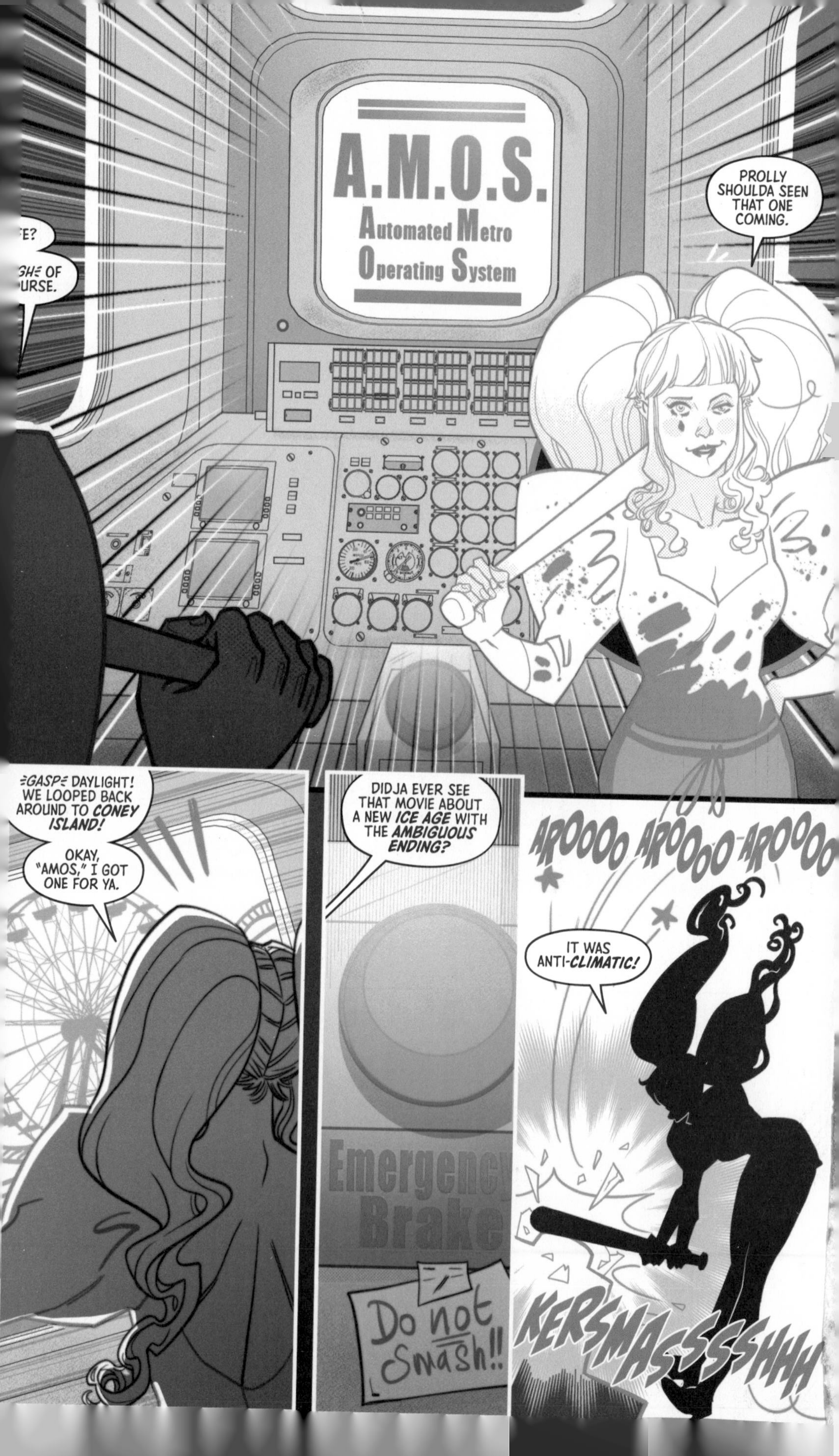
A.M.O.S.
Automated Metro Operating System
PROLLY SHOULDA SEEN THAT ONE COMING.
GASP DAYLIGHT! WE LOOPED BACK AROUND TO CONEY ISLAND!
OKAY, "AMOS," I GOT ONE FOR YA.
DIDJA EVER SEE THAT MOVIE ABOUT A NEW ICE AGE WITH THE AMBIGUOUS ENDING?
Emergency Brake
Do not Smash!!
AROOOO AROOOO-AROOOO
IT WAS ANTI-CLIMATIC!
KERSMASSSSHHH

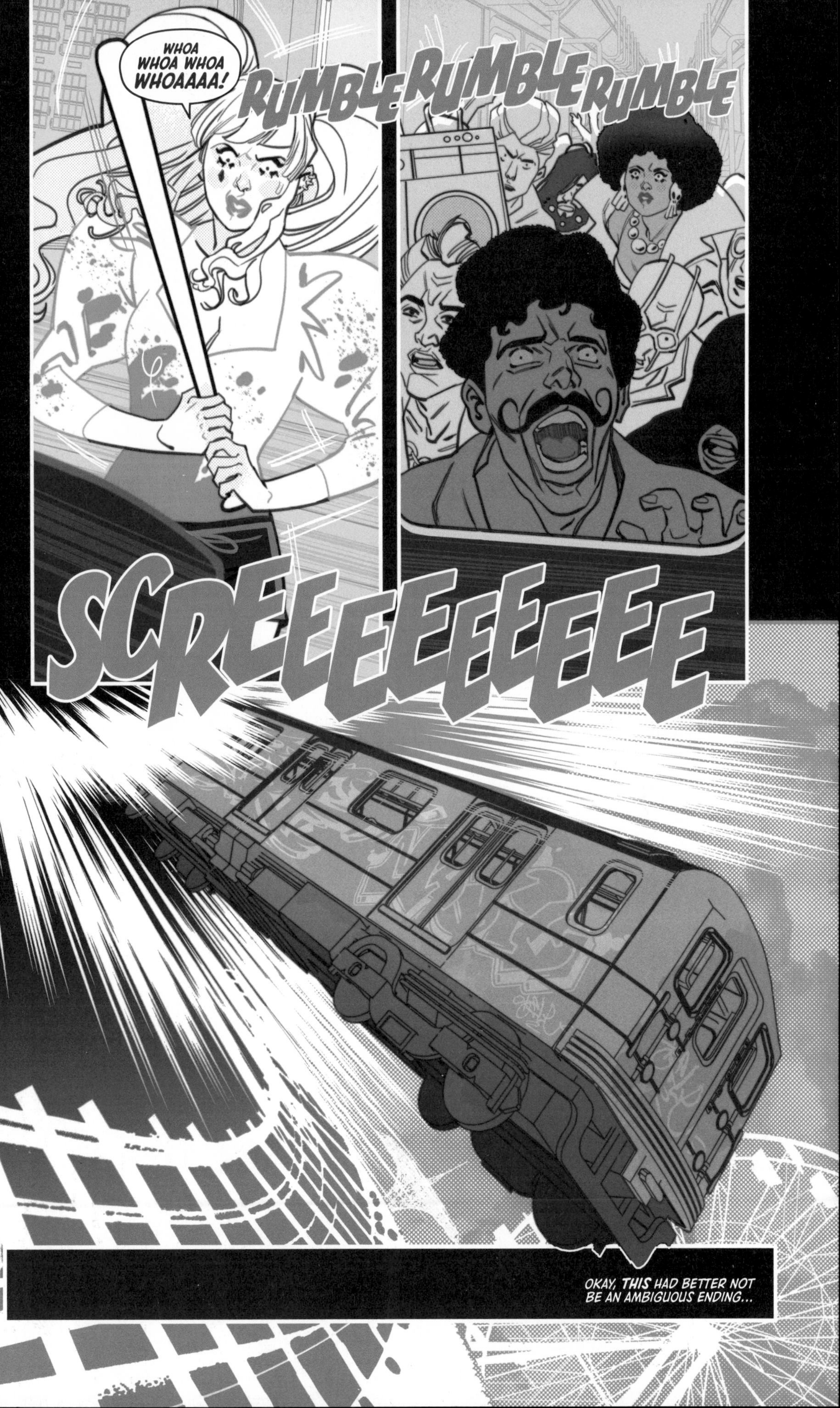
WHOA WHOA WHOA WHOAAAA!
RUMBLE RUMBLE RUMBLE
SCREEEEEEEEEE
OKAY, THIS HAD BETTER NOT BE AN AMBIGUOUS ENDING...

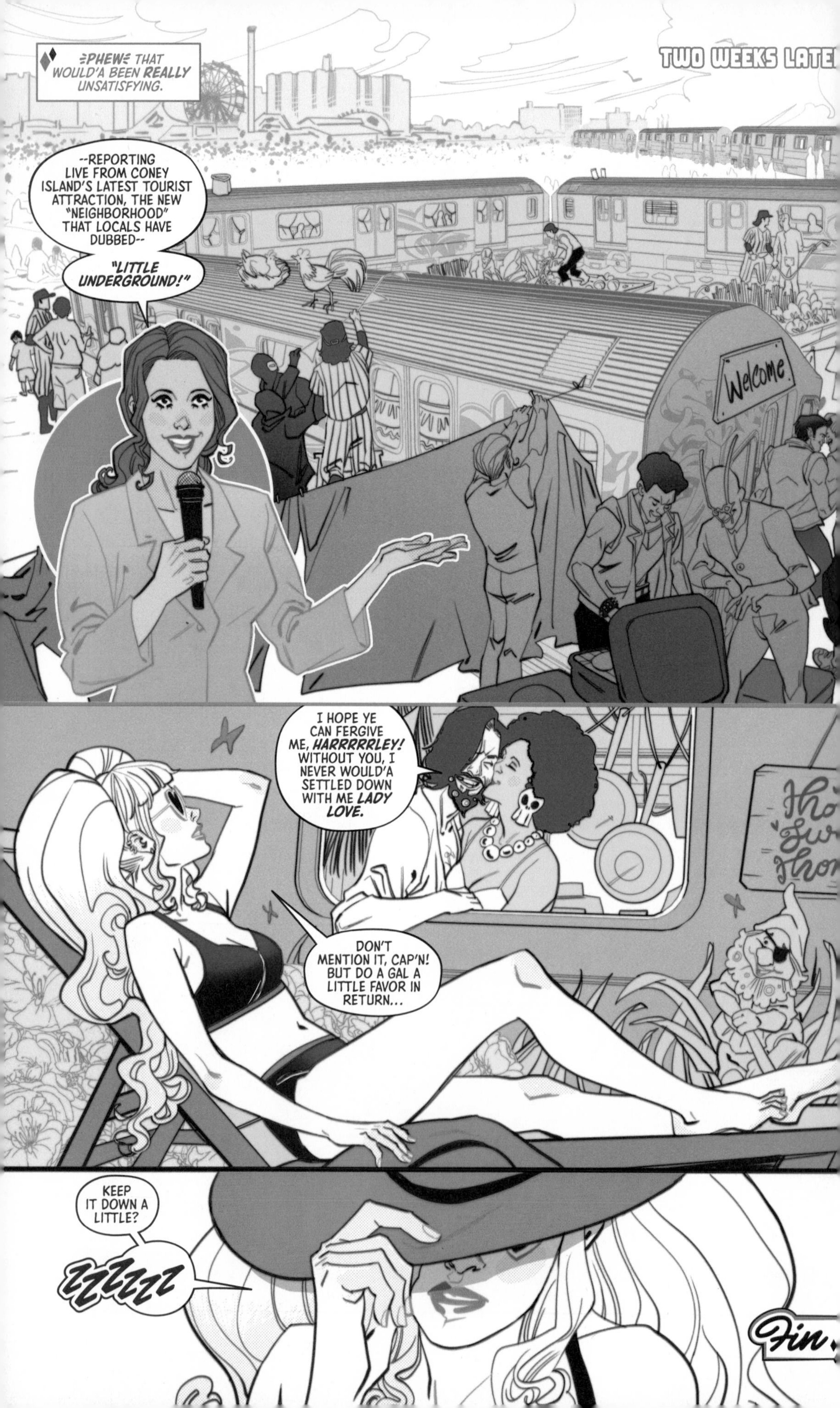

TWO WEEKS LATE
PHEW THAT WOULD'A BEEN REALLY UNSATISFYING.
--REPORTING LIVE FROM CONEY ISLAND'S LATEST TOURIST ATTRACTION, THE NEW "NEIGHBORHOOD" THAT LOCALS HAVE DUBBED--
"LITTLE UNDERGROUND!"
Welcome
I HOPE YE CAN FERGIVE ME, HARRRRRLEY! WITHOUT YOU, I NEVER WOULD'A SETTLED DOWN WITH ME LADY LOVE.
DON'T MENTION IT, CAP'N! BUT DO A GAL A LITTLE FAVOR IN RETURN...
KEEP IT DOWN A LITTLE?
ZZZZZZ
Fin.

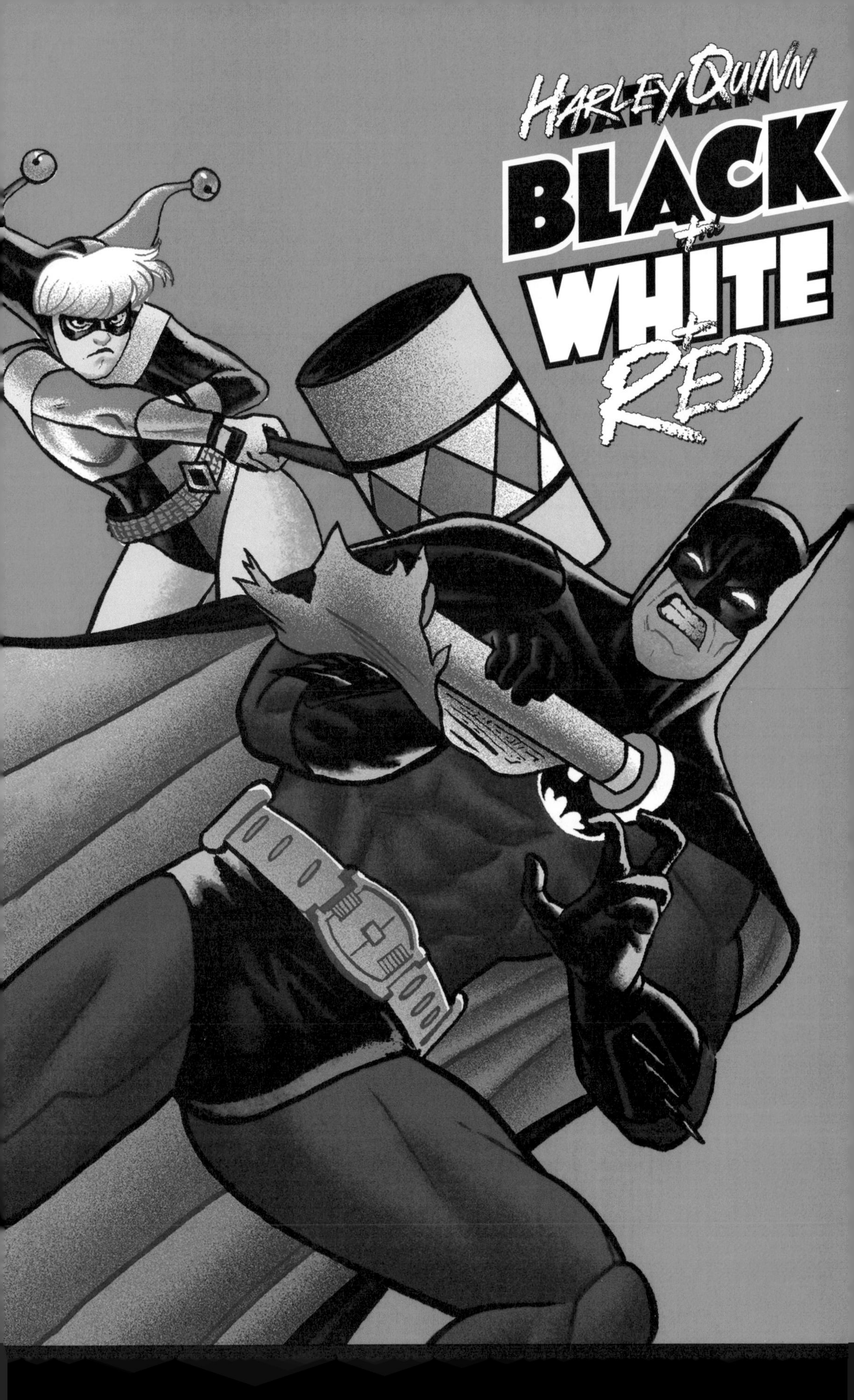
HARLEY QUINN
BLACK
+
WHITE
+
RED

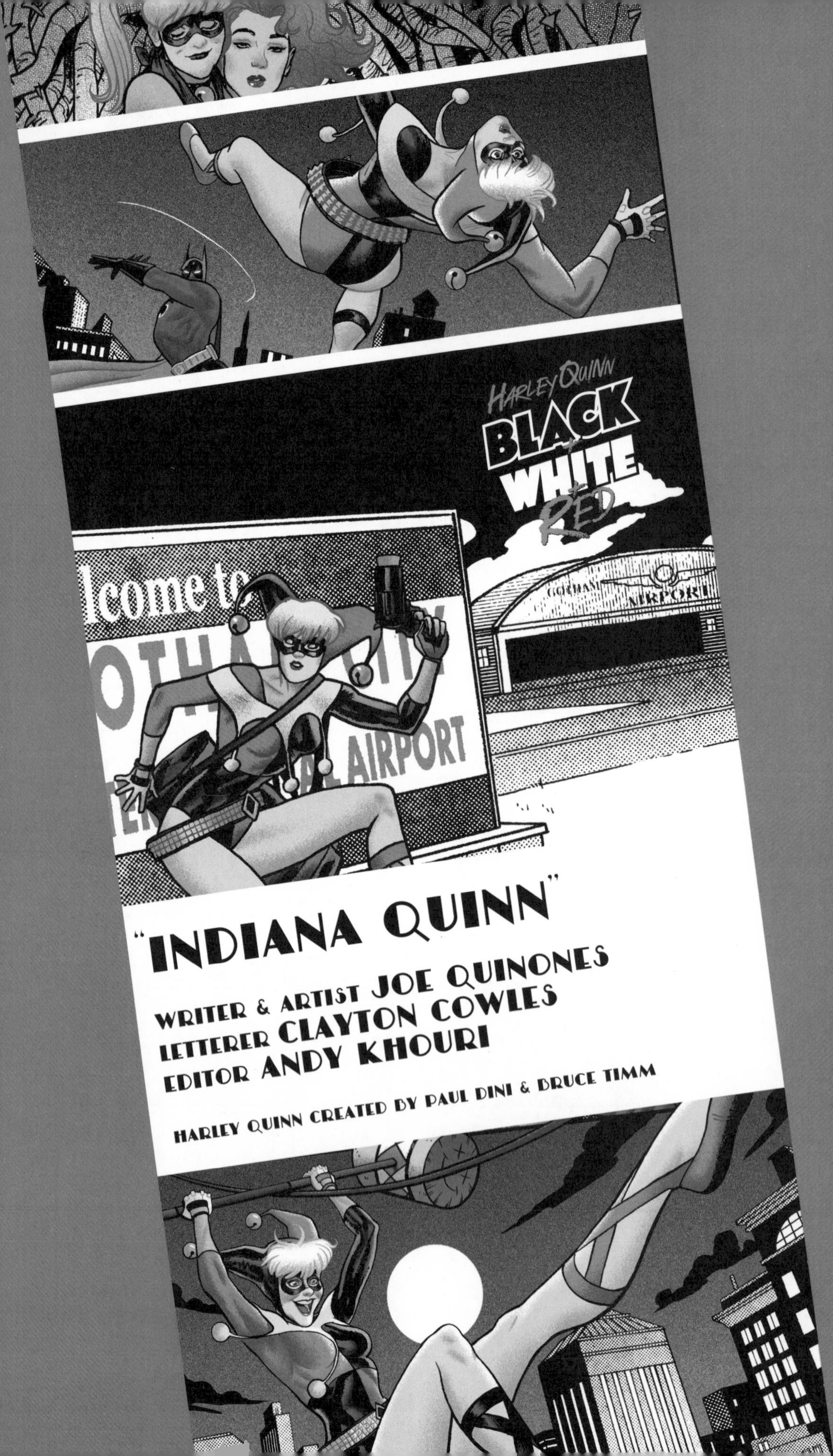
HARLEY QUINN
BLACK + WHITE + RED
lcome to
OTHA CITY
AIRPORT
GOTHAM AIRPORT
"INDIANA QUINN"
WRITER & ARTIST JOE QUINONES
LETTERER CLAYTON COWLES
EDITOR ANDY KHOURI
HARLEY QUINN CREATED BY PAUL DINI & BRUCE TIMM

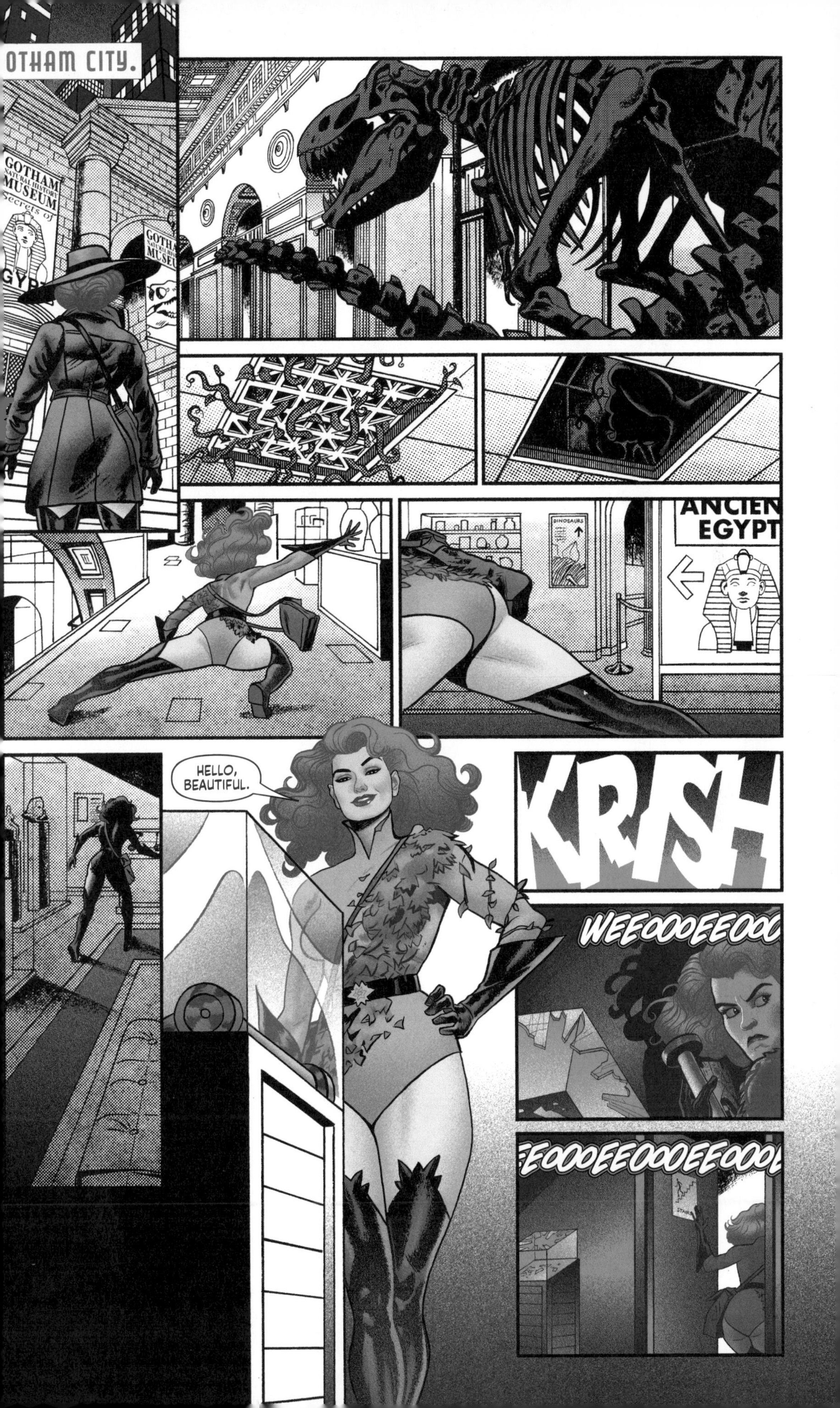
OTHAM CITY.
GOTHAM NATURAL HISTORY MUSEUM
Secrets of
GYPT
GOTHAM NATURAL HISTORY MUSEUM
ANCIENT EGYPT
DINOSAURS
HELLO, BEAUTIFUL.
KRISH
WEEOOOEEOOO
EEOOOEEOOOEEOOOE

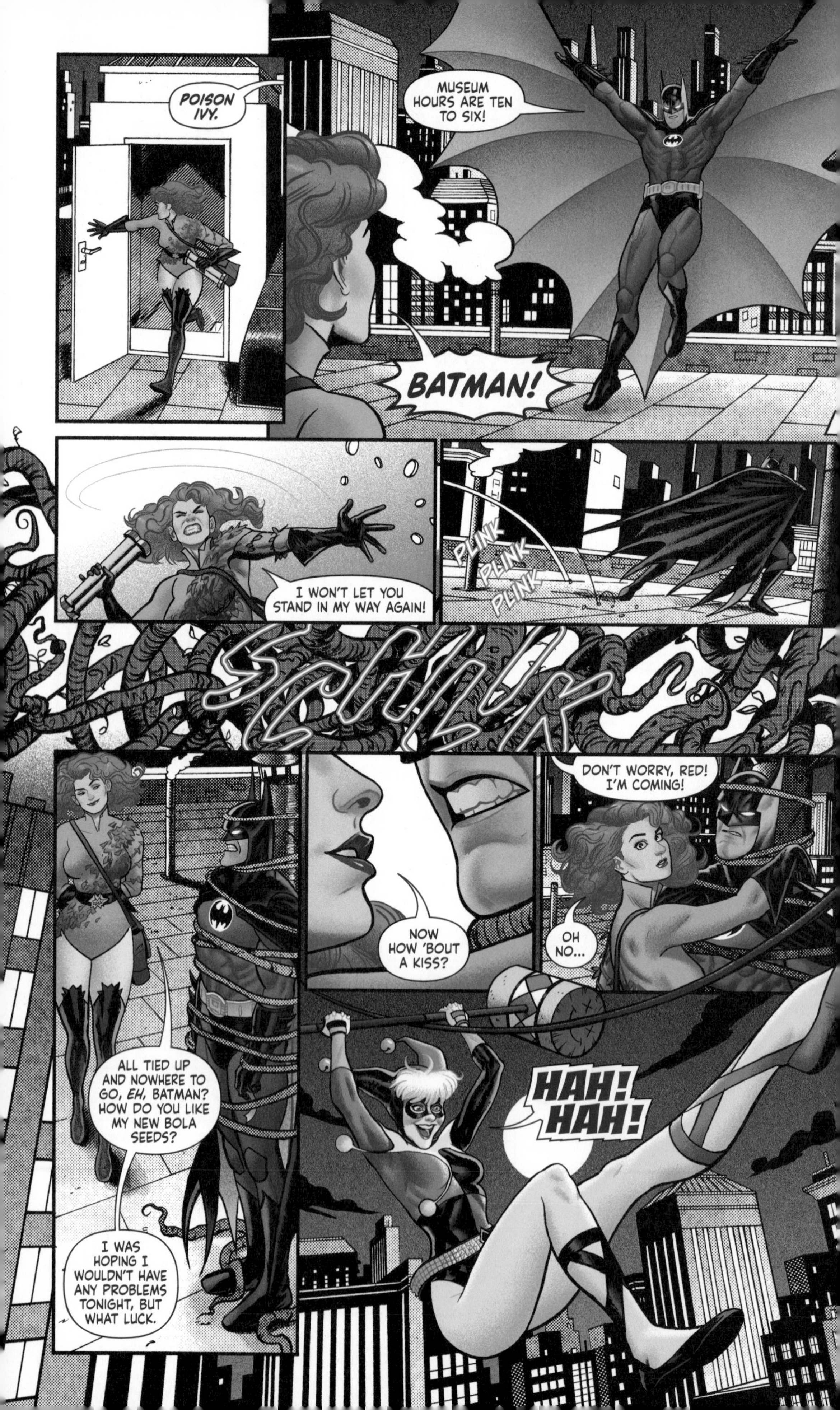
POISON IVY.
MUSEUM HOURS ARE TEN TO SIX!
BATMAN!
I WON'T LET YOU STAND IN MY WAY AGAIN!
PLINK
PLINK
PLINK
SCHLUK
ALL TIED UP AND NOWHERE TO GO, EH, BATMAN? HOW DO YOU LIKE MY NEW BOLA SEEDS?
I WAS HOPING I WOULDN'T HAVE ANY PROBLEMS TONIGHT, BUT WHAT LUCK.
NOW HOW 'BOUT A KISS?
DON'T WORRY, RED! I'M COMING!
OH NO...
HAH! HAH!

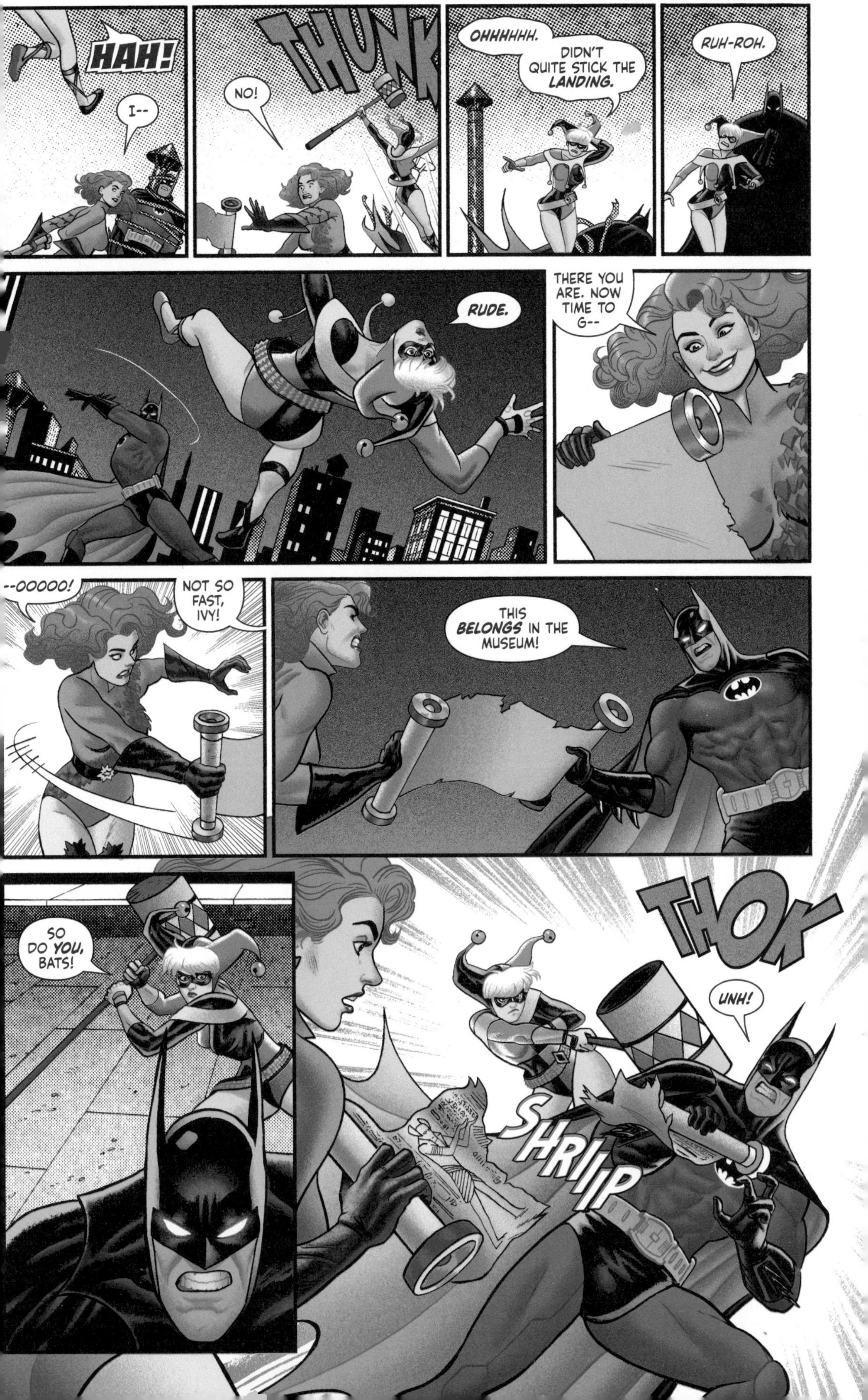
HAH!
I--
THUNK
NO!
OHHHHHH.
DIDN'T QUITE STICK THE LANDING.
RUH-ROH.
RUDE.
THERE YOU ARE. NOW TIME TO G--
--OOOOO!
NOT SO FAST, IVY!
THIS BELONGS IN THE MUSEUM!
SO DO YOU, BATS!
THOK
UNH!
SHRIIIP

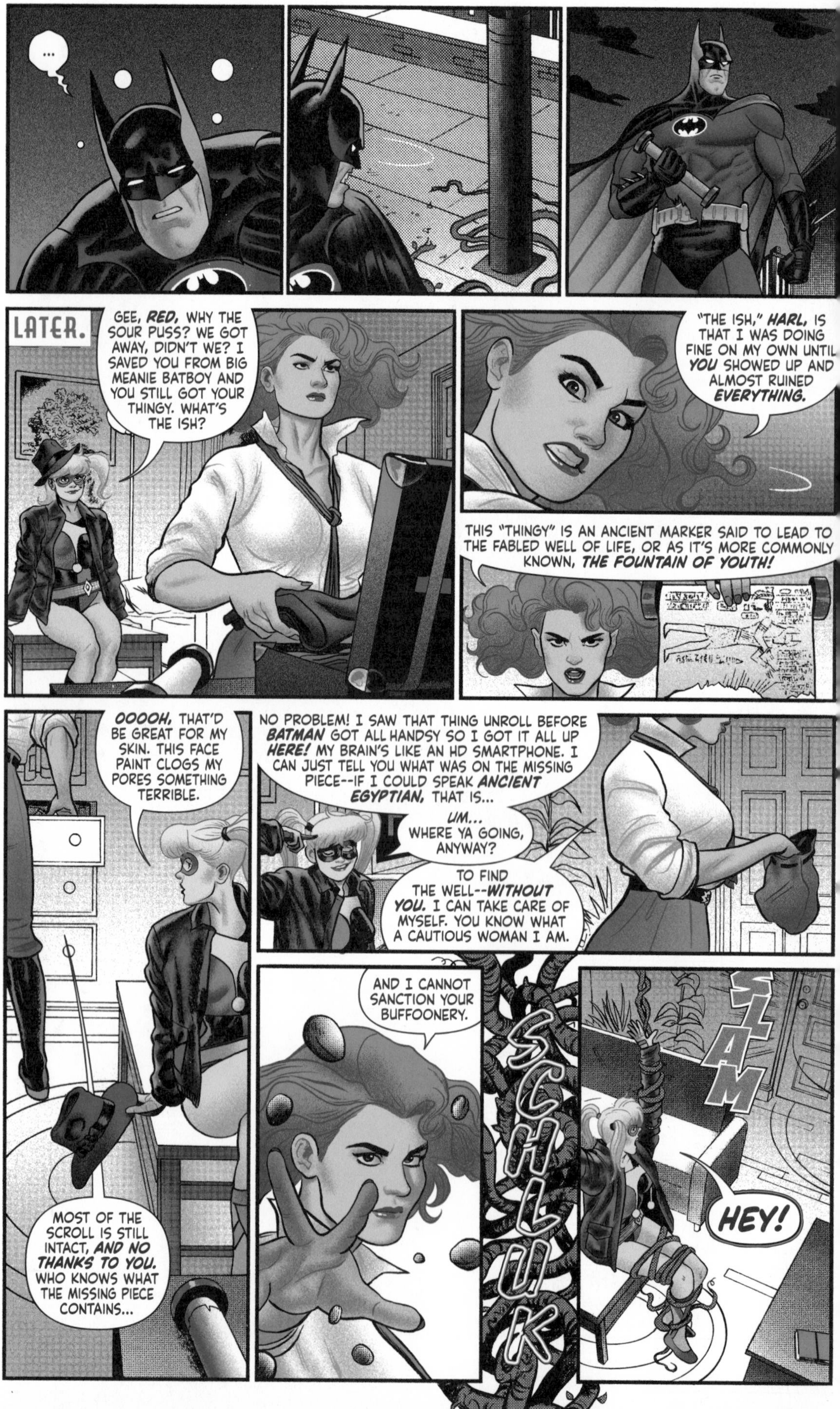
...
LATER.
GEE, RED, WHY THE SOUR PUSS? WE GOT AWAY, DIDN'T WE? I SAVED YOU FROM BIG MEANIE BATBOY AND YOU STILL GOT YOUR THINGY. WHAT'S THE ISH?
"THE ISH," HARL, IS THAT I WAS DOING FINE ON MY OWN UNTIL YOU SHOWED UP AND ALMOST RUINED EVERYTHING.
THIS "THINGY" IS AN ANCIENT MARKER SAID TO LEAD TO THE FABLED WELL OF LIFE, OR AS IT'S MORE COMMONLY KNOWN, THE FOUNTAIN OF YOUTH!
OOOOH, THAT'D BE GREAT FOR MY SKIN. THIS FACE PAINT CLOGS MY PORES SOMETHING TERRIBLE.
MOST OF THE SCROLL IS STILL INTACT, AND NO THANKS TO YOU. WHO KNOWS WHAT THE MISSING PIECE CONTAINS...
NO PROBLEM! I SAW THAT THING UNROLL BEFORE BATMAN GOT ALL HANDSY SO I GOT IT ALL UP HERE! MY BRAIN'S LIKE AN HD SMARTPHONE. I CAN JUST TELL YOU WHAT WAS ON THE MISSING PIECE--IF I COULD SPEAK ANCIENT EGYPTIAN, THAT IS...
UM... WHERE YA GOING, ANYWAY?
TO FIND THE WELL--WITHOUT YOU. I CAN TAKE CARE OF MYSELF. YOU KNOW WHAT A CAUTIOUS WOMAN I AM.
AND I CANNOT SANCTION YOUR BUFFOONERY.
SCHLUK
SLAM
HEY!

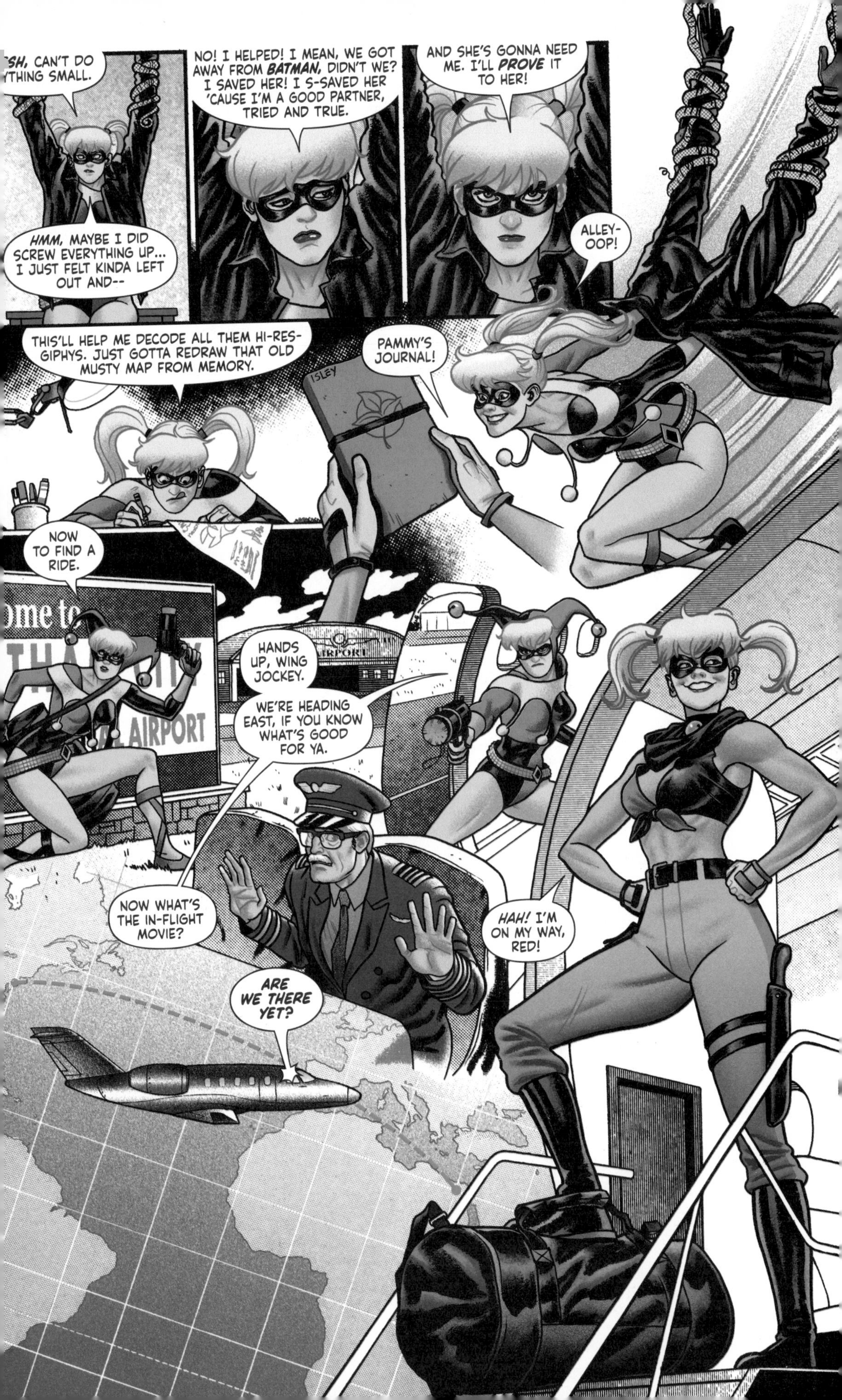

SH, CAN'T DO
YTHING SMALL.
HMM, MAYBE I DID SCREW EVERYTHING UP... I JUST FELT KINDA LEFT OUT AND--
NO! I HELPED! I MEAN, WE GOT AWAY FROM BATMAN, DIDN'T WE? I SAVED HER! I S-SAVED HER 'CAUSE I'M A GOOD PARTNER, TRIED AND TRUE.
AND SHE'S GONNA NEED ME. I'LL PROVE IT TO HER!
ALLEY-OOP!
PAMMY'S JOURNAL!
ISLEY
THIS'LL HELP ME DECODE ALL THEM HI-RES-GIPHYS. JUST GOTTA REDRAW THAT OLD MUSTY MAP FROM MEMORY.
NOW TO FIND A RIDE.
ome to
AIRPORT
HANDS UP, WING JOCKEY.
WE'RE HEADING EAST, IF YOU KNOW WHAT'S GOOD FOR YA.
NOW WHAT'S THE IN-FLIGHT MOVIE?
HAH! I'M ON MY WAY, RED!
ARE WE THERE YET?

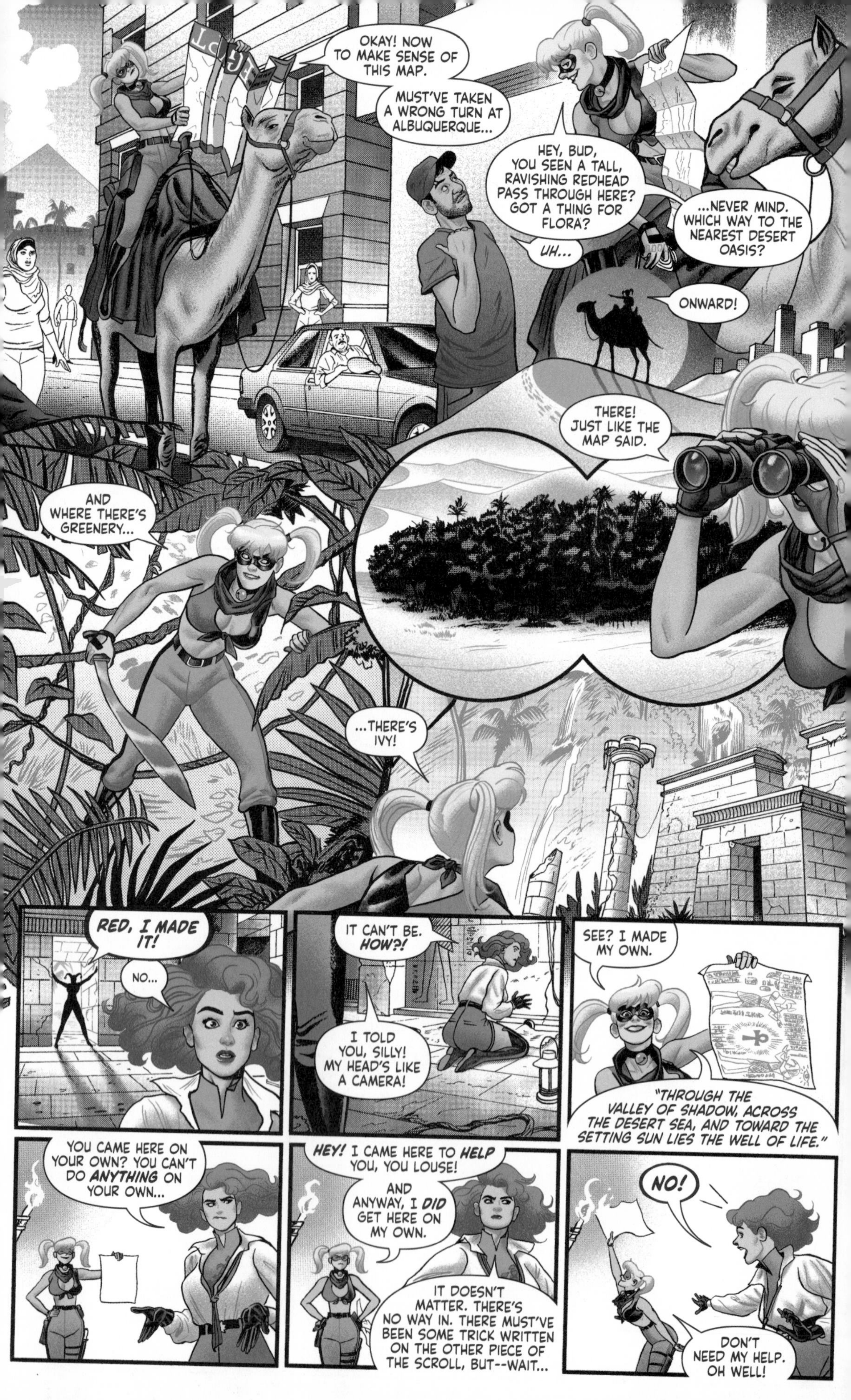
OKAY! NOW TO MAKE SENSE OF THIS MAP.
MUST'VE TAKEN A WRONG TURN AT ALBUQUERQUE...
HEY, BUD, YOU SEEN A TALL, RAVISHING REDHEAD PASS THROUGH HERE? GOT A THING FOR FLORA?
UH...
...NEVER MIND. WHICH WAY TO THE NEAREST DESERT OASIS?
ONWARD!
THERE! JUST LIKE THE MAP SAID.
AND WHERE THERE'S GREENERY...
...THERE'S IVY!
RED, I MADE IT!
NO...
IT CAN'T BE. HOW?!
I TOLD YOU, SILLY! MY HEAD'S LIKE A CAMERA!
SEE? I MADE MY OWN.
"THROUGH THE VALLEY OF SHADOW, ACROSS THE DESERT SEA, AND TOWARD THE SETTING SUN LIES THE WELL OF LIFE."
YOU CAME HERE ON YOUR OWN? YOU CAN'T DO ANYTHING ON YOUR OWN...
HEY! I CAME HERE TO HELP YOU, YOU LOUSE!
AND ANYWAY, I DID GET HERE ON MY OWN.
IT DOESN'T MATTER. THERE'S NO WAY IN. THERE MUST'VE BEEN SOME TRICK WRITTEN ON THE OTHER PIECE OF THE SCROLL, BUT--WAIT...
NO!
DON'T NEED MY HELP. OH WELL!

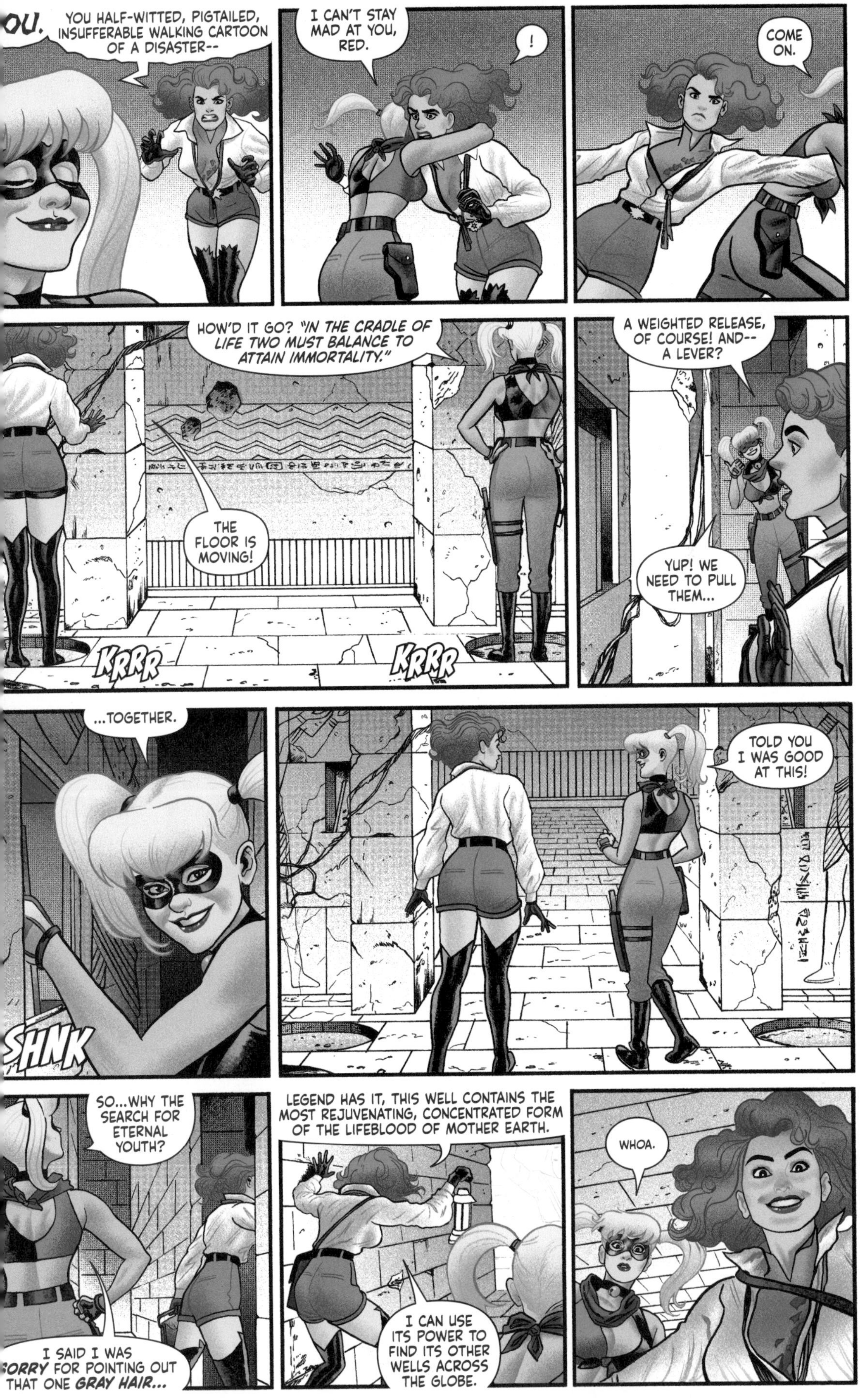
OU.
YOU HALF-WITTED, PIGTAILED, INSUFFERABLE WALKING CARTOON OF A DISASTER--
I CAN'T STAY MAD AT YOU, RED.
!
COME ON.
HOW'D IT GO? "IN THE CRADLE OF LIFE TWO MUST BALANCE TO ATTAIN IMMORTALITY."
THE FLOOR IS MOVING!
KRRR
KRRR
A WEIGHTED RELEASE, OF COURSE! AND-- A LEVER?
YUP! WE NEED TO PULL THEM...
...TOGETHER.
SHNK
TOLD YOU I WAS GOOD AT THIS!
SO...WHY THE SEARCH FOR ETERNAL YOUTH?
I SAID I WAS SORRY FOR POINTING OUT THAT ONE GRAY HAIR...
LEGEND HAS IT, THIS WELL CONTAINS THE MOST REJUVENATING, CONCENTRATED FORM OF THE LIFEBLOOD OF MOTHER EARTH.
I CAN USE ITS POWER TO FIND ITS OTHER WELLS ACROSS THE GLOBE.
WHOA.

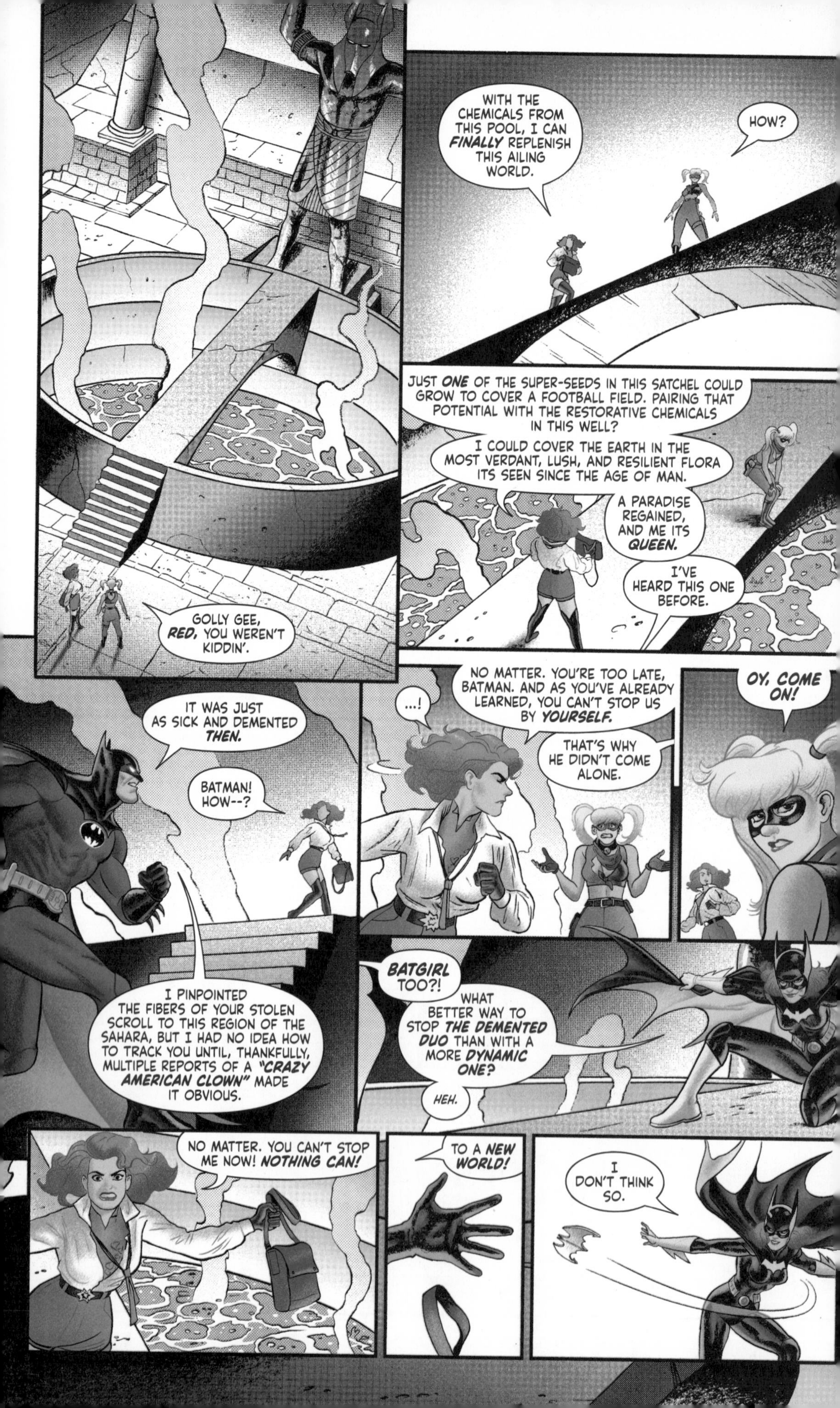
GOLLY GEE, RED, YOU WEREN'T KIDDIN'.
WITH THE CHEMICALS FROM THIS POOL, I CAN FINALLY REPLENISH THIS AILING WORLD.
HOW?
JUST ONE OF THE SUPER-SEEDS IN THIS SATCHEL COULD GROW TO COVER A FOOTBALL FIELD. PAIRING THAT POTENTIAL WITH THE RESTORATIVE CHEMICALS IN THIS WELL?
I COULD COVER THE EARTH IN THE MOST VERDANT, LUSH, AND RESILIENT FLORA ITS SEEN SINCE THE AGE OF MAN.
A PARADISE REGAINED, AND ME ITS QUEEN.
I'VE HEARD THIS ONE BEFORE.
IT WAS JUST AS SICK AND DEMENTED THEN.
BATMAN! HOW--?
I PINPOINTED THE FIBERS OF YOUR STOLEN SCROLL TO THIS REGION OF THE SAHARA, BUT I HAD NO IDEA HOW TO TRACK YOU UNTIL, THANKFULLY, MULTIPLE REPORTS OF A "CRAZY AMERICAN CLOWN" MADE IT OBVIOUS.
...!
NO MATTER. YOU'RE TOO LATE, BATMAN. AND AS YOU'VE ALREADY LEARNED, YOU CAN'T STOP US BY YOURSELF.
THAT'S WHY HE DIDN'T COME ALONE.
OY, COME ON!
BATGIRL TOO?!
WHAT BETTER WAY TO STOP THE DEMENTED DUO THAN WITH A MORE DYNAMIC ONE?
HEH.
NO MATTER. YOU CAN'T STOP ME NOW! NOTHING CAN!
TO A NEW WORLD!
I DON'T THINK SO.

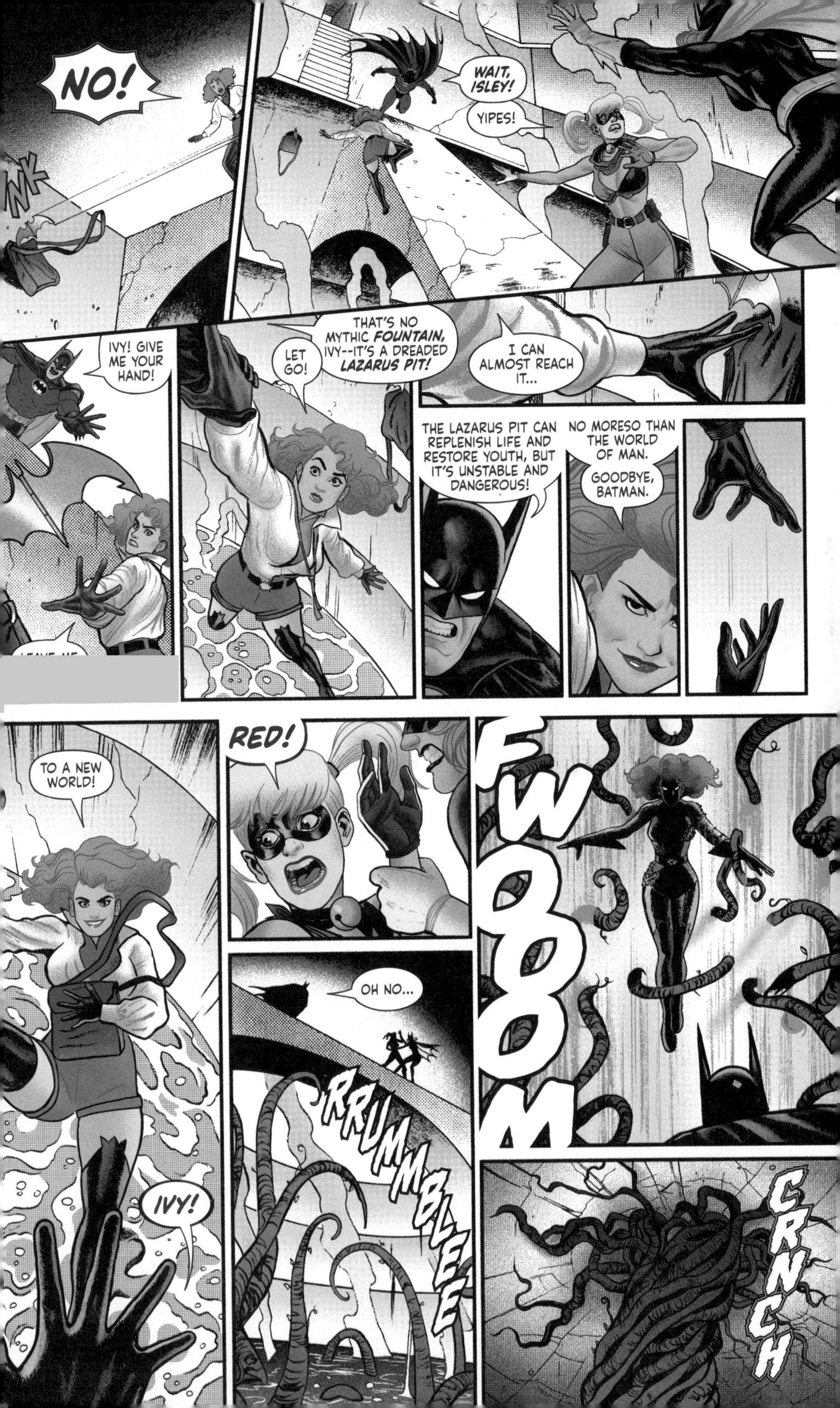
NO!
WAIT, ISLEY!
YIPES!
IVY! GIVE ME YOUR HAND!
THAT'S NO MYTHIC *FOUNTAIN,* IVY--IT'S A DREADED *LAZARUS PIT!*
LET GO!
I CAN ALMOST REACH IT...
THE LAZARUS PIT CAN REPLENISH LIFE AND RESTORE YOUTH, BUT IT'S UNSTABLE AND DANGEROUS!
NO MORESO THAN THE WORLD OF MAN.
GOODBYE, BATMAN.
TO A NEW WORLD!
IVY!
RED!
OH NO...
RRUMMBLEE
FWOOOM
CRNCH

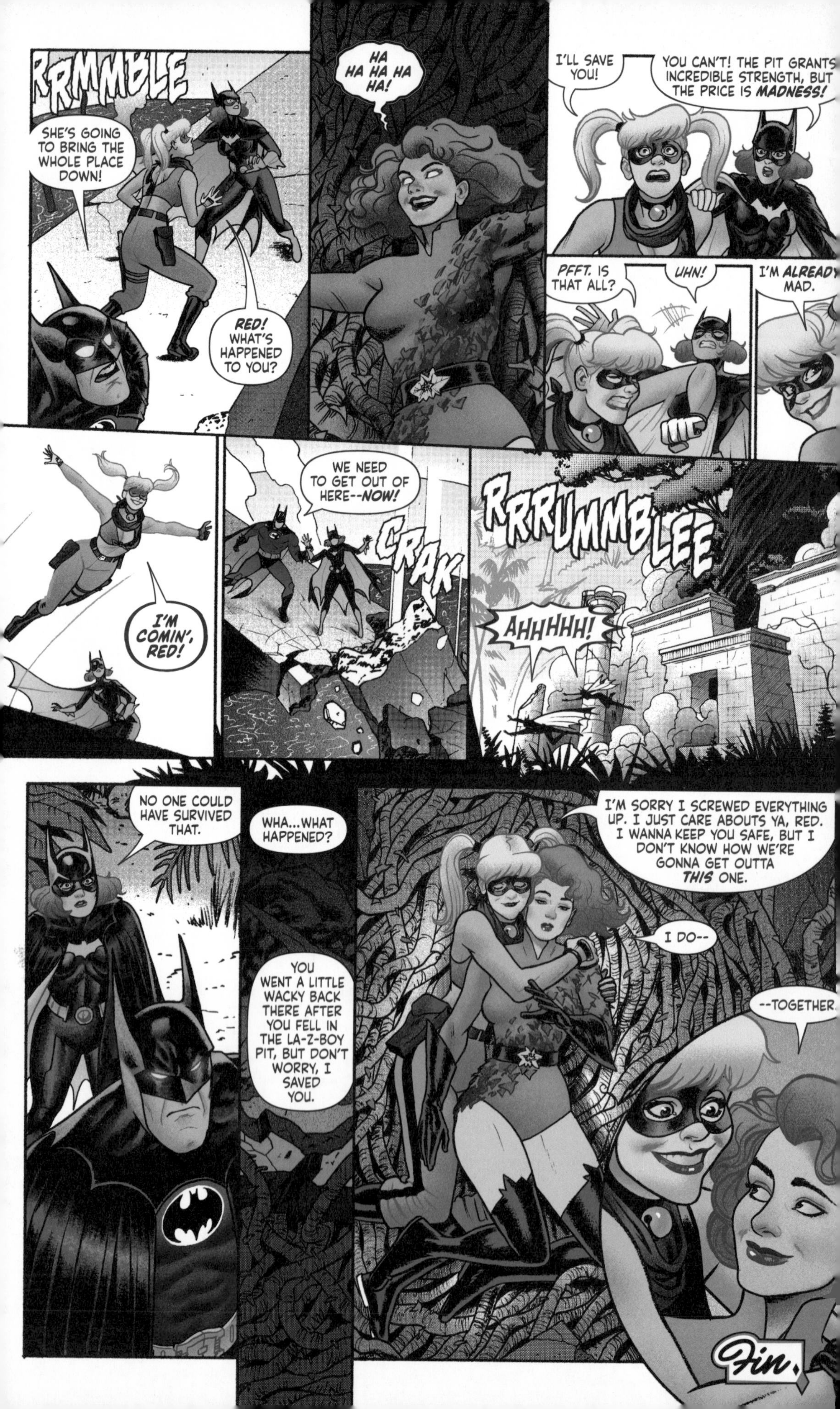

RRMMBLE
SHE'S GOING TO BRING THE WHOLE PLACE DOWN!
RED! WHAT'S HAPPENED TO YOU?
HA HA HA HA HA!
I'LL SAVE YOU!
YOU CAN'T! THE PIT GRANTS INCREDIBLE STRENGTH, BUT THE PRICE IS MADNESS!
PFFT. IS THAT ALL?
UHN!
I'M ALREADY MAD.
I'M COMIN', RED!
WE NEED TO GET OUT OF HERE--NOW!
CRAK
RRRUMMBLEE
AHHHHH!
NO ONE COULD HAVE SURVIVED THAT.
WHA...WHAT HAPPENED?
YOU WENT A LITTLE WACKY BACK THERE AFTER YOU FELL IN THE LA-Z-BOY PIT, BUT DON'T WORRY, I SAVED YOU.
I'M SORRY I SCREWED EVERYTHING UP. I JUST CARE ABOUTS YA, RED. I WANNA KEEP YOU SAFE, BUT I DON'T KNOW HOW WE'RE GONNA GET OUTTA THIS ONE.
I DO--
--TOGETHER.
Fin.

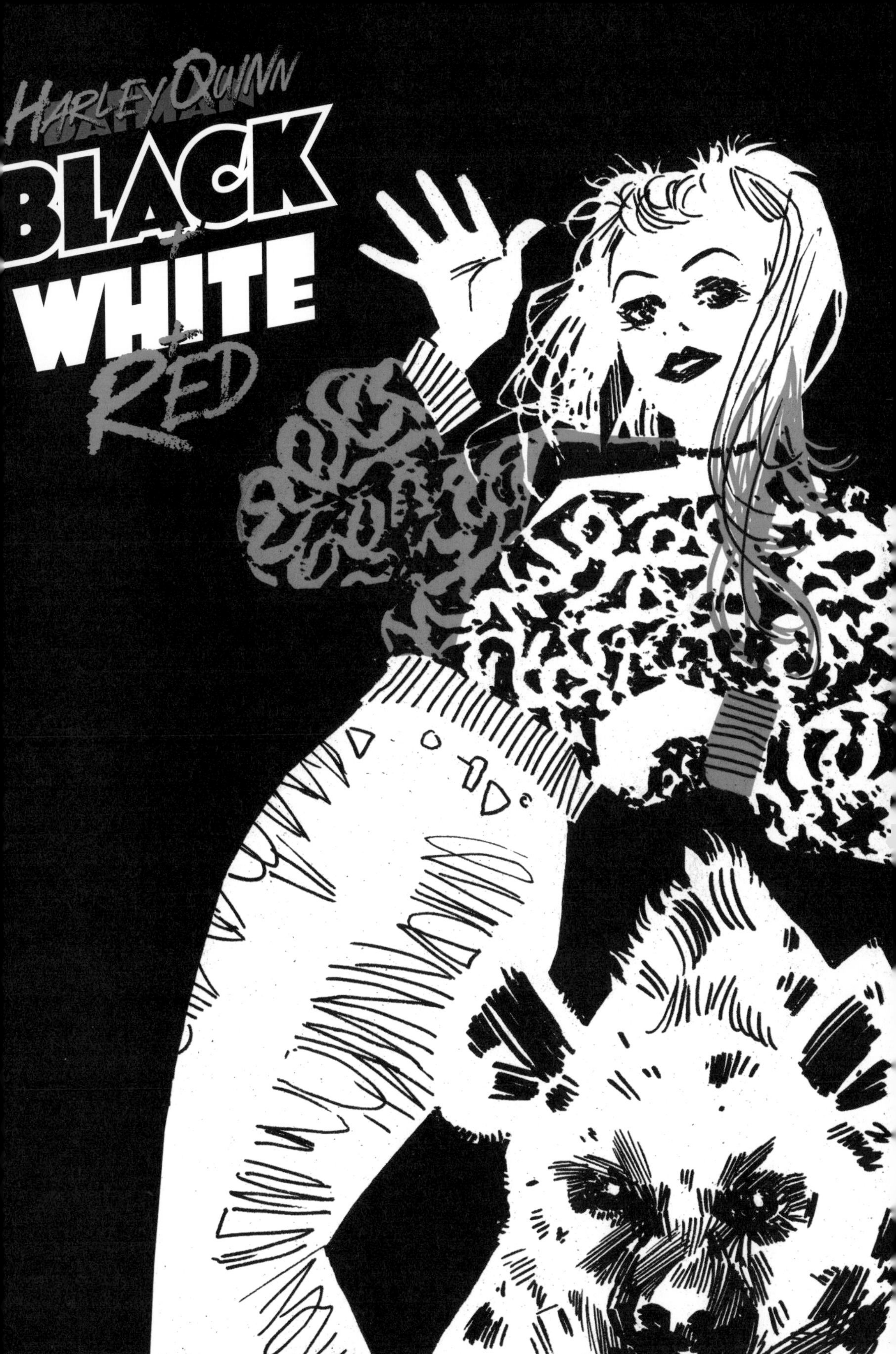
HARLEY QUINN
BLACK + WHITE + RED

CHAPTER TEN

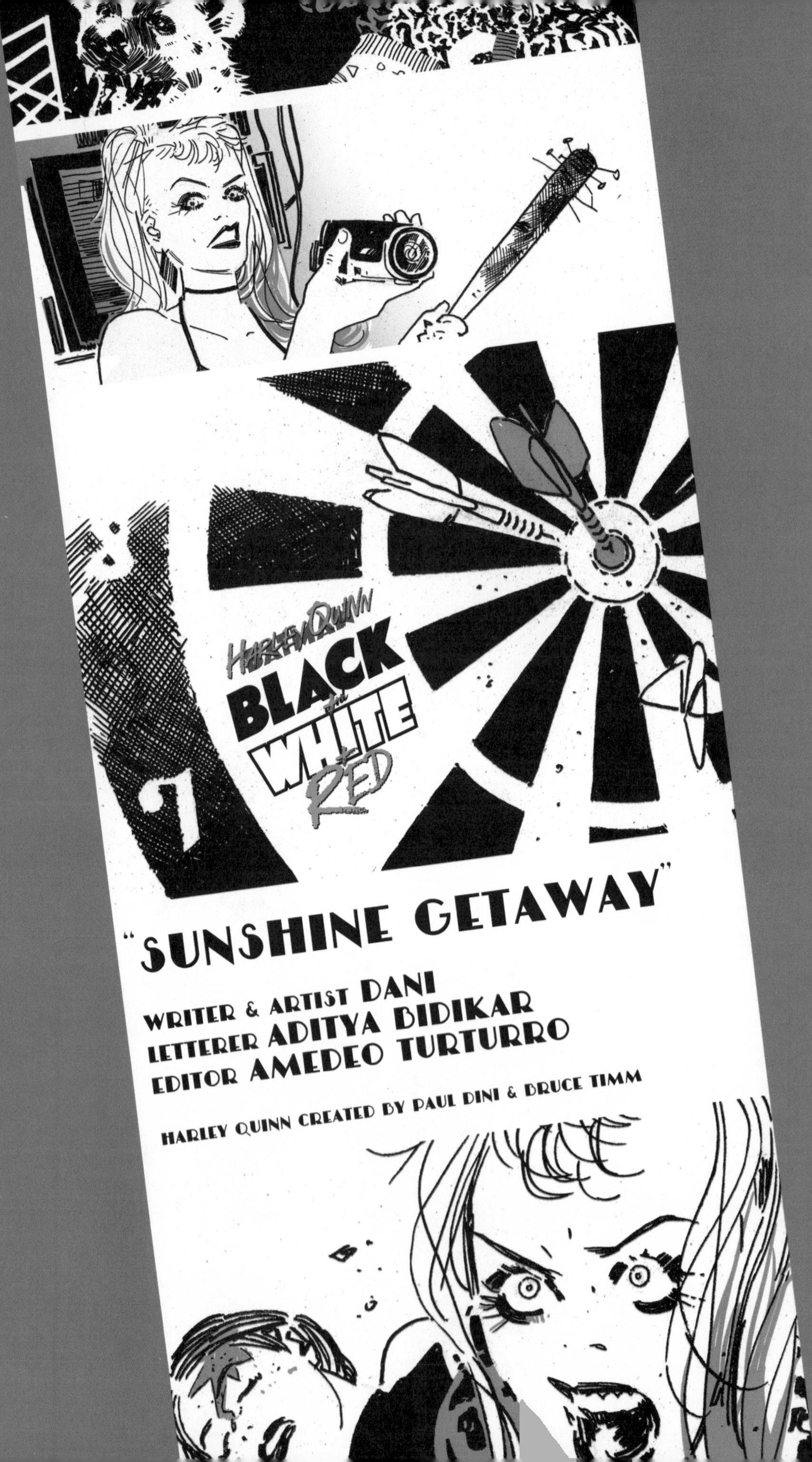
HARLEY QUINN
BLACK + WHITE + RED
"SUNSHINE GETAWAY"
WRITER & ARTIST DANI
LETTERER ADITYA BIDIKAR
EDITOR AMEDEO TURTURRO
HARLEY QUINN CREATED BY PAUL DINI & BRUCE TIMM

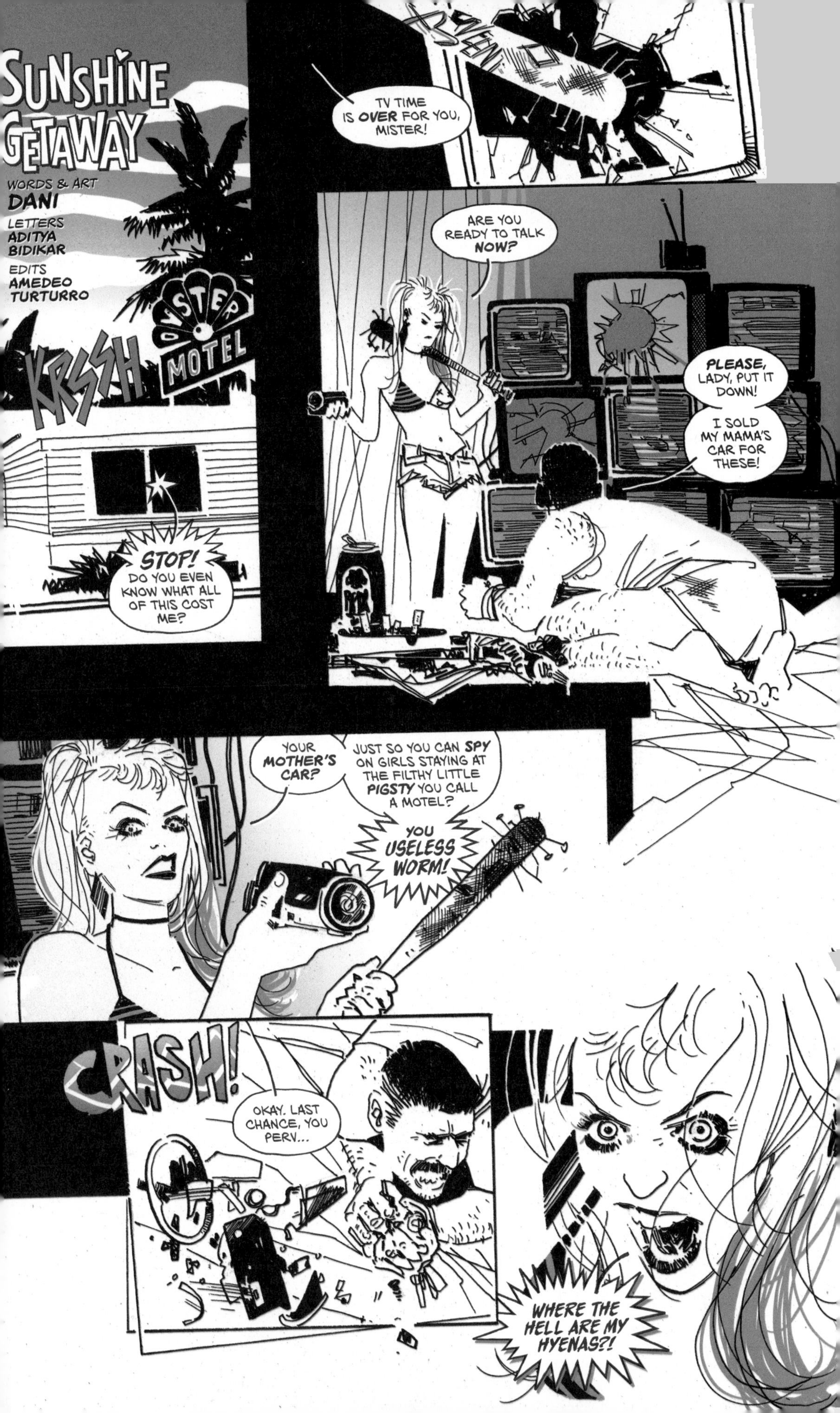
SUNSHINE GETAWAY
WORDS & ART DANI
LETTERS ADITYA BIDIKAR
EDITS AMEDEO TURTURRO
OYSTER MOTEL
KRSSH
STOP! DO YOU EVEN KNOW WHAT ALL OF THIS COST ME?
TV TIME IS OVER FOR YOU, MISTER!
ARE YOU READY TO TALK NOW?
PLEASE, LADY, PUT IT DOWN!
I SOLD MY MAMA'S CAR FOR THESE!
YOUR MOTHER'S CAR?
JUST SO YOU CAN SPY ON GIRLS STAYING AT THE FILTHY LITTLE PIGSTY YOU CALL A MOTEL?
YOU USELESS WORM!
CRASH!
OKAY. LAST CHANCE, YOU PERV...
WHERE THE HELL ARE MY HYENAS?!

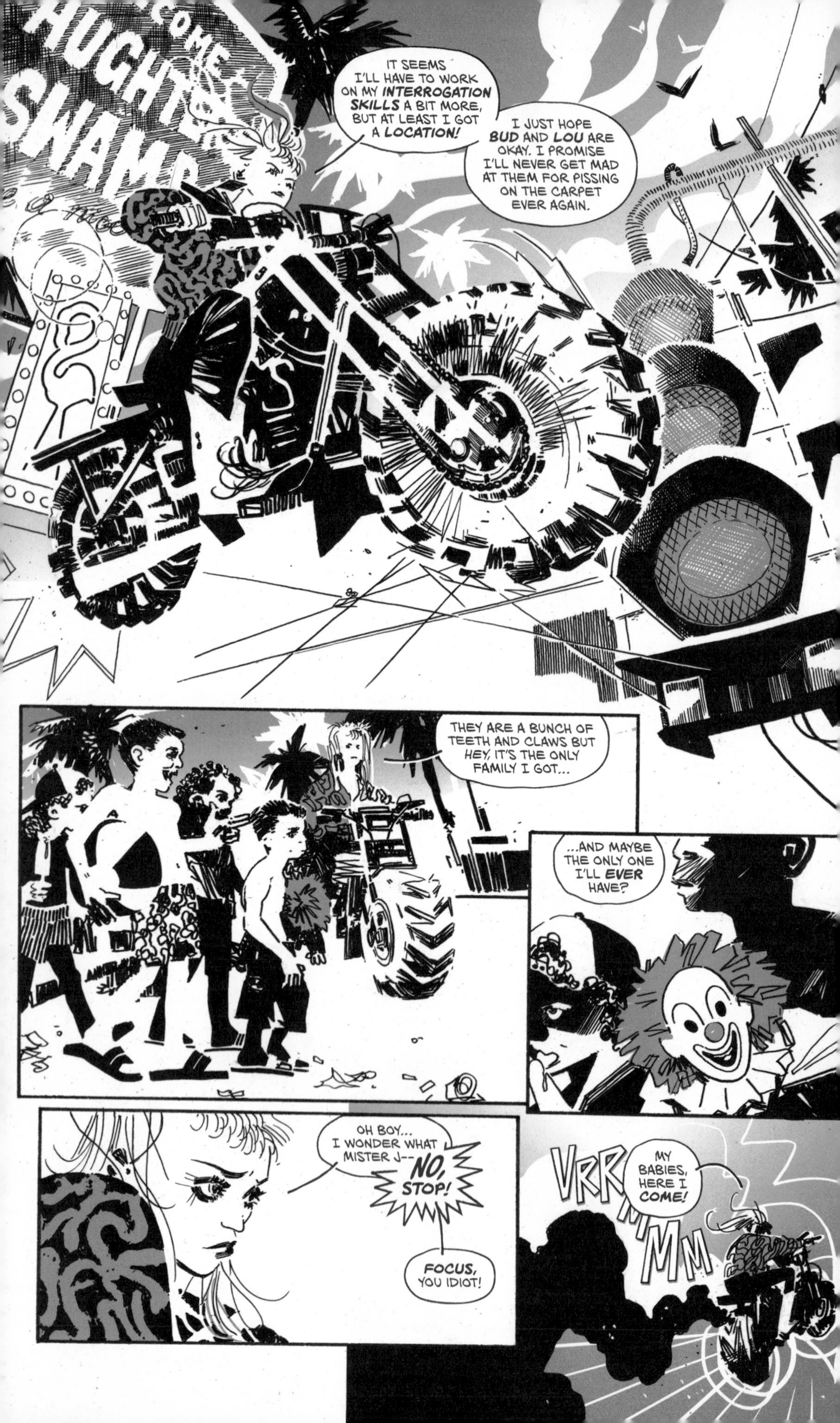

IT SEEMS I'LL HAVE TO WORK ON MY INTERROGATION SKILLS A BIT MORE, BUT AT LEAST I GOT A LOCATION!
I JUST HOPE BUD AND LOU ARE OKAY. I PROMISE I'LL NEVER GET MAD AT THEM FOR PISSING ON THE CARPET EVER AGAIN.
THEY ARE A BUNCH OF TEETH AND CLAWS BUT HEY, IT'S THE ONLY FAMILY I GOT...
...AND MAYBE THE ONLY ONE I'LL EVER HAVE?
OH BOY... I WONDER WHAT MISTER J--
NO, STOP!
FOCUS, YOU IDIOT!
VRRRMMMM
MY BABIES, HERE I COME!

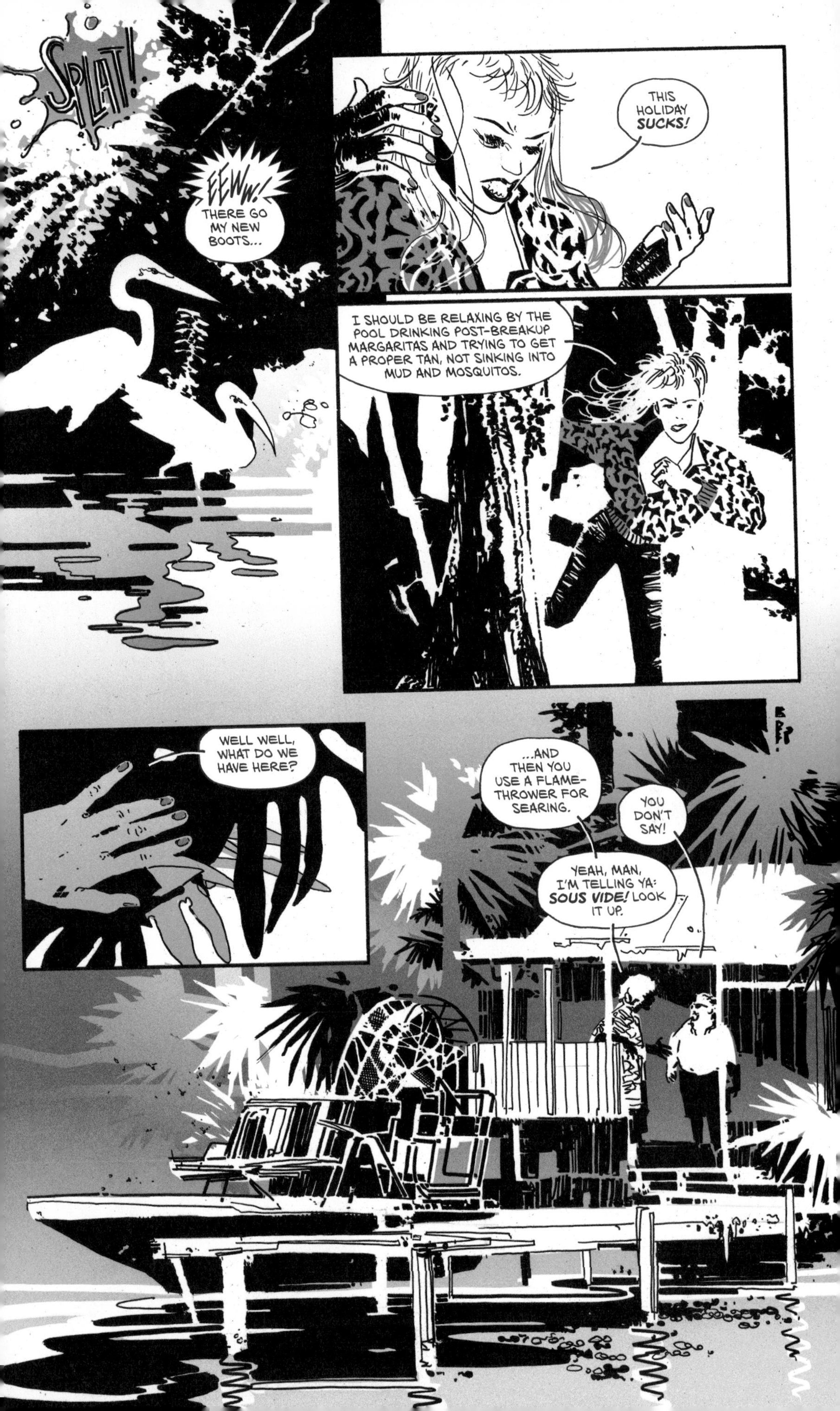
SPLAT!
EEWW! THERE GO MY NEW BOOTS...
THIS HOLIDAY SUCKS!
I SHOULD BE RELAXING BY THE POOL DRINKING POST-BREAKUP MARGARITAS AND TRYING TO GET A PROPER TAN, NOT SINKING INTO MUD AND MOSQUITOS.
WELL WELL, WHAT DO WE HAVE HERE?
...AND THEN YOU USE A FLAME-THROWER FOR SEARING.
YOU DON'T SAY!
YEAH, MAN, I'M TELLING YA: SOUS VIDE! LOOK IT UP.

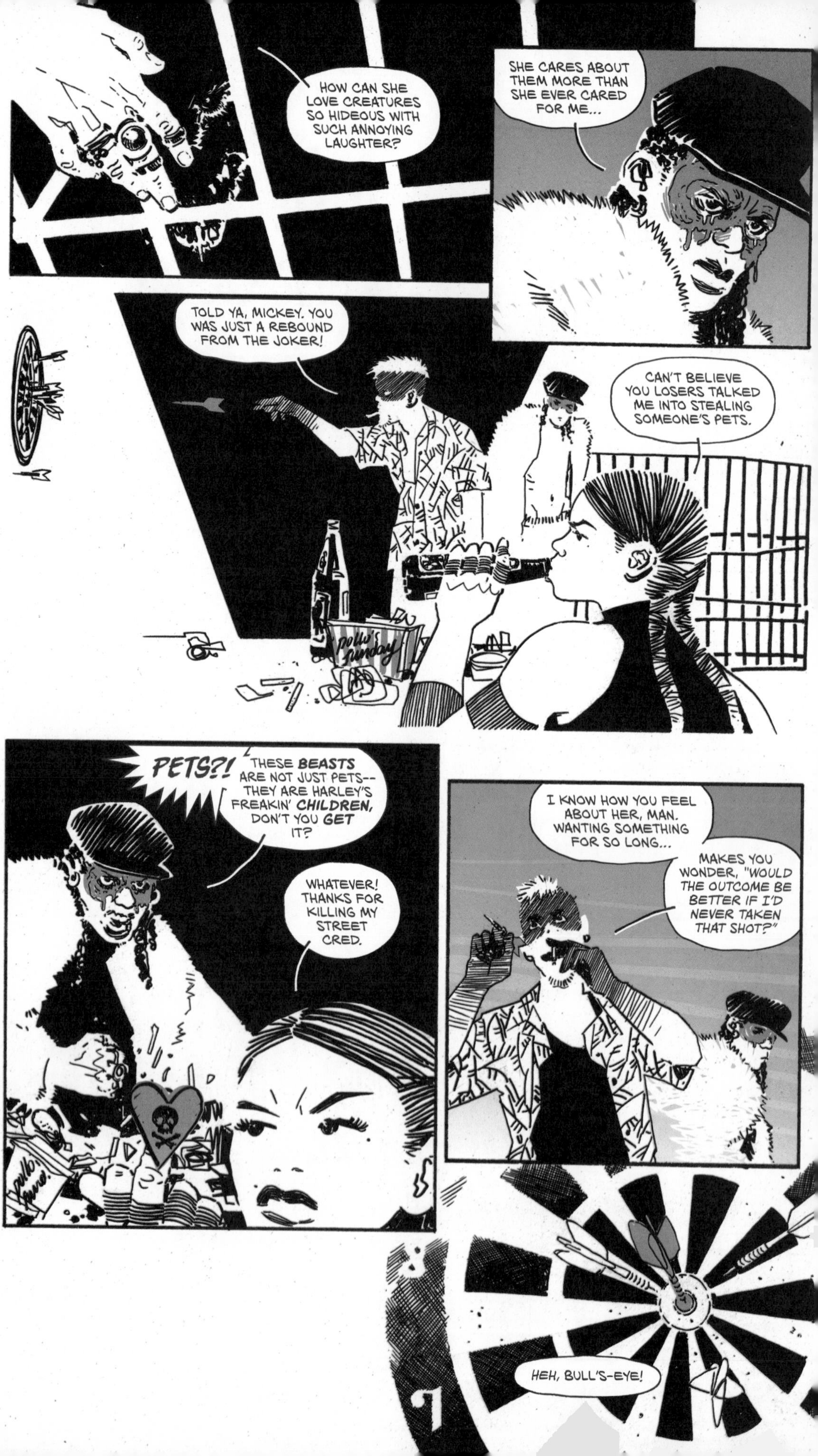
HOW CAN SHE LOVE CREATURES SO HIDEOUS WITH SUCH ANNOYING LAUGHTER?
SHE CARES ABOUT THEM MORE THAN SHE EVER CARED FOR ME...
TOLD YA, MICKEY. YOU WAS JUST A REBOUND FROM THE JOKER!
CAN'T BELIEVE YOU LOSERS TALKED ME INTO STEALING SOMEONE'S PETS.
PETS?!
THESE BEASTS ARE NOT JUST PETS-- THEY ARE HARLEY'S FREAKIN' CHILDREN, DON'T YOU GET IT?
WHATEVER! THANKS FOR KILLING MY STREET CRED.
I KNOW HOW YOU FEEL ABOUT HER, MAN. WANTING SOMETHING FOR SO LONG...
MAKES YOU WONDER, "WOULD THE OUTCOME BE BETTER IF I'D NEVER TAKEN THAT SHOT?"
HEH, BULL'S-EYE!

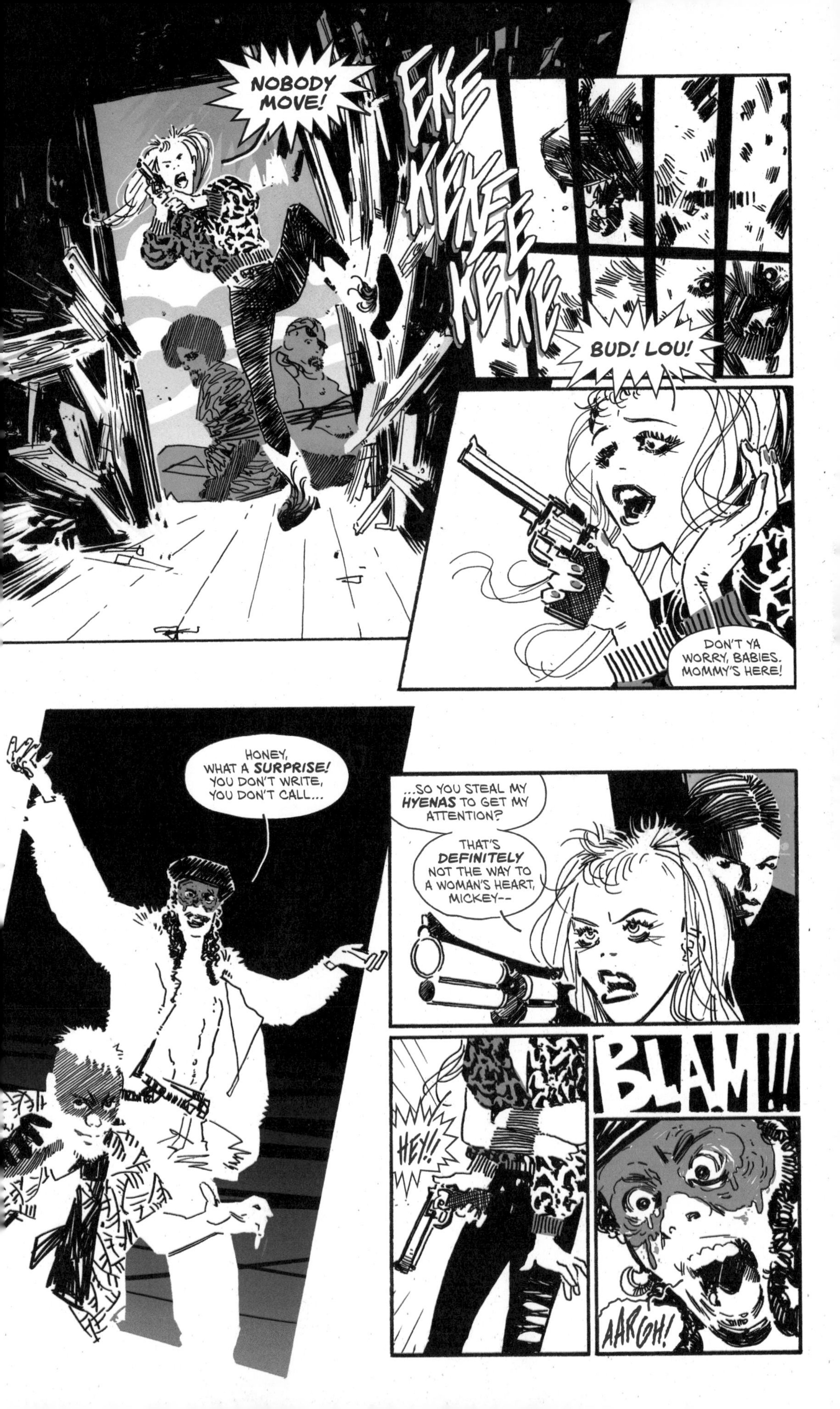
NOBODY MOVE!
EKE KEKEE KEKE
BUD! LOU!
DON'T YA WORRY, BABIES. MOMMY'S HERE!
HONEY, WHAT A *SURPRISE!* YOU DON'T WRITE, YOU DON'T CALL...
...SO YOU STEAL MY *HYENAS* TO GET MY ATTENTION?
THAT'S *DEFINITELY* NOT THE WAY TO A WOMAN'S HEART, MICKEY--
BLAM!!!
HEY!!
AARGH!

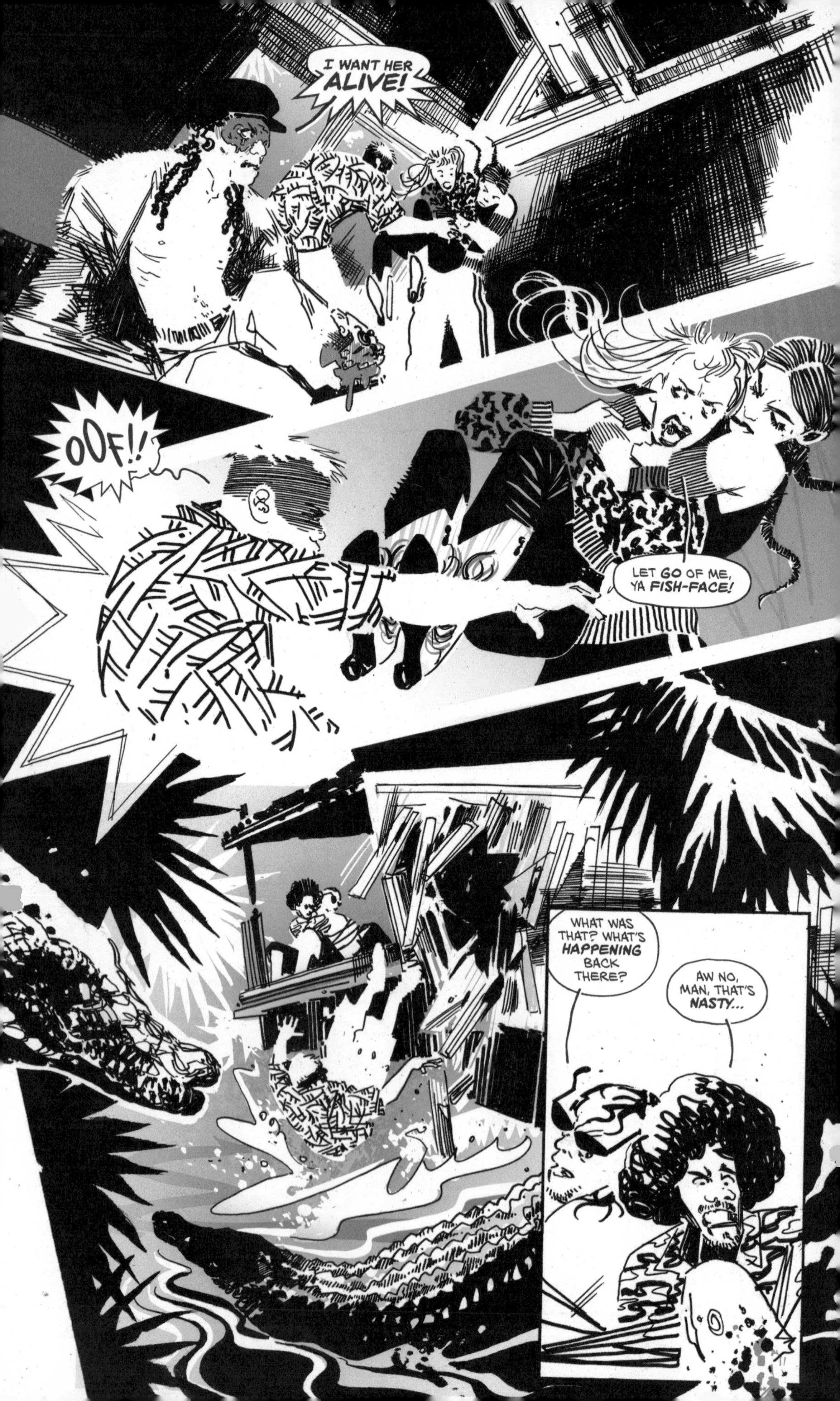
I WANT HER ALIVE!
OOF!!
LET GO OF ME, YA FISH-FACE!
WHAT WAS THAT? WHAT'S HAPPENING BACK THERE?
AW NO, MAN, THAT'S NASTY...

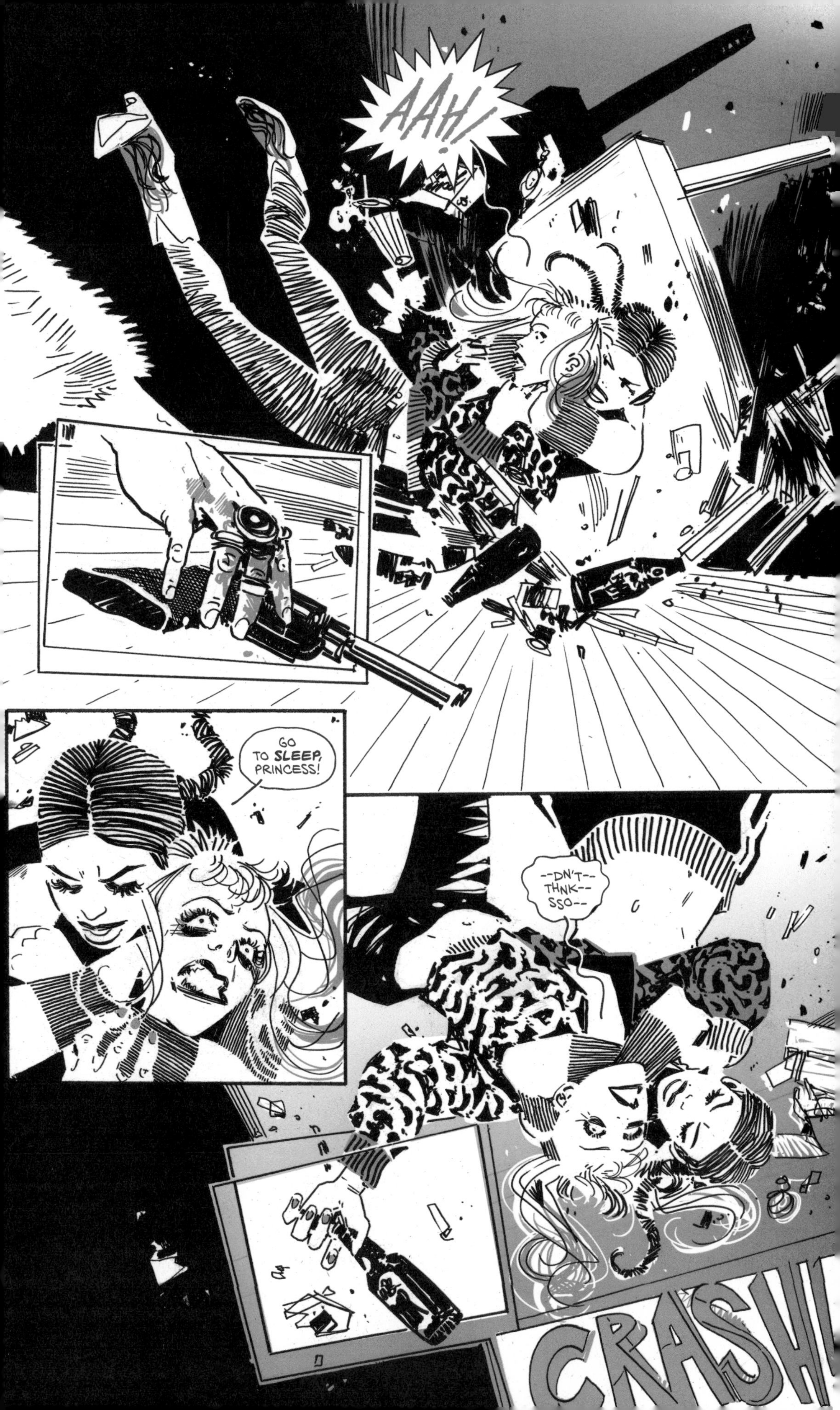
AAH!
GO TO SLEEP, PRINCESS!
--DN'T-- THNK-- SSO--
CRASH

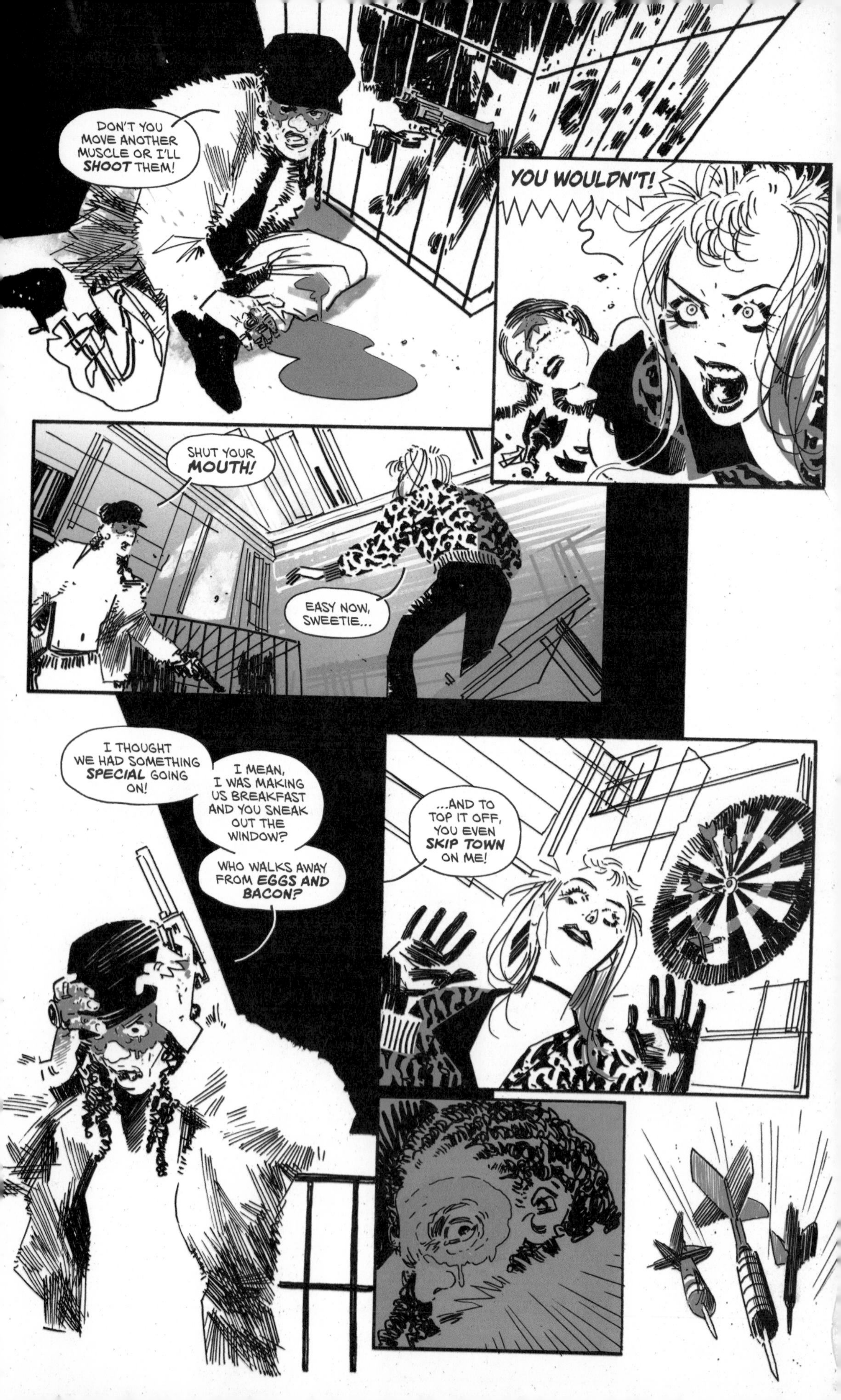
DON'T YOU MOVE ANOTHER MUSCLE OR I'LL **SHOOT** THEM!
YOU WOULDN'T!
SHUT YOUR **MOUTH!**
EASY NOW, SWEETIE...
I THOUGHT WE HAD SOMETHING **SPECIAL** GOING ON!
I MEAN, I WAS MAKING US BREAKFAST AND YOU SNEAK OUT THE WINDOW?
WHO WALKS AWAY FROM **EGGS AND BACON?**
...AND TO TOP IT OFF, YOU EVEN **SKIP TOWN** ON ME!

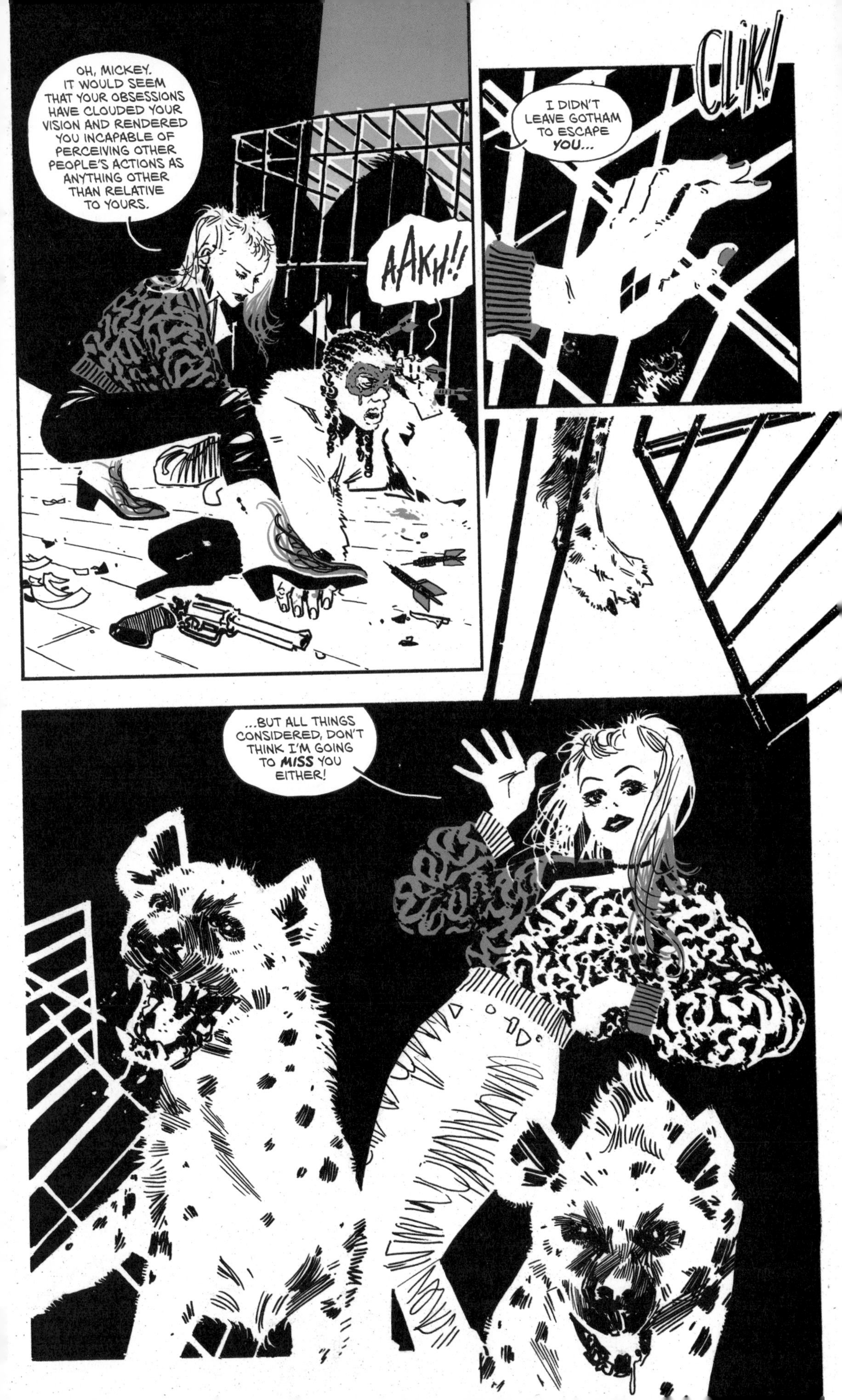
OH, MICKEY. IT WOULD SEEM THAT YOUR OBSESSIONS HAVE CLOUDED YOUR VISION AND RENDERED YOU INCAPABLE OF PERCEIVING OTHER PEOPLE'S ACTIONS AS ANYTHING OTHER THAN RELATIVE TO YOURS.
AAKH!!
CLIK!
I DIDN'T LEAVE GOTHAM TO ESCAPE *YOU*...
...BUT ALL THINGS CONSIDERED, DON'T THINK I'M GOING TO *MISS* YOU EITHER!

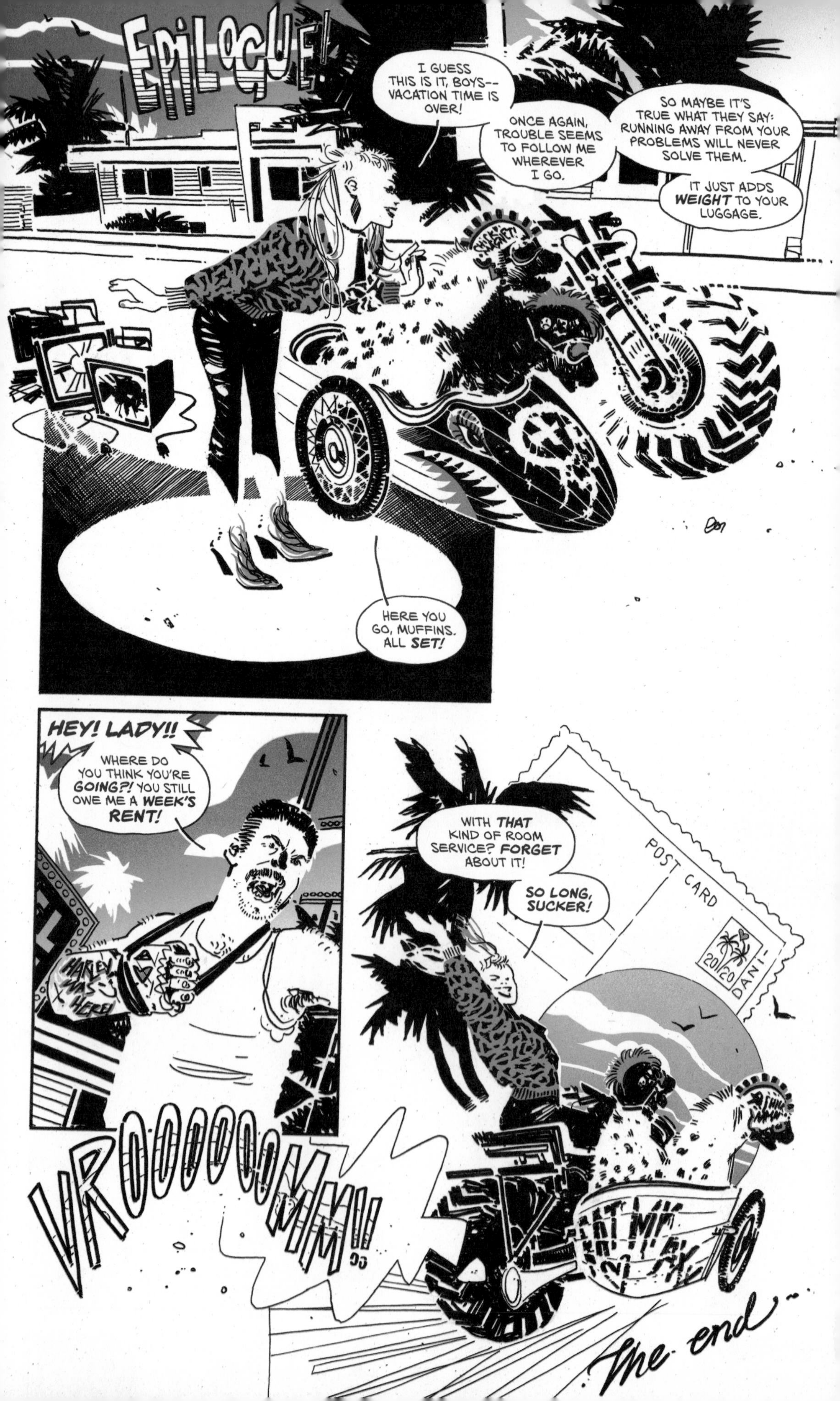
EPILOGUE!
I GUESS THIS IS IT, BOYS-- VACATION TIME IS OVER!
ONCE AGAIN, TROUBLE SEEMS TO FOLLOW ME WHEREVER I GO.
SO MAYBE IT'S TRUE WHAT THEY SAY: RUNNING AWAY FROM YOUR PROBLEMS WILL NEVER SOLVE THEM.
IT JUST ADDS **WEIGHT** TO YOUR LUGGAGE.
HERE YOU GO, MUFFINS. ALL **SET!**
HEY! LADY!!
WHERE DO YOU THINK YOU'RE **GOING?!** YOU STILL OWE ME A **WEEK'S RENT!**
HARLEY WAS HERE!
WITH **THAT** KIND OF ROOM SERVICE? **FORGET** ABOUT IT!
SO LONG, SUCKER!
POST CARD
2020 DANI
VROOOOOOMMM!!
the end...

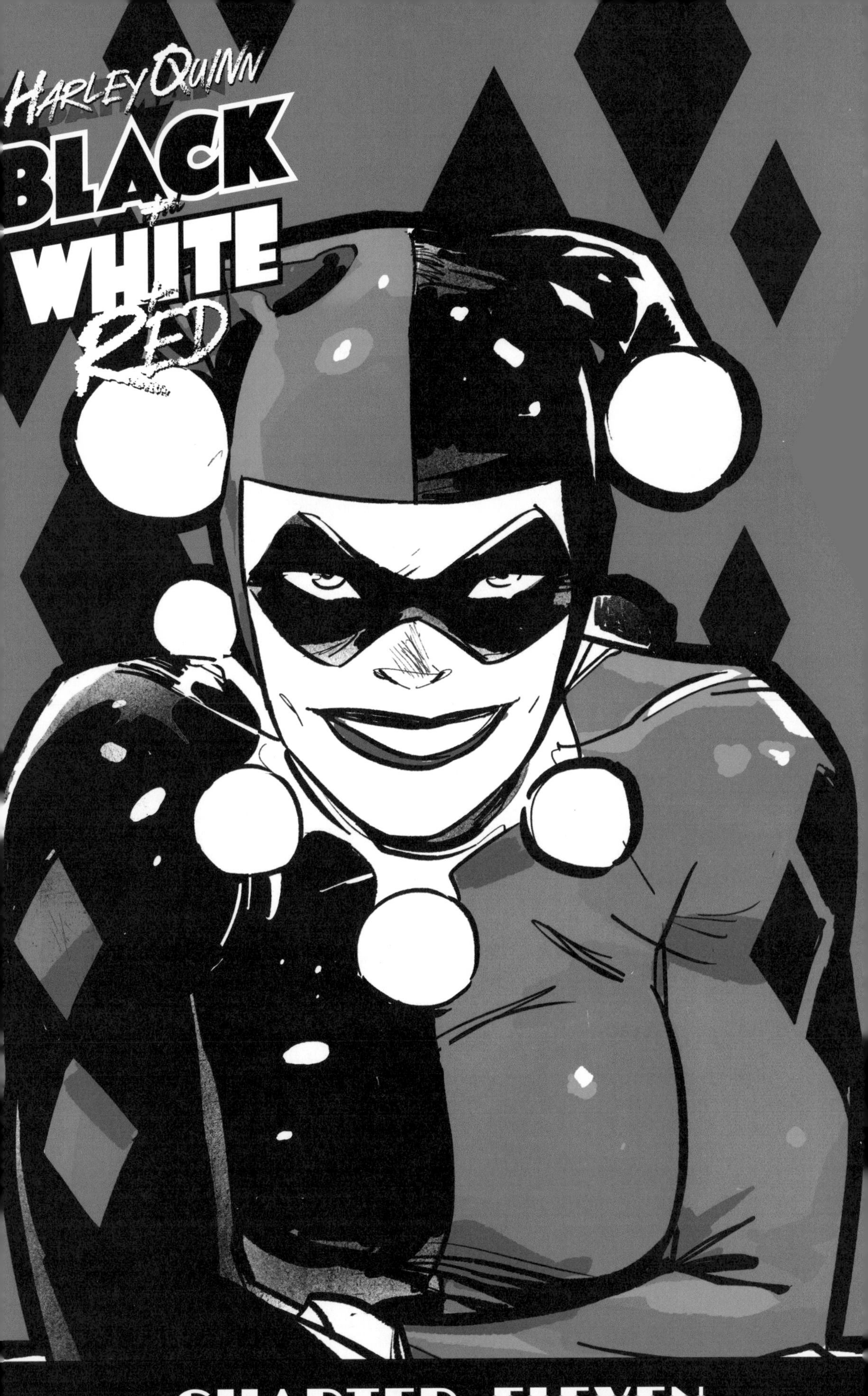

CHAPTER ELEVEN

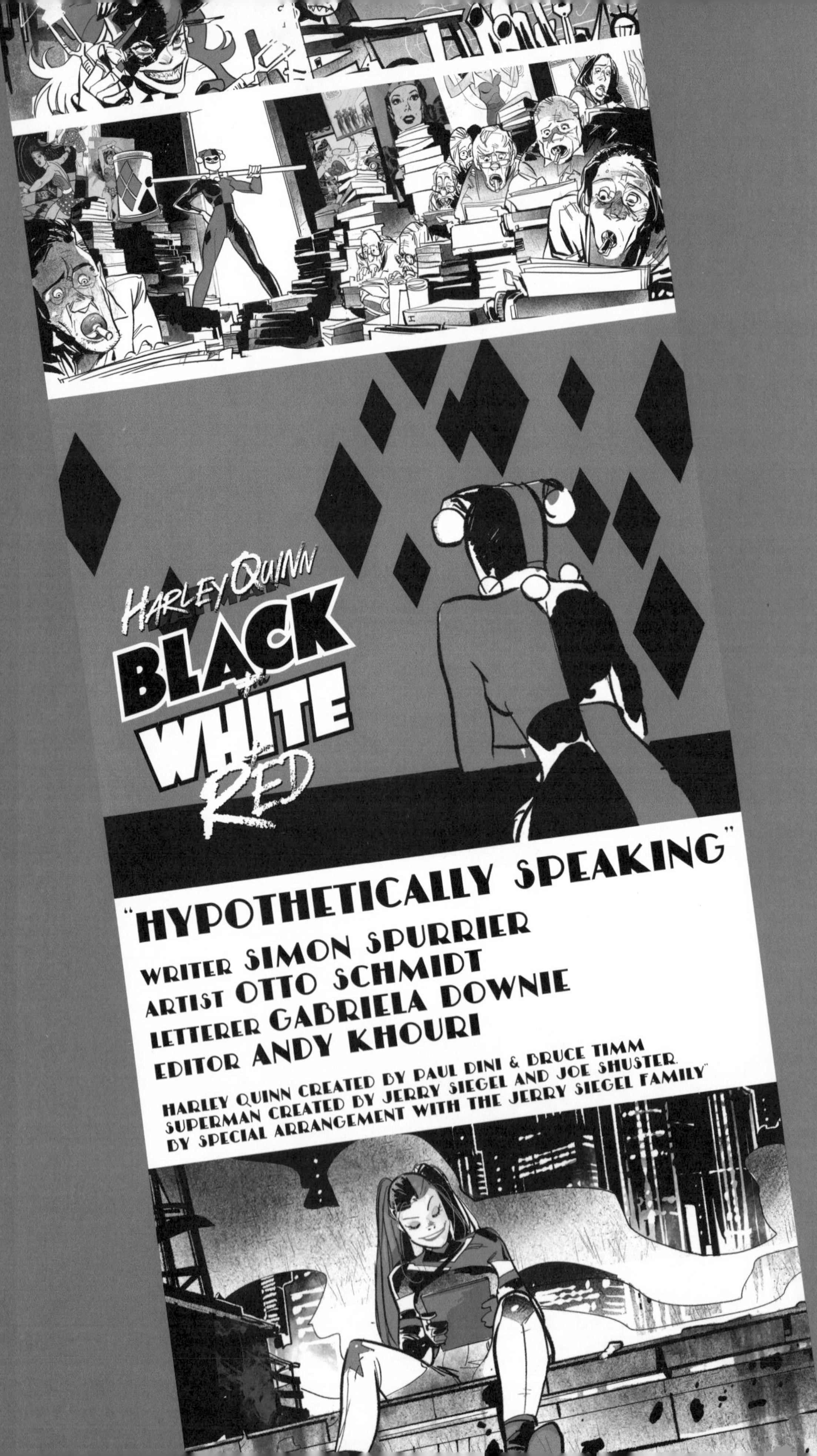
HARLEY QUINN
BLACK
WHITE
RED
"HYPOTHETICALLY SPEAKING"
WRITER SIMON SPURRIER
ARTIST OTTO SCHMIDT
LETTERER GABRIELA DOWNIE
EDITOR ANDY KHOURI
HARLEY QUINN CREATED BY PAUL DINI & BRUCE TIMM
SUPERMAN CREATED BY JERRY SIEGEL AND JOE SHUSTER.
BY SPECIAL ARRANGEMENT WITH THE JERRY SIEGEL FAMILY"

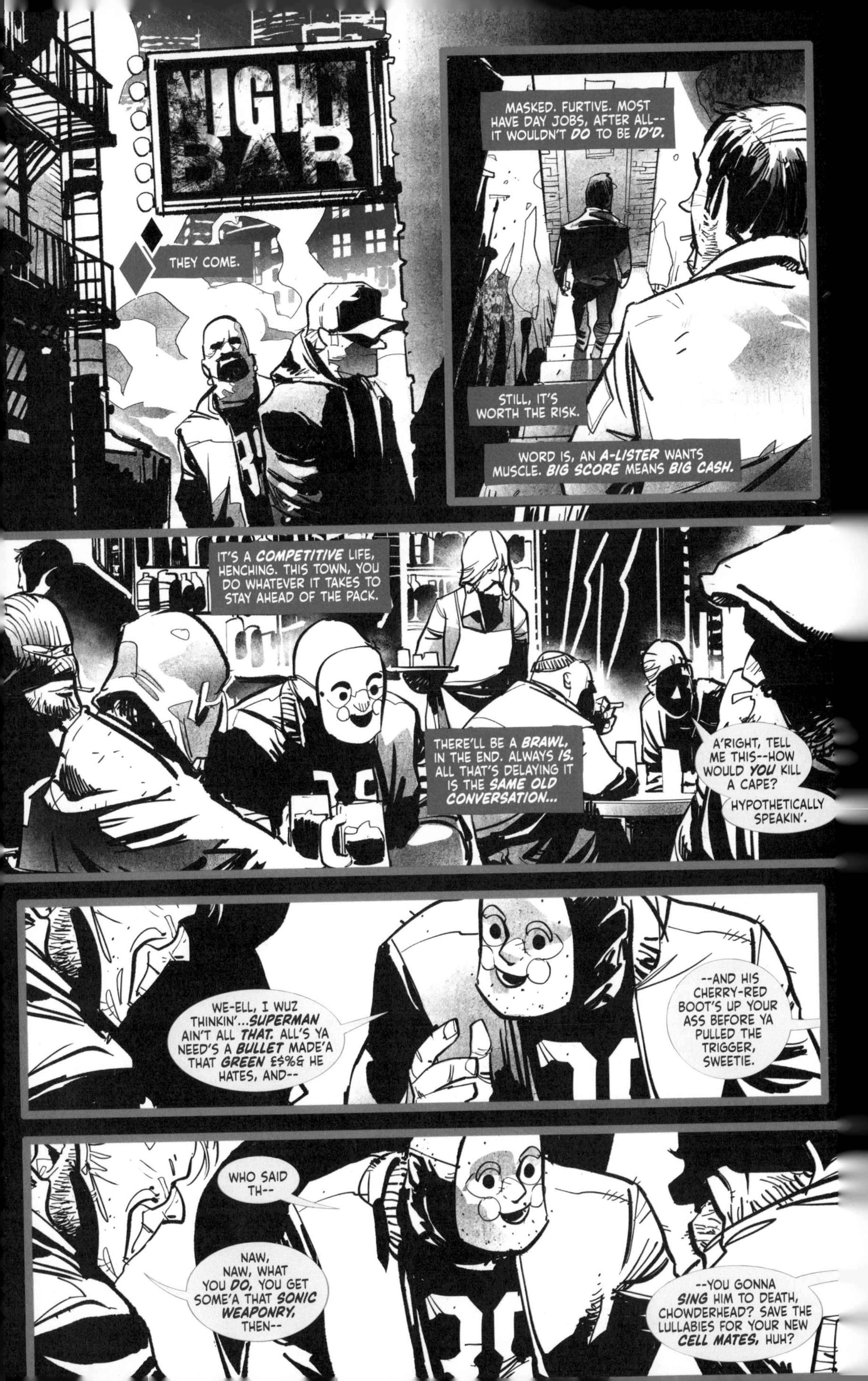
NIGHT BAR
THEY COME.
MASKED. FURTIVE. MOST HAVE DAY JOBS, AFTER ALL-- IT WOULDN'T DO TO BE ID'D.
STILL, IT'S WORTH THE RISK.
WORD IS, AN A-LISTER WANTS MUSCLE. BIG SCORE MEANS BIG CASH.
IT'S A COMPETITIVE LIFE, HENCHING. THIS TOWN, YOU DO WHATEVER IT TAKES TO STAY AHEAD OF THE PACK.
THERE'LL BE A BRAWL, IN THE END. ALWAYS IS. ALL THAT'S DELAYING IT IS THE SAME OLD CONVERSATION...
A'RIGHT, TELL ME THIS--HOW WOULD YOU KILL A CAPE?
HYPOTHETICALLY SPEAKIN'.
WE-ELL, I WUZ THINKIN'...SUPERMAN AIN'T ALL THAT. ALL'S YA NEED'S A BULLET MADE'A THAT GREEN £$%& HE HATES, AND--
--AND HIS CHERRY-RED BOOT'S UP YOUR ASS BEFORE YA PULLED THE TRIGGER, SWEETIE.
WHO SAID TH--
NAW, NAW, WHAT YOU DO, YOU GET SOME'A THAT SONIC WEAPONRY, THEN--
--YOU GONNA SING HIM TO DEATH, CHOWDERHEAD? SAVE THE LULLABIES FOR YOUR NEW CELL MATES, HUH?

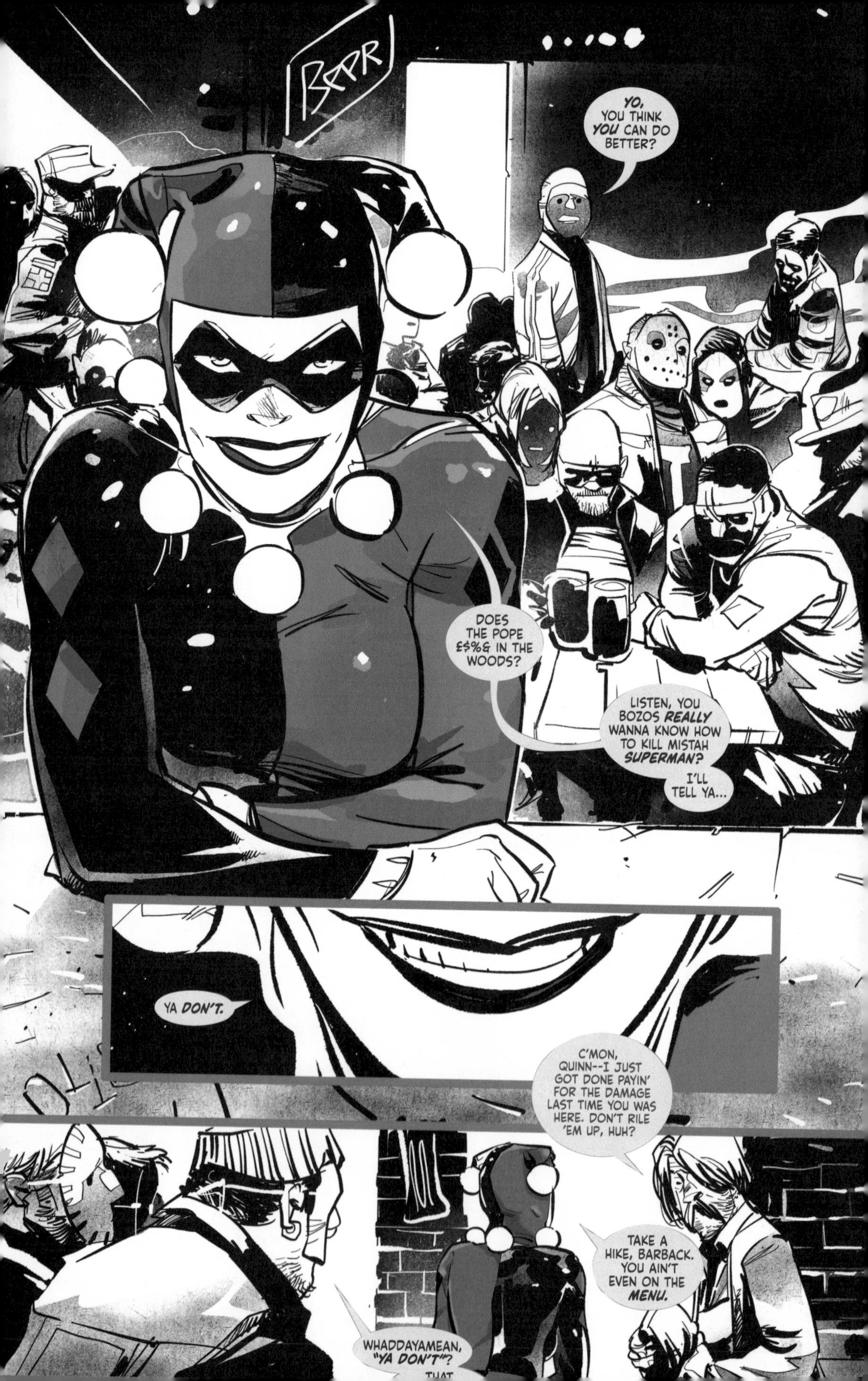

YO, YOU THINK YOU CAN DO BETTER?
DOES THE POPE £$%& IN THE WOODS?
LISTEN, YOU BOZOS REALLY WANNA KNOW HOW TO KILL MISTAH SUPERMAN?
I'LL TELL YA...
YA DON'T.
C'MON, QUINN--I JUST GOT DONE PAYIN' FOR THE DAMAGE LAST TIME YOU WAS HERE. DON'T RILE 'EM UP, HUH?
TAKE A HIKE, BARBACK. YOU AIN'T EVEN ON THE MENU.
WHADDAYAMEAN, "YA DON'T"?

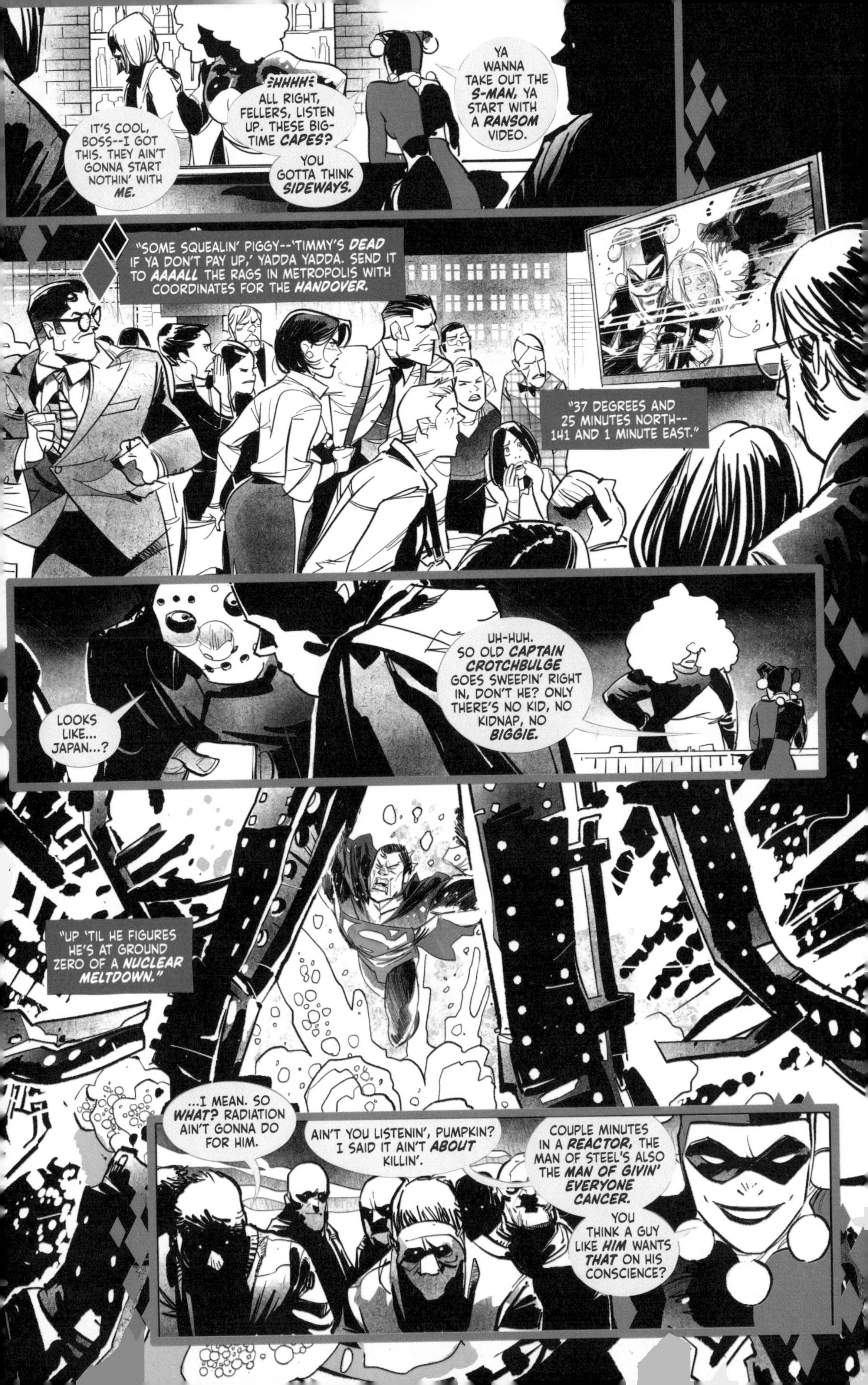
IT'S COOL, BOSS--I GOT THIS. THEY AIN'T GONNA START NOTHIN' WITH ME.
HHHH! ALL RIGHT, FELLERS, LISTEN UP. THESE BIG-TIME CAPES?
YOU GOTTA THINK SIDEWAYS.
YA WANNA TAKE OUT THE S-MAN, YA START WITH A RANSOM VIDEO.
"SOME SQUEALIN' PIGGY--'TIMMY'S DEAD IF YA DON'T PAY UP,' YADDA YADDA. SEND IT TO AAAALL THE RAGS IN METROPOLIS WITH COORDINATES FOR THE HANDOVER.
"37 DEGREES AND 25 MINUTES NORTH-- 141 AND 1 MINUTE EAST."
LOOKS LIKE... JAPAN...?
UH-HUH. SO OLD CAPTAIN CROTCHBULGE GOES SWEEPIN' RIGHT IN, DON'T HE? ONLY THERE'S NO KID, NO KIDNAP, NO BIGGIE.
"UP 'TIL HE FIGURES HE'S AT GROUND ZERO OF A NUCLEAR MELTDOWN."
...I MEAN. SO WHAT? RADIATION AIN'T GONNA DO FOR HIM.
AIN'T YOU LISTENIN', PUMPKIN? I SAID IT AIN'T ABOUT KILLIN'.
COUPLE MINUTES IN A REACTOR, THE MAN OF STEEL'S ALSO THE MAN OF GIVIN' EVERYONE CANCER.
YOU THINK A GUY LIKE HIM WANTS THAT ON HIS CONSCIENCE?

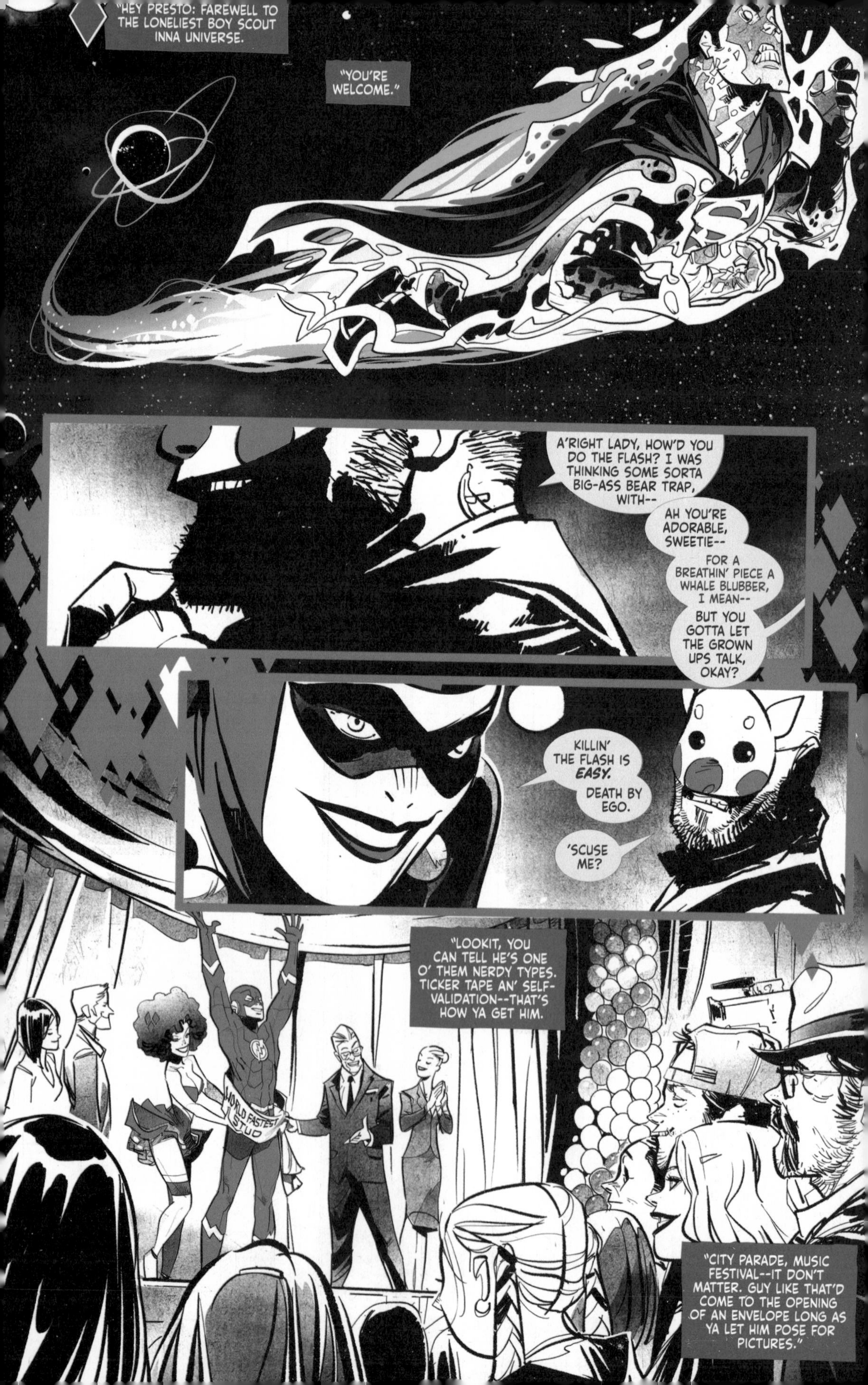
"HEY PRESTO: FAREWELL TO THE LONELIEST BOY SCOUT INNA UNIVERSE.
"YOU'RE WELCOME."
A'RIGHT LADY, HOW'D YOU DO THE FLASH? I WAS THINKING SOME SORTA BIG-ASS BEAR TRAP, WITH--
AH YOU'RE ADORABLE, SWEETIE--
FOR A BREATHIN' PIECE A WHALE BLUBBER, I MEAN--
BUT YOU GOTTA LET THE GROWN UPS TALK, OKAY?
KILLIN' THE FLASH IS *EASY.*
DEATH BY EGO.
'SCUSE ME?
"LOOKIT, YOU CAN TELL HE'S ONE O' THEM NERDY TYPES. TICKER TAPE AN' SELF-VALIDATION--THAT'S HOW YA GET HIM.
WORLD FASTEST STUD
"CITY PARADE, MUSIC FESTIVAL--IT DON'T MATTER. GUY LIKE THAT'D COME TO THE OPENING OF AN ENVELOPE LONG AS YA LET HIM POSE FOR PICTURES."

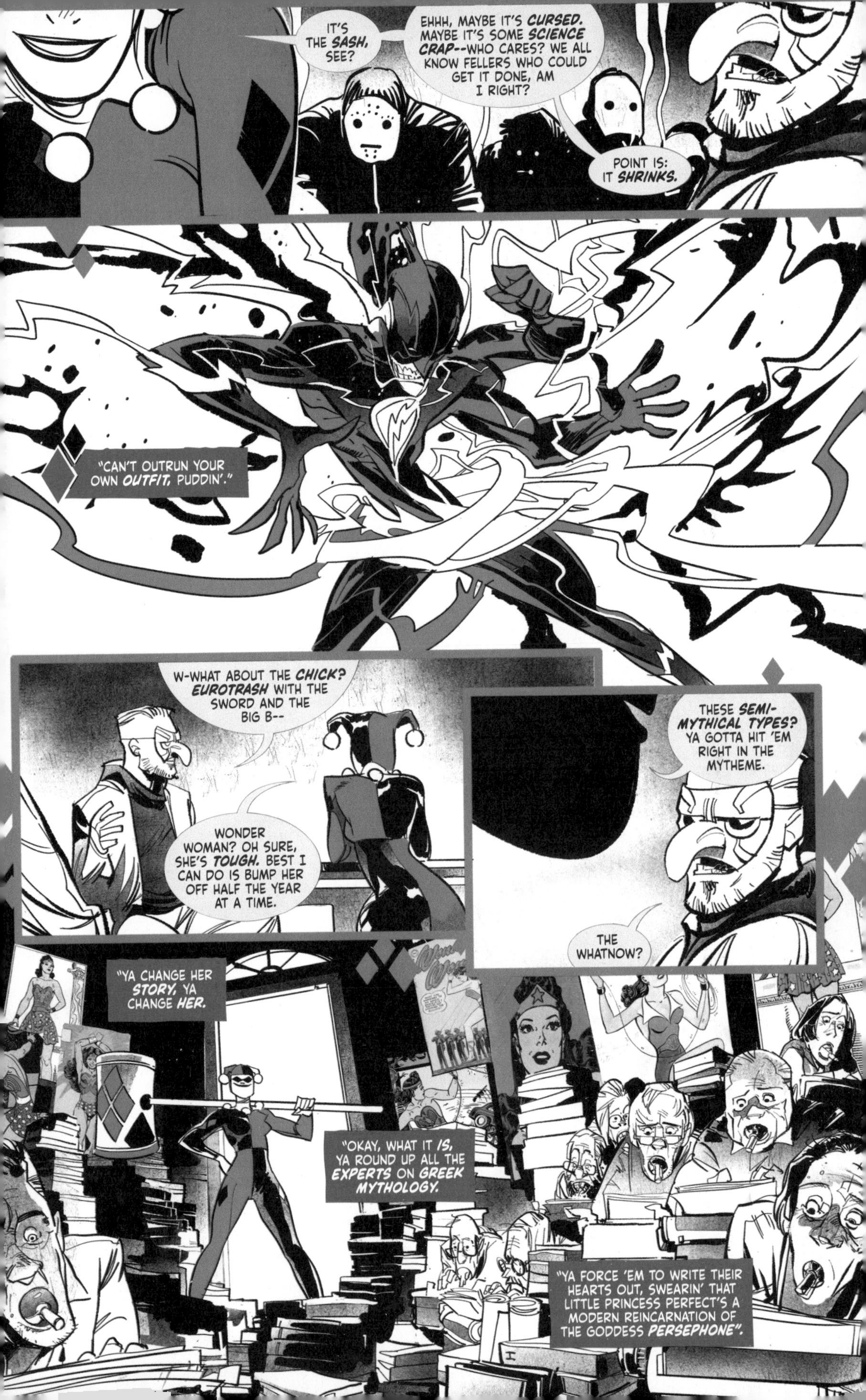
IT'S THE SASH, SEE?
EHHH, MAYBE IT'S CURSED. MAYBE IT'S SOME SCIENCE CRAP--WHO CARES? WE ALL KNOW FELLERS WHO COULD GET IT DONE, AM I RIGHT?
POINT IS: IT SHRINKS.
"CAN'T OUTRUN YOUR OWN OUTFIT, PUDDIN'."
W-WHAT ABOUT THE CHICK? EUROTRASH WITH THE SWORD AND THE BIG B--
WONDER WOMAN? OH SURE, SHE'S TOUGH. BEST I CAN DO IS BUMP HER OFF HALF THE YEAR AT A TIME.
THESE SEMI-MYTHICAL TYPES? YA GOTTA HIT 'EM RIGHT IN THE MYTHEME.
THE WHATNOW?
"YA CHANGE HER STORY, YA CHANGE HER.
"OKAY, WHAT IT IS, YA ROUND UP ALL THE EXPERTS ON GREEK MYTHOLOGY.
"YA FORCE 'EM TO WRITE THEIR HEARTS OUT, SWEARIN' THAT LITTLE PRINCESS PERFECT'S A MODERN REINCARNATION OF THE GODDESS PERSEPHONE".

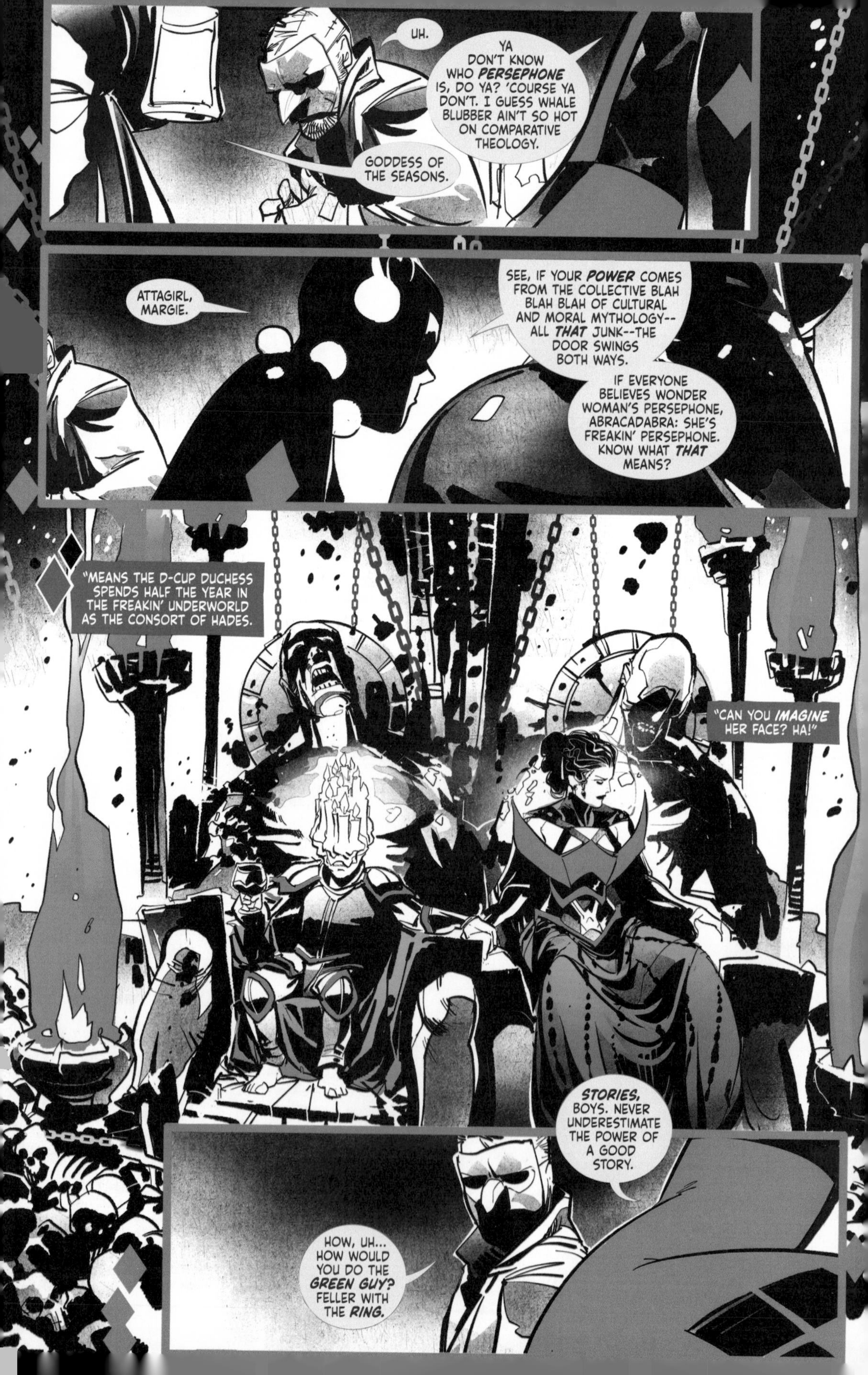
UH.
YA DON'T KNOW WHO PERSEPHONE IS, DO YA? 'COURSE YA DON'T. I GUESS WHALE BLUBBER AIN'T SO HOT ON COMPARATIVE THEOLOGY.
GODDESS OF THE SEASONS.
ATTAGIRL, MARGIE.
SEE, IF YOUR POWER COMES FROM THE COLLECTIVE BLAH BLAH BLAH OF CULTURAL AND MORAL MYTHOLOGY--ALL THAT JUNK--THE DOOR SWINGS BOTH WAYS.
IF EVERYONE BELIEVES WONDER WOMAN'S PERSEPHONE, ABRACADABRA: SHE'S FREAKIN' PERSEPHONE. KNOW WHAT THAT MEANS?
"MEANS THE D-CUP DUCHESS SPENDS HALF THE YEAR IN THE FREAKIN' UNDERWORLD AS THE CONSORT OF HADES.
"CAN YOU IMAGINE HER FACE? HA!"
STORIES, BOYS. NEVER UNDERESTIMATE THE POWER OF A GOOD STORY.
HOW, UH... HOW WOULD YOU DO THE GREEN GUY? FELLER WITH THE RING.

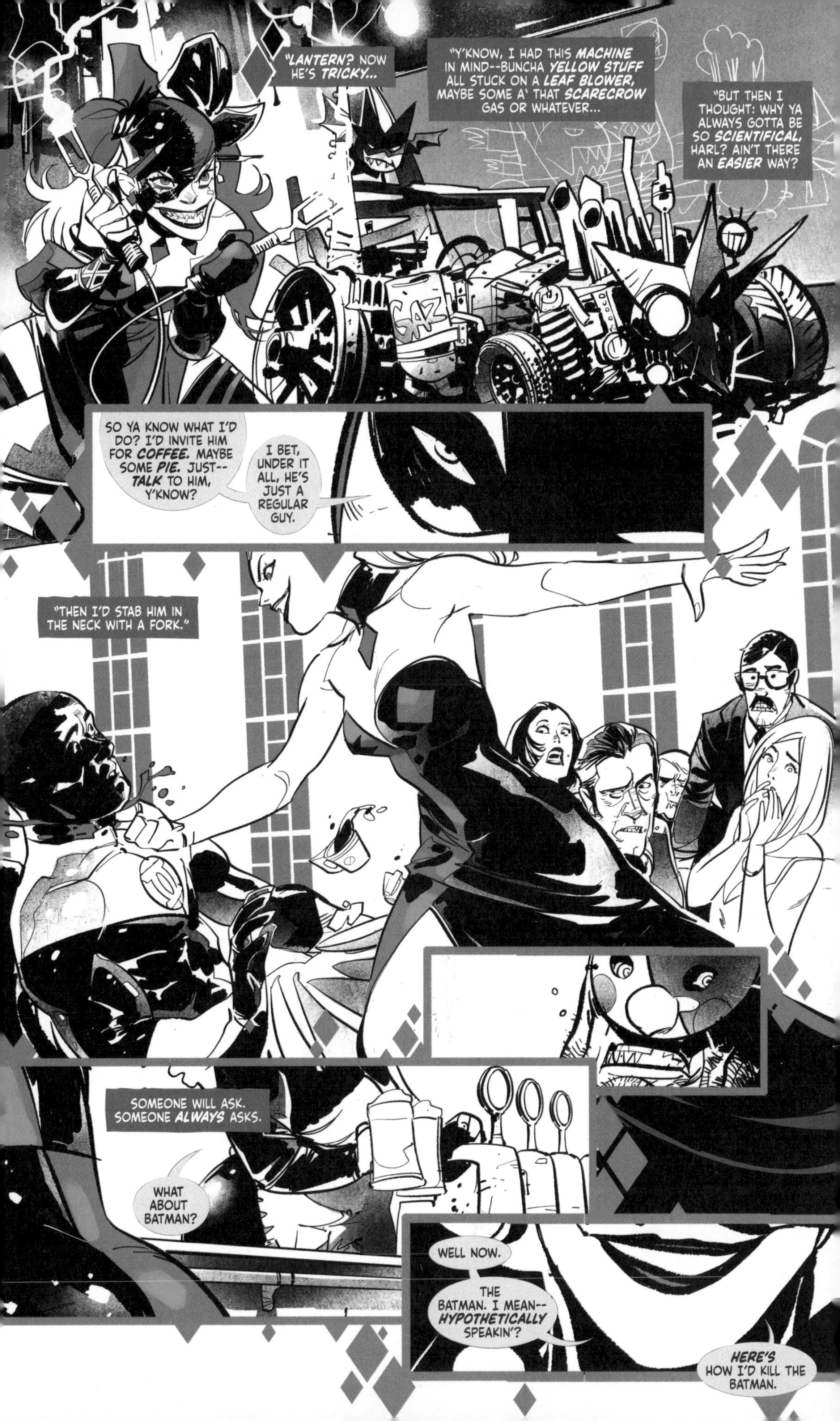
"LANTERN? NOW HE'S TRICKY...
"Y'KNOW, I HAD THIS MACHINE IN MIND--BUNCHA YELLOW STUFF ALL STUCK ON A LEAF BLOWER, MAYBE SOME A' THAT SCARECROW GAS OR WHATEVER...
"BUT THEN I THOUGHT: WHY YA ALWAYS GOTTA BE SO SCIENTIFICAL, HARL? AIN'T THERE AN EASIER WAY?
SO YA KNOW WHAT I'D DO? I'D INVITE HIM FOR COFFEE. MAYBE SOME PIE. JUST-- TALK TO HIM, Y'KNOW?
I BET, UNDER IT ALL, HE'S JUST A REGULAR GUY.
"THEN I'D STAB HIM IN THE NECK WITH A FORK."
SOMEONE WILL ASK. SOMEONE ALWAYS ASKS.
WHAT ABOUT BATMAN?
WELL NOW.
THE BATMAN. I MEAN-- HYPOTHETICALLY SPEAKIN'?
HERE'S HOW I'D KILL THE BATMAN.

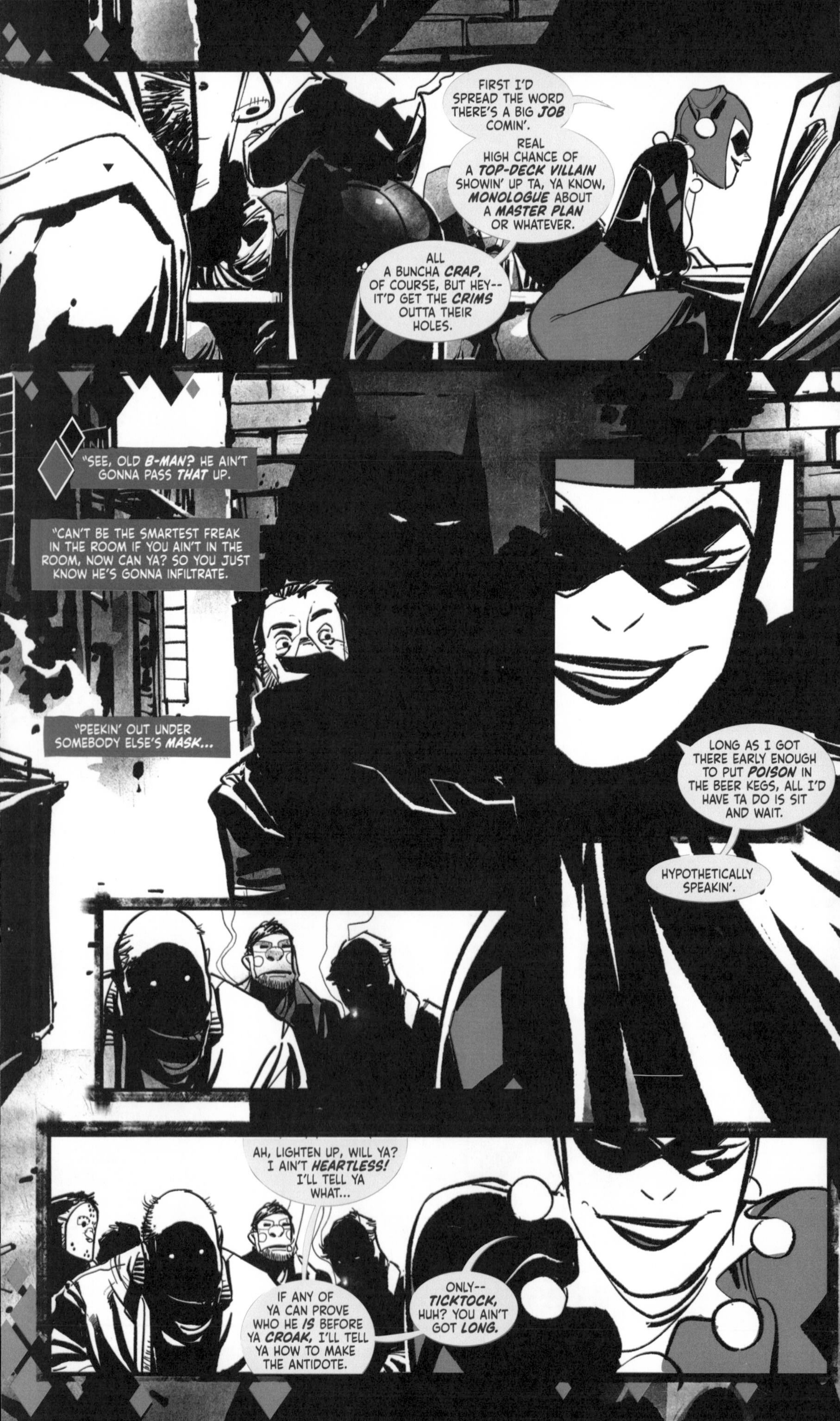
FIRST I'D SPREAD THE WORD THERE'S A BIG JOB COMIN'.
REAL HIGH CHANCE OF A TOP-DECK VILLAIN SHOWIN' UP TA, YA KNOW, MONOLOGUE ABOUT A MASTER PLAN OR WHATEVER.
ALL A BUNCHA CRAP, OF COURSE, BUT HEY-- IT'D GET THE CRIMS OUTTA THEIR HOLES.
"SEE, OLD B-MAN? HE AIN'T GONNA PASS THAT UP.
"CAN'T BE THE SMARTEST FREAK IN THE ROOM IF YOU AIN'T IN THE ROOM, NOW CAN YA? SO YOU JUST KNOW HE'S GONNA INFILTRATE.
"PEEKIN' OUT UNDER SOMEBODY ELSE'S MASK...
LONG AS I GOT THERE EARLY ENOUGH TO PUT POISON IN THE BEER KEGS, ALL I'D HAVE TA DO IS SIT AND WAIT.
HYPOTHETICALLY SPEAKIN'.
AH, LIGHTEN UP, WILL YA? I AIN'T HEARTLESS! I'LL TELL YA WHAT...
IF ANY OF YA CAN PROVE WHO HE IS BEFORE YA CROAK, I'LL TELL YA HOW TO MAKE THE ANTIDOTE.
ONLY-- TICKTOCK, HUH? YOU AIN'T GOT LONG.

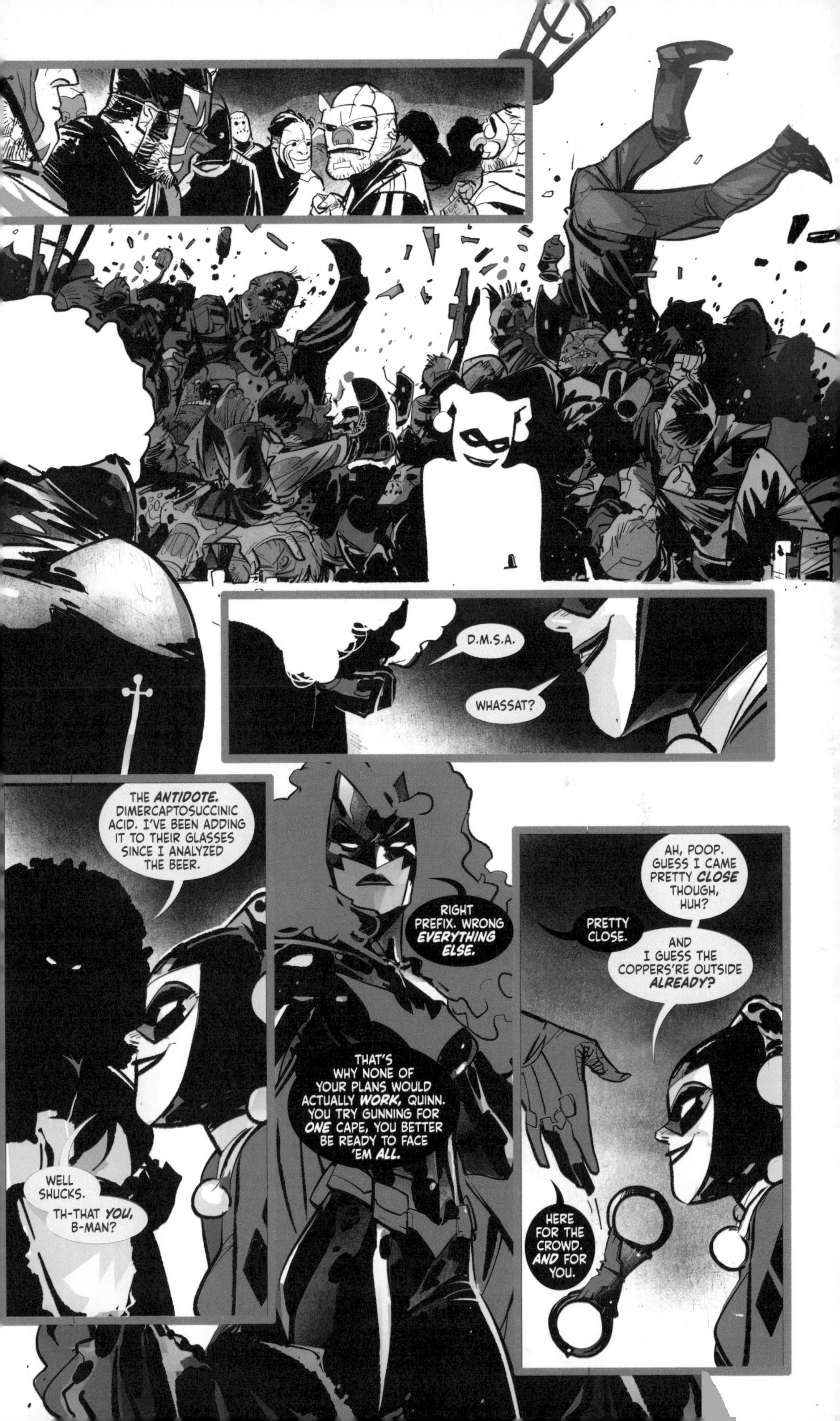
D.M.S.A.
WHASSAT?
THE ANTIDOTE. DIMERCAPTOSUCCINIC ACID. I'VE BEEN ADDING IT TO THEIR GLASSES SINCE I ANALYZED THE BEER.
WELL SHUCKS.
TH-THAT YOU, B-MAN?
RIGHT PREFIX. WRONG EVERYTHING ELSE.
THAT'S WHY NONE OF YOUR PLANS WOULD ACTUALLY WORK, QUINN. YOU TRY GUNNING FOR ONE CAPE, YOU BETTER BE READY TO FACE 'EM ALL.
AH, POOP. GUESS I CAME PRETTY CLOSE THOUGH, HUH?
PRETTY CLOSE.
AND I GUESS THE COPPERS'RE OUTSIDE ALREADY?
HERE FOR THE CROWD. AND FOR YOU.

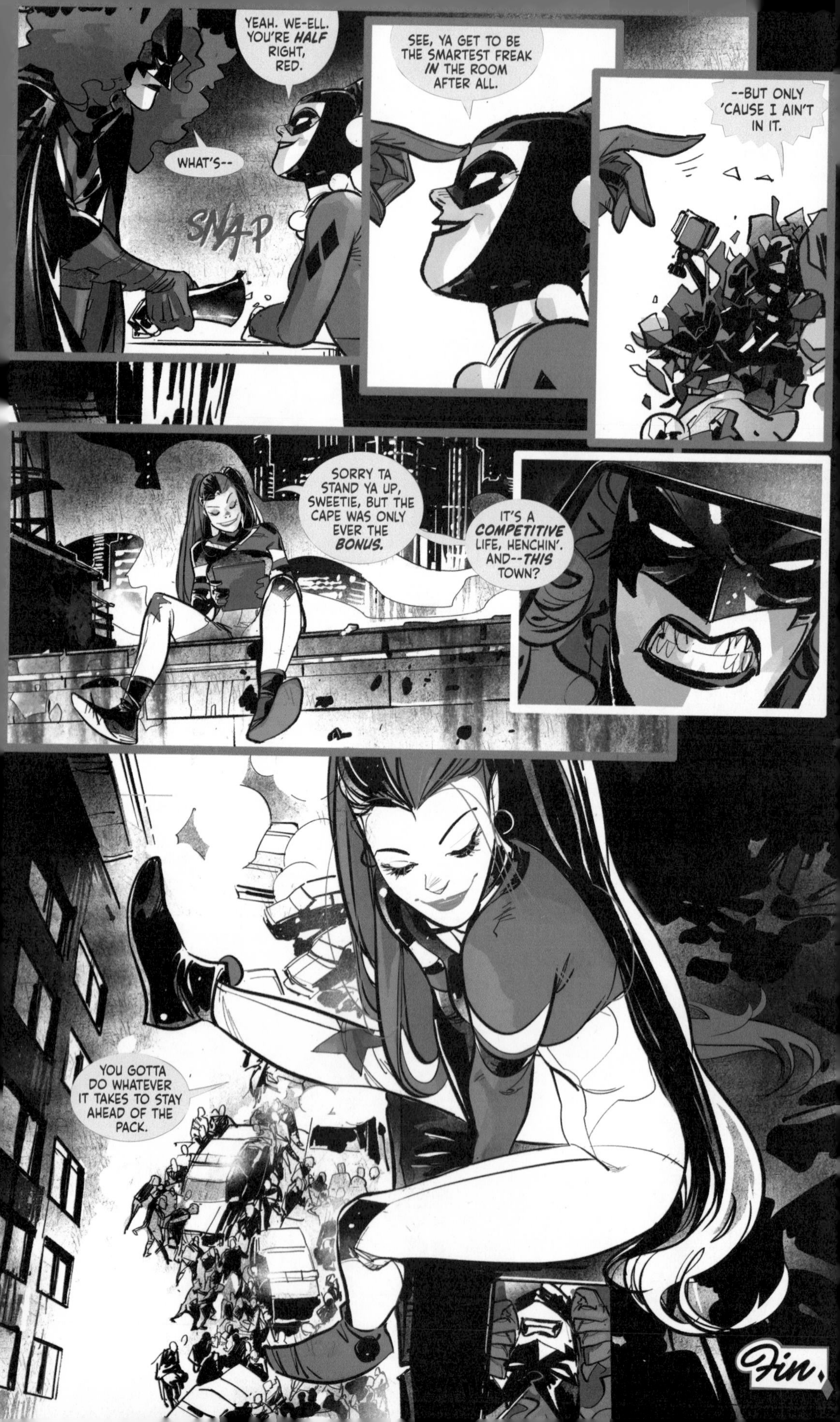
YEAH. WE-ELL. YOU'RE *HALF* RIGHT, RED.
WHAT'S--
SNAP
SEE, YA GET TO BE THE SMARTEST FREAK *IN* THE ROOM AFTER ALL.
--BUT ONLY 'CAUSE I AIN'T IN IT.
SORRY TA STAND YA UP, SWEETIE, BUT THE CAPE WAS ONLY EVER THE *BONUS.*
IT'S A *COMPETITIVE* LIFE, HENCHIN'. AND--*THIS* TOWN?
YOU GOTTA DO WHATEVER IT TAKES TO STAY AHEAD OF THE PACK.
Fin.

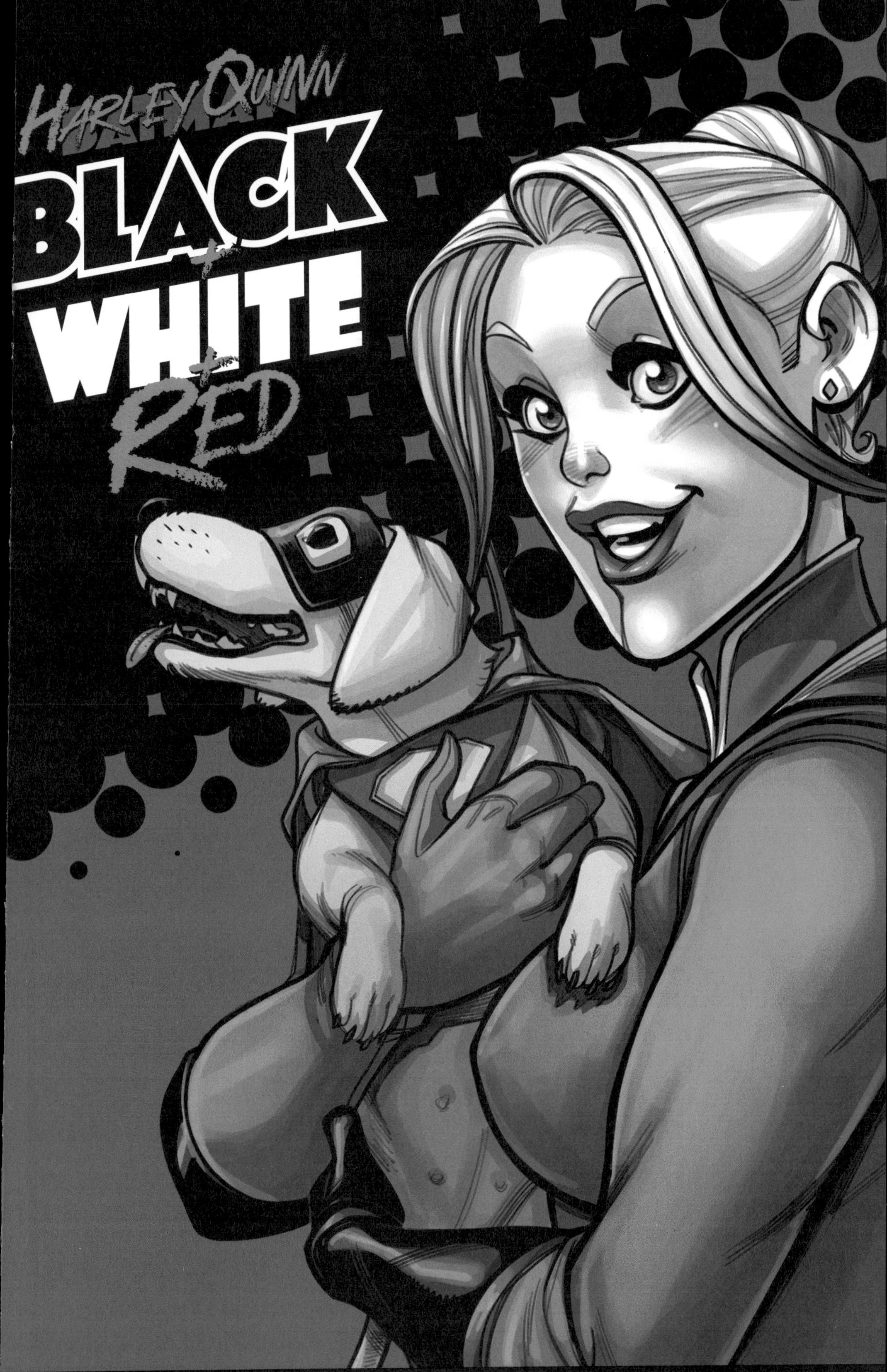
HARLEY QUINN
BLACK
+
WHITE
+
RED

CHAPTER TWELVE

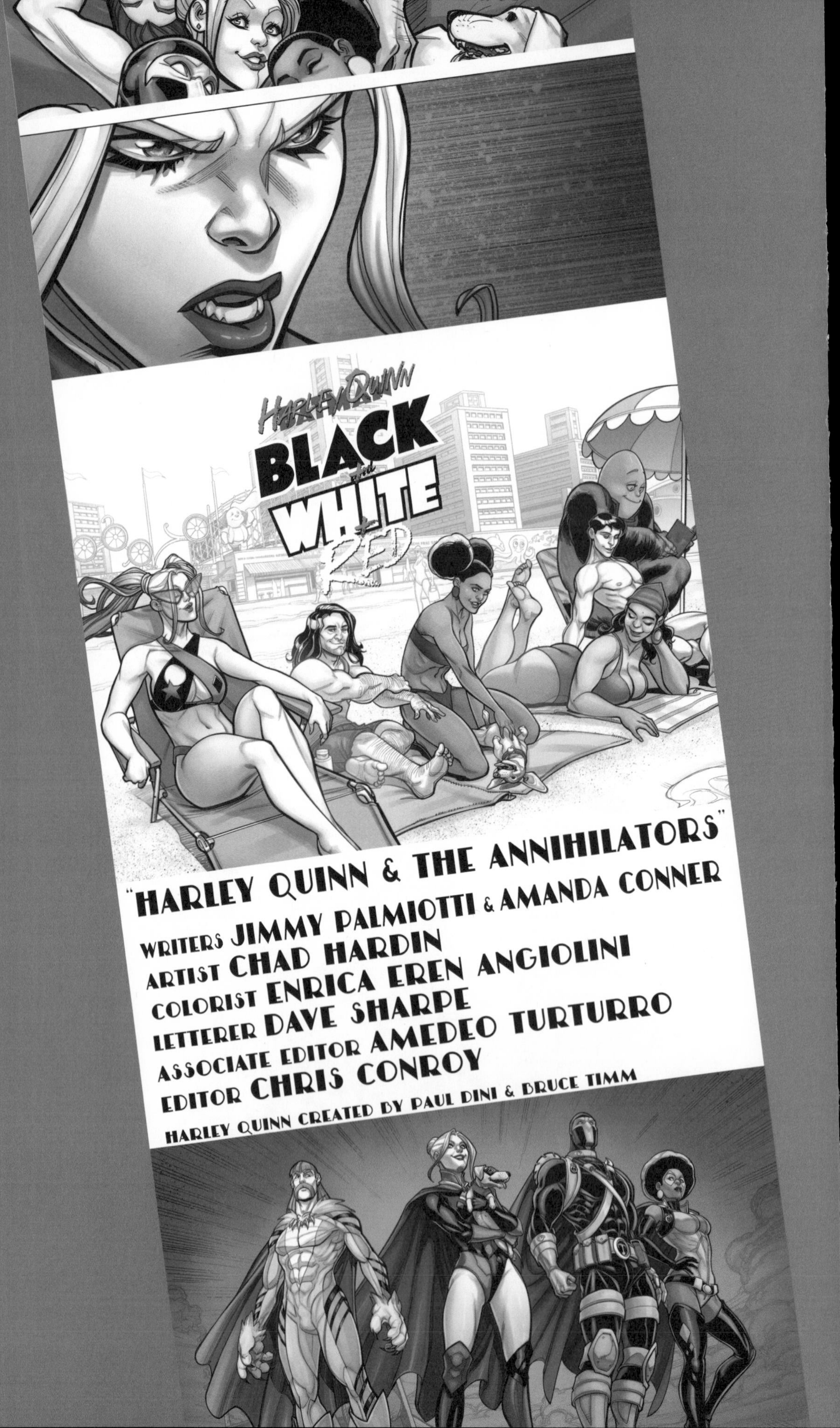
HARLEY QUINN
BLACK + WHITE + RED
"HARLEY QUINN & THE ANNIHILATORS"
WRITERS JIMMY PALMIOTTI & AMANDA CONNER
ARTIST CHAD HARDIN
COLORIST ENRICA EREN ANGIOLINI
LETTERER DAVE SHARPE
ASSOCIATE EDITOR AMEDEO TURTURRO
EDITOR CHRIS CONROY
HARLEY QUINN CREATED BY PAUL DINI & BRUCE TIMM

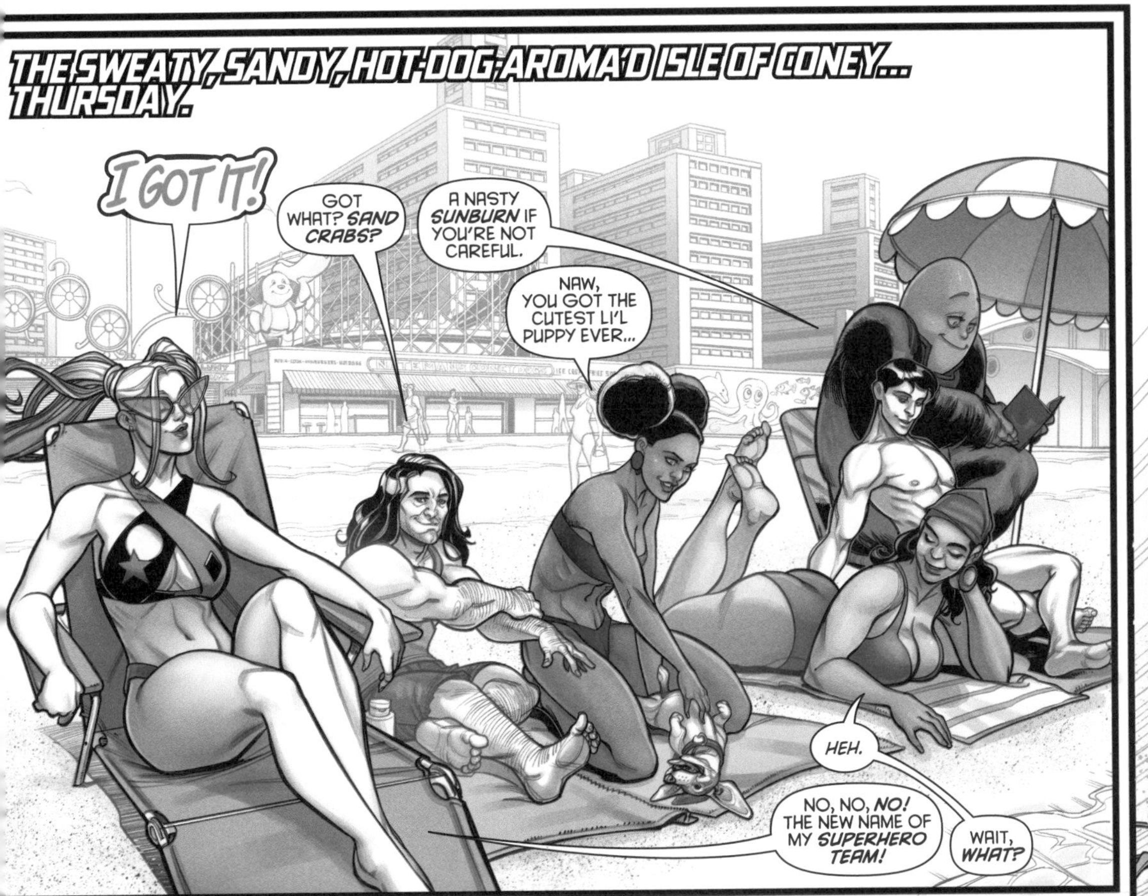
THE SWEATY, SANDY, HOT-DOG-AROMA'D ISLE OF CONEY... THURSDAY.
I GOT IT!
GOT WHAT? SAND CRABS?
A NASTY SUNBURN IF YOU'RE NOT CAREFUL.
NAW, YOU GOT THE CUTEST LI'L PUPPY EVER...
HEH.
NO, NO, NO! THE NEW NAME OF MY SUPERHERO TEAM!
WAIT, WHAT?
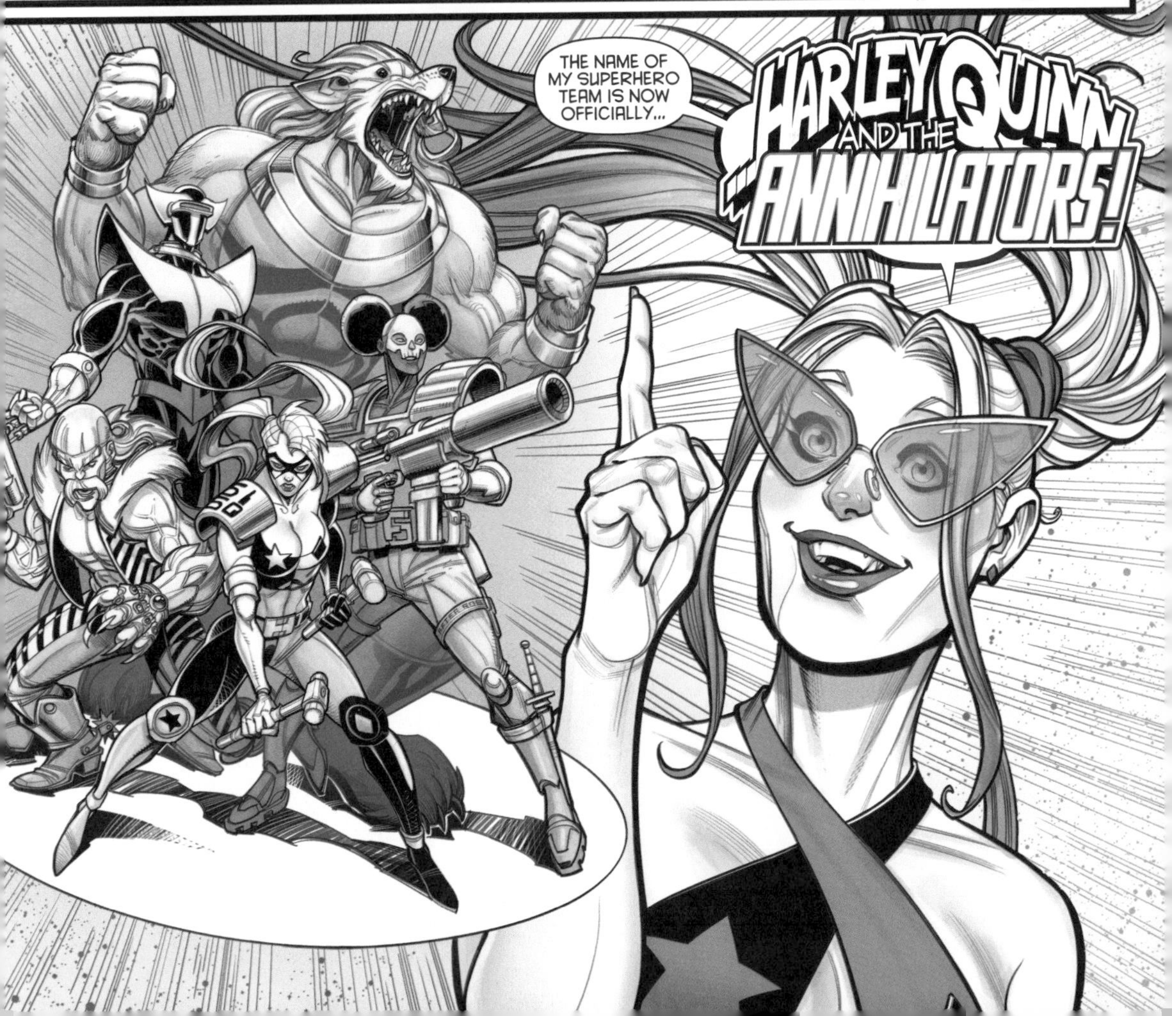
THE NAME OF MY SUPERHERO TEAM IS NOW OFFICIALLY...
HARLEY QUINN AND THE ANNIHILATORS!

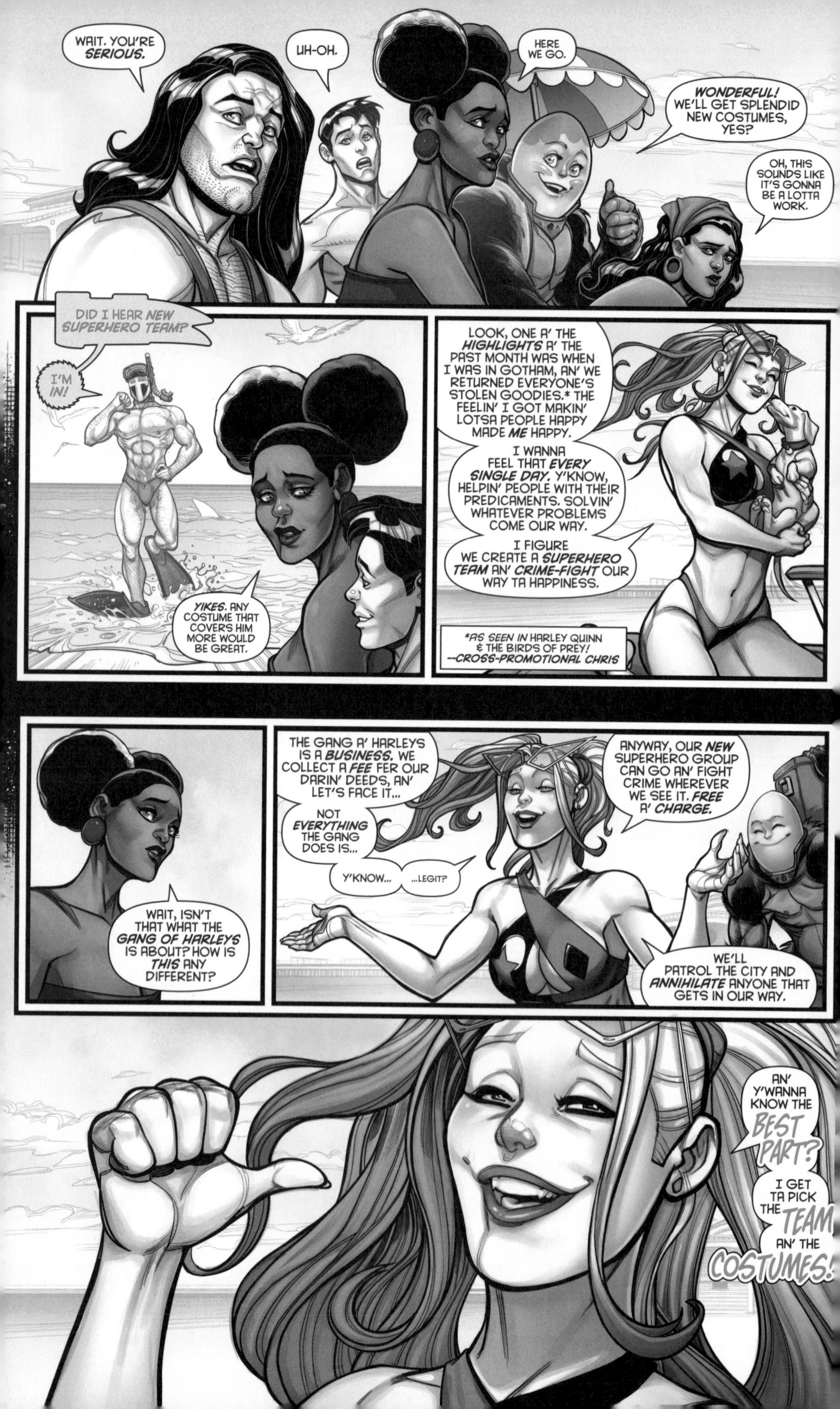

WAIT. YOU'RE SERIOUS.
UH-OH.
HERE WE GO.
WONDERFUL! WE'LL GET SPLENDID NEW COSTUMES, YES?
OH, THIS SOUNDS LIKE IT'S GONNA BE A LOTTA WORK.
DID I HEAR NEW SUPERHERO TEAM?
I'M IN!
YIKES. ANY COSTUME THAT COVERS HIM MORE WOULD BE GREAT.
LOOK, ONE A' THE HIGHLIGHTS A' THE PAST MONTH WAS WHEN I WAS IN GOTHAM, AN' WE RETURNED EVERYONE'S STOLEN GOODIES.* THE FEELIN' I GOT MAKIN' LOTSA PEOPLE HAPPY MADE ME HAPPY.
I WANNA FEEL THAT EVERY SINGLE DAY. Y'KNOW, HELPIN' PEOPLE WITH THEIR PREDICAMENTS. SOLVIN' WHATEVER PROBLEMS COME OUR WAY.
I FIGURE WE CREATE A SUPERHERO TEAM AN' CRIME-FIGHT OUR WAY TA HAPPINESS.
*AS SEEN IN HARLEY QUINN & THE BIRDS OF PREY! --CROSS-PROMOTIONAL CHRIS
WAIT, ISN'T THAT WHAT THE GANG OF HARLEYS IS ABOUT? HOW IS THIS ANY DIFFERENT?
THE GANG A' HARLEYS IS A BUSINESS. WE COLLECT A FEE FER OUR DARIN' DEEDS, AN' LET'S FACE IT...
NOT EVERYTHING THE GANG DOES IS...
Y'KNOW...
...LEGIT?
ANYWAY, OUR NEW SUPERHERO GROUP CAN GO AN' FIGHT CRIME WHEREVER WE SEE IT. FREE A' CHARGE.
WE'LL PATROL THE CITY AND ANNIHILATE ANYONE THAT GETS IN OUR WAY.
AN' Y'WANNA KNOW THE BEST PART?
I GET TA PICK THE TEAM AN' THE COSTUMES!

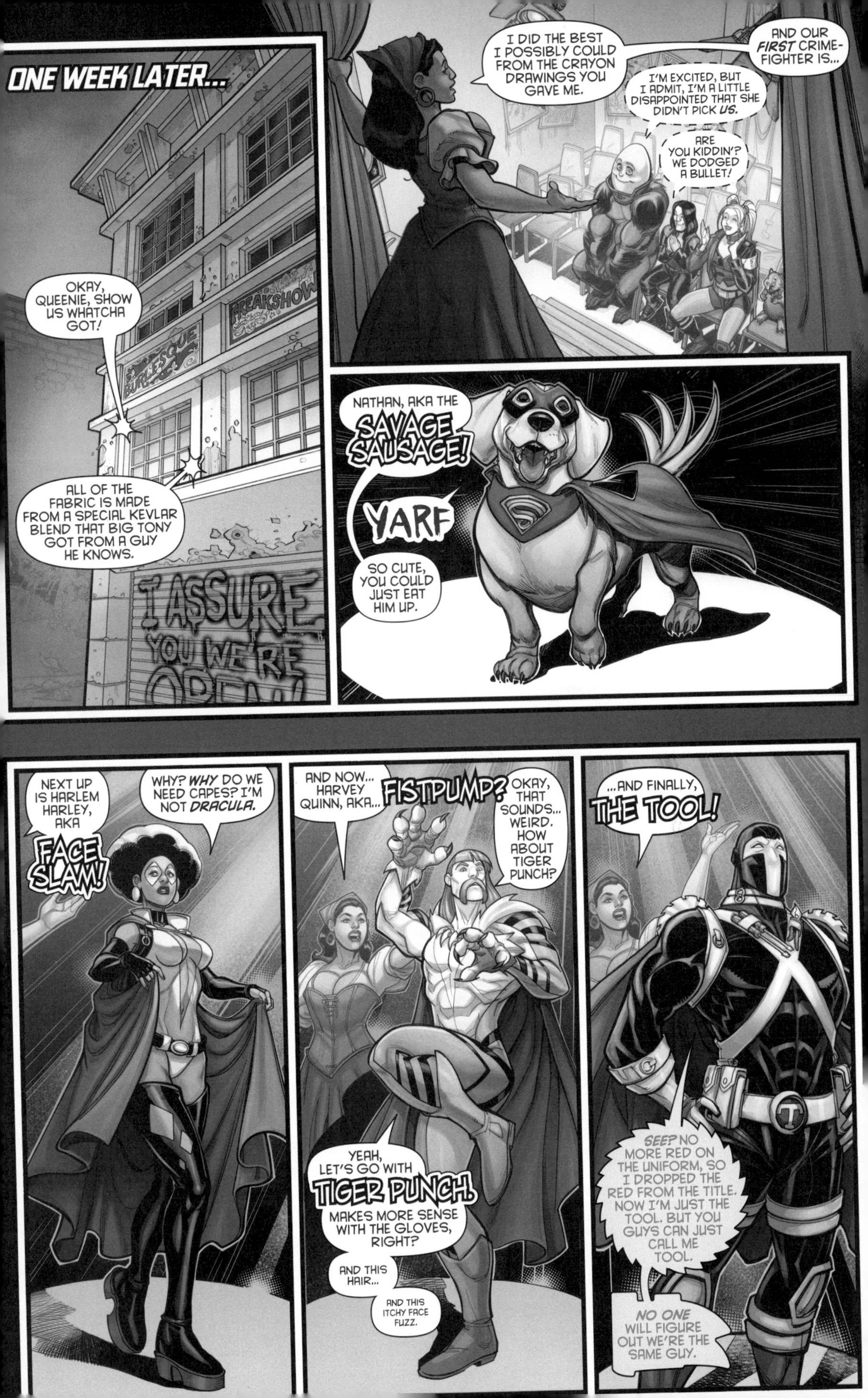
ONE WEEK LATER...
OKAY, QUEENIE, SHOW US WHATCHA GOT!
ALL OF THE FABRIC IS MADE FROM A SPECIAL KEVLAR BLEND THAT BIG TONY GOT FROM A GUY HE KNOWS.
FREAKSHOW
BURLESQUE
I ASSURE YOU WE'RE
I DID THE BEST I POSSIBLY COULD FROM THE CRAYON DRAWINGS YOU GAVE ME.
AND OUR FIRST CRIME-FIGHTER IS...
I'M EXCITED, BUT I ADMIT, I'M A LITTLE DISAPPOINTED THAT SHE DIDN'T PICK US.
ARE YOU KIDDIN'? WE DODGED A BULLET!
NATHAN, AKA THE SAVAGE SAUSAGE!
YARF
SO CUTE, YOU COULD JUST EAT HIM UP.
NEXT UP IS HARLEM HARLEY, AKA FACE SLAM!
WHY? WHY DO WE NEED CAPES? I'M NOT DRACULA.
AND NOW... HARVEY QUINN, AKA... FISTPUMP?
OKAY, THAT SOUNDS... WEIRD. HOW ABOUT TIGER PUNCH?
YEAH, LET'S GO WITH TIGER PUNCH. MAKES MORE SENSE WITH THE GLOVES, RIGHT?
AND THIS HAIR...
AND THIS ITCHY FACE FUZZ.
...AND FINALLY, THE TOOL!
SEE? NO MORE RED ON THE UNIFORM, SO I DROPPED THE RED FROM THE TITLE. NOW I'M JUST THE TOOL. BUT YOU GUYS CAN JUST CALL ME TOOL.
NO ONE WILL FIGURE OUT WE'RE THE SAME GUY.

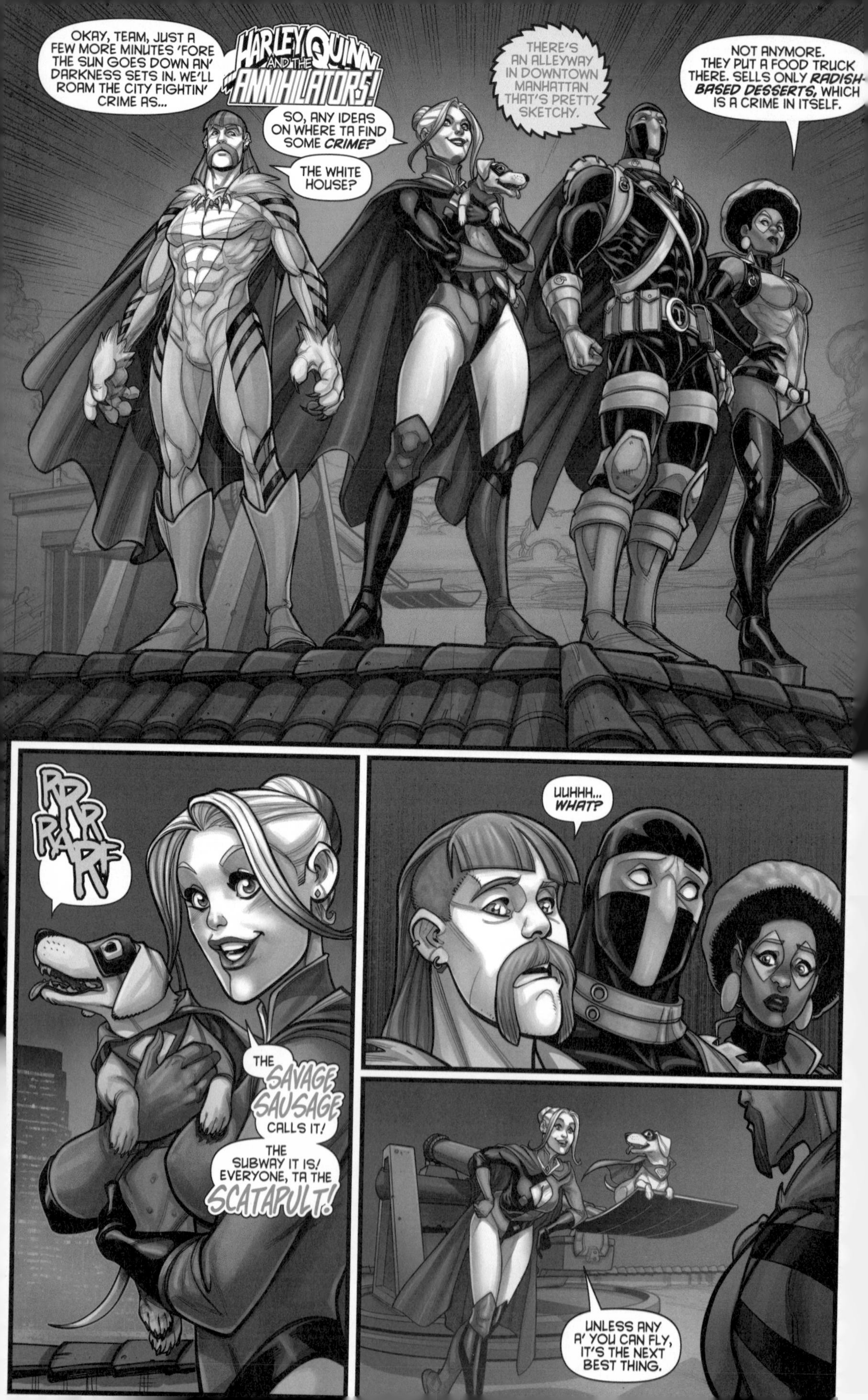

OKAY, TEAM, JUST A FEW MORE MINUTES 'FORE THE SUN GOES DOWN AN' DARKNESS SETS IN. WE'LL ROAM THE CITY FIGHTIN' CRIME AS...
HARLEY QUINN AND THE ANNIHILATORS!
SO, ANY IDEAS ON WHERE TA FIND SOME *CRIME?*
THE WHITE HOUSE?
THERE'S AN ALLEYWAY IN DOWNTOWN MANHATTAN THAT'S PRETTY SKETCHY.
NOT ANYMORE. THEY PUT A FOOD TRUCK THERE. SELLS ONLY ***RADISH-BASED DESSERTS,*** WHICH IS A CRIME IN ITSELF.
RRRRARF
THE SAVAGE SAUSAGE CALLS IT!
THE SUBWAY IT IS! EVERYONE, TA THE SCATAPULT!
UUHHH... *WHAT?*
UNLESS ANY A' YOU CAN FLY, IT'S THE NEXT BEST THING.

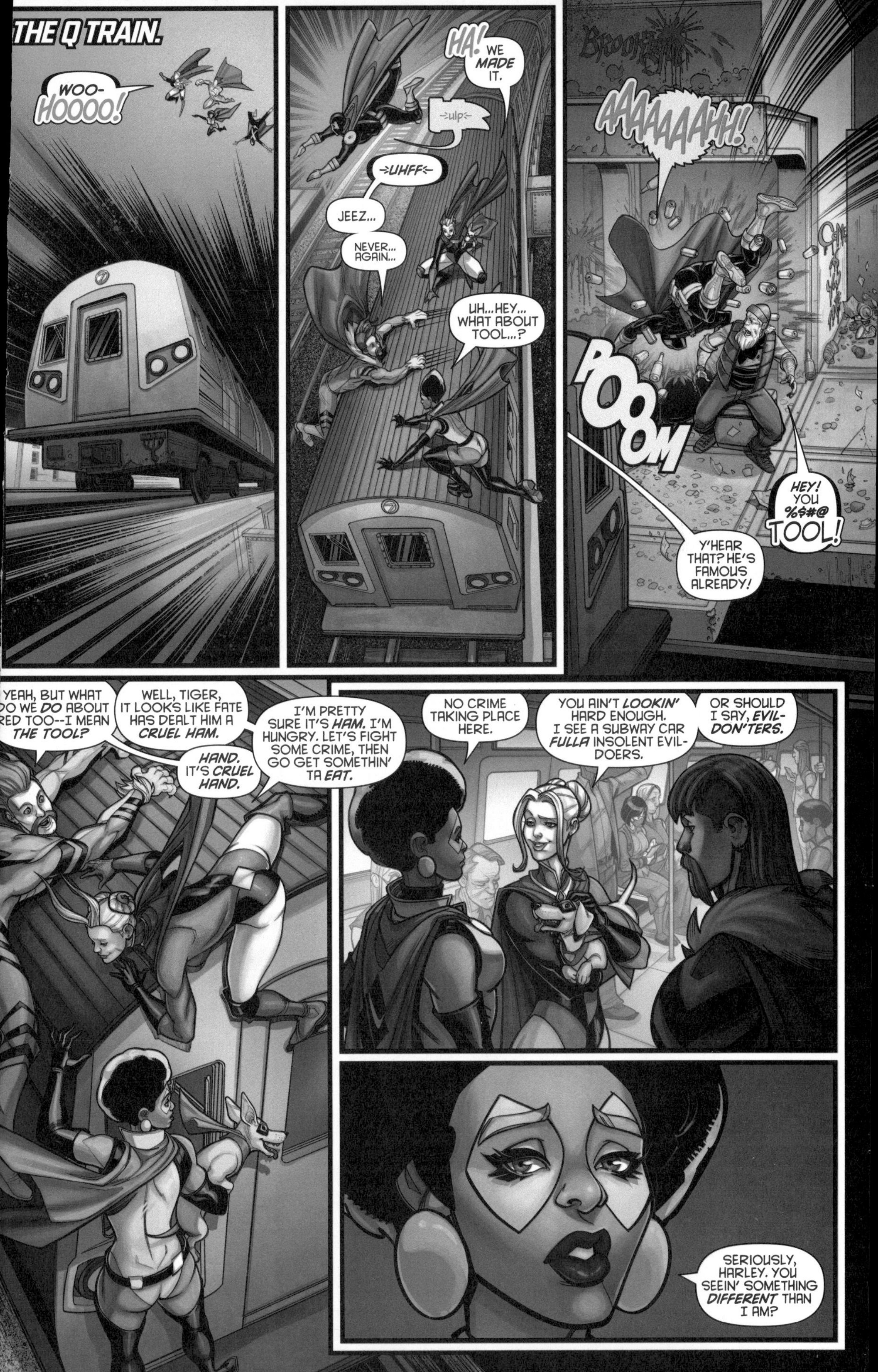
THE Q TRAIN.
WOO-HOOOO!
HA! WE MADE IT.
ulp
UHFF
JEEZ...
NEVER... AGAIN...
UH...HEY... WHAT ABOUT TOOL...?
AAAAAAAAHH!
POOOOM
HEY! YOU %$#@ TOOL!
Y'HEAR THAT? HE'S FAMOUS ALREADY!
YEAH, BUT WHAT DO WE DO ABOUT RED TOO--I MEAN THE TOOL?
WELL, TIGER, IT LOOKS LIKE FATE HAS DEALT HIM A CRUEL HAM.
HAND. IT'S CRUEL HAND.
I'M PRETTY SURE IT'S HAM. I'M HUNGRY. LET'S FIGHT SOME CRIME, THEN GO GET SOMETHIN' TA EAT.
NO CRIME TAKING PLACE HERE.
YOU AIN'T LOOKIN' HARD ENOUGH. I SEE A SUBWAY CAR FULLA INSOLENT EVIL-DOERS.
OR SHOULD I SAY, EVIL-DON'TERS.
SERIOUSLY, HARLEY. YOU SEEIN' SOMETHING DIFFERENT THAN I AM?

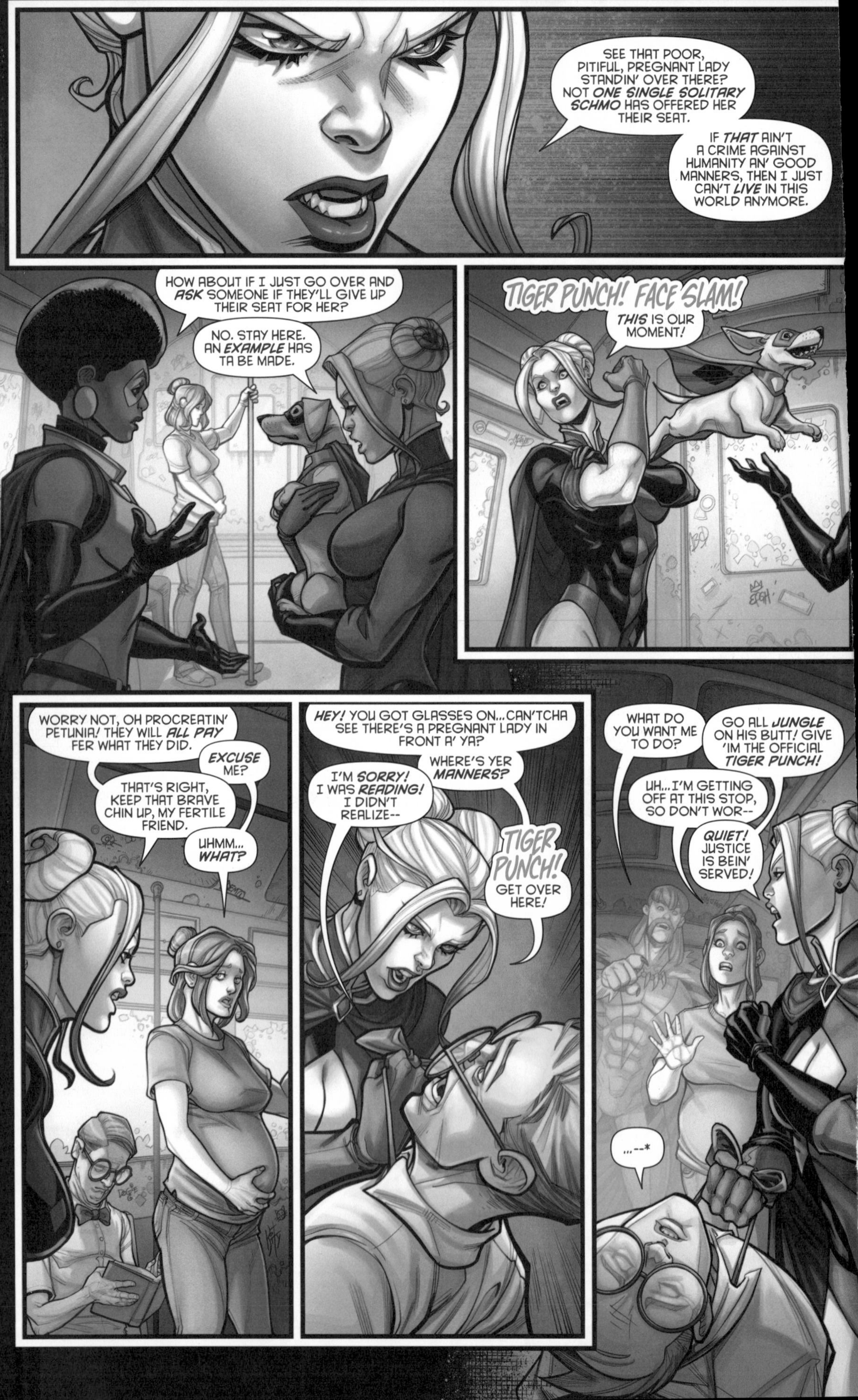

SEE THAT POOR, PITIFUL, PREGNANT LADY STANDIN' OVER THERE? NOT ONE SINGLE SOLITARY SCHMO HAS OFFERED HER THEIR SEAT.
IF THAT AIN'T A CRIME AGAINST HUMANITY AN' GOOD MANNERS, THEN I JUST CAN'T LIVE IN THIS WORLD ANYMORE.
HOW ABOUT IF I JUST GO OVER AND ASK SOMEONE IF THEY'LL GIVE UP THEIR SEAT FOR HER?
NO. STAY HERE. AN EXAMPLE HAS TA BE MADE.
TIGER PUNCH! FACE SLAM!
THIS IS OUR MOMENT!
WORRY NOT, OH PROCREATIN' PETUNIA! THEY WILL ALL PAY FER WHAT THEY DID.
EXCUSE ME?
THAT'S RIGHT, KEEP THAT BRAVE CHIN UP, MY FERTILE FRIEND.
UHMM... WHAT?
HEY! YOU GOT GLASSES ON...CAN'TCHA SEE THERE'S A PREGNANT LADY IN FRONT A' YA?
WHERE'S YER MANNERS?
I'M SORRY! I WAS READING! I DIDN'T REALIZE--
TIGER PUNCH! GET OVER HERE!
WHAT DO YOU WANT ME TO DO?
GO ALL JUNGLE ON HIS BUTT! GIVE 'IM THE OFFICIAL TIGER PUNCH!
UH...I'M GETTING OFF AT THIS STOP, SO DON'T WOR--
QUIET! JUSTICE IS BEIN' SERVED!
...--*

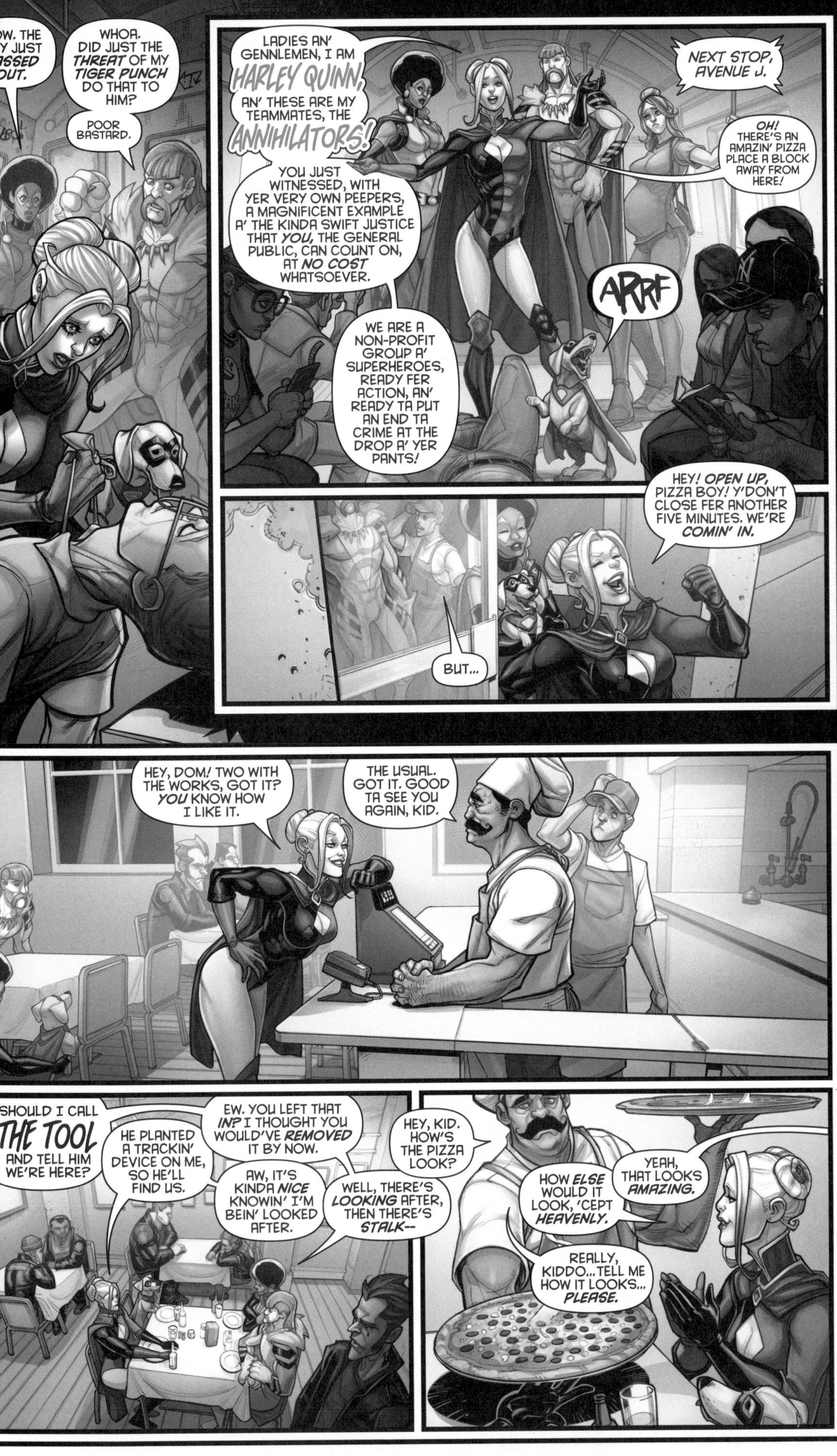

OW. THE
Y JUST
ASSED
OUT.
WHOA. DID JUST THE THREAT OF MY TIGER PUNCH DO THAT TO HIM?
POOR BASTARD.
LADIES AN' GENNLEMEN, I AM HARLEY QUINN, AN' THESE ARE MY TEAMMATES, THE ANNIHILATORS!
YOU JUST WITNESSED, WITH YER VERY OWN PEEPERS, A MAGNIFICENT EXAMPLE A' THE KINDA SWIFT JUSTICE THAT YOU, THE GENERAL PUBLIC, CAN COUNT ON, AT NO COST WHATSOEVER.
WE ARE A NON-PROFIT GROUP A' SUPERHEROES, READY FER ACTION, AN' READY TA PUT AN END TA CRIME AT THE DROP A' YER PANTS!
NEXT STOP, AVENUE J.
OH! THERE'S AN AMAZIN' PIZZA PLACE A BLOCK AWAY FROM HERE!
ARRF
HEY! OPEN UP, PIZZA BOY! Y'DON'T CLOSE FER ANOTHER FIVE MINUTES. WE'RE COMIN' IN.
BUT...
HEY, DOM! TWO WITH THE WORKS, GOT IT? YOU KNOW HOW I LIKE IT.
THE USUAL. GOT IT. GOOD TA SEE YOU AGAIN, KID.
SHOULD I CALL THE TOOL AND TELL HIM WE'RE HERE?
HE PLANTED A TRACKIN' DEVICE ON ME, SO HE'LL FIND US.
EW. YOU LEFT THAT IN? I THOUGHT YOU WOULD'VE REMOVED IT BY NOW.
AW, IT'S KINDA NICE KNOWIN' I'M BEIN' LOOKED AFTER.
WELL, THERE'S LOOKING AFTER, THEN THERE'S STALK--
HEY, KID. HOW'S THE PIZZA LOOK?
YEAH, THAT LOOKS AMAZING.
HOW ELSE WOULD IT LOOK, 'CEPT HEAVENLY.
REALLY, KIDDO... TELL ME HOW IT LOOKS... PLEASE.

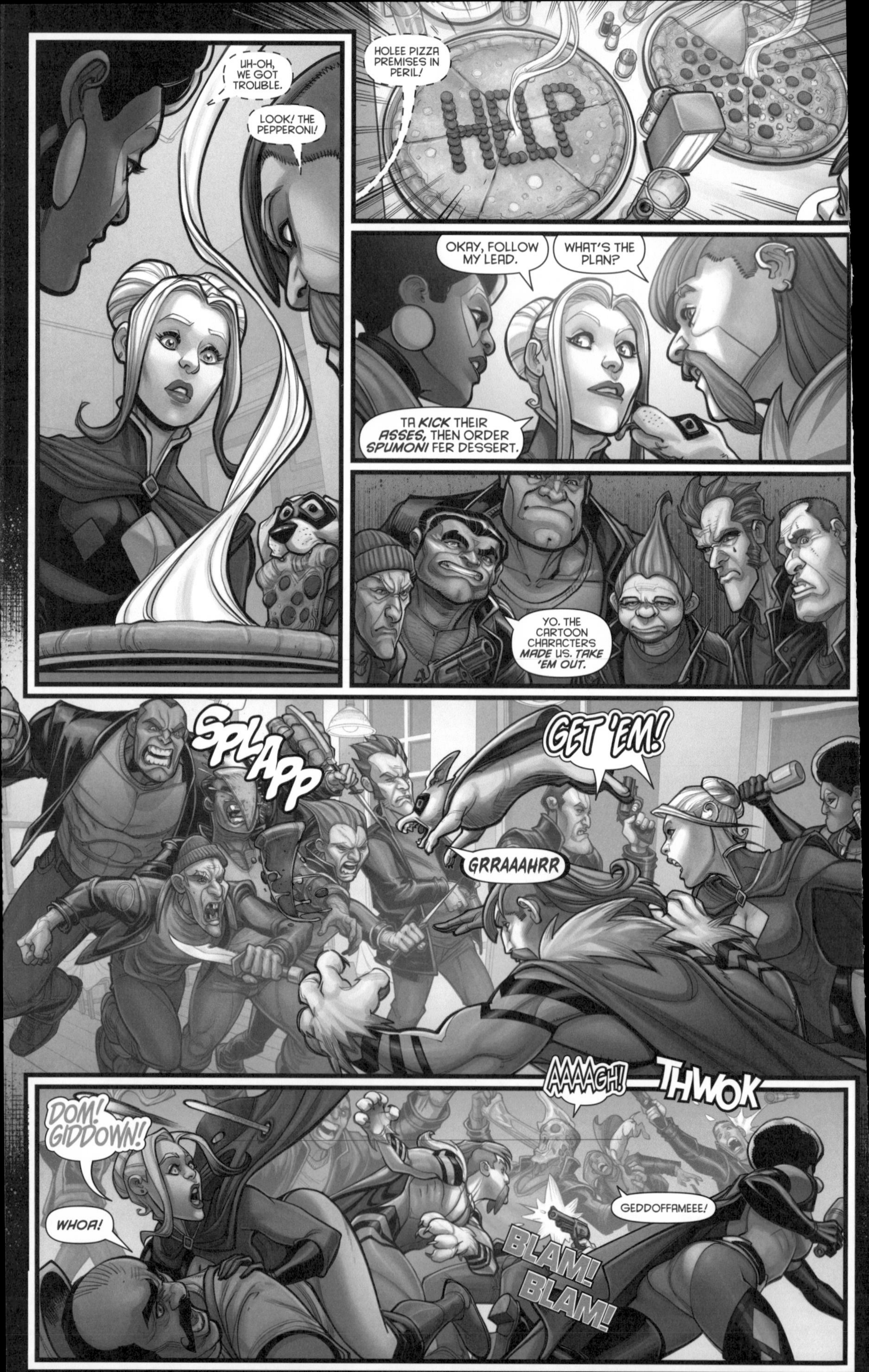
UH-OH, WE GOT TROUBLE.
LOOK! THE PEPPERONI!
HOLEE PIZZA PREMISES IN PERIL!
HELP
OKAY, FOLLOW MY LEAD.
WHAT'S THE PLAN?
TA KICK THEIR ASSES, THEN ORDER SPUMONI FER DESSERT.
YO. THE CARTOON CHARACTERS MADE US. TAKE 'EM OUT.
SPLAPP
GET 'EM!
GRRAAAHRR
AAAAGH!
THWOK
DOM! GIDDOWN!
WHOA!
GEDDOFFAMEEE!
BLAM!
BLAM!

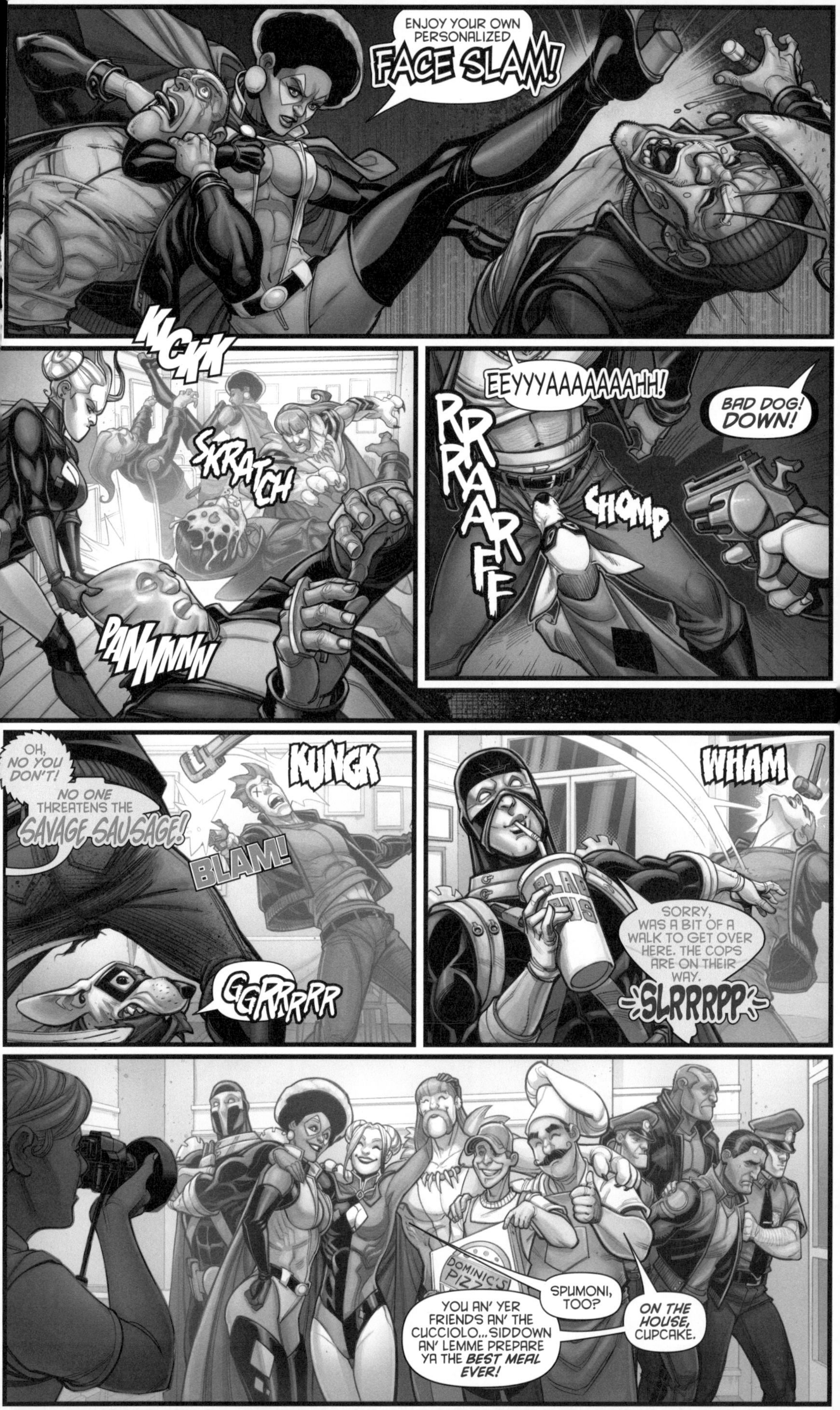

ENJOY YOUR OWN PERSONALIZED FACE SLAM!
KICKK
SKRATCH
PANNNNNN
EEYYYAAAAAAAHH!
RRRAARFF
CHOMP
BAD DOG! DOWN!
OH, NO YOU DON'T!
NO ONE THREATENS THE SAVAGE SAUSAGE!
KUNGK
BLAM!
GGRRRRR
WHAM
SORRY, WAS A BIT OF A WALK TO GET OVER HERE. THE COPS ARE ON THEIR WAY.
SLRRRPP
DOMINIC'S PIZZ
YOU AN' YER FRIENDS AN' THE CUCCIOLO... SIDDOWN AN' LEMME PREPARE YA THE BEST MEAL EVER!
SPUMONI, TOO?
ON THE HOUSE, CUPCAKE.

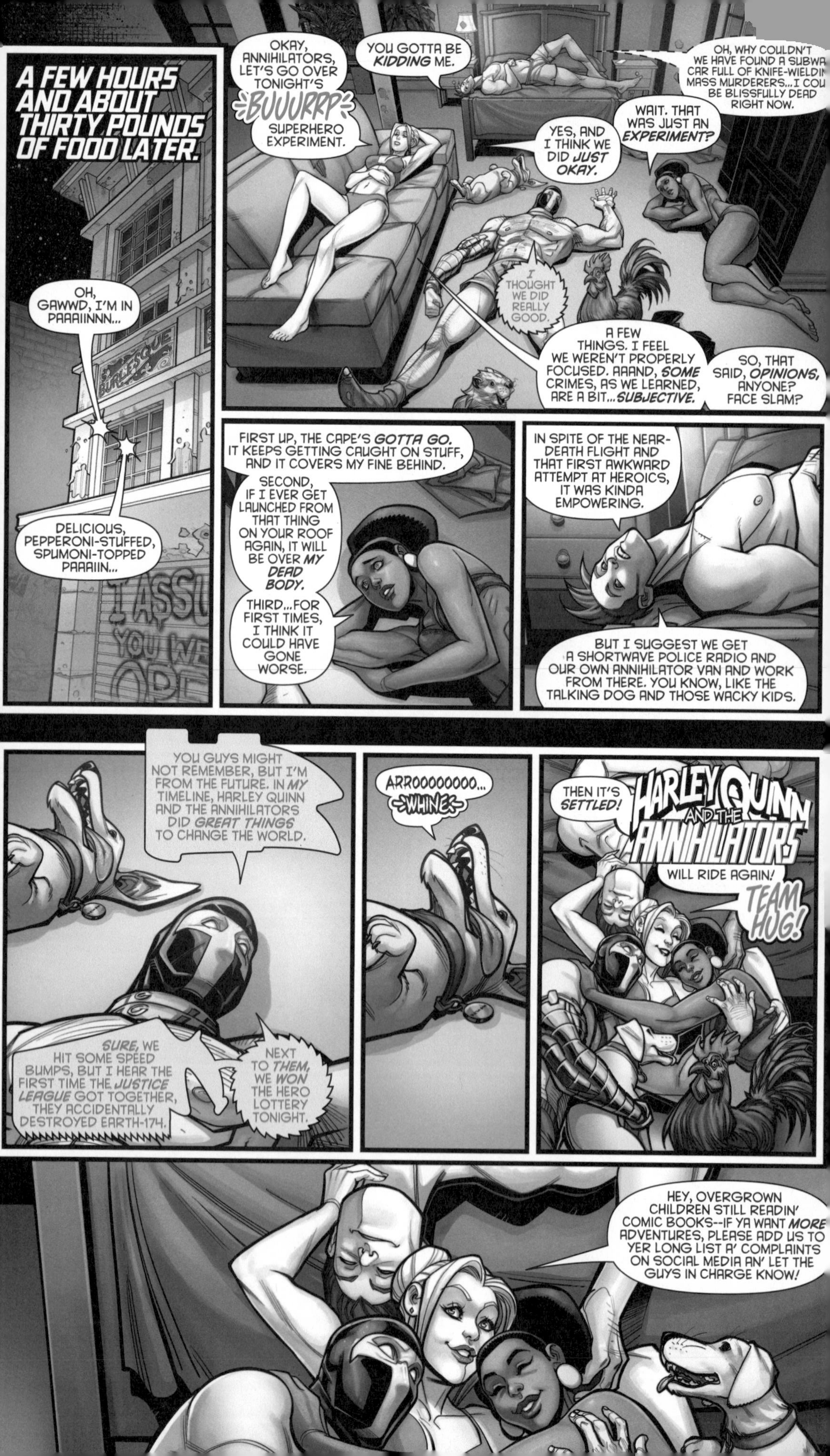
A FEW HOURS AND ABOUT THIRTY POUNDS OF FOOD LATER.
OH, GAWWD, I'M IN PAAAIINN...
DELICIOUS, PEPPERONI-STUFFED, SPUMONI-TOPPED PAAAIIN...
BURLESQUE
OKAY, ANNIHILATORS, LET'S GO OVER TONIGHT'S BUUURRP SUPERHERO EXPERIMENT.
YOU GOTTA BE KIDDING ME.
OH, WHY COULDN'T WE HAVE FOUND A SUBWA CAR FULL OF KNIFE-WIELDIN MASS MURDERERS...I COU BE BLISSFULLY DEAD RIGHT NOW.
WAIT. THAT WAS JUST AN EXPERIMENT?
YES, AND I THINK WE DID JUST OKAY.
I THOUGHT WE DID REALLY GOOD.
A FEW THINGS. I FEEL WE WEREN'T PROPERLY FOCUSED. AAAND, SOME CRIMES, AS WE LEARNED, ARE A BIT...SUBJECTIVE.
SO, THAT SAID, OPINIONS, ANYONE? FACE SLAM?
FIRST UP, THE CAPE'S GOTTA GO. IT KEEPS GETTING CAUGHT ON STUFF, AND IT COVERS MY FINE BEHIND.
SECOND, IF I EVER GET LAUNCHED FROM THAT THING ON YOUR ROOF AGAIN, IT WILL BE OVER MY DEAD BODY.
THIRD...FOR FIRST TIMES, I THINK IT COULD HAVE GONE WORSE.
IN SPITE OF THE NEAR-DEATH FLIGHT AND THAT FIRST AWKWARD ATTEMPT AT HEROICS, IT WAS KINDA EMPOWERING.
BUT I SUGGEST WE GET A SHORTWAVE POLICE RADIO AND OUR OWN ANNIHILATOR VAN AND WORK FROM THERE. YOU KNOW, LIKE THE TALKING DOG AND THOSE WACKY KIDS.
YOU GUYS MIGHT NOT REMEMBER, BUT I'M FROM THE FUTURE. IN MY TIMELINE, HARLEY QUINN AND THE ANNIHILATORS DID GREAT THINGS TO CHANGE THE WORLD.
SURE, WE HIT SOME SPEED BUMPS, BUT I HEAR THE FIRST TIME THE JUSTICE LEAGUE GOT TOGETHER, THEY ACCIDENTALLY DESTROYED EARTH-174.
NEXT TO THEM, WE WON THE HERO LOTTERY TONIGHT.
ARROOOOOOOO... WHINE
THEN IT'S SETTLED!
HARLEY QUINN AND THE ANNIHILATORS
WILL RIDE AGAIN!
TEAM HUG!
HEY, OVERGROWN CHILDREN STILL READIN' COMIC BOOKS--IF YA WANT MORE ADVENTURES, PLEASE ADD US TO YER LONG LIST A' COMPLAINTS ON SOCIAL MEDIA AN' LET THE GUYS IN CHARGE KNOW!

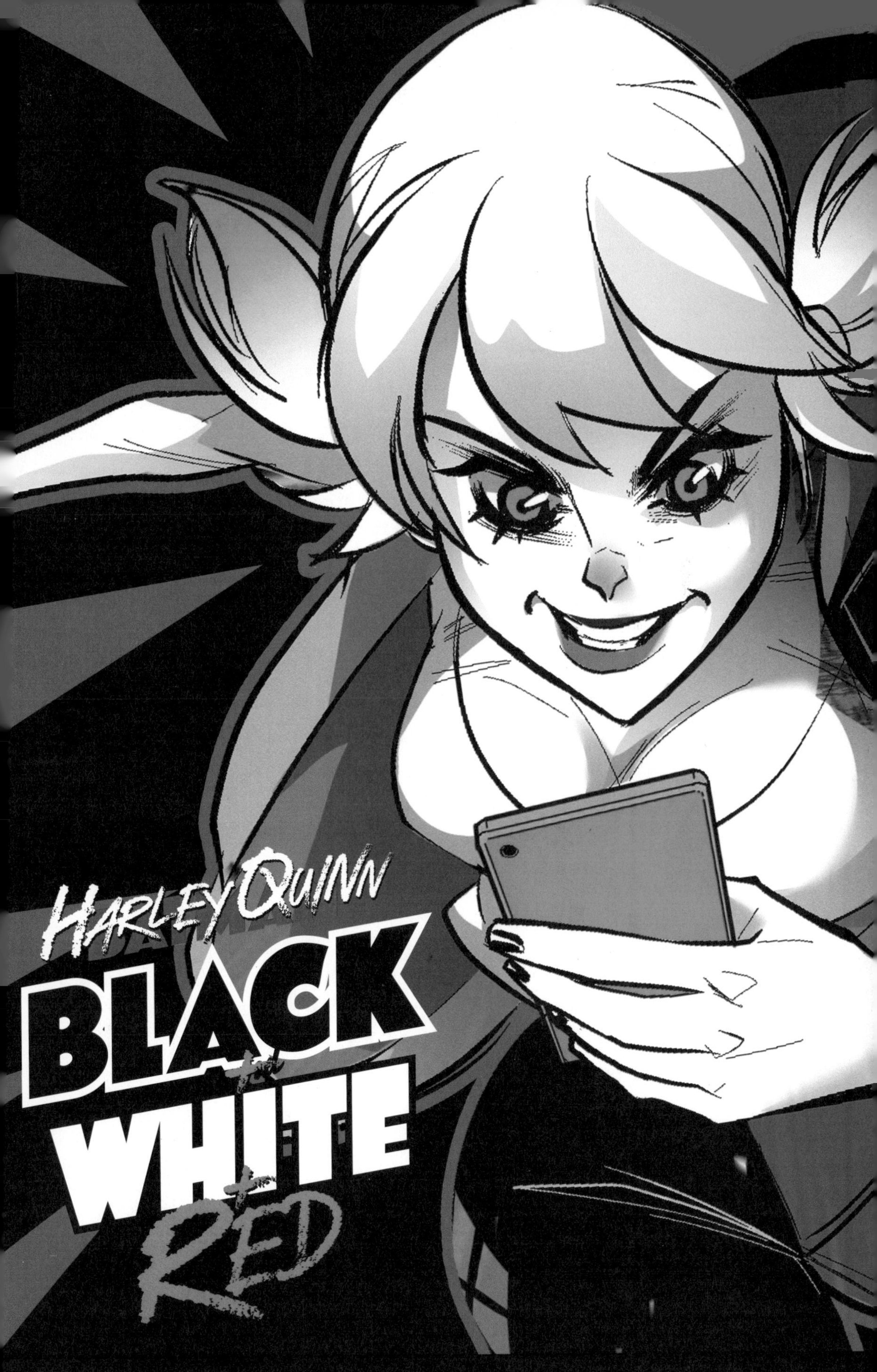
HARLEY QUINN
BLACK + WHITE + RED

CHAPTER THIRTEEN

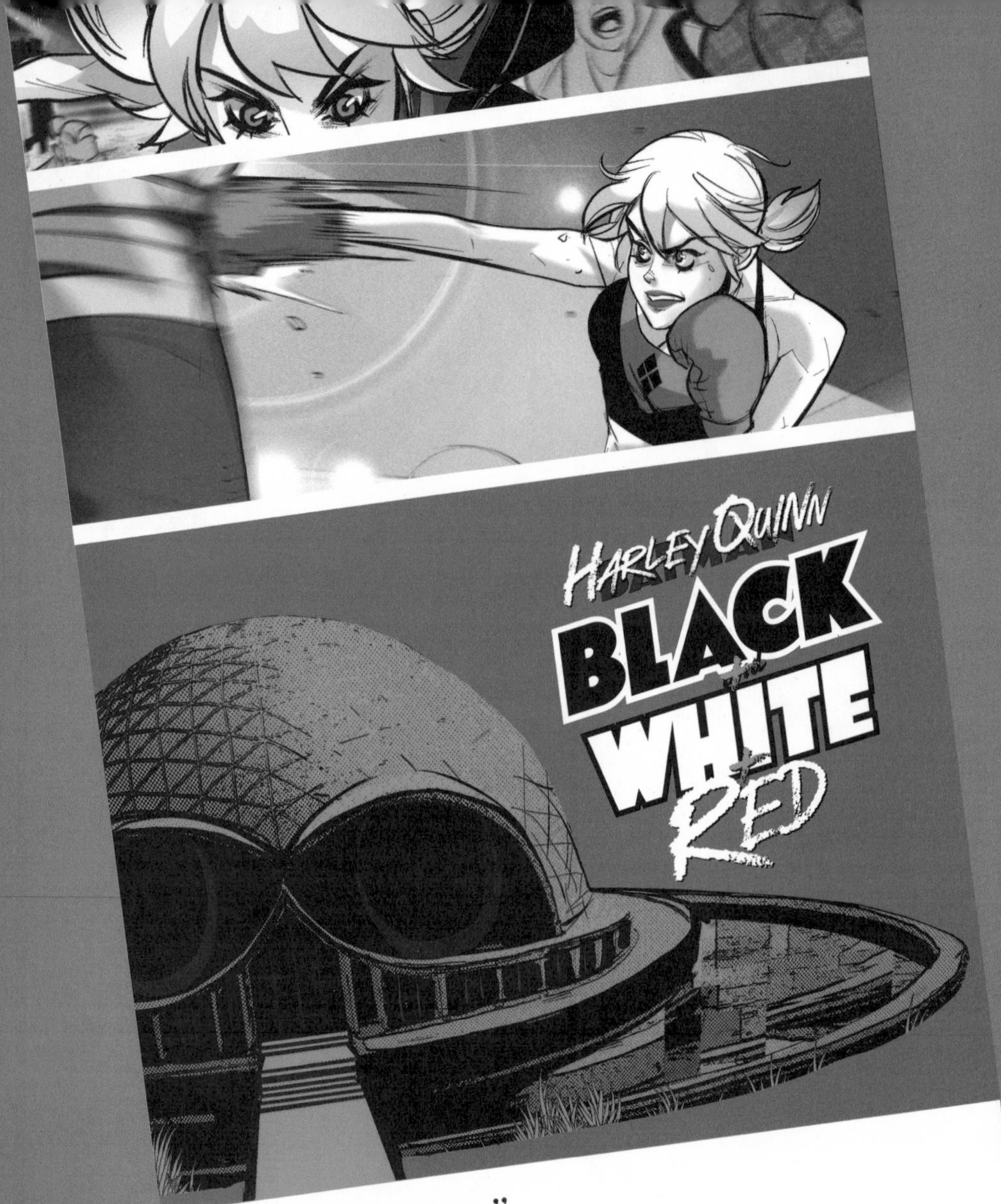
HARLEY QUINN
BLACK + WHITE + RED

"RED INK"

WRITER **PATRICK SCHUMACKER**
ARTIST **ELEONORA CARLINI**
LETTERER **TOM NAPOLITANO**
ASSOCIATE EDITOR **AMEDEO TURTURRO**
EDITOR **CHRIS CONROY**
HARLEY QUINN CREATED BY PAUL DINI & BRUCE TIMM

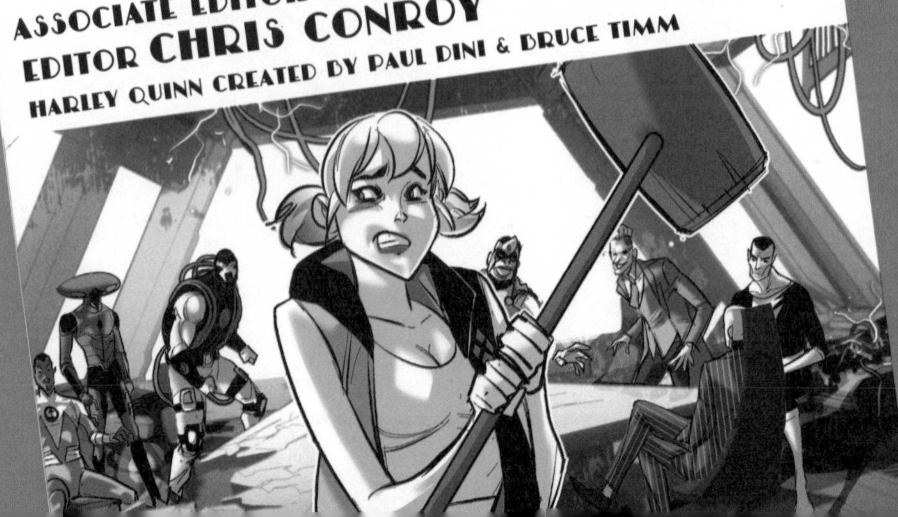

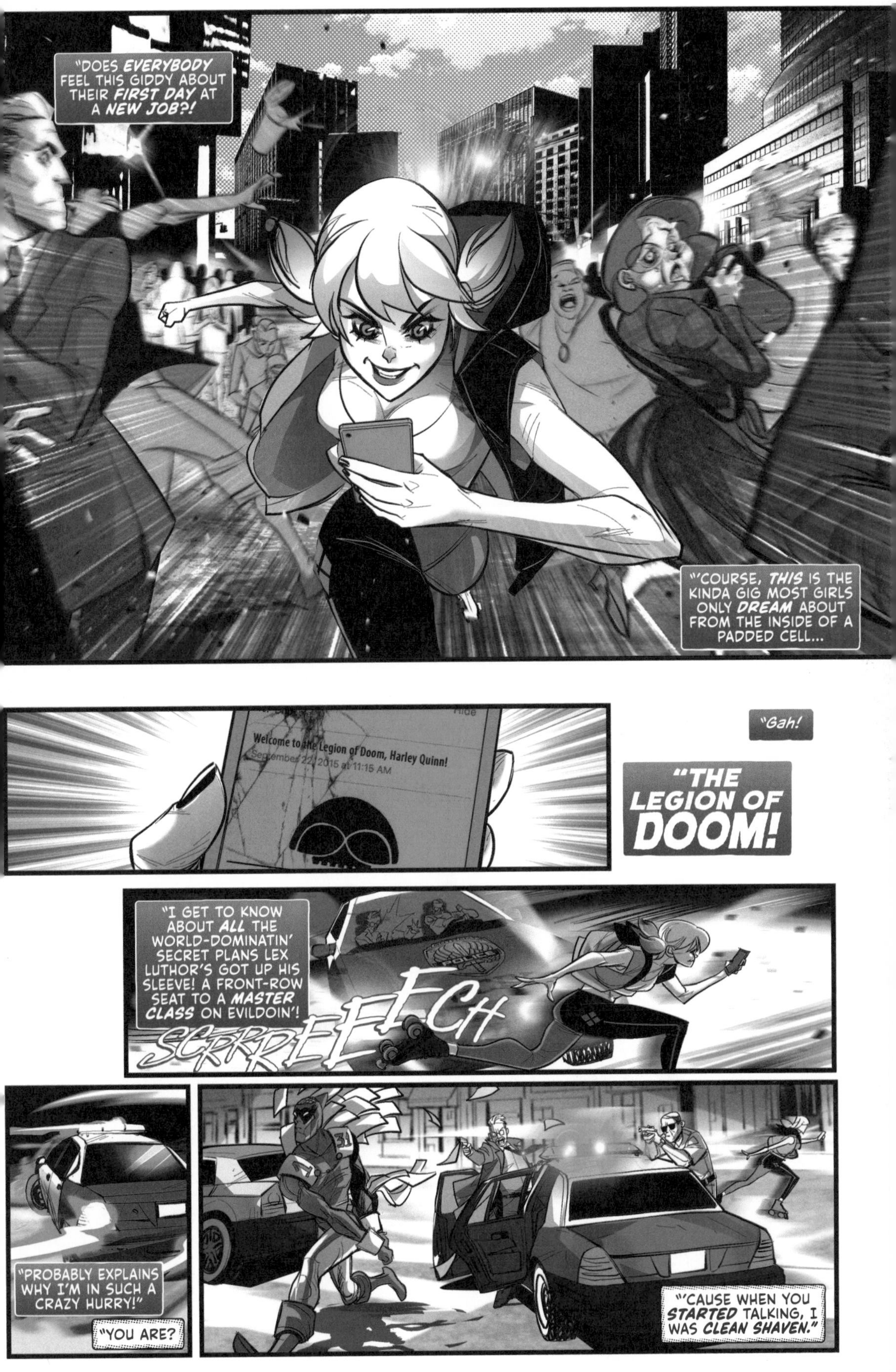

"DOES EVERYBODY FEEL THIS GIDDY ABOUT THEIR FIRST DAY AT A NEW JOB?!
"'COURSE, THIS IS THE KINDA GIG MOST GIRLS ONLY DREAM ABOUT FROM THE INSIDE OF A PADDED CELL...
Welcome to the Legion of Doom, Harley Quinn!
September 22, 2015 at 11:15 AM
"Gah!
"THE LEGION OF DOOM!
"I GET TO KNOW ABOUT ALL THE WORLD-DOMINATIN' SECRET PLANS LEX LUTHOR'S GOT UP HIS SLEEVE! A FRONT-ROW SEAT TO A MASTER CLASS ON EVILDOIN'!
SCRRREEEECH
"PROBABLY EXPLAINS WHY I'M IN SUCH A CRAZY HURRY!"
"YOU ARE?
"'CAUSE WHEN YOU STARTED TALKING, I WAS CLEAN SHAVEN."

Y'KNOW, I COULD *END YOU,* SMARTASS.

BUT I'M GONNA LET *THAT* ONE *SLIDE.*

WHEAT PRIVILEGE
A SOCIALLY CONSCIOUS BAKERY

'CAUSE IT'S TIME TO *CELEBRATE!*

"HARLEY QUINN'S HIT THE *BIG TIME!*"

THE HALL OF DOOM
(LEGION OF DOOM GLOBAL HEADQUARTERS.)

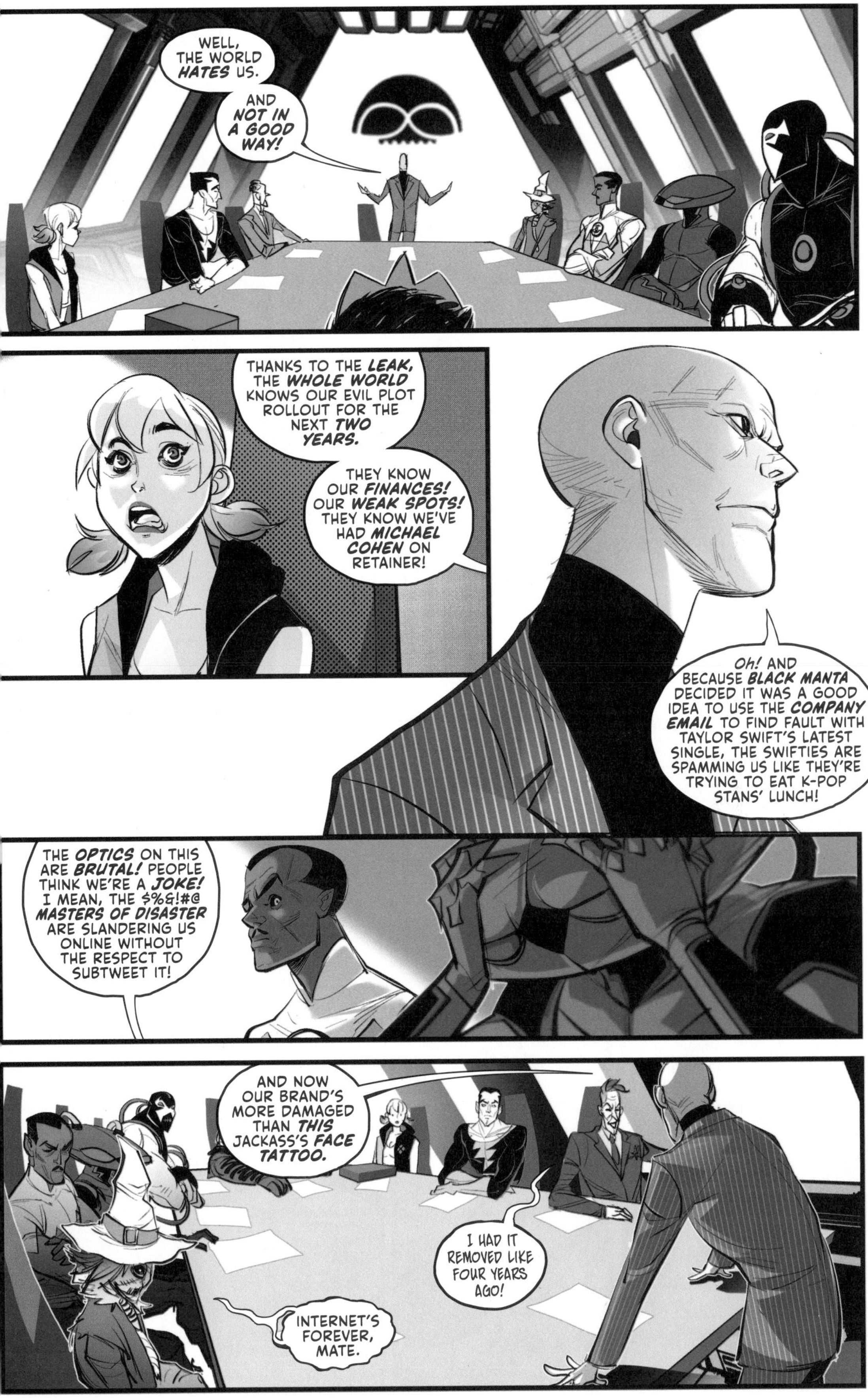
WELL, THE WORLD HATES US.
AND NOT IN A GOOD WAY!
THANKS TO THE LEAK, THE WHOLE WORLD KNOWS OUR EVIL PLOT ROLLOUT FOR THE NEXT TWO YEARS.
THEY KNOW OUR FINANCES! OUR WEAK SPOTS! THEY KNOW WE'VE HAD MICHAEL COHEN ON RETAINER!
Oh! AND BECAUSE BLACK MANTA DECIDED IT WAS A GOOD IDEA TO USE THE COMPANY EMAIL TO FIND FAULT WITH TAYLOR SWIFT'S LATEST SINGLE, THE SWIFTIES ARE SPAMMING US LIKE THEY'RE TRYING TO EAT K-POP STANS' LUNCH!
THE OPTICS ON THIS ARE BRUTAL! PEOPLE THINK WE'RE A JOKE! I MEAN, THE $%&!#@ MASTERS OF DISASTER ARE SLANDERING US ONLINE WITHOUT THE RESPECT TO SUBTWEET IT!
AND NOW OUR BRAND'S MORE DAMAGED THAN THIS JACKASS'S FACE TATTOO.
I HAD IT REMOVED LIKE FOUR YEARS AGO!
INTERNET'S FOREVER, MATE.

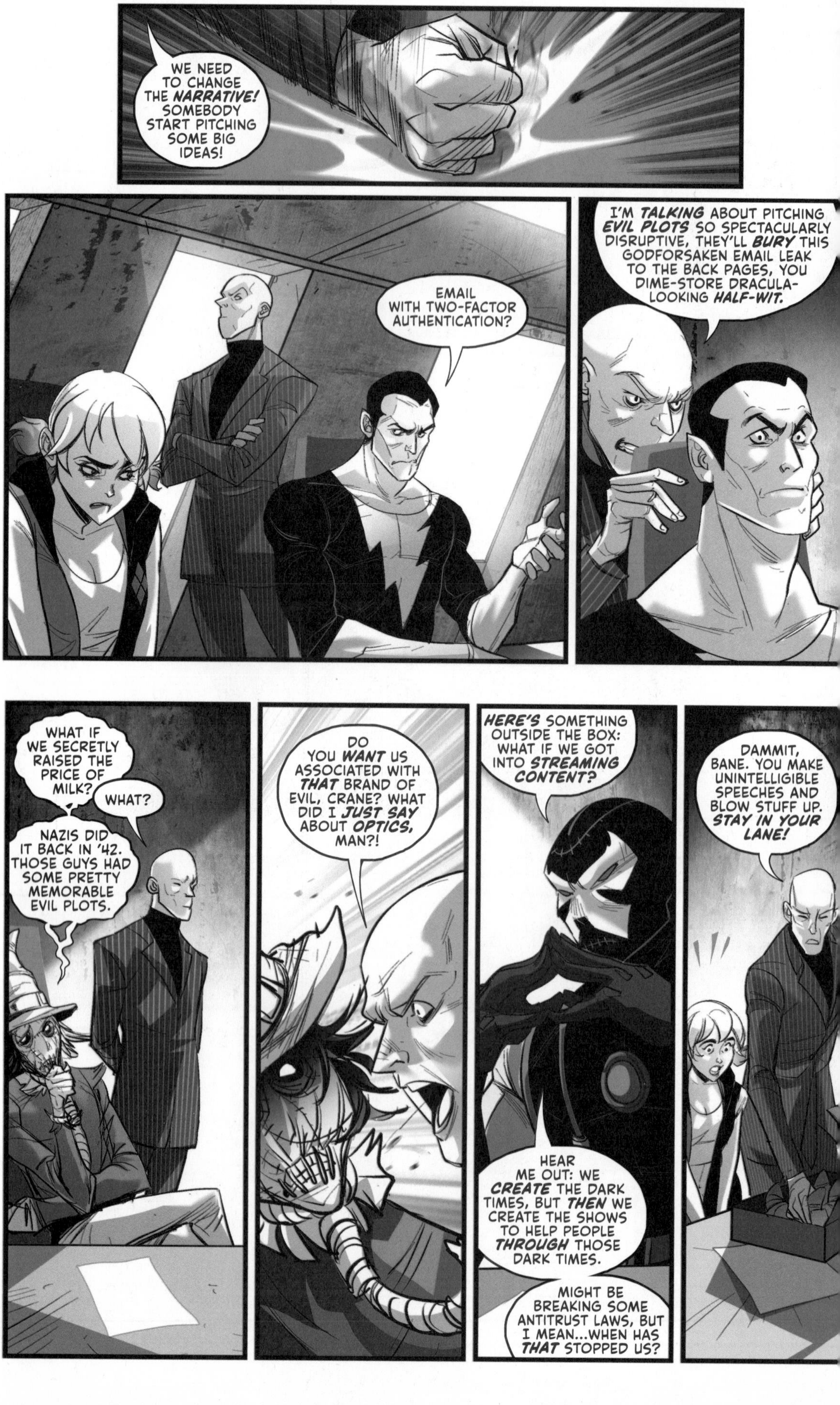
WE NEED TO CHANGE THE NARRATIVE! SOMEBODY START PITCHING SOME BIG IDEAS!
EMAIL WITH TWO-FACTOR AUTHENTICATION?
I'M TALKING ABOUT PITCHING EVIL PLOTS SO SPECTACULARLY DISRUPTIVE, THEY'LL BURY THIS GODFORSAKEN EMAIL LEAK TO THE BACK PAGES, YOU DIME-STORE DRACULA-LOOKING HALF-WIT.
WHAT IF WE SECRETLY RAISED THE PRICE OF MILK?
WHAT?
NAZIS DID IT BACK IN '42. THOSE GUYS HAD SOME PRETTY MEMORABLE EVIL PLOTS.
DO YOU WANT US ASSOCIATED WITH THAT BRAND OF EVIL, CRANE? WHAT DID I JUST SAY ABOUT OPTICS, MAN?!
HERE'S SOMETHING OUTSIDE THE BOX: WHAT IF WE GOT INTO STREAMING CONTENT?
HEAR ME OUT: WE CREATE THE DARK TIMES, BUT THEN WE CREATE THE SHOWS TO HELP PEOPLE THROUGH THOSE DARK TIMES.
MIGHT BE BREAKING SOME ANTITRUST LAWS, BUT I MEAN...WHEN HAS THAT STOPPED US?
DAMMIT, BANE. YOU MAKE UNINTELLIGIBLE SPEECHES AND BLOW STUFF UP. STAY IN YOUR LANE!

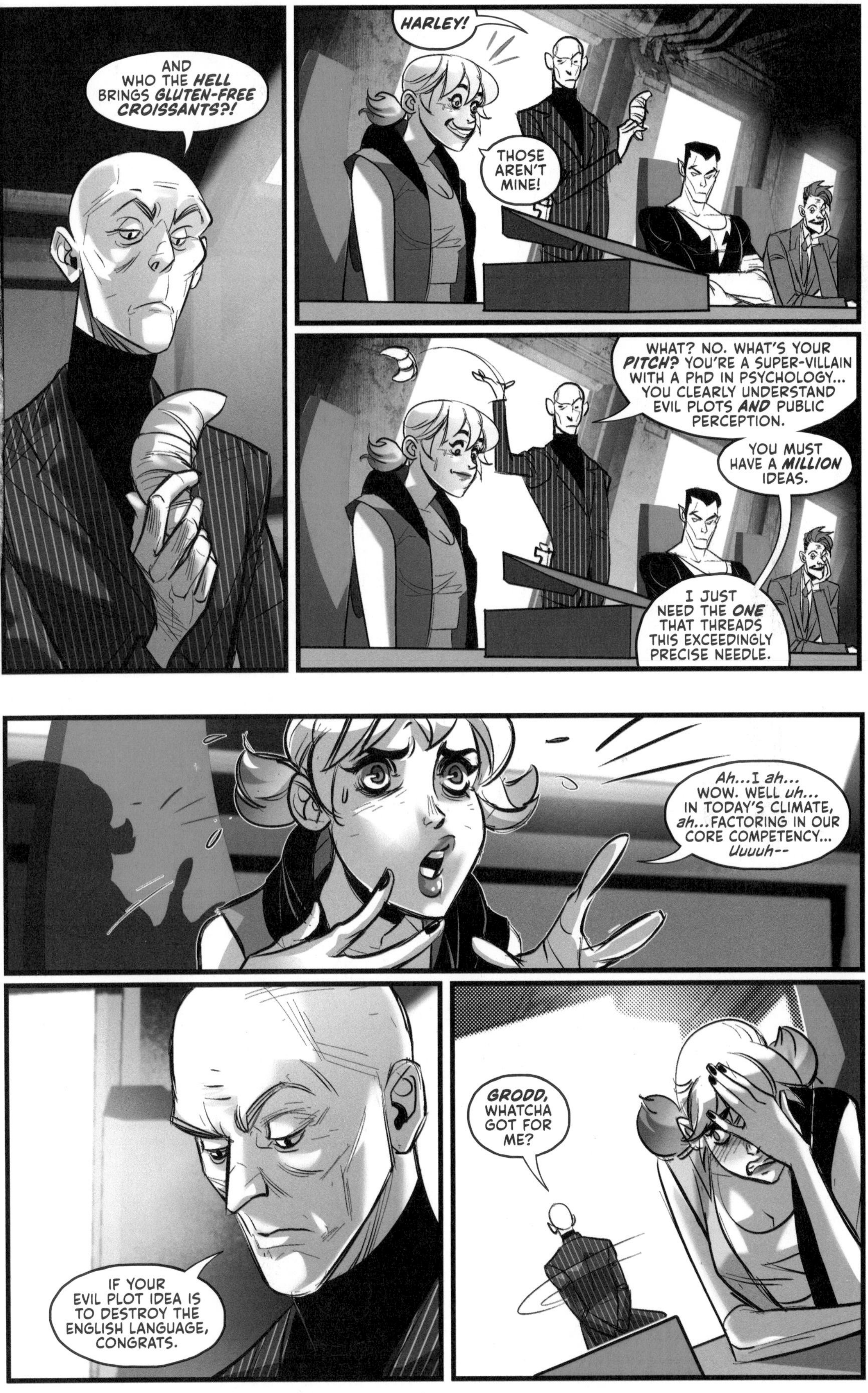
AND WHO THE HELL BRINGS GLUTEN-FREE CROISSANTS?!
HARLEY!
THOSE AREN'T MINE!
WHAT? NO. WHAT'S YOUR PITCH? YOU'RE A SUPER-VILLAIN WITH A PhD IN PSYCHOLOGY... YOU CLEARLY UNDERSTAND EVIL PLOTS AND PUBLIC PERCEPTION.
YOU MUST HAVE A MILLION IDEAS.
I JUST NEED THE ONE THAT THREADS THIS EXCEEDINGLY PRECISE NEEDLE.
Ah...I ah... WOW. WELL uh... IN TODAY'S CLIMATE, ah...FACTORING IN OUR CORE COMPETENCY... Uuuuh--
IF YOUR EVIL PLOT IDEA IS TO DESTROY THE ENGLISH LANGUAGE, CONGRATS.
GRODD, WHATCHA GOT FOR ME?

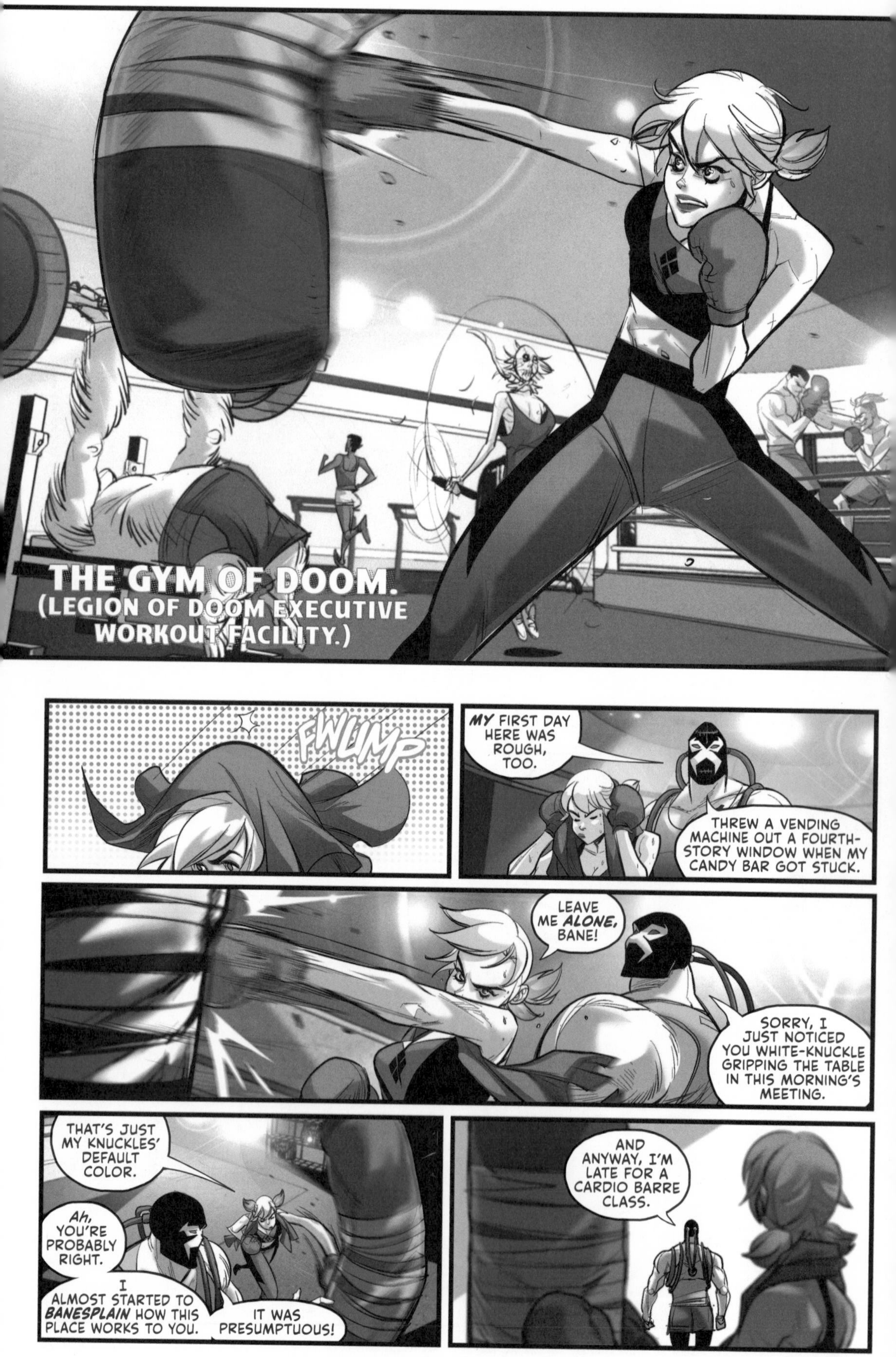
THE GYM OF DOOM.
(LEGION OF DOOM EXECUTIVE WORKOUT FACILITY.)
FWUMP
MY FIRST DAY HERE WAS ROUGH, TOO.
THREW A VENDING MACHINE OUT A FOURTH-STORY WINDOW WHEN MY CANDY BAR GOT STUCK.
LEAVE ME ALONE, BANE!
SORRY, I JUST NOTICED YOU WHITE-KNUCKLE GRIPPING THE TABLE IN THIS MORNING'S MEETING.
THAT'S JUST MY KNUCKLES' DEFAULT COLOR.
Ah, YOU'RE PROBABLY RIGHT.
I ALMOST STARTED TO BANESPLAIN HOW THIS PLACE WORKS TO YOU.
IT WAS PRESUMPTUOUS!
AND ANYWAY, I'M LATE FOR A CARDIO BARRE CLASS.

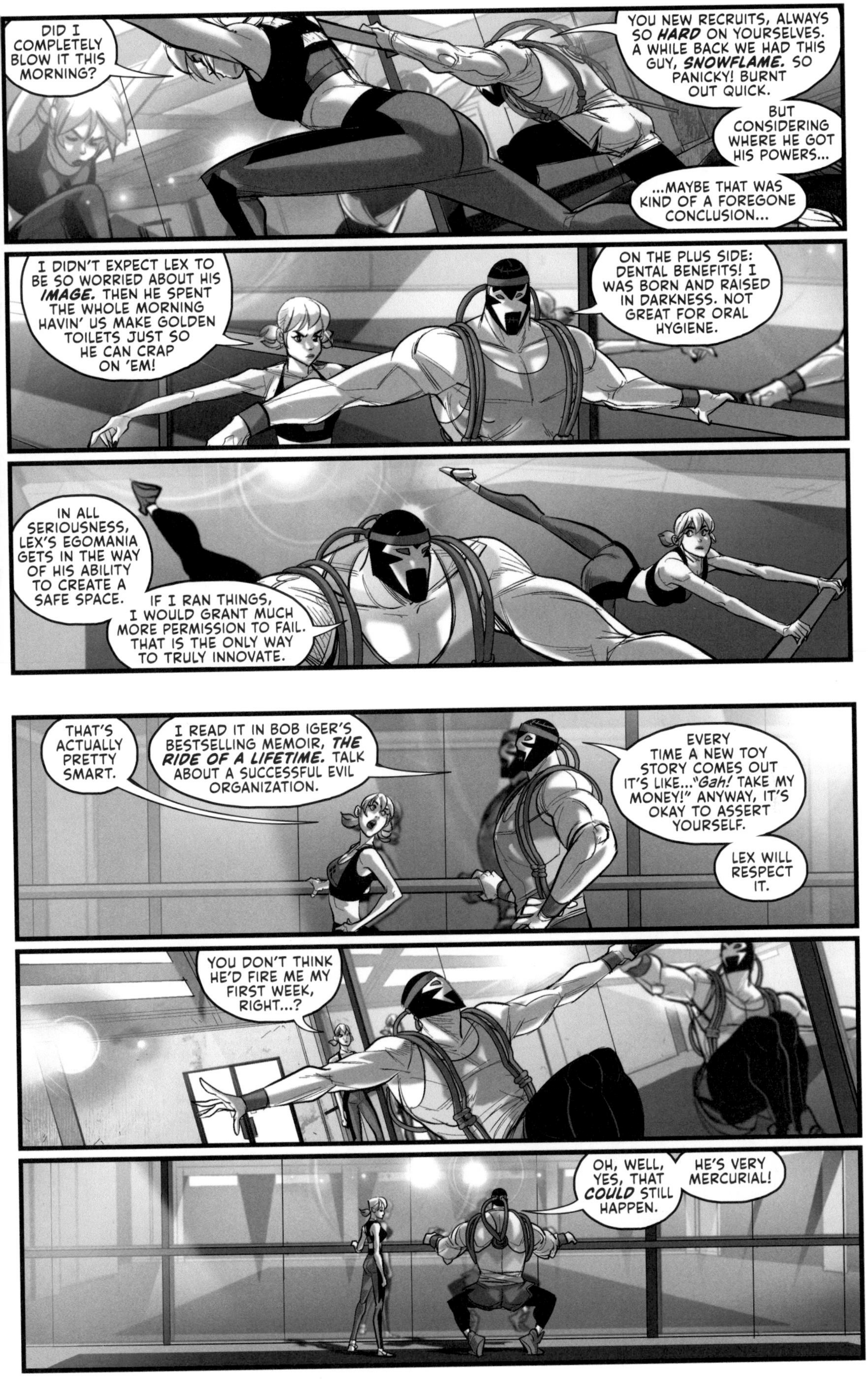

DID I COMPLETELY BLOW IT THIS MORNING?
YOU NEW RECRUITS, ALWAYS SO HARD ON YOURSELVES. A WHILE BACK WE HAD THIS GUY, SNOWFLAME. SO PANICKY! BURNT OUT QUICK.
BUT CONSIDERING WHERE HE GOT HIS POWERS...
...MAYBE THAT WAS KIND OF A FOREGONE CONCLUSION...
I DIDN'T EXPECT LEX TO BE SO WORRIED ABOUT HIS IMAGE. THEN HE SPENT THE WHOLE MORNING HAVIN' US MAKE GOLDEN TOILETS JUST SO HE CAN CRAP ON 'EM!
ON THE PLUS SIDE: DENTAL BENEFITS! I WAS BORN AND RAISED IN DARKNESS. NOT GREAT FOR ORAL HYGIENE.
IN ALL SERIOUSNESS, LEX'S EGOMANIA GETS IN THE WAY OF HIS ABILITY TO CREATE A SAFE SPACE.
IF I RAN THINGS, I WOULD GRANT MUCH MORE PERMISSION TO FAIL. THAT IS THE ONLY WAY TO TRULY INNOVATE.
THAT'S ACTUALLY PRETTY SMART.
I READ IT IN BOB IGER'S BESTSELLING MEMOIR, THE RIDE OF A LIFETIME. TALK ABOUT A SUCCESSFUL EVIL ORGANIZATION.
EVERY TIME A NEW TOY STORY COMES OUT IT'S LIKE..."Gah! TAKE MY MONEY!" ANYWAY, IT'S OKAY TO ASSERT YOURSELF.
LEX WILL RESPECT IT.
YOU DON'T THINK HE'D FIRE ME MY FIRST WEEK, RIGHT...?
OH, WELL, YES, THAT COULD STILL HAPPEN.
HE'S VERY MERCURIAL!

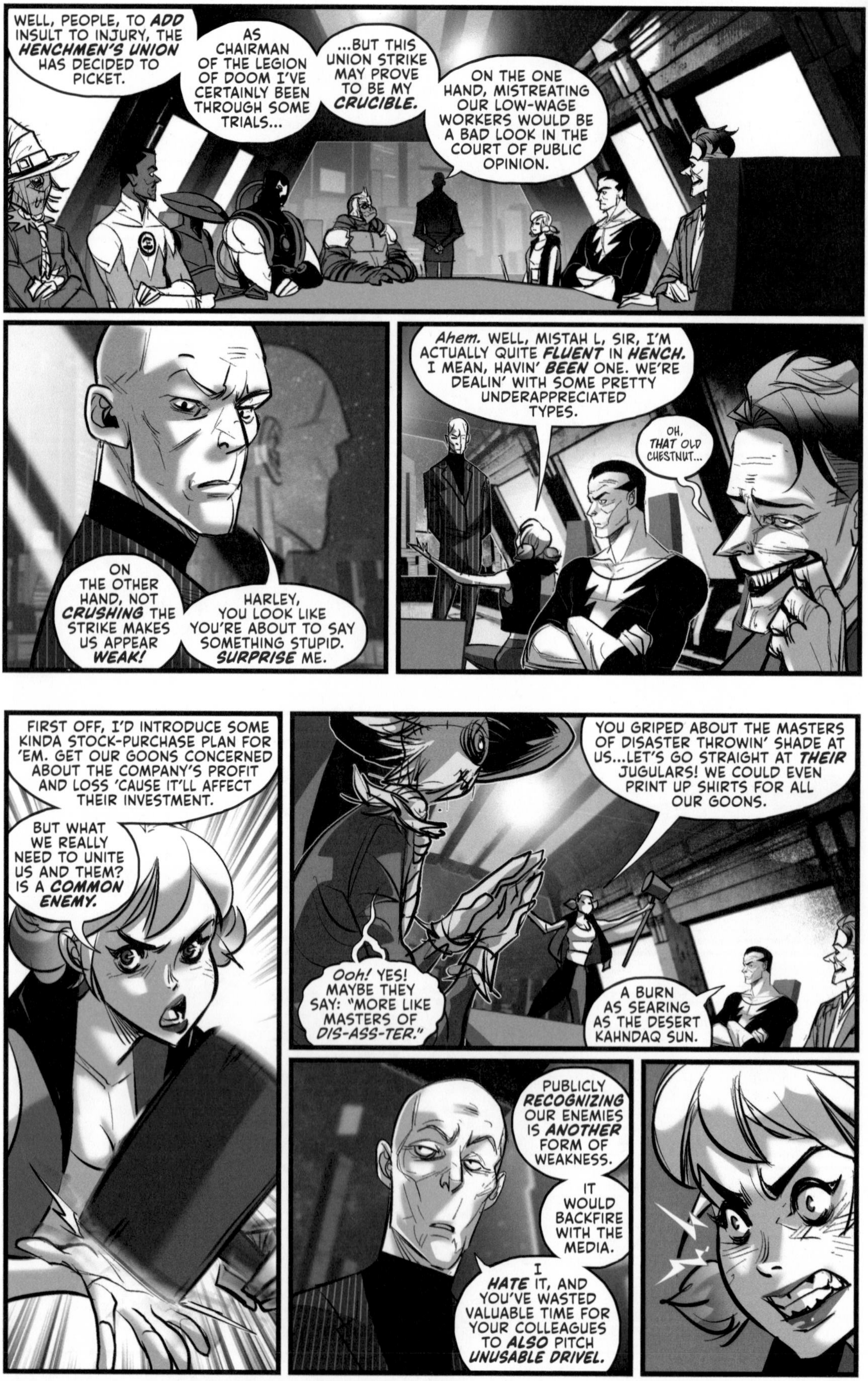

WELL, PEOPLE, TO ADD INSULT TO INJURY, THE HENCHMEN'S UNION HAS DECIDED TO PICKET.
AS CHAIRMAN OF THE LEGION OF DOOM I'VE CERTAINLY BEEN THROUGH SOME TRIALS...
...BUT THIS UNION STRIKE MAY PROVE TO BE MY CRUCIBLE.
ON THE ONE HAND, MISTREATING OUR LOW-WAGE WORKERS WOULD BE A BAD LOOK IN THE COURT OF PUBLIC OPINION.
ON THE OTHER HAND, NOT CRUSHING THE STRIKE MAKES US APPEAR WEAK!
HARLEY, YOU LOOK LIKE YOU'RE ABOUT TO SAY SOMETHING STUPID. SURPRISE ME.
Ahem. WELL, MISTAH L, SIR, I'M ACTUALLY QUITE FLUENT IN HENCH. I MEAN, HAVIN' BEEN ONE. WE'RE DEALIN' WITH SOME PRETTY UNDERAPPRECIATED TYPES.
OH, THAT OLD CHESTNUT...
FIRST OFF, I'D INTRODUCE SOME KINDA STOCK-PURCHASE PLAN FOR 'EM. GET OUR GOONS CONCERNED ABOUT THE COMPANY'S PROFIT AND LOSS 'CAUSE IT'LL AFFECT THEIR INVESTMENT.
BUT WHAT WE REALLY NEED TO UNITE US AND THEM? IS A COMMON ENEMY.
YOU GRIPED ABOUT THE MASTERS OF DISASTER THROWIN' SHADE AT US...LET'S GO STRAIGHT AT THEIR JUGULARS! WE COULD EVEN PRINT UP SHIRTS FOR ALL OUR GOONS.
Ooh! YES! MAYBE THEY SAY: "MORE LIKE MASTERS OF DIS-ASS-TER."
A BURN AS SEARING AS THE DESERT KAHNDAQ SUN.
PUBLICLY RECOGNIZING OUR ENEMIES IS ANOTHER FORM OF WEAKNESS.
IT WOULD BACKFIRE WITH THE MEDIA.
I HATE IT, AND YOU'VE WASTED VALUABLE TIME FOR YOUR COLLEAGUES TO ALSO PITCH UNUSABLE DRIVEL.

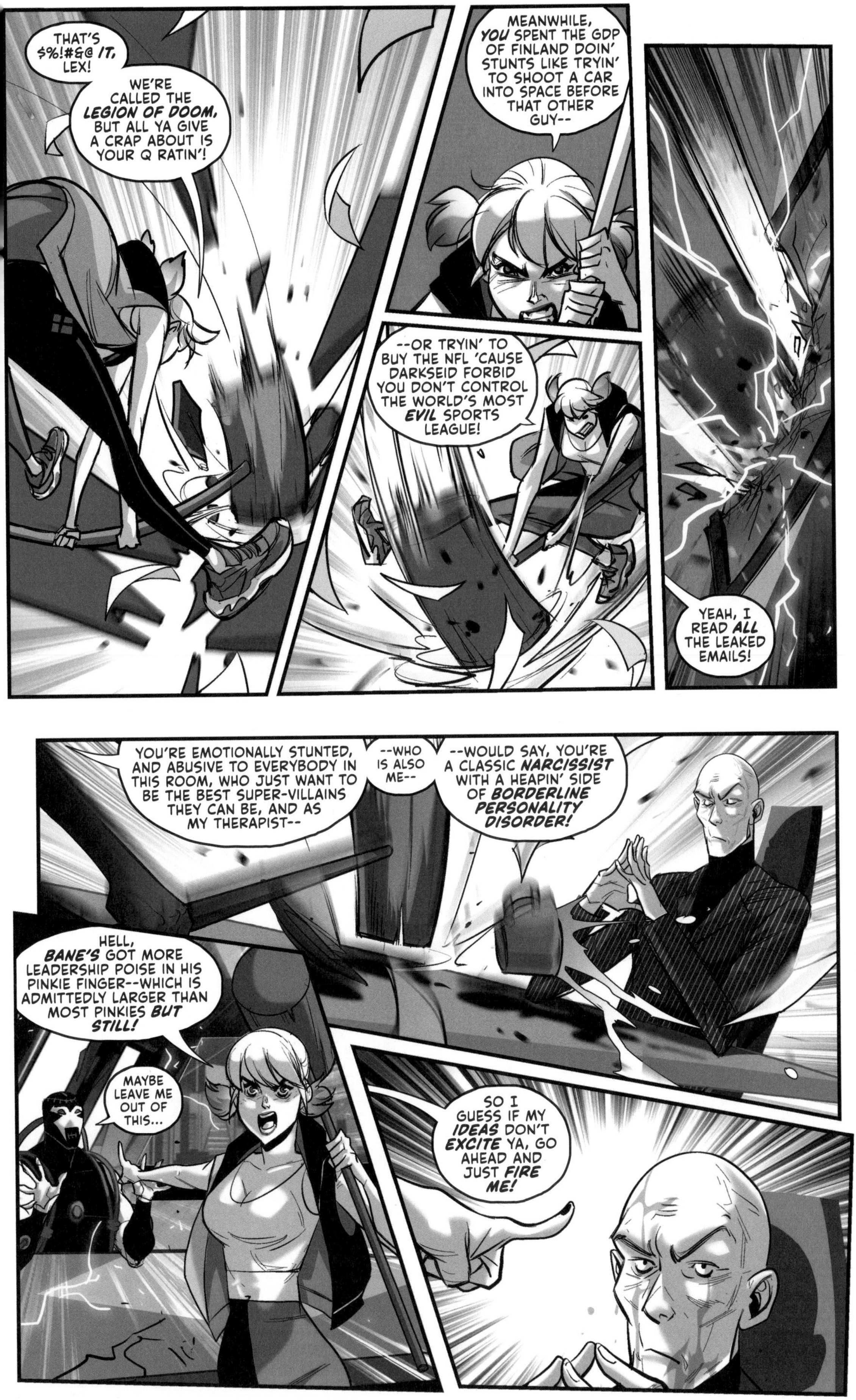
THAT'S $%!#&@ IT, LEX!
WE'RE CALLED THE LEGION OF DOOM, BUT ALL YA GIVE A CRAP ABOUT IS YOUR Q RATIN'!
MEANWHILE, YOU SPENT THE GDP OF FINLAND DOIN' STUNTS LIKE TRYIN' TO SHOOT A CAR INTO SPACE BEFORE THAT OTHER GUY--
--OR TRYIN' TO BUY THE NFL 'CAUSE DARKSEID FORBID YOU DON'T CONTROL THE WORLD'S MOST EVIL SPORTS LEAGUE!
YEAH, I READ ALL THE LEAKED EMAILS!
YOU'RE EMOTIONALLY STUNTED, AND ABUSIVE TO EVERYBODY IN THIS ROOM, WHO JUST WANT TO BE THE BEST SUPER-VILLAINS THEY CAN BE, AND AS MY THERAPIST--
--WHO IS ALSO ME--
--WOULD SAY, YOU'RE A CLASSIC NARCISSIST WITH A HEAPIN' SIDE OF BORDERLINE PERSONALITY DISORDER!
HELL, BANE'S GOT MORE LEADERSHIP POISE IN HIS PINKIE FINGER--WHICH IS ADMITTEDLY LARGER THAN MOST PINKIES BUT STILL!
MAYBE LEAVE ME OUT OF THIS...
SO I GUESS IF MY IDEAS DON'T EXCITE YA, GO AHEAD AND JUST FIRE ME!

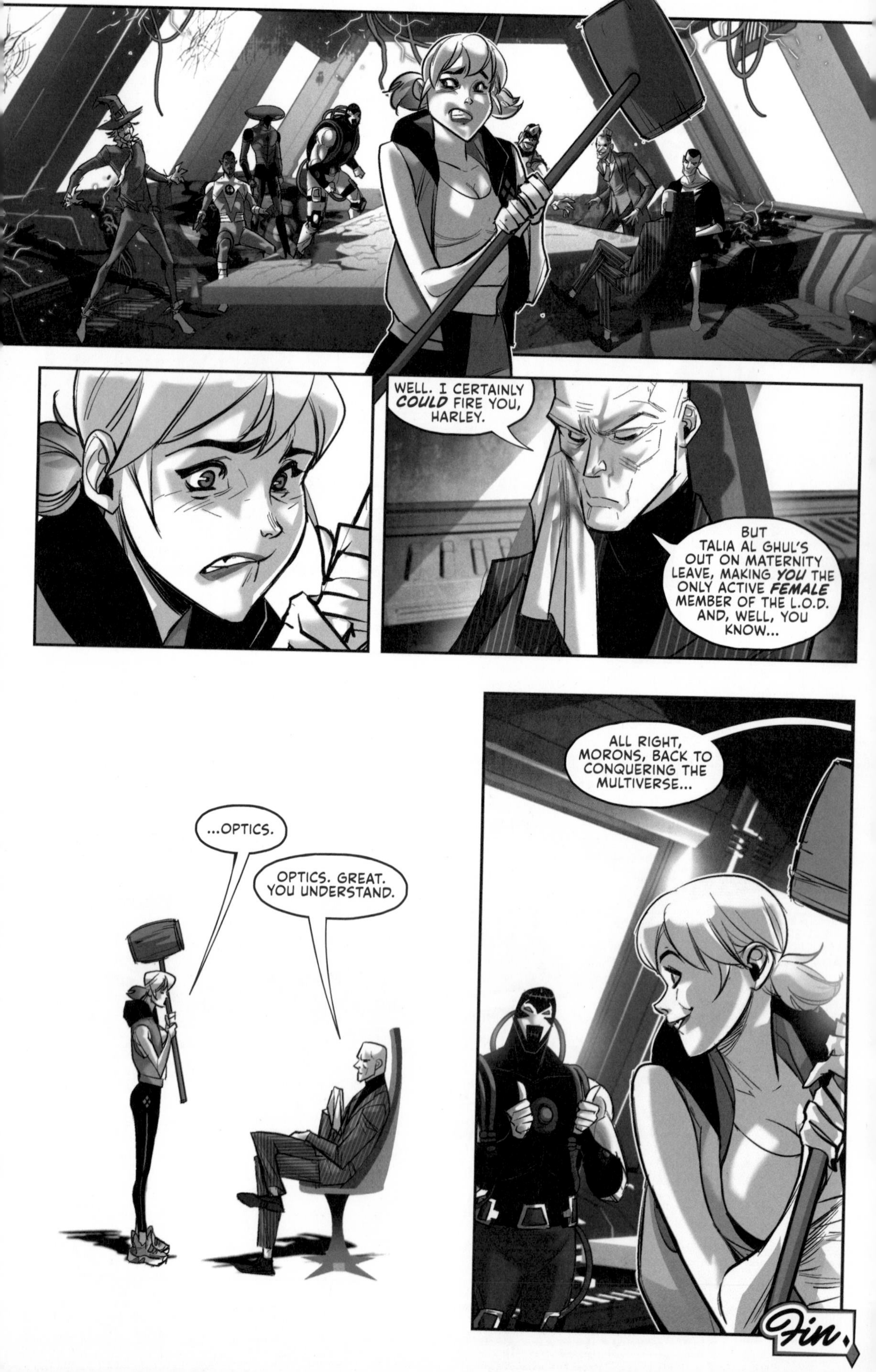
WELL. I CERTAINLY *COULD* FIRE YOU, HARLEY.
BUT TALIA AL GHUL'S OUT ON MATERNITY LEAVE, MAKING *YOU* THE ONLY ACTIVE *FEMALE* MEMBER OF THE L.O.D. AND, WELL, YOU KNOW...
...OPTICS.
OPTICS. GREAT. YOU UNDERSTAND.
ALL RIGHT, MORONS, BACK TO CONQUERING THE MULTIVERSE...
Fin.

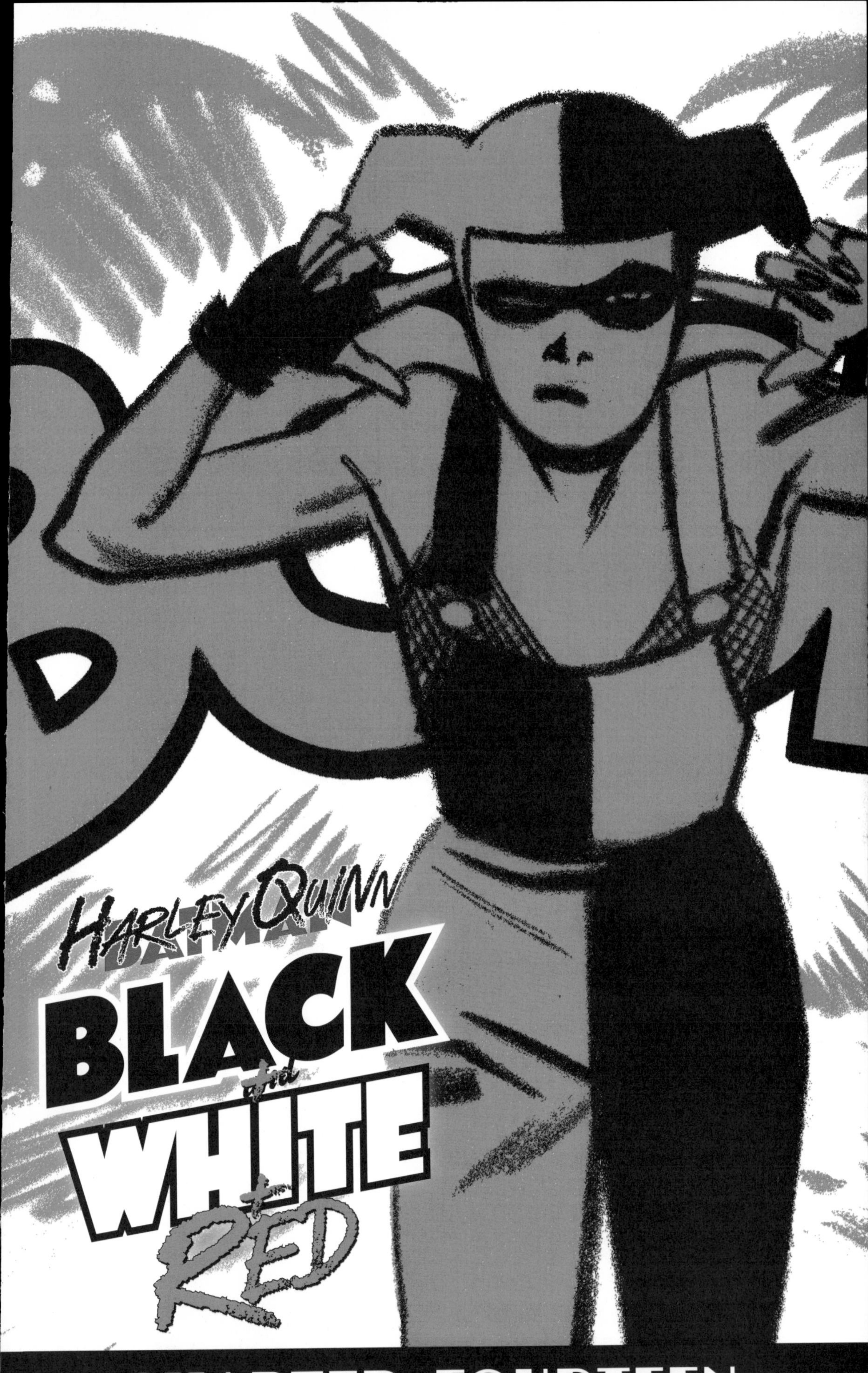
HARLEY QUINN
BLACK
and
WHITE
+
RED

CHAPTER FOURTEEN

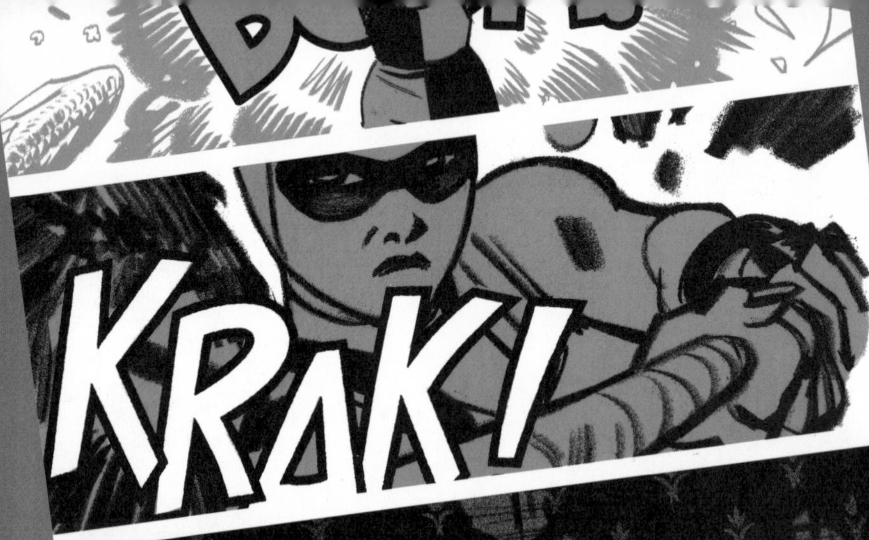
KRAK!

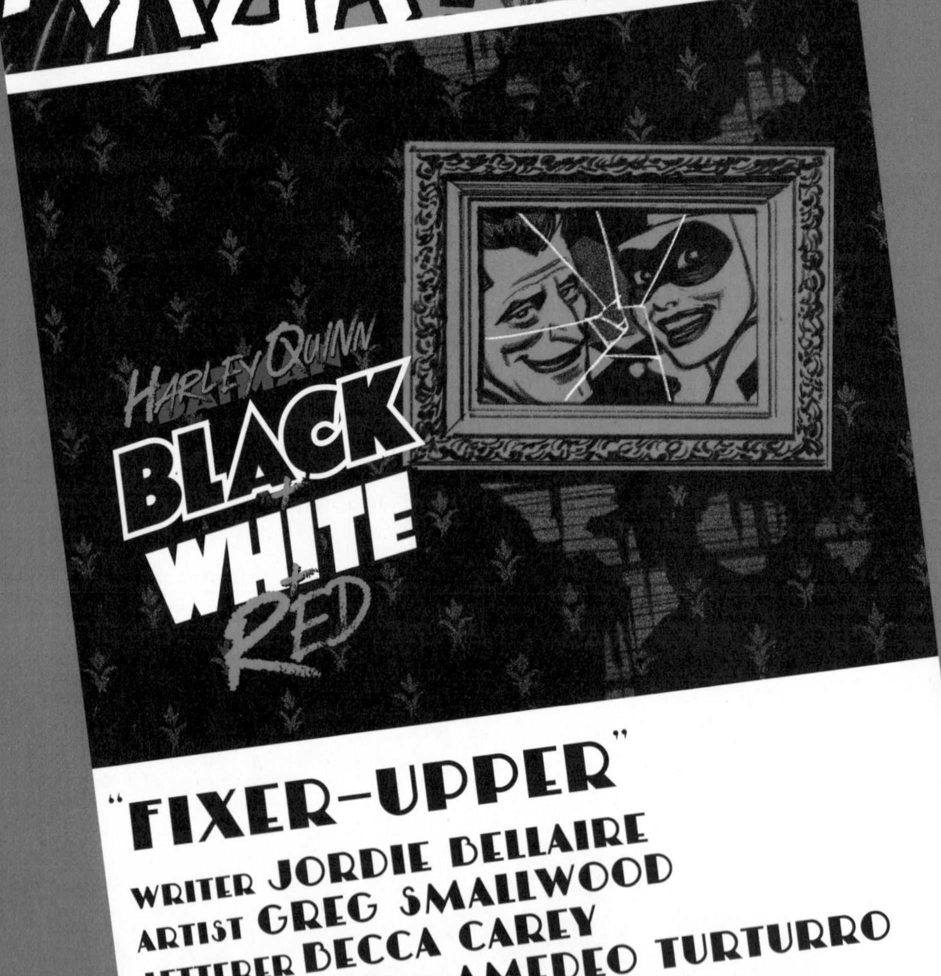
HARLEY QUINN
BLACK + WHITE + RED

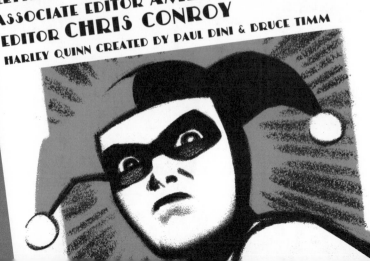

"FIXER-UPPER"

WRITER JORDIE BELLAIRE
ARTIST GREG SMALLWOOD
LETTERER BECCA CAREY
ASSOCIATE EDITOR AMEDEO TURTURRO
EDITOR CHRIS CONROY

HARLEY QUINN CREATED BY PAUL DINI & BRUCE TIMM

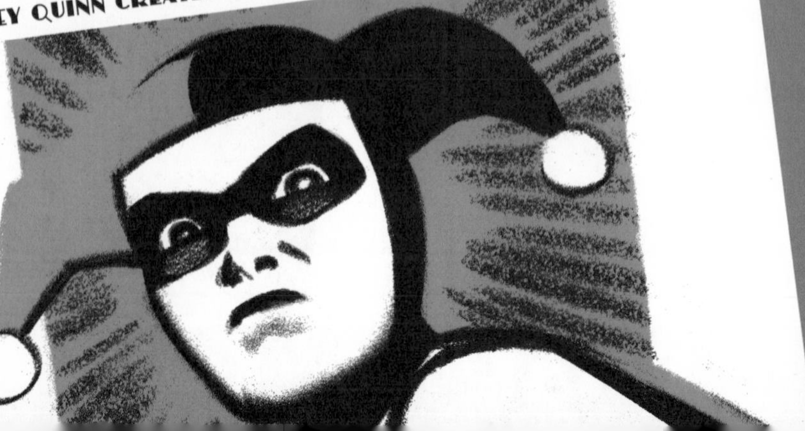

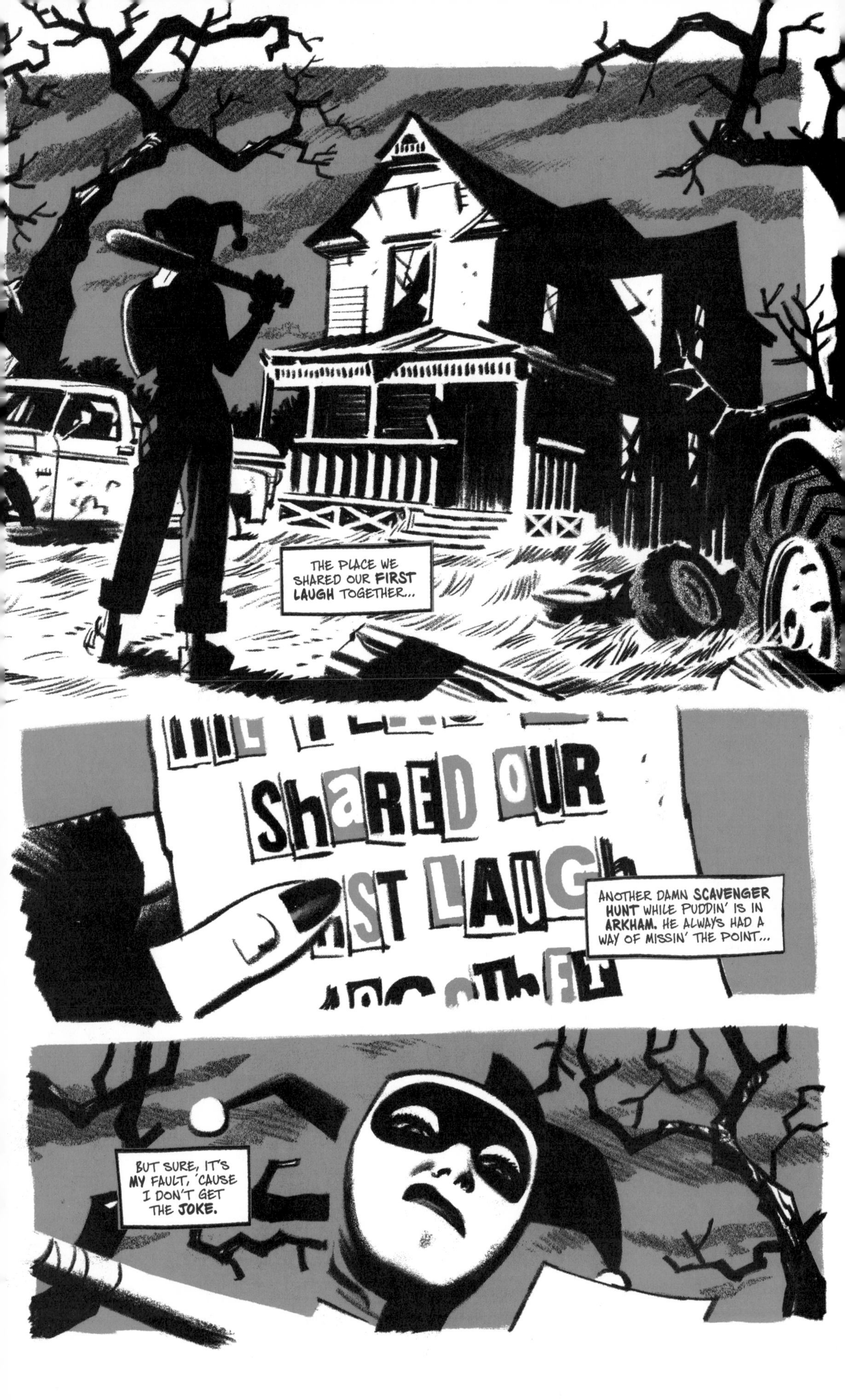

THE PLACE WE SHARED OUR **FIRST LAUGH** TOGETHER...
SHARED OUR
ST LAUGH
ANOTHER DAMN **SCAVENGER HUNT** WHILE PUDDIN' IS IN **ARKHAM.** HE ALWAYS HAD A WAY OF MISSIN' THE POINT...
BUT SURE, IT'S **MY** FAULT, 'CAUSE I DON'T GET THE **JOKE.**

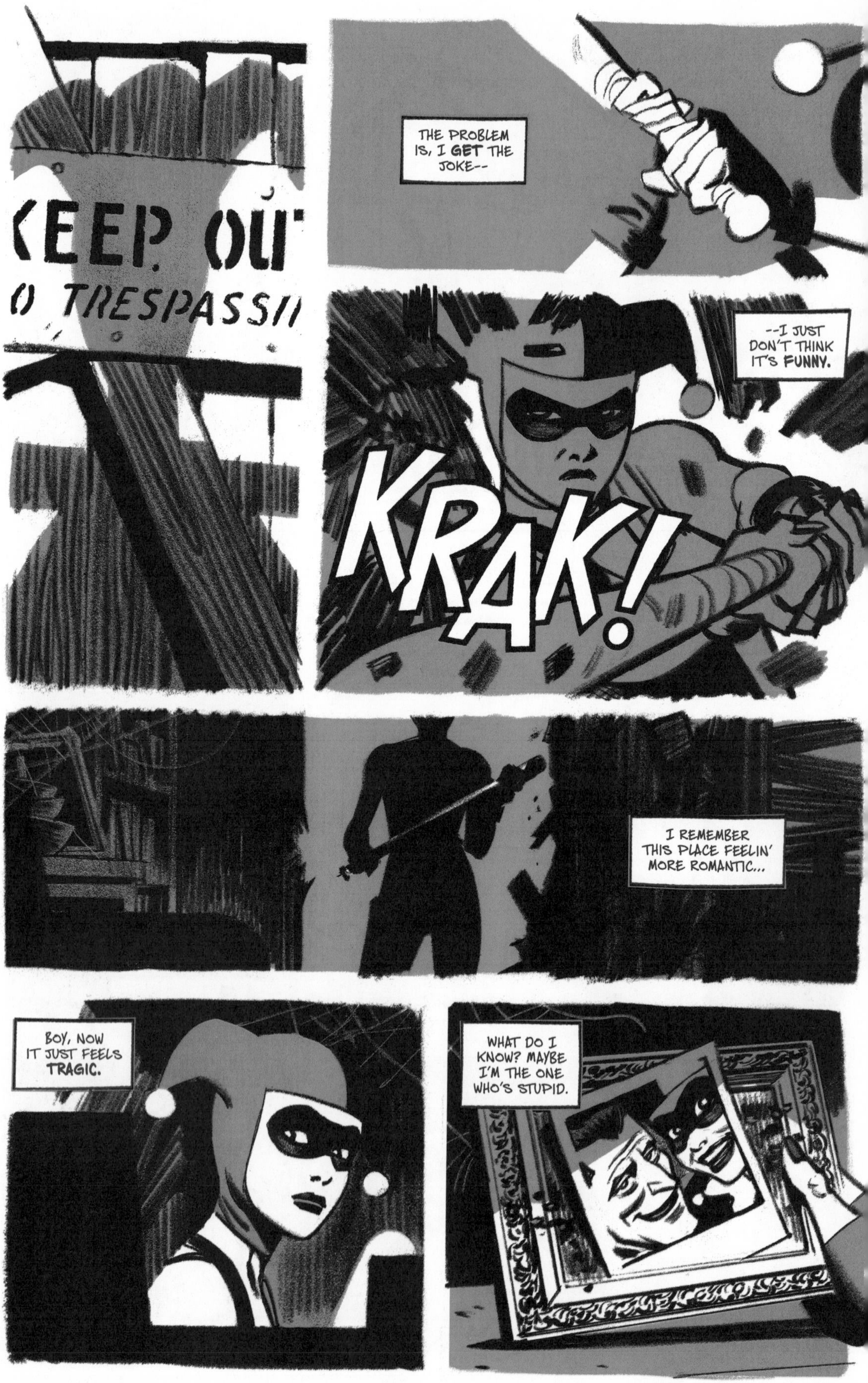
KEEP OUT
O TRESPASSI
THE PROBLEM IS, I GET THE JOKE--
--I JUST DON'T THINK IT'S FUNNY.
KRAK!
I REMEMBER THIS PLACE FEELIN' MORE ROMANTIC...
BOY, NOW IT JUST FEELS TRAGIC.
WHAT DO I KNOW? MAYBE I'M THE ONE WHO'S STUPID.

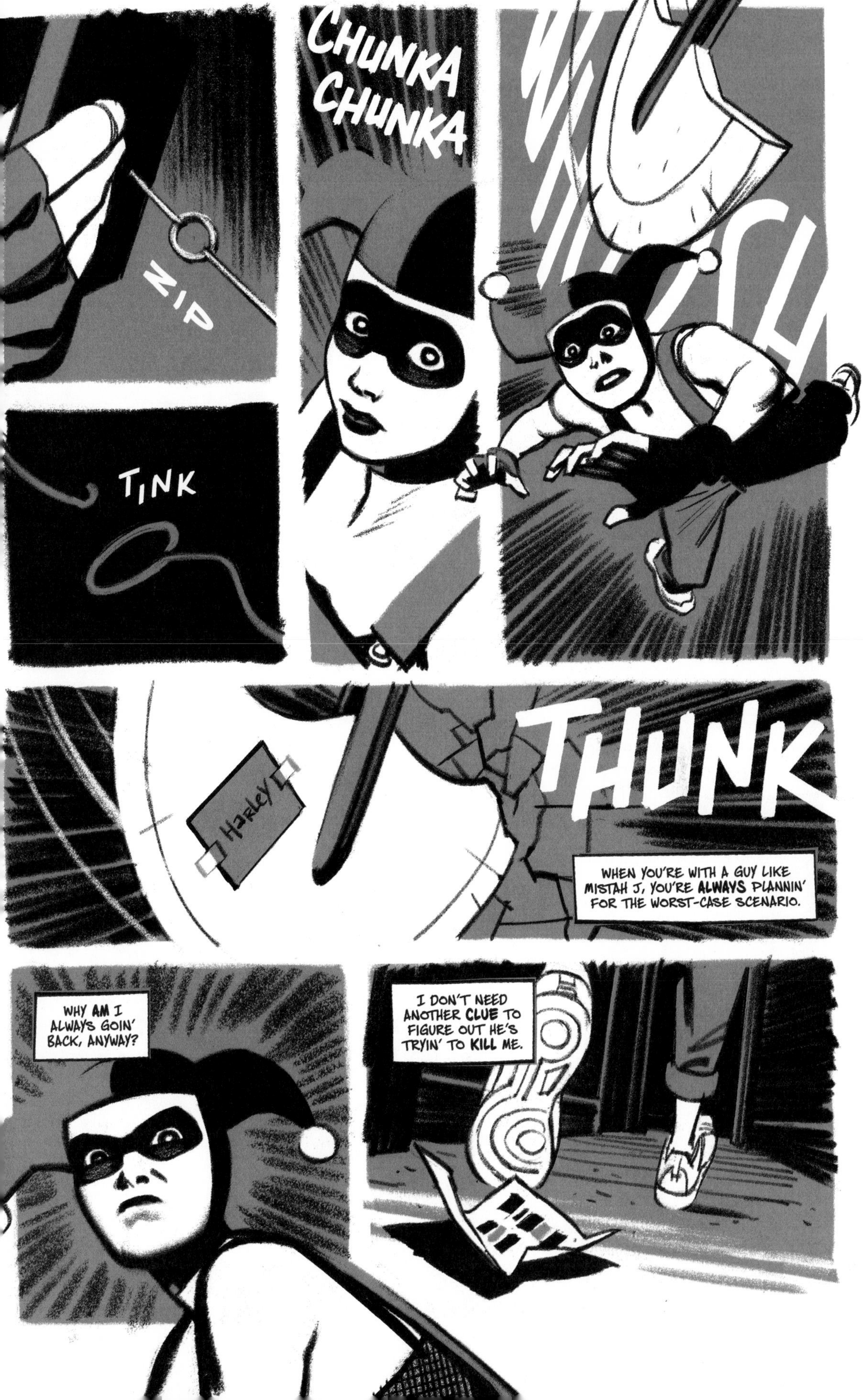
ZIP
TINK
CHUNKA CHUNKA
THUNK
Harley
WHEN YOU'RE WITH A GUY LIKE MISTAH J, YOU'RE ALWAYS PLANNIN' FOR THE WORST-CASE SCENARIO.
WHY AM I ALWAYS GOIN' BACK, ANYWAY?
I DON'T NEED ANOTHER CLUE TO FIGURE OUT HE'S TRYIN' TO KILL ME.

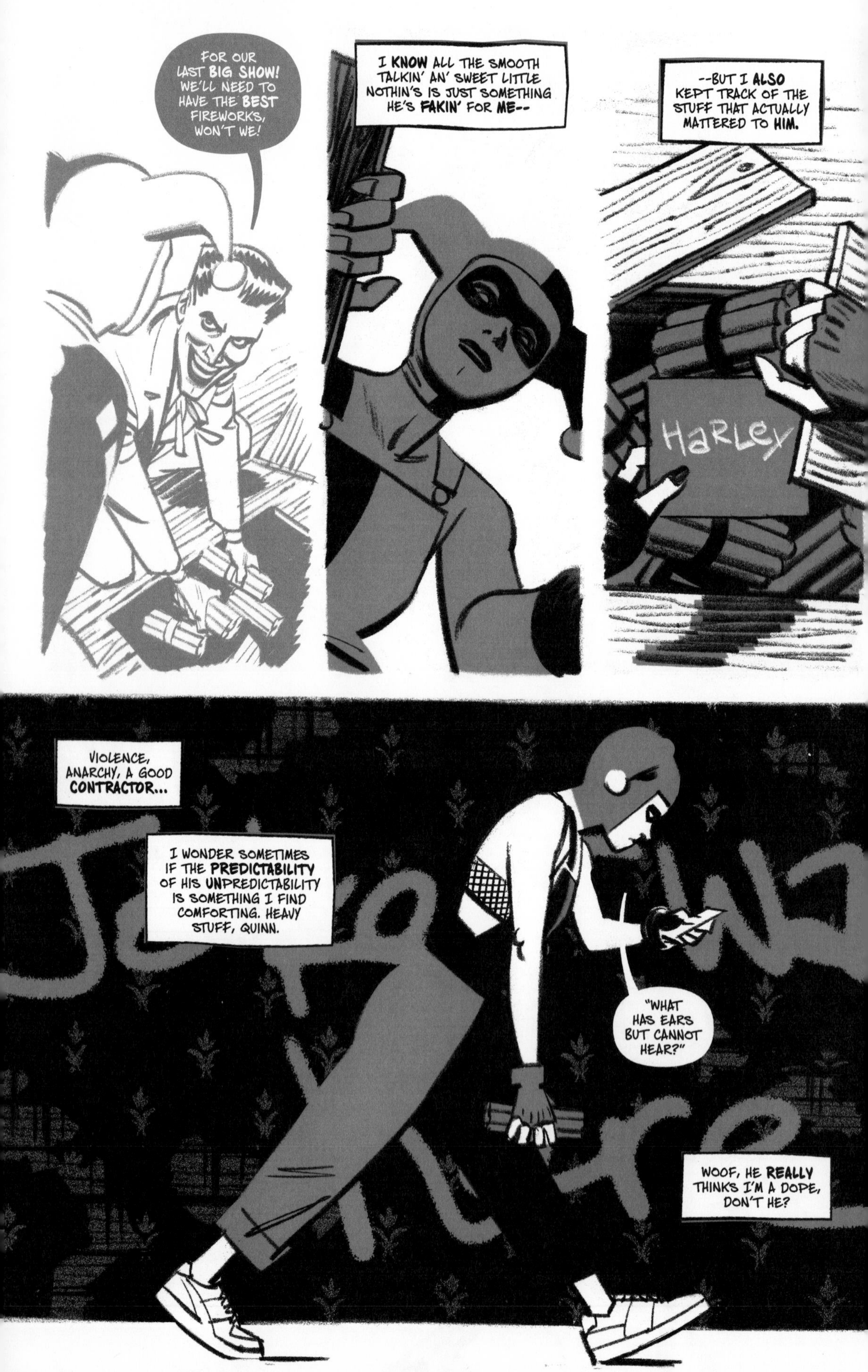

FOR OUR LAST BIG SHOW! WE'LL NEED TO HAVE THE BEST FIREWORKS, WON'T WE!
I KNOW ALL THE SMOOTH TALKIN' AN' SWEET LITTLE NOTHIN'S IS JUST SOMETHING HE'S FAKIN' FOR ME--
--BUT I ALSO KEPT TRACK OF THE STUFF THAT ACTUALLY MATTERED TO HIM.
HARLEY
VIOLENCE, ANARCHY, A GOOD CONTRACTOR...
I WONDER SOMETIMES IF THE PREDICTABILITY OF HIS UNPREDICTABILITY IS SOMETHING I FIND COMFORTING. HEAVY STUFF, QUINN.
"WHAT HAS EARS BUT CANNOT HEAR?"
WOOF, HE REALLY THINKS I'M A DOPE, DON'T HE?

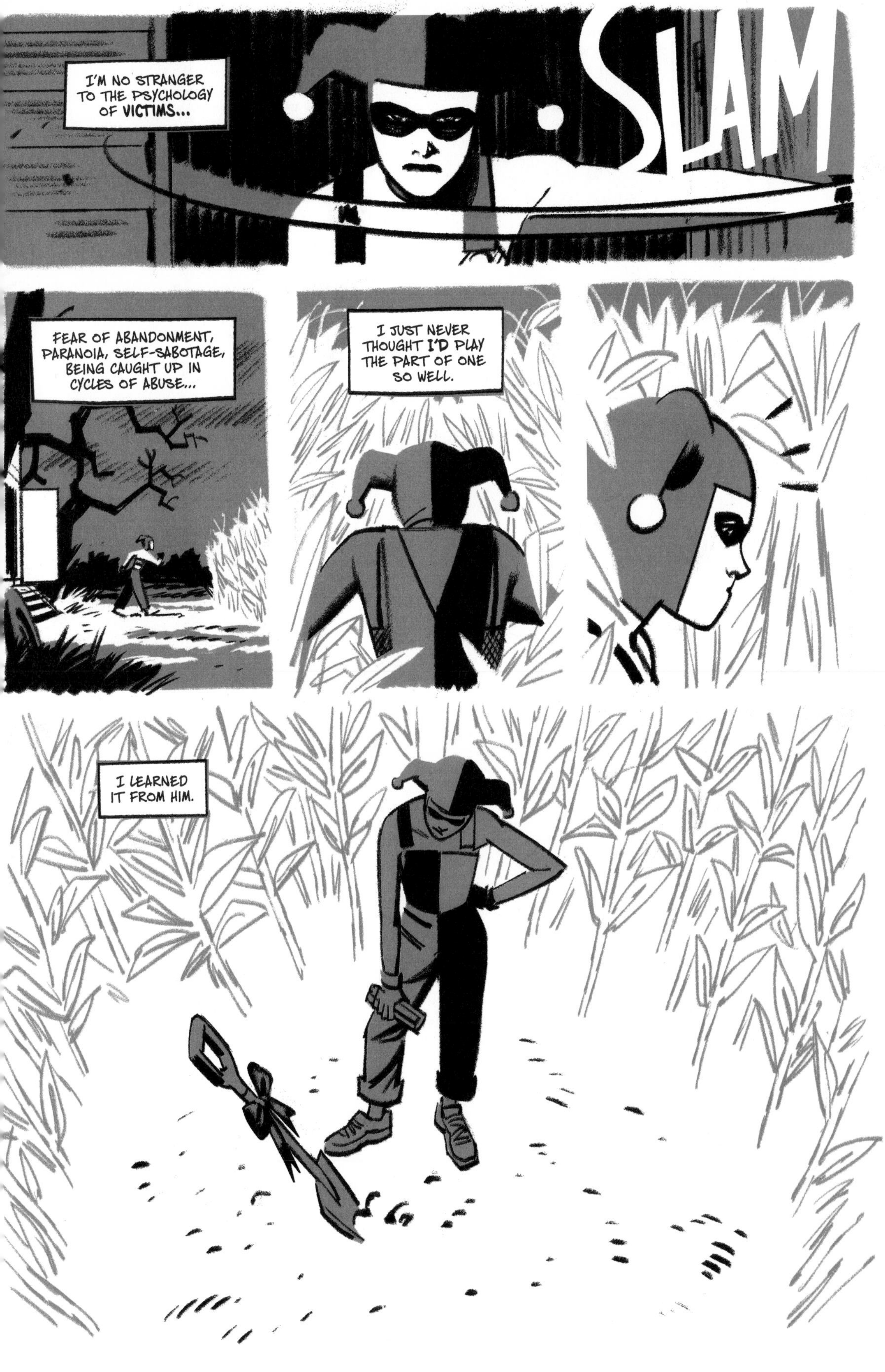
I'M NO STRANGER TO THE PSYCHOLOGY OF VICTIMS...
SLAM
FEAR OF ABANDONMENT, PARANOIA, SELF-SABOTAGE, BEING CAUGHT UP IN CYCLES OF ABUSE...
I JUST NEVER THOUGHT I'D PLAY THE PART OF ONE SO WELL.
I LEARNED IT FROM HIM.

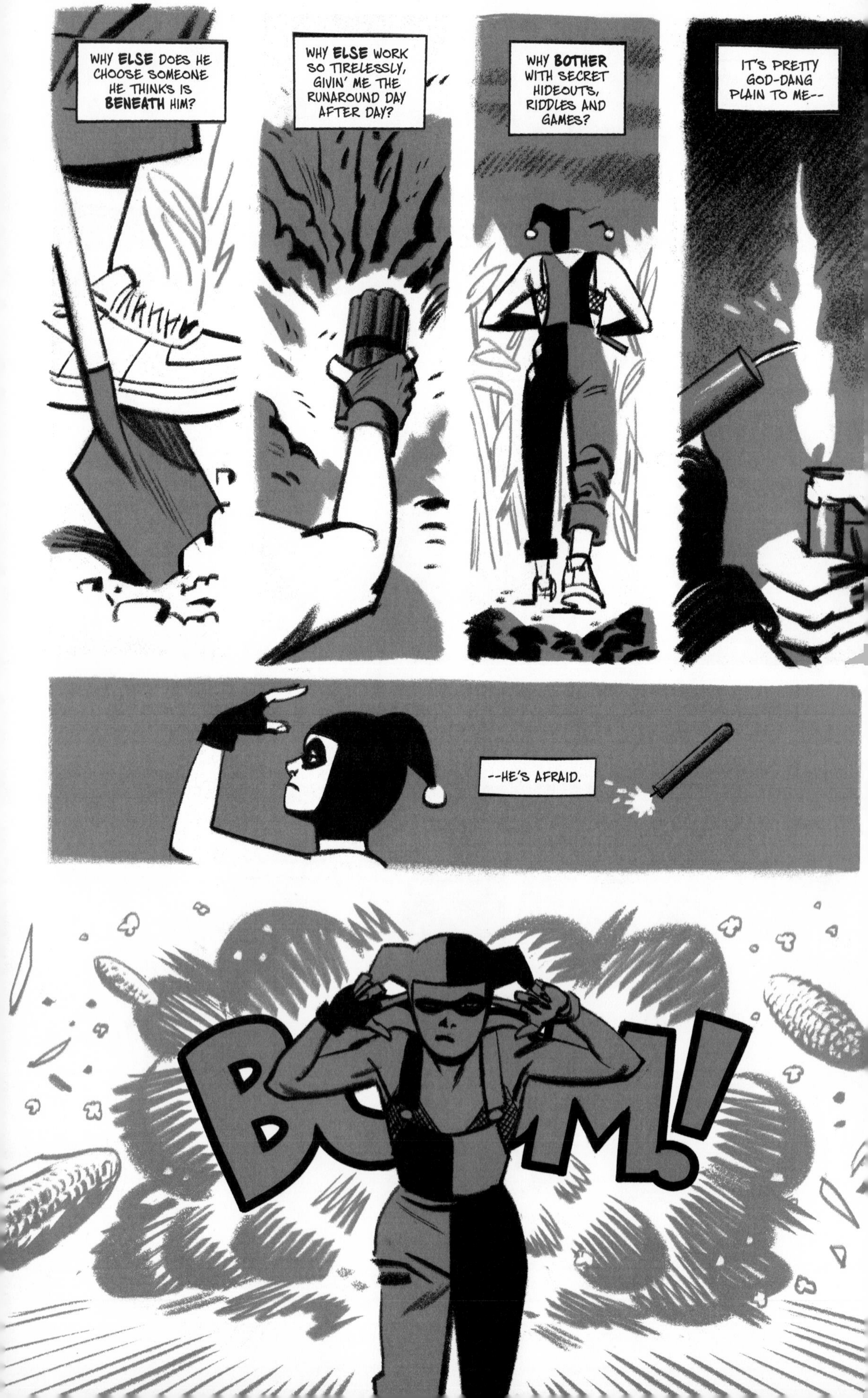
WHY ELSE DOES HE CHOOSE SOMEONE HE THINKS IS BENEATH HIM?
WHY ELSE WORK SO TIRELESSLY, GIVIN' ME THE RUNAROUND DAY AFTER DAY?
WHY BOTHER WITH SECRET HIDEOUTS, RIDDLES AND GAMES?
IT'S PRETTY GOD-DANG PLAIN TO ME--
--HE'S AFRAID.
BOOM!

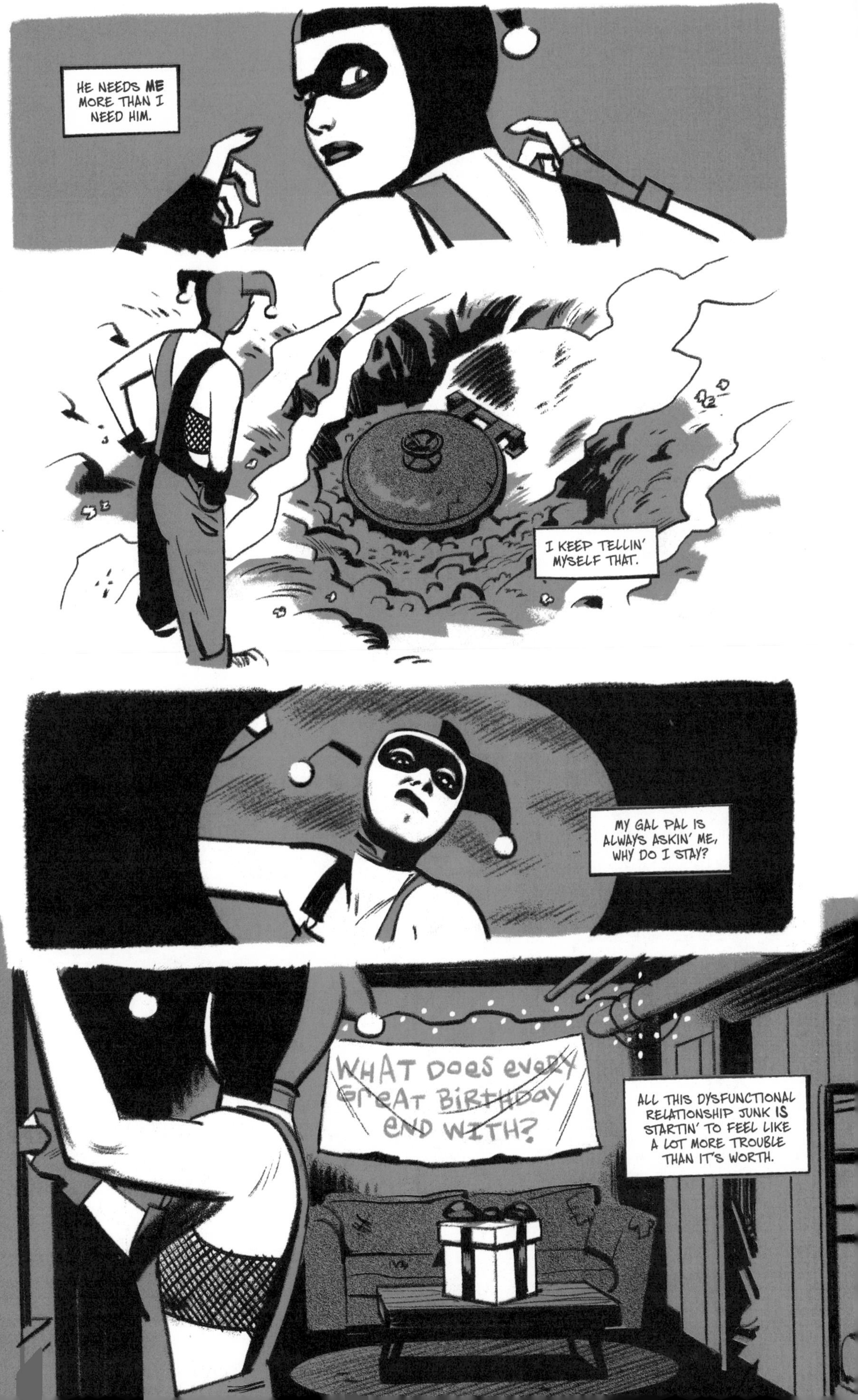
HE NEEDS ME MORE THAN I NEED HIM.
I KEEP TELLIN' MYSELF THAT.
MY GAL PAL IS ALWAYS ASKIN' ME, WHY DO I STAY?
WHAT DOes every Great BIRTHDay eND WITH?
ALL THIS DYSFUNCTIONAL RELATIONSHIP JUNK IS STARTIN' TO FEEL LIKE A LOT MORE TROUBLE THAN IT'S WORTH.

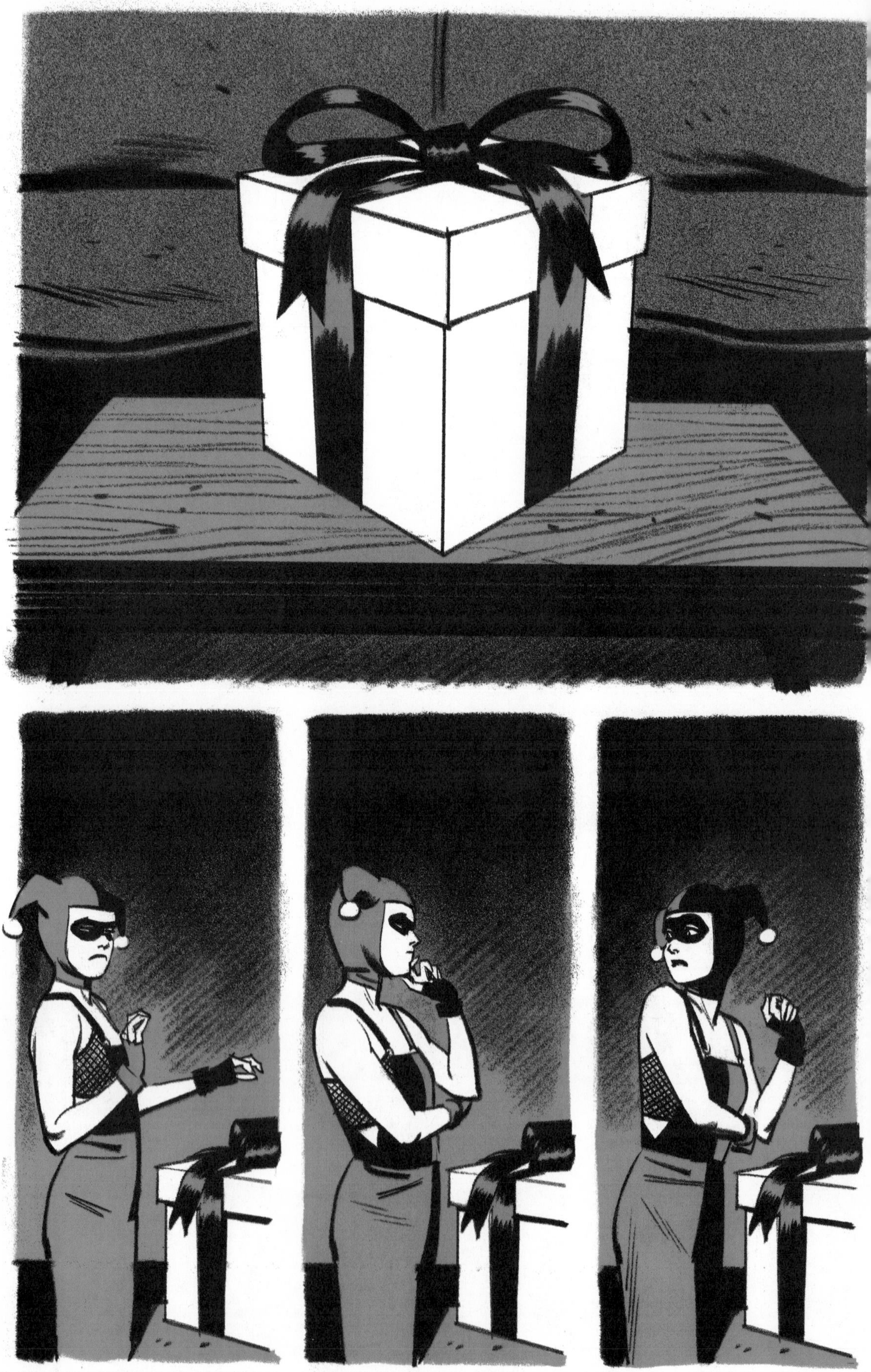

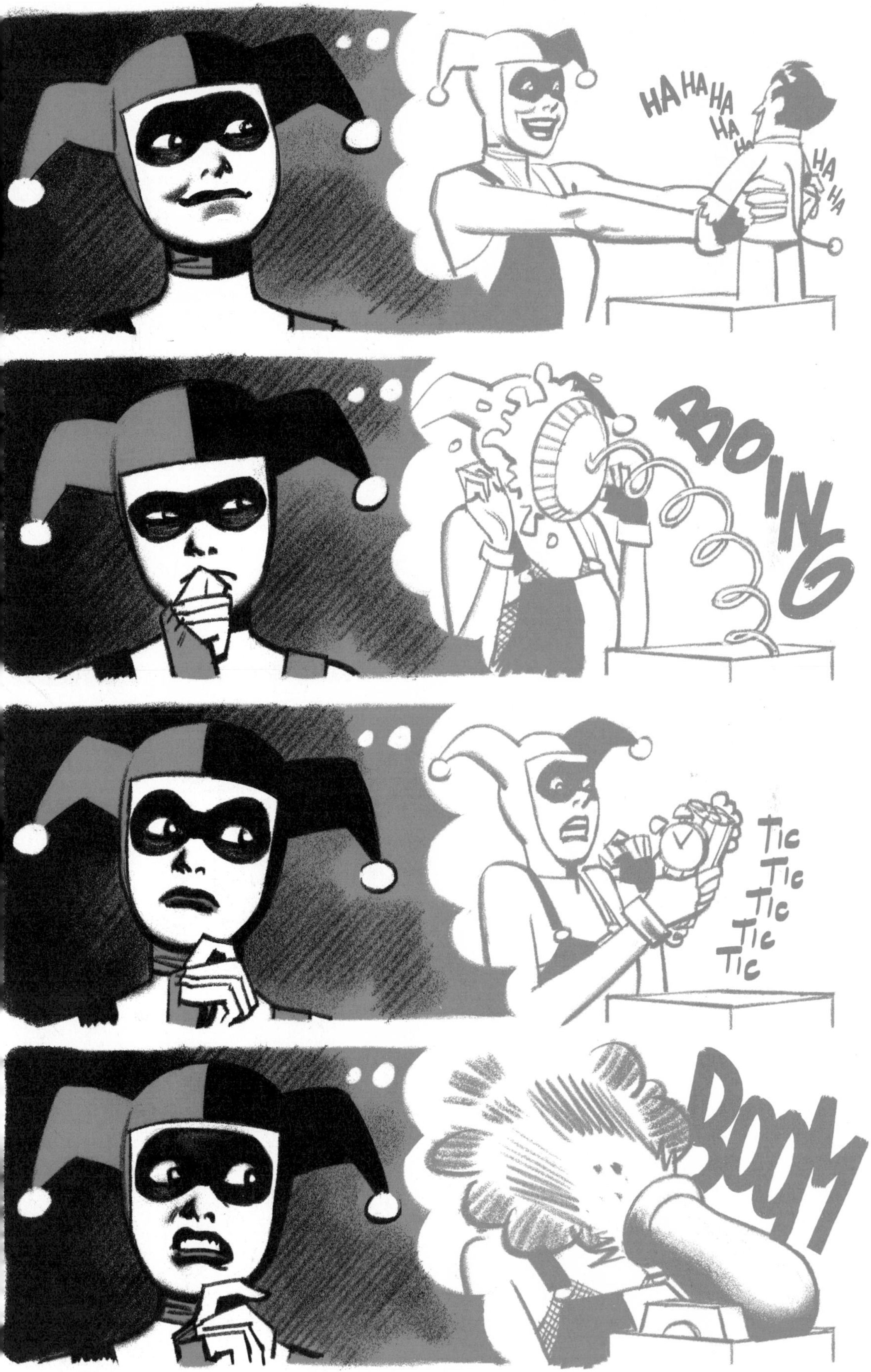

HA HA HA HA HA
HA HA HA
BOING
TIC TIC TIC TIC TIC
BOOM

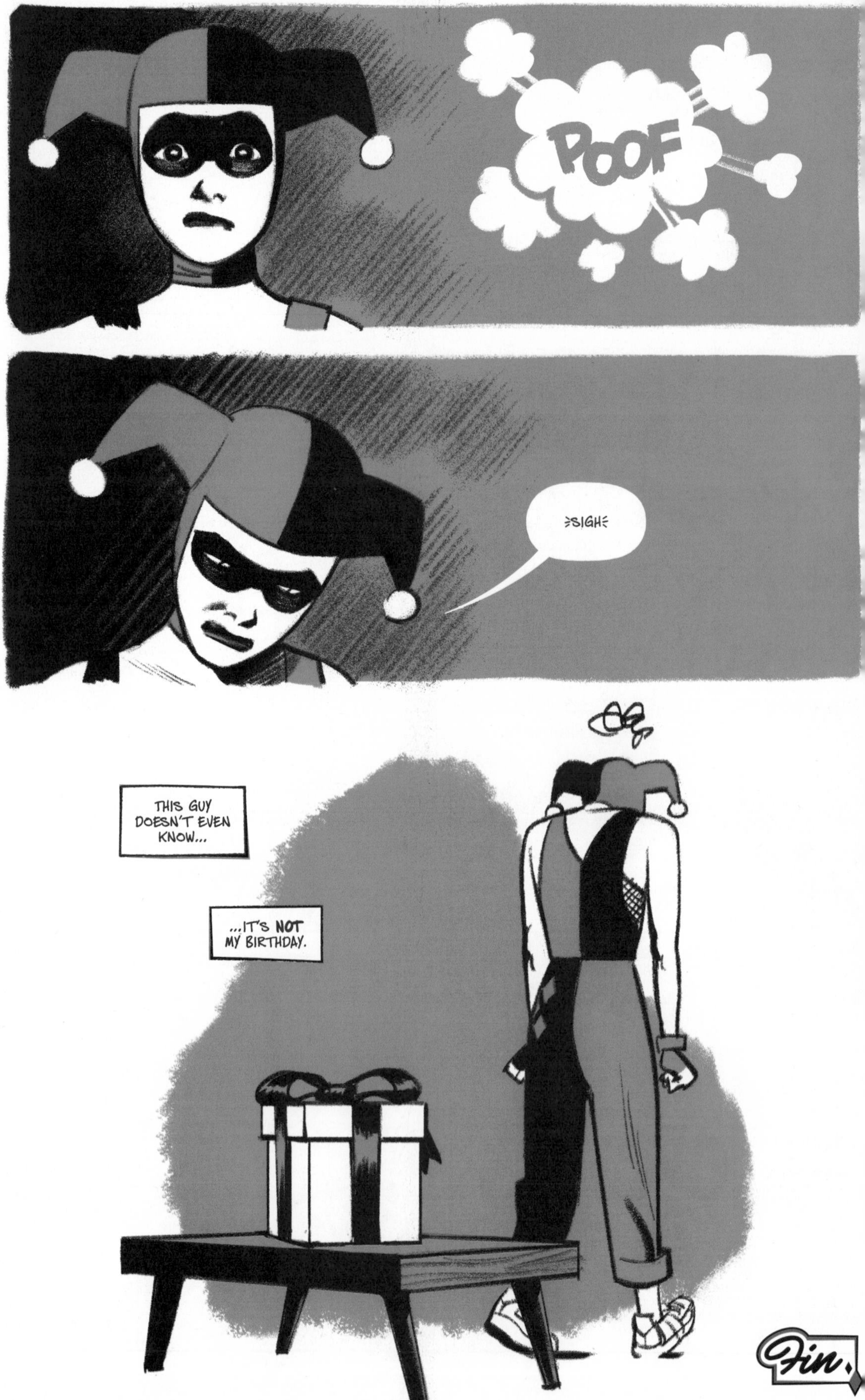
POOF
SIGH
THIS GUY DOESN'T EVEN KNOW...
...IT'S NOT MY BIRTHDAY.
Fin.

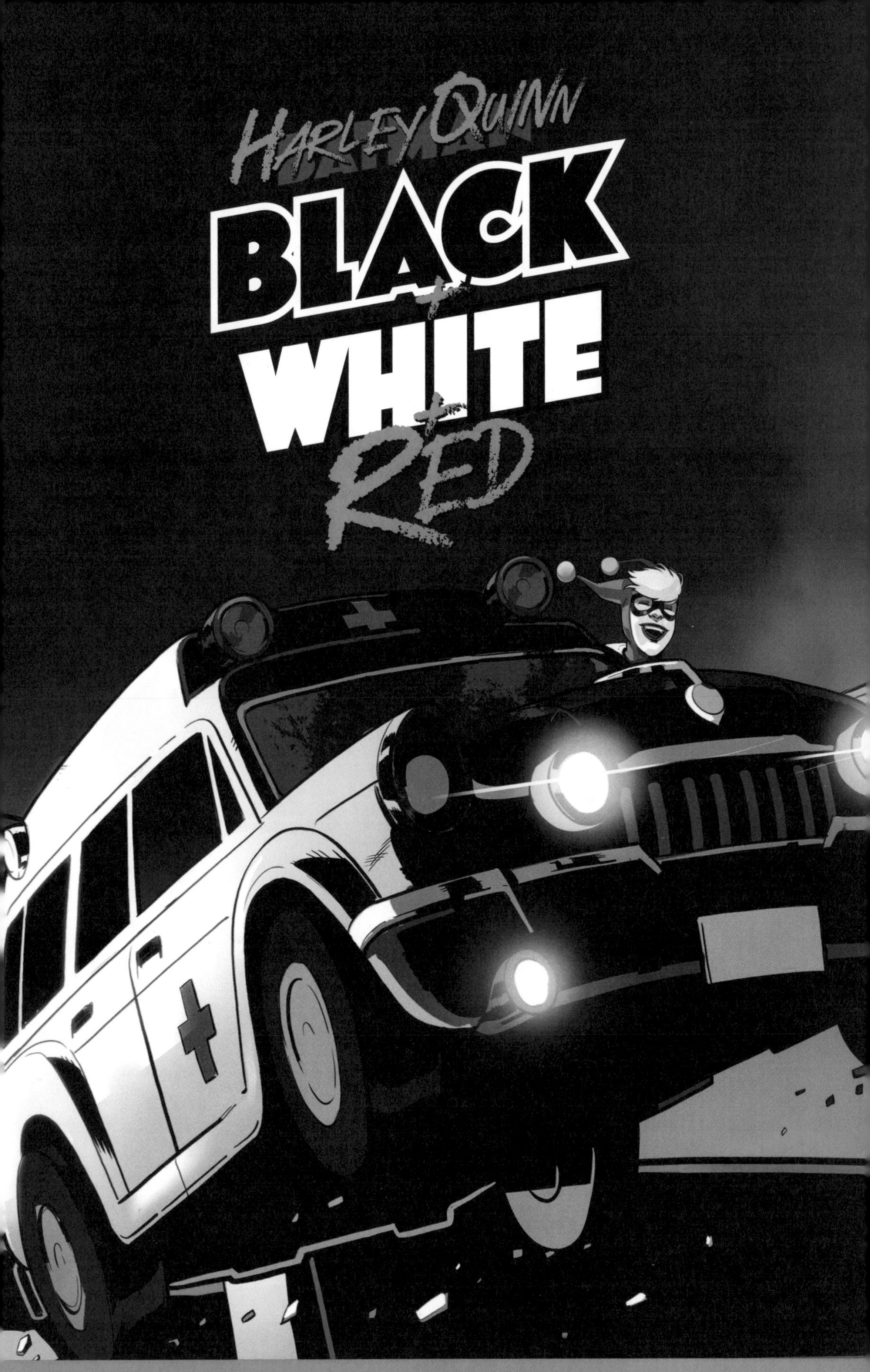
Harley Quinn
Black
+
White
+
Red

CHAPTER FIFTEEN

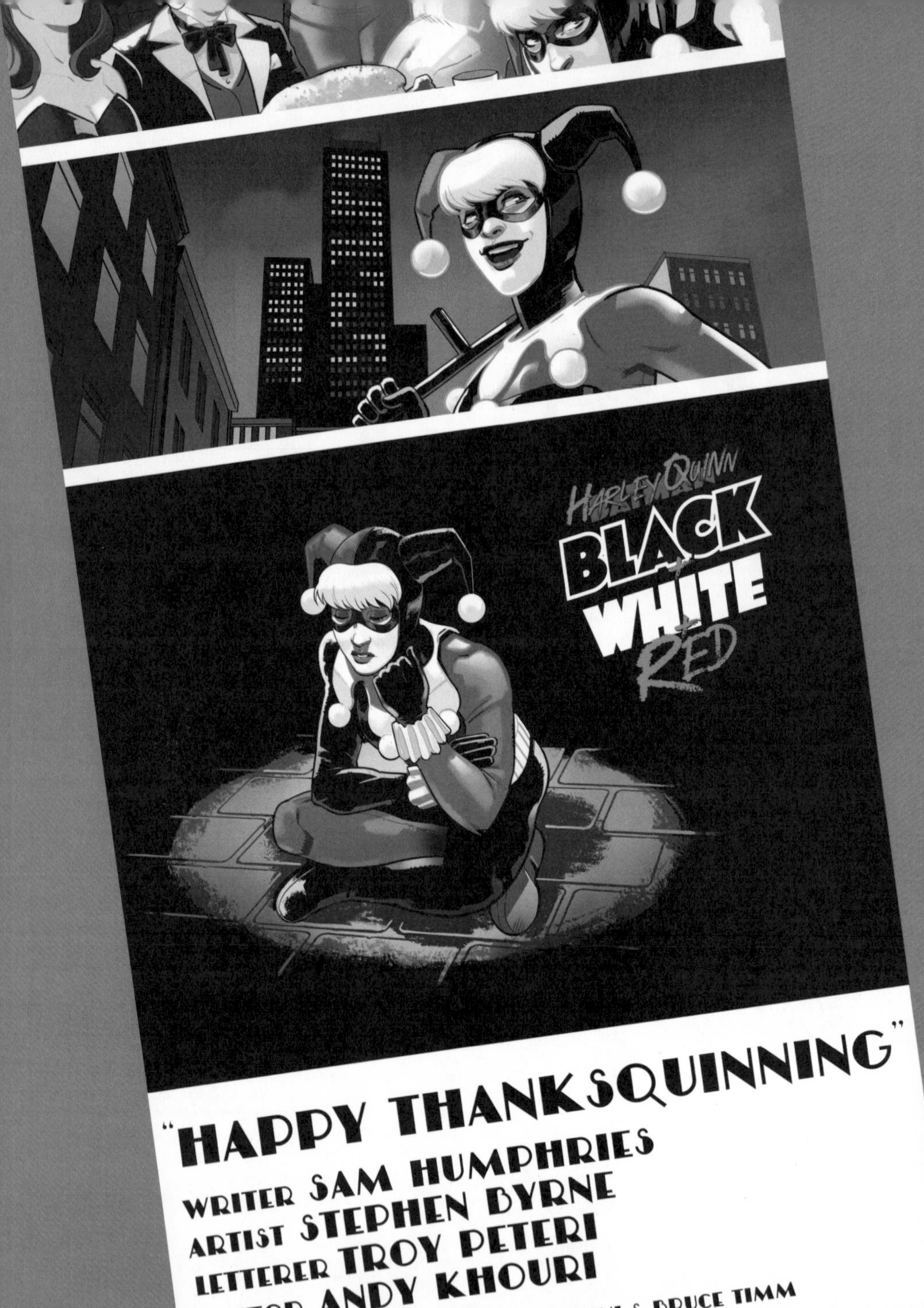
Harley Quinn
BLACK
+
WHITE
+
RED

"HAPPY THANKSQUINNING"

WRITER **SAM HUMPHRIES**
ARTIST **STEPHEN BYRNE**
LETTERER **TROY PETERI**
EDITOR **ANDY KHOURI**

HARLEY QUINN CREATED BY PAUL DINI & BRUCE TIMM

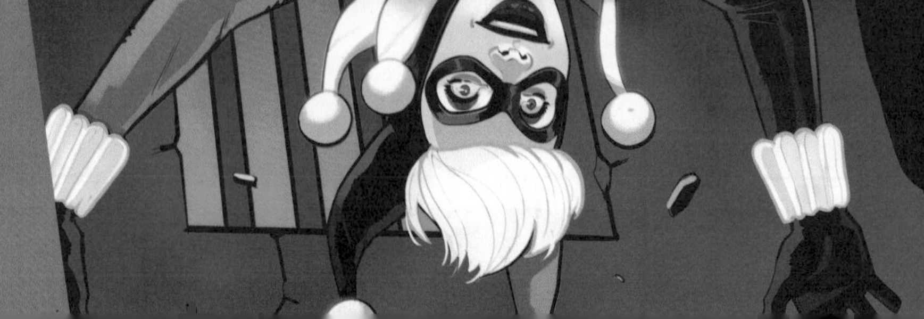

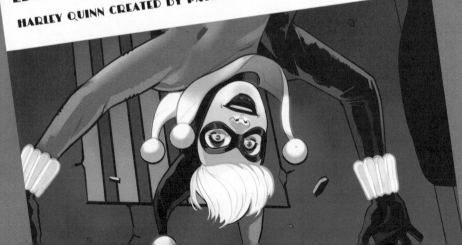

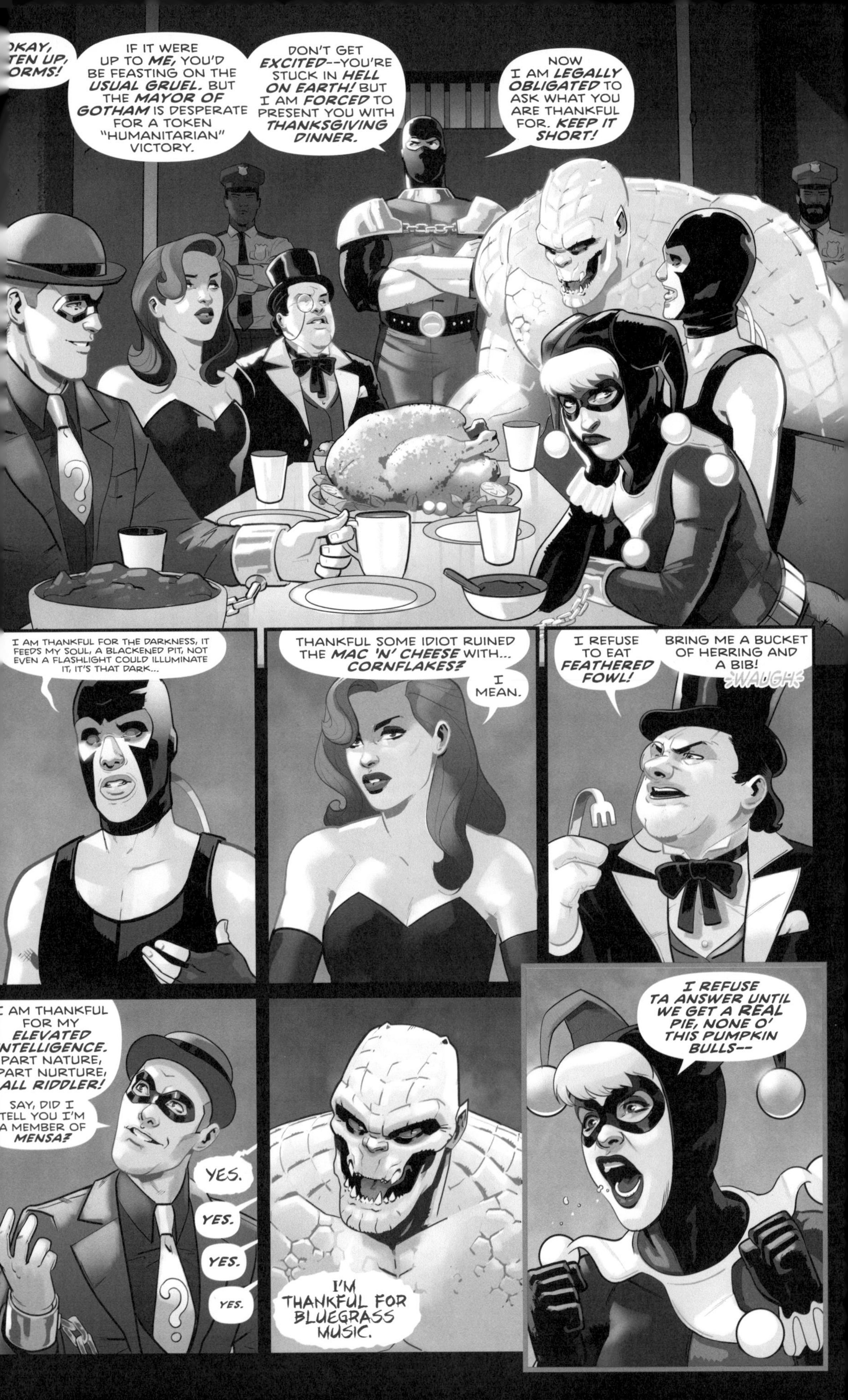
OKAY, ...TEN UP, ...ORMS!
IF IT WERE UP TO ME, YOU'D BE FEASTING ON THE USUAL GRUEL. BUT THE MAYOR OF GOTHAM IS DESPERATE FOR A TOKEN "HUMANITARIAN" VICTORY.
DON'T GET EXCITED--YOU'RE STUCK IN HELL ON EARTH! BUT I AM FORCED TO PRESENT YOU WITH THANKSGIVING DINNER.
NOW I AM LEGALLY OBLIGATED TO ASK WHAT YOU ARE THANKFUL FOR. KEEP IT SHORT!
I AM THANKFUL FOR THE DARKNESS, IT FEEDS MY SOUL, A BLACKENED PIT, NOT EVEN A FLASHLIGHT COULD ILLUMINATE IT, IT'S THAT DARK...
THANKFUL SOME IDIOT RUINED THE MAC 'N' CHEESE WITH... CORNFLAKES?
I MEAN.
I REFUSE TO EAT FEATHERED FOWL!
BRING ME A BUCKET OF HERRING AND A BIB!
WAUGH
I AM THANKFUL FOR MY ELEVATED INTELLIGENCE. PART NATURE, PART NURTURE, ALL RIDDLER!
SAY, DID I TELL YOU I'M A MEMBER OF MENSA?
YES.
YES.
YES.
YES.
I'M THANKFUL FOR BLUEGRASS MUSIC.
I REFUSE TA ANSWER UNTIL WE GET A REAL PIE, NONE O' THIS PUMPKIN BULLS--

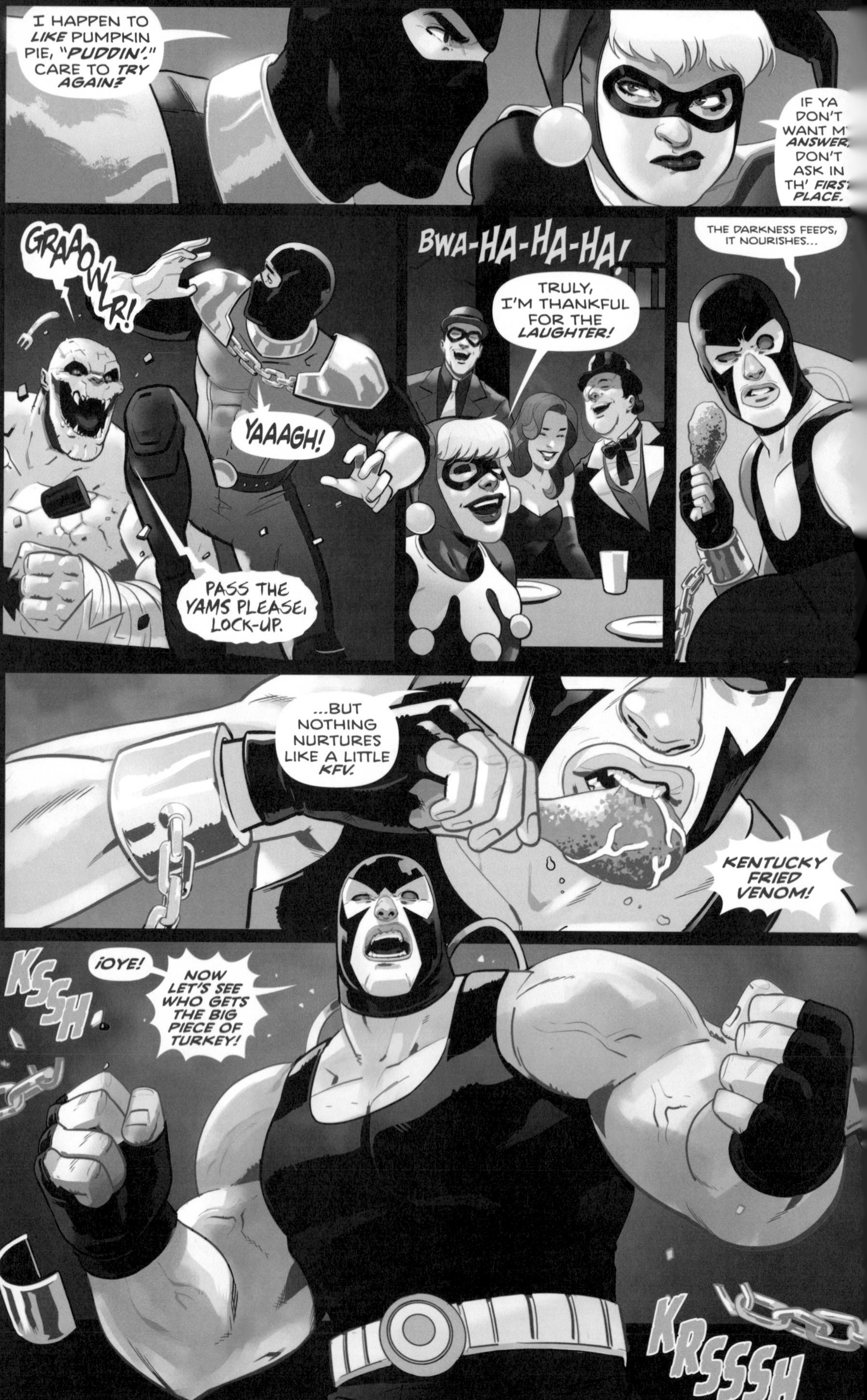

I HAPPEN TO LIKE PUMPKIN PIE, "PUDDIN'." CARE TO TRY AGAIN?
IF YA DON'T WANT M' ANSWER, DON'T ASK IN TH' FIRST PLACE.
GRAAOWLR!
YAAAGH!
PASS THE YAMS PLEASE, LOCK-UP.
BWA-HA-HA-HA!
TRULY, I'M THANKFUL FOR THE LAUGHTER!
THE DARKNESS FEEDS, IT NOURISHES...
...BUT NOTHING NURTURES LIKE A LITTLE KFV.
KENTUCKY FRIED VENOM!
KSSH
¡OYE!
NOW LET'S SEE WHO GETS THE BIG PIECE OF TURKEY!
KRSSSH

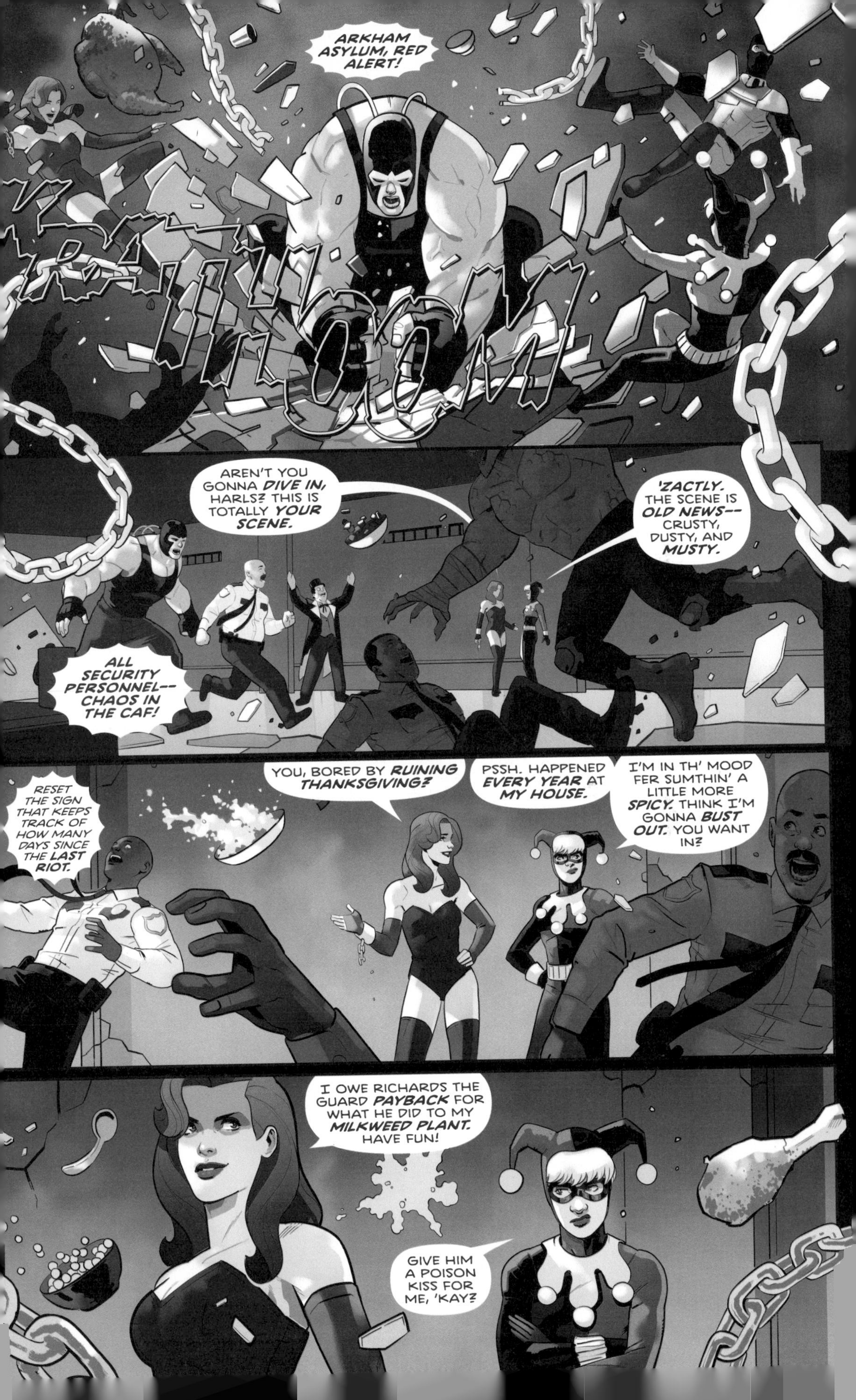

ARKHAM ASYLUM, RED ALERT!
KRA-THOOOM!
AREN'T YOU GONNA DIVE IN, HARLS? THIS IS TOTALLY YOUR SCENE.
'ZACTLY. THE SCENE IS OLD NEWS-- CRUSTY, DUSTY, AND MUSTY.
ALL SECURITY PERSONNEL-- CHAOS IN THE CAF!
RESET THE SIGN THAT KEEPS TRACK OF HOW MANY DAYS SINCE THE LAST RIOT.
YOU, BORED BY RUINING THANKSGIVING?
PSSH. HAPPENED EVERY YEAR AT MY HOUSE.
I'M IN TH' MOOD FER SUMTHIN' A LITTLE MORE SPICY. THINK I'M GONNA BUST OUT. YOU WANT IN?
I OWE RICHARDS THE GUARD PAYBACK FOR WHAT HE DID TO MY MILKWEED PLANT. HAVE FUN!
GIVE HIM A POISON KISS FOR ME, 'KAY?

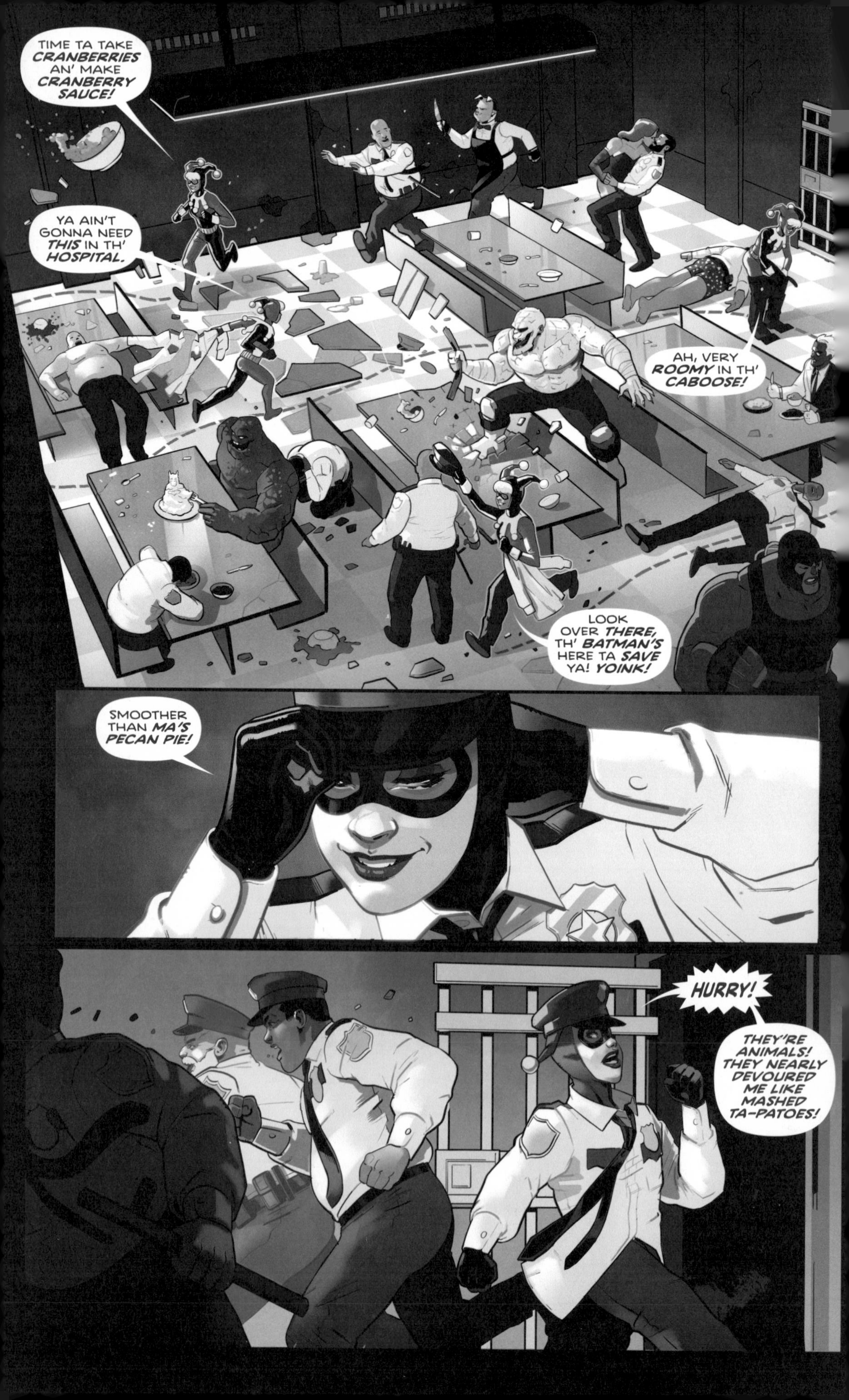
TIME TA TAKE CRANBERRIES AN' MAKE CRANBERRY SAUCE!
YA AIN'T GONNA NEED THIS IN TH' HOSPITAL.
AH, VERY ROOMY IN TH' CABOOSE!
LOOK OVER THERE, TH' BATMAN'S HERE TA SAVE YA! YOINK!
SMOOTHER THAN MA'S PECAN PIE!
HURRY!
THEY'RE ANIMALS! THEY NEARLY DEVOURED ME LIKE MASHED TA-PATOES!

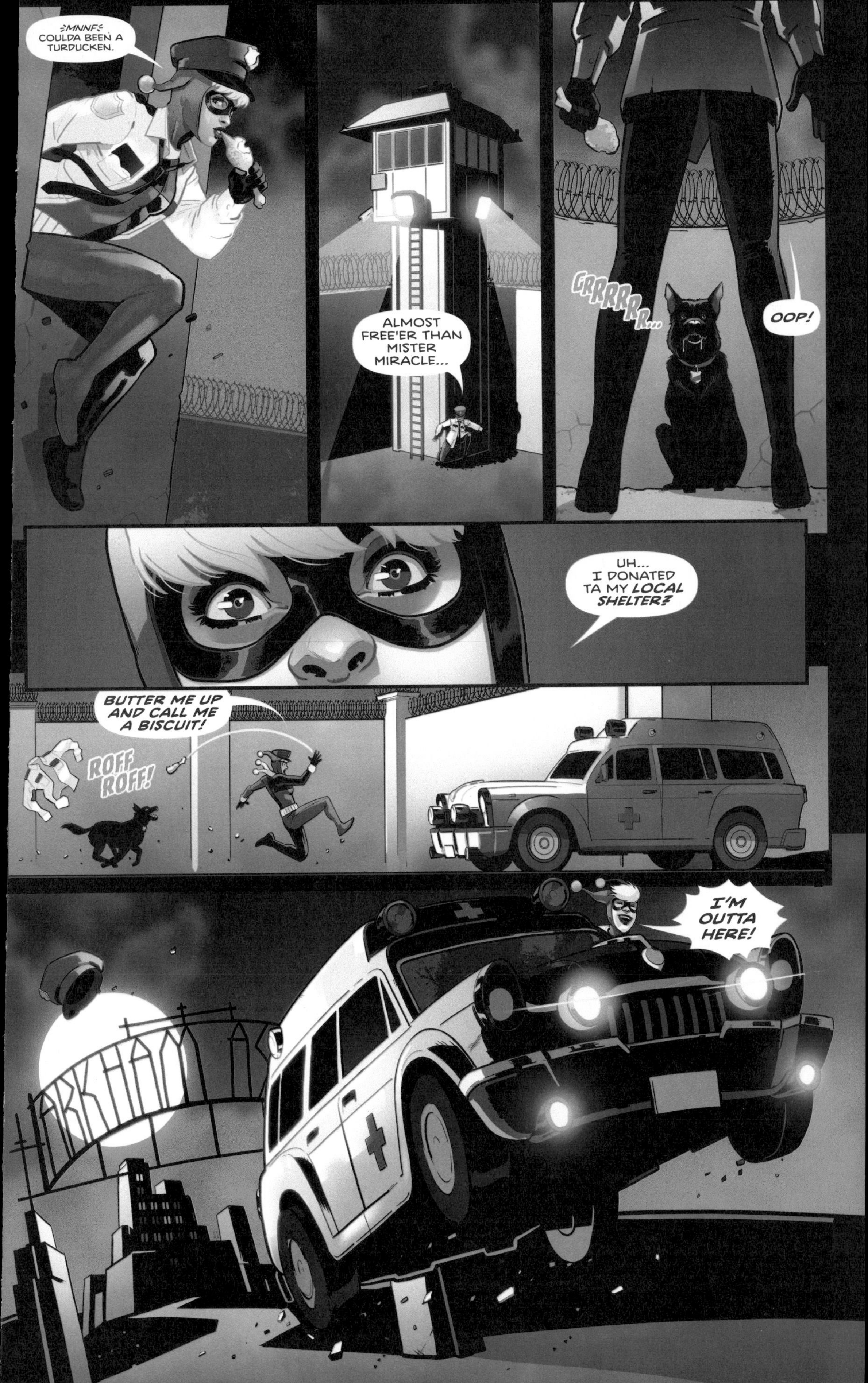

MNNF
COULDA BEEN A TURDUCKEN.
ALMOST FREE'ER THAN MISTER MIRACLE...
GRRRRRR...
OOP!
UH... I DONATED TA MY LOCAL SHELTER?
BUTTER ME UP AND CALL ME A BISCUIT!
ROFF ROFF!
I'M OUTTA HERE!
ARKHAM

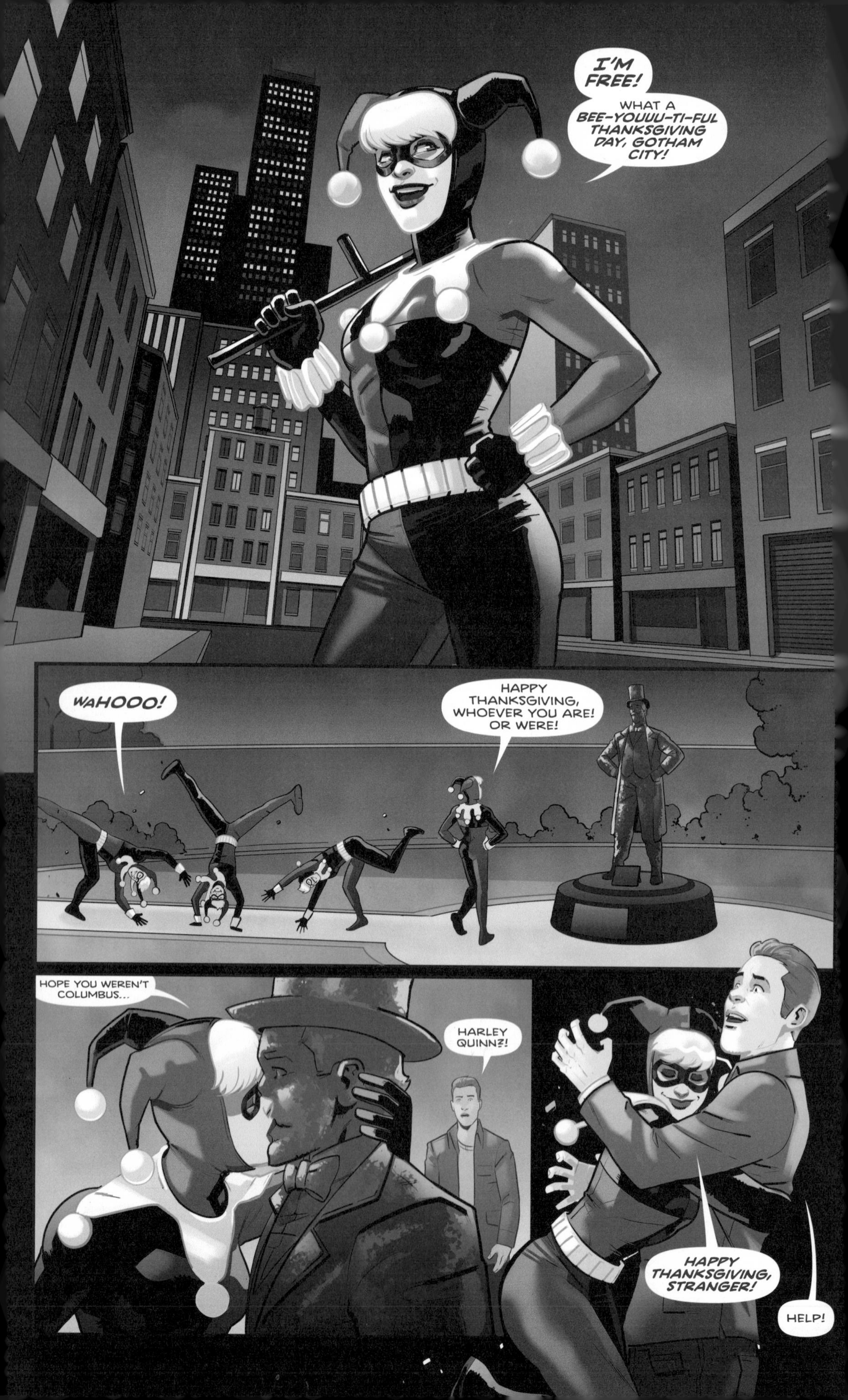
I'M FREE!
WHAT A BEE-YOUUU-TI-FUL THANKSGIVING DAY, GOTHAM CITY!
WAHOOO!
HAPPY THANKSGIVING, WHOEVER YOU ARE! OR WERE!
HOPE YOU WEREN'T COLUMBUS...
HARLEY QUINN?!
HAPPY THANKSGIVING, STRANGER!
HELP!

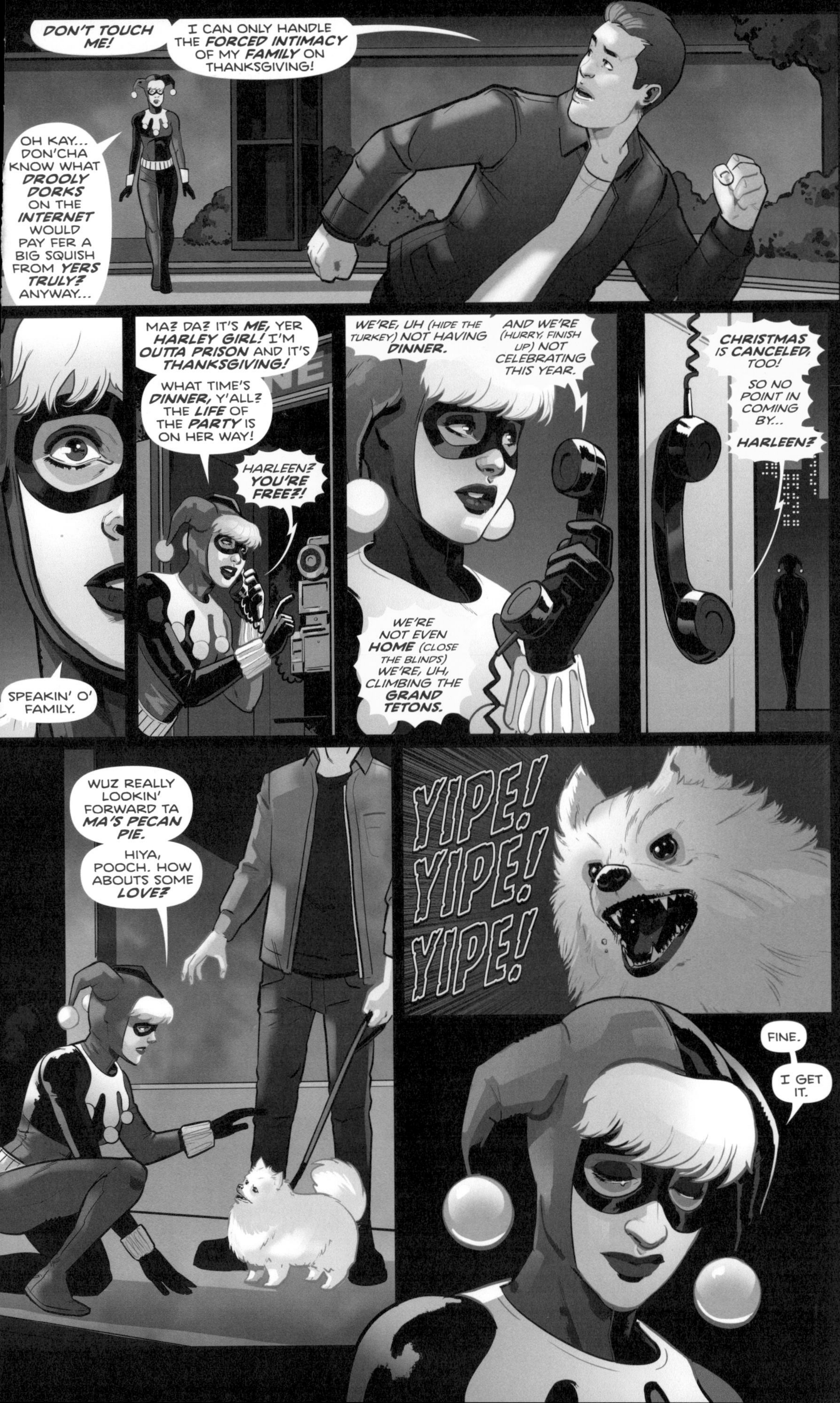

DON'T TOUCH ME!
I CAN ONLY HANDLE THE FORCED INTIMACY OF MY FAMILY ON THANKSGIVING!
OH KAY... DON'CHA KNOW WHAT DROOLY DORKS ON THE INTERNET WOULD PAY FER A BIG SQUISH FROM YERS TRULY? ANYWAY...
SPEAKIN' O' FAMILY.
MA? DA? IT'S ME, YER HARLEY GIRL! I'M OUTTA PRISON AND IT'S THANKSGIVING!
WHAT TIME'S DINNER, Y'ALL? THE LIFE OF THE PARTY IS ON HER WAY!
HARLEEN? YOU'RE FREE?!
WE'RE, UH (HIDE THE TURKEY) NOT HAVING DINNER.
AND WE'RE (HURRY, FINISH UP) NOT CELEBRATING THIS YEAR.
WE'RE NOT EVEN HOME (CLOSE THE BLINDS) WE'RE, UH, CLIMBING THE GRAND TETONS.
CHRISTMAS IS CANCELED, TOO!
SO NO POINT IN COMING BY...
HARLEEN?
WUZ REALLY LOOKIN' FORWARD TA MA'S PECAN PIE.
HIYA, POOCH. HOW ABOUTS SOME LOVE?
YIPE! YIPE! YIPE!
FINE.
I GET IT.

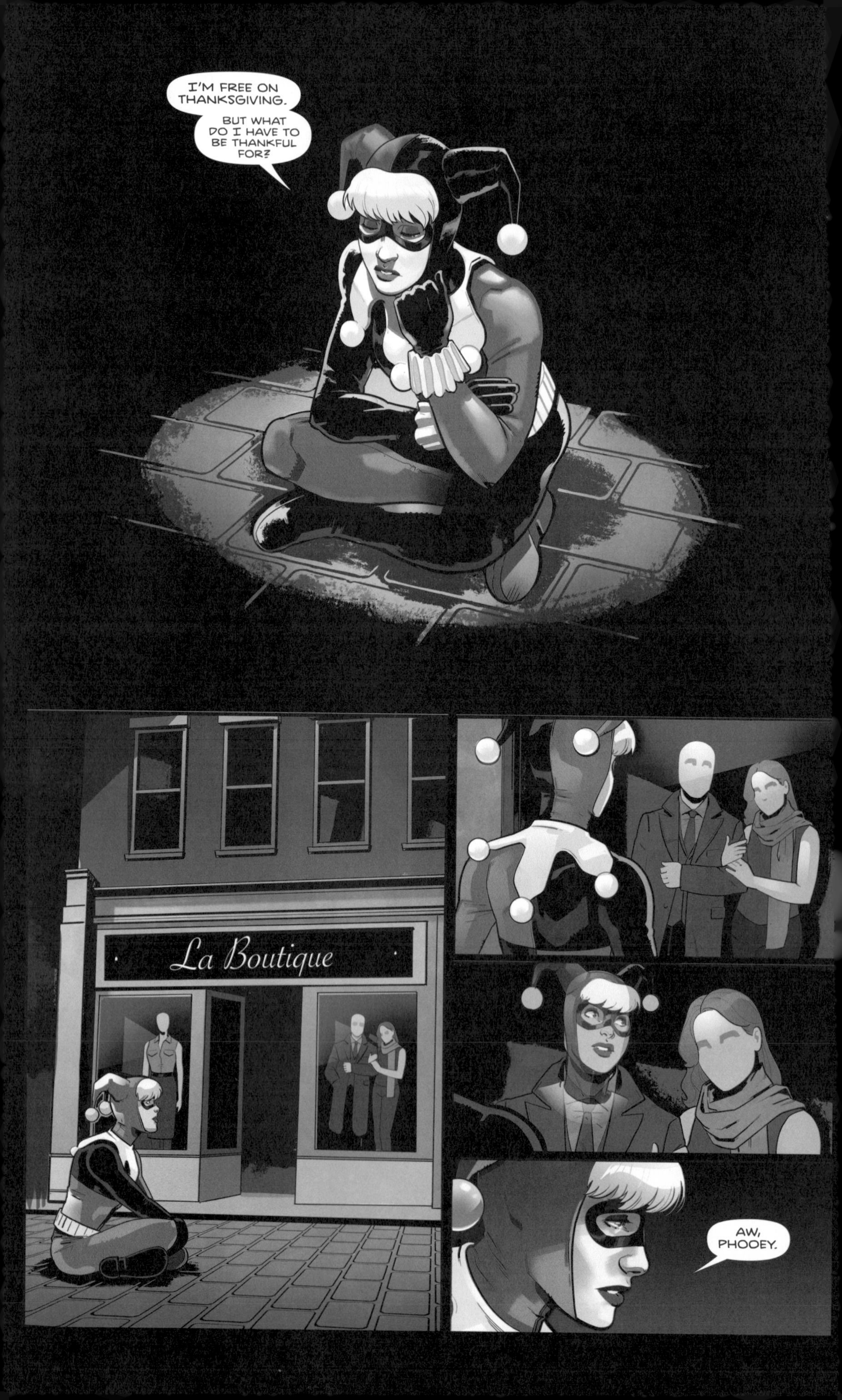
I'M FREE ON THANKSGIVING.
BUT WHAT DO I HAVE TO BE THANKFUL FOR?
La Boutique
AW, PHOOEY.

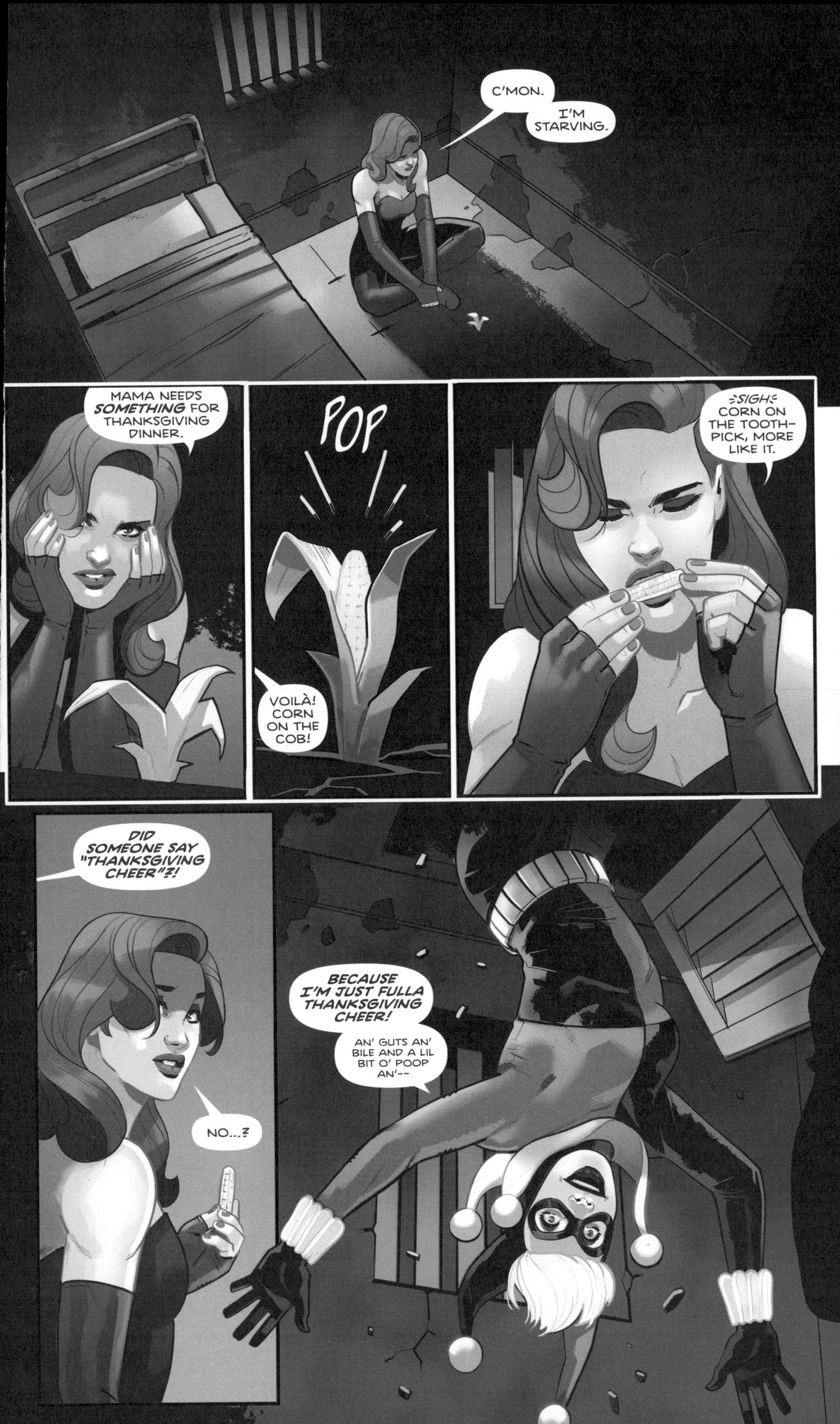
C'MON.
I'M STARVING.
MAMA NEEDS SOMETHING FOR THANKSGIVING DINNER.
POP
VOILÀ! CORN ON THE COB!
SIGH
CORN ON THE TOOTH-PICK, MORE LIKE IT.
DID SOMEONE SAY "THANKSGIVING CHEER"?!
NO...?
BECAUSE I'M JUST FULLA THANKSGIVING CHEER!
AN' GUTS AN' BILE AND A LIL BIT O' POOP AN'--

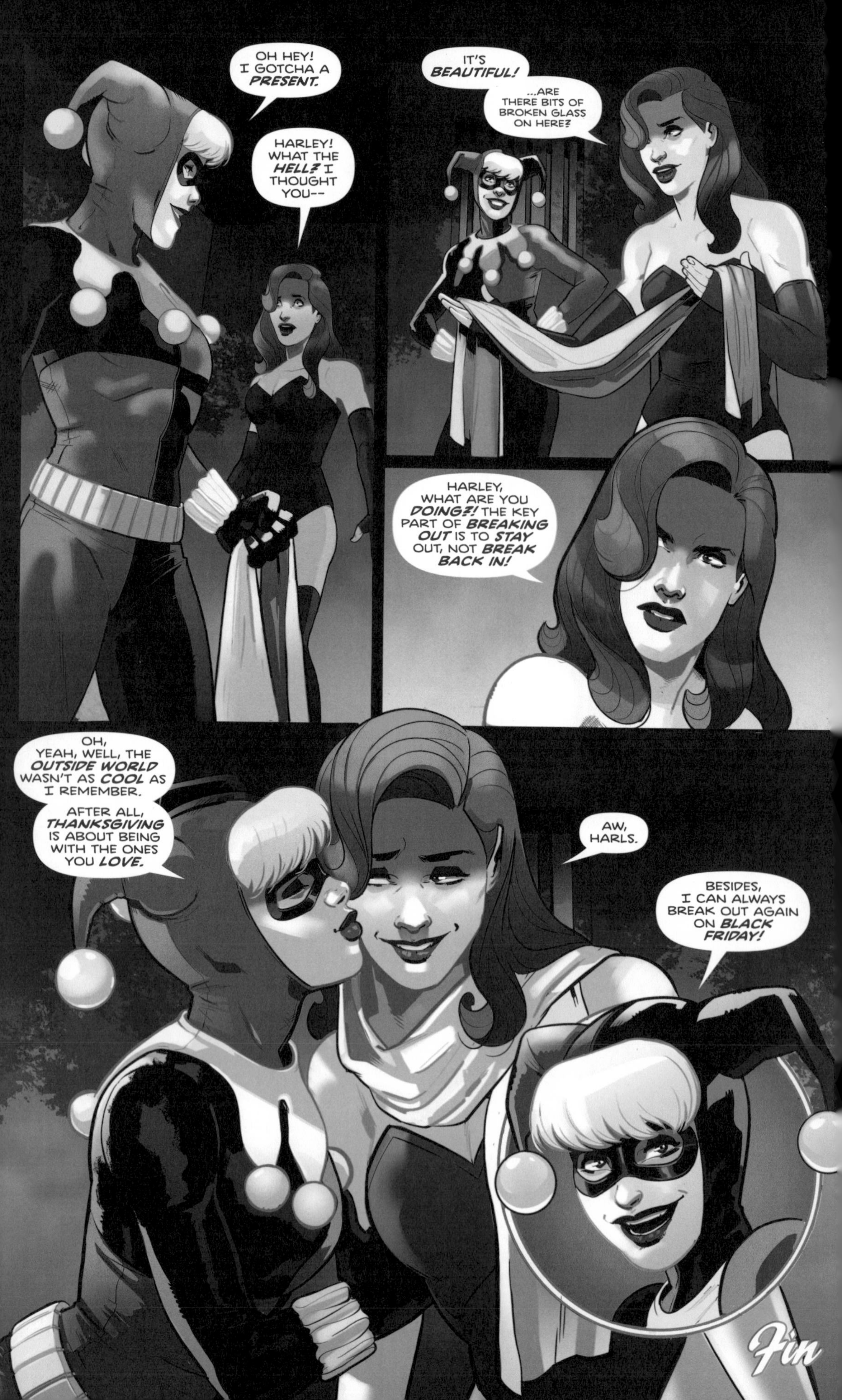
OH HEY! I GOTCHA A PRESENT.
HARLEY! WHAT THE HELL? I THOUGHT YOU--
IT'S BEAUTIFUL!
...ARE THERE BITS OF BROKEN GLASS ON HERE?
HARLEY, WHAT ARE YOU DOING?! THE KEY PART OF BREAKING OUT IS TO STAY OUT, NOT BREAK BACK IN!
OH, YEAH, WELL, THE OUTSIDE WORLD WASN'T AS COOL AS I REMEMBER.
AFTER ALL, THANKSGIVING IS ABOUT BEING WITH THE ONES YOU LOVE.
AW, HARLS.
BESIDES, I CAN ALWAYS BREAK OUT AGAIN ON BLACK FRIDAY!
Fin

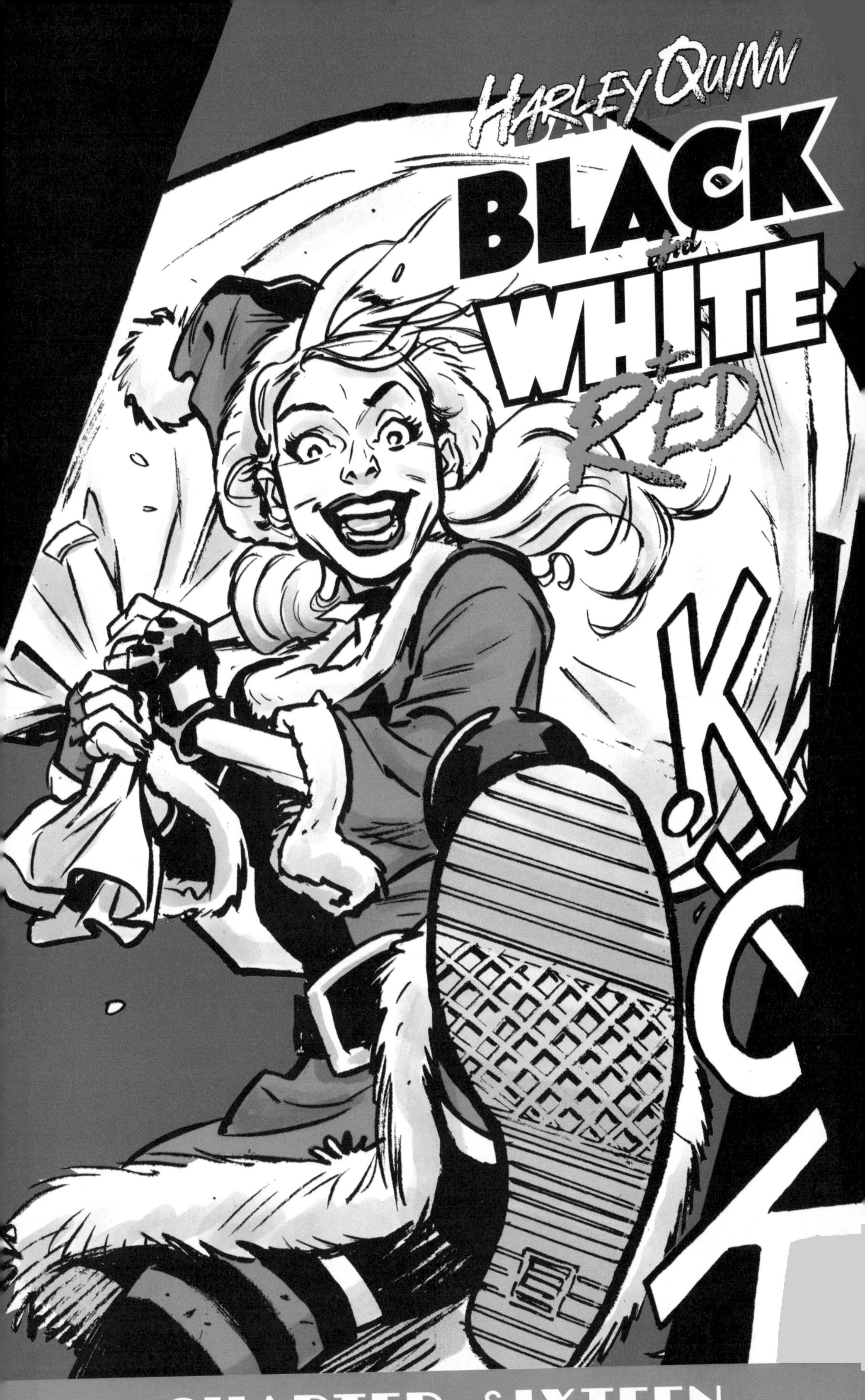
HARLEY QUINN
BLACK and WHITE + RED
KICK

CHAPTER SIXTEEN

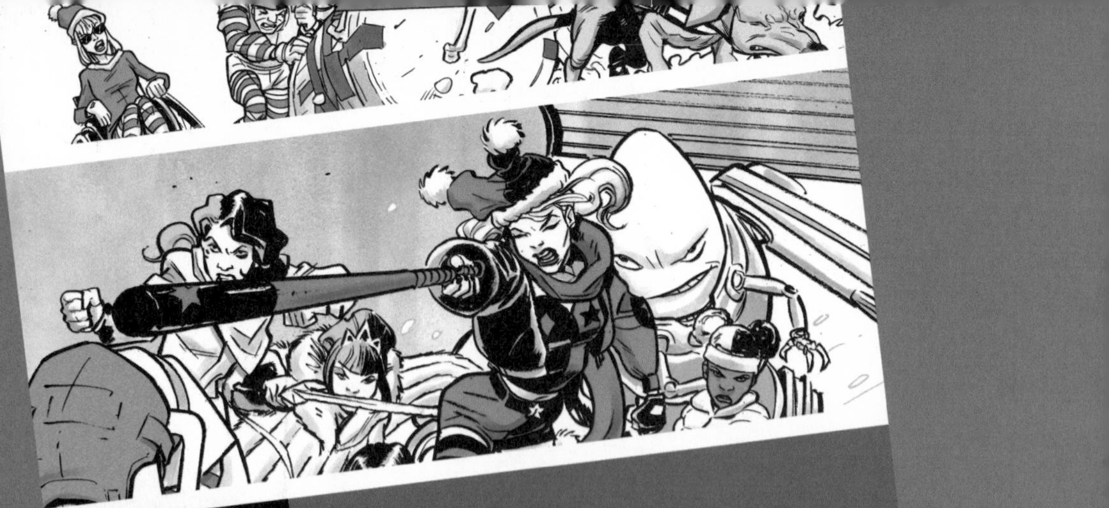

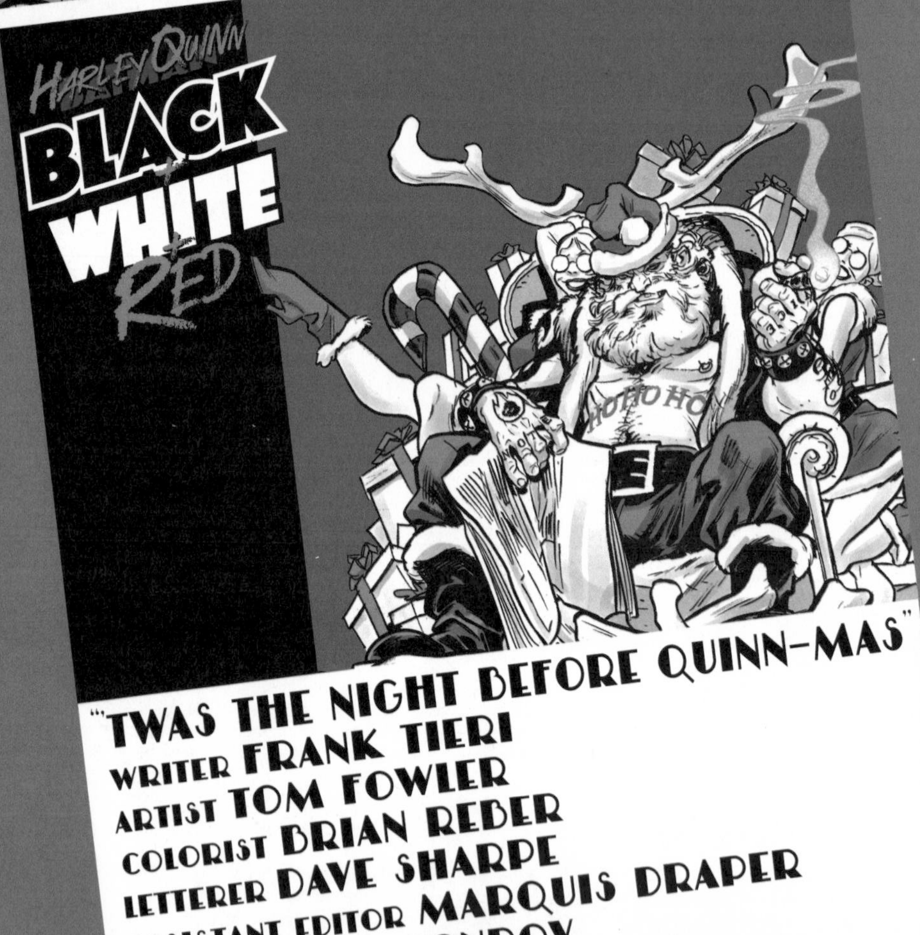
HARLEY QUINN
BLACK
WHITE
RED

"'TWAS THE NIGHT BEFORE QUINN-MAS"

WRITER FRANK TIERI
ARTIST TOM FOWLER
COLORIST BRIAN REBER
LETTERER DAVE SHARPE
ASSISTANT EDITOR MARQUIS DRAPER
EDITOR CHRIS CONROY

HARLEY QUINN CREATED BY PAUL DINI & BRUCE TIMM

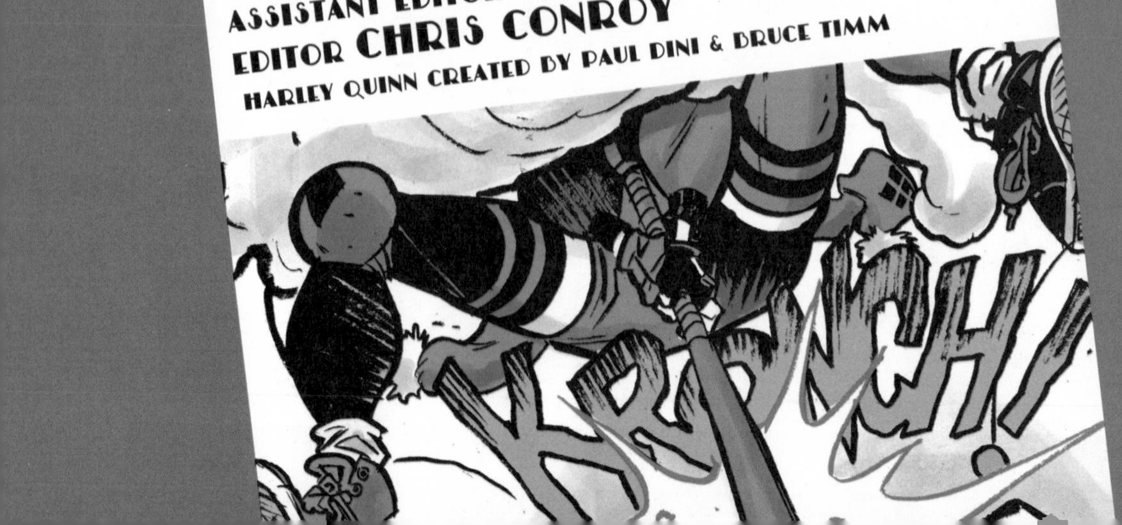

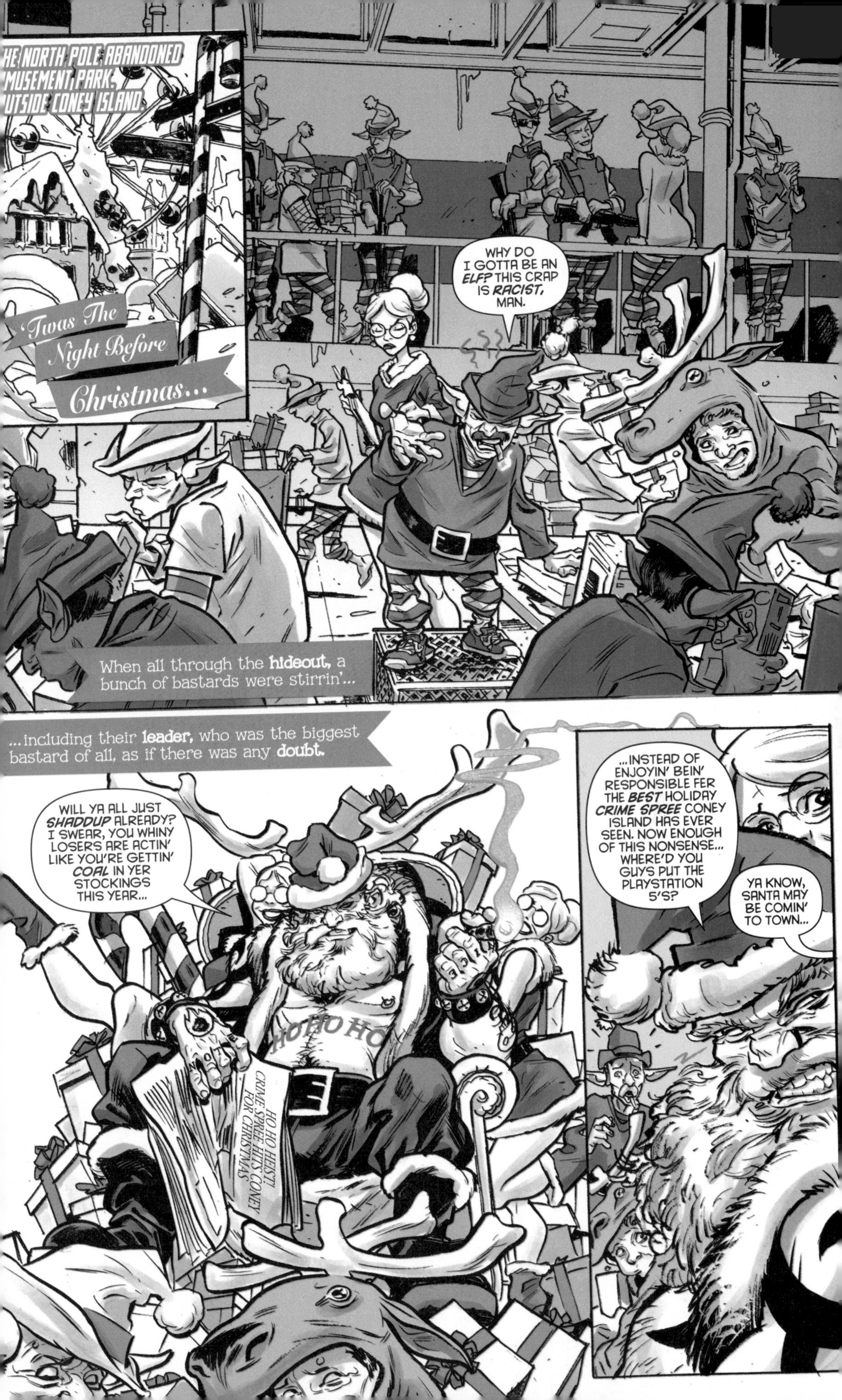

HE NORTH POLE ABANDONED MUSEMENT PARK, UTSIDE CONEY ISLAND.
'Twas The Night Before Christmas...
WHY DO I GOTTA BE AN ELF? THIS CRAP IS RACIST, MAN.
When all through the hideout, a bunch of bastards were stirrin'...
...including their leader, who was the biggest bastard of all, as if there was any doubt.
WILL YA ALL JUST SHADDUP ALREADY? I SWEAR, YOU WHINY LOSERS ARE ACTIN' LIKE YOU'RE GETTIN' COAL IN YER STOCKINGS THIS YEAR...
HO HO HO
HO HO HEIST! CRIME SPREE HITS CONEY FOR CHRISTMAS
...INSTEAD OF ENJOYIN' BEIN' RESPONSIBLE FER THE BEST HOLIDAY CRIME SPREE CONEY ISLAND HAS EVER SEEN. NOW ENOUGH OF THIS NONSENSE... WHERE'D YOU GUYS PUT THE PLAYSTATION 5'S?
YA KNOW, SANTA MAY BE COMIN' TO TOWN...

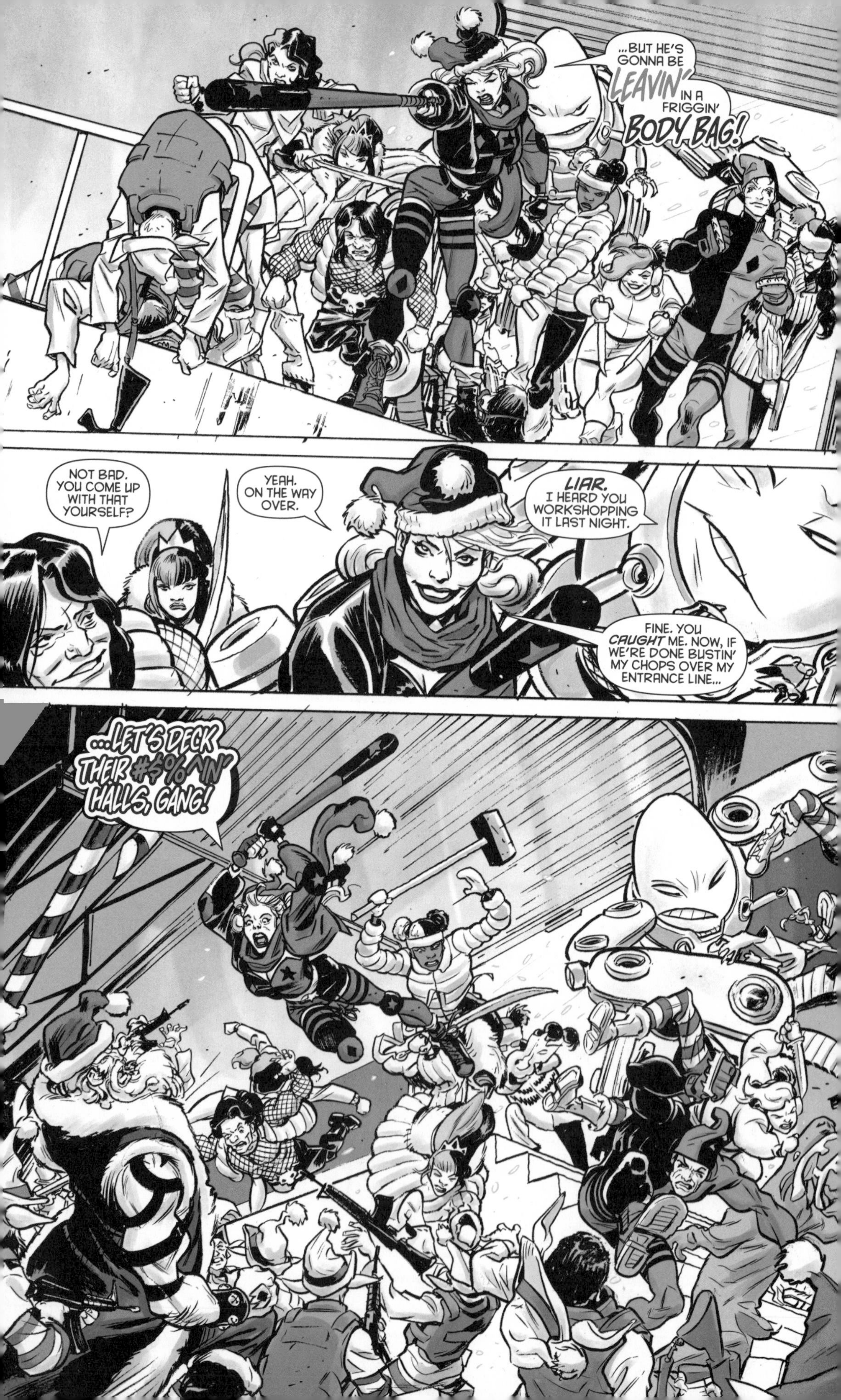
...BUT HE'S GONNA BE LEAVIN' IN A FRIGGIN' BODY BAG!
NOT BAD. YOU COME UP WITH THAT YOURSELF?
YEAH. ON THE WAY OVER.
LIAR. I HEARD YOU WORKSHOPPING IT LAST NIGHT.
FINE. YOU CAUGHT ME. NOW, IF WE'RE DONE BUSTIN' MY CHOPS OVER MY ENTRANCE LINE...
...LET'S DECK THEIR #$%^IN' HALLS, GANG!

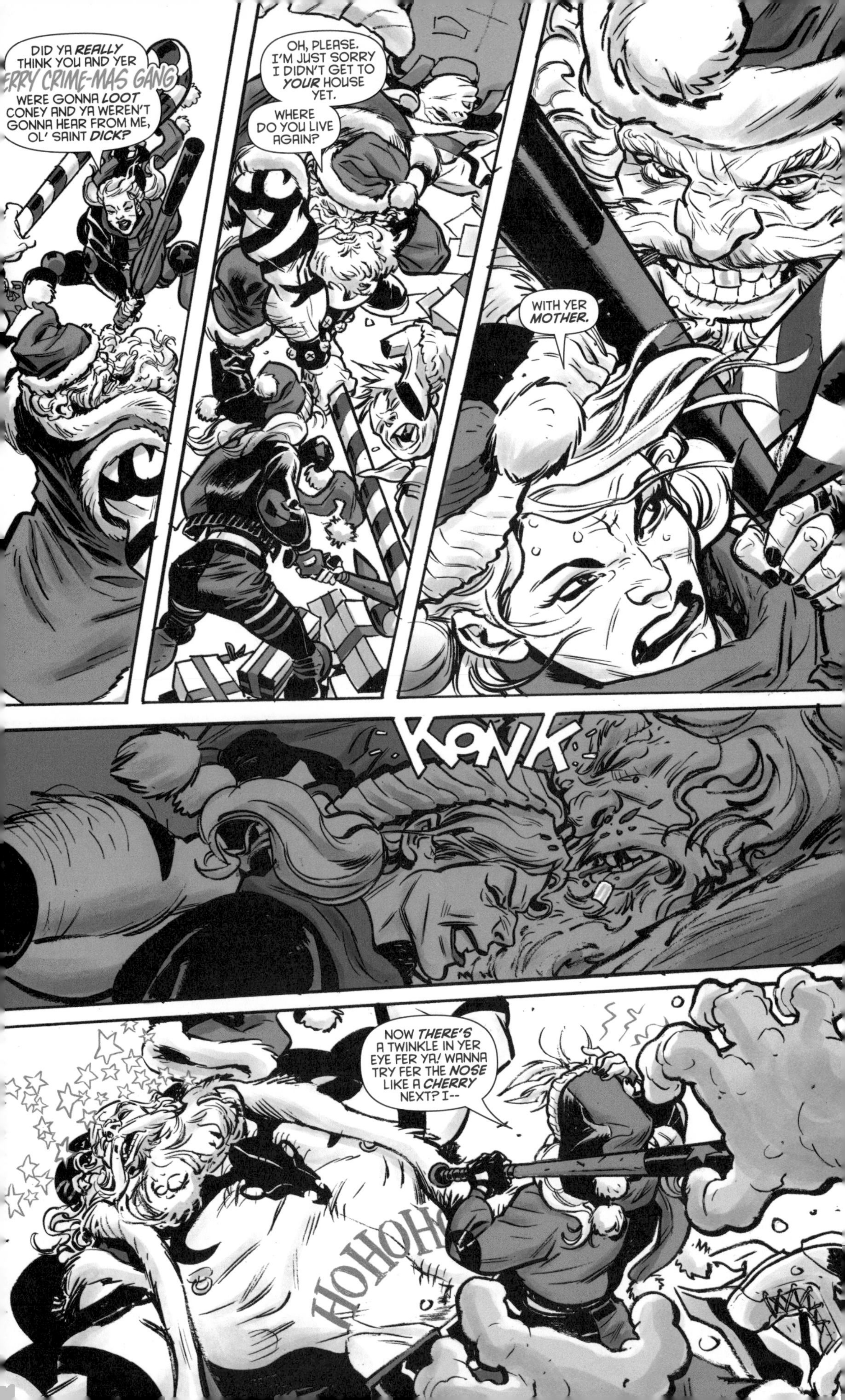
DID YA REALLY THINK YOU AND YER
ERRY CRIME-MAS GANG
WERE GONNA LOOT CONEY AND YA WEREN'T GONNA HEAR FROM ME, OL' SAINT DICK?
OH, PLEASE. I'M JUST SORRY I DIDN'T GET TO YOUR HOUSE YET.
WHERE DO YOU LIVE AGAIN?
WITH YER MOTHER.
KONK
NOW THERE'S A TWINKLE IN YER EYE FER YA! WANNA TRY FER THE NOSE LIKE A CHERRY NEXT? I--
HOHOHO

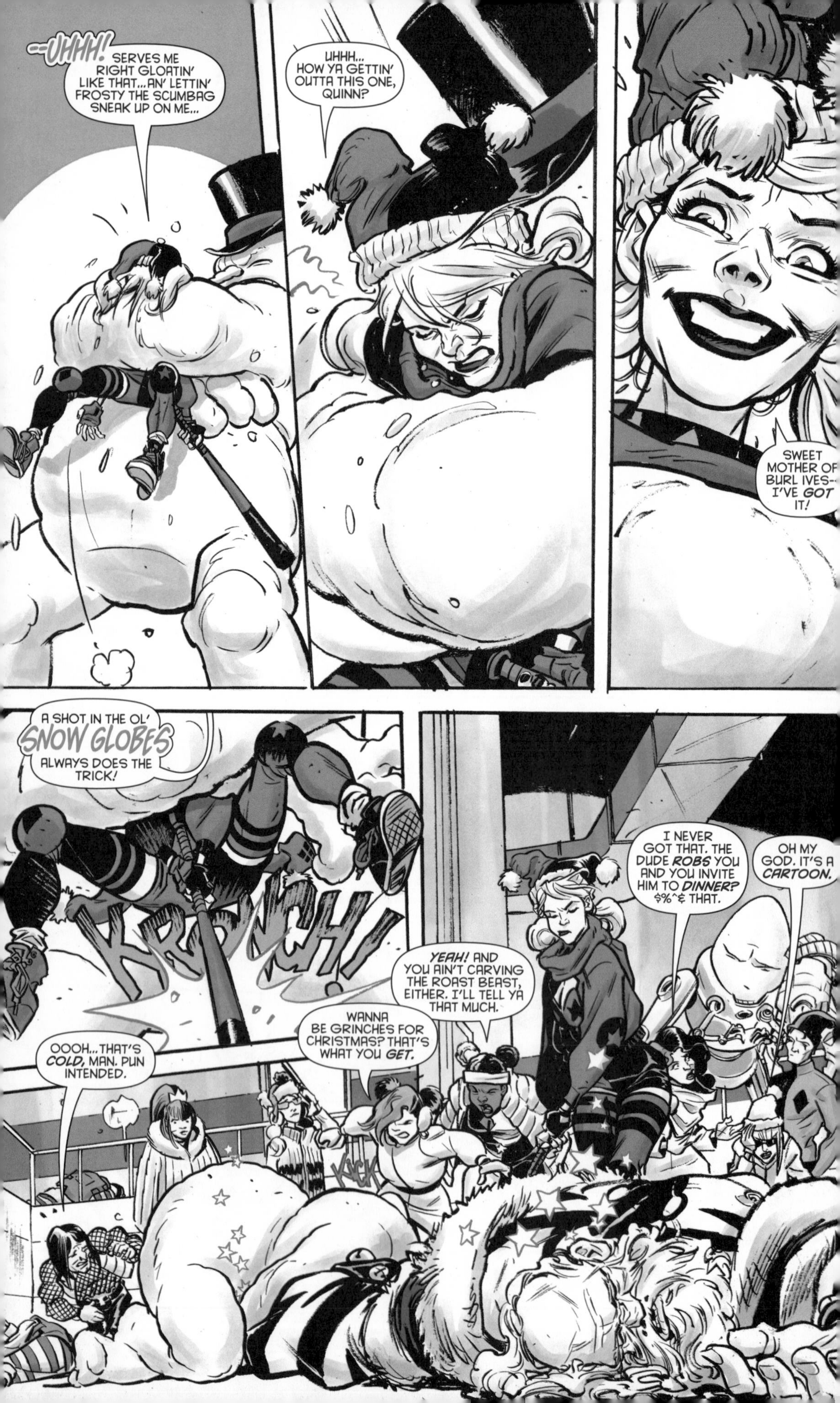
--UHHH!
SERVES ME RIGHT GLOATIN' LIKE THAT...AN' LETTIN' FROSTY THE SCUMBAG SNEAK UP ON ME...
UHHH... HOW YA GETTIN' OUTTA THIS ONE, QUINN?
SWEET MOTHER OF BURL IVES-- I'VE GOT IT!
A SHOT IN THE OL' SNOW GLOBES ALWAYS DOES THE TRICK!
KRUNCH!
I NEVER GOT THAT. THE DUDE ROBS YOU AND YOU INVITE HIM TO DINNER? $%^& THAT.
OH MY GOD. IT'S A CARTOON.
YEAH! AND YOU AIN'T CARVING THE ROAST BEAST, EITHER. I'LL TELL YA THAT MUCH.
WANNA BE GRINCHES FOR CHRISTMAS? THAT'S WHAT YOU GET.
OOOH...THAT'S COLD, MAN. PUN INTENDED.
KICK

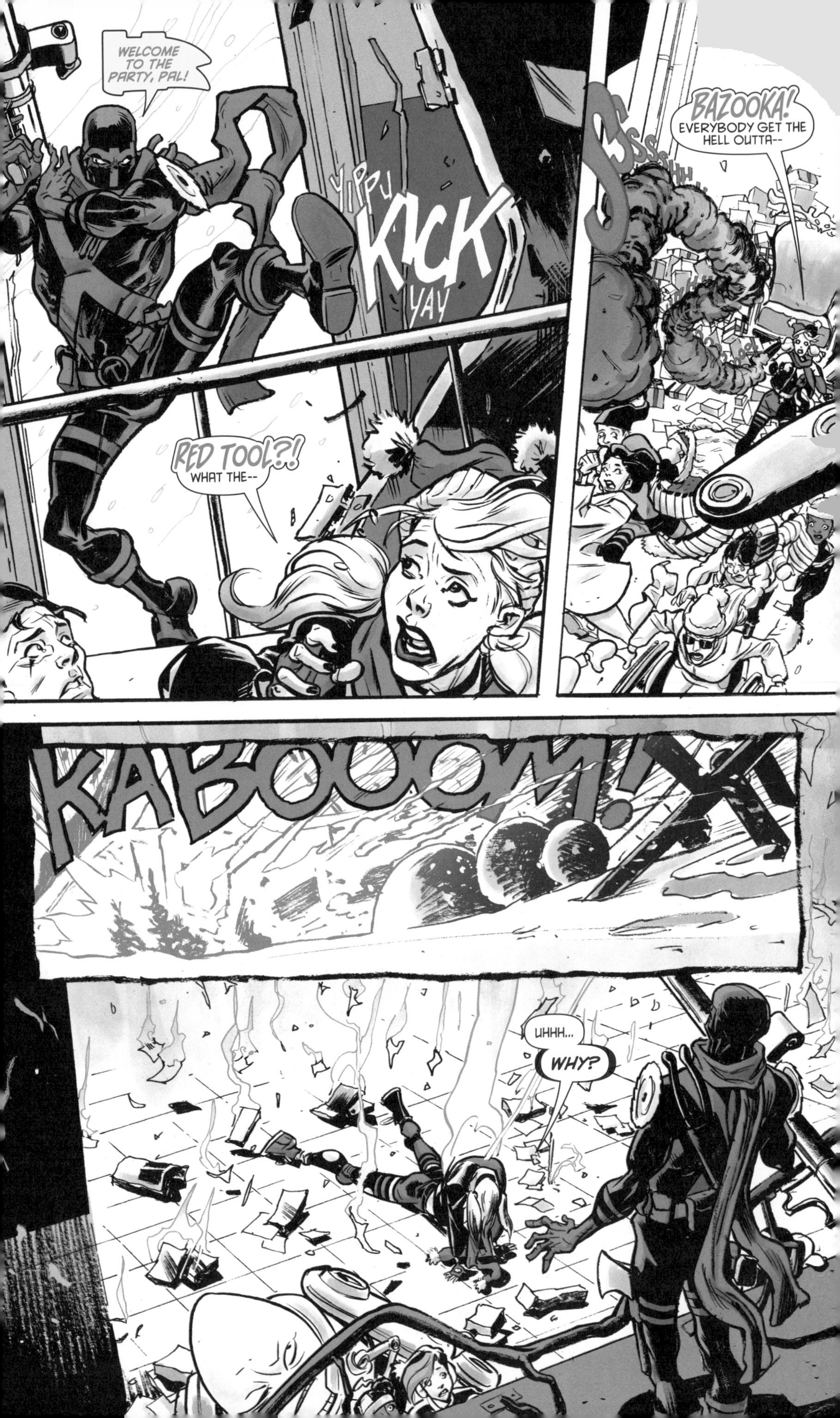

WELCOME TO THE PARTY, PAL!
YIPPY KICK YAY
RED TOOL?! WHAT THE--
SSSSSHHH
BAZOOKA! EVERYBODY GET THE HELL OUTTA--
KABOOOM!
UHHH...
WHY?

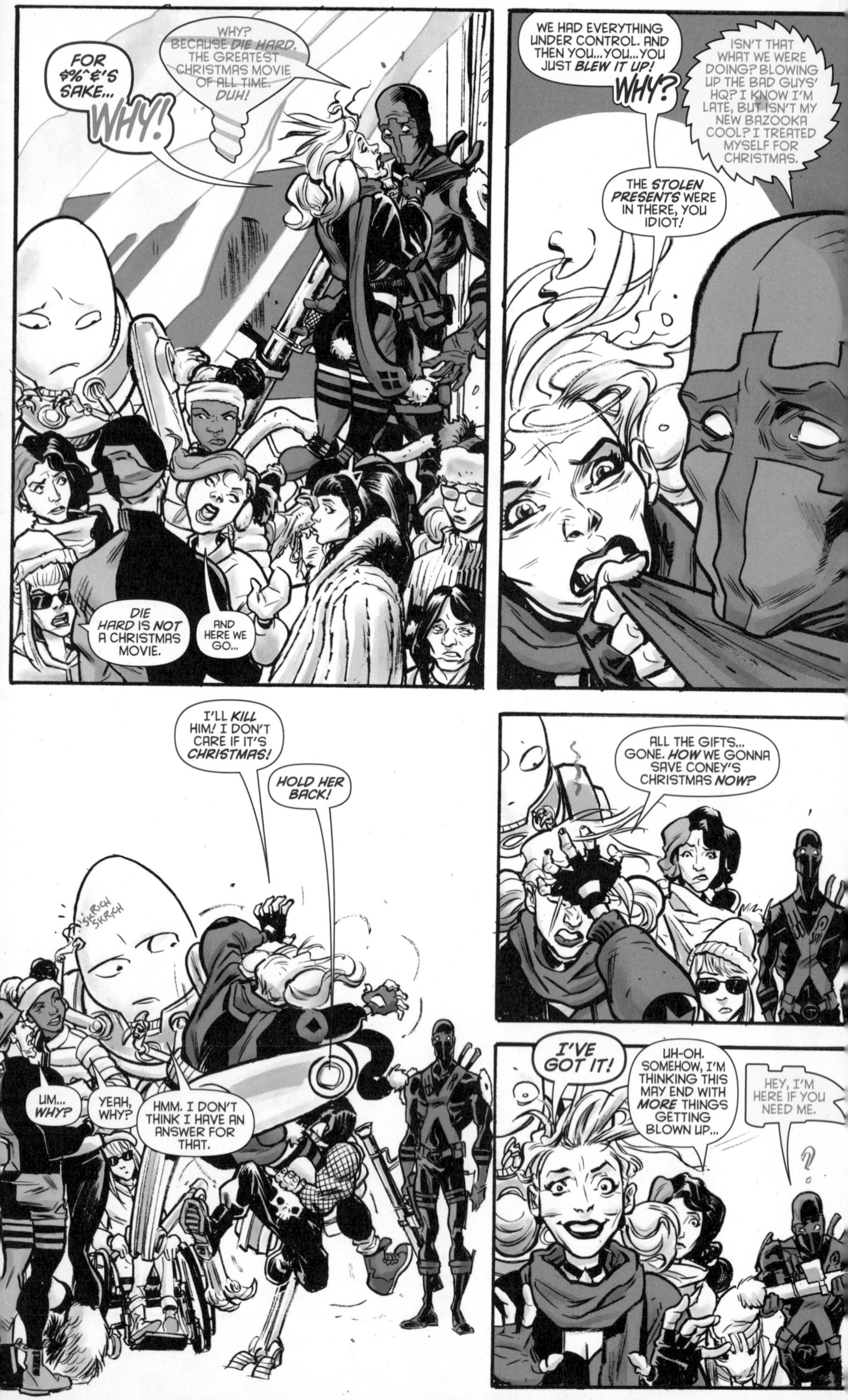
FOR $%^&'S SAKE... WHY!
WHY? BECAUSE DIE HARD. THE GREATEST CHRISTMAS MOVIE OF ALL TIME. DUH!
DIE HARD IS NOT A CHRISTMAS MOVIE.
AND HERE WE GO...
WE HAD EVERYTHING UNDER CONTROL. AND THEN YOU...YOU...YOU JUST BLEW IT UP! WHY?
ISN'T THAT WHAT WE WERE DOING? BLOWING UP THE BAD GUYS' HQ? I KNOW I'M LATE, BUT ISN'T MY NEW BAZOOKA COOL? I TREATED MYSELF FOR CHRISTMAS.
THE STOLEN PRESENTS WERE IN THERE, YOU IDIOT!
I'LL KILL HIM! I DON'T CARE IF IT'S CHRISTMAS!
HOLD HER BACK!
SKRICH SKRYCH
UM... WHY?
YEAH, WHY?
HMM. I DON'T THINK I HAVE AN ANSWER FOR THAT.
ALL THE GIFTS... GONE. HOW WE GONNA SAVE CONEY'S CHRISTMAS NOW?
I'VE GOT IT!
UH-OH. SOMEHOW, I'M THINKING THIS MAY END WITH MORE THINGS GETTING BLOWN UP...
HEY, I'M HERE IF YOU NEED ME.
?

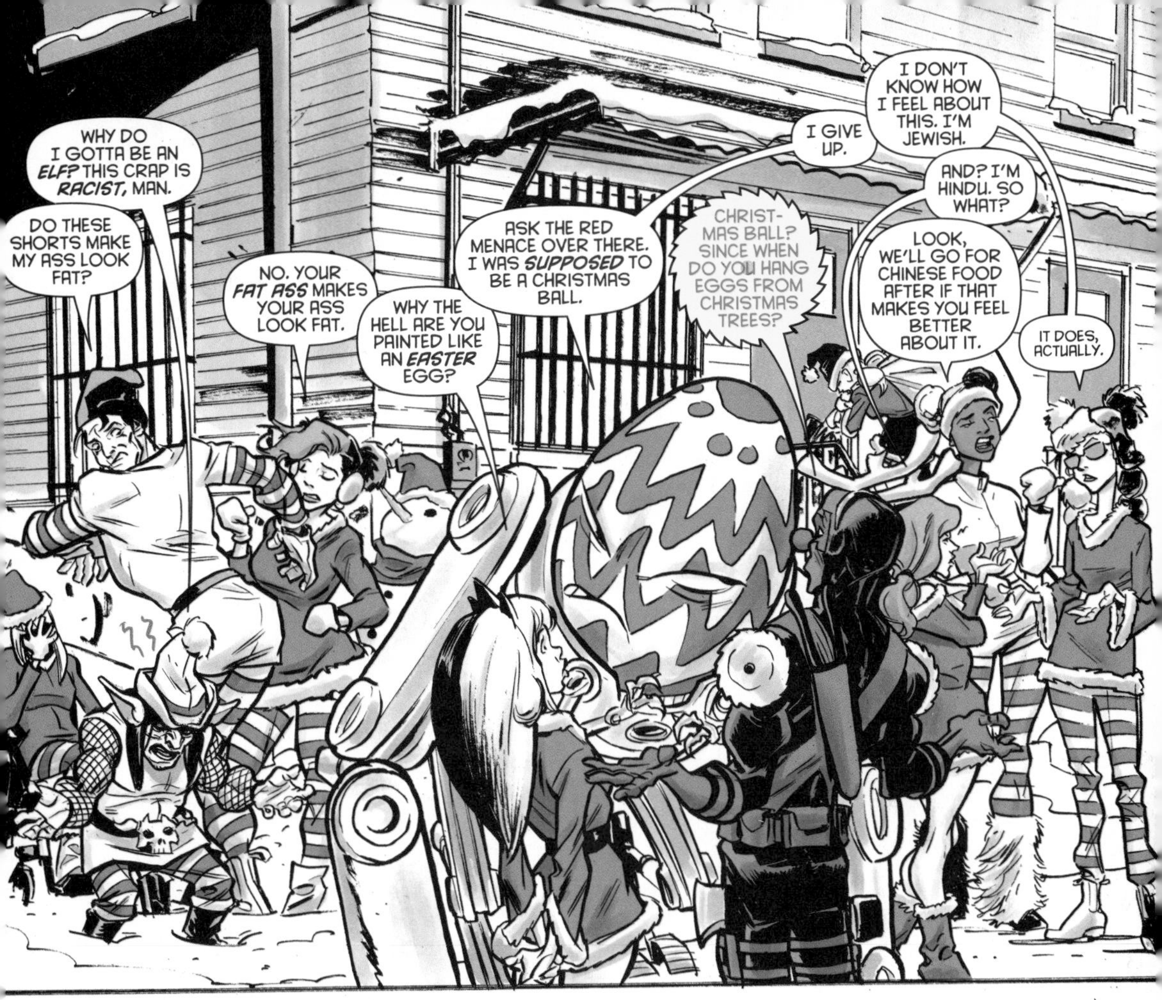
WHY DO I GOTTA BE AN *ELF?* THIS CRAP IS *RACIST,* MAN.
DO THESE SHORTS MAKE MY ASS LOOK FAT?
NO. YOUR *FAT ASS* MAKES YOUR ASS LOOK FAT.
WHY THE HELL ARE YOU PAINTED LIKE AN *EASTER* EGG?
ASK THE RED MENACE OVER THERE. I WAS *SUPPOSED* TO BE A CHRISTMAS BALL.
CHRISTMAS BALL? SINCE WHEN DO YOU HANG EGGS FROM CHRISTMAS TREES?
I GIVE UP.
I DON'T KNOW HOW I FEEL ABOUT THIS. I'M JEWISH.
AND? I'M HINDU. SO WHAT?
LOOK, WE'LL GO FOR CHINESE FOOD AFTER IF THAT MAKES YOU FEEL BETTER ABOUT IT.
IT DOES, ACTUALLY.
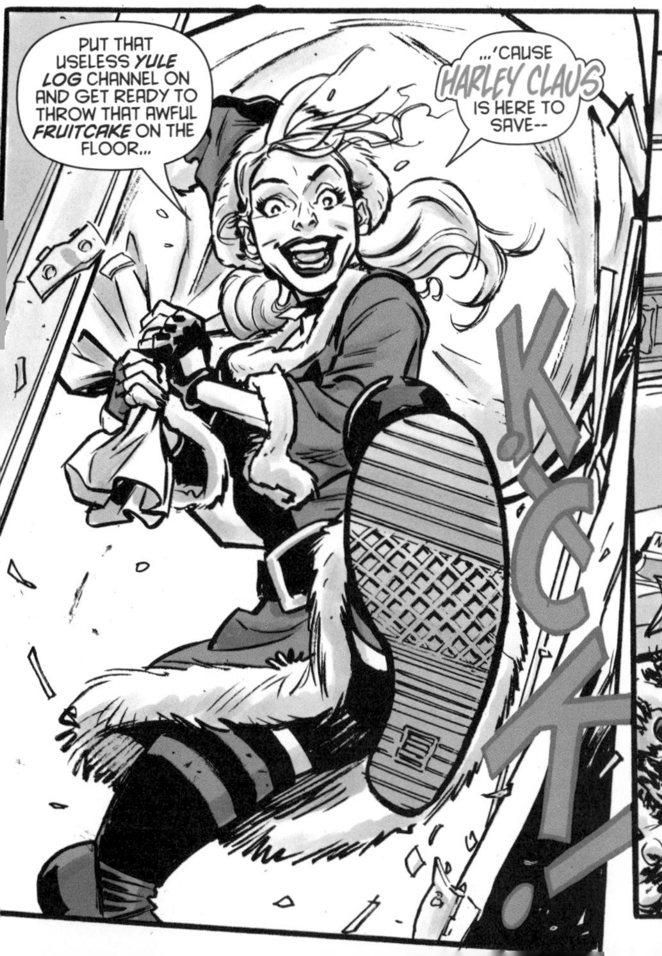
PUT THAT USELESS *YULE LOG* CHANNEL ON AND GET READY TO THROW THAT AWFUL *FRUITCAKE* ON THE FLOOR...
...'CAUSE HARLEY CLAUS IS HERE TO SAVE--
KICK!
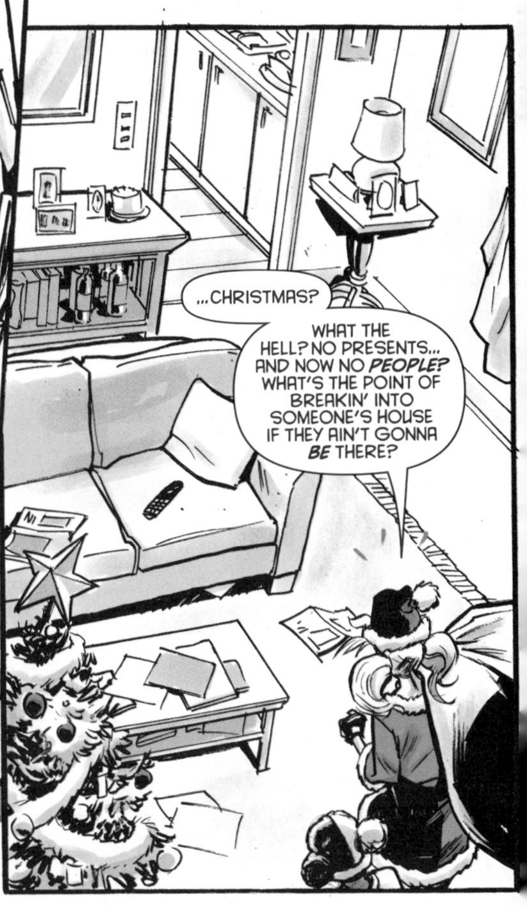
...CHRISTMAS?
WHAT THE HELL? NO PRESENTS... AND NOW NO *PEOPLE?* WHAT'S THE POINT OF BREAKIN' INTO SOMEONE'S HOUSE IF THEY AIN'T GONNA *BE* THERE?

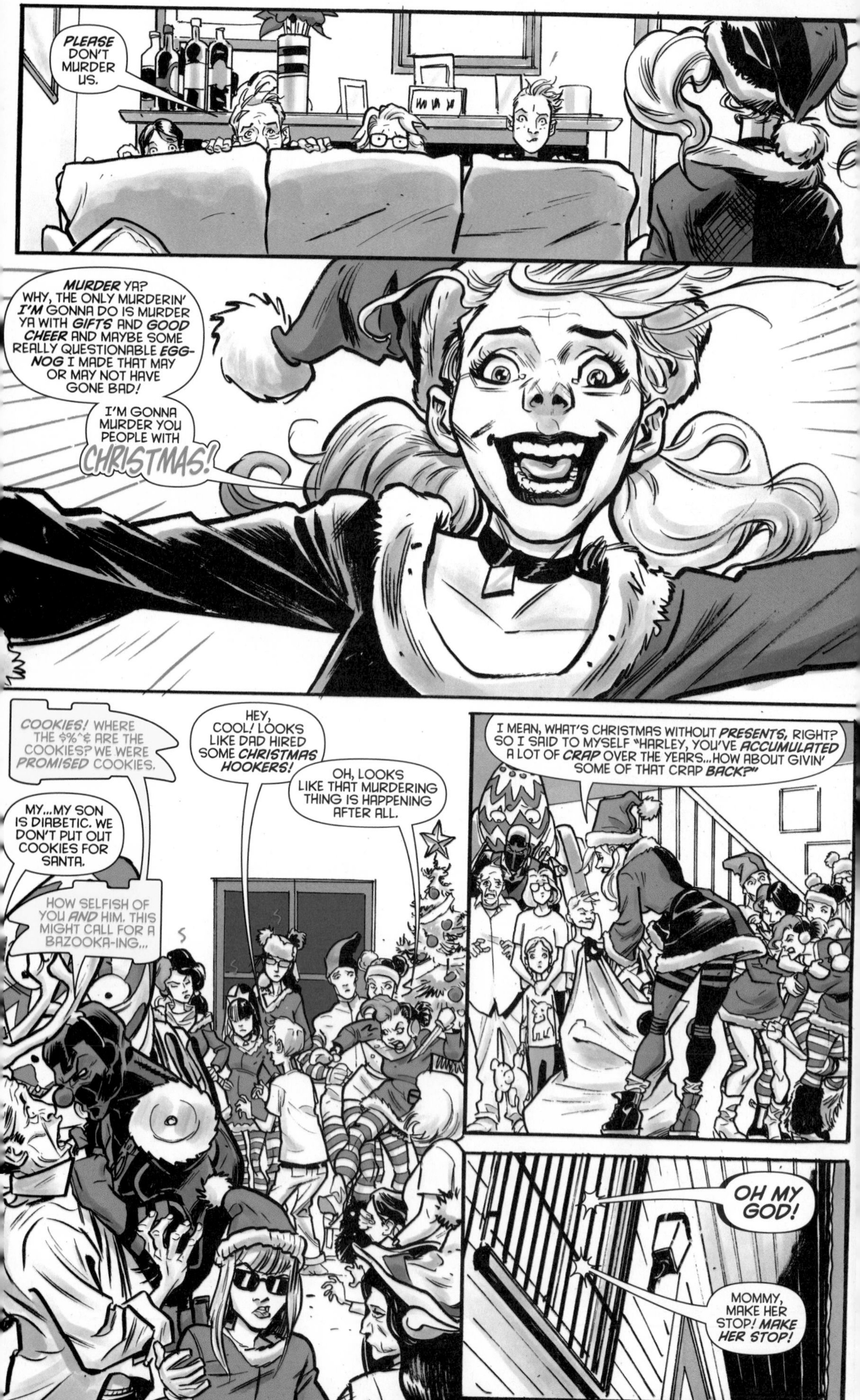
PLEASE DON'T MURDER US.
MURDER YA? WHY, THE ONLY MURDERIN' I'M GONNA DO IS MURDER YA WITH GIFTS AND GOOD CHEER AND MAYBE SOME REALLY QUESTIONABLE EGG-NOG I MADE THAT MAY OR MAY NOT HAVE GONE BAD!
I'M GONNA MURDER YOU PEOPLE WITH CHRISTMAS!
COOKIES! WHERE THE $%^& ARE THE COOKIES? WE WERE PROMISED COOKIES.
MY... MY SON IS DIABETIC. WE DON'T PUT OUT COOKIES FOR SANTA.
HOW SELFISH OF YOU AND HIM. THIS MIGHT CALL FOR A BAZOOKA-ING...
HEY, COOL! LOOKS LIKE DAD HIRED SOME CHRISTMAS HOOKERS!
OH, LOOKS LIKE THAT MURDERING THING IS HAPPENING AFTER ALL.
I MEAN, WHAT'S CHRISTMAS WITHOUT PRESENTS, RIGHT? SO I SAID TO MYSELF "HARLEY, YOU'VE ACCUMULATED A LOT OF CRAP OVER THE YEARS...HOW ABOUT GIVIN' SOME OF THAT CRAP BACK?"
OH MY GOD!
MOMMY, MAKE HER STOP! MAKE HER STOP!

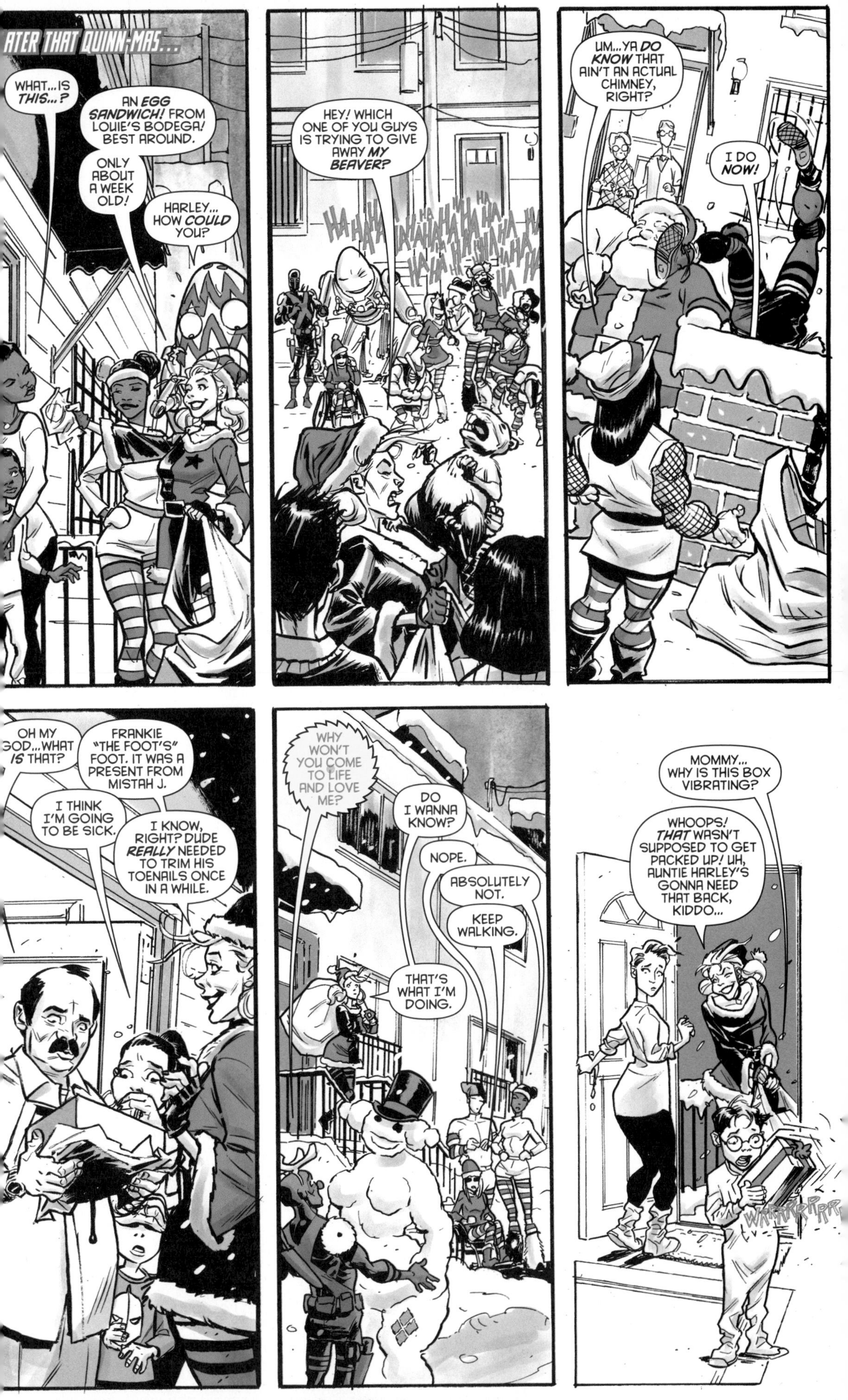
ATER THAT QUINN-MAS...
WHAT...IS THIS...?
AN EGG SANDWICH! FROM LOUIE'S BODEGA! BEST AROUND.
ONLY ABOUT A WEEK OLD!
HARLEY... HOW COULD YOU?
HEY! WHICH ONE OF YOU GUYS IS TRYING TO GIVE AWAY MY BEAVER?
HA HA HA HA HA HA HA HA HA HA HA HA HA HA HA HA HA HA HA HA
UM...YA DO KNOW THAT AIN'T AN ACTUAL CHIMNEY, RIGHT?
I DO NOW!
OH MY GOD...WHAT IS THAT?
FRANKIE "THE FOOT'S" FOOT. IT WAS A PRESENT FROM MISTAH J.
I THINK I'M GOING TO BE SICK.
I KNOW, RIGHT? DUDE REALLY NEEDED TO TRIM HIS TOENAILS ONCE IN A WHILE.
WHY WON'T YOU COME TO LIFE AND LOVE ME?
DO I WANNA KNOW?
NOPE.
ABSOLUTELY NOT.
KEEP WALKING.
THAT'S WHAT I'M DOING.
MOMMY... WHY IS THIS BOX VIBRATING?
WHOOPS! THAT WASN'T SUPPOSED TO GET PACKED UP! UH, AUNTIE HARLEY'S GONNA NEED THAT BACK, KIDDO...
WRRRRRRRR

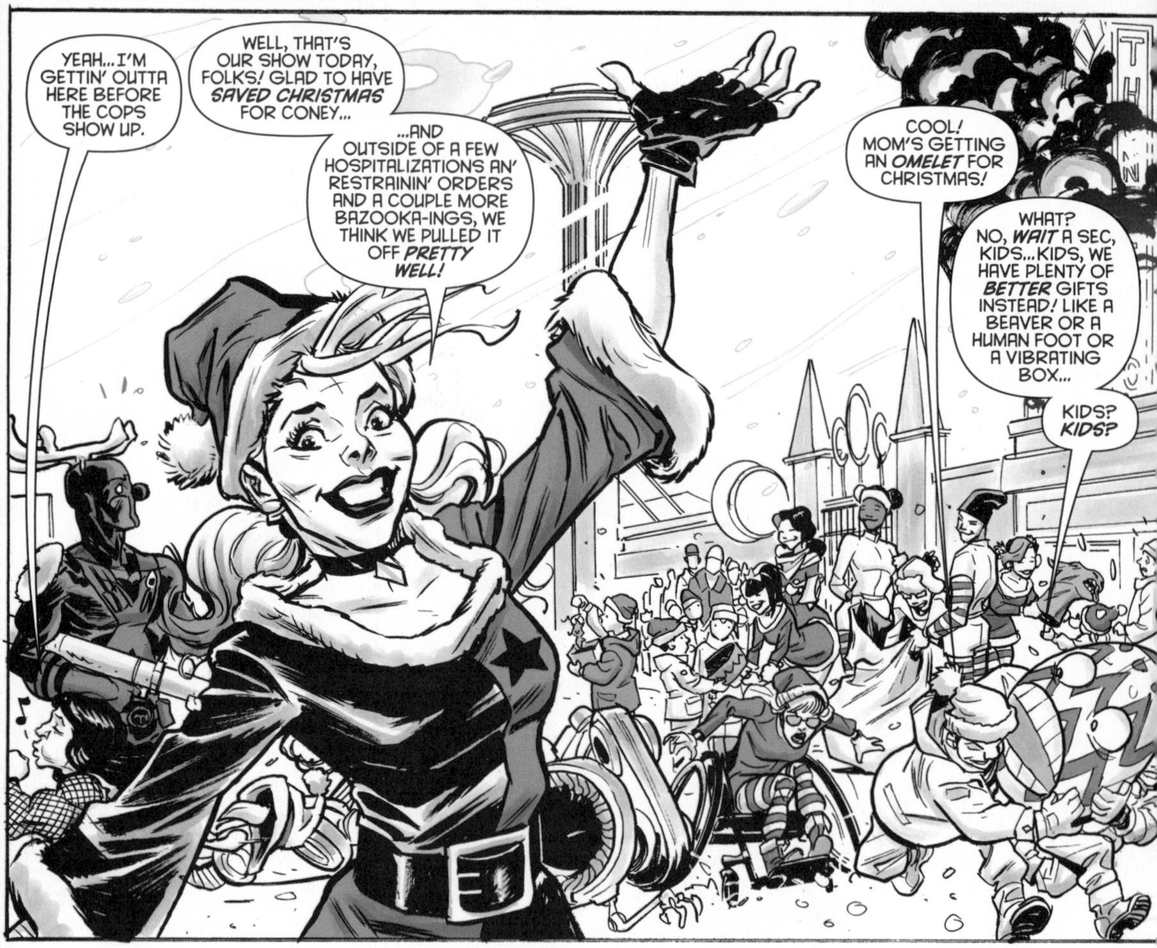
YEAH...I'M GETTIN' OUTTA HERE BEFORE THE COPS SHOW UP.
WELL, THAT'S OUR SHOW TODAY, FOLKS! GLAD TO HAVE *SAVED CHRISTMAS* FOR CONEY...
...AND OUTSIDE OF A FEW HOSPITALIZATIONS AN' RESTRAININ' ORDERS AND A COUPLE MORE BAZOOKA-INGS, WE THINK WE PULLED IT OFF *PRETTY WELL!*
COOL! MOM'S GETTING AN *OMELET* FOR CHRISTMAS!
WHAT? NO, *WAIT* A SEC, KIDS...KIDS, WE HAVE PLENTY OF *BETTER* GIFTS INSTEAD! LIKE A BEAVER OR A HUMAN FOOT OR A VIBRATING BOX...
KIDS? *KIDS?*

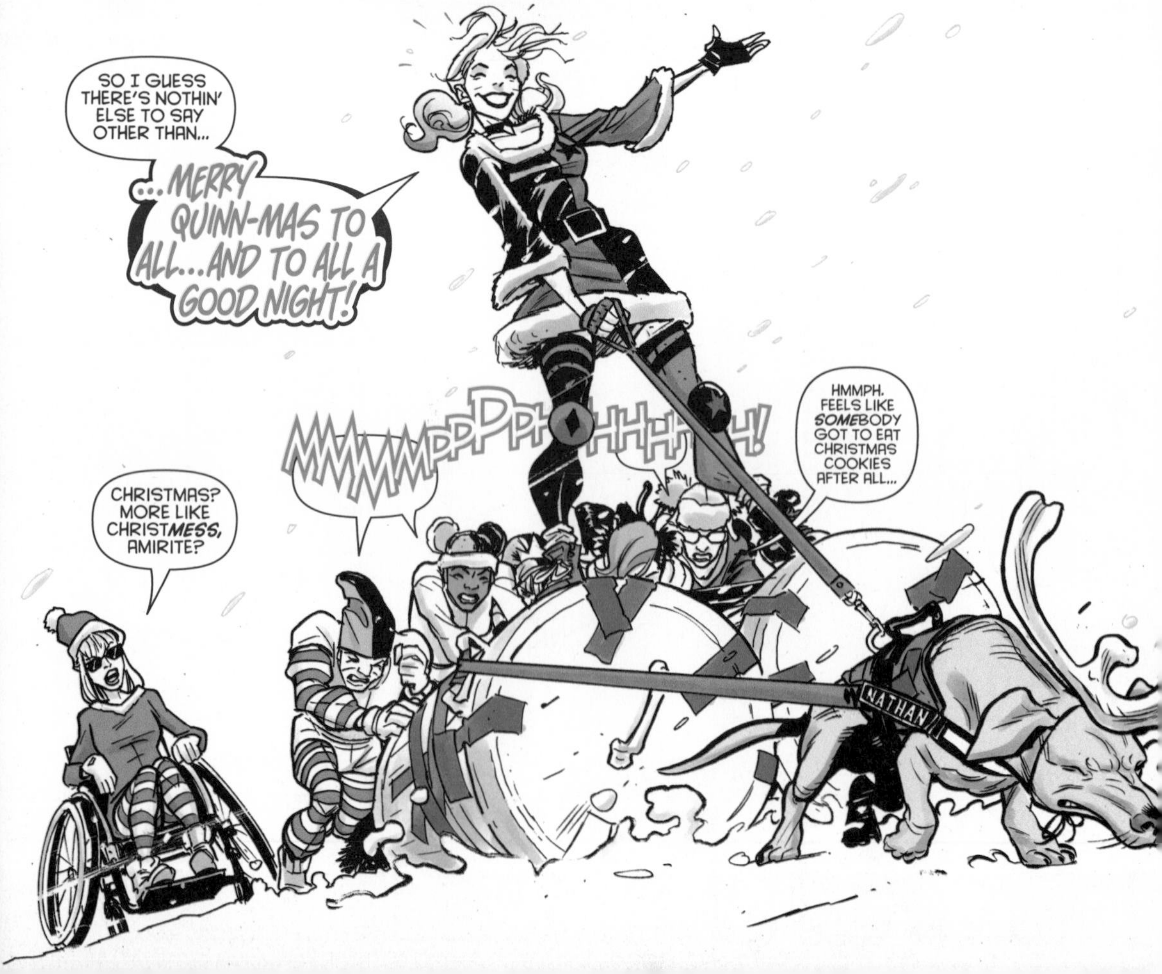
SO I GUESS THERE'S NOTHIN' ELSE TO SAY OTHER THAN...
...MERRY QUINN-MAS TO ALL...AND TO ALL A GOOD NIGHT!
MMMMMPPPPHHHHHH!
HMMPH. FEELS LIKE *SOME*BODY GOT TO EAT CHRISTMAS COOKIES AFTER ALL...
CHRISTMAS? MORE LIKE CHRIST*MESS*, AMIRITE?
NATHAN

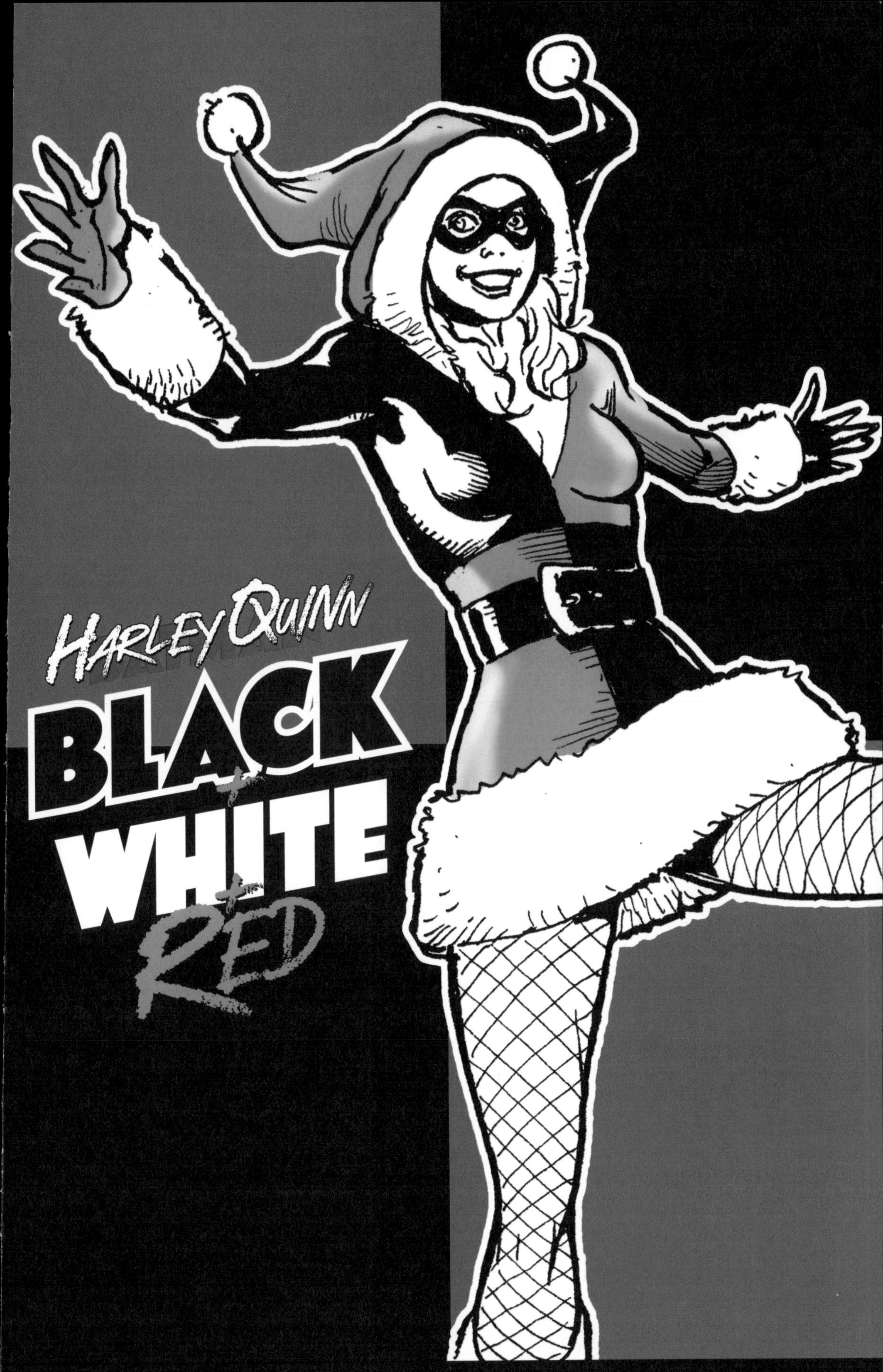
HARLEY QUINN
BLACK + WHITE + RED

CHAPTER SEVENTEEN

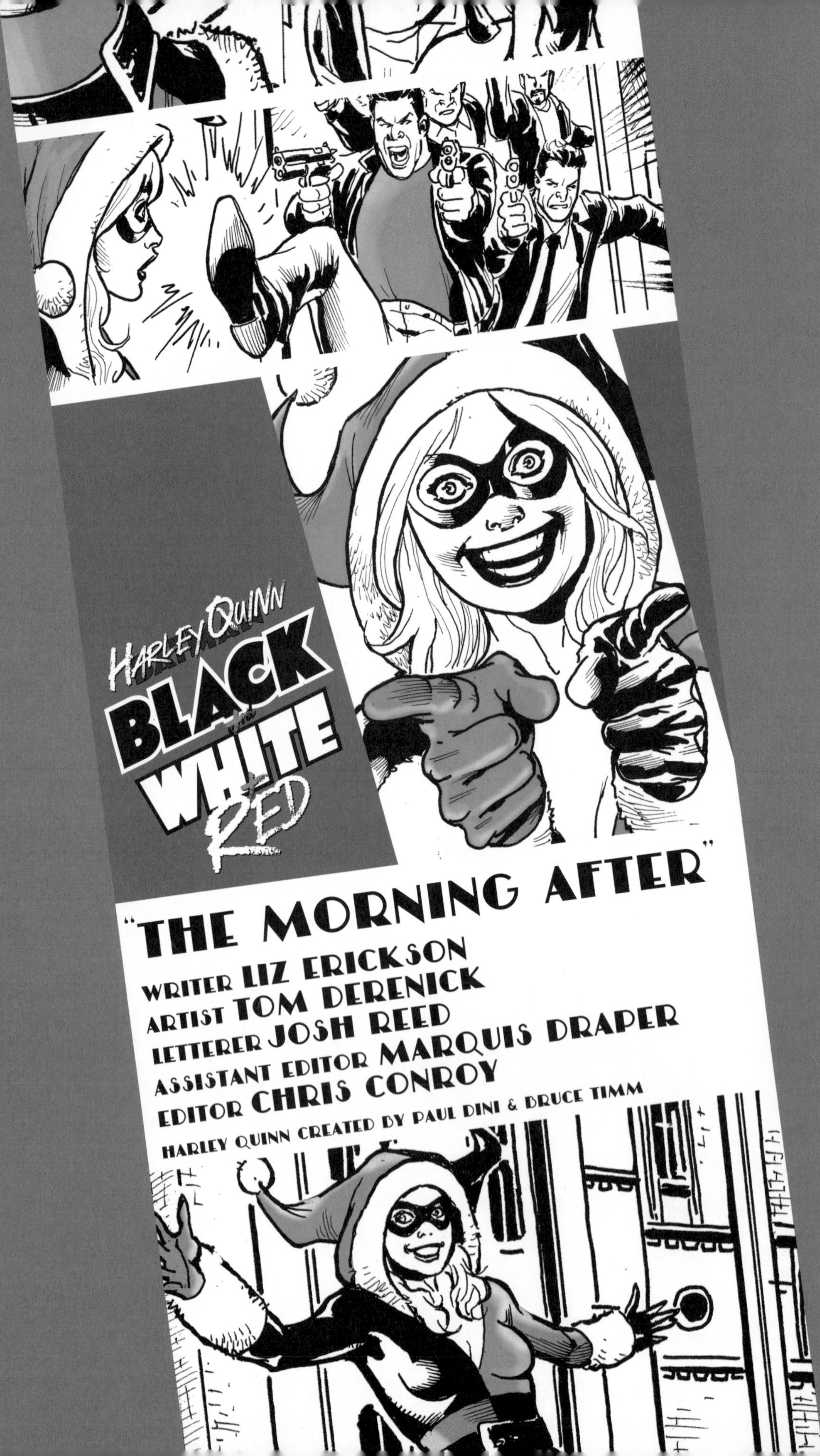
HARLEY QUINN
BLACK
WHITE
RED
"THE MORNING AFTER"
WRITER LIZ ERICKSON
ARTIST TOM DERENICK
LETTERER JOSH REED
ASSISTANT EDITOR MARQUIS DRAPER
EDITOR CHRIS CONROY
HARLEY QUINN CREATED BY PAUL DINI & BRUCE TIMM

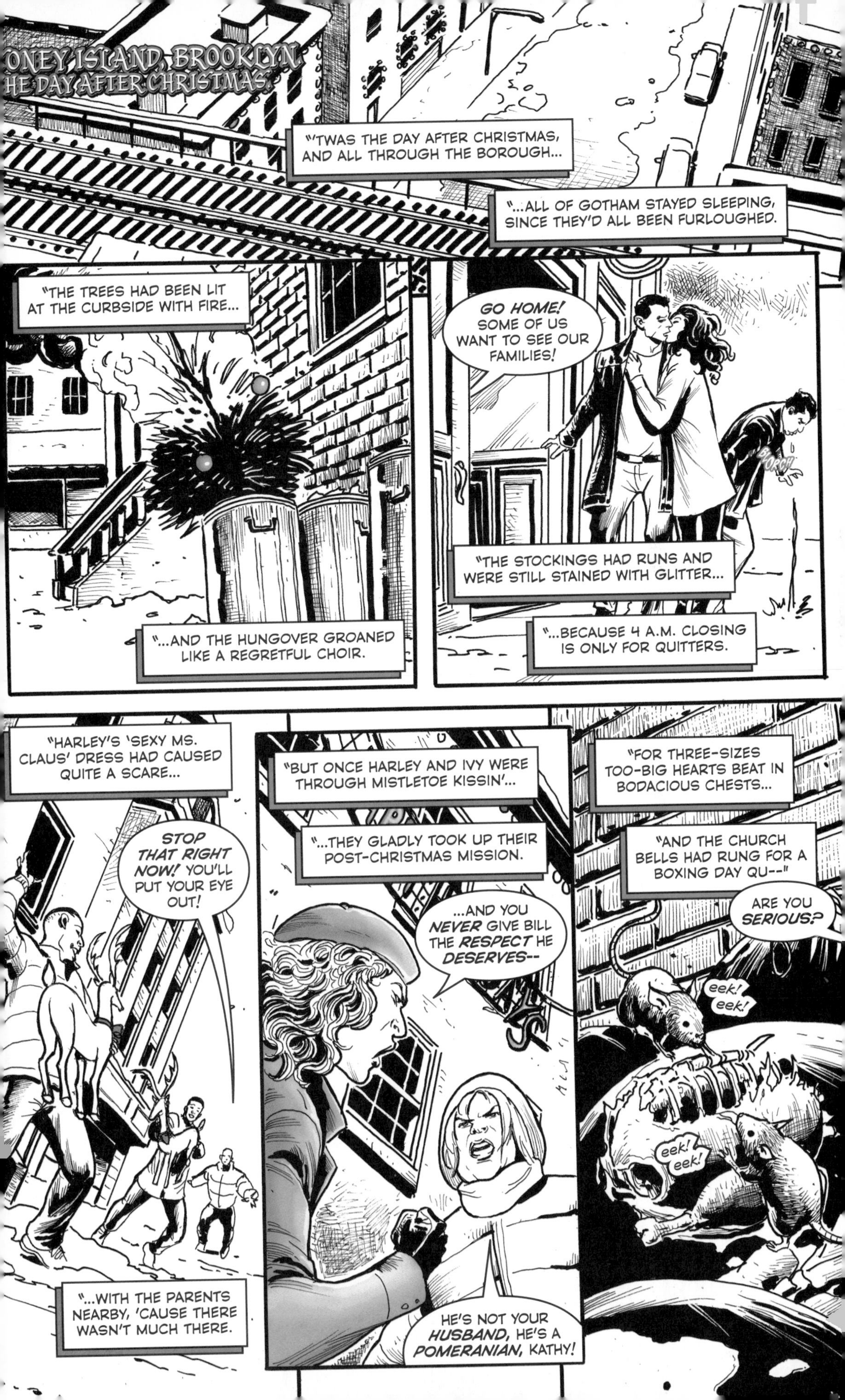
ONEY ISLAND, BROOKLYN
HE DAY AFTER CHRISTMAS
"TWAS THE DAY AFTER CHRISTMAS, AND ALL THROUGH THE BOROUGH...
"...ALL OF GOTHAM STAYED SLEEPING, SINCE THEY'D ALL BEEN FURLOUGHED.
"THE TREES HAD BEEN LIT AT THE CURBSIDE WITH FIRE...
"...AND THE HUNGOVER GROANED LIKE A REGRETFUL CHOIR.
GO HOME! SOME OF US WANT TO SEE OUR FAMILIES!
"THE STOCKINGS HAD RUNS AND WERE STILL STAINED WITH GLITTER...
"...BECAUSE 4 A.M. CLOSING IS ONLY FOR QUITTERS.
"HARLEY'S 'SEXY MS. CLAUS' DRESS HAD CAUSED QUITE A SCARE...
STOP THAT RIGHT NOW! YOU'LL PUT YOUR EYE OUT!
"...WITH THE PARENTS NEARBY, 'CAUSE THERE WASN'T MUCH THERE.
"BUT ONCE HARLEY AND IVY WERE THROUGH MISTLETOE KISSIN'...
"...THEY GLADLY TOOK UP THEIR POST-CHRISTMAS MISSION.
...AND YOU NEVER GIVE BILL THE RESPECT HE DESERVES--
HE'S NOT YOUR HUSBAND, HE'S A POMERANIAN, KATHY!
"FOR THREE-SIZES TOO-BIG HEARTS BEAT IN BODACIOUS CHESTS...
"AND THE CHURCH BELLS HAD RUNG FOR A BOXING DAY QU--"
ARE YOU SERIOUS?
eek! eek!
eek! eek!

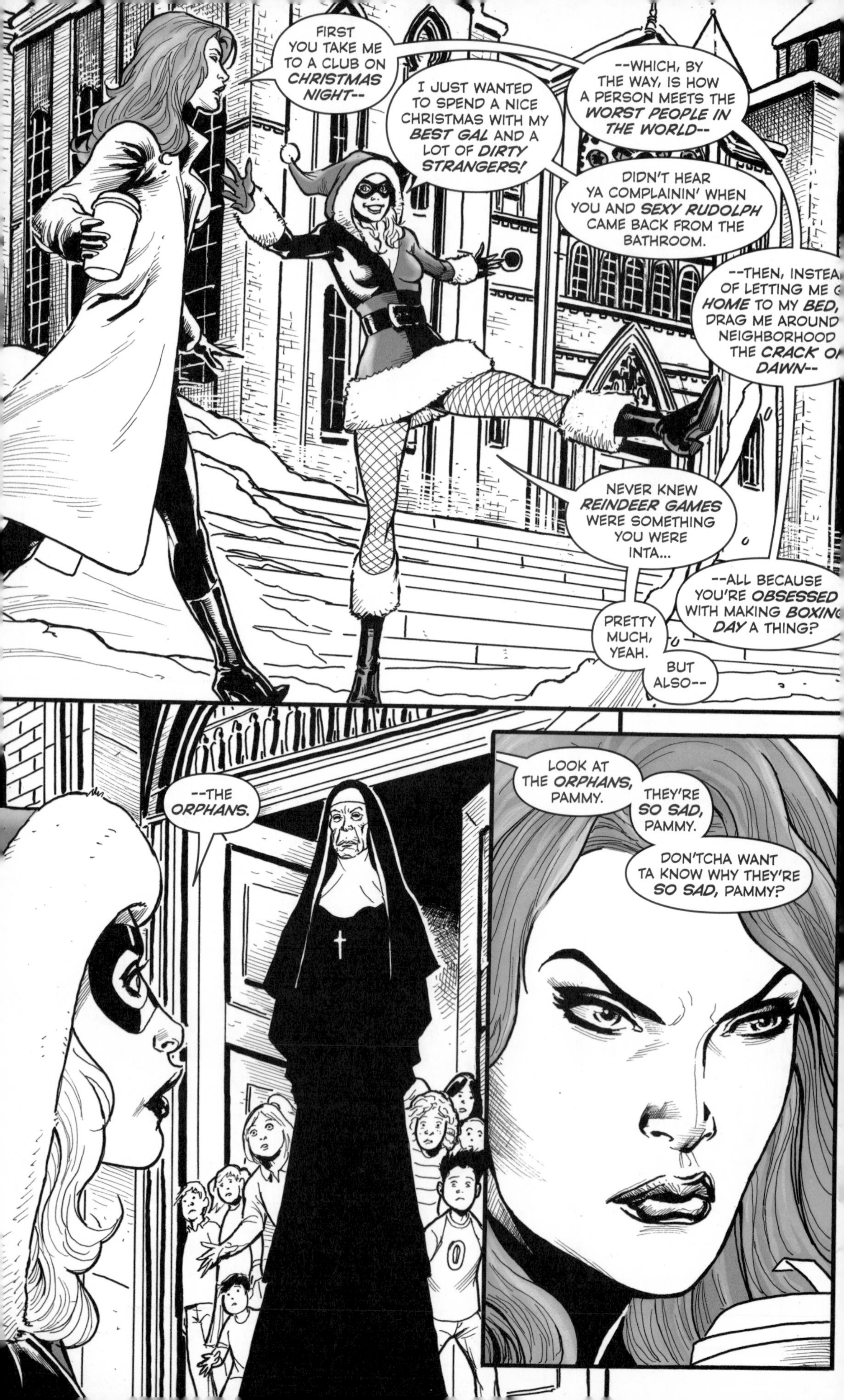

FIRST YOU TAKE ME TO A CLUB ON *CHRISTMAS NIGHT*--
I JUST WANTED TO SPEND A NICE CHRISTMAS WITH MY *BEST GAL* AND A LOT OF *DIRTY STRANGERS!*
--WHICH, BY THE WAY, IS HOW A PERSON MEETS THE *WORST PEOPLE IN THE WORLD*--
DIDN'T HEAR YA COMPLAININ' WHEN YOU AND *SEXY RUDOLPH* CAME BACK FROM THE BATHROOM.
--THEN, INSTEA OF LETTING ME G *HOME* TO MY *BED,* DRAG ME AROUND NEIGHBORHOOD THE *CRACK O DAWN*--
NEVER KNEW *REINDEER GAMES* WERE SOMETHING YOU WERE INTA...
--ALL BECAUSE YOU'RE *OBSESSED* WITH MAKING *BOXIN DAY* A THING?
PRETTY MUCH, YEAH.
BUT ALSO--
--THE *ORPHANS.*
LOOK AT THE *ORPHANS,* PAMMY.
THEY'RE *SO SAD,* PAMMY.
DON'TCHA WANT TA KNOW WHY THEY'RE *SO SAD,* PAMMY?

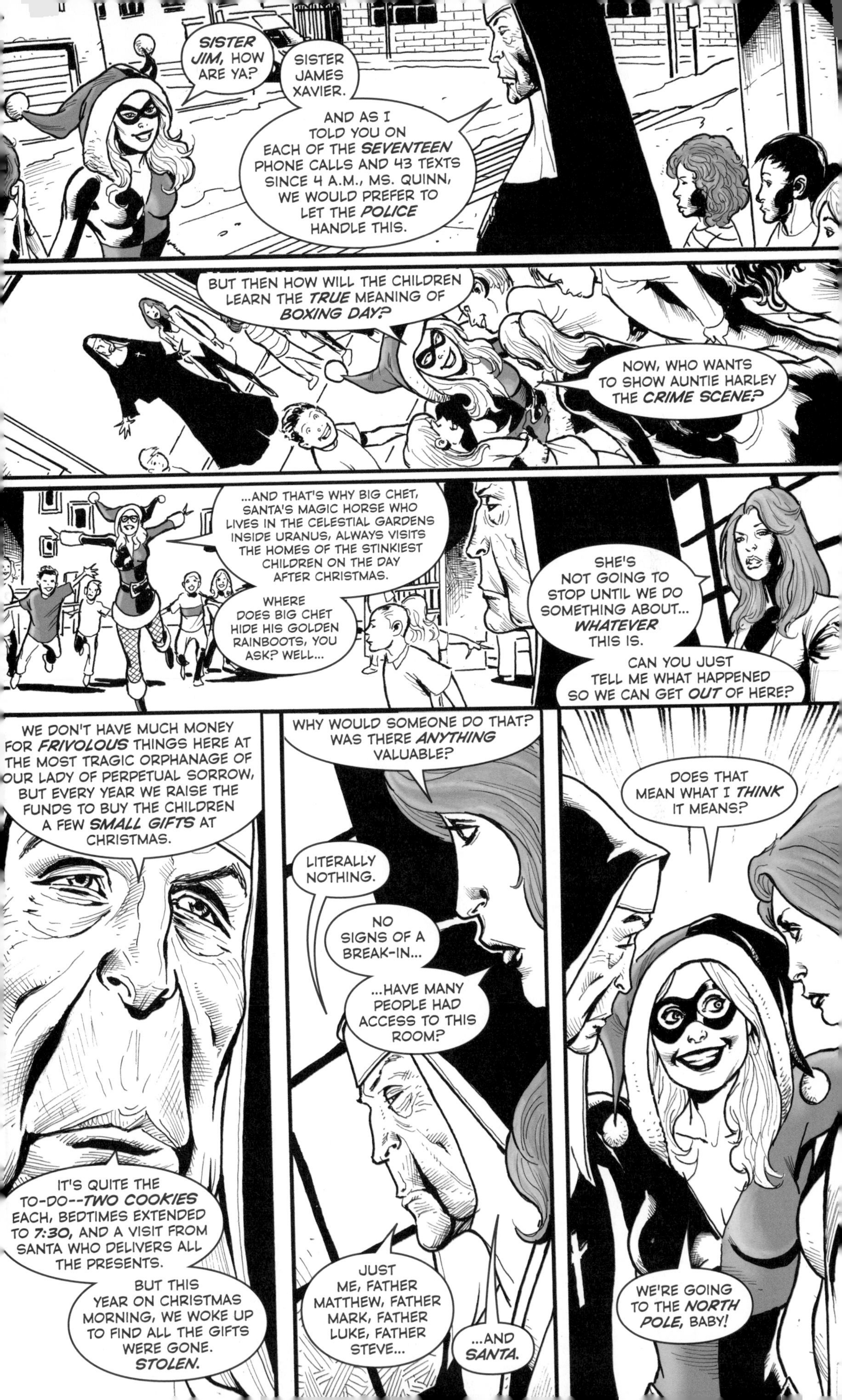
SISTER JIM, HOW ARE YA?
SISTER JAMES XAVIER.
AND AS I TOLD YOU ON EACH OF THE SEVENTEEN PHONE CALLS AND 43 TEXTS SINCE 4 A.M., MS. QUINN, WE WOULD PREFER TO LET THE POLICE HANDLE THIS.
BUT THEN HOW WILL THE CHILDREN LEARN THE TRUE MEANING OF BOXING DAY?
NOW, WHO WANTS TO SHOW AUNTIE HARLEY THE CRIME SCENE?
...AND THAT'S WHY BIG CHET, SANTA'S MAGIC HORSE WHO LIVES IN THE CELESTIAL GARDENS INSIDE URANUS, ALWAYS VISITS THE HOMES OF THE STINKIEST CHILDREN ON THE DAY AFTER CHRISTMAS.
WHERE DOES BIG CHET HIDE HIS GOLDEN RAINBOOTS, YOU ASK? WELL...
SHE'S NOT GOING TO STOP UNTIL WE DO SOMETHING ABOUT... WHATEVER THIS IS.
CAN YOU JUST TELL ME WHAT HAPPENED SO WE CAN GET OUT OF HERE?
WE DON'T HAVE MUCH MONEY FOR FRIVOLOUS THINGS HERE AT THE MOST TRAGIC ORPHANAGE OF OUR LADY OF PERPETUAL SORROW, BUT EVERY YEAR WE RAISE THE FUNDS TO BUY THE CHILDREN A FEW SMALL GIFTS AT CHRISTMAS.
IT'S QUITE THE TO-DO--TWO COOKIES EACH, BEDTIMES EXTENDED TO 7:30, AND A VISIT FROM SANTA WHO DELIVERS ALL THE PRESENTS.
BUT THIS YEAR ON CHRISTMAS MORNING, WE WOKE UP TO FIND ALL THE GIFTS WERE GONE. STOLEN.
WHY WOULD SOMEONE DO THAT? WAS THERE ANYTHING VALUABLE?
LITERALLY NOTHING.
NO SIGNS OF A BREAK-IN...
...HAVE MANY PEOPLE HAD ACCESS TO THIS ROOM?
JUST ME, FATHER MATTHEW, FATHER MARK, FATHER LUKE, FATHER STEVE...
...AND SANTA.
DOES THAT MEAN WHAT I THINK IT MEANS?
WE'RE GOING TO THE NORTH POLE, BABY!

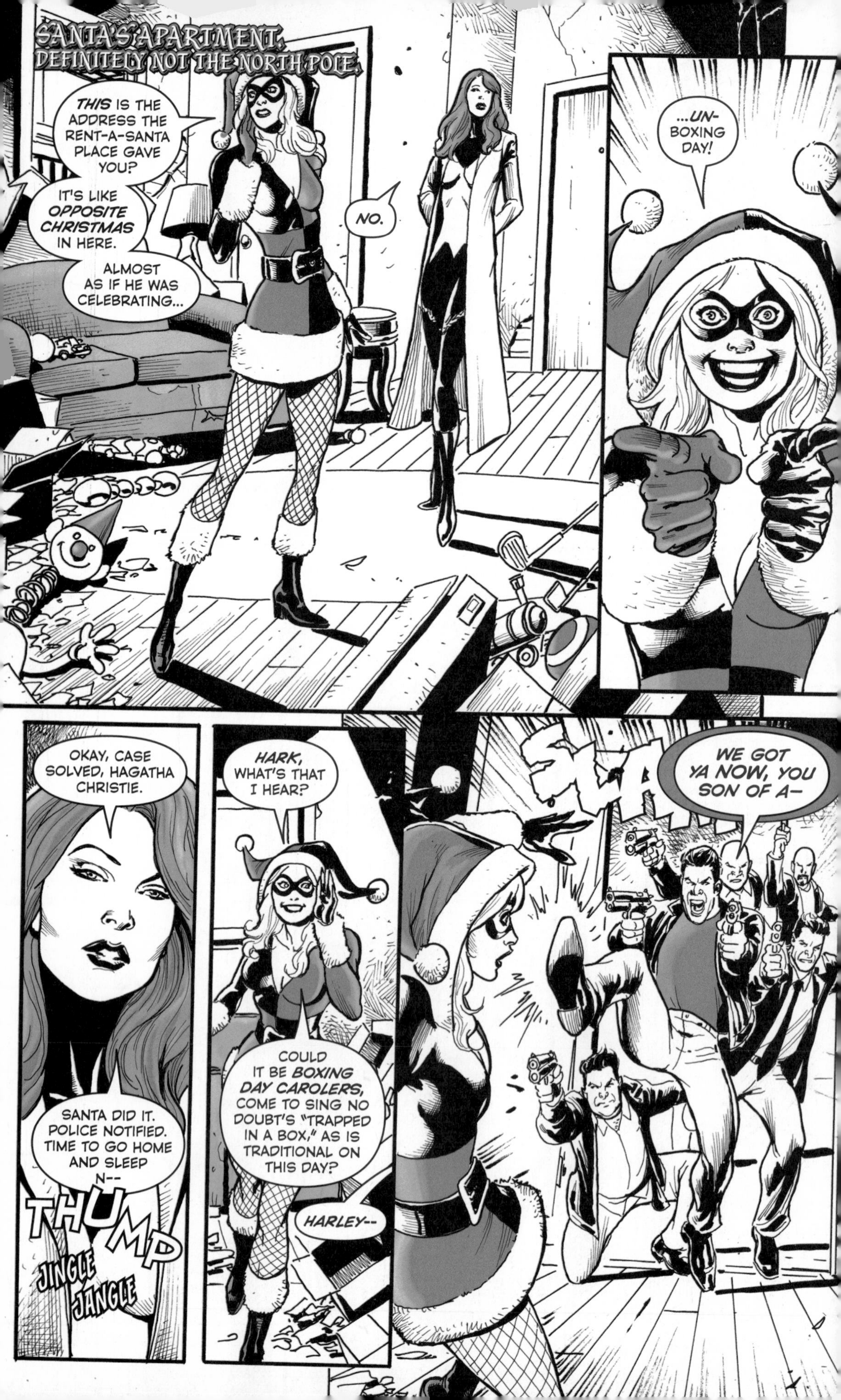

SANTA'S APARTMENT. DEFINITELY NOT THE NORTH POLE.
THIS IS THE ADDRESS THE RENT-A-SANTA PLACE GAVE YOU?
NO.
IT'S LIKE *OPPOSITE CHRISTMAS* IN HERE.
ALMOST AS IF HE WAS CELEBRATING...
...*UN*-BOXING DAY!
OKAY, CASE SOLVED, HAGATHA CHRISTIE.
SANTA DID IT. POLICE NOTIFIED. TIME TO GO HOME AND SLEEP N--
THUMP
JINGLE JANGLE
HARK, WHAT'S THAT I HEAR?
COULD IT BE *BOXING DAY CAROLERS*, COME TO SING NO DOUBT'S "TRAPPED IN A BOX," AS IS TRADITIONAL ON THIS DAY?
HARLEY--
WE GOT YA NOW, YOU SON OF A—

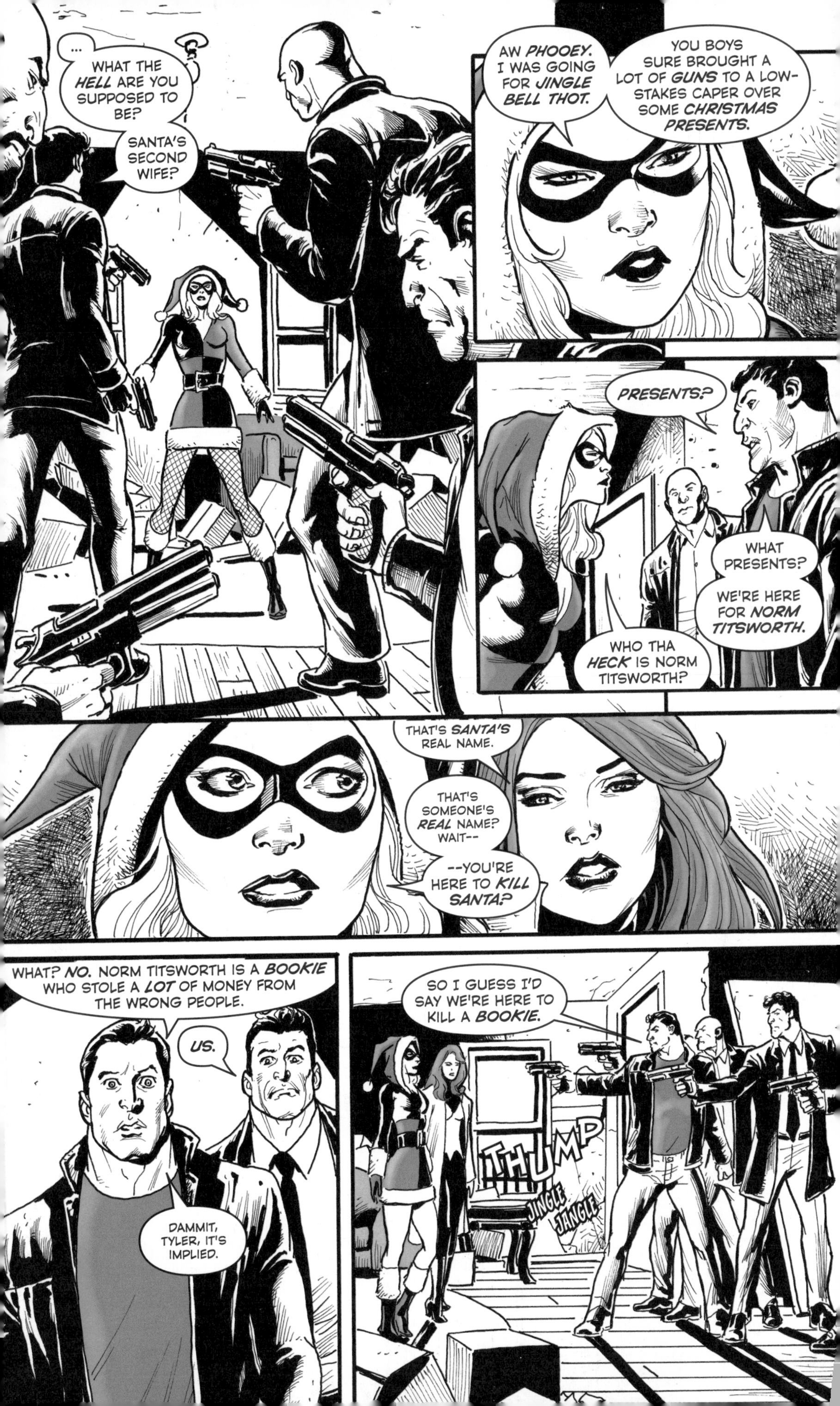
...
WHAT THE HELL ARE YOU SUPPOSED TO BE?
SANTA'S SECOND WIFE?
AW PHOOEY. I WAS GOING FOR JINGLE BELL THOT.
YOU BOYS SURE BROUGHT A LOT OF GUNS TO A LOW-STAKES CAPER OVER SOME CHRISTMAS PRESENTS.
PRESENTS?
WHAT PRESENTS?
WE'RE HERE FOR NORM TITSWORTH.
WHO THA HECK IS NORM TITSWORTH?
THAT'S SANTA'S REAL NAME.
THAT'S SOMEONE'S REAL NAME? WAIT--
--YOU'RE HERE TO KILL SANTA?
WHAT? NO. NORM TITSWORTH IS A BOOKIE WHO STOLE A LOT OF MONEY FROM THE WRONG PEOPLE.
US.
DAMMIT, TYLER, IT'S IMPLIED.
SO I GUESS I'D SAY WE'RE HERE TO KILL A BOOKIE.
THUMP
JINGLE
JANGLE

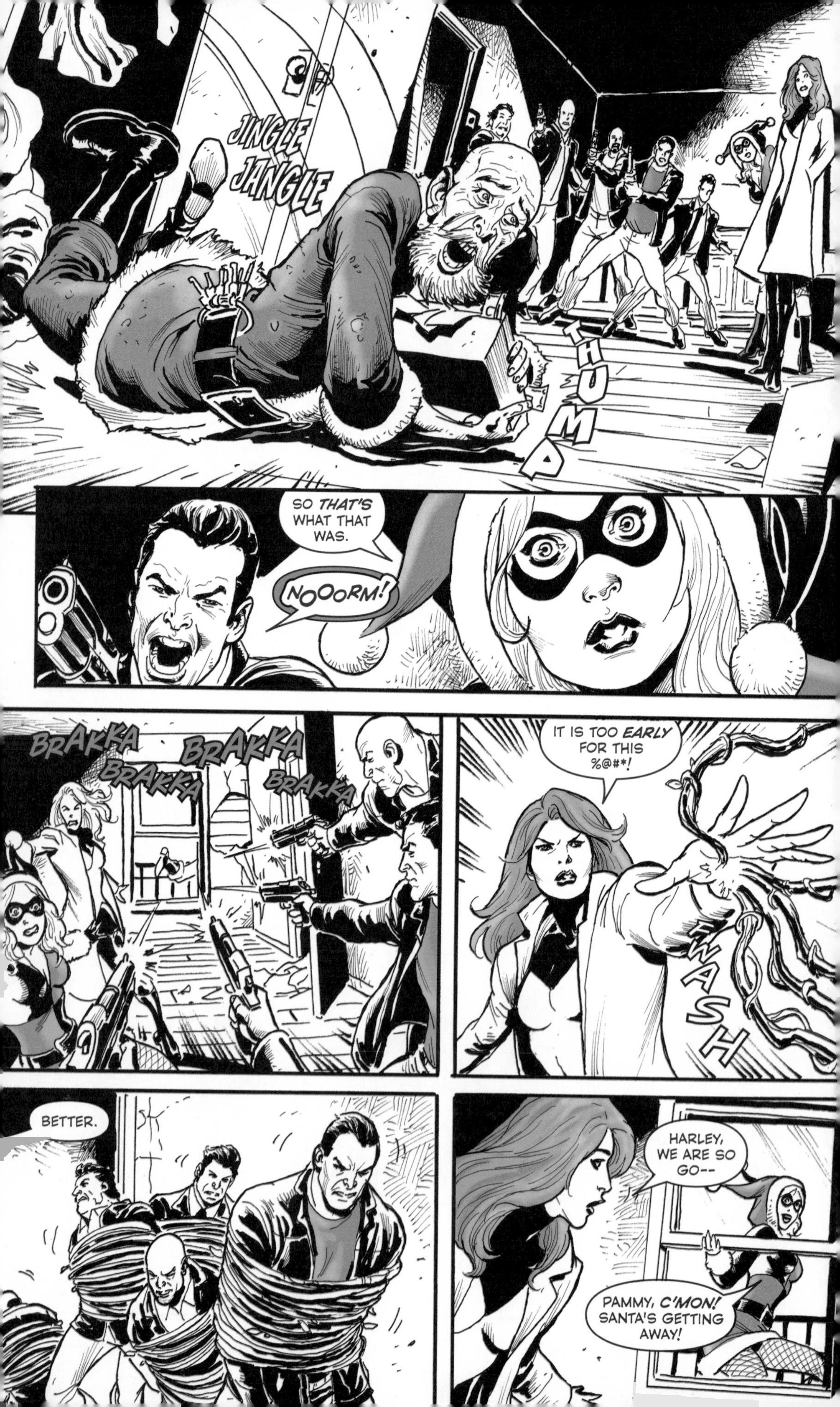
JINGLE
JANGLE
THUMP
SO THAT'S WHAT THAT WAS.
NOOORM!
BRAKKA
BRAKKA
BRAKKA
BRAKKA
IT IS TOO EARLY FOR THIS %@#*!
FWASH
BETTER.
HARLEY, WE ARE SO GO--
PAMMY, C'MON! SANTA'S GETTING AWAY!

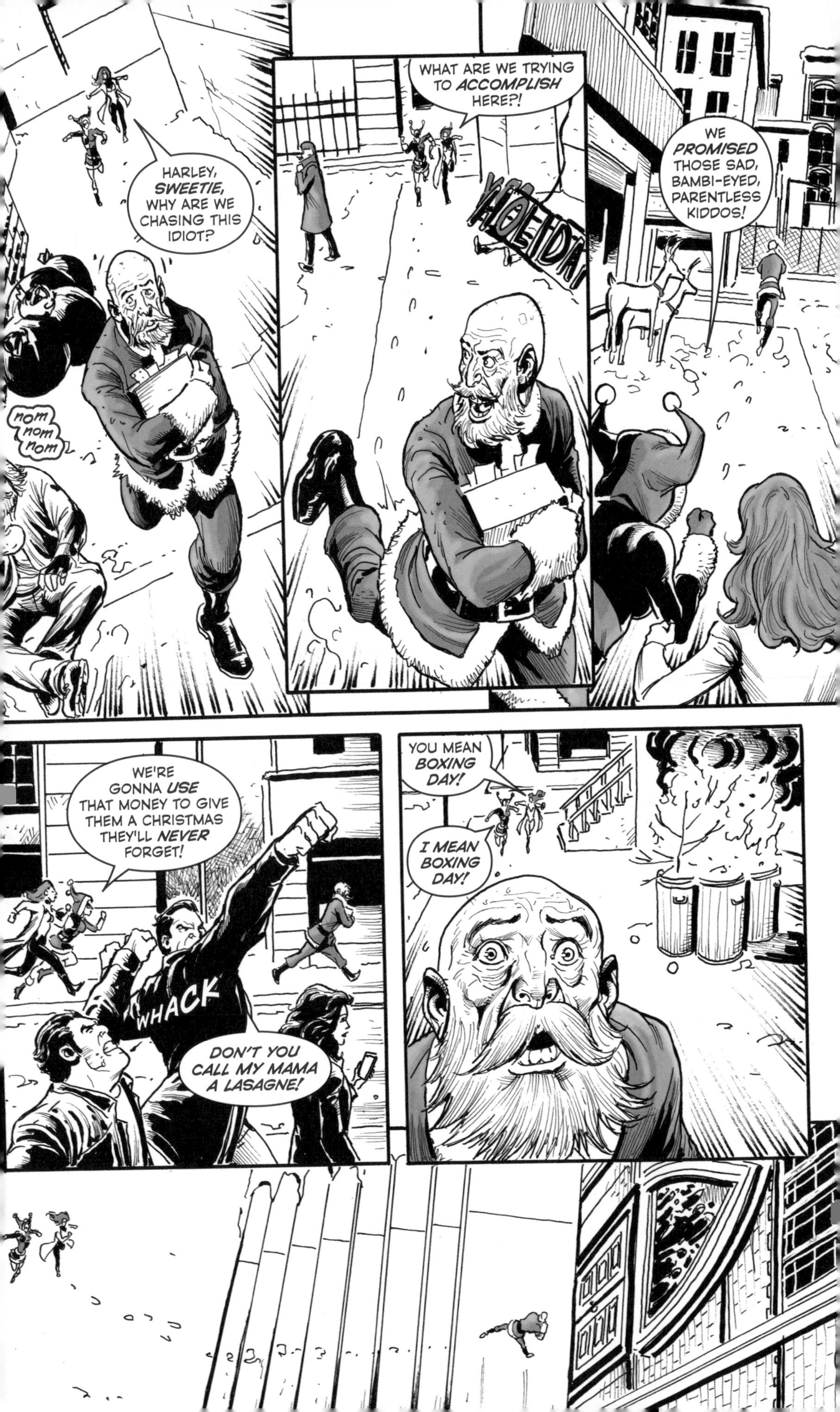
HARLEY, SWEETIE, WHY ARE WE CHASING THIS IDIOT?
nom nom nom
WHAT ARE WE TRYING TO ACCOMPLISH HERE?!
WE PROMISED THOSE SAD, BAMBI-EYED, PARENTLESS KIDDOS!
WE'RE GONNA USE THAT MONEY TO GIVE THEM A CHRISTMAS THEY'LL NEVER FORGET!
WHACK
DON'T YOU CALL MY MAMA A LASAGNE!
YOU MEAN BOXING DAY!
I MEAN BOXING DAY!

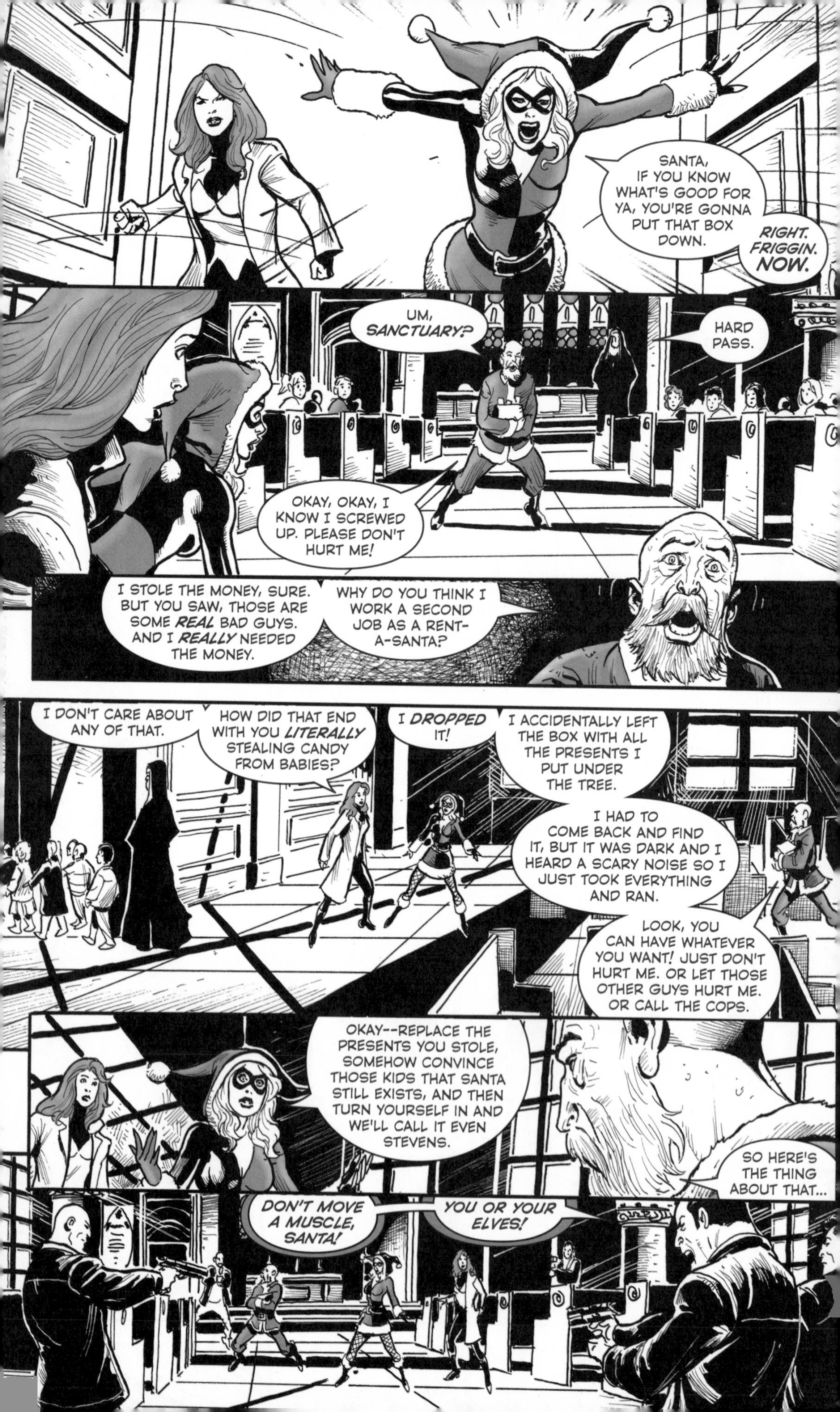
SANTA, IF YOU KNOW WHAT'S GOOD FOR YA, YOU'RE GONNA PUT THAT BOX DOWN.
RIGHT. FRIGGIN. NOW.
UM, SANCTUARY?
HARD PASS.
OKAY, OKAY, I KNOW I SCREWED UP. PLEASE DON'T HURT ME!
I STOLE THE MONEY, SURE. BUT YOU SAW, THOSE ARE SOME REAL BAD GUYS. AND I REALLY NEEDED THE MONEY.
WHY DO YOU THINK I WORK A SECOND JOB AS A RENT-A-SANTA?
I DON'T CARE ABOUT ANY OF THAT.
HOW DID THAT END WITH YOU LITERALLY STEALING CANDY FROM BABIES?
I DROPPED IT!
I ACCIDENTALLY LEFT THE BOX WITH ALL THE PRESENTS I PUT UNDER THE TREE.
I HAD TO COME BACK AND FIND IT, BUT IT WAS DARK AND I HEARD A SCARY NOISE SO I JUST TOOK EVERYTHING AND RAN.
LOOK, YOU CAN HAVE WHATEVER YOU WANT! JUST DON'T HURT ME. OR LET THOSE OTHER GUYS HURT ME. OR CALL THE COPS.
OKAY--REPLACE THE PRESENTS YOU STOLE, SOMEHOW CONVINCE THOSE KIDS THAT SANTA STILL EXISTS, AND THEN TURN YOURSELF IN AND WE'LL CALL IT EVEN STEVENS.
SO HERE'S THE THING ABOUT THAT...
DON'T MOVE A MUSCLE, SANTA!
YOU OR YOUR ELVES!

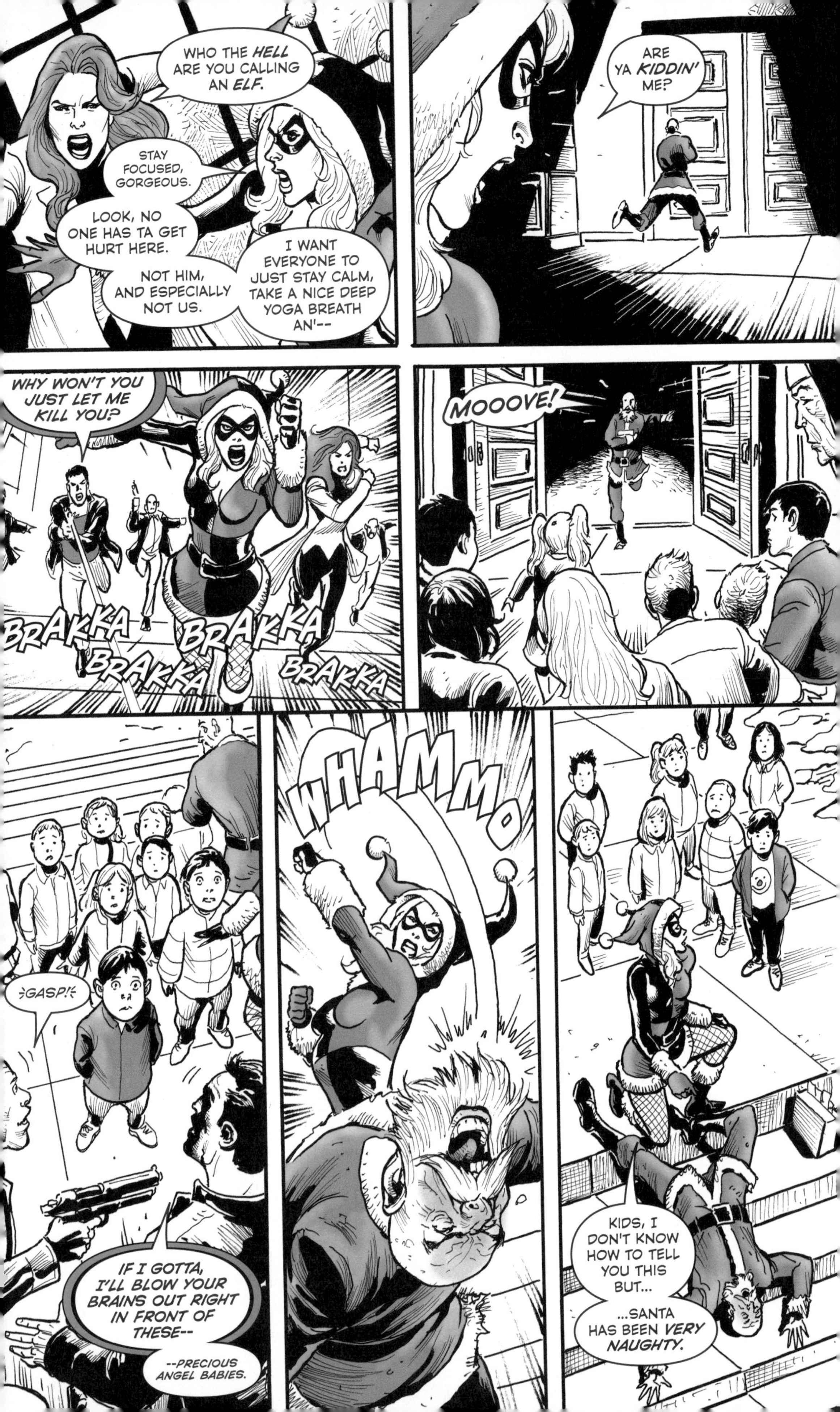
WHO THE HELL ARE YOU CALLING AN ELF.
STAY FOCUSED, GORGEOUS.
LOOK, NO ONE HAS TA GET HURT HERE.
NOT HIM, AND ESPECIALLY NOT US.
I WANT EVERYONE TO JUST STAY CALM, TAKE A NICE DEEP YOGA BREATH AN'--
ARE YA KIDDIN' ME?
WHY WON'T YOU JUST LET ME KILL YOU?
BRAKKA
BRAKKA
BRAKKA
BRAKKA
MOOOVE!
GASP!
IF I GOTTA, I'LL BLOW YOUR BRAINS OUT RIGHT IN FRONT OF THESE--
--PRECIOUS ANGEL BABIES.
WHAMMO
KIDS, I DON'T KNOW HOW TO TELL YOU THIS BUT...
...SANTA HAS BEEN VERY NAUGHTY.

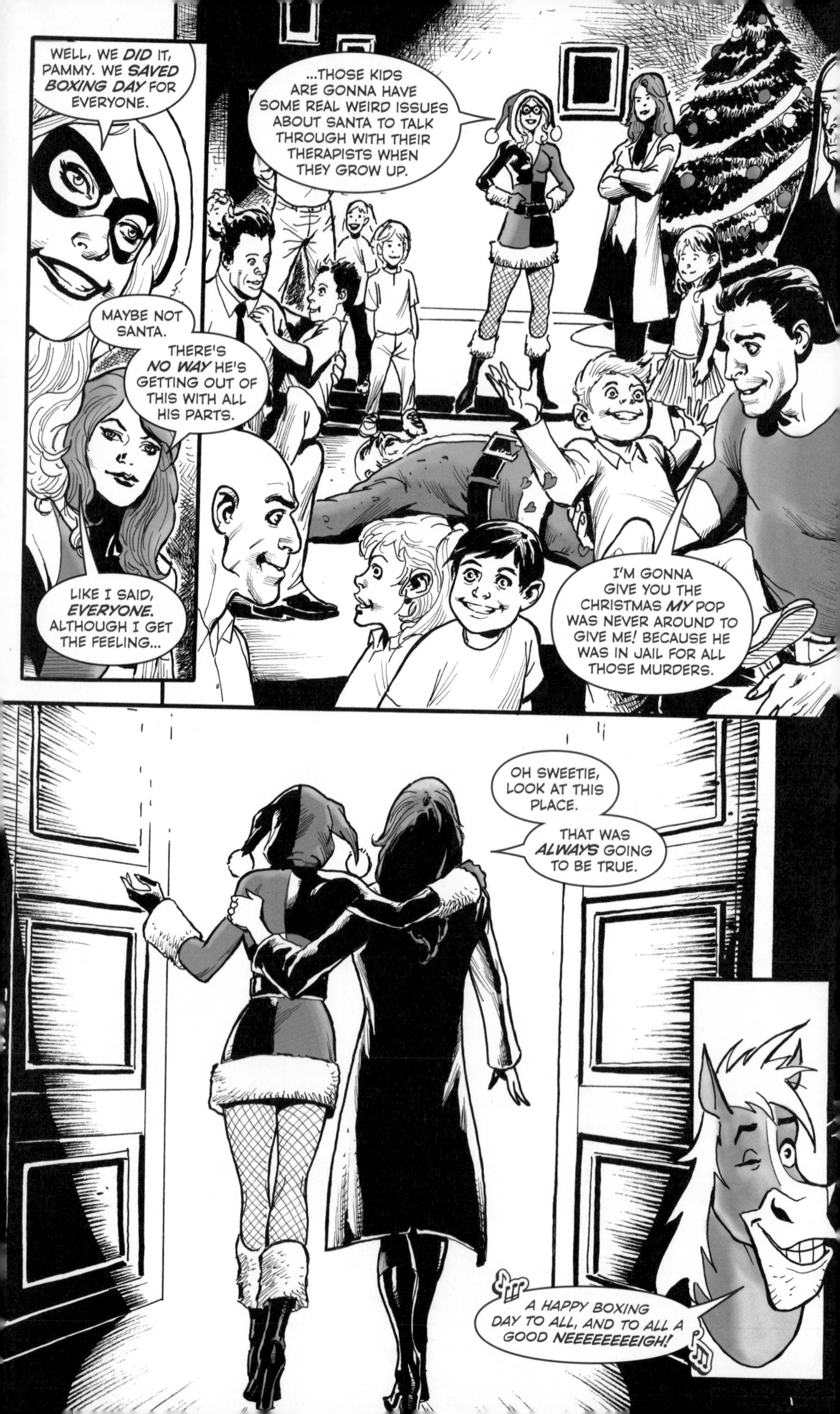
WELL, WE DID IT, PAMMY. WE SAVED BOXING DAY FOR EVERYONE.
MAYBE NOT SANTA.
THERE'S NO WAY HE'S GETTING OUT OF THIS WITH ALL HIS PARTS.
LIKE I SAID, EVERYONE. ALTHOUGH I GET THE FEELING...
...THOSE KIDS ARE GONNA HAVE SOME REAL WEIRD ISSUES ABOUT SANTA TO TALK THROUGH WITH THEIR THERAPISTS WHEN THEY GROW UP.
I'M GONNA GIVE YOU THE CHRISTMAS MY POP WAS NEVER AROUND TO GIVE ME! BECAUSE HE WAS IN JAIL FOR ALL THOSE MURDERS.
OH SWEETIE, LOOK AT THIS PLACE.
THAT WAS ALWAYS GOING TO BE TRUE.
A HAPPY BOXING DAY TO ALL, AND TO ALL A GOOD NEEEEEEEEIGH!

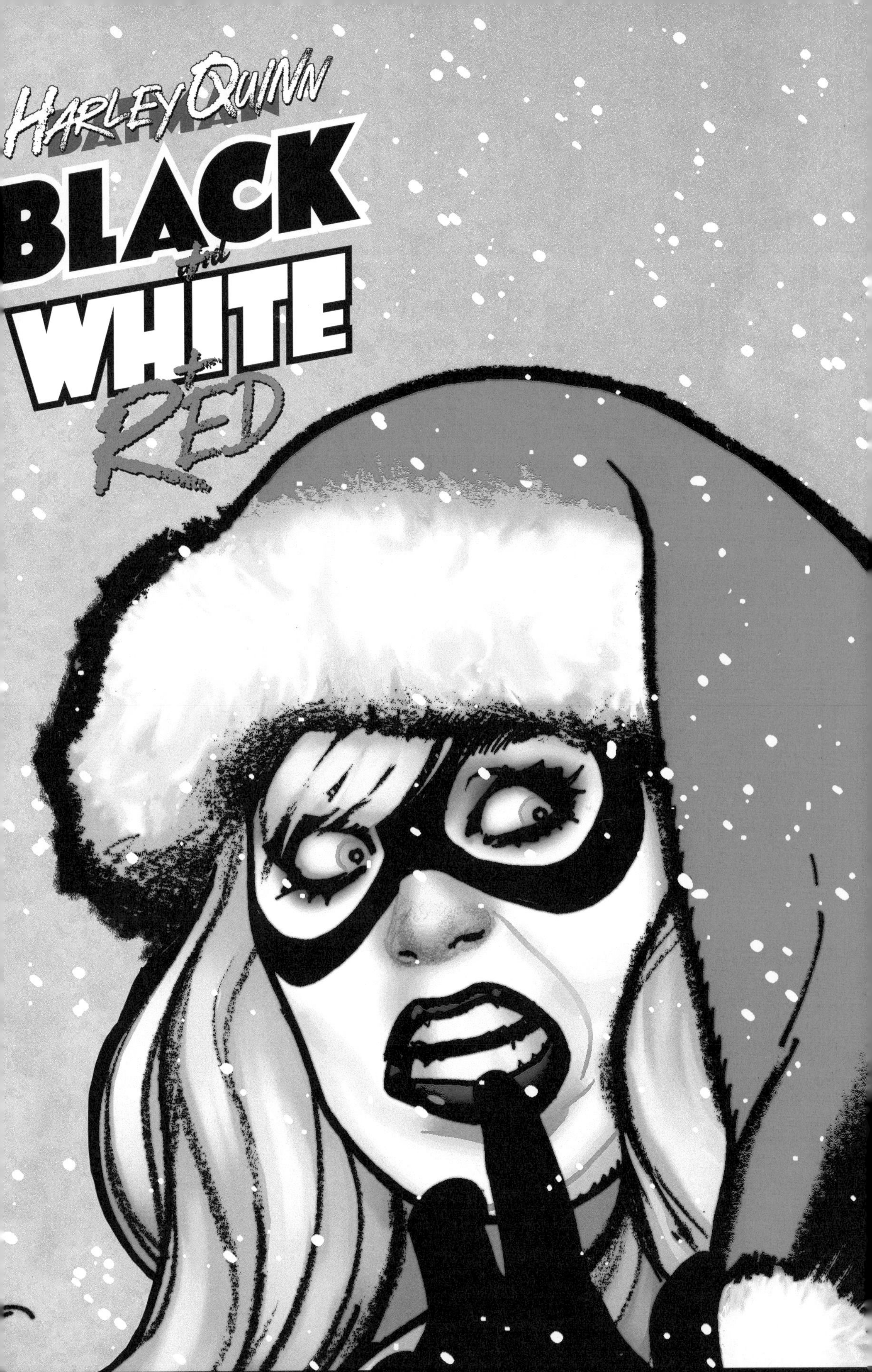

CHAPTER EIGHTEEN

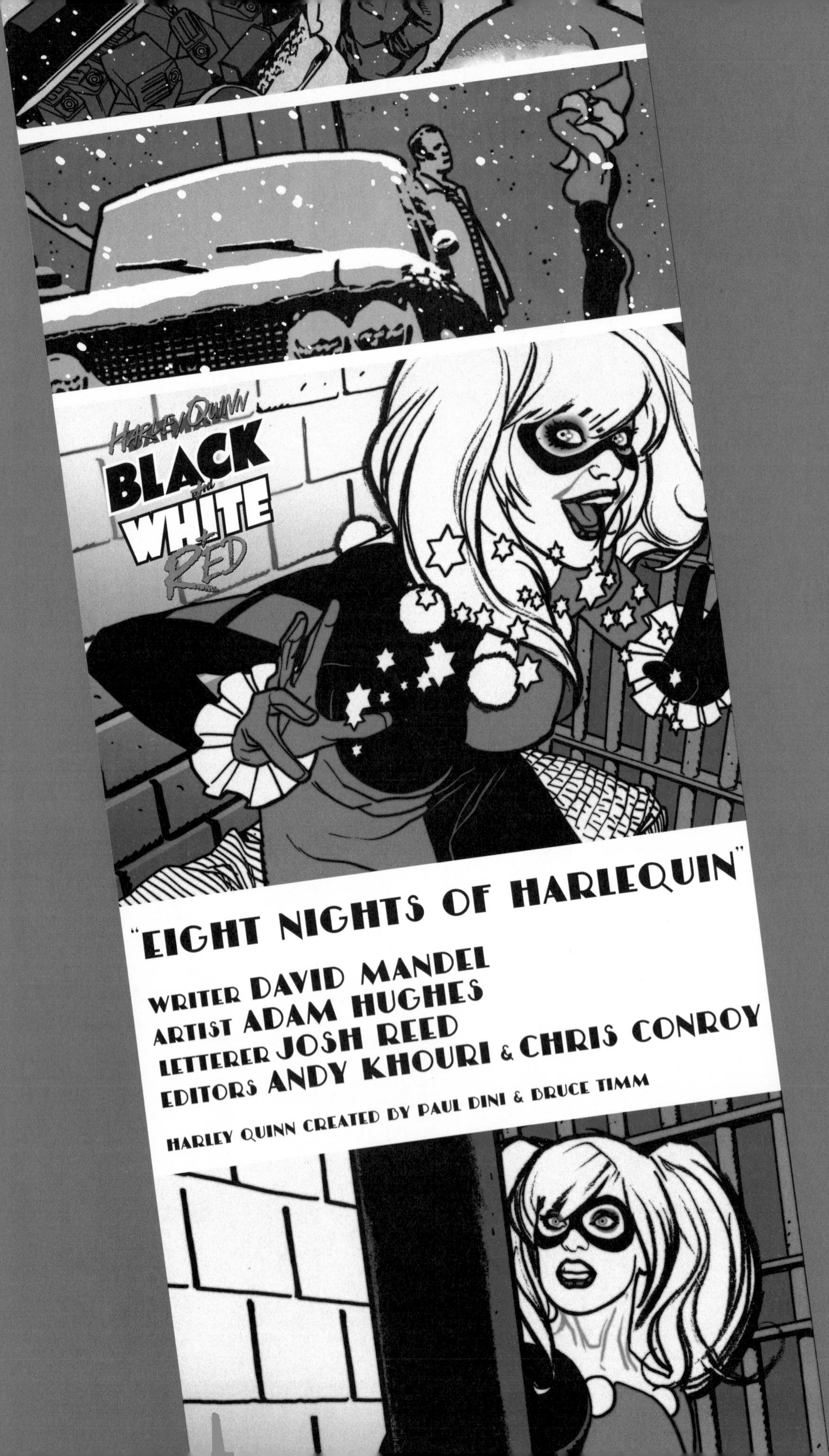
HARLEY QUINN
BLACK and WHITE + RED
"EIGHT NIGHTS OF HARLEQUIN"
WRITER DAVID MANDEL
ARTIST ADAM HUGHES
LETTERER JOSH REED
EDITORS ANDY KHOURI & CHRIS CONROY
HARLEY QUINN CREATED BY PAUL DINI & BRUCE TIMM

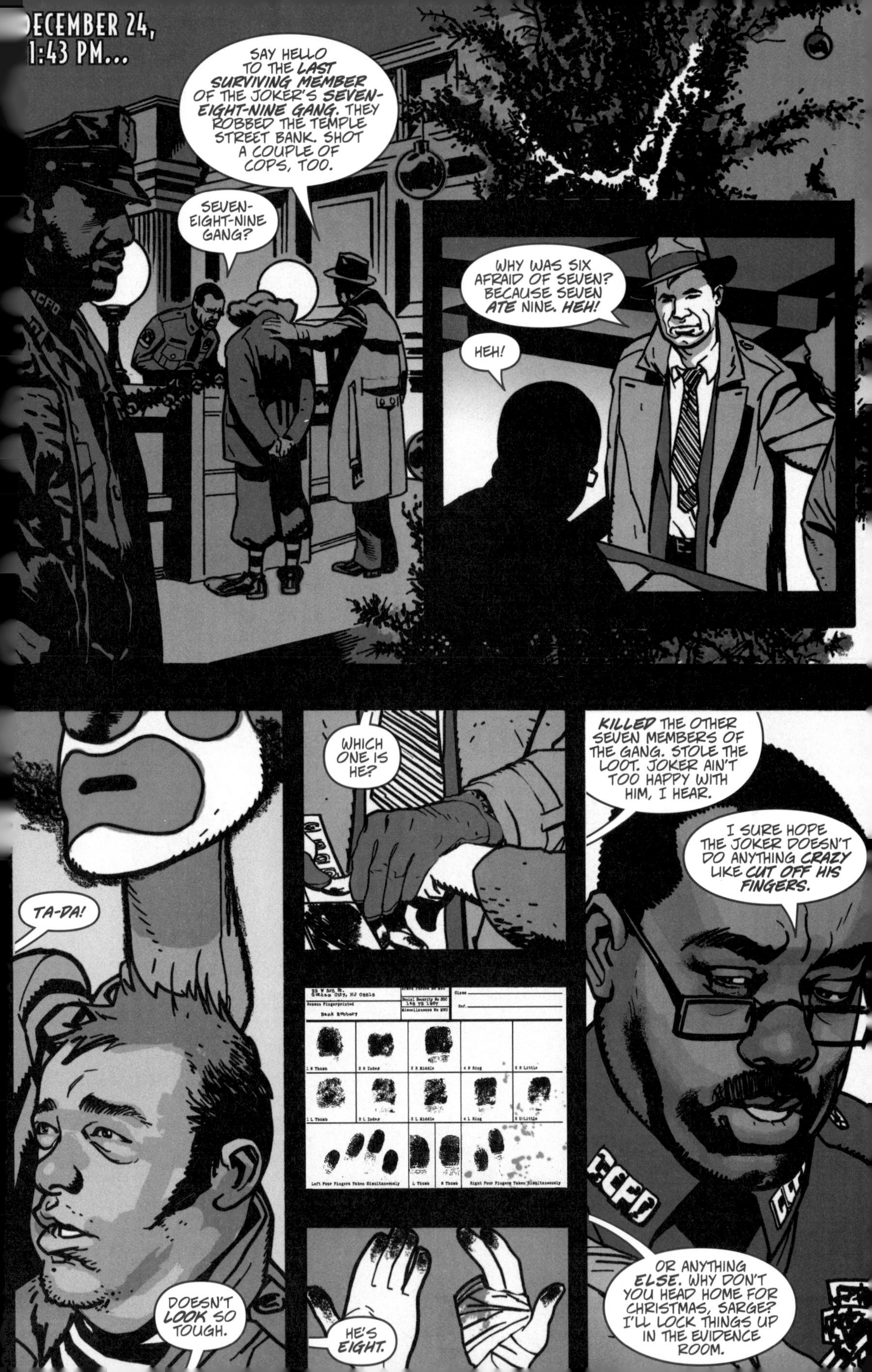
DECEMBER 24, 1:43 PM...
SAY HELLO TO THE LAST SURVIVING MEMBER OF THE JOKER'S SEVEN-EIGHT-NINE GANG. THEY ROBBED THE TEMPLE STREET BANK. SHOT A COUPLE OF COPS, TOO.
SEVEN-EIGHT-NINE GANG?
WHY WAS SIX AFRAID OF SEVEN? BECAUSE SEVEN ATE NINE. HEH!
HEH!
TA-DA!
DOESN'T LOOK SO TOUGH.
WHICH ONE IS HE?
HE'S EIGHT.
KILLED THE OTHER SEVEN MEMBERS OF THE GANG. STOLE THE LOOT. JOKER AIN'T TOO HAPPY WITH HIM, I HEAR.
I SURE HOPE THE JOKER DOESN'T DO ANYTHING CRAZY LIKE CUT OFF HIS FINGERS.
OR ANYTHING ELSE. WHY DON'T YOU HEAD HOME FOR CHRISTMAS, SARGE? I'LL LOCK THINGS UP IN THE EVIDENCE ROOM.

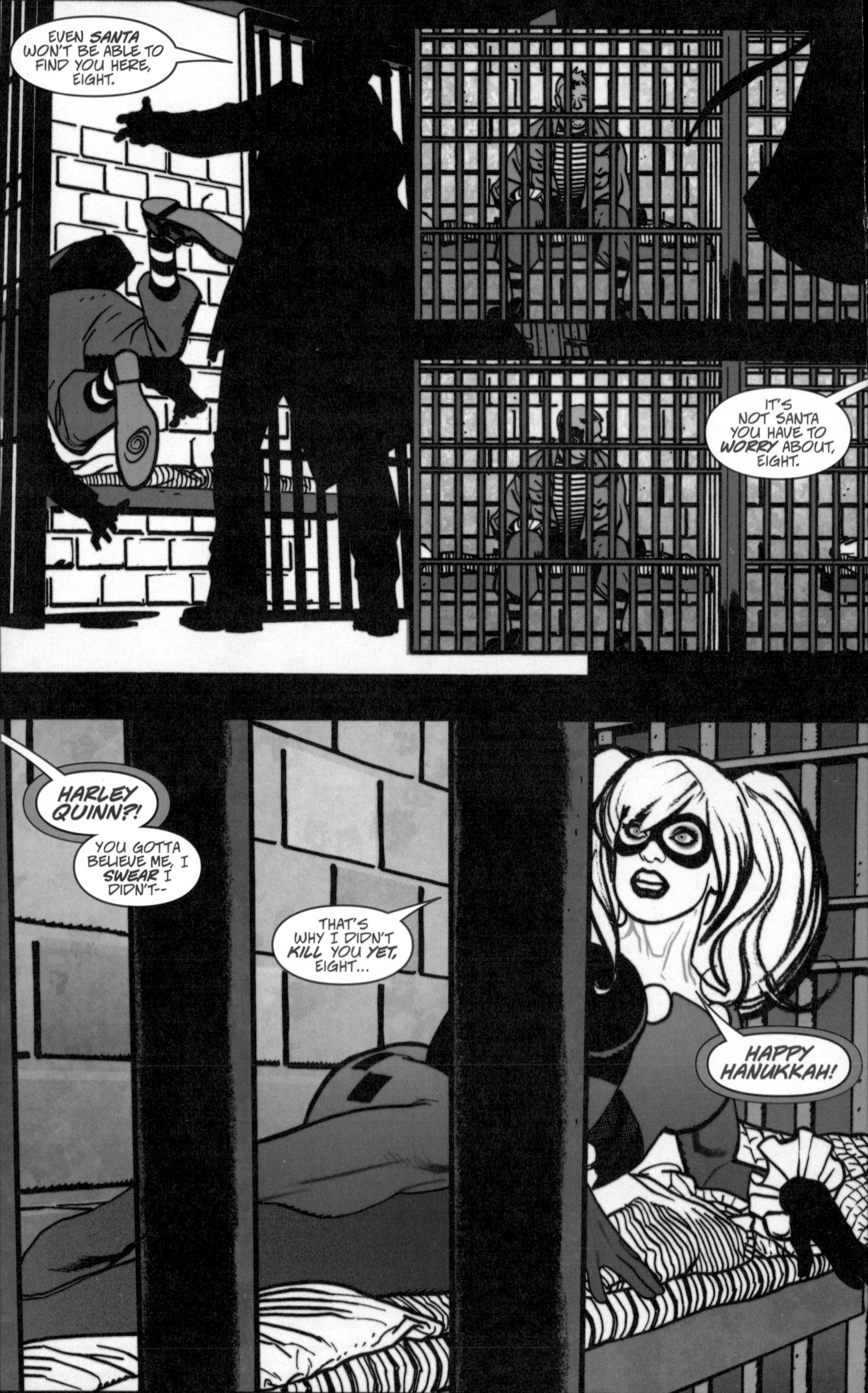
EVEN SANTA WON'T BE ABLE TO FIND YOU HERE, EIGHT.
IT'S NOT SANTA YOU HAVE TO WORRY ABOUT, EIGHT.
HARLEY QUINN?!
YOU GOTTA BELIEVE ME, I SWEAR I DIDN'T--
THAT'S WHY I DIDN'T KILL YOU YET, EIGHT...
HAPPY HANUKKAH!

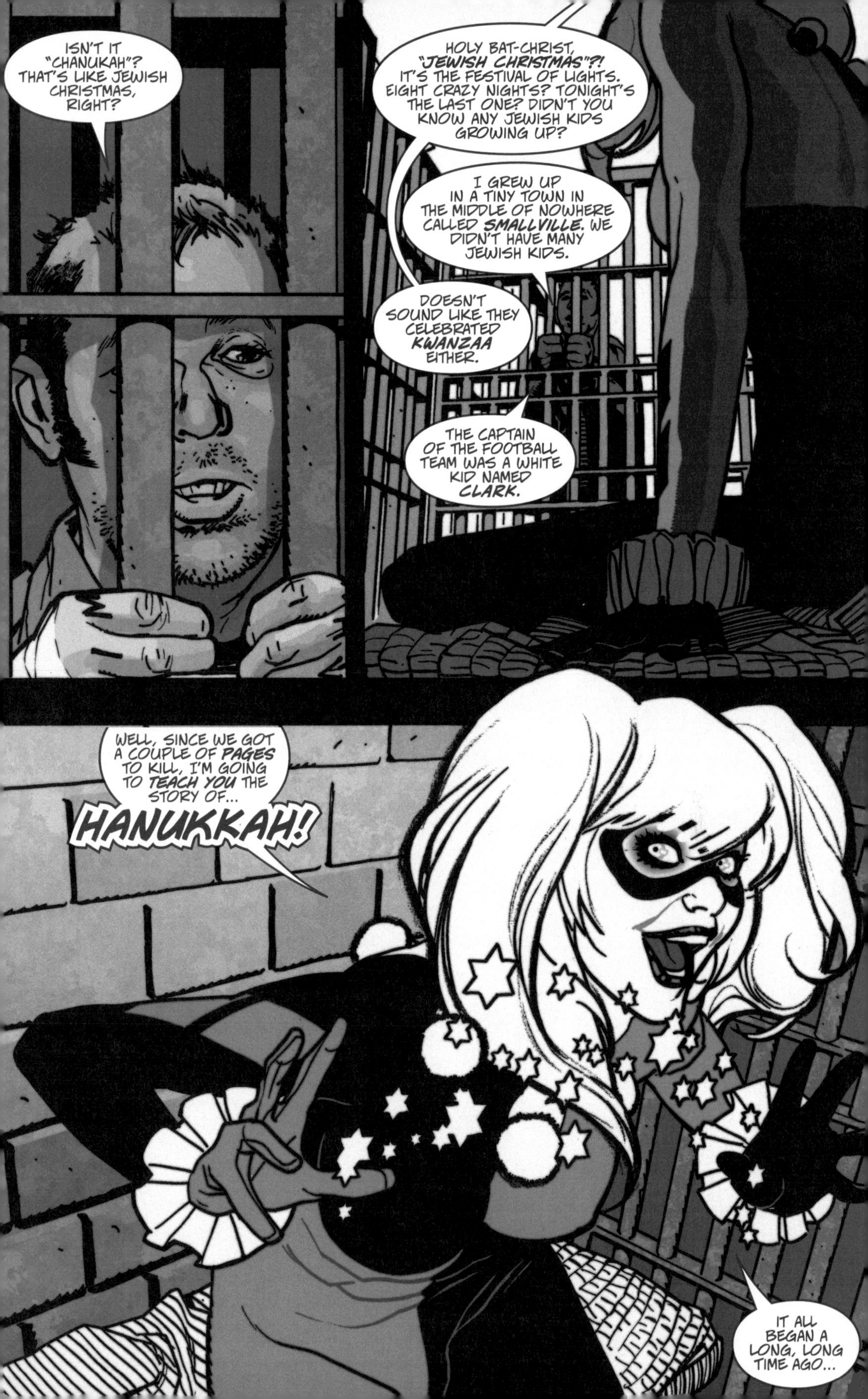

ISN'T IT "CHANUKAH"? THAT'S LIKE JEWISH CHRISTMAS, RIGHT?
HOLY BAT-CHRIST, "JEWISH CHRISTMAS"?! IT'S THE FESTIVAL OF LIGHTS. EIGHT CRAZY NIGHTS? TONIGHT'S THE LAST ONE? DIDN'T YOU KNOW ANY JEWISH KIDS GROWING UP?
I GREW UP IN A TINY TOWN IN THE MIDDLE OF NOWHERE CALLED SMALLVILLE. WE DIDN'T HAVE MANY JEWISH KIDS.
DOESN'T SOUND LIKE THEY CELEBRATED KWANZAA EITHER.
THE CAPTAIN OF THE FOOTBALL TEAM WAS A WHITE KID NAMED CLARK.
WELL, SINCE WE GOT A COUPLE OF PAGES TO KILL, I'M GOING TO TEACH YOU THE STORY OF...
HANUKKAH!
IT ALL BEGAN A LONG, LONG TIME AGO...

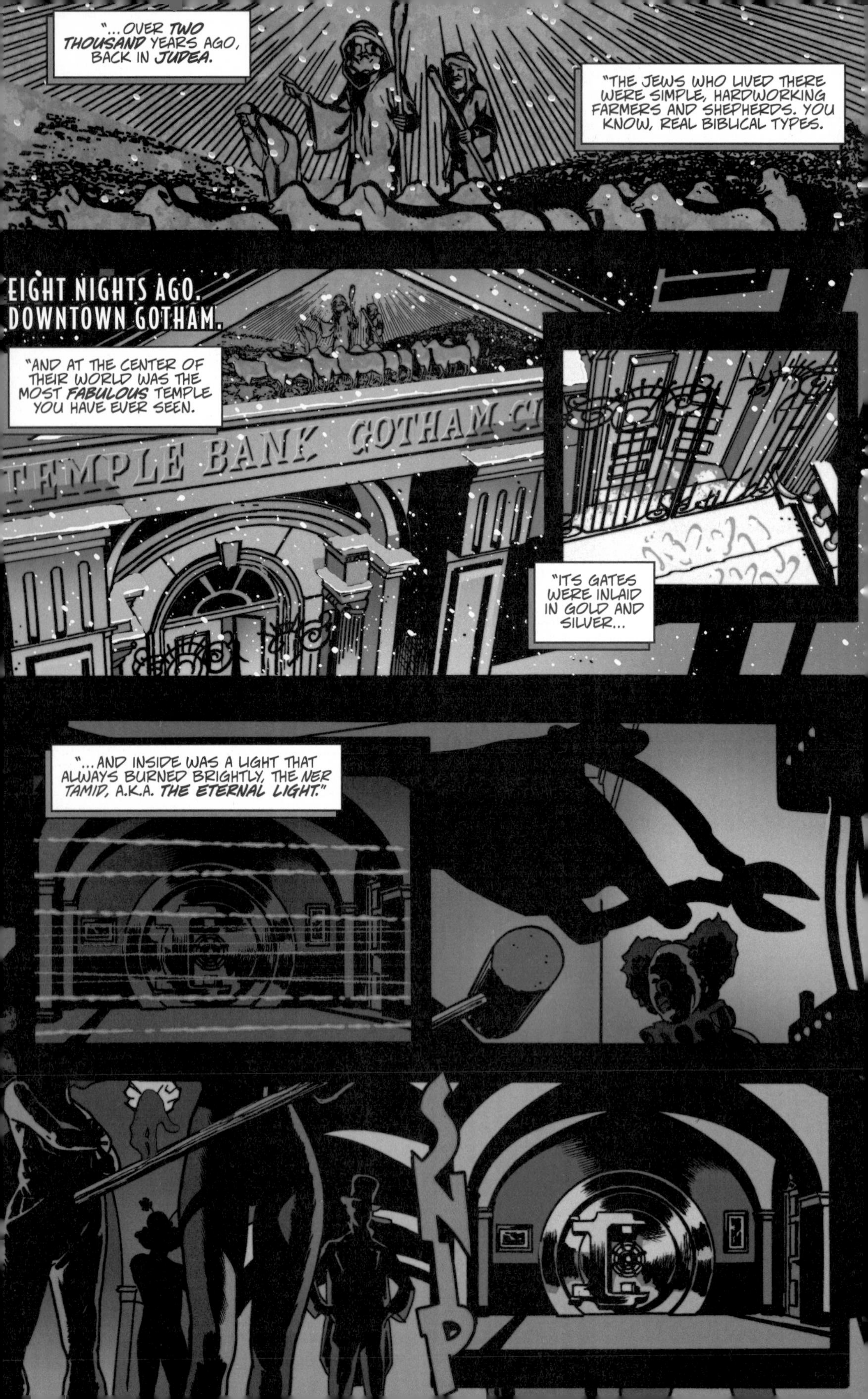
"...OVER TWO THOUSAND YEARS AGO, BACK IN JUDEA.
"THE JEWS WHO LIVED THERE WERE SIMPLE, HARDWORKING FARMERS AND SHEPHERDS. YOU KNOW, REAL BIBLICAL TYPES.
EIGHT NIGHTS AGO. DOWNTOWN GOTHAM.
"AND AT THE CENTER OF THEIR WORLD WAS THE MOST FABULOUS TEMPLE YOU HAVE EVER SEEN.
TEMPLE BANK GOTHAM CI
"ITS GATES WERE INLAID IN GOLD AND SILVER...
"...AND INSIDE WAS A LIGHT THAT ALWAYS BURNED BRIGHTLY, THE NER TAMID, A.K.A. THE ETERNAL LIGHT."
SNIP

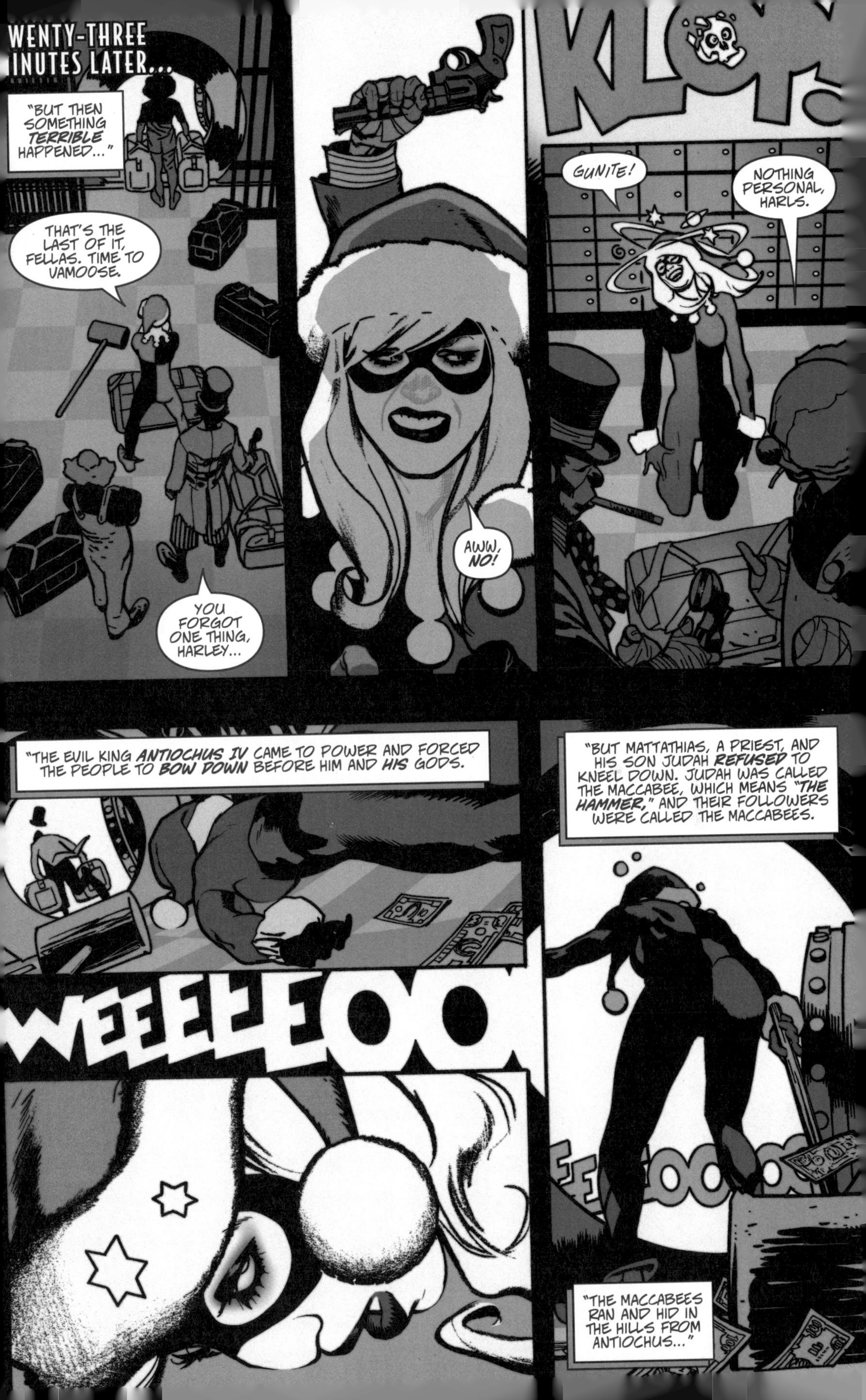
WENTY-THREE INUTES LATER...
"BUT THEN SOMETHING TERRIBLE HAPPENED..."
THAT'S THE LAST OF IT, FELLAS. TIME TO VAMOOSE.
YOU FORGOT ONE THING, HARLEY...
AWW, NO!
KLOP!
GUNITE!
NOTHING PERSONAL, HARLS.
"THE EVIL KING ANTIOCHUS IV CAME TO POWER AND FORCED THE PEOPLE TO BOW DOWN BEFORE HIM AND HIS GODS.
WEEEEEOO
"BUT MATTATHIAS, A PRIEST, AND HIS SON JUDAH REFUSED TO KNEEL DOWN. JUDAH WAS CALLED THE MACCABEE, WHICH MEANS "THE HAMMER," AND THEIR FOLLOWERS WERE CALLED THE MACCABEES.
"THE MACCABEES RAN AND HID IN THE HILLS FROM ANTIOCHUS..."

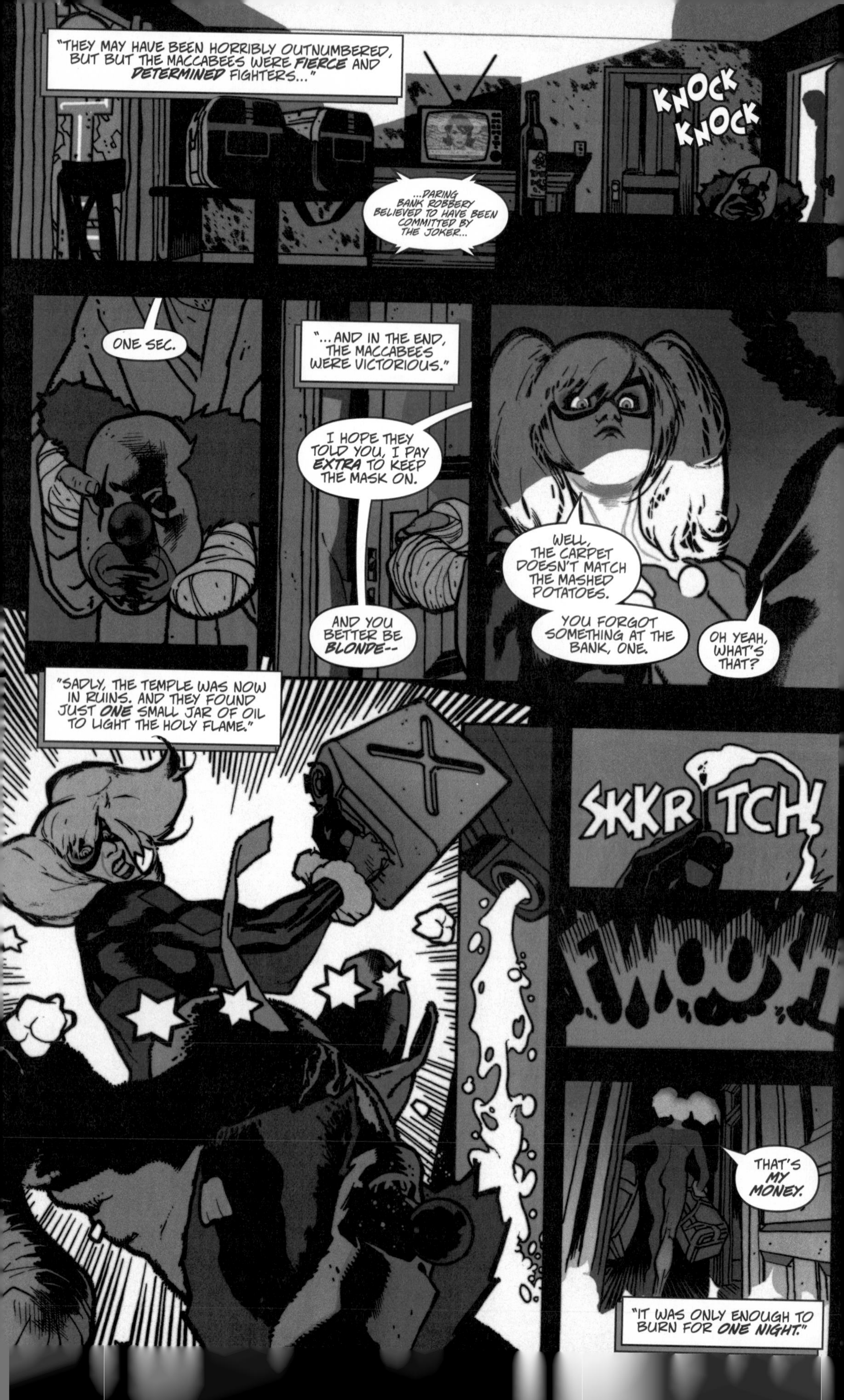
"THEY MAY HAVE BEEN HORRIBLY OUTNUMBERED, BUT BUT THE MACCABEES WERE FIERCE AND DETERMINED FIGHTERS..."
...DARING BANK ROBBERY BELIEVED TO HAVE BEEN COMMITTED BY THE JOKER...
KNOCK KNOCK
ONE SEC.
"...AND IN THE END, THE MACCABEES WERE VICTORIOUS."
I HOPE THEY TOLD YOU, I PAY EXTRA TO KEEP THE MASK ON.
AND YOU BETTER BE BLONDE--
WELL, THE CARPET DOESN'T MATCH THE MASHED POTATOES.
YOU FORGOT SOMETHING AT THE BANK, ONE.
OH YEAH, WHAT'S THAT?
"SADLY, THE TEMPLE WAS NOW IN RUINS. AND THEY FOUND JUST ONE SMALL JAR OF OIL TO LIGHT THE HOLY FLAME."
SKKRITCH!
FWOOSH
THAT'S MY MONEY.
"IT WAS ONLY ENOUGH TO BURN FOR ONE NIGHT."

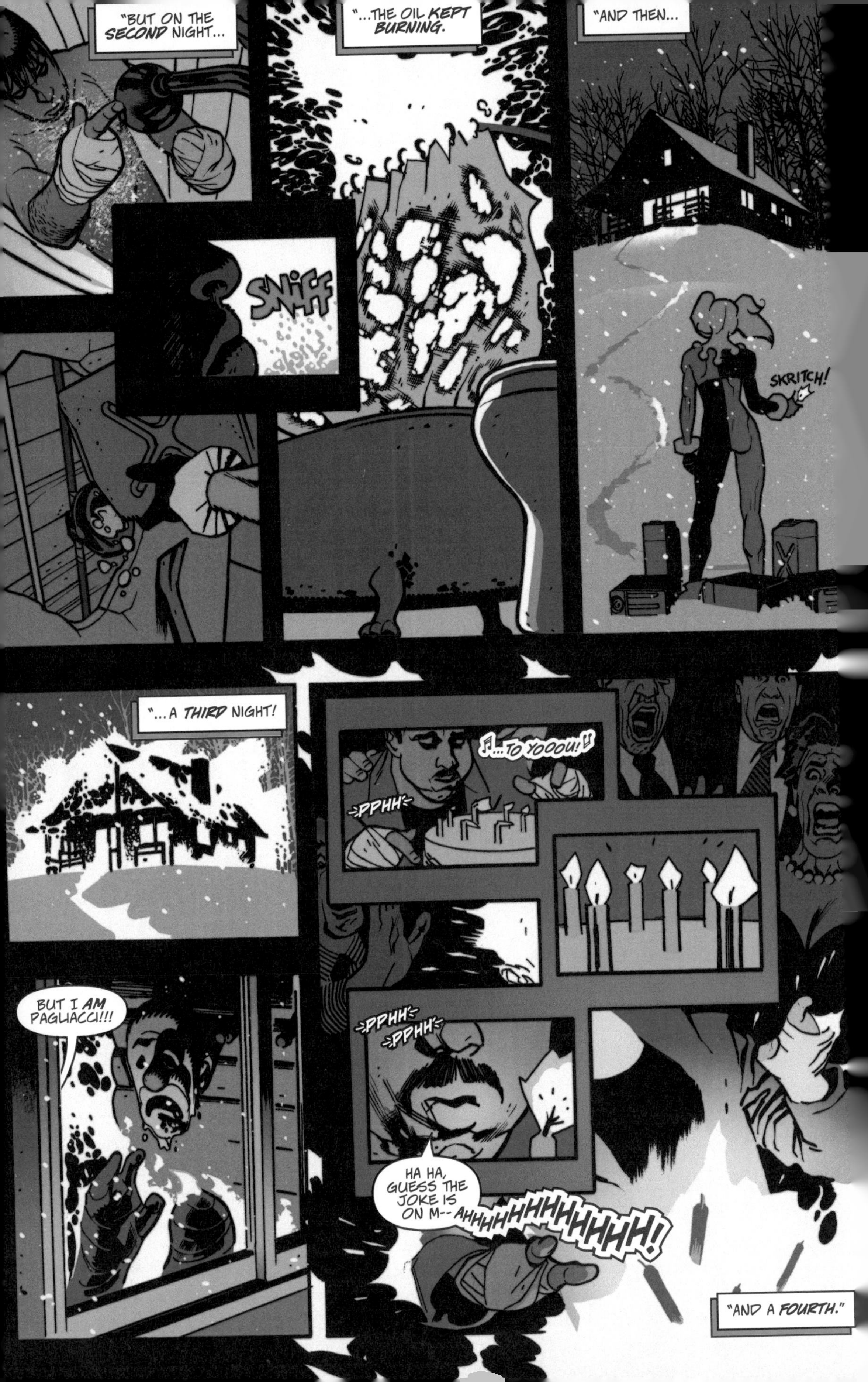
"BUT ON THE SECOND NIGHT...
SNIFF
"...THE OIL KEPT BURNING.
"AND THEN...
SKRITCH!
"...A THIRD NIGHT!
♫...TO YOOOU!♫
PPHH
BUT I AM PAGLIACCI!!!
PPHH
PPHH
HA HA, GUESS THE JOKE IS ON M-- AHHHHHHHHHHHHH!
"AND A FOURTH."

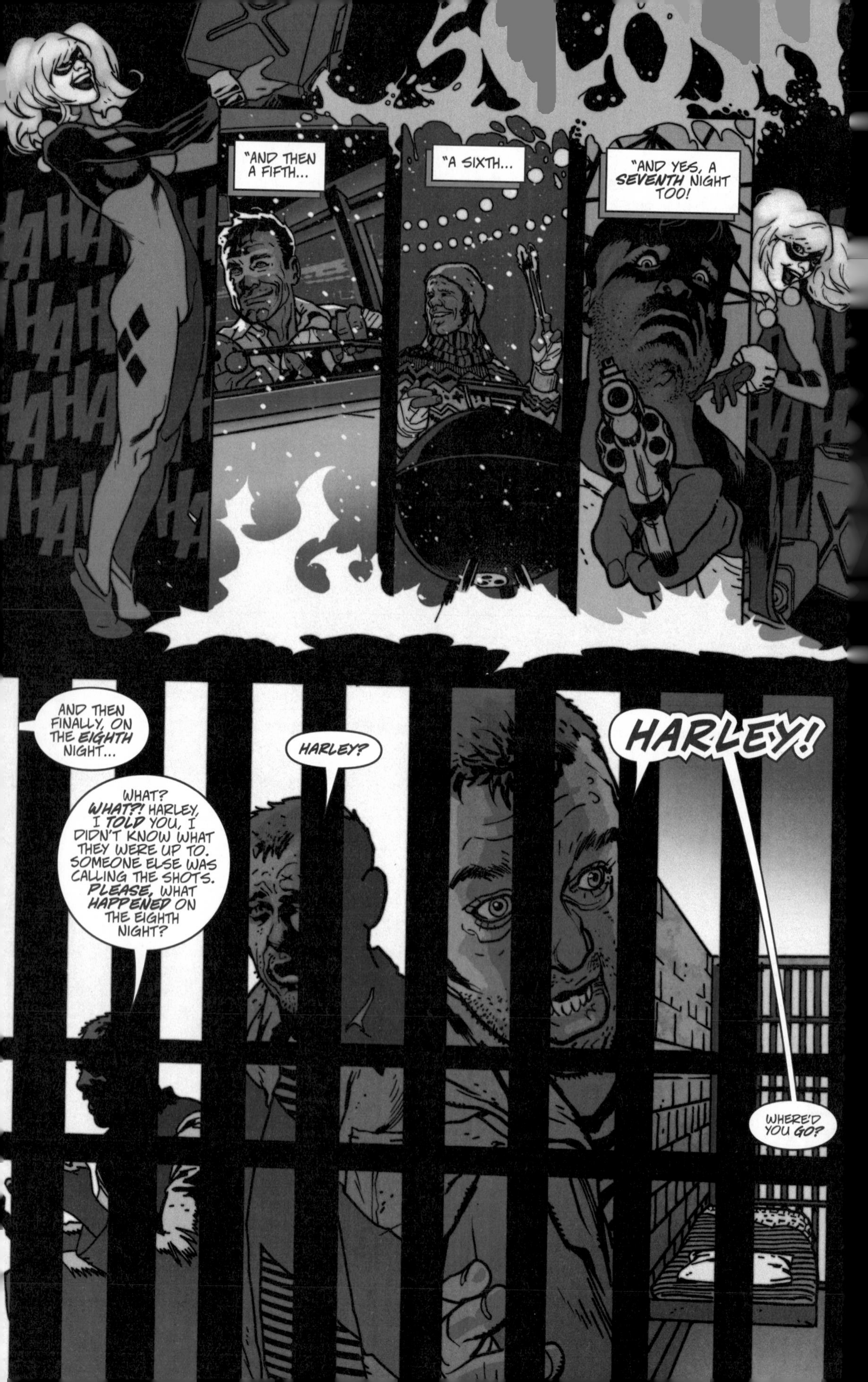
SPLOOSH
HAHAHAHAHAHAHAHAHA
"AND THEN A FIFTH...
"A SIXTH...
"AND YES, A SEVENTH NIGHT TOO!
AND THEN FINALLY, ON THE EIGHTH NIGHT...
WHAT? WHAT?! HARLEY, I TOLD YOU, I DIDN'T KNOW WHAT THEY WERE UP TO. SOMEONE ELSE WAS CALLING THE SHOTS. PLEASE, WHAT HAPPENED ON THE EIGHTH NIGHT?
HARLEY?
HARLEY!
WHERE'D YOU GO?

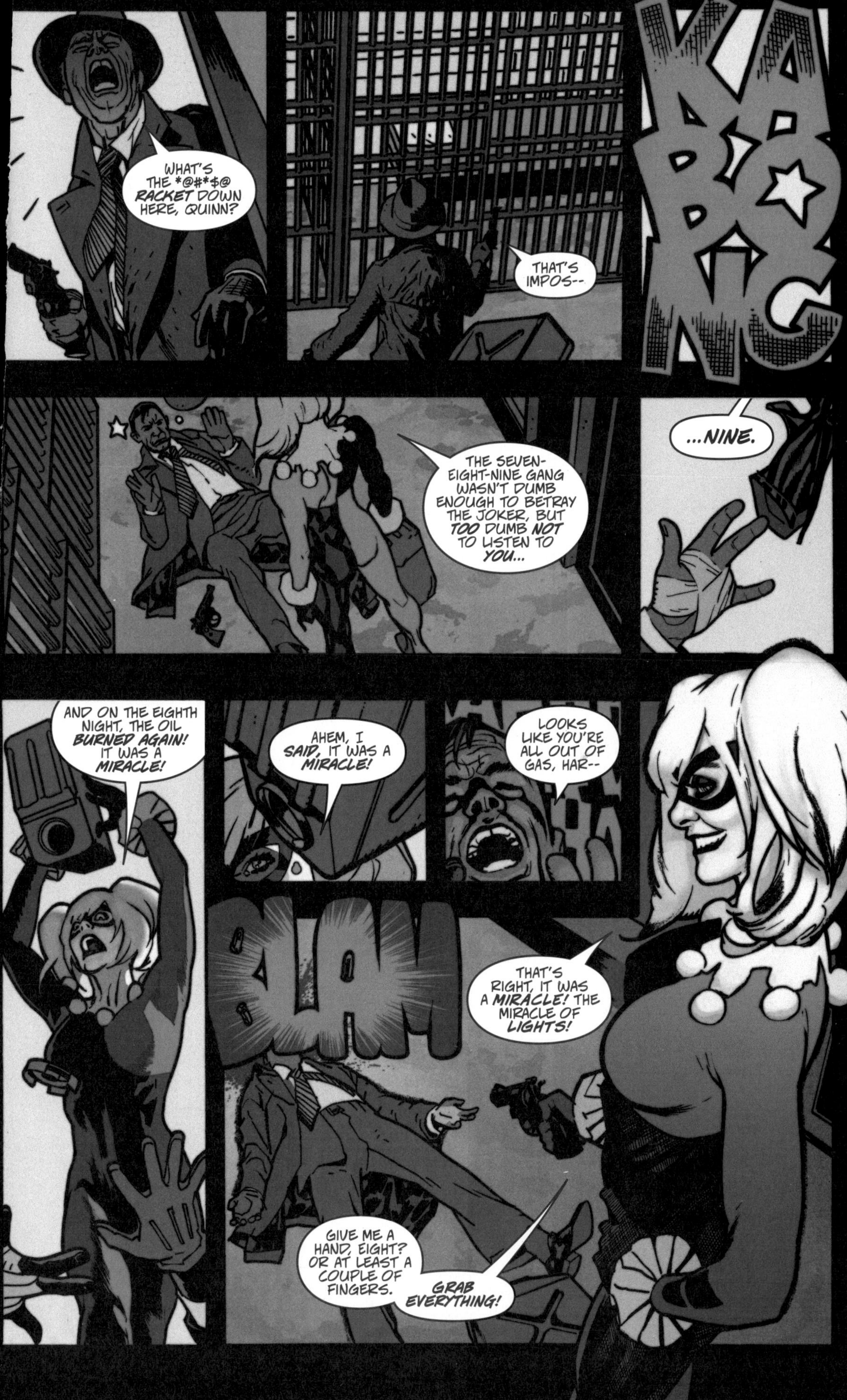
WHAT'S THE *@#*$@ RACKET DOWN HERE, QUINN?
THAT'S IMPOS--
THE SEVEN-EIGHT-NINE GANG WASN'T DUMB ENOUGH TO BETRAY THE JOKER, BUT TOO DUMB NOT TO LISTEN TO YOU...
...NINE.
AND ON THE EIGHTH NIGHT, THE OIL BURNED AGAIN! IT WAS A MIRACLE!
AHEM, I SAID, IT WAS A MIRACLE!
LOOKS LIKE YOU'RE ALL OUT OF GAS, HAR--
THAT'S RIGHT, IT WAS A MIRACLE! THE MIRACLE OF LIGHTS!
GIVE ME A HAND, EIGHT? OR AT LEAST A COUPLE OF FINGERS.
GRAB EVERYTHING!

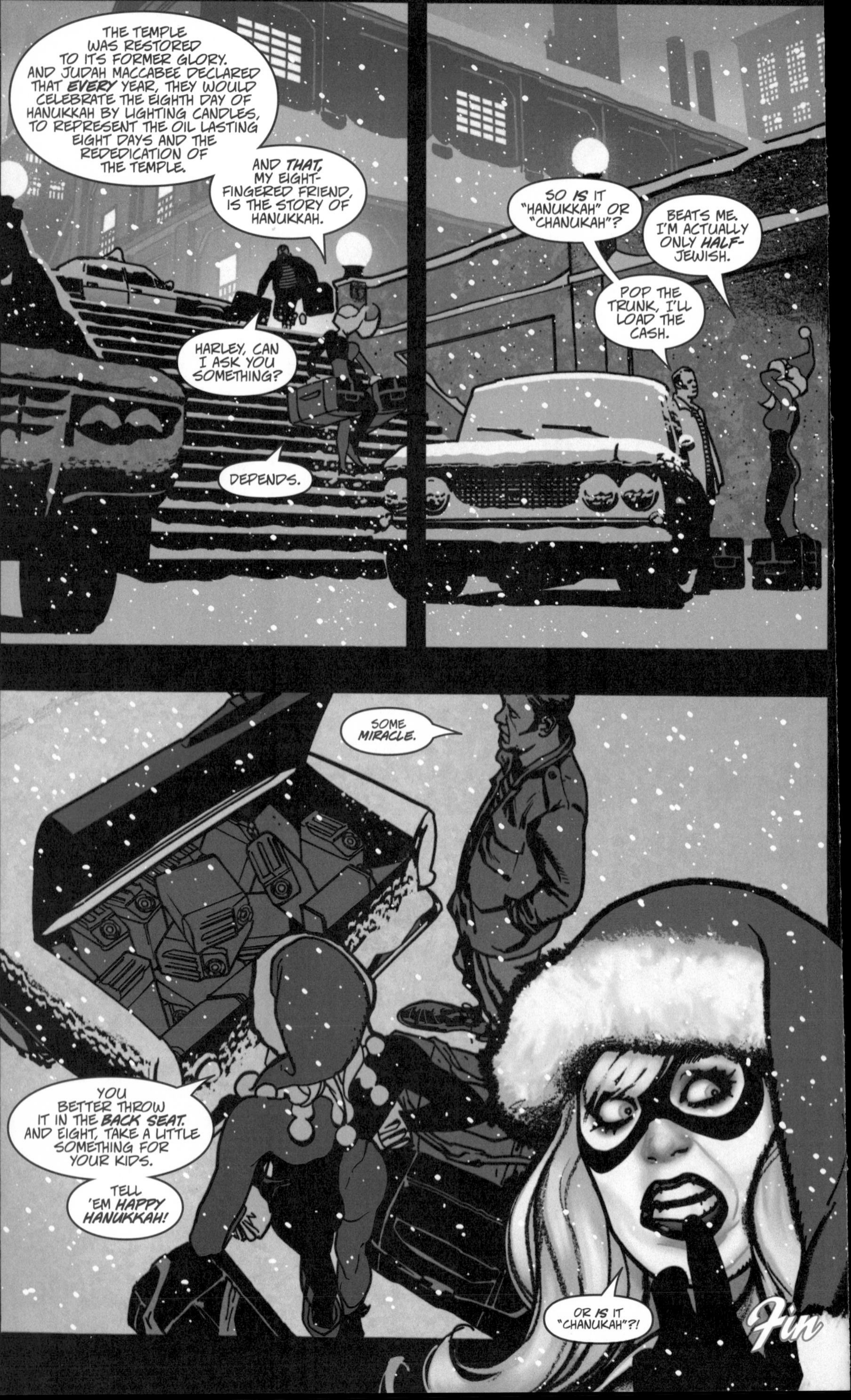
THE TEMPLE WAS RESTORED TO ITS FORMER GLORY. AND JUDAH MACCABEE DECLARED THAT EVERY YEAR, THEY WOULD CELEBRATE THE EIGHTH DAY OF HANUKKAH BY LIGHTING CANDLES, TO REPRESENT THE OIL LASTING EIGHT DAYS AND THE REDEDICATION OF THE TEMPLE.
AND THAT, MY EIGHT-FINGERED FRIEND, IS THE STORY OF HANUKKAH.
HARLEY, CAN I ASK YOU SOMETHING?
DEPENDS.
SO IS IT "HANUKKAH" OR "CHANUKAH"?
BEATS ME. I'M ACTUALLY ONLY HALF-JEWISH.
POP THE TRUNK, I'LL LOAD THE CASH.
SOME MIRACLE.
YOU BETTER THROW IT IN THE BACK SEAT. AND EIGHT, TAKE A LITTLE SOMETHING FOR YOUR KIDS.
TELL 'EM HAPPY HANUKKAH!
OR IS IT "CHANUKAH"?!
Fin

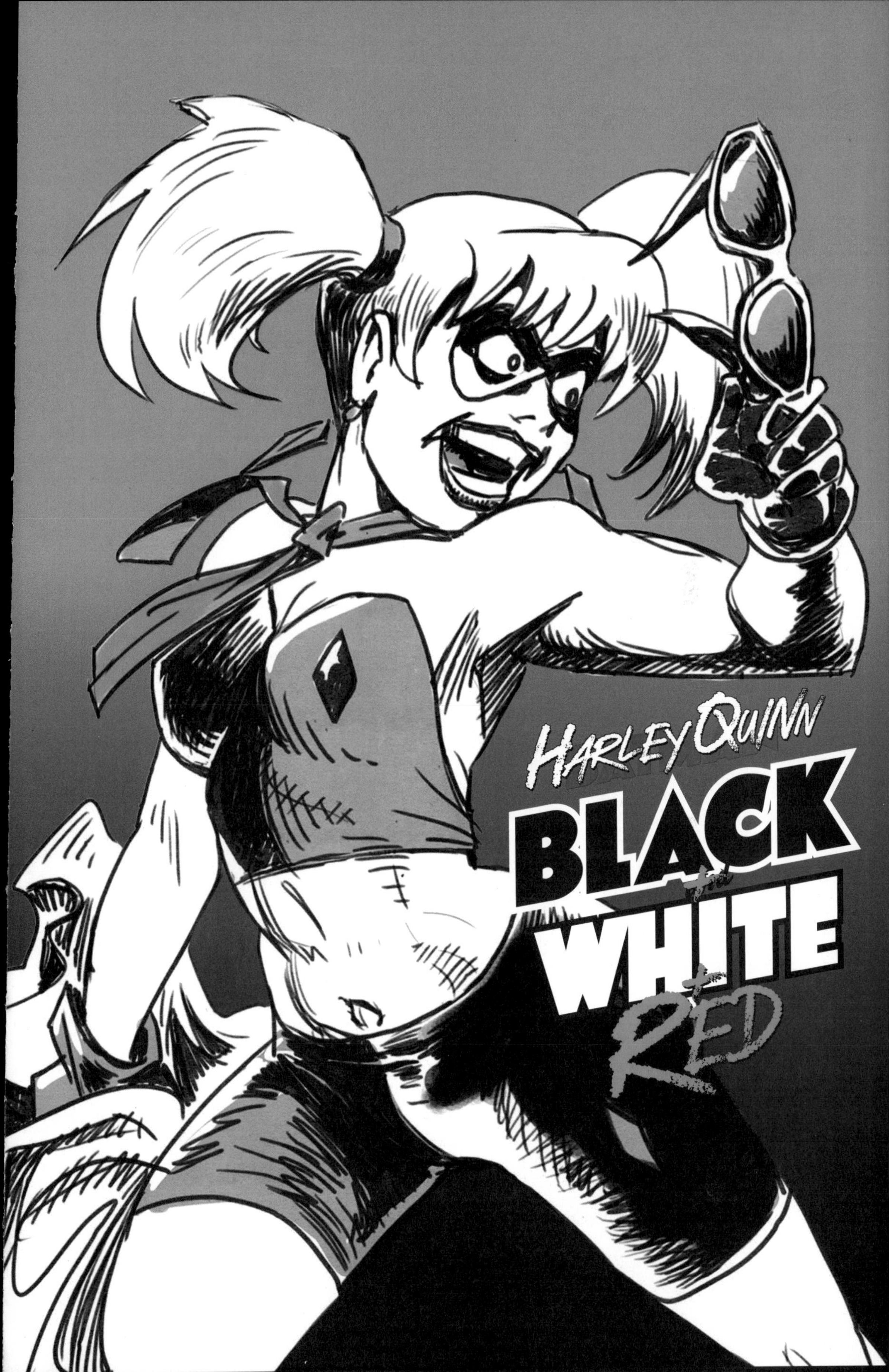
HARLEY QUINN
BLACK
+
WHITE
+
RED

CHAPTER NINETEEN

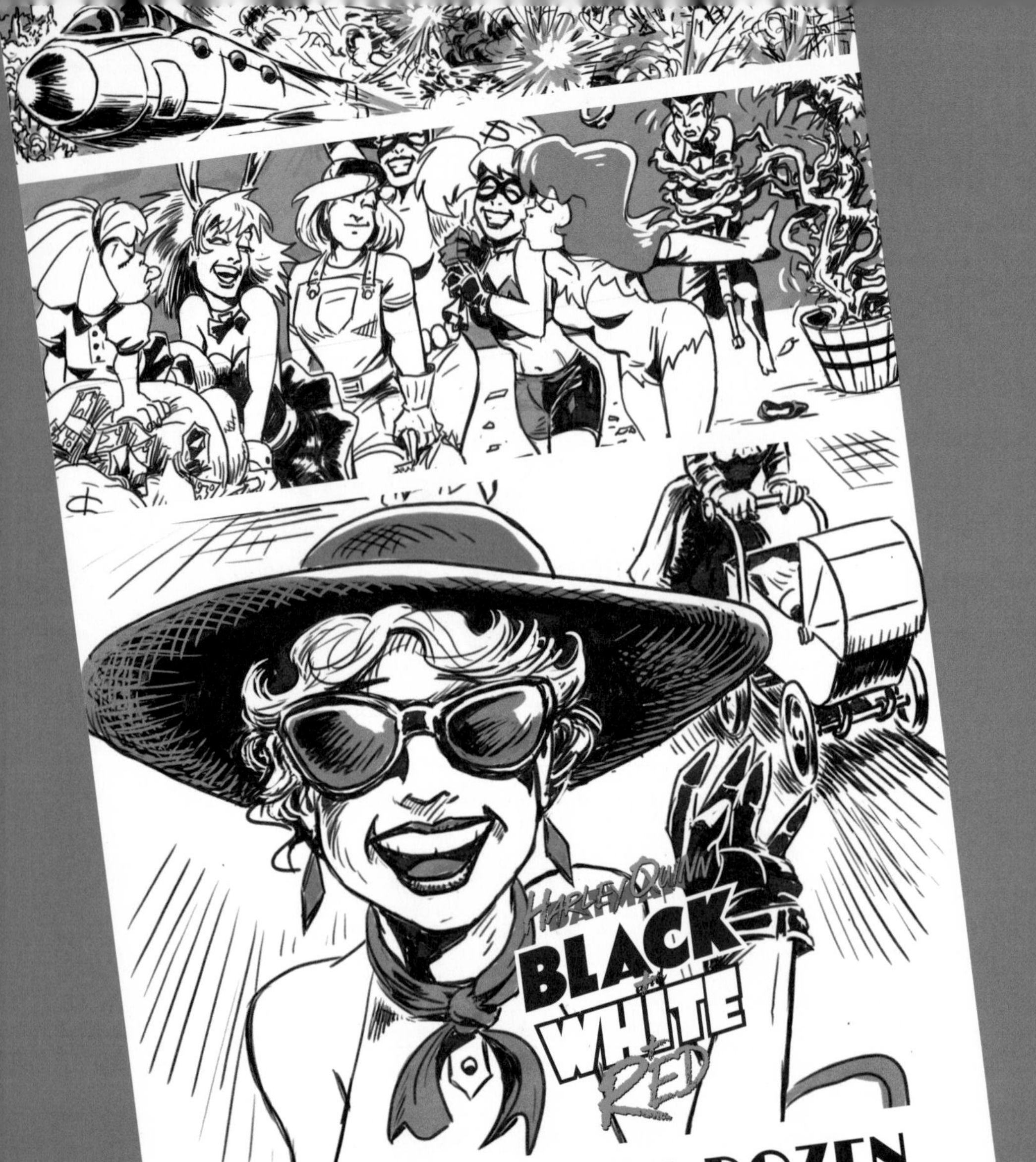
HARLEY QUINN
BLACK
WHITE
RED

"HARLEEN'S HALF DOZEN (PLUS ONE)"

WRITER **PAUL DINI**
ARTIST **KEVIN ALTIERI**
LETTERER **JOSH REED**
EDITOR **CHRIS CONROY**

HARLEY QUINN CREATED BY PAUL DINI & BRUCE TIMM

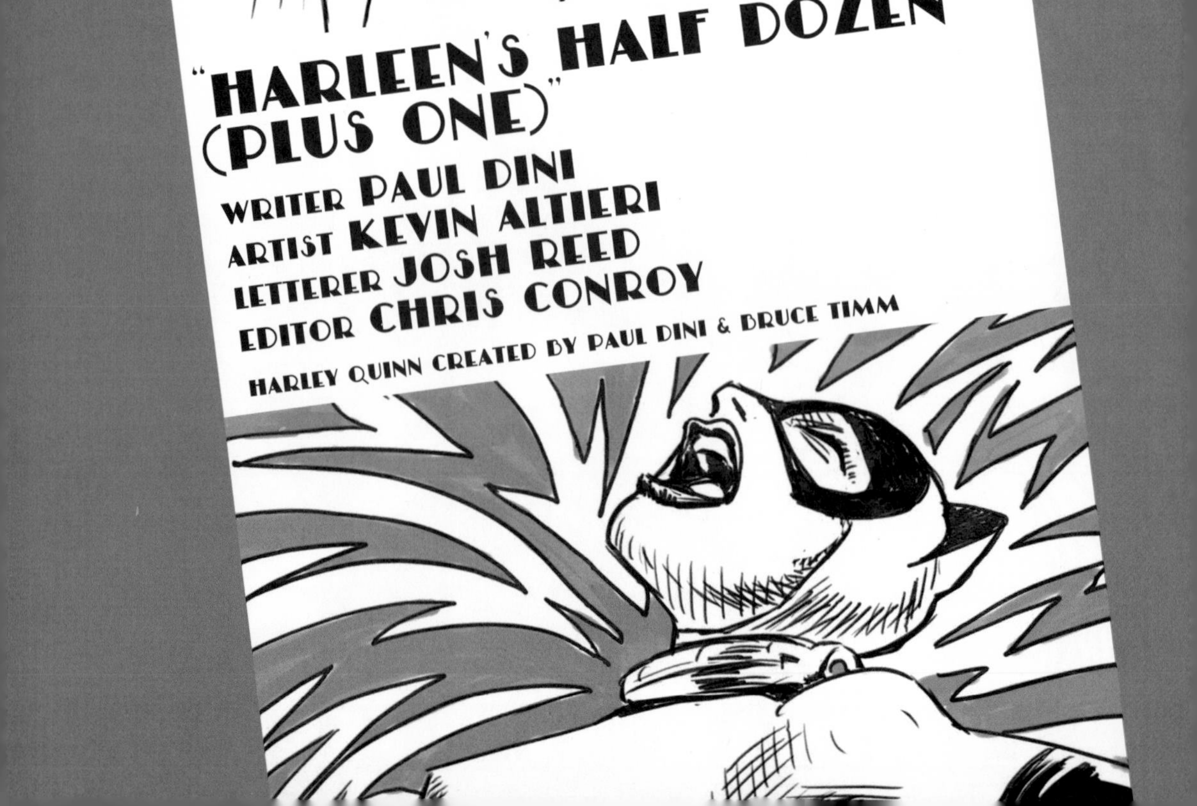

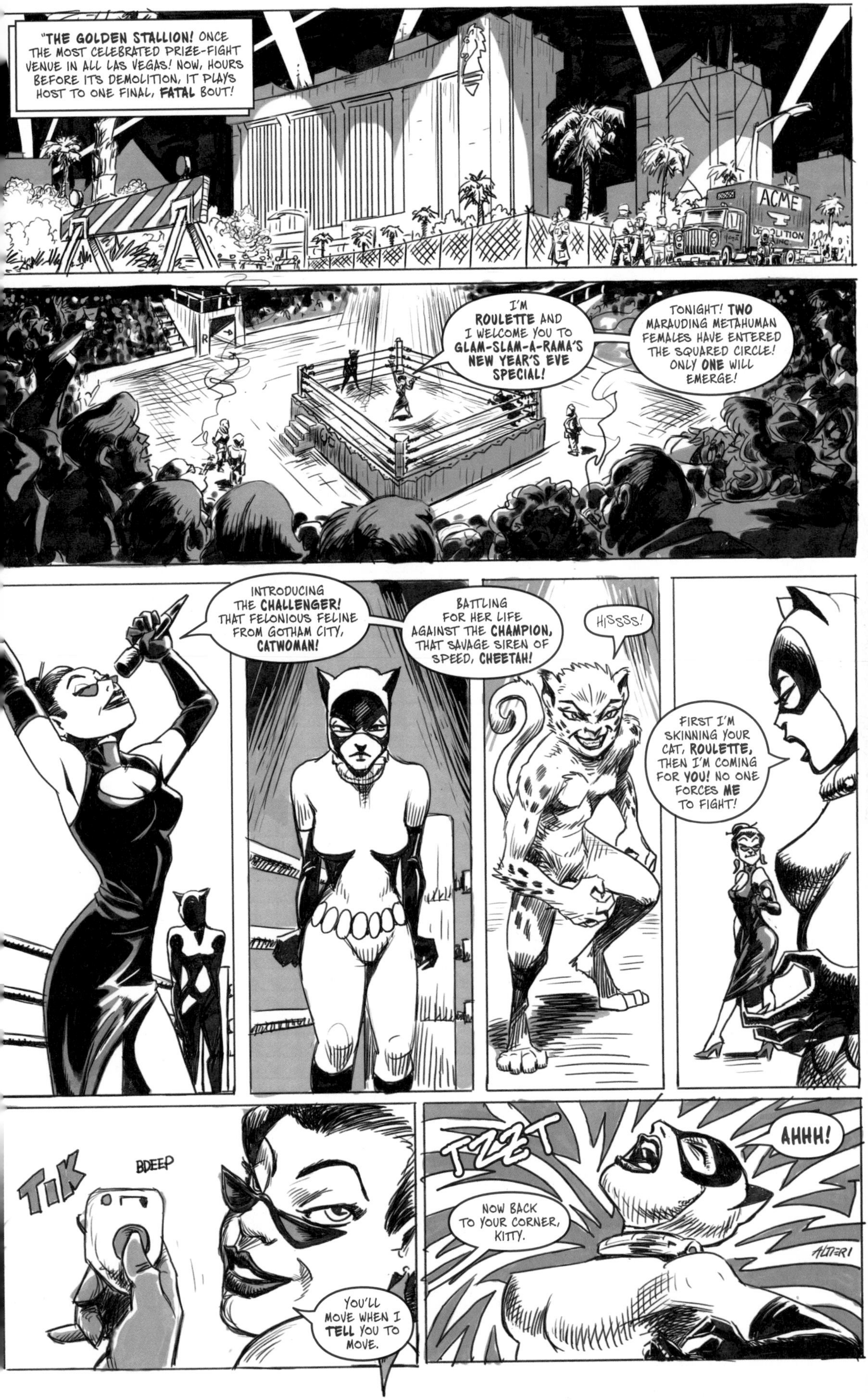
"THE GOLDEN STALLION! ONCE THE MOST CELEBRATED PRIZE-FIGHT VENUE IN ALL LAS VEGAS! NOW, HOURS BEFORE ITS DEMOLITION, IT PLAYS HOST TO ONE FINAL, FATAL BOUT!
ACME
DEMOLITION INC.
I'M ROULETTE AND I WELCOME YOU TO GLAM-SLAM-A-RAMA'S NEW YEAR'S EVE SPECIAL!
TONIGHT! TWO MARAUDING METAHUMAN FEMALES HAVE ENTERED THE SQUARED CIRCLE! ONLY ONE WILL EMERGE!
INTRODUCING THE CHALLENGER! THAT FELONIOUS FELINE FROM GOTHAM CITY, CATWOMAN!
BATTLING FOR HER LIFE AGAINST THE CHAMPION, THAT SAVAGE SIREN OF SPEED, CHEETAH!
HISSSS!
FIRST I'M SKINNING YOUR CAT, ROULETTE, THEN I'M COMING FOR YOU! NO ONE FORCES ME TO FIGHT!
TIK
BDEEP
YOU'LL MOVE WHEN I TELL YOU TO MOVE.
TZZT
AHHH!
NOW BACK TO YOUR CORNER, KITTY.
ALTIERI

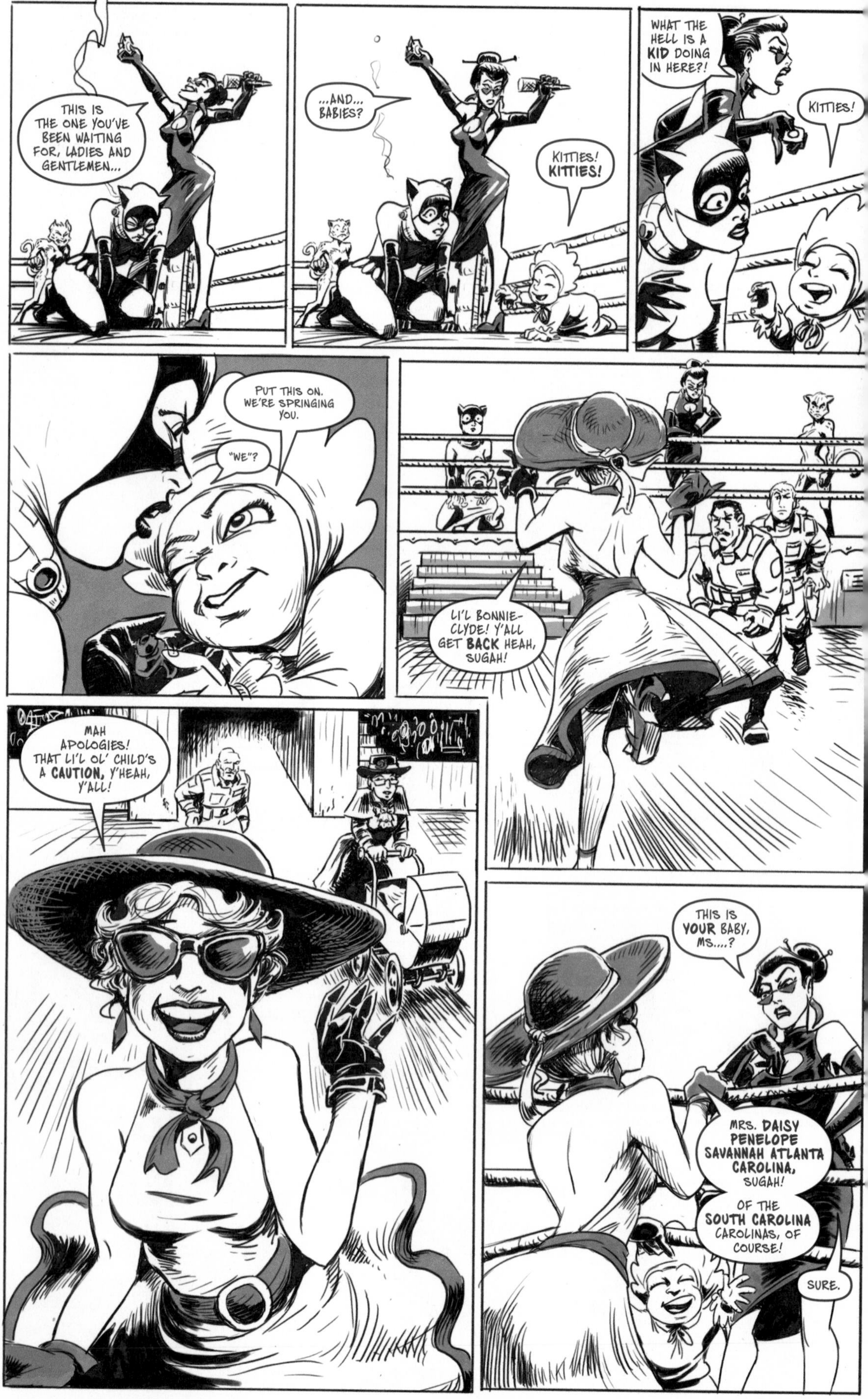
THIS IS THE ONE YOU'VE BEEN WAITING FOR, LADIES AND GENTLEMEN...
...AND... BABIES?
KITTIES! KITTIES!
WHAT THE HELL IS A KID DOING IN HERE?!
KITTIES!
PUT THIS ON. WE'RE SPRINGING YOU.
"WE"?
LI'L BONNIE-CLYDE! Y'ALL GET BACK HEAH, SUGAH!
MAH APOLOGIES! THAT LI'L OL' CHILD'S A CAUTION, Y'HEAH, Y'ALL!
THIS IS YOUR BABY, MS....?
MRS. DAISY PENELOPE SAVANNAH ATLANTA CAROLINA, SUGAH!
OF THE SOUTH CAROLINA CAROLINAS, OF COURSE!
SURE.

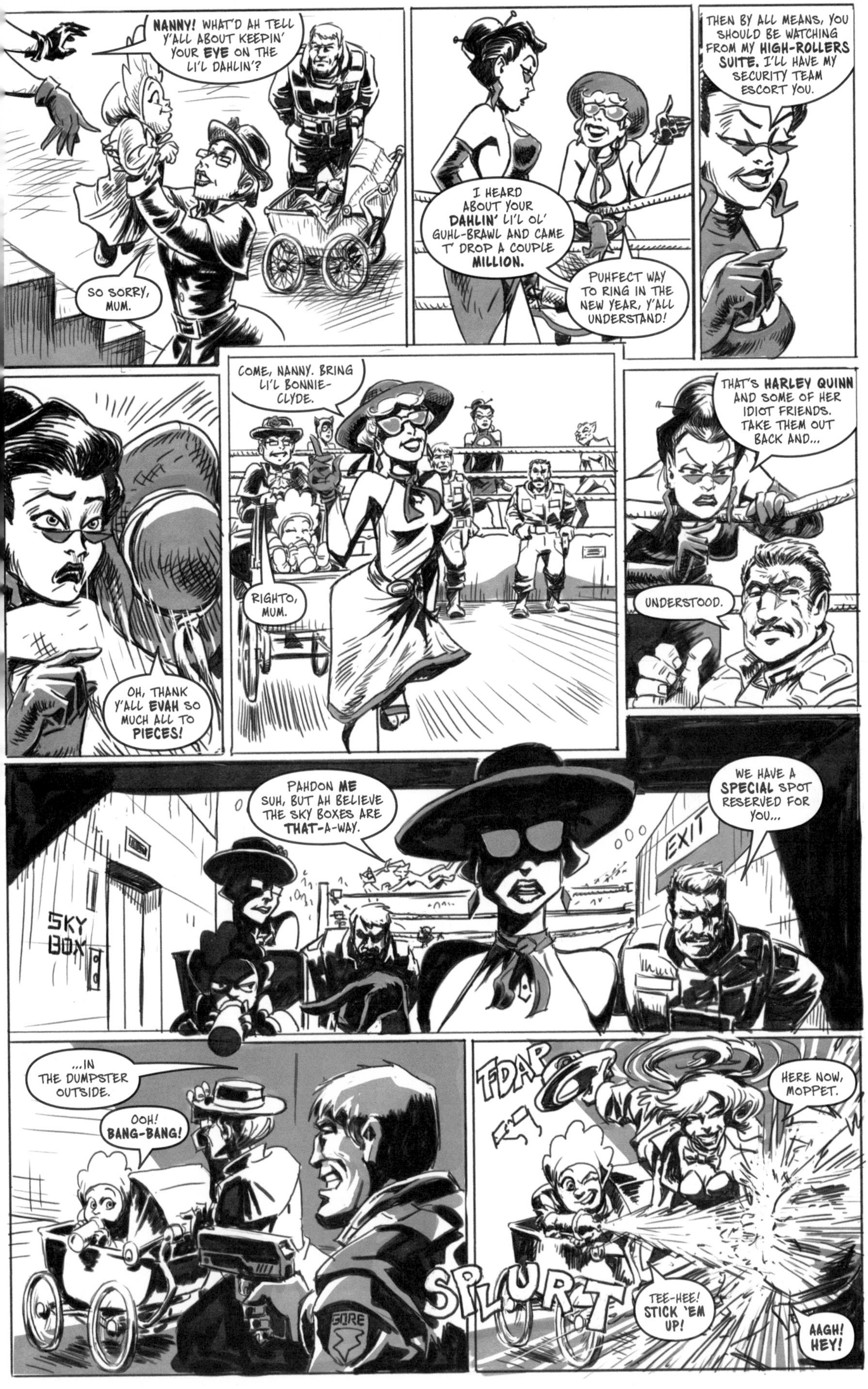
NANNY! WHAT'D AH TELL Y'ALL ABOUT KEEPIN' YOUR EYE ON THE LI'L DAHLIN'?
SO SORRY, MUM.
I HEARD ABOUT YOUR DAHLIN' LI'L OL' GUHL-BRAWL AND CAME T' DROP A COUPLE MILLION.
PUHFECT WAY TO RING IN THE NEW YEAR, Y'ALL UNDERSTAND!
THEN BY ALL MEANS, YOU SHOULD BE WATCHING FROM MY HIGH-ROLLERS SUITE. I'LL HAVE MY SECURITY TEAM ESCORT YOU.
OH, THANK Y'ALL EVAH SO MUCH ALL TO PIECES!
COME, NANNY. BRING LI'L BONNIE-CLYDE.
RIGHTO, MUM.
THAT'S HARLEY QUINN AND SOME OF HER IDIOT FRIENDS. TAKE THEM OUT BACK AND...
UNDERSTOOD.
PAHDON ME SUH, BUT AH BELIEVE THE SKY BOXES ARE THAT-A-WAY.
WE HAVE A SPECIAL SPOT RESERVED FOR YOU...
SKY BOX
EXIT
...IN THE DUMPSTER OUTSIDE.
OOH! BANG-BANG!
TFDAP
HERE NOW, MOPPET.
SPLURT
TEE-HEE! STICK 'EM UP!
AAGH! HEY!

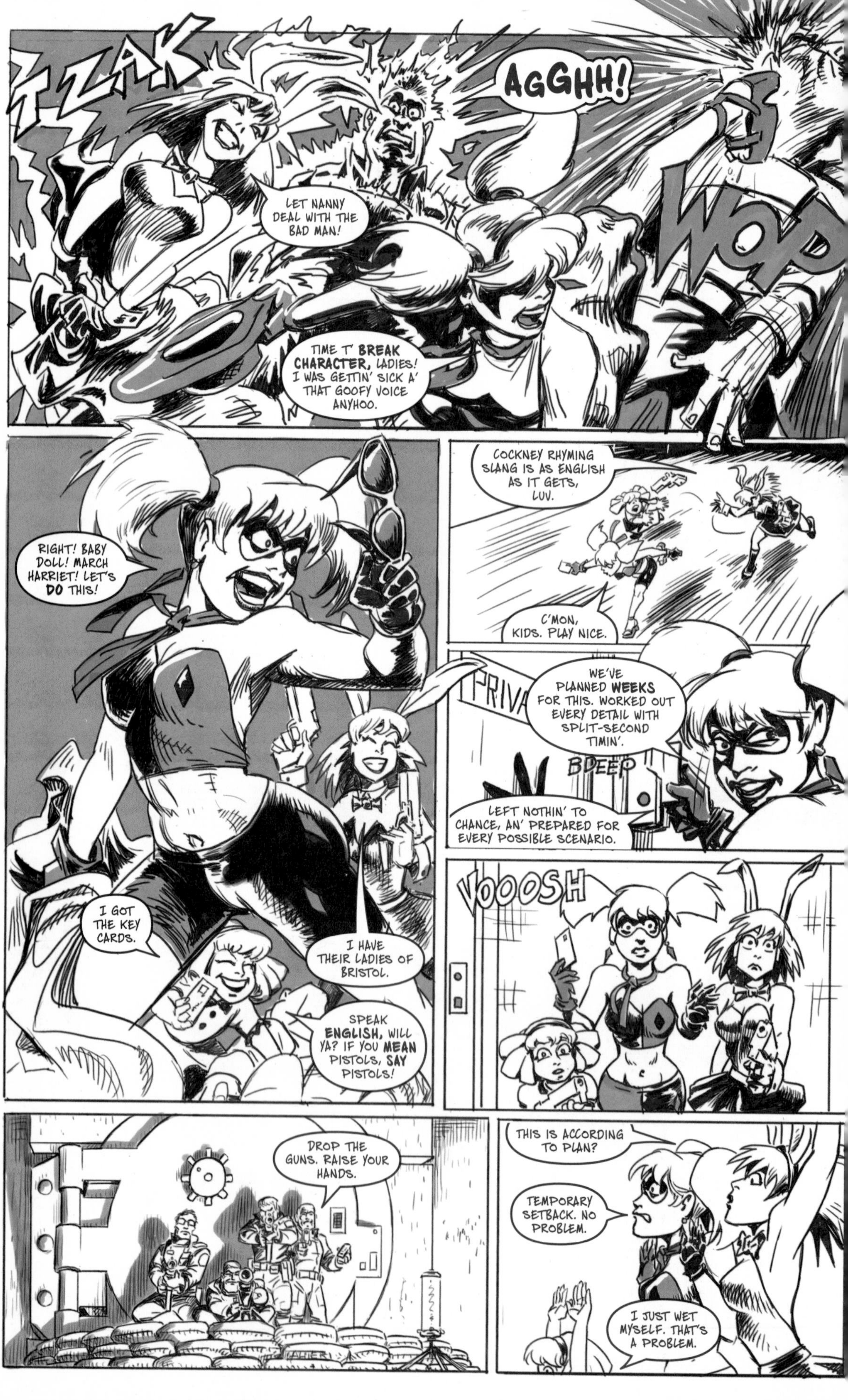

TZZAK
AGGHH!
LET NANNY DEAL WITH THE BAD MAN!
WOP
TIME T' BREAK CHARACTER, LADIES! I WAS GETTIN' SICK A' THAT GOOFY VOICE ANYHOO.
RIGHT! BABY DOLL! MARCH HARRIET! LET'S DO THIS!
I GOT THE KEY CARDS.
I HAVE THEIR LADIES OF BRISTOL.
SPEAK ENGLISH, WILL YA? IF YOU MEAN PISTOLS, SAY PISTOLS!
COCKNEY RHYMING SLANG IS AS ENGLISH AS IT GETS, LUV.
C'MON, KIDS. PLAY NICE.
PRIVA
WE'VE PLANNED WEEKS FOR THIS. WORKED OUT EVERY DETAIL WITH SPLIT-SECOND TIMIN'.
BDEEP
LEFT NOTHIN' TO CHANCE, AN' PREPARED FOR EVERY POSSIBLE SCENARIO.
VOOOSH
DROP THE GUNS. RAISE YOUR HANDS.
THIS IS ACCORDING TO PLAN?
TEMPORARY SETBACK. NO PROBLEM.
I JUST WET MYSELF. THAT'S A PROBLEM.

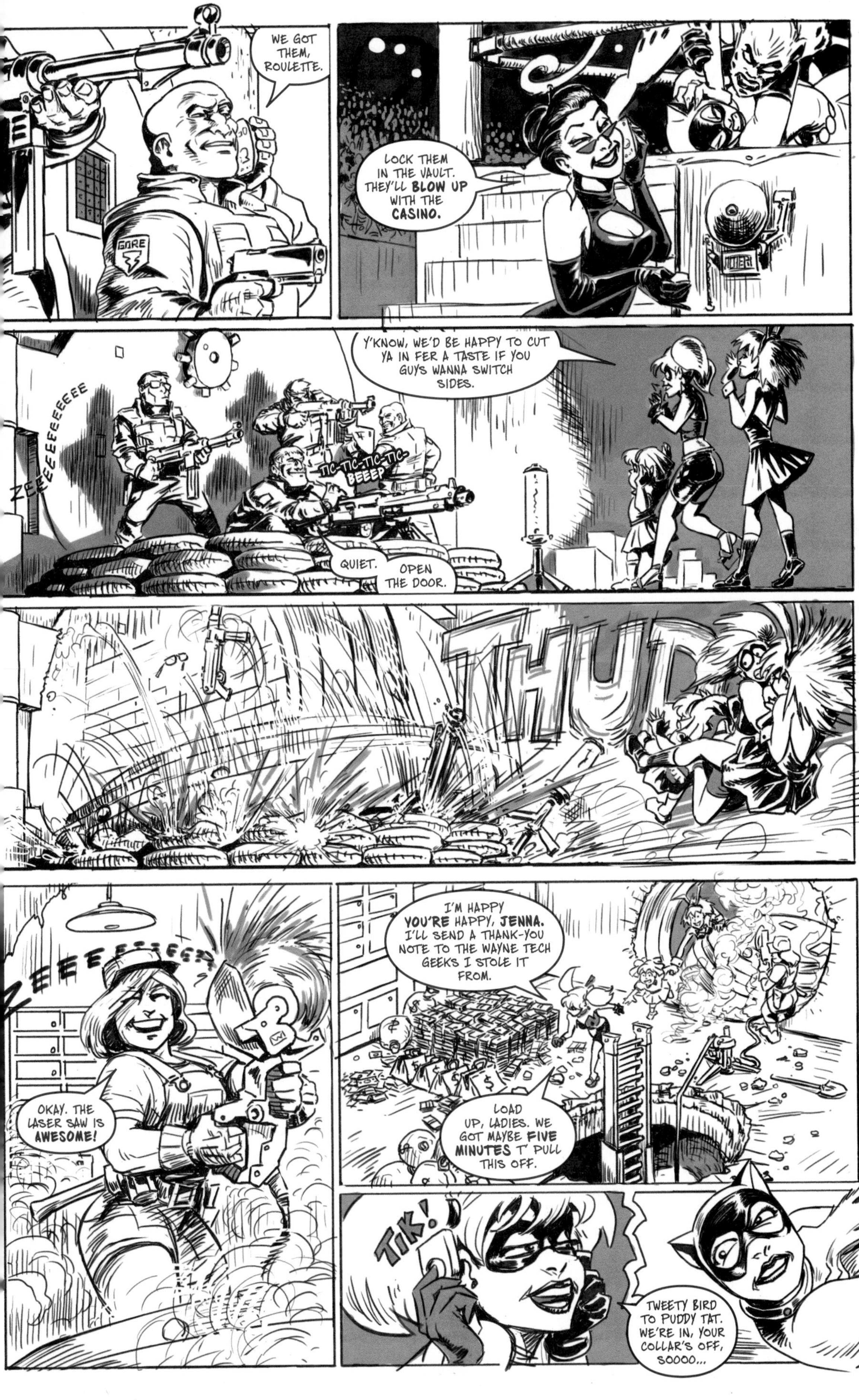

WE GOT THEM, ROULETTE.
LOCK THEM IN THE VAULT. THEY'LL **BLOW UP** WITH THE **CASINO.**
Y'KNOW, WE'D BE HAPPY TO CUT YA IN FER A TASTE IF YOU GUYS WANNA SWITCH SIDES.
ZEEEEEEEEEEE
TIC-TIC-TIC-TIC BEEEP
QUIET.
OPEN THE DOOR.
THUD
ZEEEEEEEEEE
OKAY. THE LASER SAW IS **AWESOME!**
I'M HAPPY **YOU'RE** HAPPY, **JENNA.** I'LL SEND A THANK-YOU NOTE TO THE WAYNE TECH GEEKS I STOLE IT FROM.
LOAD UP, LADIES. WE GOT MAYBE **FIVE MINUTES** T' PULL THIS OFF.
TIK!
TWEETY BIRD TO PUDDY TAT. WE'RE IN, YOUR COLLAR'S OFF, SOOOO...

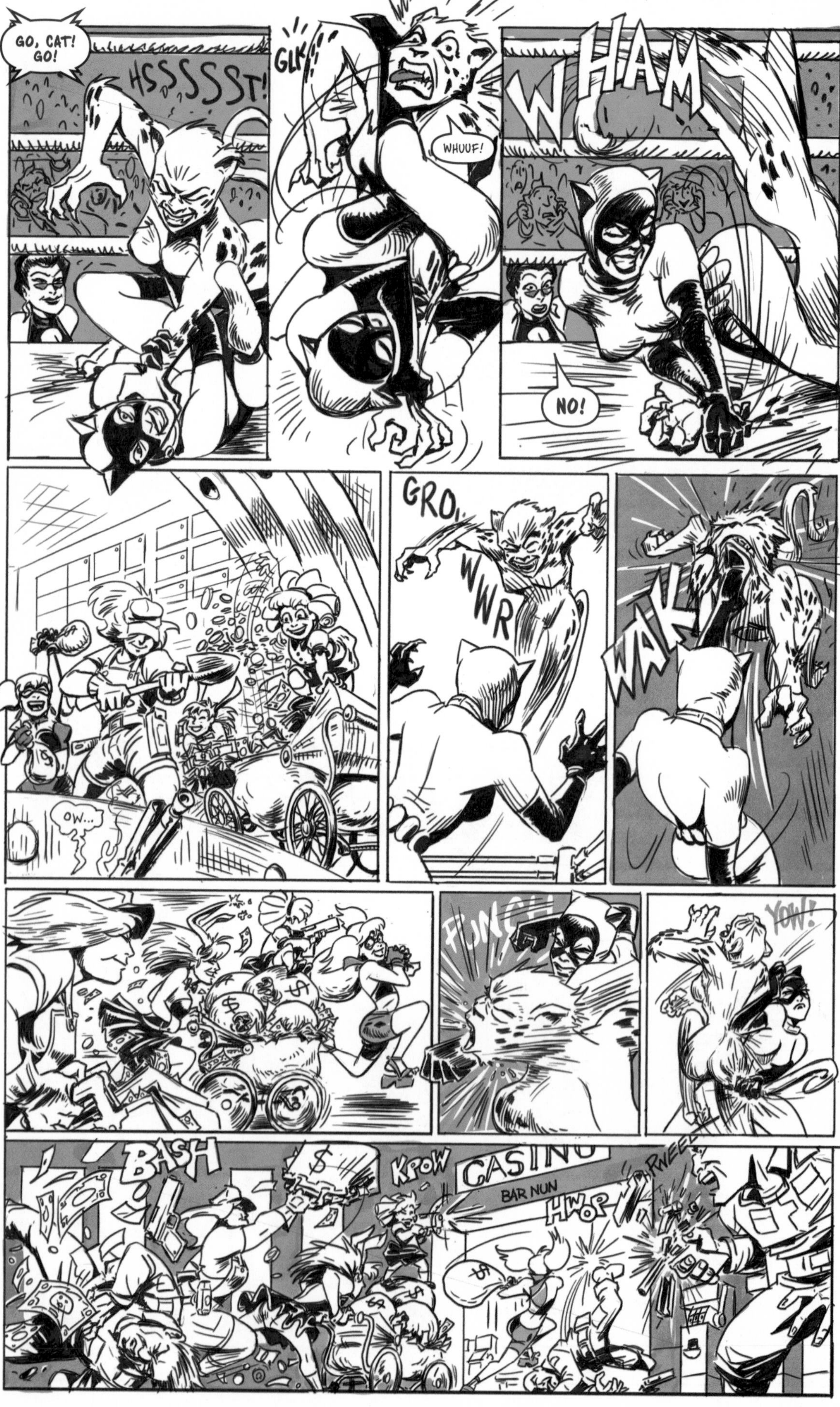
GO, CAT! GO!
HSSSSST!
GLK
WHUUF!
WHAM
NO!
OW...
GROWWR
WAK
PUNCH
YOW!
BASH
KPOW
CASINO
BAR NUN
HWOP
PWEE

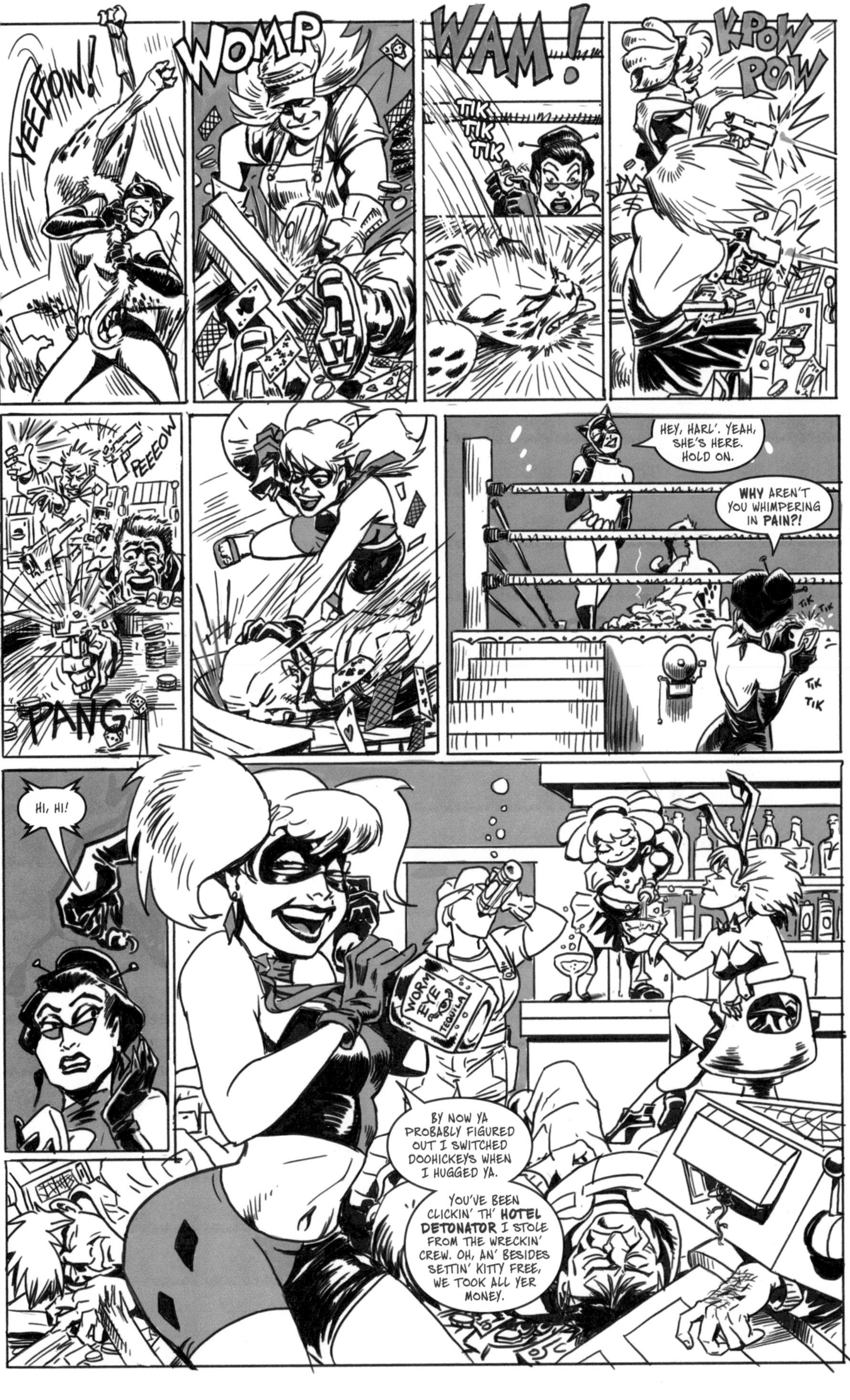
YEEEOW!
WOMP
WAM!
TIK TIK TIK
KPOW POW
PEEEOW
PANG
HEY, HARL'. YEAH, SHE'S HERE. HOLD ON.
WHY AREN'T YOU WHIMPERING IN **PAIN?!**
TIK TIK
TIK TIK
HI, HI!
WORM EYE TEQUILA
BY NOW YA PROBABLY FIGURED OUT I SWITCHED DOOHICKEYS WHEN I HUGGED YA.
YOU'VE BEEN CLICKIN' TH' **HOTEL DETONATOR** I STOLE FROM THE WRECKIN' CREW. OH, AN' BESIDES SETTIN' KITTY FREE, WE TOOK ALL YER MONEY.

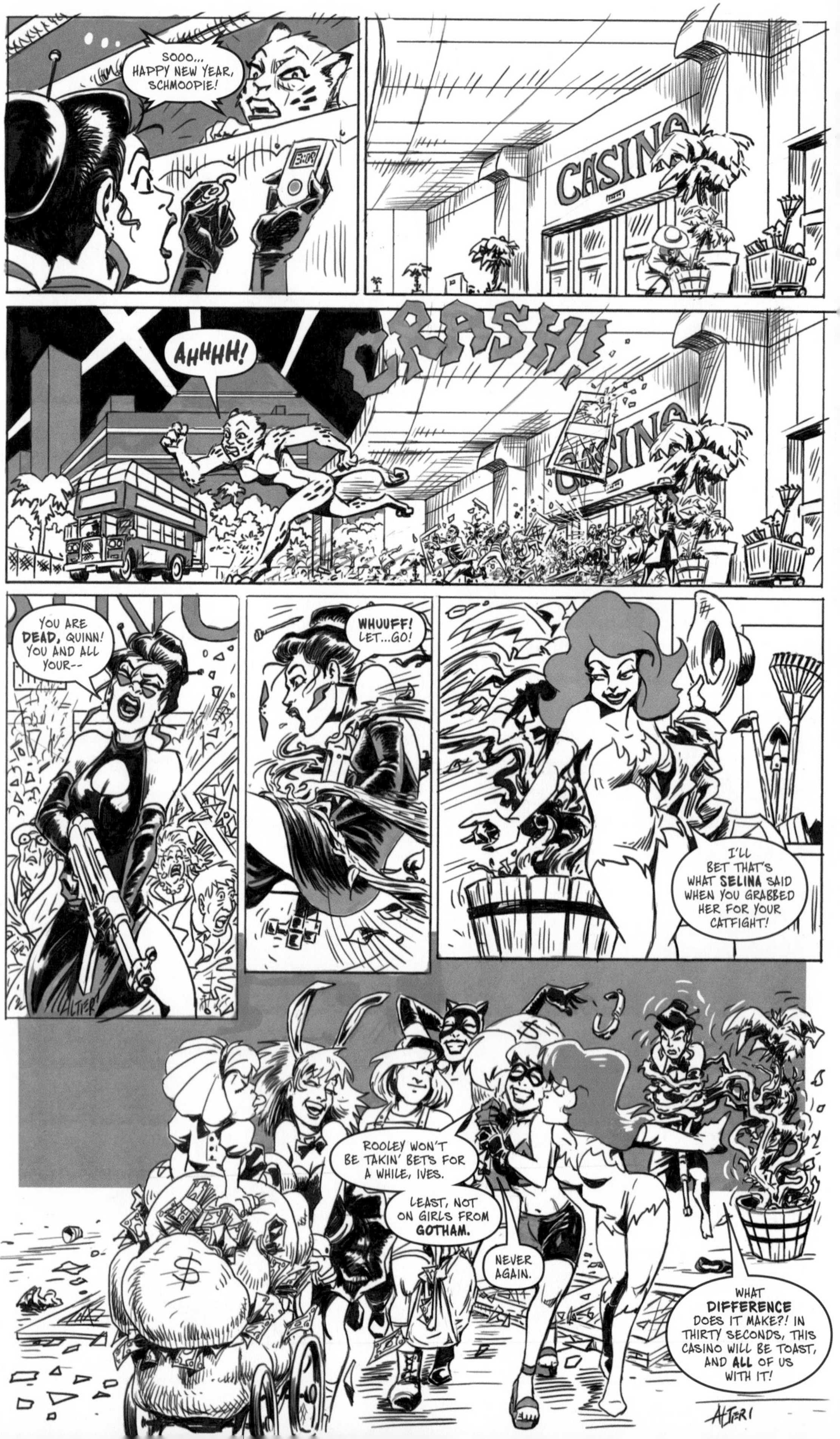
SOOO... HAPPY NEW YEAR, SCHMOOPIE!
CASINO
CRASH!
AHHHH!
YOU ARE DEAD, QUINN! YOU AND ALL YOUR--
WHUUFF! LET...GO!
I'LL BET THAT'S WHAT SELINA SAID WHEN YOU GRABBED HER FOR YOUR CATFIGHT!
ROOLEY WON'T BE TAKIN' BETS FOR A WHILE, IVES.
LEAST, NOT ON GIRLS FROM GOTHAM.
NEVER AGAIN.
WHAT DIFFERENCE DOES IT MAKE?! IN THIRTY SECONDS, THIS CASINO WILL BE TOAST, AND ALL OF US WITH IT!
ALTIERI

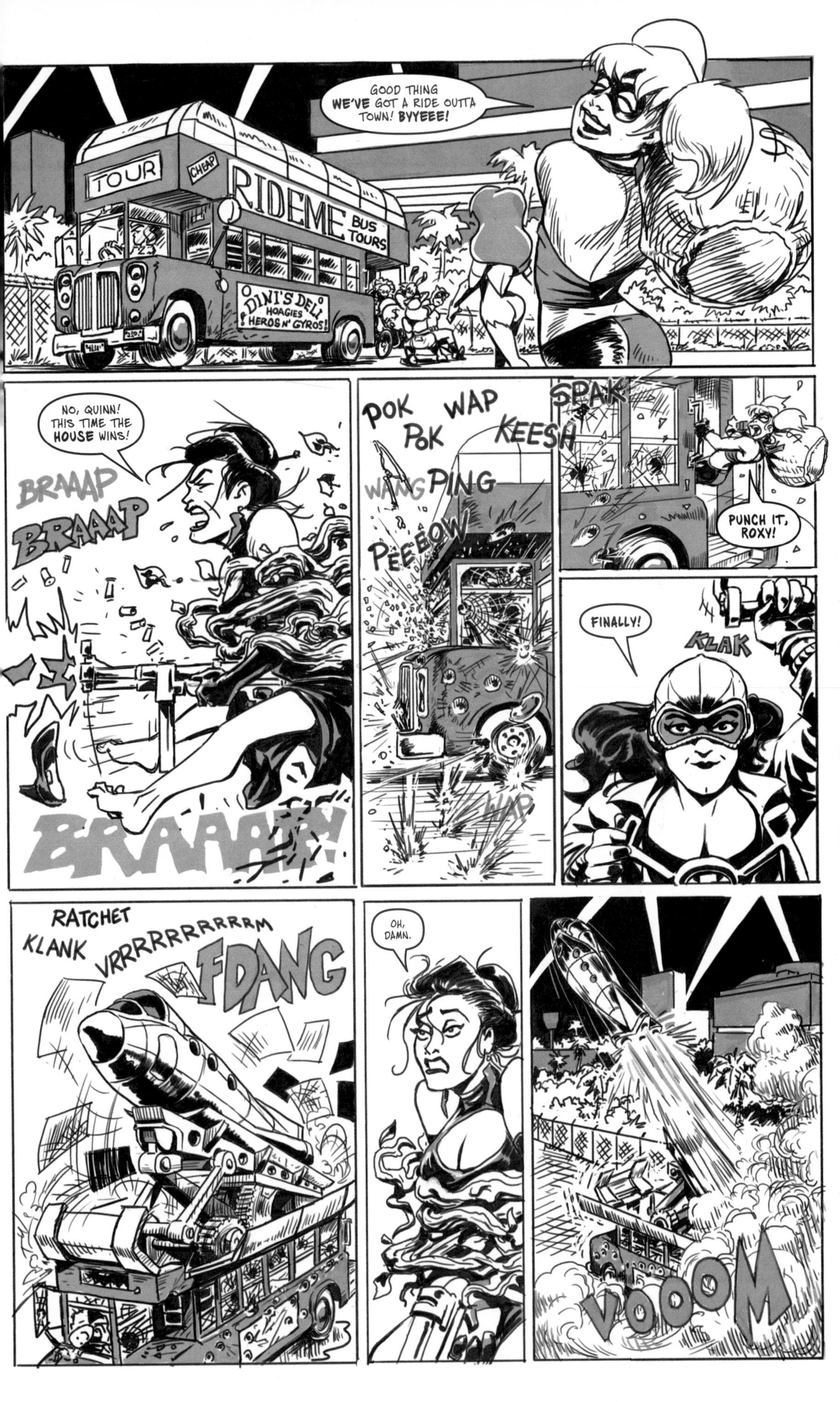

GOOD THING WE'VE GOT A RIDE OUTTA TOWN! BYYEEE!
TOUR
CHEAP
RIDEME BUS TOURS
DINI'S DELI HOAGIES HEROS N' GYROS!
NO, QUINN! THIS TIME THE HOUSE WINS!
BRAAAP
BRAAAP
BRAAAP!
POK
WAP
POK
KEESH
WANG
PING
PEEBOW
WAP
SPAK
PUNCH IT, ROXY!
FINALLY!
KLAK
RATCHET
KLANK
VRRRRRRRRRRM
FDANG
OH, DAMN.
VOOOM

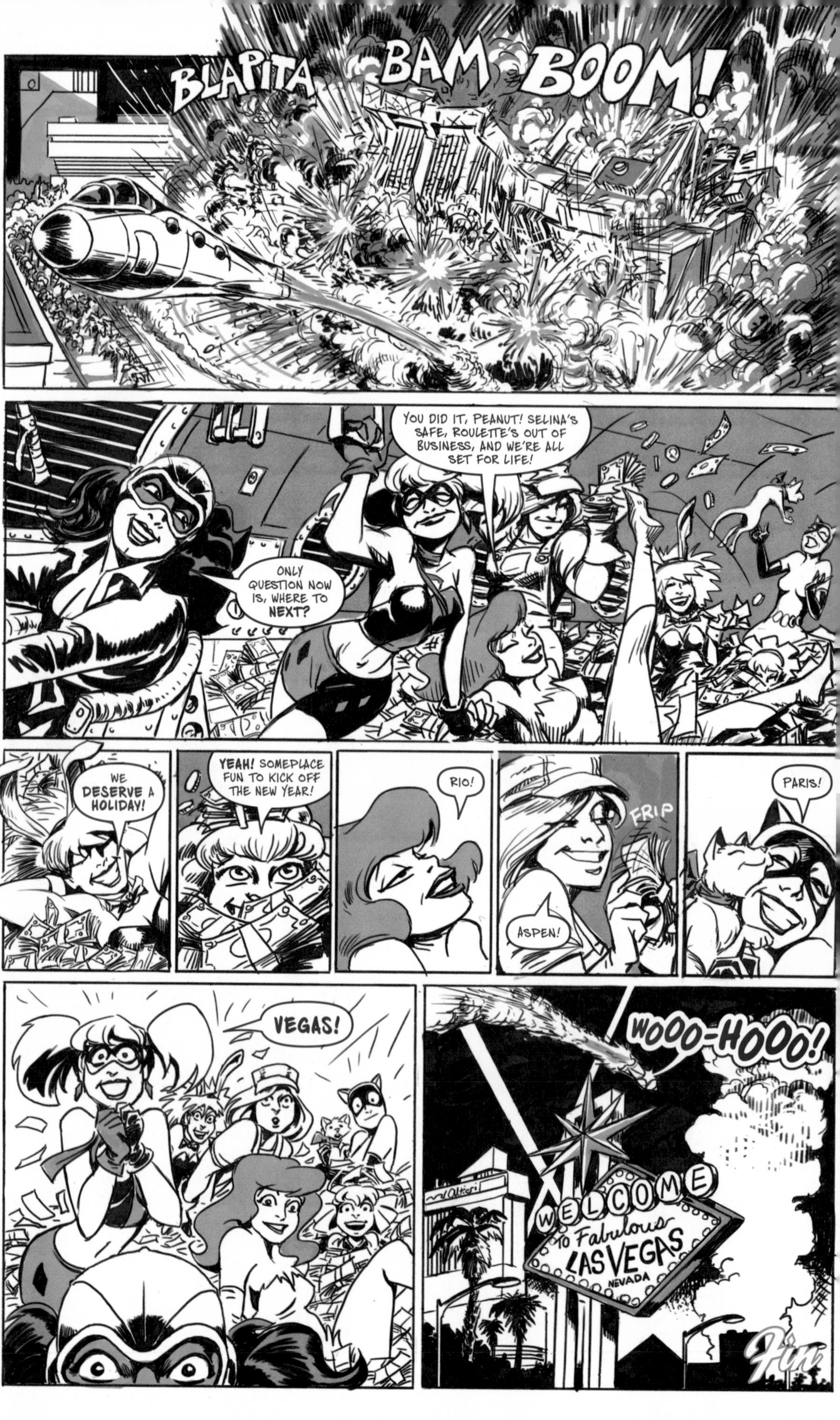
BLAPITA BAM BOOM!
YOU DID IT, PEANUT! SELINA'S SAFE, ROULETTE'S OUT OF BUSINESS, AND WE'RE ALL SET FOR LIFE!
ONLY QUESTION NOW IS, WHERE TO NEXT?
WE DESERVE A HOLIDAY!
YEAH! SOMEPLACE FUN TO KICK OFF THE NEW YEAR!
RIO!
FRIP
ASPEN!
PARIS!
VEGAS!
WOOO-HOOOO!
WELCOME to Fabulous LAS VEGAS NEVADA
Fin